ONE WEEK LOAN

Forensic Criminology

Forensic Criminology

Wayne A. Petherick
Brent E. Turvey
Claire E. Ferguson

AMSTERDAM • BOSTON • HEIDELBERG • LONDON
NEW YORK • OXFORD • PARIS • SAN DIEGO
SAN FRANCISCO • SINGAPORE • SYDNEY • TOKYO

Academic Press is an imprint of Elsevier

ELSEVIER

Elsevier Academic Press
30 Corporate Drive, Suite 400, Burlington, MA 01803, USA
525 B Street, Suite 1900, San Diego, California 92101-4495, USA
84 Theobald's Road, London WC1X 8RR, UK

This book is printed on acid-free paper. ∞

Library of Congress Cataloging-in-Publication Data
Forensic criminology / [edited by] Wayne A. Petherick, Brent E. Turvey, Claire E. Ferguson.
    p. cm.
  ISBN 978-0-12-375071-6 (hard cover: alk. paper) 1. Forensic sciences. 2. Criminology.
3. Criminal investigations. I. Petherick, Wayne. II. Turvey, Brent E. III. Ferguson,
Claire E.
  HV8073.F562 2009
  363.25–dc22

2009021294

British Library Cataloguing in Publication Data
A catalogue record for this book is available from the British Library

ISBN 13: 978-0-12-375071-6

For all information on all Elsevier Academic Press publications
visit our Web site at www.elsevierdirect.com

Printed in the United States of America

09 10 11 12 9 8 7 6 5 4 3 2 1

Contents

Acknowledgments

The authors wish to thank their friends, families, and loved ones for being supportive and patient during the creation of this work.

- W.A.P., C.E.F., and B.E.T.

About the Authors

Craig M. Cooley, M.S., J.D.

Craig Cooley received his law degree from Northwestern University School of Law (2004), his M.S. in forensic science from the University of New Haven (2000), and his B.S. in psychology from the University of Pittsburgh (1996). Mr. Cooley's research and writings have been published in law journals such as *George Mason University Civil Rights Law Journal*, *New England Law Review*, *Indiana University Law Journal*, *Stanford Law & Policy Review*, *Oklahoma City University Law Review*, and *Southern Illinois University Law Journal*, and books such as *Crime Reconstruction* (Academic Press, 2006) and *Criminal Profiling: An Introduction to Behavioral Evidence Analysis*, 3rd Edition (Academic Press, 2008).

Mr. Cooley joined the Innocence Project as a Staff Attorney in August 2007. He represents clients in various states seeking access to post-conviction DNA testing and/or relief from their conviction based on exculpatory DNA evidence. Prior to his work with the Innocence Project, Mr. Cooley worked as an Assistant Federal Defender in Las Vegas, Nevada (2005–2007), where he (and the Capital Habeas Unit) represented Nevada death row inmates in federal and state post-conviction proceedings. Prior to this, Mr. Cooley worked as an Investigator in Harrisburg, Pennsylvania (2004–2005), where he (and the Capital Habeas Unit) represented Pennsylvania death row inmates in federal and state post-conviction proceedings. Prior to joining the Harrisburg Capital Habeas Unit, Mr. Cooley served as an Investigator with the Office of the State Appellate Defenders, Death Penalty Trial Assistance Division in Chicago, Illinois (2001–2004), where he worked on various cases affected by Governor George Ryan's death row pardons and commutations.

He can be reached via email at ccooley@innocenceproject.org.

Stan Crowder, Ph.D.

Stan Crowder is a retired U.S. Army Military Police Colonel. During his 35 years of military service, Dr. Crowder has held numerous positions, including MP Commander, Chief of Investigations for the Inspector General of Georgia, Counterdrug Coordinator, Battalion Commander, and Chief of Personnel. He also served seven years as a civilian police officer. He currently teaches in the Criminal Justice Program at Kennesaw State University in Kennesaw, Georgia, where he has been since 1999. In 2007 he was the recipient of the Betty Siegel teaching award. Dr. Crowder holds a Ph.D. in Criminal Justice, as well as an M.B.A. He can be reached via email at scrowder@kennesaw.edu.

Claire E. Ferguson, M.Crim.

Claire Ferguson holds her Bachelor of Arts degree in Honors Psychology from the University of Western Ontario in Canada and a Master of Criminology from Bond University in Australia. She is currently a Doctoral Candidate in the Criminology Department at Bond University, where she is studying staged crime scenes. Ms. Ferguson worked for St. Leonard's Society in 2006, writing a narrative to be used for training purposes about homicide cases. In 2007, she undertook an internship with Queensland Fire and Rescue in the Fire Investigation Unit. She completed a crime scene analysis internship with Forensic Solutions in 2008. Ms. Ferguson also works at Bond University as an adjunct teaching fellow in the Criminology Department. She can be contacted via email at clfergus@staff.bond.edu.au.

David Field, L.L.B.

David Field is an Associate Professor of Law at Bond University in Gold Coast, Australia. His positions include Former Solicitor for Prosecutions for Queensland, stipendiary magistrate for Glasgow, also former prosecutor and defense trial attorney in both Scotland and Australia (Queensland and New South Wales). He is the author of *Evidence Law in Queensland*, as well as numerous textbook chapters relating to law and evidence.

Kind to children, considerate toward animals, and environmentally friendly. Available for funerals and bah mitzvas. Happily married, although my wife may not be.

Terry Goldsworthy, Ph.D.

Terry Goldsworthy is a Detective Senior Sergeant in the Queensland Police Service with over 24 years of law enforcement experience in Australia. He has served in general duties, including watch house and traffic branch, before moving to the Criminal Investigation Branch (CIB) in 1994. He is currently stationed at the Gold Coast CIB, where he is responsible for the management of serious investigations.

Dr. Goldsworthy has completed a Bachelor of Commerce, Bachelor of Laws, Advanced Diploma of Investigative Practice, and a Diploma of Policing. As a result of his law studies, Dr. Goldsworthy was admitted to the bar as a barrister in the Queensland and Federal Courts in 1999. Dr. Goldsworthy then completed a Master of Criminology at Bond University. He later undertook his Ph.D., focusing on the concept of evil and its relevance from a criminological and sociological viewpoint. In particular, Dr. Goldsworthy looked at the link between evil and armed conflicts using the Waffen-SS as a case study.

Dr. Goldsworthy's first book, titled *Valhalla's Warriors*, examines the genocidal actions of the SS in Russia during World War II. He has also contributed a chapter to the tertiary textbook, *Serial Crime*, published by Academic Press.

Ben Ihle, L.L.B., B.A.

Ben Ihle is a barrister (trial advocate) based in Victoria, Australia. Formerly, he worked as a solicitor for the Victorian Office of Public Prosecutions primarily prosecuting serious indictable offenses. In his practice, Mr. Ihle regularly appears in criminal (for both prosecution and defense) and civil trials before various state and federal courts and tribunals around Australia. He also, on occasion, appears in international tribunals.

From its inception (until its discontinuance), Mr. Ihle was the professional supervisor of the University of Melbourne's Innocence Project, where he worked with students in reviewing cases of alleged miscarriages of justice. He may be contacted at benihle@vicbar.com.au.

Carole McCartney, Ph.D.

Carole McCartney holds an M.A. by research in Criminology and a Ph.D. from the University of Leeds. She is a lecturer in criminal law and criminal justice at the University of Leeds, previously of Bond University, Queensland, Australia. Dr. McCartney has written on Australian justice, Innocence Projects, and DNA and criminal justice, authoring *Forensic Identification and Criminal Justice: Forensic Science, Justice and Risk* (2006). She established an Innocence Project at the University of Leeds in 2005, of which she remains Director. She was project manager for the Nuffield Council on Bioethics report "The Forensic Uses of Bio-information: Ethical Issues" and is currently leading a Nuffield Foundation project on "The Future of Forensic Bioinformation," a teaching project on forensic science education and researching forensic regulation. She has recently secured an EU Marie Curie international research fellowship (2009–2012) on "Forensic Identification Frontiers." She may be contacted by email at lawcim@leeds.ac.uk.

Michael McGrath, M.D.

Michael McGrath is a Board Certified Forensic Psychiatrist, licensed in the State of New York. He is a Clinical Associate Professor in the Department of Psychiatry, University of Rochester School of Medicine and Dentistry, Rochester, New York, and Medical Director & Chair, Department of Behavioral Health, Unity Health System, Rochester, New York.

Dr. McGrath divides his time among administrative, clinical, research, and teaching activities. His areas of expertise include forensic psychiatry and criminal profiling. He has lectured on three continents and is a founding member of the Academy of Behavioral Profiling. He can be contacted at mmcgrath@profiling.org.

Ronald J. Miller, M.S.

Ron Miller holds a Bachelor of Forensic Science from the University of California at Berkeley, where he studied under Dr. Paul L. Kirk and Dr. John I. Thornton. He also holds a Master in Public Service, a Master in Clinical Mental Health, and is a Licensed Marriage and Family Therapist. He loved "working the street" as a police officer and as a crime scene investigator, detective, and EOD team member in the 1970s and 1980s in the San Francisco Bay Area. He left law enforcement due to a vision disorder, and it was then that he sought his graduate education. He found himself continuing to work in the judicial arena doing mental health evaluations and treatment for the courts and critical incident debriefings for public safety and industry. Eventually, he shifted his focus to felony investigations, specializing in homicides, death penalty mitigation investigations, and post-conviction appellate work in state and federal courts as a licensed private investigator in the Pacific Northwest. He can be contacted at rjmiller@behavioralforensics.com.

Wayne A. Petherick, Ph.D.

Wayne Petherick, Ph.D., is Assistant Professor of Criminology at Bond University on Australia's Gold Coast. Dr. Petherick teaches criminal profiling, Behavioral Evidence Analysis, criminal motivations, forensic criminology, and crime and deviance, among other subjects. He also consults to private clients on matters of risk and threat, stalking, miscarriages of justice, and crime prevention.

Dr. Petherick is the author of *Serial Crime: Theoretical and Practical Issues in Behavioral Profiling*, 2nd Edition (2009), and coauthor of *Forensic Victimology* (2008), both with Elsevier Science. He has also published numerous articles on profiling and stalking. Dr. Petherick is a board member of the Academy of Behavioral Profiling and Assistant Editor of the *Journal of Behavioral Profiling*. He can be reached via email at wpetheri@staff.bond.edu.au or wpetheri@profiling.org.

Angela N. Torres, Ph.D.

Angela Torres received her B.A. in Psychology from the University of California at Berkeley and then her Ph.D. in Clinical Psychology from Sam Houston State University. She also completed a one-year internship in clinical psychology at the Federal Medical Center, Federal Bureau of Prisons, in Rochester, Minnesota. Subsequently, she completed a one-year fellowship in forensic psychology. Currently, Dr. Torres is a Licensed Clinical Psychologist and Forensic Evaluator at Central State Hospital, the maximum-security forensic hospital in Petersburg, Virginia. In this capacity, Dr. Torres completes forensic evaluations for the court, such as competency to stand trial and mental status at the time of the offense evaluations. She may be contacted at Angela.Torres@csh.dmhmrsas.virginia.gov.

Brent E. Turvey, M.S.

Brent E. Turvey spent his first years in college on a pre-med track only to change his course of study once his true interests took hold. He received a Bachelor of Science degree from Portland State University in Psychology, with an emphasis on Forensic Psychology, and an additional Bachelor of Science degree in History. He went on to receive his Master's of Science in Forensic Science after studying at the University of New Haven, in West Haven, Connecticut.

Since graduating in 1996, Mr. Turvey has consulted with many agencies, attorneys, and police departments in the United States, Australia, China, Canada, Barbados, and Korea on a range of rapes, homicides, and serial/multiple rape/death cases, as a forensic scientist and criminal profiler. He has also been court qualified as an expert in the areas of criminal profiling, forensic science, victimology, and crime reconstruction.

In August of 2002, he was invited by the Chinese People's Police Security University (CPPSU) in Beijing to lecture before groups of detectives at the Beijing, Wuhan, Hanzou, and Shanghai police bureaus. In 2005, he was invited back to China again, to lecture at the CPPSU, and to the police in Beijing and Xian—after the translation of the second edition of his text into Chinese for the university. In 2007, he was invited to lecture at the First Behavioral Sciences Conference at the Home Team (Police) Academy in Singapore, where he also provided training to their Behavioral Science Unit.

Mr. Turvey is the author of *Criminal Profiling: An Introduction to Behavioral Evidence Analysis*, 1st, 2nd, and 3rd Editions (1999, 2002, 2008); and coauthor of *Rape Investigation Handbook* (2004), *Crime Reconstruction* (2006), and *Forensic Victimology* (2008)—all with Elsevier Science. He is currently a full partner, Forensic Scientist, Criminal Profiler, and Instructor with Forensic Solutions, LLC, and an Adjunct Professor of Justice Studies at Oklahoma City University. He can be contacted via email at bturvey@forensic-science.com.

Foreword

Daniel B. Kennedy
Emeritus Professor of Sociology and Criminal Justice
University of Detroit Mercy

It is with great pleasure that I welcome you to what may be the only contemporary textbook devoted to an explication of forensic criminology. I suspect that many of you already have practiced forensic criminology for some time now or will do so in the future even if you would not normally characterize your efforts by this name. In other words, while the criminological subspecialty known as forensic criminology has not been widely known or readily identified as such, its actual practice permeates both criminal and civil justice courts throughout the common law world. This innovative text will not only help clarify this reality, but I expect it will also provide a basis for future scholar-practitioner contributions to forensic criminology for years to come. At this point, however, discussion of some concepts seems to be in order.

Criminology is concerned with the social and functional origins of law, the etiology and patterns of criminal behavior, and societal responses to and control of this behavior. In other words, criminology is the scientific study of the making of law, the breaking of law, and control of the lawbreakers. Criminology may be academic, as when it is taught and studied. It may be practical, as evidenced by the daily efforts of legislators, law enforcement officers, prosecutors, and defense attorneys, the judiciary, and corrections professionals both in the field and in correctional institutions. Criminology is also forensic, as when criminological knowledge is provided to and utilized by both criminal and civil courts in order to decide the issues before them. It is this last application, of course, which constitutes the substance of this impressive text.

As an evolving field of study, forensic criminology is currently multidisciplinary in nature. Its continuing evolution, however, will no doubt take it to a truly interdisciplinary and perhaps even transdisciplinary level. Even now I am impressed with the abundant common ground I am able to find with my colleagues in psychology, anthropology, political science, law, biology, physics, and even information technology as we discuss forensic criminological issues of mutual interest. Further evidence of the multidisciplinarity of forensic criminology may be gleaned from a review of the impressive biographies of those who contributed to this book.

It should be noted, however, that the practice of forensic criminology is not for everyone. Given the volatility of the issues under litigation, the gravity of the stakes, and the powerful personalities which dominate court systems world-wide, forensic criminologists can be subjected to a great deal of stress. To effectively render professional analyses and opinions under these circumstances, forensic criminologists are advised to remain both flexible and principled. Although they are subject matter specialists within some area of criminology, effective forensic scientists must be able to value and appreciate the contributions offered by a variety of other disciplines. Disciplinary boundaries must willingly be crossed. This flexibility is further demonstrated by the forensic scientist who remembers that while he or she may rule the lab or the classroom, the courtroom is ruled by judges and lawyers. As forensic scientists, we prepare evidence; the judges and lawyers control its application.

By principled, I mean simply that the forensic criminologist should clearly limit himself or herself to the role of expert rather than advocate. Our role is to apply criminological analysis to the issues at hand through the use of mainstream methodologies. Effective forensic criminologists will avoid the pitfalls of advocacy research and emotive statistics. Although some attorneys will readily accept demonstrably slanted testimony, the vast majority of legal professionals want simply to know the ground truth so they can best prepare their cases from that foundation.

The publication of *Forensic Criminology* could not have come at a more exciting and propitious time for this evolving field. As knowledge in the physical sciences, life sciences, and social sciences accumulate at an increasing pace, courts in the United States and other common law countries are demanding an improvement in the reliability of scientific testimony. The *Daubert*, *Kumho*, and *Joiner* cases decided by the U.S. Supreme Court have gone a long way toward keeping junk science out of the courtroom, much to my delight and to the delight of the contributors to this volume. As the evidentiary quality of forensic criminology continues to improve, it may be possible to stem the troubling growth of cases involving miscarriages of justice. However, just as the innocent must be set free, the guilty must be appropriately sanctioned. Likewise, the goals of civil justice are to compensate those who suffer unjustly while at the same time denying enrichment to the undeserving. The continually improving contributions of forensic criminology to both criminal and civil courts go a long way toward achieving these goals.

Finally, I must point out that forensic criminology does more than respond to criminal depredations by providing both knowledge and opinions to criminal and civil courts. Effective forensic criminology also deters criminal and tortious acts by assisting the courts in their attempts to dispense justice in a timely, efficient, and appropriate manner. Forensic criminology allows for both general and specific crime deterrence. Forensic criminology encourages professionalism in police and correctional services by ensuring that the truth of their actions will be known while at the same time discouraging frivolous litigation against public servants. Forensic criminology is a driving force behind the continued improvement in the security posture of mass private property, particularly as the civilized world faces the threat of terrorism. The value of this volume to those endeavors should be readily apparent to those who are perspicacious enough to read and learn from it.

Preface

The Origins of Forensic Criminology

Brent E. Turvey and Wayne A. Petherick

Criminology is generally defined as the scientific study of crime and criminals. If this comes across as overly inclusive, that's because it is meant to. This definition, which is consistent with the majority of criminology texts in use around the world, indeed swells the jurisdiction of criminology further than most outside the community are generally prepared to acknowledge. As described in Reckless (1955, pp. 6–7):

> ...[I]t is clear that criminology is not only a behavioral science but also an applied science and science of manipulation and social control.

> ...It receives contributions from experts in such disciplines as biology, anthropology, physiology, medicine, psychiatry, psychology, social administration, economics, law, political science, and penology and corrections.

A similar and contemporary view is found in McMillan and Roberts (2003, pp. 317–318):

> On one view, criminology characteristically addresses itself to the discipline-defining question: what is crime? Other researchers and theorists would extend the definition to cover all or most aspects of official responses to crime, including policing, prosecution, trial and penal treatment. One might break down this expansive conception of criminology into subdisciplines such as criminal process, penology or victimology, or reconstitute its component parts in terms of intersecting and overlapping concepts such as regulation, risk, trust or restorative justice. The simple rule to remember when confronted with this apparent riot of theorizing is that disciplinary differentiation and rival conceptualizations should be retained and employed if, and only to the extent that, they serve to promote understanding of the issues, questions or phenomena under discussion. The present project calls for a broad, inclusive conception of 'criminology', to set against traditional conceptions of international legal scholarship.

So, setting possibly idiosyncratic terminological preferences and quibbles aside, our advocacy of criminology in ICrimJ [International Criminal Justice] will extend to research on law enforcement, criminal proceedings and penal treatment, in addition to core work on the definition, meaning and causes of crime. Moreover, we mean this conception to embrace pertinent empirical research and theorizing across the broad spectrum of the social and behavioural sciences, regardless of whether particular researchers consider themselves to be 'criminologists' rather than, say, anthropologists, social historians or political sociologists.

This view is repeated in Reid (2003, p. 20) which explains:

Criminology is the scientific study of crime, criminals, criminal behavior, and efforts to regulate crime.

…

Most early teachers of criminology and related subjects were educated in sociology, psychology, political science, or some other related discipline or were practitioners in various fields of criminal justice. Today many professors in the field have a Ph.D. in criminal justice or criminology, although the emphasis on interdisciplinary studies remains strong among many scholars. Perhaps, however, we will never dispute the statement of noted theorist Thorsten Sellin, who stated in 1938 that the "criminologist does not exist who is an expert in all the disciplines which converge in the study of crime."

These conceptual definitions of criminology create myriad intersections between crime, criminality, and scientific study that have made criminologists out of practitioners and researchers from almost every background—some intentionally and some otherwise. For professionals who engage in the study of crime environments and causes, criminology is a social science; for those who study the actions, choices, psychology or personality of criminals, it is a cognitive or behavioral science; and for those who study the correlations between biological factors and criminal behavior, it is a science rendered from chemistry and genetics. To the subject of this textbook, for those seeking to answer investigative and legal questions, criminology is a forensic behavioral science. Each type of scientist approaches crime and criminals within the limits of their scope and means, sometimes crossing purposes with that of another.

This is an excellent time to point out that because the study of crime and criminals is multidisciplinary, no one profession, discipline, or type of scientist may lay a sole claim to the vestments of criminology.

The objective of this textbook is to provide readers with the basic tenets and core disciplinary relationships within *Forensic Criminology*: the scientific study of crime and criminals for the purposes of addressing investigative and legal issues. The vast majority of criminology literature is statistical and theoretical in nature. It deals with groups of offenders and broad crime theory as opposed to applied case examination. This textbook is intended to educate students in an applied fashion regarding the nature and extent of forensic casework that is supported by, dependent on, and interactive with research, theory, and knowledge derived from criminology. It is also intended to act as a preliminary guide for criminologist practitioners working with and within related criminal justice professions—particularly when they are involved with assisting investigations, administrative inquiries, legal proceedings or providing expert findings or testimony under oath. It is offered as an applied scientific subdiscipline within the domain of general criminology, as well as a roadmap to the forensic realm for the uninitiated.

Forensic criminology exists as a discipline within criminology separate from any legal system that may employ its practitioners. It is a science, it is a behavioral science, and it is a forensic science. The underlying theories and methods are not meant to be constructs developed in the courts of law but rather in the courts of science (Thornton, 1994). Like any other scientific practice, it exists beyond legal or national borders as a realm unto itself as it must to be a true discipline. While the scope of its practice and admissibility by different courts around the world can and does vary, the core of forensic criminology and its best practices do not change.

The authors have collaborated on this work with the contributors of this text for the following reasons: despite numerous courses on the subject at colleges and universities all over the world, there is much excitement yet confusion about the specific nature and place of forensic criminology—with no unifying philosophy or guide. Moreover, criminology subjects are often taught by theoretical sociologists without a forensic orientation to large groups of students seeking employment in the areas of forensic science, corrections, law enforcement, and the law. In other words, it is often taught by an abstract group with one philosophy to an applied group that requires another—which can lead to miscommunication, uncertainty, and ignorance. When taught criminology subjects by pure academics and theoreticians (sociologists and criminal justice researchers), students are left without a sense of the practical forensic nature of their work; when taught solely by criminal justice practitioners (law enforcement, lawyers, and forensic technicians), those same students are left without a sense of the relevant theoretical and even scientific underpinnings. The mismatch should be clear, and it is the purpose of this text to bridge this gap in a way that no other has, with a diverse collection of contributors that none other has assembled. Forensic criminology is a bridge between the broad construct of multidisciplinary criminology and forensic examination of individual cases.

Let us explain.

DEFINING THE PROBLEM

Criminology in general suffers from a number of ills that we have long observed and now recognize as both serious and pathological. First, we have observed that many criminologists no longer have a sense of where they came from, or why that is important (let alone that they are even criminologists). Second, we have observed that criminology has been conceptualized and presented at university in the same general fashion for at least 60 years, perhaps more, with few significant developments or advancements. Third, as already mentioned, criminology has an applied forensic component despite being taught in large numbers by nonforensic theoretical social scientists. This means students get only a limited picture of criminology, and sometimes without the high standards and ethical mandates that forensic practice requires. We have also observed a level of forensic ignorance regarding the nature, extent, and implications of criminological research and opinions. That is, if the forensic component of criminology is acknowledged at all. The net result of these conditions at colleges and universities around the world is an ever-growing population of criminology graduates—whether they be police officers, forensic scientists, corrections officers, paralegals, lawyers, or criminological experts—with little or no comprehension of their forensic roots, roles, responsibilities, and opportunities.

These problems have been allowed to suffuse because, over the years, we criminologists have forgotten where we came from, we have forgotten how to act like scientists, and we have repeatedly chosen the path of least political resistance and consequently the least intellectual advancement within the study of crime and criminals. As the reader will soon understand, these problems are pathological, interconnected, and solvable.

The Problem of Origins

In discussing the basic issue of origins with our contemporaries, it becomes clear that we criminologists have forgotten who we are and where we come from.

For example, recently, in a discussion about forensic evidence on a forensic science listserv, a seasoned forensic chemist responded to a news article about crime lab ethics and integrity wherein a crime lab worker was referred to by a reporter as a "criminologist." The forensic chemist offered the following correction: "For the uninformed, Criminalists are physical/natural scientists who analyze physical evidence in forensic labs. Criminologists are social scientists who have nothing to do with the analysis of physical evidence, and do not usually work in crime labs." This response belies a narrow view of the relationship between criminology and forensic science. There are many forensic sciences. A *criminalist* is a particular type of forensic scientist who performs objective testing on physical evidence in a crime lab. Indeed, there are more than a few different subspecialties within laboratory criminalistics. So in fairness this part of the explanation is accurate and even helpful. However, the reference to criminologists being purely social scientists is false. All the forensic sciences are, in fact, subdisciplines of criminology.

Criminology owes its existence to a diverse convergence of professions that attempted to join and then ultimately fractured, causing a broken consensus of precisely what it was and is. Today's students, enrolled in criminology coursework, need only look at the title of their degree program to get a sense of the community: criminology and criminal justice programs tend to be housed within sociology departments, within law schools, or within schools of social science. Full-time instructors tend to be social scientists; part-time faculty tend to be current and ex-law enforcement adjuncts. And that is pretty much how things have been in recent history. However, that's not how things started out.

The origins of criminology as they intersect with formal scientific inquiry are found in a blend of medicine, psychiatry, and criminal anthropology. We are, of course, referring to the work of Cesare Lombroso (1835–1909), an Italian professor of legal medicine at the University of Turin. Lombroso's research in the area of criminal physical and psychological types has led many to refer to him as the "father" of criminology. This history is presented in every introductory criminology text and does not need repeating here.

Shortly after Lombroso published his theories, from the perspective of criminal anthropology and psychiatry, the Austrian Jurist and Professor of Criminology Dr. Hans Gross published his treatises on *Criminal Investigation* (1906) and *Criminal Psychology* (1911).[1] These two works provide explicit instruction for the general investigation of crime, the scientific examination of physical evidence, and the classification of criminal behavior; in addition, they discuss crime causes and criminal motives. Dr. Gross is in essence the "grandfather" of forensic criminology, which includes subspecialties such as criminalistics and criminal profiling (Turvey, 2008). His works remain of utmost importance to both theoreticians and practitioners alike.

[1]These works were originally published in the late 1800s, in Gross's native Austrian-German. The dates given refer to the first editions of English translations.

As shown in Figure 1, the field of criminology was defined by Gross as broad and inclusive. In *Criminal Investigation*, Gross (1906, p. xxvii) argues, "We may remind our readers that the subject with which this book deals in part, Criminal Phenomenology, is but one branch of the wider science of *Criminology*."

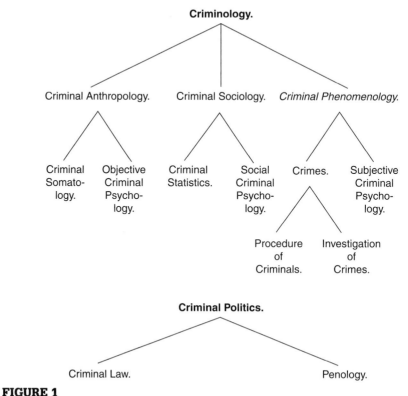

FIGURE 1
The Branches of Criminology, taken from Gross (1906, p. xxvii).

This same philosophy was also adopted to great extent by August Vollmer (1876–1955), the first chief of police in Berkeley, California, and the leading figure behind early efforts to professionalize and modernize law enforcement training and criminal justice education in the United States.

Law Enforcement Education
The true origins of criminal justice education in the United States are found in the groundwork laid by law enforcement educators as they attempted to professionalize the vocation of policing in the early twentieth century (Morn, 1995).

It is indisputable that "the history of policing in the nineteenth-century was characterized by corruption, inefficiency, and partisan politics" (Morn, 1995, p. 26). In an attempt to gain control over this chaos in their individual jurisdictions, some joined forces in the International Association of Chiefs of Police (IACP) to mandate acceptance of scientific advances in crime detection and more rigorous training regimens for police recruits. This was in no small part owing to the negative portrayal of police officers as "keystone cops" in the burgeoning genre of motion pictures. Joined with corruption, cronyism, nepotism, and the long-held practice of hiring officers based on their size rather than ability, an unfavorable public image had emerged, and unfortunately it wasn't far off the mark. Something needed to be done, and that something was formal education and training.

One of those seeking this kind change within policing was August Vollmer, a progressive reformer who believed that law enforcement could and should be professionalized to meet its mandates (see "Key Historical Figures" in Chapter 1 of this text). Vollmer developed police training academies and courses of study by fostering relationships with a number of different colleges and universities over the span of his career, but in the end he was frustrated by the academic community. Two things in specific caused friction. First was the tendency of academics to focus on social work as a primary function of policing while investigations and investigative concerns were sidelined. Vollmer held the opposite to be true: he wanted to train crime fighters. Second was the tendency of academics to be critical of every aspect of policing despite knowing very little about its actual practice (Morn, 1995). While he was not above criticizing the obvious shortcomings and even laziness among his fellow police chiefs, along with the rank and file, Vollmer had little use for those who did nothing else.

Regardless, colleges and university were viewed as necessary for the professionalization of law enforcement—to alter general perception of police officers as ignorant, unprincipled, and heavy handed. This situation posed a problem of control. Understandably, those in law enforcement wanted to maintain control over the instruction of any future applicants. They wanted to regulate and dictate the subjects students were being taught, how they were being taught to view the world of crime and policing, and also to engender a sense of loyalty to police culture. College and university programs, on the other hand, tend to be populated by academic scholars who have been taught to think critically and with no allegiance to law enforcement traditions. Few in law enforcement had sufficient credentials to teach in higher education, but if they handed the reins over to those in academia, then graduates would not necessarily be all that desirable. This conflict in higher education remains a problem to this day and will be discussed further throughout this text.

Despite their ignorance of the practical concerns of police officers and police culture, Vollmer still maintained a healthy respect for academic scholars because he understood both the necessity and the merits of involvement in higher education. As a consequence, in 1941, when he agreed to participate with a group of his former students (by then well-respected police educators in their own right) in the formation of an organization to effect the professionalization of law enforcement by virtue of advancement in education and training, he lobbied for the involvement of those outside law enforcement. There was open disagreement, as explained in Morn (1995, pp. 70–71):

> Almost immediately Vollmer and [William] Wiltberger[2] split over the fundamental direction of the proposed organization. The San Jose contingent felt that association membership should be restricted to the heads of college police schools. Vollmer, on the other hand, with strong support from [O. W.] Wilson and [V. A.] Leonard [well established "V-Men"], felt "that we should include outstanding professors in the social sciences and criminology," a position that was given face acceptance but was modified in the bylaws by limiting membership to those working in police training programs in accredited colleges.

The organization that formed was to become the American Society of Criminology. Originally, it was called the Association of Heads of Police Schools. Wiltberger hated the name change, arguing to Vollmer in 1949, "My interest is in turning out expert police officers, not criminologists" (Morn, 1995 p. 71). It could be argued that he saw the coming struggle for control over both the organization and the professional education of police officers and sought to avoid it. Or it could be argued that he simply had no use for those in academia. Either way, he couldn't stop what was to come.

The American Society of Criminology (ASC)

The organizational meeting of the National Association of College Police Training Officials (originally called the Association of Heads of Police Schools, and later to become the American Society of Criminology) was held during the last days of December 1941 in Berkeley, California—at the home of August Vollmer. It was attended by Vollmer, who was by then a retired Professor of Police Administration at the University of California; Robert L. Drexel, Chief Investigator of the District Attorney's Office in San Jose, California; Vivian A. Leonard, Professor and Head of the Department of Police Science and Administration at Washington State College in Pullman, Washington; Benjamin W. Pavone, Chairman of the Peace Officers Training Division at San Francisco Junior College in San Francisco, California; Willard E. Schmidt, Director of Police Training at Sacramento Junior College in Sacramento, California; Orlando W. Wilson, Professor of Police Administration and Director of the Bureau of Criminology at the University California, Berkeley; William Wiltberger, Director of the Police School at San Jose State College in San Jose, California; and Frank Lee, formerly Director of the National Police

[2] Wiltberger was one of Vollmer's early students (referred to as "V-Men" or "college cops"). At the time of this meeting, he already had a long career in both law enforcement and academia, and served as head of the two-year police school program at San Jose State. He practiced what has been referred to as a "Wiltbergering Model" of education wherein police schools exist at a college or university separate from the bureaucracy and student body of scholarly programs in order to "train people to do police work, to act as a placement service for its graduates, and to be a center of service for the various police departments in the area" (Morn, 1995, p. 45).

Academy in China (Morris, 1975). It was first and foremost a gathering of "Police Science"[3] educators—old friends and students of Vollmer who shared a common interest in teaching students entering or working in law enforcement. As explained in Morris (1975):

> The organization, thus started, attracted to membership officers of rank concerned with police training from the major police forces of California and some neighboring states, as well as those engaged in college teaching in the field. But if its focus was on police training it was with the conviction that the professionalism of police forces was its goal and that this required that police—and especially police administrators become broadly informed in the entire area of criminology and in the principles of such related areas as public administration, political science, psychology, and sociology.

> Vollmer's interest in developing a formal organization, concerned with the extension and improvement of police training, was an almost inevitable step in his own long-existing personal commitment to that objective. Probably the most widely known and most innovative police chief in American police history, August Vollmer (1876–1955) had been Marshal of Berkeley (1905–1909) the first Police Chief of Berkeley (1909–1932) and Professor of Police Administration at the University of California at Berkeley (1932–1937), and was widely sought as a consultant in police administration. He was physically an imposing person (6′4″ tall and weighing about 190 lbs.) who always seemed to be in top physical condition. He was a broadly informed and creative man with a contagious enthusiasm for making police work a profession with a highly trained core of persons who had college degrees and who could teach at the college level. As early as 1916, Vollmer, in collaboration with law professor Alexander Marsden Kidd, developed a summer session

---

[3]*Police science* is a generic term that is used in reference to any study or discipline that intersects with or informs police work. It was developed by law enforcement instructors to further delineate police study programs from scholarly criminal justice programs. As discussed in Williams (1995, p. 181):

> …[P]olice science departments preceded criminology departments in colleges and universities. While often difficult to distinguish from each other, police science departments usually focus more on the technical aspects of police: administration, management, crime analysis, and the "doing" of law enforcement. Criminology, when it deals with the police province, more often uses the "system in action" focus. Thus criminological approaches to the problem of policing are apt to be sociological in nature and to focus on informal structures and relationships.

Those studying police science at college or university are necessarily preparing for careers associated with the process of policing and not the scientific study or examination of evidence. Police science subjects and texts intersect only somewhat with forensic science in terms of police use of technology. This relationship will be discussed further in the first chapter, as well as in the chapter on forensic science.

program in criminology at the Berkeley campus in which courses were given from 1916 to 1931, with the exception of the 1927 session.

It was Vollmer and Kidd who in 1928 proposed the establishment of a school of criminology, a proposal that led in 1931 to criminology course in the regular school year sessions at the University of California at Berkeley, the development of a major in criminology in 1933, a Bureau of Criminology in the Department of Political Science in 1939, a Master's program in Criminology in 1947, and the establishment of the nation's first and only formally designated university "School of Criminology" in 1950.

Vollmer regarded the absence of education and proper qualification as law enforcement's greatest weakness, as detailed in Vollmer (1971, pp. 3–4):

The poor quality of the personnel is perhaps the greatest weakness of police departments in the United States. In departments of all sizes, the percentage of men suited to police work is woefully small. Far too many policemen are purely political appointees, with no technical knowledge of the work and quite unsuited to it. Even among those who may be considered fit, some have been unable to get all the training that is requisite to the adequate discharge of their functions.... The greater number of these men are badly placed and inadequately trained, yet they are charged with a task that would be difficult for men of the highest quality and skill.

Thus, Vollmer not only sought to professionalize the ranks of law enforcement and its many support staff, he sought the development and nurturing of university programs that would ensure educated police applicants with an appreciation for all that logic and science could bring to bear in their work. It was holistic, it was forward thinking, and it was inclusive. Scientific analysis and rational problem solving were things that police officers should understand and incorporate into their methods of operation. Consequently, a college education was something to be viewed with high regard and not ridiculed as irrelevant to the task of policing.

This was the legacy of August Vollmer, and it can still be found in the work of many criminology practitioners to this day.

Unfortunately, within a decade the ASC became overrun with academic sociologists—the very ones that Vollmer had invited over the protestations of those in support of a "Wiltbergerian Model" of police education. Consequently, by the early 1960s, more than a few police professors felt "sufficiently alienated from the Society they had helped to found that they contemplated forming a new one" (Morn, 1995, p. 81). The organization that they formed was the International Association of Police Professors, which later became the Academy of Criminal Justice Sciences (ACJS), and it became home to the displaced Vollmerites.

Presently, criminal justice educators remain critical of the ASC, arguing that it is an organization of "Ivory Tower" sociology-oriented intellectuals and statisticians consumed by theoretical empiricism that lacks real-world application or utility. This is a far cry from where it began—as a practitioner's organization governed by caseworkers who were grounded by the relevance of their education on the one hand and the breadth of their experience on the other. The organizational shift has been so great that it has changed the way that we conceive, culturally, of criminology and criminologists in our immediate present.

There are more than a few reasons for this, and they are related to the *problem of authority* to be discussed presently. In essence, there was a shift away from formal education within law enforcement. Many of those in the rank and file did not respect those at university and consequently did not want to be educated by them. They viewed college courses as a waste of time and experience as the only true teacher of anything. Education was viewed with disdain in no small part by those who had done the job for years without it. They sought to "professionalize" themselves with "law enforcement only" professional organizations, often excluding those teaching or educated at university. Shades of this unfortunate attitude and practice remain for some to the present day.

Theoretical Criminology vs. Crime Fighting

The separation between theorist and practitioner is often nothing short of contemptuous. Law-enforcement-oriented practitioners see themselves at odds with those they view as working only with theory, and those who study theory see themselves as intellectually superior to the variety of practitioners they are meant to provide research support for. Too often, neither side seems to appreciate that they are working toward the same goal: to enrich the scientific study of crime and criminals to be able to detect, identify, apprehend, and adjudicate suspected criminal offenders.

Perhaps this is owing to the utter ignorance of crime theorists about the true nature of crime and the everyday needs of those seeking to investigate it for lack of actual exposure to either.

Perhaps, also, the reason is that the methods and assumptions of these opposing groups are at odds. Law-enforcement-oriented practitioners seek to "build cases" against suspects through the lenses of authority and suspicion, while the scientist seeks to understand events and is meant to embrace the scientific examination of criminal behavior. Law enforcement practitioners seek to create an aura of certainty and confirmation regarding their theories; scientists are intended to be skeptical and expose doubt. When suspects must ultimately be convicted by court-worthy evidence, beyond a reasonable doubt, it is not impossible to understand why scientific inquiry has been generally unwelcome by many criminal justice practitioners.

Early on, this division left those working in police crime labs with a problem of branding. They needed a scientific education; they needed police science, criminology, and criminal justice programs offered at university. But unfortunately, they were operating under a label that officers on the street had lost respect for: that of criminologist.

Criminologists and Criminalists

As we mentioned at the beginning of this section on the problem of origins, the current popular view is that criminologists as professionals are limited to the ranks of theoretical sociologists. By now it is evident that this perception is overly narrow and uninformed by the diverse history of criminology practice. Criminology was and remains an applied discipline for many, as we will demonstrate throughout this text.

Truth be told, the first crime laboratory scientists were actually referred to by job title and general description as "criminologists." This is reflected in the pages of what is arguably the very first forensic science textbook published in the United States, *Crime's Nemesis* (May, 1936). In this groundbreaking text, the author refers to the practice of crime detection and evidence examination as the field of "scientific criminology" (p. ix) and to those working in it as "scientific criminologists" (p. 2). He further refers to himself, in bold letters on the cover page, as "LUKE S. MAY, CRIMINOLOGIST, Director, The Scientific Detective Laboratories; President, The Institute of Scientific Criminology." The word *criminalist* is absent, while the works of Hans Gross are cited repeatedly within.

As explained by the late criminalist Lowell Bradford (1918–2007) in his paper regarding the origins of the California Association of Criminalists, founded in 1954 (Bradford, 2007, p. 5):

> ...I first entered into the field of criminalistics in 1947 in the California State Crime Laboratory in Sacramento.... In those days, the terms criminalistics and criminalist were not in use. Those of us in the state crime laboratory had civil service position titles of criminologist. It remained for James P. Osterburg to publish "An Introduction to Criminalistics" in 1949, which marked the beginning of the usage of the terms in this country. "Crime Investigation" by Paul L. Kirk in 1953 closely followed and gave full meaning to "criminalistics."

Duayne Dillon, then Chief of the Criminalistics Laboratory for the Office of the Sheriff-Coroner in Contra Costa County, California, wrote the foreword to the second printing of Osterburg's text mentioned in Bradford (2007). He sheds light on the issue of precisely how the *criminalist* is defined as separate from the *criminologist*, while crediting the authors of *An Introduction to Criminalistics* with helping engender community acceptance for the term (Dillon, 1972):

The authors were not only responsible for introducing many of the principles and practices of Criminalistics in an organized manner, but were a prime factor in the subsequent acceptance of the term "criminalistics" to describe the profession engaged in the examination, evaluation, and interpretation of physical evidence.

Most forensic science authors have actually credited the formulation of modern criminalistics as a discipline to the aforementioned Jurist and Professor of Criminology Hans Gross, in no small part because he coined the term *Kriminalistik*, from which our use of the terms *criminalistics* and *criminalist* were derived (Chisum and Turvey, 2007; DeForest, Gaennslen, and Lee, 1983; Inman and Rudin, 2000; Turner, 1995). However, it must be admitted that the term *Kriminalistic* translates literally from Austrian-German to English as *Criminology*. Moreover a *Kriminalist*, by Gross's definition, was a generalist who studied the causes of crime, the behaviors and motives of criminals, and the scientific methods of their identification, apprehension, and prosecution (Gross, 1906). The concept was intended to be inclusive of police officers, investigators, crime lab personnel, forensic pathologists, and forensic psychologists—anyone involved in the practice of applying criminology to casework (criminal investigation, forensic detection and identification, etc.). It was wholly mimicked and repeated by early criminology practitioners in the United States such as Luke May upon the publication of English translations of Gross's works.

Regardless of the original definition and intent, the term *criminalistics* was borrowed from the works of Gross in the late 1940s. The burgeoning forensic science community needed a way to conceptually separate those criminologists working in police crime labs from future police officers (and social scientists) studying in criminology, criminal justice, and police science programs at university. Their aim was to help professionalize the scientific examination and interpretation of physical evidence with specific principles and practice borrowed from criminology as well as the natural sciences. They began referring to themselves as criminalists and to their work as criminalistics. This rebranding was widely accepted within the police lab community, as evidenced by the literature and the formation of associated professional organizations, including the California Association of Criminalists.

All of this bears mentioning because modern-day criminalists and criminologists alike appear to have forgotten their history of association and interdependence. As a result there has been confusion within both communities and inconsistencies in reference to either by those professions looking in from the outside.

Criminology, it must be understood, is a vast field with many subdisciplines. History teaches us that forensic science and the subdiscipline of criminalistics are among them, alongside others such as criminal investigation, forensic psychology, victimology, criminal profiling, and many, many more. The failure to recognize and embrace these relationships is a manifestation of professional dissociation and isolationism that fosters interdisciplinary ignorance and prevents professional development.

The Problem of Authority

Compounding the problem of professional identity among criminologists is the ignorance of those who are generally asked to teach it. Unfortunately, the vast majority of university-based criminologists who lecture on the subject, largely from a narrow theoretical perspective, reinforce the view that criminology is limited to the confines of a theoretical sociological discipline. This oversimplifies things dramatically. As warned by Vollmer (1949, p. 19): "Absence of a clear understanding of the vastly complex nature of crime and criminality is not confined to the layman." Consider further the admonition offered regarding the contemporary characterization of criminology in Williams (1995, p. 179):

> Criminology is generally understood to be an offspring of the discipline of sociology. While this is arguably the case, such a statement slights both the history of criminology and the various disciplines that comprise the breadth of the field… in spite of this sociological focus, it should be recognized that criminology is characterized by a relative integration of materials from several disciplines. The advent and rise, through the last three decades, of the multidisciplinary field of criminal justice has challenged sociology as the training round for criminology, and many criminologists are now either working in or receiving their academic training from criminal justice departments. This movement promises to more directly integrate sociological criminology with other disciplines.

We regard Williams's perspective as optimistic, as he does not speak to the consequences of multidisciplinary integration—which we saw with the formation and fracturing of the ASC.

In the modern university there are indeed few full and distinct criminology departments—especially in the United States. Rather it is more common for small criminology programs to be housed within a larger sociology department or to exist in concert within a criminal justice program. Full-time faculty instructors therefore tend to be drawn from a pool of Ph.D.-educated theoretical sociologists or criminal justice educators. Part-time faculty, conversely, tend to be current and ex-law enforcement employees with and without formal education in order to round out the applied subjects. Under the best circumstances, these instructors would compare notes and curricula, augmenting each other's shortcomings. This kind of cooperation and mutual respect within criminology is, to put it gently, unusual.

As previously mentioned, there is often enmity between the social scientist and the criminal justice practitioner. The Ph.D. tends to think that the practitioner is uneducated, cynical, and even pedantic—acting without knowing; the practitioner tends to think that the Ph.D. is out of touch with real-life problems and solutions—consumed with all things intellectual and impractical. One is concerned with investigating crime causes and social issues as prescribed by the mandates of good science; the other enters higher education having spent a career concerned with the day-to-day function of protecting citizens and investigating crime as prescribed by the legal community. Keeping the scholar and the crime-fighter from working together in higher education is the fact that both have completely different agendas and harbor well-founded criticism of each other.

Such a teaching environment, which is common, facilitates a practical disconnect between many students and their intended careers. Students who seek degrees in criminology, criminal justice, or criminal justice administration are very often navigating directly toward a career in law enforcement, forensic science, corrections, or law. These are applied professions with practical as opposed to theoretical issues and concerns. Learning about crime theory, law enforcement, corrections, and law from a theoretical sociologist with limited applied knowledge or case experience in these areas can be confusing if not completely frustrating—especially to the student who is already a professional.

Students of criminology and criminal justice need a strong foundation in science and crime theory as part of their holistic liberal arts education. That is a given. However, with respect to criminology, they also need the benefit of an instructor's case-based knowledge and experience so that theory can be given context, meaning, and ultimately be of use when they hit the streets or start examining cases. If students are taught about crime and criminals only by instructors inexperienced with casework involving either, for having spent a life entirely within university, something important is lost. Additionally, when teaching staff lack the educational and even scientific foundation to effectively organize and convey the lessons they have learned in the field, all the experience in the world will not help them teach a classroom full of students.[4]

What we are left with is the realization that not everyone who teaches criminology is actually a practicing criminologist, even though he or she may be employed within a criminology department at a well-regarded university. Vollmer (1949, pp. 38–39) correctly explains that

> Every person who writes or lectures about crime, or who occupies a position which requires him to deal with crime or criminals is mislabeled a criminologist. It is assumed, therefore, that he is able to speak with authority on all phases of the subject. Nothing could be further from the truth.

Authority and ability in the area of criminology, given its applied origins and subject matter, must come from an amalgam of education and experience. This is especially

[4]Best practice, as proscribed in the recent National Academy of Science (NAS) Report, "Strengthening Forensic Science in the United States: A Path Forward," embraces the fact that experience and on-the-job training are an inadequate substitute for a formal scientific education (Edwards and Gotsonis, 2009).

true when teaching students who are intent upon entering the many applied professions associated with it, to be discussed at length in this text. Currently, this is an area where many criminology and criminal justice programs may be lacking—being too heavy in one direction or the other. The consequences to students, particularly in light of the forensic landscape awaiting them, can be dire.

The Death of Real Magic

The forefathers of modern criminology, and subsequently forensic criminology, were practitioners concerned with the peculiar needs of case examination rather than just broad social research. They were defined by the problems presented to them in criminal and even civil cases. How, then, did we criminologists start down the path of studying groups rather than individuals, or broad theoretical constructs rather than the degree to which they apply in a given case? The answer, it seems, is magic.

While undoubtedly metaphorical, one of the authors (Petherick) was once told a story regarding "the death of real magic." This story has, as its central premise, the notion that magic was once a reality, and that the "magician" was a real person who could bend space and time, materialize objects out of thin air, and transmute the mundane into precious treasure. The story goes that, over time, the skills of magicians stopped being passed from one generation to the next. Perhaps this was because of a loss of interest in magic itself, an increase in the study of the tangible (so a change of focus), religious pressure, or, in the extreme, the active hunting and eradication of witches or magicians (occurring during the "witch hunts" around the world). The story can involve any or all of these.

Regardless of reason or cause, magicians lost their skills over successive generations. This happened to the point that modern "magicians" are so bereft of actual magical skills that they are, irrespective of technical talent, left to sleight of hand and misdirection rather than the magic of old.

To the critical thinker or skeptic, the possibility of real magic is absurd. It is, some will scoff, nothing more than a bedtime story or the ability of one to fool the eye of another. All of this is true—but there is more to it than that.

Consider that this story regarding "magic" is actually a metaphor for how skills are lost over time. Consider now not the magician, but the forensic practitioner; consider also the history of criminology, where we are now, and where it seems we may be going. The story becomes less and less far-fetched as we progress.

When criminology was born as a formal area of study, impetus came from the need to examine particular cases, requiring those involved to bring all that science could bear in its understanding. The practice was about the gathering of knowledge; the determination of scientific fact; the answering questions to determine and contextualize criminal identity and behavior. These practitioners were, for our comparative purposes, the magicians of old.

Over time, with the establishment of forensic units in police agencies and government crime labs, private forensic practitioners and those teaching "scientific criminology" at university were sidelined in what was and remains a turf war over authority and expertise in criminology—as already discussed. Fearing the education that they did not have, which highlighted their lack of knowledge and proficiency, those involved in law enforcement all but barricaded themselves away from formal education. The university educators that followed lost their law enforcement connections and hence their applied component. Successive generations could only become researchers and academics focused not on individual cases (which they no longer had access to), but rather on broad social problems—such as why one group commits more crime than another, or why females often commit different crimes than males. Law enforcement practitioners became entrenched in knowledge drawn from experience; academics, conversely, became entrenched in empirical research and theoretical knowledge. Each became irrelevant to the ends of the other—or so they perceive and are content to repeat as gospel.[5] This is a myth that we hope to expose.

The Problem of Development in Criminology

Another problem we observe in the field of general criminology is the absence of development. As mentioned, criminology is largely taught by academics to current and would-be practitioners, or by those without the educational dexterity to go beyond their training. As a direct consequence, there has been little stake in advancing the core theories and literature of criminology outside specialized research projects on certain crimes and criminals, let alone an ability among practitioners to do so. This can be established by opening a sample of any five criminology textbooks published over the past 40 to 50 years—starting with the oldest. They will generally have the same chapter sections and even titles, with only the names of authors varying. In truth, significant developments in the area of criminology during this time frame are limited to the origination of critical criminology, victimology, forensic victimology, and recent research focused on miscarriages of justice by the legal community. However, the core theories and subject matter in criminology remain the same, with few criminology texts covering these burgeoning areas.

This needs to change for the literature to remain relevant and for the field to advance.

[5]The exception which proves this rule are those criminology, criminal justice, and police science programs that are designed essentially as trade or vocational schools for law-enforcement-related employment. In such programs, the average student either works in law enforcement of some kind or intends to. Not all programs are like this, but many are.

FAILED EDUCATION

We should begin by explaining to students up front that a failed education is not your fault. You have been prepared inadequately, rewarded inappropriately, and shaped ineptly with respect to thought and reason. But upon being shown what is needed in the sciences and in the forensic realm, you are responsible for engaging in and setting a new educational heading.

The vast majority of students encountered by the authors, even at university, do not know how to think rationally. Theirs is a world of belief, emotions, and reactions—not of deliberate analytical thought. They have, in general, been pitched into what should be the crucible of higher education based on a "teach to test" model of instruction that has failed them in every meaningful way. They often lack the ability to perform meaningful research or understand why that might be important; they often lack the skill to write a basic thesis paper in comprehensible language or to support that thesis in a meaningful fashion with calculated argumentation; and they often lack the intellectual dexterity to comprehend what they have read or the patience to be bothered with reading at all. When students are confronted with these limitations, their responses range from entitlement to hostility, an appreciation of personal responsibility being the least common. If anything, students arrive at university having become experts at concealing how little knowledge they have accumulated, even from themselves.

For those who might suggest such statements are over the top, consider a 2007 study conducted by The State Education Agency, formed by the U.S. Department of Education, which found that 36% of Washington, D.C., residents are functionally illiterate. This contrasts with the national rate of functional illiteracy at around 21% (Montent, 2007). Functional illiteracy refers to those who can read and write, but have difficulty with basic everyday reading and writing tasks such as understanding bus schedules or navigating the newspaper, and filling out government forms or resumes.

These findings are even more significant when viewed in the light of results from a nationwide writing test published in 2008, which found "[a]bout one-third of America's eighth-grade students, and about one in four high school seniors, are proficient writers" (Dillon, 2008). A number of educators and education administrators have defended these and similar numbers as a success story. However, that seems a deeply misplaced, and also self-preserving, characterization. Put another way, two-thirds of eighth-grade students and three in four high school seniors lack basic essay writing proficiency. When discussing these results, the librarian of Congress felt compelled to question what U.S. students were and were not being taught that they should achieve so poorly on something so basic (Dillon, 2008):

> James H. Billington, the librarian of Congress, drew laughs when he expressed concern about what he called "the slow destruction of the basic unit of human thought, the sentence," because young Americans are doing most of their writing in disjointed prose composed in Internet chat rooms or in cellphone text messages.

> "The sentence is the biggest casualty," Mr. Billington said. "To what extent is students' writing getting clearer? Is that still being taught?"

The authors would argue, as both frontline university educators as well as parents of children in public schools, that this is no laughing matter. A high school student who cannot write coherently will necessarily fail to meet the mandates of good scientific practice—to say nothing of the student who graduates and is also functionally illiterate. Therefore, it is more than fair to say that high school education currently stands in the way of academic scholarship rather than being something that naturally produces it.

Students are, to be fair, products of more than one imperfect educational environment. At primary and secondary school, they may have learned from teachers not to deviate from the letter of their assignments in order to receive a passing grade. At home, they may have learned from parents not to question authority so they may receive spending money or the keys to the car. At church, they may have learned not to doubt so they may receive fellowship and forgiveness. Among their peers, they may have learned to conform so they may receive social acceptance and companionship. It is fair to say that any knowledge or insight that gets in the way of the requirements prescribed in these often-competing cultures is met with hostility or denial and then summarily closeted. It is the rare individual who transcends these crushing influences to become his or her own free and critical thinking person.

Even at university, students are met with intellectual intolerance by the smallest of professorial minds. They are too often rewarded for pedantic regurgitating of dated or hastily assembled material fed to them in the classroom, and punished for seeking information or knowledge that is outside or above the abilities of their lecturers. Lecturers, we would add, that are too frequently drawn from graduate students incapable of advanced appreciation of any subject matter for lack of applied experience with it. This is to say nothing of receiving out-of-date lectures from prominent university minds that have simply failed to keep up with developments in their respective fields.

As the product of such environments, many students are incapable of knowing when they are thinking competently. They are all the more incapable of knowing when they are wrong, or even whether that possibility exists. Worse, if they have routinely achieved a desired outcome in a particular setting—such as passing grades or social acceptance—they may actually come to believe that they are performing reasonably well.

These circumstances of widespread functional illiteracy, a general lack of proficiency in writing, institutional hostility toward critical thinking, and rewards for conformity in thought and practice have gathered and combined to institute a crisis of ignorant overconfidence in students and professionals alike—as the first group becomes the second. This is something that the mandates of good science cannot afford. Science requires doubt and skepticism.

Science requires analytical and objective practice. Science requires literacy. Working within the forensic domain requires even more.

THE FORENSIC REALM

As already discussed, criminology and criminal justice programs around the world are primarily attended by students seeking eventual employment within the fields of law enforcement, corrections, forensic science, and the law. Or by those inside these same professions who are working toward advancement and pay raises within their respective agencies by virtue of increasing individual educational holdings. In other words, the students and professionals attending these programs must develop a working knowledge of investigative and/or legal issues, practices, and standards to do their work and get promoted. This is the forensic realm: the world of investigations, courts, and law.

Achieving basic forensic knowledge is not a simple matter, as the mandates of the forensic realm place students at crossed purposes with scientific, public safety, and legal mandates. They must learn to distinguish scientific fact from legal truth; to appreciate how investigative thresholds for evidence are a great deal less than scientific standards, and a great deal different from legal ones; and to understand the role that they seek to uphold in the criminal justice system—be that of factual witness, impartial examiner, or zealous advocate—as well as the importance of each to the others.

The varying issues, practices, and standards peculiar to the forensic realm are nothing short of vital to student survival and prosperity once employment has been secured. However, the authors have routinely observed that these same issues are too often all but foreign to those teaching coursework within criminology and criminal justice programs. Not all of the time, but more often than not. For example, while crime theory and criminal motivation may be within a particular instructor's grasp from a research or law enforcement perspective, that instructor may have no appreciation for the limits of expert forensic testimony, the admissibility issues related to expert forensic findings, and the case law which governs the circumstances around which such testimony is more probative than prejudicial—let alone why all of this is important to consider before an officer, investigator, or forensic examiner writes a report or a lawyer files a motion. This remains true whether this instructor holds a Ph.D. in sociology and full professorship, is an adjunct lecturer retired after 25 years on the job as a police detective, or works for the state crime lab as a hair and fiber analyst and offers guest lectures once or twice a semester for a local community college. Criminal justice practitioners such as these know their own narrow section of the river and seldom venture into the upper reaches—for whatever reason.

In short, those teaching in criminology and criminal justice programs are seldom thinking forensically about the instruction of their subjects because they are unaware that they should. They largely come to teach subjects either as theoreticians, as law enforcement, or as the guests of either. Subsequently, the mandates of the forensic realm are not front and center, and the necessity of imprinting students with a forensic mindset is not understood.

As a consequence of all these things working against each other, the problems with criminology and criminal justice programs have been inherited by the professions they ultimately serve. Students are generally unprepared, philosophically and otherwise, for the work they seek because they are being taught by those with limited knowledge of its nature, and little or no investment in its future. And, in particular, the enmity between law enforcement and academia is perpetuated.

A MULTIDISCIPLINARY SOLUTION

To help resolve some of these issues, to educate criminology and criminal justice educators, and to give them a tool in their constant struggle to connect with the forensic disciplines on a practical level, the authors and contributors of this text seek primarily to define the nature and scope of the subject of *Forensic Criminology*. It is best conceived as the applied case examination aspect of criminology and criminal justice, concerned with studying crime and criminals for the explicit purposes of addressing investigative and legal issues. It also provides the rationale for teaching current and future forensic professionals within the criminology and criminal justice programs that are currently in existence. That is, so long as they begin to embrace an applied, scientific, and forensic aspect to their instruction.

Along with our primary ambition, two additional goals are reached with this text. First, it provides students of criminology and criminal justice with an introduction to the forensic realm. It exposes them to the various disciplines they will encounter at work in the criminal justice system from the perspective of practitioners currently in the field. It also exposes them to the major applied forensic issues they must face and resolve no matter what path they choose within the myriad professions that comprise forensic criminology. Rather than being primarily a text full of theory, it effectively bridges the world of general criminology with the applied world of the criminal justice system. Second, this text will ultimately serve as a career guide for students of criminology and criminal justice. It will let them know not only the professions that exist, but also their roles and responsibilities. In terms of deciding their future, there has been no better introduction and no clearer guide.

REFERENCES

Bradford, L., 2007. The Genesis of the CAC [California Association of Criminalists]. CAC News 3rd Quarter, 5 (Originally presented at the 100th Semiannual Seminar of the CAC, Huntington Beach, Fall 2002).

Chisum, W.J., Turvey, B., 2006. Crime Reconstruction. Elsevier Science, Boston.

DeForest, P., Gaennslen, R., Lee, H., 1983. Forensic Science: An Introduction to Criminalistics. McGraw-Hill, New York.

Dillon, D., 1972. Foreword. In: O'Hara, C., Osterburg, J. (Ed.), Criminalistics: The Application of Physical Sciences to the Detection of Crime, Second Printing. Indiana University Press, Bloomington, IN.

Dillon, S., 2008. In Test, Few Students Are Proficient Writers. The New York Times April 3.

Edwards, H., Gotsonis, C., 2009. Strengthening Forensic Science in the United States: A Path Forward. National Academies Press, Washington, D.C.

Gross, H. (1906) Criminal Investigation. G. Ramasawmy Chetty & Co., Madras.

Gross, H., 1911. Criminal Psychology. Little, Brown, & Co, New York.

Inman, K., Rudin, N., 2000. Principles and Practice of Criminalistics: The Profession of Forensic Science. CRC Press, Boca Raton, FL.

May, L., 1936. Crime's Nemesis. MacMillan Company, New York.

McMillan, N., Roberts, P., 2003. For Criminology in International Criminal Justice. Journal of International Criminal Justice 1 (1), 315–338.

Montent, M., 2007. More Than One-Third of Washington D.C. Residents Are Functionally Illiterate. Associated Content. Available at http://www.associatedcontent.com/article/183792/more_than_onethird_of_washington_dc.html

Morris, A., 1975. The American Society of Criminology: A History, 1941–1974. Criminology (August), 123–167.

Morn, F., 1995. Academic Politics and the History of Criminal Justice Education. Greenwood Press, Westport, CT.

Reckless, W., 1955. The Crime Problem, second ed. Appleton-Century-Crofts, Inc., New York.

Reid, S., 2003. Crime and Criminology, tenth ed., McGraw Hill, Boston.

Thornton, J.I. 1994. Courts of Law v. Courts of Science: A Forensic Scientist's Reaction to Daubert. Shepard's Scientific and Evidence Quarterly, 1 (3), 475–485.

Turner, R., 1995. Forensic Science. In: Bailey, W. (Ed.), The Encyclopedia of Police Science. Garland Publishing, New York, pp. 321–326.

Turvey, B., 2008. Criminal Profiling, third ed., Elsevier Science, San Diego.

Vollmer, A., 1949. The Criminal. Foundation Press, Brooklyn.

Vollmer, A., 1971. The Police and Modern Society. Patterson Smith, Montclair, NJ. Reprint of Vollmer, A., 1936. The Police and Modern Society. University of California Press, Berkeley.

Williams, F., (1995) Criminology. In: Bailey, W. (Ed.), The Encyclopedia of Police Science. Garland Publishing, New York, pp. 178–184.

PART

1

Forensic Criminology, the Forensic Criminologist, and the Law

CHAPTER 1

An Introduction to Forensic Criminology

Brent E. Turvey and Wayne Petherick

The only guarantee that the administration of justice is truly democratic from initiation to conclusion is that the value systems of those who administer such justice are indeed democratic. The most effective means ever found to insure the inculcation of such a value system is analytic education.

Hoover (1995, p. 247)

KEY TERMS

Adversarial System: A legal system in which at least two opposing sides contend against each other for a result most favorable to themselves.

Applied Criminology: The application of criminological theory to criminal justice practice. This includes the application of criminological knowledge to the making of laws, the management of police agencies, the management of prisoners, and the treatment of victims.

Corrections: The branch of the criminal justice system that deals with the probation, incarceration, management, rehabilitation, treatment, parole, and execution of convicted criminals.

Criminal Justice System: The network of government and private agencies that deal with accused and convicted criminals.

Criminologist: An individual who studies and interprets the biological, social, behavioral, and/or cognitive aspects of crime and criminality.

Criminology: The scientific study of crime and criminals, including biological factors, psychological factors, victim traits, punishments, and the control and prevention of crime.

Forensic Criminology: The scientific study of crime and criminals for the purpose of addressing investigative and legal questions.

Forensic Services: The branch of the criminal justice system that deals with the examination and interpretation of evidence, be it physical, behavioral, or testimonial.

CONTENTS

3

Judiciary: The branch of the criminal justice system that deals with the adjudication and exoneration or punishment of criminal defendants.

Law Enforcement: The branch of the criminal justice system that deals with reported crime.

Police Science: A general term referring to the narrow collection of subjects and disciplines specifically related to police work. It does not refer to scientific policing or to the police as scientists.

Science: An orderly body of knowledge with principles that are clearly enunciated which is reality oriented and whose conclusions are susceptible to testing.

Scientific Knowledge: Any knowledge, enlightenment, or awareness that comes from examining events or problems through the lens of the scientific method.

Scientific Method: An approach to knowledge building and problem solving employed by scientists in which how or why something works or how something happened is investigated through the development of hypotheses and subsequent attempts at falsification through testing and other accepted means.

This textbook is intended to provide readers with an applied understanding of the principles and practice of *forensic criminology*, to outline its value within investigative and forensic purposes, and to impart the necessary scientific and forensic philosophies required for casework and analysis in these environments. In doing so, we will discuss the various kinds of forensic criminologists currently in practice, the types of analyses they perform in their forensic duties, and their professional interactions with, and even dependence upon, each other.

First, however, we must generally discuss the nature and scope of *criminology*; the domain of the *criminologist*; and the relationship of both to the criminal justice system. Then we will discuss forensic criminology and its distinguishing features. We will close with a discussion of key historical figures and modern architects of the profession.

This entire text is written in the language of *science*. While forensic criminologists may practice in different jurisdictions, and even in different countries, under varying legal codes, they are scientists first. That science and its practice must exist independent of any court before it is worthy of legal service. Therefore, the methods discussed, the research cited, and the practices advocated are universal—they are not bound by province, culture, or the borders around nations. As will be made clear throughout this work, the law cannot dictate what science is or is not; it can only rule on its admissibility.

CRIMINOLOGY

Criminology presents a terminological quagmire to the neophyte.

MacMillan and Roberts (2003, p. 317)

Criminology is the scientific study of crime and criminals. As described in Terblanche (1999, p. 10), "Criminology, broadly speaking, studies crime, criminals, victims, punishment and the prevention and control of crime. The most important role of a criminologist is to study crime, and to interpret and explain crime." It is also multidisciplinary in both theory and practice.

This inclusive definition brings many researchers and practitioners from a variety of disciplines under the same aegis. However, it also sets strict limits on what criminology is and who practices it. This is owing to the caveat that a criminologist must also be a scientist—involved in the application of the *scientific method* to problem solving and the subsequent development of *scientific knowledge*. A useful discussion regarding the relationship between scientific knowledge, the scientific method, and the scientist is provided in Chisum and Turvey (2006; pp. 86–87):

> Education in the sciences and specialized training help define a *scientist*, not just experience, and even this is not enough. Though it often escapes notice, a scientist is actually defined by their adherence to the scientific method when solving problems such as how something works, why something does not work, or how something happened. Anyone who fully comprehends and diligently employs the scientific method is a scientist, lab coat or not. Though these seemingly limited criteria may appear to the uninitiated as a lowering of the bar, they actually raise it. A degree requirement, for example, even in the hard sciences, in no way ensures student exposure to, or comprehension of, the scientific method.
>
> …
>
> The *scientific method* is a way to investigate how or why something works, or how something happened, through the development of hypotheses and subsequent attempts at falsification through testing and other accepted means. It is a structured process designed to build scientific knowledge by way of answering specific questions about observed events through analysis and critical thinking. Observations are used to form testable hypotheses, and with sufficient testing

hypotheses can become scientific theories. Eventually, over much time, with precise testing marked by a failure to falsify, scientific theories can become scientific principles. The scientific method is the particular approach to knowledge building and problem solving employed by scientists.

Scientific knowledge is any knowledge, enlightenment, or awareness that comes from examining events or problems through the lens of the scientific method. The accumulation of scientific knowledge in a particular subject or discipline leads to its development as a *science*. The classic definition of a *science*, as provided by Thornton (1997, p. 12), is "an orderly body of knowledge with principles that are clearly enunciated," as well as being reality oriented and having conclusions susceptible to testing.

A strong cautionary is needed here. The use of statistics does not make something scientific. The use of a computer does not make something scientific. The use of chemicals does not make something scientific. The use of technology does not make something scientific. Science is found in the interpretations. Was the scientific method used to synthesize the knowledge at hand, and has that knowledge been applied correctly to render interpretations, with the necessary humility. The relationship of scientists, the scientific method, and science is thus: Scientists employing the scientific method can work within a particular discipline to help create and build a body of scientific knowledge to the point where its theories become principles, and the discipline as a whole eventually becomes a science. And the discipline remains a science through the continued building of scientific knowledge.

Given the requirement of scientific practice, not all of those who study and then go to work in the milieu of crime and criminals are necessarily criminologists. For instance, this prohibition excludes those who perform work within the *criminal justice system* without both a scientific background and an interpretive mandate.

THE CRIMINAL JUSTICE SYSTEM

"For the way we administer justice is by the adversary proceeding, which is to say, we set the parties fighting."
　　　　Charles P. Curtis, Legal Ethicist (from Curran and Shapiro, 1970, p. 32)

The *criminal justice system* in most western countries is the network of government and private agencies that deal with accused and convicted criminals. It is adversarial in nature. In an *adversarial system,* there are always at least two sides in each criminal matter: a prosecution representing the government and its citizens, and a defense representing the accused. As defined in Black (1990, p. 53):

> [An adversary system is a] jurisprudential network of laws, rules and procedures characterized by opposing parties who contend against each other for a result favorable to themselves. In such a system, the judge acts as an independent magistrate rather than prosecutor; distinguished from an inquisitorial system.

Ultimately, each side of this legal contest works to convince a judge or a jury that its position is the most correct.

In an adversarial system, all defendants are entitled to an adequate defense and due process, while the burden of proof is on the prosecution. The prosecutor must prove guilt beyond a reasonable doubt rather than the defense being required to prove innocence. Alternatively, the defense must prove only that there is reasonable doubt with respect to the prosecution's theories regarding their client's guilt. If a defendant is convicted of a crime, that person may continue to have or need legal representation as he or she moves through the criminal justice system, or he or she may not. This type of system is also found in Australia, Canada, the United Kingdom, and parts of Europe as well.

In the United States, attorneys for the prosecution work exclusively for the government at the county, state, or federal level. They are charged with seeking the truth regarding criminal matters on behalf of the citizenry. Unfortunately, prosecutors are often elected, appointed, promoted, or otherwise advanced based on their conviction rate. This can cause some to be less interested in "truth seeking" and more interested in what they can prove in court to obtain a politically desirable legal outcome. This agenda may also explain why "get tough on crime" strategies are political gold for those who can only gain, and justice system kryptonite for those who have everything to lose (the wrongfully convicted, the wrongfully accused, and any other victims of an errant criminal justice system).

In opposition, attorneys for the defense are not necessarily interested in the truth, but rather are ethically bound to zealously advocate for the best interests of the accused—their client. Some defense attorneys work for the government as county, state, or federal public defenders. Others work in private practice. Defendants with the financial means must hire a private attorney. However, doing so can be prohibitively expensive. Indigent defendants, being financially unable to afford private counsel, are represented by the public defender. In states or counties without a public defender system, the court appoints legal representatives to indigent defendants from a list of available local attorneys referred to as "appointed counsel."

Adversarial Friction

These adversarial roles have created a great deal of friction within the criminal justice system and related educational efforts. Criminal justice educators tend to be associated with law enforcement and prosecutorial agencies—as this facilitates research opportunities, student internships, and future employment. Subsequently, criminal justice students tend to be taught and encouraged in that direction—that there are right and wrong or good and bad sides to the justice system. This bias is reflected in the general under-representation of defense-oriented or science-oriented counterbalance in criminology texts and criminal justice curriculum. Friction is created when this attitude is taken to the workplace, as those taught in such an environment may treat non-law enforcement-oriented efforts in the criminal justice system with derision or even hostility.

Both authors have witnessed firsthand how pervasive and damaging this attitude can be to the administration of justice. From instructors who convey a very one-sided view of the justice system; to police officers who hold a rigid "us-and-them" attitude; to prosecutors who see everything as black and white—perceiving that anyone who is not on their side, supporting their cause or theory, is an enemy of the state. From the start to finish, there are those who take sides and coerce others to do the same—often to no good end.

For example, one of the authors (Petherick) was involved in the examination of a case involving a police officer who had accused his former girlfriend of stalking him. She was subsequently arrested and charged, and had several related court appearances. The cost to the accused and her family was rising, and the risk of losing her liberty swung back and forth. The family called the author for assistance, and, upon scrutiny, more than a few inconsistencies became evident.

As a matter of course and due diligence, a number of witnesses in relation to the case were contacted and further information sought. During one inquiry about the alleged behavior of the complainant (a police officer, recall), the author was asked the question "What have you got against the cops?" Of course, there was no agenda against the police as a whole, but a concern about the behavior of one member alone.

However belligerent and unyielding it might sound, a widespread attitude within law enforcement is that "if you're not with us, you're against us." Consequently, any action or criticism taken against one may well be viewed as being against the group as a whole. This issue will be discussed further throughout the text. Of course, to the vast majority of ethical, law-abiding, and professional law enforcement officers, this view is absurd. To the professional law enforcement officer, any individual actions that harm the citizenry or reflect poorly on policing as a whole are appropriately regarded as cancerous, to be screened for regularly, and removed upon discovery.

Composition of the Criminal Justice System

The criminal justice system itself is often characterized as being composed of "agencies responsible for enforcing criminal laws, including legislatures, police, courts, and corrections," (Reid, 2003, p. 355). This is similar to the perspective offered in Sullivan (1977, p. 157): "The general view of criminal justice reflects a system of three separately organized functions: the *police*, the *courts*, and *corrections*. Each has a distinct role, yet they are interrelated." This conceptualization, while generally accurate in most countries, is prosecution oriented. As it prevails, many texts and courses on the subject of police science and criminal justice administration have, historically, failed to acknowledge the non-law enforcement and non-prosecutorial components of the justice system. That is to say, they fail to adequately discuss the role of the defense and private forensic examiners—if they are mentioned at all.

With respect to forensic practitioners, this one-sided view of adversarial systems dates back to the time when forensic services, such as evidence examination, death investigation, and mental health evaluation, were housed almost exclusively within government institutions and police agencies. While a community of independent forensic practitioners has long existed in private practice, they were until recently "available only to individuals willing or able to pay for them or those having an attorney or other advocate to secure the services of an expert" (Anderson and Winfree, 1987, p. xx). Consequently, they were few in number. Now the use of private forensic practitioners of all kinds is widespread and even commonplace in criminal and civil courts—especially in the United States. The reason for this change will be discussed later in the upcoming section on forensic criminology.

Suffice it to say that the modern criminal justice system consists of the following major branches: *law enforcement, forensic services, judiciary,* and *corrections*. These remain generally the same whether one is in the United States, the United Kingdom, Canada, or Australia. Only the laws and their interpretation vary.

Law enforcement is the branch of the criminal justice system that deals with reported crime. Law enforcement agencies are intended to enforce the law— to ensure that citizens act lawfully and to investigate the nature and extent of unlawful acts. In that capacity they are meant to investigate criminal complaints to establish what happened. When they believe a crime has been committed, law enforcement seek to identify and arrest available suspects. In some cases this may also involve the collection, submission, and/or storage of physical evidence by crime scene investigators. As explained in Sullivan (1977, p. 149):

> It is the job of the police to enforce the law. Thus, officers must remember that they are primarily fact-finders for their department and have no authority or control over the judicial or legislative branches of government. If the police effectively enforce the law, they have done all that is expected.

What is the sequence of events in the criminal justice system?

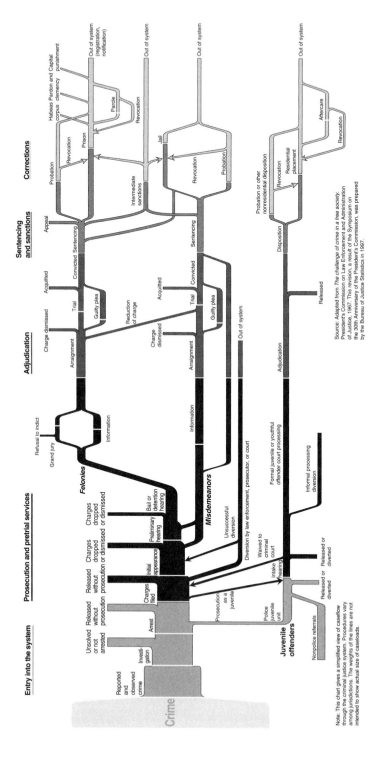

Note: This chart gives a simplified view of caseflow through the criminal justice system. Procedures vary among jurisdictions. The weights of the lines are not intended to show actual size of caseloads.

Source: Adapted from *The challenge of crime in a free society*, President's Commission on Law Enforcement and Administration of Justice, 1967. This revision, a result of the Symposium on the 30th Anniversary of the President's Commission, was prepared by the Bureau of Justice Statistics in 1997.

The Sequence of Events in the United States Criminal Justice System. From the reporting of crime, to its investigation and adjudication with related sentencing and the involvement of corrections to release or capital punishment. Taken from BJS (2004).

This conceptualization has changed little since criminologist and police reformer Elmer Graper wrote of law enforcement duties in the early 1920s (1969, p. 5):

> Upon the policeman we depend for protection. He is expected to preserve the public peace. His presence acts as a restraining influence upon the lawless elements who would endanger life and property. When crimes are committed the policeman must bring offenders into court.

Law enforcement officers and investigators work for government entities as dictated by jurisdiction and statute, to include federal (i.e., national), state, county/boroughs, and municipal (e.g., city, village) authorities.

Forensic services refers to the branch of the criminal justice system that deals with the examination and interpretation of evidence—physical, behavioral, and testimonial alike. Government-employed analysts, technicians, criminalists, pathologists, and forensic mental health experts perform a wide variety of forensic services on behalf of the state, generally for the police and prosecution. In the United Kingdom, this is done by Forensic Science Services (FSS; see http://www.forensic.gov.uk), which is a government-owned company that exists independent of law enforcement authority. FSS has contracts to provide forensic examinations for law enforcement in England, Wales, and even the Royal Canadian Mounted Police (RCMP). In Australia, government forensic services are provided as an adjunct to the health department. For example, Queensland Health Forensic and Scientific Services are responsible for performing autopsies and forensic analyses out of the John Tonge Centre in Brisbane. Each state has its own regional forensic center. However, law enforcement officers still perform evidence collections and certain kinds of forensic analyses in both countries.

In the United States, however, a large number of forensic professionals work directly for government law enforcement agencies, causing a potential conflict of interest that must be acknowledged and carefully managed. In Australia and the United Kingdom, most government agencies performing forensic services are independent of law enforcement affiliation and oversight.

Another distinguishing feature of the forensic community in the United States is the large number of privately employed, independent forensic examiners. They are regularly engaged to perform examinations for the prosecution and the defense alike. When state or private funds are available, as happens in major cases or those involving financially capable defendants, this community of forensic professionals may be hired to provide a necessary counterbalance within the adversarial system, though access is by no means equal and varies from state to state. It is therefore reasonable to explain that not every available forensic service is an adjunct of the government, though it is more often the case than not.

The availability of forensic expertise is a definite issue within the justice system, as it is a scarce resource. In some jurisdictions (Australia, for example) there are few if any nongovernment forensic labs, and even attorneys in civil cases may rely on state government labs for analyses. It is also fair to say that the lack of available government forensic services, private practitioners, and related funds for either has caused serious case backlogs and delays of justice worldwide.

The *judiciary* is the branch of the criminal justice system that deals with the adjudication and exoneration or punishment of criminal defendants. This includes everything from arraignment to acquittal; from sentencing to appeal. A judge or jury, referred to as the *trier of fact*, determines the legal guilt or innocence of a criminal defendant. Subsequently, the trier also decides the terms of punishment, also referred to as the *sentence*. A short list of those involved in the judiciary includes government prosecutors and public defenders, private defense attorneys, magistrates, judges, investigators for the prosecution, investigators for the defense, investigators for the court, paralegals, court reporters, court clerks, court bailiffs, and the jury, which is drawn from the local citizenry.

Corrections is the branch of the criminal justice system that deals with the probation, incarceration, management, rehabilitation, treatment, parole, and sometimes execution of convicted criminals. Many law enforcement agencies and courthouses have on-site jail facilities to enable short-term incarceration of offenders involved in lesser crimes, or to accommodate the local court appointments of felons "visiting" from other correctional institutions. However, federal, state, and county penitentiaries are designed to facilitate the long-term sentences of convicted felons. Additionally, there are hospitals outside correctional institutes that have forensic units providing offender mental evaluations, treatment, and residency. Some of these institutions are government owned and operated (county, state, and federal), whereas others are privately contracted. A short list of those professionals involved in corrections includes probation officers, corrections officers, corrections investigators, corrections counselors, parole officers, intelligence officers, social workers, and members of various parole boards.

Employment in the Criminal Justice System

Most of those students enrolled in undergraduate criminology and criminal justice programs at college or university do so to seek employment or advancement within the criminal justice system[1]. Students work toward associate and bachelor degrees in criminology, criminal justice, and criminal justice

[1] The authors have noted that the vast majority of criminology and criminal justice programs in the United States, the United Kingdom, and Australia teach essentially the same core subjects. In many instances, to conserve budgetary resources, criminology and criminal justice programs have been combined into one entity as a "school of criminology and criminal justice." Because of its affiliation with law enforcement, this is also where you find the majority of university-based forensic science programs.

administration with the following occupations in mind, either immediately or pursuant to specialized postgraduate and graduate education (with assistance from Hoover, 1995):

- Police officer/law enforcement
- Military police/investigations
- Federal investigator
- Evidence technician (a.k.a. Crime Scene Investigator)
- Medico-legal investigator
- Forensic scientist
- Legal aide
- Paralegal
- Prosecutor
- Defense attorney
- Court administrator
- Correctional officer
- Probation officer
- Parole officer
- Social worker

Ironically, none of the preceding professionals are actually criminologists (save those in the forensic sciences, such as the criminalist—as they are by definition scientists working in subdisciplines of criminology). However, success in their work relies in large part on peculiar knowledge of criminology and the criminal justice system. So while they may not become criminologists in practice, study in a related degree program is highly recommended if not required for proficiency, pay raises, and promotions.

This is a good time to point out that criminology itself isn't just an amalgam of semirelated disciplines. Rather, many disciplines benefit greatly from those with criminological knowledge. As a consequence, professionals with related degrees can often be found putting them to good use in a variety of fields and occupations, from human resources, to corporate security, to insurance and beyond. The reason is that the study of criminology provides a multidisciplinary foundation relating to government, people, behavior, and law—which effects everything and everyone. So just because one studies criminology does not mean he or she is locked in to a particular career track with limited options. In fact, precisely the opposite is true.

THE DOMAIN OF CRIMINOLOGY
AND CRIMINOLOGISTS

Strange as it may seem, the contents and boundaries of criminology have never been adequately defined.

Reckless (1955, p. 6)

No matter which authority, text, or reference one looks to for guidance, the response is generally the same: the boundaries of criminology, as a field, are broadly and poorly drawn. This hasn't kept it from being a reliable and valid enterprise when actual scientists are involved, or from providing useful theories and references to those working in the criminal justice system. But it has caused more than enough confusion.

One critical omission from criminology that has helped to restrain vagaries in other professions is the lack of a governing or accrediting body whose purpose is to ensure that standards are met and maintained. While there are a number of criminological organizations around the world, few if any actually dictate membership to the profession through a vetting of educational and professional achievements. This, undoubtedly, has resulted in no small amount of deception and brigandry among its practitioners and may have gone a long way in undermining criminology (and specifically, forensic criminology) as a discipline capable of addressing complex social and legal problems.

The Domain

The domain of criminology is vast, involving any field or practice that intersects with the scientific study of crime and criminality. It looks at these issues from any available angle. As shown in the preceding section, criminology is therefore a field of study that is composed of and informed by an amalgam of subdisciplines. As explained in Reckless (1955, p. 7):

> Although criminology is a behavioral science as well as an applied science, it is also a highly synthetic science and not at all an exact science like physics and mathematics. It receives it contributions from experts in such disciplines as biology, anthropology, physiology, medicine, psychiatry, psychology, social administration, sociology, economics, law, political science, and penology and corrections.

Another similar short list of those disciplines that have contributed to the development of criminological theory and research includes "philosophy, history, anthropology, psychology, psychiatry, medicine, biology, genetics, endocrinology, neurochemistry, political science, economics, social work, jurisprudence, geography, urban planning, architecture, and statistics" (Williams, 1995, p. 179). Aside from the obvious, these refer to professionals such as the historian who studies criminal patterns of the past, the neurochemist researching neurotransmitter activity in the criminal brain, the economist who studies crime and poverty trends, and the architect who studies and designs prisons. All these professionals, their methods, and more, comprise or inform the multidisciplinary fabric of criminology as a composite field of study.

A useful way to define some of the discrete edges of that fabric, to identify the domain of criminology itself as it is woven, is to categorize the major areas of criminological research apart from professionals and their methods, including:

- The study and development of methods of crime detection and reconstruction
- The study and development of methods of criminal identification
- The study of the motives, causes, and consequences of crime
- The study of crime and deviant behavior
- The study of crime rates
- The study of crime victims
- The study of criminal justice system processes, interactions, and outcomes
- The study of crime patterns and deterrence

For example, crime may be detected by the criminalist identifying evidence from a scene and then reconstructed by a forensic scientist combining the results of several other forensic analysts; a criminal may be identified by a crime analyst using modus operandi patterns, or by a criminalist using DNA from the criminal's blood; criminal motives may be inferred by a profiler, and deviant sadistic tendencies may be inferred by a forensic psychologist; burglary rates in a given neighborhood may be compiled and interpreted by a statistician; victim occupational risk factors may be studied by a sociologist; and the wrongful conviction rate of a particular race may be studied by a legal scholar. Each of these professionals contributes to criminology as a scientific body of knowledge, puts criminological knowledge to use, or both.

Consider the following hierarchy of criminology subjects, featuring forensic criminology, its related subdisciplines and associated specialties:

I. Criminology
a. Applied Criminology
- **i.** Community Policing
- **ii.** Corrections/Penology
- **iii.** Criminal Justice Administration/Police Science
- **iv.** Forensic Criminology
  - **1.** Criminal Investigation
    - **a.** Crime Analysis
    - **b.** Crime Scene Analysis and Case Linkage
    - **c.** Crime Scene Investigation
    - **d.** Criminal Profiling
    - **e.** Fire Scene Investigation
    - **f.** Interview/Interrogation
    - **g.** Investigative Practice and Procedure
    - **h.** Medicolegal Investigation
    - **i.** Presentencing/Mitigation Investigation
    - **j.** Polygraphy
    - **k.** Threat Assessment or Risk Assessment

    2. Forensic Mental Health
       a. Correctional Counseling and Therapy
       b. Forensic Psychology/Forensic Psychiatry
          i. Offender Competency Evaluation
          ii. Offender Diagnosis and Treatment
          iii. Offender Risk Assessment
    3. Forensic Science
       a. Crime Reconstruction
          i. Accident Reconstruction/Forensic Engineering
          ii. Bloodstain Pattern Analysis
          iii. Shooting Incident Reconstruction
          iv. Wound Pattern Analysis
       b. Criminalistics
          i. Drug Chemistry/Analysis
          ii. Forensic Biology
             1. DNA
             2. Serology
          iii. Fire Debris Analysis
          iv. Trace Evidence Analysis
             1. Commercial Materials Analysis
             2. Fiber Analysis
             3. Glass Analysis
             4. Hair Analysis
             5. Soil Analysis
       c. Digital Evidence Analysis
       d. Equivocal Death Investigation
          i. Equivocal Forensic Analysis
          ii. Psychological Autopsy
       e. Fingerprint Analysis
       f. Footwear Pattern Analysis
       g. Forensic Dentistry/Odontology
       h. Forensic Nursing
       i. Forensic Pathology
       j. Forensic Toxicology
       k. Firearms & Tool Mark Analysis
       l. Questioned Documents
    4. Forensic Victimology
    5. Law
  b. Crime and Deviance
  c. Crime Statistics
  d. Crime Theory
  e. Criminal Motivations

  f. **Policy Development**
  g. **Restorative Justice**
  h. **Victimology**

While not all-inclusive, this outline should provide readers with a threshold sense of what the authors, and many others across the centuries, are referring to when employing the word *criminology* and the relationships between its subdisciplines.

Again, and for the uninitiated, this structure relates to the field of criminology and exists separate from laws and legal systems.

The Practitioners

There are as many different types of criminology practitioners as there are of criminology and its subdisciplines. One way to distinguish this wide assortment is by their formal association with the profession. First, there are those who refer to themselves as criminologists, and those who do not.

Formally trained criminologists are for the most part social scientists with graduate- or doctoral-level education employed by universities (often dictated by institutional policy and employment requirements). As theoretical as this may seem, such positions are heavy with application, or at least its potential. As explained in van der Hoven (2006, p. 156):

> Briefly, it can be stated that criminologists are trained in the social sciences and focus mainly on the causes, explanation and prevention of criminal behaviour. The study field includes the profiling of offenders as well as of victims of crime. The main emphasis is therefore on the *individuals* involved in the criminal act.

> Dr. Irma Labuschagne (2003, p. 5) rightly points out that criminology not only focuses on individual criminal behaviour, but also on all environmental circumstances, as well as the context within which the criminal was functioning when the crime was committed.

> Criminologists specifically study the criminal in all his facets, such as causal factors contributing to the criminal event, predisposition (e.g., personality make-up, genetic factors), precipitating factors, triggering factors, the interaction between the offender and the victim, victim vulnerability, victim rights, role of the victim in the criminal justice process, the criminal justice process, the prevention of crime and victim support, et cetera. Criminological studies involve personality and sexual deviations, for example the antisocial personality, paedophilia, violent offenders, rapists, and phenomena such as domestic violence, school violence and workplace violence.

Criminologists focus on the causes, dynamics, theoretical explanation and prevention of violent behaviour. They also study the offender's patterns of criminal behaviour in the past to predict his or her behaviour in future.

Professional criminologists are easily identified by their formal education—most often at the doctoral level in criminology, sociology, or criminal justice—and by the nature and extent of their research publications. Though infrequently employed by the police in our modern justice system, "it is the police who are relying most heavily on criminological research to make substantial changes in basic structure and methods of operating" (Williams, 1995, p. 182).

As a behavioral scientist, the criminologist is distinguished from those in the mental health professions, such as the psychologist and the psychiatrist, by virtue of a focus on examining causes, interactions, and patterns of criminal behavior rather than specific diagnoses and treatment (van der Hoven, 2006).

We have already explained that some of the work in the subdisciplines of criminology is theoretical and abstract research, related to the identification and scrutiny of various criminal phenomenon. Conversely, some of it is practical and concrete, involving the hands-on application of criminological research and analytical processes to resolve questions related to criminal inquiry, legal disputes, and even social problems.

This leads us necessarily to forensic criminology.

FORENSIC CRIMINOLOGY

Quis, quid, ubi, quibus auxiliis, cur, quomodo, quando?

> Offered at the beginning of *In the Tracks of Crime* by Henry T. F. Rhodes
> (1952) as the "Maxim of a Roman Jurist"[2]

It may be argued that *forensic criminology* first appeared in U.S. literature as *scientific criminology* in the book *Crime's Nemesis* by Luke May, published in 1936. He referred to this work as the scientific detection of crime and criminals, coming from the combined perspectives of physical evidence analysis and criminal modus operandi analysis. May (1936) states (pp. vi-viii):

> The successful criminologist has no illusions about himself, despite the superman that fiction depicts. He lays no claim to psychic powers or clairvoyance. And yet, he must be more clever than the criminal. The criminologist often fights a battle of wits with diabolical cunning. His knowledge of life and men must be immense; his powers of logic and deduction, acutely developed. His must be a thirst for knowledge

[2]Translation: "Who, what, where, with what aids, why, how, when?" Rhodes took this from the Summa Theologica, written by St. Thomas Aquinas between 1265 and 1274 (though Aquinas never actually completed it). It was intended as a manual for theological scholars to contain all primary religious teachings of the era. It offers specific sections on ethics and law, from which this passage is drawn with respect to the basic questions needed to contextualize and understand human behavior—particularly criminal behavior. The roman jurist who developed this line of inquiry is Cicero, and they are referred to as "Cicero's seven circumstances" (Franzosi, 2004, p. 382).

in every field… Modern crime detection methods and the marvelous developments in the scientific detective laboratories of today bring stupendous odds against the criminal.

It is the purpose of this book to reveal these methods, bring them into the light…

Criminology demands much… Much of this work, especially its application to crime problems, was, of necessity, original; for science has only recently become the handmaiden of the criminologist.

Not surprisingly, this language is essentially an adaption of the writings of Hans Gross (to be discussed in the "Key Historical Figures" section of this chapter), which had significant influence over May, and his holistic approach to forensic casework.

The next major appearance of the concept occurred postcriminalistics, in the text *Expert Witnesses: Criminologists in the Courtroom*, published in 1987. The authors of this work come from an applied social science background: one is a professor of criminology with a Ph.D. in criminology, and one is a professor of criminal justice with a Ph.D. in sociology. Both are criminologists and both have confronted the issues of expert social science testimony in forensic casework. Their approach to criminology and expert witnessing takes a narrow but important perspective, leaving the investigative, physical evidence examination, and forensic mental health aspects entirely aside. They focused their treatment instead on criminology as it relates to "matters of policing, court processing, and prison treatment" (Anderson and Winfree, 1987, p. ix), where research, theoretical, and process-oriented expertise in criminology becomes important to legal questions and court proceedings, often in a civil context. They explain that (p. 13):

The presence of criminologists in the court as expert witnesses offering testimony on a broad range of criminal justice practices and procedures, or criminological testimony in criminal trials, has included, and continues to include evidence provided by forensic criminologists trained in criminalistics… Experts are a available for every imaginable type of physical evidence and are usually qualified as expert witnesses based on training and experience.

…

More recently, owing largely to the expansion of the academic field of criminal justice…, to the increased liability of actions of its criminal justice personnel…, and to social issues on key constitutional issues…, behavioral scientists and social scientists with criminological or criminal justice expertise have increasingly been asked to appear as expert witnesses.

> The university-based criminologist, therefore, generally provides expert testimony based on research which transcends and precedes the events or matters before the court and which the expert applies to such matters.

The authors of this earlier work provide deep and useful insight into the role of expert criminologists and social science testimony, which are important threads in the overall fabric of forensic criminology.

Based on the long history of criminology, and the multidisciplinary literature cited thus far, the authors of this text define *forensic criminology* as the scientific study of crime and criminals for the purpose of addressing investigative and legal questions. This is very similar to the equally broad definition offered in van der Hoven (2006, p. 153): "Forensic criminology refers to the actions of a criminologist in collecting, analysing and presenting evidence in the interest of objective proceedings in the judicial process." It is an applied subcategory of general criminology where the abstract and the theoretical meet the practical and the concrete. It involves the proficient, critical, and objective examination of criminal cases and related evidence, featuring the scientific method and subsequent evidentiary interpretations. While there are a number of forensic criminologists in private practice, this field also encompasses many forensic subdisciplines.

In terms of forensic criminology practitioners (a.k.a. forensic criminologists), it quickly becomes evident that there are *generalists* and there are *specialists*. As with any profession, the specialist is highly proficient and informed regarding a very restricted area of practice. Forensic criminology specialists might focus entirely on a single subject matter, such as police use of force, risk assessments, security, criminal profiling, threat assessment, presentencing assessments, or an area of physical evidence examination such as criminalistics. Forensic criminology generalists, on the other hand, have a broad spectrum of knowledge from multiple areas of study and will have multiple areas of expertise. They are fluent in the theory and application of a broad range of criminology subjects without necessarily knowing all there is to know about a given subdiscipline. There are also forensic criminology generalists with speciality areas of concentration—hybrids of a sort. While being knowledgeable about many areas in general, they have localized strengths by virtue of greater research, skill, or experience in particular areas over the course of their career.

The distinction between generalist and specialist forensic practitioner is made clearer by a discussion provided in Chisum and Turvey (2007) regarding forensic scientists (pp. ix–x):

> Forensic generalists and forensic specialists alike are a requirement for informed forensic case examination, laboratory testing, and crime reconstruction to occur. A forensic generalist is a particular kind of

forensic scientist who is broadly educated and trained in a variety of forensic specialties. They are "big picture" people who can help reconstruct a crime from work performed with the assistance of other forensic scientists and then direct investigators to forensic specialists as needed. They are experts not in all areas, but in the specific area of evidence interpretation. According to DeForest et al. (1983, p. 17),

> Because of the depth and complexity of criminalistics, the need for specialists is inescapable. There can be serious problems, however, with overspecialization. Persons who have a working knowledge of a broad range of criminalistics problems and techniques are also necessary. These people are called generalists. The value of generalists lies in their ability to look at all of the aspects of a complex case and decide what needs to be done, which specialists should be involved, and in which order to carry out the required examinations.

> Specialization occurs when a forensic scientist has been trained in a specific forensic subspecialty, such as an area of criminalistics, forensic toxicology, forensic pathology, or forensic anthropology. Specialists are an important part of forensic science casework, with an important role to fill. Traditionally, forensic specialists provide the bricks, and forensic generalists have traditionally provided the blueprints.

The forensic generalist in criminology, therefore, understands that informed case analysis is the result of objectively examining a whole related system of evidence rather than a narrow, specialized portion. The forensic generalist considers the totality of the known physical and behavioral evidence and only then frames theories regarding the behavior and circumstances related to a crime. He or she is steered by good science and the scientific method, holding no investment in the outcome. The forensic generalist then tests those theories and the theories of others against the evidence, using a framework of analytical logic and critical thinking to distinguish facts, assumptions, opinions, and inference.

DISTINGUISHING FORENSIC CRIMINOLOGY

The single distinguishing feature of forensic criminologists, with respect to any other type of criminologist, is the expectation that their findings will be submitted as evidence within the context of a formal investigation or legal proceeding. That is to say, their findings are not only bound by adherence to the scientific method, but are also intended to be of sufficient quality and certainty for courtroom use. To that end, they must be prepared to offer their conclusions under penalty of perjury, whether in a written declaration or affidavit, a forensic report, or sworn expert testimony.

While the majority of university-based criminologists are concerned with crime and criminality from a research, process, or theoretical perspective, forensic criminologists have a particular type of examination to perform or a particular set of questions to answer. They are interested in research or theory only inasmuch as it can be applied to forensic analyses or the subsequent interpretations of results in casework. Generally, this will relate to the detection, investigation, reconstruction, and analysis of crime and criminal behavior, as well as to the identification, apprehension, examination, and adjudication of criminals. In civil cases, this will relate to areas of liability as defined by law.

It is necessary at this point to delineate forensic criminology from other like areas of criminology. This includes its "mother," *applied criminology*, as well as the areas of *police science* and *criminal justice administration*.

Applied criminology is a term that "refers to the application of criminological theory to criminal justice practice" (Helfgott, 2008, p. 419). It is also argued that "Applied Criminology should have a critical edge, casting a discriminating analytical gaze over the processes of criminalization, crime enforcement, and the criminal justice system" (Stout, Yates, and Williams, 2008, p. 6). Using these descriptions, applied criminology is an appropriate term for characterizing *any* application of criminological knowledge to *any* process related to the criminal justice system as we have defined it. This encompasses many areas, including the application of criminological knowledge to the making of laws, the management of police agencies, the management of prisoners, and the treatment of victims, to name but a few. It also includes, as a subcategory, the area of forensic criminology.

Forensic criminology is, as defined, a particular type of applied criminology involving the scientific study of crime and criminals for the purpose of addressing investigative and legal questions. This distinction involves an appreciation of applied criminology as a form of macro-analysis: it tends to involve the nomothetic (group) examination of systems, processes, and their relationships. Alternatively, forensic criminology is a form of micro-analysis: it tends to involve the idiographic (individual) examination of one or more related cases and consideration of its internal issues.

Police science, on the other hand, is a general term referring to those subjects relating to the process of policing. Despite the misunderstanding of some, it does not refer to scientific policing or to police officers who are acting in the capacity of scientists. This is in fact a contradiction because police culture cannot house or cultivate the flower of science—science and law enforcement exist at cross-purposes (Edwards and Gotsonis, 2009). However, it is easy to see why those outside the community would make this mistake. It is also easy to see the advantage to those within the community who do not correct these kinds of misapprehensions for fear of losing the aura of scientific certainty with respect to what they know and do.

The term *police science* was in fact coined by law enforcement affiliated instructors working as educators at colleges and university. It was intended to separate educational programs run by scholarly criminal justice and criminology professors from those run by educators with a background in law enforcement. In other words, its use was initially crafted to signal the existence of a culture of law enforcement within educational institutions that excluded "outsiders" concerned with research and development of knowledge. Though antithetical to university culture, it remains in use within some criminal justice programs that are more vocational than scholarly (see generally Morn, 1995).

Regardless, modern textbooks on police science focus not on scientific analysis of evidence or even scientific methodology, but rather on police administration, covering such general subjects as "a career in law enforcement," "criminal law," "police organization," and "criminal justice functions" (Sullivan, 1977, p. ix). Police science, then, is a course of study intended specifically to educate the future police officer. This is why "police science departments usually focus more on the technical aspects of policing: administration, management, crime analysis, and the 'doing' of law enforcement" (Williams, 1995, p. 181), and not on criminology, forensic science, or criminalistics per se.

As defined, the term *police science* involves the word *science* in reference to the technical aspects of policing and is in no way meant to suggest that there is a scientific component to the work of police officers or the graduates of such programs. The concept of police science is essentially synonymous with other process-oriented terms covering the same subject areas such as *police administration* and *criminal justice administration* (Graper, 1969; Sullivan, 1977; Vollmer, 1971). While it certainly falls under the aegis of applied criminology, its technical process orientation, strict law enforcement alignment, and lack of emphasis on scientific analysis or scientific interpretation of anything combine to separate it decisively from forensic criminology. In short, *police science* refers to a course of study that is specially designed to teach police officers about the criminal justice system and their work in relation to it; *forensic criminology* refers to scientific case examination and evidence interpretation for the purpose of providing expert findings in legal proceedings.

[3]Some portions of this section have been adapted from Chisum and Turvey (2006), Turvey (2008), and Turvey and Petherick (2008).

KEY HISTORICAL FIGURES[3]

There are certain individuals whose work, theories, and publications have been of considerable foundational value to the development of modern forensic criminology, not to mention their enormous contributions to its related subdisciplines. They include European influences in the late nineteenth century, as well as "a small group of people at Berkeley who were endeavoring to establish scientific criminology as an academic discipline" in the first half of the twentieth century (Thorwald, 1966, p. 149). These forensic generalists, who used "scientific criminology," social science, and behavioral science to answer investigative and legal questions, were the forbearers of modern forensic criminology.

Dr. Johann (Hans) Baptist Gustav Gross

A thousand mistakes of every description would be avoided if people did not base their conclusions upon premises furnished by others, take as established fact what is only possibility, or as a constantly recurring incident what has only been observed once.

—Dr. Hans Gross (1906)

Hans Gross was born in 1847, in Graz, Austria. He studied criminology and the law, and he eventually came to serve as an examining magistrate of the Criminal Court at Czernovitz. It was during this time that Dr. Gross observed firsthand the failings of apathetic and incompetent criminal investigators, as well as criminal identifications made by flawed and biased eyewitness accounts. He also became painfully familiar with the continuous stream of false suspect, eyewitness, and alleged victim accounts that poured into his office as a regular matter of course.

Dr. Hans Gross (1847–1915). He is regarded by the authors as the Grandfather of Forensic Criminology.

These experiences led him to the conclusion that because people were essentially unreliable, and investigators were often their own worst enemy, a methodical, systematic way of determining the facts of a case was needed. In 1893, Gross finished work on his seminal work, *Handbuch fur Untersuchunsrichter, als System der Kriminalistik* [*Criminal Investigation, A Practical Textbook for Magistrates, Police Officers, and Lawyers* (Gross, 1906)]. It was a watershed event in which Dr. Gross proclaimed the virtues of science against intuition, and a systematic approach to holistic criminology and criminal investigation against uninformed experience and overspecialization.

The success of this groundbreaking textbook was, without exaggeration, unparalleled in the history of applied criminology.

The forensic community, as it existed, enthusiastically devoured *System der Kriminalistik*. It achieved a fifth edition and was translated into eight languages by 1907. This included versions in French, Spanish, Danish, Russian, Hungarian, Serbian, English, and Japanese, each with an overwhelmingly supportive foreword written by a forensic contemporary impatient to see it printed and adopted in his respective country. As described in Thorwald (1966, pp. 234–235):

> You had only to open Gross's book to see the dawning of a new age....
> Each of his chapters was an appeal to examining magistrates (his word
> for criminologists) to avail themselves of the potentialities of science
> and technology far more than they had done so far.

Dr. Gross became a professor of Criminal Law at the University of Czernovitz, a professor of Criminology at the University of Prague, and later a professor of Criminal Law at the University of Graz. With the success of *System der Kriminalistik* as a platform, he launched other professional ventures that continue to contribute significantly to the development of forensic science. In 1898, Dr. Gross began serving as the editor for the *Archiv fur Kriminalanthropologie und Kriminalistik*, a journal to which he was a frequent contributor. He also introduced the forensic journal *Kriminologie*, which still serves as a respected medium for reporting improved methods of scientific crime detection. In 1912, he established the Museum of Criminology, the *Kriminalmuseum*, at the University of Graz.

Dr. Edmond Locard
(1877–1966).

The significance of *System der Kriminalistik* to criminology, forensic and otherwise, cannot be understated. It was the first comprehensive textbook to systematically cover the integrated philosophy and practice of scientific criminal investigation, forensic analysis, crime reconstruction, and criminal profiling. Its philosophies have not been diminished by the passage of time and should be required reading for any student of these subjects.

Dr. Hans Gross was a criminologist in the classic sense, a forensic generalist, and he changed the world with his multidisciplinary, scientific approach to criminal investigation and forensic analysis.

Dr. Edmond Locard

Dr. Alexandre Lacassagne (1843–1924) was a professor of Forensic Medicine with the faculty of medicine at the University of Lyon, France. In 1880, he became the director of the Lyons Institute of Forensic Medicine. He was a

[4]Sir Arthur Conan Doyle was an author and creator of the fictional character Sherlock Holmes, but he was also far more. He was a medical doctor and scientist. He was a forensic practitioner and forensic reformer who overturned several cases involving miscarriages of justice. He also believed in logic, he believed in the scientific examination of evidence, and he taught these philosophies through his stories, which remain inspirational to forensic scientists of modern day. Students would be well served to revisit his works often.

[5]The Institut de Police Scientifique (IPS) remains to this day at the University of Lausanne, offering undergraduate and graduate education in forensic science and criminology.

[6]The French Surete Nationale was a plainclothes undercover unit developed to keep strict surveillance over all ex-convicts and known criminals living in and migrating into the city; to pursue all lawbreakers and make arrests; and to prevent criminal activity before it occurred. In Dr. Locard's day, the Surete Nationale, which was separate from the local police, was assuming a lot of police functions, and this alliance protected his lab politically.

medical doctor, an anthropologist, and a fervent advocate of combining science with criminology. Dr. Lacassagne also planted very specific ideas in the minds of his students about the potential importance of what we now refer to as *trace and transfer evidence* in the investigation and reconstruction of a crime (Thorwald, 1966, p. 281):

> He had encouraged some of his students to make studies on clues that few or no criminologists had hitherto considered. Thus, he proposed the idea that the dust on clothing, or on people's ears, noses, and fingernails, could provide information on the occupations and whereabouts of suspects.

Edmond Locard was born in 1877 in Saint-Chamond, France. He was a student of Dr. Lacassagne. In time, he became a doctor of medicine and a master of law, and he would eventually replace Lacassagne as the director of the Lyons Institute of Forensic Medicine.

In 1908, having been inspired by the works of Dr. Hans Gross and Sir Arthur Conan Doyle,[4] Dr. Locard traveled the world to better study how police agencies in major cities were incorporating the scientific method and trace evidence analysis into their investigation and reconstruction of crime. During the next two years, he would visit agencies and colleagues in Paris, Lausanne, Rome, Berlin, Brussels, New York, and Chicago. To his dismay, he found no true police crime labs or even scientific detectives, and the majority of police agencies remained steeped in *Bertillonage* (a form of personal identification based on a system of body measurements and photography of features).

In 1909, the Institut de Police Scientifique et de Criminologie was formally created at the University of Lausanne, Switzerland, under the direction of Professor Rudolph A. Reiss (1875–1929). It was the first university to deliver a degree in forensic science covering all major subjects.[5] Professor Reiss had originally offered courses in forensic photography, scene of crime investigation, and identification, and he had been involved in forensic casework since at least 1903. The institute developed from the success of those courses and his tireless efforts.

In the summer of 1910, after having visited with Professor Reiss, Dr. Locard returned to Lyon and persuaded the prefects of the Rhone Department to provide him with two rooms in an attic of the Law Courts and two *Surete* officials as assistants.[6] The arrangement was desirable but the accommodations were not the best, as described in Thorwald (1966, p. 283):

> The laboratory was reached through a gloomy entrance hall from which one corridor led to the prison and a dirt-stained door into the dusty caves and archives. Every day Locard climbed the steep winding staircase leading to his laboratory four floors up.

This marked the creation of what has become regarded as the world's first police crime laboratory, as it was housed under the auspices of law enforcement and staffed by law enforcement agents. However, contrary to some publications, this was not the world's first forensic science laboratory. The first forensic science labs were not government owned, were often highly specialized, and were commonly housed in universities, as Dr. Locard had experienced in Switzerland with Reiss.

In any event, once in place at his lab at Lyon, Dr. Locard took to the task of implementing everything he had learned from the publications of Dr. Hans Gross, from the stories of Sir Arthur Conan Doyle, from his study and travels, and from his devotion to forensic science and crime reconstruction. These efforts included foundational research, publications, and the development of practice standards in dust analysis, detailed in Locard (1929), and fingerprint examination.

Dr. Locard also helped establish one of the first forensic science professional organizations. In 1929, after the death of Professor Reiss, Locard returned to Lausanne and gathered with his European forensic scientist colleagues to form The International Academy of Criminalistics. His contributions to scientific criminology and the forensic sciences were nothing short of massive, as summarized in Söderman (1957, p. 25):

> He put the analysis of handwriting on a firmer footing, systematized the analysis of the dust in the clothes of suspects, invented a modified method of analyzing blood stains, and invented poroscopy, whereby the pores in the papillary ridges of fingerprints are used as a means of identification.

However, Dr. Locard is most famous for the forensic axiom that bears his name: Locard's Exchange Principle. It has been misstated, misrepresented, and misattributed over the years by those lecturing and writing authoritatively on the subject. Confusion in the forensic science community and among students has resulted.

A reference from Locard found in *La Police et Les Methodes Scientifiques*, in the original French, may be of use to understand what he actually meant (Locard, 1934, pp. 7–8):

> [A] recherche des traces n'est pas, autant qu'on pourrait le croire, une innovation des criminalistes modernes. C'est une occupation probablement aussi vieille que 1'humanité.

> Le principe est celui-ci. Toute action de l'homme, et *a fortiori*, l'action violente qu'est un crime, ne peut pas se derouler sans laisser quelque marque. L'admirable est la variete de ces marques. Tantot ce seront des empreintes, tantot de simples traces, tantot des taches.

Rough translation:

> Searching for traces is not, as much as one could believe it, an innovation of modern criminal jurists. It is an occupation probably as old as humanity.

> The principle is this one. Any action of an individual, and obviously, the violent action constituting a crime, cannot occur without leaving a mark. What is admirable is the variety of these marks. Sometimes they will be prints, sometimes simple traces, and sometimes stains.

In 1935, a Spanish translation of this same general principle was provided in Locard (1935, p. 107):

> Al malhechor le es imposible actuar, y sobre todo actuar con la intensidad que supone la accion criminal, sin dejar indicios de su paso.

Rough translation:

> To the criminal, it is impossible for him to act, and mainly to act with the intensity that supposes criminal action, without leaving indications of his step.

This principle has been adapted and adopted in its English translation by the forensic science community in the United States. As stated by Dr. John Thornton, a practicing criminalist and a former professor of Forensic Science at the University of California (UC) at Berkeley (Thornton, 1997, p. 29):

> Forensic scientists have almost universally accepted the Locard Exchange Principle. This doctrine was enunciated early in the 20th century by Edmund Locard, the director of the first crime laboratory, in Lyon, France. Locard's Exchange Principle states that with contact between two items, there will be an exchange of microscopic material. This certainly includes fibers, but extends to other microscopic materials such as hair, pollen, paint, and soil.

By recognizing, documenting, and examining the nature and extent of evidentiary traces and exchanges in a crime scene, Dr. Locard postulated that criminals could be tracked down and then later associated with particular locations, items of evidence, and persons (i.e., victims).

Dr. Locard regarded this postulation as both obvious and ancient, and likened the recognition and examination of trace evidence to hunting behavior as old as mankind (Locard, 1934, p. 7). Prey, for example, in the normal course of drinking at a watering hole, leave tracks and spoor and other signs that betray their presence and direction; the hunter deliberately seeks out this evidence, picks up the trail, and follows. Every contact leaves a trace that may be discovered and understood. The detection and identification of exchanged materials is interpreted to mean that two objects have been in contact. This is the cause-and-effect principle reversed; the effect is observed and the cause is concluded. Understanding and accepting this principle of evidentiary exchange makes possible the reconstruction of contacts between objects and persons. Consequently, the incorporation of this principle into evidentiary interpretations is perhaps one of the most important considerations in the reconstruction of crime.

It is true that Dr. Locard concerned himself chiefly with organizing and systematizing methods of analyzing prints, traces, and stains. He wrote extensively on how to identify and individuate dust, how to identify and individuate fingerprints, how to analyze and interpret handwriting, how to analyze and interpret bloodstains, and the like. However, a careful read of his publications reveals that his goals were ultimately those of reconstructing crime through the skills brought to bear by a forensic generalist. As Locard (1934, p. 6) explains, "Criminalistics seeks tools everywhere, in biology, physics, and more particularly chemistry, and proposes solutions to every problem brought up by the criminal investigation." Consequently, he organized and systematized methods of physical evidence analysis in order that criminology might be a scientific endeavor, and well-founded reconstruction interpretations would be possible.

Dr. Edmond Locard was a criminologist in the classic sense, a forensic generalist, and he educated and changed the world with his multidisciplinary and scientific approach to systematic evidence analysis.

August Vollmer

August Vollmer taught his students that criminology was not just about research. It necessarily involved the application of knowledge regarding crime and criminals in order to reduce either. He was, not surprisingly, heavily influenced by the works of Hans Gross, and wrote (Vollmer, 1949; pp. 39–40):

August Vollmer (1876–1955) was the first Chief of Police in Berkeley, California. He is known for his advocacy of both scientific education and investigations in law enforcement. Having helped accomplished more to professionalize and reform law enforcement than any other single figure in the history of criminology, Vollmer committed suicide with a bullet to the head November 4, 1955.

Among the several branches of criminology, one of them—criminalistics or scientific crime investigation—does employ the tools and techniques of the scientist.... Criminology belongs with the arts, and particularly does this statement apply to that entire field which concerns itself with the study of the causes and prevention of crime. Criminology as an art has probably existed since the beginning of civilization, but its development as a system is comparatively recent....

This is to say Vollmer believed that forensic examination of crime scenes and evidence was and should be scientific, while determining precise social causes and remedies for the problem of crime and criminals is less exact—drawn with imprecision and uncertainty given the general ignorance regarding criminology in his day.

A modest biography is offered in MacNamara (1995, pp. 811–812):

[Vollmer] was elected marshal of Berkeley, California, in 1905.... In 1907 he was elected president of the California Police Chiefs Association; from 1909 to 1932 he served as chief of Police for Berkeley; in 1922 he accepted the presidency of the International Association of Chiefs of Police; and from 1932 until his death he was an educator, professor of police administration at the University of California....

Vollmer was an innovator in an extremely conservative profession. He was an early advocate of college education for police officers.... He instituted an in-service training program of such rigor and effectiveness that it was copied by numerous police agencies in the United States and other countries.... As early as 1922 he inaugurated a single fingerprint classification system and a simple but effective method of classifying handwriting specimens. He also initiated the modus operandi approach to criminal investigation. In the 1920s and early 1930s, the Berkeley police laboratory became the model and training ground for police laboratory technicians throughout the country.

...Vollmer was at home with academic criminologists and he respected them.... As founder and president of the organization now known as the American Society of Criminology (which presents annually the August Vollmer Award to a distinguished criminologist), he extended his influence considerably. A faithful student of scientific management and public administration, he ceaselessly reeducated himself.

As a consequence of his scientifically oriented policing philosophy, Vollmer focused his career on the education and training of police officers and investigators as professionals. This meant a need for formal educational programs at colleges and universities, as well as professional organizations to provide a sense of community and guidance from those more knowledgeable, skilled, and experienced. Further background is provided in "Finest of the Finest" (1966):

> In 1905, August Vollmer, a self-educated criminologist, noticed that the then 130-year-old city had no police force and decided to start one. His name is still legend in law enforcement circles for the methods that he pioneered. His stiff rules of conduct are now standardized as a code of ethics for police across the country. His department was the first to use blood, fiber and soil analysis in detection (1907); the first to use the lie detector (a Berkeley cop collaborated in inventing the polygraph in 1921); it was an early developer of a fingerprint classification system (1924) and the first to use radio-equipped squad cars (1928).
>
> Perhaps most significant of all, Vollmer established a school of criminology on the Berkeley campus in 1916, and he sent his men to it. Early detractors used to laugh at the "college cops," but Vollmer's emphasis on an educated policeman has been carried forward and expanded under each of the three men who have succeeded him.

To see his vision through, police officers needed to be educated at university where they were to be schooled in modern methods of crime detection, criminal investigation, and criminal identification. What followed from Vollmer, at least in the United States, was a succession of professional gatherings related to police and forensic science education. These took shape as the result of the combined efforts of academic, legal, forensic, and law enforcement practitioners who met and shared knowledge regarding their common interests. Primarily these interests revolved around the study of crime and criminals, and the methods of their detection, identification, and apprehension. This included the development of the American Society of Criminology, as was discussed in the Preface of this work.

His legacy continued through the tremendous efforts of his students for at least a generation.

Edward Oscar Heinrich

The camera never lies, but a camera in the hands of a liar is a dangerous instrument.
　—Edward O. Heinrich (as quoted in Block, 1958, p. 37)

Edward Oscar Heinrich was born in 1881 in Clintonville, Wisconsin. At age 18, he became a licensed pharmacist in Tacoma, Washington; he worked hard and saved his money, aspiring to a college education and becoming a

Edward O. Heinrich, a.k.a. "The Wizard of Berkeley" (1881–1953).

chemist. In 1908, he realized that goal and graduated from the University of California at Berkeley with a bachelor's degree in chemistry. Soon thereafter, he moved back to Tacoma, where he worked for the city as a chemist and sanitary engineer for the next nine years. This position gave Heinrich his first exposure to forensic casework—it involved frequent requests for investigative assistance from both the police and the coroner's office.

Applying chemistry to casework taught Heinrich the limits of specializing. He learned that to be of use—to fully reconstruct events—a forensic scientist must have at least a general working knowledge of as many forensic specialties as possible. As a result, he continually made a study of ballistics, geology, physics, photography, hairs, handwriting, paper, and inks; he read every reference text and article he could get his hands on. In essence, he made of himself a forensic generalist, and his reputation grew with the successful employment of his methods to both criminal and civil cases.

In 1916, Heinrich became the chief of police in Alameda, California, and reorganized the department from top to bottom in terms of criminal files, fingerprints, and the employment of more modern investigative techniques. During that time, after the onset of World War I, he also lent his services to U.S. Army intelligence, providing training and performing forensic analysis.

Only a few years later, Heinrich would open his own private lab in Berkeley. To augment his practice, he became a member of the U.C. Berkeley faculty where he lectured on the subject of criminal investigation and served as a research associate in police science. When Heinrich began his private forensic casework, his methods were the exception and not the rule (Block, 1958, pp. 41–42):

> Scientific work was little known and often ridiculed. Plodding, without definite direction, took its place—chasing here and there for information, trying to find someone who might know something about the crime.

> In every way Heinrich's approach was quite opposite.

> That approach—his methodology—was one of the unique features of his whole career.

> "Understand this first," he usually said. "Crime analysis is an orderly procedure. It's precise and it follows always the same questions . . .

> "Precisely *what* happened? Precisely *when* did is happen? Precisely *where* did it happen? *Why* did it happen? *Who* did it?"

> . . .

"It's all like a mosaic, and every fact must be evaluated before it can
be fitted into the pattern. In that way, every fact as it is developed and
equated becomes a clue."

Heinrich would dedicate his life to advancing the cause of scientific investigation through the employment of his methods—working for the prosecution and the defense throughout his career. As recalled in Walton (2004, p. 5):

In Berkeley, the work of Edward Oscar Heinrich laid the foundation for
the future of professional forensic sciences. From his laboratory, Heinrich
repeatedly demonstrated the value of scientific examination of trace
evidence as his meticulous inspections provided the necessary links
between the crime and suspects. As a result, his work was in demand by
prosecutors and defense attorneys alike throughout the West.

According to Heinrich, the crime scene always contained a variety of clues, and it was up to a scientific investigator to find and accurately interpret them (Walton, 2004). Those interpretations could be combined to form a reconstruction of events that established both contacts and actions. Evidence, to Heinrich, was the only reliable witness to a crime (Block, 1958, pp. 43–44):

In the test tube and crucible or through the lens of the microscope and
camera I have found in my own practice the evidence of poison, the
traces of the deadly bullet, the identity of a clot, the source of a fiber,
the telltale fingerprint, the differing ink, the flaw in the typewriter,
the slip of the pen upon which I have turned in dramatic scenes of our
courts the rightful title to an estate, of the liberty, even the life, of an
individual.

Clues thus found and verified as physical facts definitely related to
an action become of enormous importance to clarifying erroneous
observations of eyewitnesses.

Heinrich did not regard the interpretation of evidence and its reconstruction as something within the ken of the average person or investigator. He regarded reconstruction as an ordered, disciplined, and scientific practice borne out of tireless dedication to one's personal education, experience, and research (Block, 1958, p. 44):

It is a matter of understanding the scientific aspects of ordinary
phenomena. Rarely are other than ordinary phenomena involved in the
commission of a crime. One is confronted with scrambled effects, all
parts of which separately are attributed to causes. The tracing of the
relationship between isolated points of fact, the completion of the chain
of circumstances between cause and effect, are the highest functions of
reason—to which must be added the creative imagination of the scientist.

Heinrich died in 1953 at the age of 72, with many of the techniques and philosophies that he had practiced having been adopted in police crime labs throughout the United States. Before his passing, he wondered at his life and purpose, writing (Block, 1958, p. 253):

> I am not positive that I am doing yet that which I was created for. Life is a series of frustrations but no man can spend his life with the atoms of chemistry without becoming convinced, that, though infinitesimally small, given the proper environment he will fulfill his function. Out of such observations has grown my hope that I, too, may find my purpose. In the meantime I try to approach it by using what training and talent I may have to make my community better to live in, helping where I can.

Edward Heinrich was a criminologist in the classic sense, a self-educated forensic generalist, and his development of scientific techniques and criminal identification revolutionized forensic science and its instruction in the United States.

Dr. Paul L. Kirk

This is evidence that does not forget. It is not confused by the excitement of the moment. It is not absent because human witnesses are. It is factual evidence. Physical evidence cannot be wrong; it cannot perjure itself; it cannot be wholly absent. Only its interpretation can err.

—Dr. Paul Kirk (1953, p. 4)

Dr. Paul Leland Kirk (1902–1970). *Source:* John E. Murdock, ATF Forensic Lab, Walnut Creek, California.

Paul Leland Kirk was born in Colorado Springs, Colorado, in 1902. He was first and foremost a scientist, but he was also a man of practical application as opposed to pure theory. He was educated at Ohio State University, where he received a B.A. in Chemistry; the University of Pittsburgh, where he received an M.S. in Chemistry; and the University of California, where he received a Ph.D. in Biochemistry. From 1929 to 1945, Dr. Kirk served as a professor of Biochemistry at the University of California at Berkeley.

Later in his career, he would tell students that he was initially drawn to forensic science in his early teaching days when a biochemistry student approached him with a question about a deceased dog and whether it could be determined if the dog had been poisoned. Investigating this issue piqued Kirk's forensic curiosities. Soon after, authorities contacted him to examine the clothing of a rape victim; they wanted to know whether anything on the clothing could be found, at the microscopic level, to associate the victim with her attacker.

Kirk's discovery of fibers from the attacker's shirt and the conviction of the rapist sealed his interest in forensic science and secured his reputation for solid results based on careful examinations. As described in Thorwald (1966, p. 150): "Kirk was a practical man rather than a theoretician. As early as 1934 he had concerned himself with the application of biochemistry to criminological questions.... He had also dealt with questions of blood testing for many years. He and his pupils published innumerable studies on investigation of blood clues and blood group determinations."

In 1937, Dr. Kirk, while remaining a professor of Biochemistry, assumed leadership of the Criminology program at U.C. Berkeley. He is widely credited with having saved this program from extinction. As described in Turner (1995, p. 323):

> August Vollmer, pioneering police administrator in Berkeley,
> California, was influential in developing university courses dealing
> with police matters, among them forensic science. At the outset
> these programs were offered in the criminology context, with the
> University of California, Berkeley, offering a curriculum in criminology
> as early as 1933. Dr. Paul Kirk subsequently developed the program in
> criminalistics at Berkeley....

The program gained momentum and grew in its reputation under his charge.

In 1953, after the completion of his work on the Manhattan Project during World War II, Kirk published the first edition of *Crime Investigation*, a treatise on criminal investigation, crime reconstruction, and forensic examination that endures to this day as a foundational industry standard with few equals (Kirk, 1953).

Kirk took a much bolder, holistic position on the importance of crime reconstruction and criminal behavior than most are aware. He repeatedly discussed what could only be referred to as criminal profiling in both editions of his seminal forensic textbook, *Crime Investigation* (Kirk, 1953, 1974). He more or less viewed criminal profiling as the natural outcome of physical evidence examination (Kirk, 1974, pp. 4–5):

> The study of physical evidence can be a material aid in locating the
> perpetrator of a crime....

> Physical evidence is often very useful to the police investigator before
> he has a suspect in custody or, in fact, before he even has suspicion
> of a possible perpetrator. If, for instance, the laboratory can describe
> the clothes worn by the criminal, give an idea of his stature, age, hair
> color, or similar information, the officer's search is correspondingly
> narrowed.

Frequently it is possible to indicate a probable occupation, or to describe a habitat with remarkable accuracy from careful examination of some apparently trifling object found at the scene of the crime. Such facts do not necessarily constitute proof of guilt of any particular person, but they may give a background that is of the greatest value....

As an illustration of the possibilities and the pitfalls attendant upon deductions from laboratory findings, the following example is illuminating. From the examination of a glove left at the scene of a burglary, the following inferences were drawn:

1. The culprit was a laborer associated with building construction.
2. His main occupation was pushing a wheelbarrow.
3. He lived outside the town proper, on a small farm or garden plot.
4. He was a southern European.
5. He raised chickens, and kept a cow or a horse.

As suggested by this passage, Kirk was an advocate of the investigative use of criminal profiling well before its potential was formally recognized by even the criminal investigators of his time. This advocacy continued in the first edition of *Fire Investigation* (1969), in which Kirk provided a basic guideline for crime reconstruction and criminal profiling that has not been significantly eroded by developments in either field.

Dr. Marvin Wolfgang (1924–1998), a pioneer in the fields of applied criminology and victimology, died of pancreatic cancer the age of 73.

Paul Kirk was a criminologist in the classic sense, a legendary forensic science educator, a forensic generalist, and "one of the foremost pioneers of scientific criminology" and criminalistics in the world (Thorwald, 1966, p. 149).

Dr. Marvin E. Wolfgang

...[W]hen a social scientist steps into the arena of adversary games, confronts role conflicts, and subjects the presentation of research to the cross-examination of his mind, he faces problems in the drama that are different from those described in textbooks.

Dr. Marvin Wolfgang (1987, p. 21)

Dr. Marvin Wolfgang was a professor of Criminology, Legal Studies, and Law at the Wharton School, and founding director of the Sellin Center for Studies in Criminology and Criminal Law, at the University of Pennsylvania. A brief biography, useful to understanding his tremendous contributions to all of criminology, including victimology, was written upon his death by Kaufman (1998):

Professor Wolfgang, a Philadelphia resident, was acknowledged in 1994 by the *British Journal of Criminology* as "the most influential criminologist in the English-speaking world."

He expanded the field of criminology by introducing and perfecting a methodology in which great masses of data like arrest records are analyzed over years to discern patterns of violence and crime. Through such longitudinal studies, now common in social sciences beyond criminology, he was able to portray criminal behavior in specific ways, examining subjects like the scale of juvenile delinquency, the relations of murderers and their victims and the extent of racial imbalances in sentencing.

For much of this century, academic criminology had concerned itself almost exclusively with psychological studies of the criminal mind and the amassing of anecdotal material. That emphasis was irrevocably altered in 1958 when Mr. Wolfgang produced a study, "Patterns of Criminal Homicide," a deep analysis of 588 Philadelphia murders.

"With that work Professor Wolfgang virtually defined modern criminology," said Richard Rosenfeld, a professor of criminology at the University of Missouri. Mr. Rosenfeld is serving as editor of a forthcoming edition of the *Journal of Criminal Homicide* that is dedicated to Mr. Wolfgang to mark the 40th anniversary of his work.

One of the more significant findings in that study was that 150 of the Philadelphia murders were what Mr. Wolfgang termed, in the neutral language of sociologists, "victim-precipitated homicides"—cases in which the eventual victim was "the first one in the homicide drama to use physical force."

He spelled it out even more clearly with a typical example: "A drunken husband, beating his wife in their kitchen, gave her a butcher knife and dared her to use it on him. She claimed that if he would strike her once more, she would use the knife, whereupon he slapped her in the face and she fatally stabbed him."

At the time, terms like "spouse abuse" were unknown, and Mr. Wolfgang did not use it. But with the evidence he had found from the police reports, he was able to define the shape and determine the scale of a not uncommon form of violence that few if any before him had studied in detail. Findings of a similar magnitude emerged from another remarkable longitudinal study, "Delinquency in a Birth Cohort," which was published in 1972 and is generally regarded as Professor Wolfgang's crowning scholarly achievement.

For this study, which, like all his work, was written by hand with a pen, Mr. Wolfgang obtained from schools in Philadelphia the names of 10,000 boys who were born in 1945. After 1963, when the boys turned 18, he and his team of researchers pored through police and court records to determine how many of the boys had police records. They found that 3,400 of the boys, or just over one-third, had records by the time they were 18.

He also determined that it was the youths whose records showed five or more offenses who together accounted for 52 percent of all offenses recorded in the study, and that this group amounted to only 6 percent of the total.

Mr. Wolfgang's conclusion that a few chronic offending juveniles account for a disproportionate amount of crime has strongly influenced legislative bodies and criminal justice policy makers around the world.

…

Neil Weiner, once his student and now a senior research associate at the Center for the Study of Youth Policy at Penn, said Mr. Wolfgang was often asked to testify in courts and before legislative commissions. "He routinely responded to such requests, but, in seeming contradiction, he rarely laid out policy recommendations, whether specific or general. Such things he left to others to infer from his dispassionate and objective studies."

However dispassionate was the form of his testimony, its content was sufficiently stirring to provoke any number of mailed threats. "We kept a folder of these loony letters," said Esther Lafair, who had been Mr. Wolfgang's secretary for 27 years.

She said the letters came in whenever he offered reasons that the death penalty should not be used or how the distribution of handguns should be curbed. Mr. Wolfgang was proud that his research findings were used in the Supreme Court's decision in Furman v. Georgia, which held in 1972 that the death penalty as then applied by states was unconstitutional.

The career of Dr. Wolfgang as it laid the foundation for future forensic criminologists with a social science orientation is best summarized by his own writing, penned just prior to his death (Wolfgang, 1987, pp. 20–21):

My experiences began in 1965 with the NAACP Legal Defense and Educational Fund, Inc. I gave my first testimony in Federal District Court in Little Rock, Arkansas, in connection with the famous case of Maxwell v. Bishop (1966), which was later pursued through the United States Supreme Court.... Alabama and Georgia followed, all dealing with blacks who, like Maxwell, had been convicted of rape and sentenced to death. My last major court experience was as a witness in Gregory v. Litton Systems, Inc. in Los Angeles in 1970, a case involving denial of a job because of a "substantial" arrest record....

I am a sociologist and criminologist, opposed to the death penalty, in favor of equality of opportunities and opposed to discrimination, whether on the street, in the factory, or in the courts.

...[W]hen a social scientist steps into the arena of adversary games, confronts role conflicts, and subjects the presentation of research to the cross-examination of his mind, he faces problems in the drama that are different from those described in textbooks.

Wolfgang also wrote thoughtfully about the ethics of forensic criminological testimony, explaining that science and scientific practice must exist separately from the law in order to serve it. He urged that "[t]he social scientist should not try to convert his design, his data, or his conclusions to conform to the litigation process," (Wolfgang, 1987, p. 31). However, he also appreciated that the aims and rules of litigation were different from those of scientific inquiry. He saw these challenges as well met by able scientific minds, and the expansion of expert testimony by criminologists as inevitable.

PAST TO PRESENT

In the past, the majority of forensic criminologists were government-employed civil servants like Hans Gross and August Vollmer—working for law enforcement, the courts, government agencies, or publicly funded crime labs adjunct to law enforcement. After retirement, there is every indication that the greater number had little option other than to live out their life on a government pension, or take up a second career in teaching or security work. There was, as previously mentioned, little perceived need, let alone funding, for independent forensic expertise of any kind.

In many parts of the world, independent forensic expertise is still available only to those who can afford it. In many systems, such as Australia, Canada, and the United Kingdom, there is even a prevailing attitude that if forensic experts are good enough for the government, they are good enough for the defense. Hence, the defense bar does not often perceive the need to, nor can it often afford to, hire privately employed forensic examiners of any kind. This reality hides the quality of forensic examinations in such systems, as there is no real peer review of findings and subsequent criticisms: we simply have no impartial measure regarding the quality of forensic work being done when private examinations are not performed.

In the United States, however, this changed radically upon the Supreme Court decision in *Ake v. Oklahoma* (1985). This decision held that

> This Court has long recognized that when a State brings its judicial power to bear on an indigent defendant in a criminal proceeding, it must take steps to assure that the defendant has a fair opportunity to present his defense. This elementary principle, grounded in significant part on the Fourteenth Amendment's due process guarantee of fundamental fairness, derives from the belief that justice cannot be equal where, simply as a result of his poverty, a defendant is denied the opportunity to participate meaningfully in a judicial proceeding in which his liberty is at stake. In recognition of this right, this Court held almost 30 years ago that once a State offers to criminal defendants the opportunity to appeal their cases, it must provide a trial transcript to an indigent defendant if the transcript is necessary to a decision on the merits of the appeal. Griffin v. Illinois, 351 U.S. 12 (1956). Since then, this Court has held that an indigent defendant may not be required to pay a fee before filing a notice of appeal of his conviction, Burns v. Ohio, 360 U.S. 252 (1959), that an indigent defendant is entitled to the assistance of counsel at trial, Gideon v. Wainwright, 372 U.S. 335 (1963), and on his first direct appeal as of right, Douglas v. California, 372 U.S. 353 (1963), and that such assistance must be effective. See Evitts v. Lucey, 469 U.S. 387 (1985); Strickland v. Washington, 466 U.S. 668 (1984); McMann v. Richardson, 397 U.S. 759, 771, n. 14 (1970). 3 Indeed, in Little v. Streater, 452 U.S. 1 (1981), we extended this principle of meaningful participation to a "quasi-criminal" proceeding and held that, in a paternity action, the State cannot deny the putative father blood grouping tests, if he cannot otherwise afford them. [470 U.S. 68, 77]

> Meaningful access to justice has been the consistent theme of these cases. We recognized long ago that mere access to the courthouse doors does not by itself assure a proper functioning of the adversary process, and that a criminal trial is fundamentally unfair if the State proceeds against an indigent defendant without making certain that he has access to the raw materials integral to the building of an effective defense. Thus, while the Court has not held that a State must purchase for the indigent defendant all the assistance that his wealthier counterpart might buy, see Ross v. Moffitt, 417 U.S. 600 (1974), it has often reaffirmed that fundamental fairness entitles indigent defendants to "an adequate opportunity to present their claims fairly within the adversary system," id., at 612. To implement this principle, we have focused on identifying the "basic tools of an adequate defense or appeal," Britt v. North Carolina, 404 U.S. 226, 227 (1971), and we have

required that such tools be provided to those defendants who cannot afford to pay for them.

To say that these basic tools must be provided is, of course, merely to begin our inquiry.

This decision basically held that because the government has overwhelming access to manpower, money, and forensic experts, the defense must be given parity for the adversary system to function fairly. The ruling is of course an ideal. The reality is that not every lawyer and court understands and invokes *Ake* appropriately or consistently, as explained in Findley (2008, pp. 929–931):

> …[T]he government has significantly greater access to forensic science services and experts than do most criminal defendants. Crime laboratories exist to provide such services to prosecutors; no corresponding institutions exist for defendants. And, because most defendants are indigent, their ability to hire experts is dependent on public funding of legal services to the indigent, which is abysmally inadequate in virtually every jurisdiction. Because funding for indigent defense is so inadequate, defense services are rationed in ways that put innocents at risk; rationing disfavors expensive, substantive innocence claims (such as expensive litigation about the validity of forensic evidence), and instead favors more inexpensive procedural constitutional claims. While the Supreme Court in Ake v. Oklahoma recognized a constitutional right to publicly funded experts for the indigent, exercise of that right is dependent on the willingness of a local judge to order the expenditure of scarce local resources, and on a cumbersome case-by-case, expert-by-expert process for requesting funding. Any risk of failure of that case-by-case process to provide adequate expert services falls on the defendant, and courts have tended to apply Ake narrowly.

> That system comes nowhere close to providing the level of forensic sciences assistance that is needed, or that is available to the prosecution.

In any case, the rendering of *Ake* changed the forensic realm in the United States dramatically by requiring the state to fund expert forensic analyses for indigent defendants. It increased the demand for independent forensic expertise of every relevant type, and directly acknowledged the legitimacy of private forensic practice as a necessary part of due process. Despite the majority of key historical figures in forensic criminology having already originated outside government employment, this was a major development because it enabled the number of private forensic practitioners, and private forensic labs, to increase beyond a select few. This reality was foreseen in Anderson and Winfree (1987) when they correctly recognized *Ake* as a "portent of things to come" (p. xx) with respect to the development of forensic criminology.

MODERN ARCHITECTS

There are certain individuals whose work and publications over the past 30 years have been of considerable architectural value to the continued existence of modern forensic criminology. They exist in pockets of multidisciplinary professional collaboration around the world, at universities and in private practice in the United States, Australia, the United Kingdom, and even South Africa. Some of these contemporary framers have had a tremendous impact on the authors of this text. This includes Dr. Paul Wilson, a professor of criminology at Bond University on the Gold Coast, Australia; Dr. John I. Thornton, an emeritus professor of Forensic Science at the University of California at Berkeley; and Dr. Daniel Kennedy who was kind enough to provide a foreword to this text. Their continued work and contribution bear mentioning for future generations.

Dr. Daniel B. Kennedy

Dr. Daniel Kennedy, Emeritus Professor of Sociology and Criminal Justice, University of Detroit-Mercy.

Dr. Daniel Kennedy holds an M.A. in Sociology, a Ph.D. in Educational Sociology, and is currently an emeritus professor of Sociology and Criminal Justice at the University of Detroit-Mercy. He began his career as a civilian crime analyst with the Detroit Police Department in 1966. Over the next decade, he also served as a counselor for the Federal Bureau of Prisons, as a probation officer in Detroit, and as a senior administrator of two police academies in southeastern Michigan.

Dr. Kennedy has been a practicing forensic criminologist since the 1980s, and is frequently called to court to testify in cases involving state police agencies, municipal police departments, and county sheriffs' departments. His testimony generally involves explaining the appropriate standards of care for the use of deadly force, vehicle pursuits, emergency psychiatric evaluations, prisoner health care, prevention of prisoner suicide, positional asphyxia/excited delirium, and "suicide by cop." Also, he evaluates lawsuits concerning premises' liability for negligent security in the private sector involving properties both in the United States and overseas. He specializes in crime foreseeability issues, appropriate standards of care in the security industry, and analyses of the behavioral aspects of proximate causation.

The authors regard Dr. Kennedy's most influential works to include the textbook *Applied Sociology for Police* (Kennedy and Kennedy, 1972); and his extensive body of research publications on the subjects of criminal profiling, negligent security, and premises liability, including "Premises Liability for Negligent Security" (Kennedy, 1993); "Role of the Criminologist in Negligent Security Cases" (Homant and Kennedy, 1996); "Problems with the Use of Criminal Profiling in Premises Security Litigation" (Homant and Kennedy, 1997); and "Psychological Aspects of Crime Scene Profiling: Validity Research" (Homant and Kennedy, 1998).

Dr. Kennedy's current research focus includes terrorist behavior and sleeper cells.

Dr. John I. Thornton

Dr. John I. Thornton holds a doctorate in Criminalistics, and is an emeritus professor of Forensic Science at the University of California at Berkeley. In a career that has spanned more than 45 years, he has authored more than 185 publications in the areas related to forensic science, to include methods of evidence analysis and interpretation, crime reconstruction, and professional ethics. He has also examined more than 800 homicide cases and testifed in court as an expert on more than several hundred occasions.

Dr. John I. Thornton, emeritus professor of forensic science at the University of California at Berkeley.

Dr. Thornton was a student of the late Dr. Paul Kirk, mentioned previously. Upon Kirk's death, Thornton assisted with editing the completed manuscript for the second edition of Kirk's seminal text *Crime Investigation* (1974). He also worked in California at the Contra Costa Sheriff's Department crime lab for nine years as a criminalist, several more years as the supervising criminalist, and then for one year as laboratory director. Following that, he taught as a professor of forensic science at the University of California at Berkeley for 24 years.

To the benefit of his profession, Dr. Thornton has served as president of the California Association of Criminalists, chairman of the Criminalistics Section of the American Academy of Forensic Sciences, and chairman of the Ethics Committee of the California Association of Criminalists.

The authors regard his most influential works to include "Uses and Abuses of Forensic Science" (Thornton, 1983); "Courts of Law v. Courts of Science: A Forensic Scientist's Reaction to Daubert" (Thornton, 1994); and "The General Assumptions and Rationale of Forensic Identification" (Thornton, 1997). Among his most recent contributions to forensic criminology is an ethical canon for crime reconstructionists published in Chisum and Turvey (2007).

Dr. Thornton is currently semiretired, working as an evidence specialist and crime scene investigator for the Napa County Sheriff's Department, just north of San Francisco.

Dr. Paul Wilson

Professor Paul Wilson is a criminologist and forensic psychologist who describes himself as a "generalist" in terms of his academic work but has developed an interest in recent years in forensic criminology issues. He has been Chairperson of Sociology at the University of Queensland, Foundation Dean of Humanities at the Queensland University of Technology, and Director of Research and Acting Director at the Australian Institute of Criminology. For eight years he was Dean of Humanities at Bond University and is currently Chair of Criminology at the same university.

Professor Wilson has also held several appointments in North America. He has worked and lectured at the Battelle Crime and Justice Research Centre in Seattle (largely in the area of rape investigation), the University of California at Irvine (on risk assessment and medical negligence), and Simon Fraser University in Vancouver, Canada. During these appointments, he worked with

Dr. Paul Wilson, Professor of Humanities and Social Science, Bond University.

prominent American criminologists Henry Pontell and Gil Geis and published articles on medical fraud. In 1990 he spent six months as the Rutgers University Library Fellow in New Jersey, with Professor Ron Clarke working on situational crime prevention techniques, a program that led to Clarke and Wilson establishing a crime prevention unit within Australia's national telephone carrier.

Professor Wilson has coauthored, edited, or written over 30 books, including *The Two Faces of Deviance* (cowritten with the internationally acclaimed criminologist Professor John Braithwaite who was Wilson's first Ph.D. candidate, is renowned for his work on reintegrative shaming, and won the Stockholm prize for criminology in 2006). Wilson's *Black Death White Hands* was based on evidence he gave in a landmark Australian case assessing the reasons why Aboriginal Australians had such a high rate of violence. *The Other Side of Rape* was another seminal work because it was the first detailed examination of unreported rape in Australia. His coedited textbook (with Professor Duncan Chappell) *The Australian Criminal Justice System* is now in its fifth edition, and together with *Sydney Morning Herald* journalist Malcolm Brown, he cowrote *Justice and Nightmares*, a book that assessed the failures and successes of forensic science in major criminal cases in the Antipodes.

Professor Wilson is especially interested in miscarriages of justice issues. His book *Who Killed Leanne* (with Graeme Crowley) pointed to the dangers of tunnel vision in police investigations of murder cases and his recently published *Five Drops of Blood* (with Dianne McInnes) outlined the problems of convicting on DNA evidence alone. He currently teaches courses in miscarriages of justice and is working on several other cases, one of which is before the Queensland Court of Appeal for a record-breaking third time.

As well as having prepared reports and given evidence in many criminal and civil proceedings, Professor Wilson has presented evidence in some major cases. These include the Kable case, the first major test in Australia of the right of governments to extend the time that prisoners serve in prison because of their propensity to commit future violence; a number of civil cases involving the right of criminological experts to give evidence in Australian courts in premise liability actions; and several controversial cases relating to the acceptability and effects, if any, of bondage material, brothels, and adult book shops. He has also given evidence in Bali, Indonesia, in the case of Schapelle Corby, accused of smuggling drugs into the country, and is on the List of Expert Witnesses for the International Criminal Court in The Hague.

Professor Wilson has recently published on the use, and misuse, of profiling in terrorism prevention and is currently researching, with others, the effects of unscrutinized and sometimes misleading forensic evidence presented in courts. He has also recently completed a study on the effectiveness of CCTV. In 2003 he was awarded the Order of Australia Medal for his contributions to criminology.

Moving Forward

Each of these authors has contributed mightily to the purposes of forensic criminology by virtue of casework, a commitment to higher education, and extensive publications in their respective areas of criminological interest. Students are encouraged to seek out the works of these authors, read them carefully, and keep them in their personal library for future reference.

As forensic criminologists, we need to remember our roots. We need to remember those came before us—their work, their words, and their purpose. We need to remember that while the practical aspects of criminology have fallen by the wayside for many, it is a science that can be applied to real-life problems in real-life situations, especially where the law is concerned. But not lightly, and not carelessly. There are many players, and there are many rules. In the words of Marvin Wolfgang (1987, p. 34):

> The litigation process has a different set of operating procedures than does scientific inquiry. Scientific evidence is judged within the context of legal rules of evidence, especially doctrines of constitutionality, that do not always coincide with the rubrics of science in the manner in which they order knowledge of empirical reality…. The preceptors of science must be alerted to their own fallibilities and be prepared to accept challenges outside their disciplines by others trained in the parameters of law, the adequacy of logic, and the rigors of reasoning.

The remainder of this text will be dedicated to educating criminology students and the forensic criminologist practitioners in the nature of forensic criminology, the kinds of examinations performed, the types of professionals involved, and the rule of law that governs their work such that they will meet these challenges successfully.

SUMMARY

Forensic criminology is the scientific study of crime and criminals for the purposes of addressing investigative and legal questions. This chapter reviewed how this type of criminology was developed from the broader applied criminology and how it differs from police science. What a science is, what scientific knowledge is, and the importance of the scientific method were discussed at length. It was further noted that the single distinguishing feature of forensic criminologists, with respect to any other type of criminologist, is the expectation that their findings will be submitted as evidence within the context of a formal investigation or legal proceeding.

The four major branches of the criminal justice system were discussed at length, including *law enforcement, forensic services, judiciary,* and *corrections.* It was further noted that the boundaries of criminology, as a field, are broadly and poorly drawn. The vast and various subdisciplines of criminology were discussed in an attempt to illustrate this broadness and to outline these boundaries for more informed study.

The history and origins of forensic criminology were discussed, with specific mention of the major contributors: Dr. Hans Gross, Dr. Edmond Locard, August Vollmer, Edward Heinrich, Dr. Paul Kirk, and Dr. Marvin Wolfgang. The importance of, and difference between, generalists and specialists in forensic criminology was also outlined in detail, and it was explained that the specialist is highly proficient and informed regarding a very restricted area of practice, while the generalist has a broad spectrum of knowledge from multiple areas of study and has multiple areas of expertise.

Finally, the importance of precedent-setting cases in the United States was discussed, including *Ake v. Oklahoma*, where it was recognized that every individual has the right to independent forensic expertise. It was noted that this is particularly important to forensic criminologists because without such rulings the checks and balances presented in other fields for peer review are not present, and the system cannot function fairly. As mentioned, these cases have opened the door for many independent forensic criminologists to make substantial contributions to various areas of forensic criminology, allowing for the continued existence of this field.

Review Questions

1. For a discipline to fall under the banner of criminology it must be_____ .
2. Name the three elements involved in the definition of a science.
3. T/F Those who work in laboratories are considered scientists,
4. T/F In an adversarial system, the defense must prove innocence.
5. T/F Forensic services providers are most often employed privately.
6. T/F There is no governing body for criminologists.
7. Define and explain Locard's Exchange Principle as it is used today.

REFERENCES

Ake v. Oklahoma, 1985. United States Supreme Court (470 U. S. 68), February 26.

Anderson, P., Winfree, L.T., 1987. Expert Witnesses: Criminologists in the Courtroom. State University of New York Press, Albany.

Black, H.C., 1990. Black's Law Dictionary, sixth ed. West Publishing Co., St. Paul, MN.

Block, E., 1958. The Wizard of Berkeley. Coward-McCann, New York.

Bureau of Justice Statistics (BJS), 2004. What Is the Sequence of Events in the Criminal Justice System?, U. S. Department of Justice, Washington D.C. January 14; url: http://www.ojp.usdoj.gov/bjs/justsys.htm

Chisum, W.J., Turvey, B., 2006. Crime Reconstruction. Elsevier Science, Boston, MA.

Curran, W.J., Shapiro, E.D., 1970. Law, Medicine, and Forensic Science, second ed. Little, Brown, and Co., Boston; citing Curtis, C. (1954) *It's Your Law*, Harvard University Press, Cambridge.

DeForest, P., Gaennslen, R., Lee, H., 1983. Forensic Science: An Introduction to Criminalistics. McGraw-Hill, New York.

Edwards, H., Gotsonis, C., 2009. Strengthening Forensic Science in the United States: A Path Forward. National Academies Press, Washington DC.

Findley, K., 2008. Innocents at Risk: Adversary Imbalance, Forensic Science, and the Search for Truth. Seton Hall Law Rev. 38, 893–973.

Finest of the Finest, 1966. Time Magazine, February 18; url: http://www.time.com/time/printout/0,8816,899019,00.html

Franzosi, R., 2004. From Words to Numbers: Narrative, Data, and Social Science. Cambridge University Press, Cambridge, UK.

Graper, E., 1969. American Police Administration. Patterson Smith Publishing Co., Montclair, NJ, Reprint from 1921 edition.

Gross, H., 1906. Criminal Investigation. G. Ramasawmy Chetty & Co, Madras.

Gross, H., 1911. Criminal Psychology. Little, Brown, & Co, New York.

Gross, H., 1924. Criminal Investigation. Sweet & Maxwell, London.

Gross, H., 1968. Criminal Psychology. Patterson Smith, Montclaire, NJ.

Homan, R., Kennedy, D., 1996. Role of the Criminologist in Negligent Security Cases. In: Wiley Law Publications Editorial Staff (Ed.), Wiley Expert Witness Update. John Wiley and Sons, New York, pp. 151–166.

Homant, R., Kennedy, D., 1997. Problems with the Use of Criminal Profiling in Premises Security Litigation. Trial Diplomacy Journal 20, 223–229.

Homant, R., Kennedy, D., 1998. Psychological Aspects of Crime Scene Profiling: Validity Research. Criminal Justice and Behavior 25, 319–343.

Hoover, L., 1995. Education. In: Bailey, W. (Ed.), The Encyclopedia of Police Science. Garland Publishing, New York, pp. 245–248.

Kaufman, M., 1998. Marvin E. Wolfgang, 73, Dies; Leading Figure in Criminology. New York Times, April 18; url: http://query.nytimes.com/gst/fullpage.html?res=9A0DE0D8123CF93BA25757C0A96E958260&sec=&spon=&pagewanted=print

Kennedy, D., 1993. Premises Liability for Negligent Security. In: Fay, J. (Ed.), Encyclopedia of Security Management. Butterworth-Heinemann, Boston, pp. 567–570.

Kennedy, D., Kennedy, B., 1972. Applied Sociology for Police. Charles C. Thomas Publishers, Springfield.

Kirk, P., 1953. Crime Investigation. Interscience, New York.

Kirk, P., 1969. Fire Investigation. John Wiley & Sons, New York.

Kirk, P., 1974. Crime Investigation, second ed. John Wiley & Sons, New York.

Labuschagne, I.L., 2003. The Role of the Criminologist as Expert Witness in Court, in Comparison with Those of Other Specialists, such as Psychologists, Psychiatrists or Social Workers. Symposium paper presentation: "Expert Evidence in Court: Requirements and Expectations", Sunnyside Campus, University of South Africa, May 30.

Locard, E., 1929. The Analysis of Dust Traces, Part 1. Revue Internationale de Criminalistique I (4–5), 176–249.

Locard, E., 1934. La Police et Les Methodes Scientifiques. Les Editions Rieder, Paris.

Locard, E., 1935. Manuel de Tecnica Policiaca. Imprenta Claraso, Barcelona.

MacNamara, D., 1995. August Vollmer. In: Bailey, W. (Ed.), The Encyclopedia of Police Science. Garland Publishing, New York, pp. 811–812.

May, L., 1936. Crime's Nemesis. MacMillan Company, New York.

McMillan, N., Roberts, P., 2003. For Criminology in International Criminal Justice. Journal of International Criminal Justice August, 1 (1), 315–338.

Morn, F., 1995. Academic Politics and the History of Criminal Justice Education. Greenwood Press, Westport, CT.

Reckless, W., 1995. The Crime Problem, second ed. Appletan-Century-Crafts, Inc., New York.

Reid, S., 2003. Crime and Criminology, tenth ed. McGraw Hill, Boston.

Rhodes, H., 1952. In the Tracks of Crime. Turnstile Press Ltd, London.

Söderman, H., 1957. Policeman's Lot. Longmans, Green and Company, London.

Stout, B., Yates, J., Williams, B., 2008. Applied Criminology. Sage Publications, Thousand Oaks, CA.

Sullivan, J., 1977. Introduction to Police Science, third ed. McGraw Hill, New York.

Terblanche, S.S., 1999. The Guide to Sentencing in South Africa, Butterworths, Durban.

Thornton, J.I., 1983. Uses and Abuses of Forensic Science. In: Thomas, W. (Ed.), Science and Law: An Essential Alliance, Westview Press, Boulder, CO.

Thornton, J.I., 1994. Courts of Law v. Courts of Science: A Forensic Scientist's Reaction to Daubert. Shepard's Scientific and Evidence Quarterly Winter 1 (3), 475–485.

Thornton, J.I., 1997. The General Assumptions and Rationale of Forensic Identification. In: Faigman, D.L., Kaye, D.H., Saks, M.J., Sanders, J. (Eds.), Modern Scientific Evidence: The Law and Science of Expert Testimony, vol. 2, West Publishing Co., St. Paul, MN.

Thorwald, J., 1966. Crime and Science: The New Frontier in Criminology. Harcourt, Brace, & World, New York.

Turner, R., 1995. Forensic Science. In: Bailey, W. (Ed.), The Encyclopedia of Police Science. Garland Publishing, New York, pp. 321–326.

Turvey, B., 2008. Criminal Profiling: An Introduction to Behavioral Evidence Analysis, third ed. Elsevier Science, San Diego.

Turvey, B., Petherick, W., 2008. Forensic Victimology. Elsevier Science, San Diego.

Van der Hoven, A.E., 2006. The Criminologist as an Expert Witness in Court. Acta Criminologica 19 (2), 152–171.

Vollmer, A., 1949. The Criminal. Foundation Press, Brooklyn.

Vollmer, A., 1971. The Police and Modern Society. Patterson Smith, Montclaire, NJ. Reprint of Vollmer, A. (1936) The Police and Modern Society, Berkeley, University of California Press.

Walton, R., 2004. The Legacy of Edward Oscar Heinrich. Bancroftiana: The Newsletter of the Friends of the Bancroft Library, Spring, No. 124, p. 5.

Williams, F., 1995. Criminology In: Bailey, W. (Ed.), The Encyclopedia of Police Science. Garland Publishing, New York, pp. 178–184.

Wolfgang, M., 1987. The Social Scientist in Court. In: Anderson, P., Winfree, L.T. (Eds.), Expert Witnesses: Criminologists in the Courtroom. State University of New York Press, Albany.

CHAPTER 2

Anatomy of the Courtroom: A Legal Perspective

Ben Ihle

When the liberty of an individual may depend in part on physical evidence it is not unreasonable to ask that the expert witnesses who are called upon to testify, either against the defendant, or on his behalf, know what they are doing.

Dr. John Thornton in Kirk and Thornton (1974, pp. v–vi)

KEY TERMS

Adversarial System: A sytem of justice in which each side to a dispute puts arguments to an impartial and disinterested arbiter.

Civil Trial: A trial in which a party seeks money or some other remedy that may arise due to the occurrence of events such as a contractual breach, a false advertisement, or an act of alleged negligence; a suit.

Consultant Expert: One engaged by a party to litigation who provides advice and opinions behind the scenes.

Criminal Trial: A type of trial that may arise from the commission of, and subsequent detection of, a crime or alleged crime.

Discovery: The act of each party to litigation providing the other side with documents in their respective possession that relates to the claim, whether or not the documents tend to support the case of the side providing them.

Expert Witness: A witness who gives evidence designed to assist the court based on the witness's specialized training, study, or experience.

Hung Jury: The result (or more accurately, the lack of a result) of a trial whereby jurors become deadlocked in their deliberations; they are not unanimous.

Inquisitorial System: A system of justice in with the judge does not sit as an independent arbiter but acts as an investigator in search of the truth.

Jury: A group of people who decide the outcome of a case after being told as much of the law as they need to know to determine the facts of a case in dispute.

CONTENTS

51

"Not Guilty" Verdict: The outcome of a jury which unanimously finds that the prosecution has failed to discharge its burden of proof.

Scientific Method: A search for scientific truth through systematic observation and testing.

Voir Dire: A trial within trial, reserved to be considered and determined by the trial judge only.

The roles played by an expert forensic criminologist are wide and varied. From advising policy makers to aiding investigators, the forensic criminologist may need to be many things to many people, depending on the task at hand. However, never are the stakes so high, nor the immediate ramifications so dire, than when the expert is called to testify as to his or her opinion upon the trial of a person accused of a crime. It is in this arena where the product of the expert's craft (the evidence of the expert's professional opinion) may literally be the difference between another's freedom and incarceration. In some jurisdictions, it may be the difference between life and death.

When the expert is giving evidence within a courtroom setting, his or her methods and opinions are exposed to the highest level of scrutiny. The expert may be challenged as to the extent of his or her expertise, or forced to defend the validity of his or her chosen field of study against attacks that it is merely guesswork or irrelevant. The attack may not only extend to that of the expert's profession: salvos on his or her personal credibility may be launched with the expert forced to explain matters within his or her personal life, or historical indiscretions.

It is for these reasons that experts must know not only what they are doing within their chosen field of expertise, but also when called as witnesses have some appreciation of their function and province as such. The level of professional self-awareness required can only come through an appreciation of the framework in which they are performing, the roles of others within that framework, and the use that can and will be made of the experts' evidence. By gleaning some understanding of what is required of experts and of where other experts routinely fail, it is hoped that the readers of this chapter will be better equipped to prepare themselves and hone their skills in this challenging task. While it is one thing to know what one is doing within a professional office, laboratory, or classroom, it is quite another to adequately know what one is doing when being examined and cross-examined in a court of law.

ADVERSARIAL LITIGATION: SEARCH FOR TRUTH OR GLADIATORIAL ARENA?

Any discussion of the role of the expert witness must necessarily be pared back to the stage upon which that witness is called to perform: the courtroom. Most courtrooms, whether operating under the adversarial or inquisitorial systems, have several features that are common. The judge(s) (and *jury* if there is one) will have a clearly delineated area, usually with a clear view of the witness box (or stand) from where the expert and other witnesses give their evidence. The parties to the proceeding will be allocated areas that will invariably face toward the judge(s) and also have clear line of sight to the witness box.

The physical layout of the courtroom, though, is only one aspect of the setting. The most significant aspect of the setting is the historical and functional system under which the courtroom in question operates. In common law countries (such as the United States, Australia, and the United Kingdom), all criminal courts operate under the *adversarial system*.[1] In civil law jurisdictions (such as France and other mainland European countries), the *inquisitorial system* is favored.

[1] As well as most civil law courts, with a few exceptions such as the coroner's court and some tribunals and commissions.

The Adversarial System

Put simply, the adversarial system of litigation is one in which each side to a dispute puts arguments to an impartial and disinterested (as opposed to uninterested, one hopes) arbiter. The arbiter may be one who is asked to find facts, or decide on the law, or both, and come to a final decision about the dispute between the parties. The adversarial system has been applied and refined through precedent over centuries in several jurisdictions. It holds as its fundamental underpinning the philosophy that the best way to determine a dispute is for an independent adjudicator to hear and consider strong arguments on each side of the issue. It is for this reason that the adversarial system is often referred to as a contest or game between two (or more) sides with the judge(s) acting as umpire (Fairchild and Dammer, 2001, p. 140) deciding whether each side is playing by the rules. If the individual case being litigated does not involve a jury, then the judge(s) will also be required to determine the victor.

Within the adversarial system, the parties advance their case through argument and by calling witnesses to give evidence that support and tend to advance their case. At the same time the parties may seek to attack or undermine their opponent's case by demonstrating that it is flawed, misconceived, or unbelievable (Ranson, 1996, p. 29). The system is adversarial not only by name, but also by nature: a contest between two opposing sides who aim to strike blows against the other to the advancement of their case.

Critical to the adversarial system of criminal litigation is the notion of *procedural fairness* (also known as *natural justice*), which provides that the accused person is to be afforded rights[2] such as:

- The right to silence;
- The right to counsel;
- The presumption of innocence;
- The right to know the allegations leveled against him or her; and
- The right to face his or her accusers.

It is for these reasons that the adversarial system is said to afford the accused person in a criminal trial with the most advantages. The accused's counsel will attempt to use these advantages as both weapons and shield in the battle against the prosecution. Where a dispute as to the application of these principles arises, the judge will be asked to determine the dispute on that issue.

Consistent with the rights listed previously, the rules of evidence are significantly weighed in favor of the accused person in an adversarial trial. This is to ensure, as best as possible, that the accused receives a fair trial, determined on evidence that is reliable and relevant to the issue in dispute. However, the application of these rules can be of frustration to victims and prosecutors alike. Often cogent (and relevant) evidence is excluded because its admission would detrimentally impact on the fairness of the trial. Accordingly, a trial must be determined on the evidence presented within it, and that evidence only. The discourse between a barrister (counsel) and law lord (judge) in a now famous (or perhaps infamous) passage from an English case most poignantly demonstrates the extreme application of this tenet. Murphy (2002) in his tome on evidence recounts this exchange:

> A frustrated judge in an English adversarial court finally asked a barrister (counsel) after witnesses had produced conflicting accounts, "Am I never to hear the truth?"
>
> "No, my lord, merely the evidence" replied the counsel.

The Inquisitorial System

Civil law countries, such as most of those in mainland Europe, derive their inquisitorial system of justice from the most ancient traditions of justice. Stemming from the biblical times of King Solomon through Roman practices and the Napoleonic Code, inquisitorial judges do not sit as independent arbiters. Rather, judges act as a kind of "investigator" in search of the truth. They determine what evidence is to be taken into account in considering the dispute. The court calls witnesses on its own initiative and plays an active role in both the pretrial and trial processes.

Unlike the common law traditions of the adversarial process, the procedures and rules of evidence are much less rigorously applied in the inquisitorial system. As such, it is often said that the inquisitorial process arrives more readily at a finding of "truth," whereas the adversarial system merely results in the determination of a dispute upon the evidence presented. Perhaps for this reason a former U.S. Supreme Court Justice (Burger, 1968) made the following remark:

> If he were innocent, he would prefer to be tried by a civil law (i.e., Inquisitorial) court, but that if he were guilty, he would prefer to be tried by a common law (i.e., Adversarial) court.

THE EXPERT'S ROLE IN THE PROCESS: AN ADVERSARIAL PERSPECTIVE

An *expert witness* within the adversarial system will almost always be called by one side or another to the litigation.[3] In a criminal case this will involve the expert being called either by the prosecution or the defense, presumably to give evidence that is most favorable the side calling him or her. Accordingly, the expert witness needs to appreciate the audience to whom the evidence is to be presented. In criminal cases, this audience will most often be constituted by a jury.

[3]Some courts have the power to call their own experts either through their inherent jurisdiction or as provided for by statutory rules. However, these powers, where they exist, should, and are, exercised only in rare circumstances.

Juries in the Adversarial System

In cases where a jury is involved,[4] the presiding judge is asked only to determine issues of law including admissibility of evidence and fairness to the accused. This may include the admissibility of the evidence from an expert witness.

Practically, the role of arbiter (or "judge") is shared among the relevant umpires: the judge is the judge of the law, while the jury combined are the judges of the facts. To this end, the judge tells the jury as much law as they need to know to fulfill their task, determining the facts of the case in dispute.

You will recall the brief discussion at the beginning of this chapter of the common features of all courtrooms and the fact that the jury (if there is one) are positioned in an area that has "a clear view of the witness box (or stand) from where the expert and other witnesses give their evidence." The reason is that the jury's deliberations must be based exclusively upon the evidence, and the evidence in any given criminal case will be, by far and away, mostly constituted by what witnesses say in the witness box. In a jury trial it is exclusively the function of the jury to determine what parts of the presented evidence they will rely on in determining the facts in dispute. In doing this the jury must consider the weight which they will attach to any individual piece of evidence, whether

[4]Most criminal trials in common law countries are determined by juries; however, recent legislative amendments in some jurisdictions mean that issues as to criminal responsibility may be determined by a judge alone. These amendments represent a significant shift in historical adversarial processes and may be indicative of a more inquisitorial approach being taken by criminal courts traditionally operating under the adversarial system.

[5]*Viva voce* is a Latin term that means "by word of mouth."

physical or given as *viva voce*[5] evidence from a witness. For this reason, the jury is often given "the best seat in the house" with a clear view of the witness box (also referred to as the witness stand) so they can assess the evidence being given by a witness and the manner in which it is given, including the witness's demeanor under cross-examination when challenged on his or her evidence.

The Expert Witness's Role in the Adversarial System

Distinct from the rules of admissibility lies the role of the expert witness in the courtroom setting. While the rules are well recorded and explained, the role is less well defined. It will vary on a case-by-case basis, but generally, the expert witness's role is "to assist the court" in its determination of the issues in dispute.

A respected English judge, Lord President Cooper, laid down the following general formulation of the expert witness's role in his decision in *Davie v Edinburgh Magistrates*:[6]

[6](1953) SC 34 at 40.

> [The duty of the expert is to] furnish the judge or jury with the necessary scientific criteria for testing the accuracy of their conclusions, so as to enable the judge or jury to form their own independent judgement by the application of these criteria to the facts proved in evidence.

In isolation, the utility of this formulation is limited. For one, how does one adequately identify the relevant "necessary scientific criteria"?

Helpfully, Eggleston (1983) argues that the expert's role may be satisfied by performance of four separate yet related functions:

- Generalizing from experience;
- Acting as librarian;
- Acting as statistician; and
- Acting as advocate.

[7](1990) 24 FCR 313 at 350–1. Court comprising of Lockhart, Wilcox, and Gummow (later of the High Court) JJ.

While this approach is not flawless, it was approved and adopted by the Full Federal Court of Australia in *Arnotts Ltd v Trade Practices Commission*.[7]

Generalizing from Experience

Eggleston suggests that generalizations based on experience may be in the form of an assertion of fact or opinion. However, although the Federal Court has adopted this analysis, many noted authors in the area of expert evidence warn of the dangers of generalizing. Thornton (1997) argues that this type of assertion is based on inductive reasoning and merely results in a working assumption that may or may not be valid. Turvey (2002) states that inductive reasoning involves broad generalizations based on premises. However, while the premises themselves may be correct, the subsequent conclusion may be false.

The problems raised by inductive reasoning within the setting of a criminal trial are twofold: first, the conclusion if stated as a fact may actually be false; second, if the conclusion is stated as an opinion based on experience, often the premises are untestable. Therefore, the jury cannot assess the logic involved in drawing the conclusion, and the expert effectually usurps his or her own function and remains unaccountable. Gross (1898, p. 106) grappled with this issue as early as the late 1800s when he stated, "[T]he problem is the examination of how inferences have been made by another and what value his inferences may have for our own conclusions."

The critics of inductive reasoning unanimously support its antithesis, deduction.[8] Deductive reasoning takes the given premises and logically follows them through to the conclusion. It involves critical thinking and may be evaluated by an objective assessor. Implicitly, if the premises are true, then so too must be the conclusion. This is the basis of the *scientific method*.

[8]See, for example, Gross (1894), Ranson (1996), Saferstein (2001), and Turvey (2002).

The decreased potential for false conclusions based on true premises and the increased ability to evaluate the logic from which a deductive opinion results makes it more conducive to the role of the expert witness. By providing the jury with the ability to evaluate the reasoning of the expert, the witness may necessarily facilitate his or her role as expounded by Cooper LP. Moreover, as justice should be the ultimate aim of the court, the increased reliability of deduction lends itself more convincingly, and appropriately, to the process.

Acting as Librarian

One interpretation of Cooper LP's statement may be summarized thus: the role of the expert witness is to educate the triers of fact as to things beyond their ordinary knowledge. Due to the nature of the expert's training and experience, this knowledge may only be imparted by the expert "flagging" relevant literature through his or her testimony. Sometimes, the expert may not know the answer from his or her own experience or study but may know, as he or she is adequately skilled in his or her art, which works of authority provide such an answer. In this instance, the expert is not generalizing or inductively reasoning. Rather, as suggested by Freckleton and Selby (2002), the expert is using his or her knowledge and skill to find the answer from the body of literature that provides the framework for his or her field of expertise.

One such example of this within a criminal law setting can be found in the case of *R v Abadom*[9] where a scientist from the British Home Office gave evidence as to the refractive index of glass found in a suspect's shoe. The glass was the same type as that found at the scene of the crime. Although the scientist was able to offer opinion as to the match, it was only through use of a table of refractive index compiled by other scientists that he was able to highlight the low probability that the two samples of glass were unrelated. By effectively bringing

[9][1983] 1 All E R 364.

that table to the attention of the jury, the expert scientist fulfilled the role of librarian and the jury could ponder the fact as to whether the glass samples were from the same source.

Acting as Statistician

[10](1988) 83 ALR 299.

In *Trade Practices Commission v Australian Meat Holdings Pty Ltd*,[10] the Australian Federal Court held that sometimes the expert can only draw appropriate conclusions from statistical methods applied to material from other sources. The significance of this process to criminal trials can be observed through expert evidence related to DNA typing.

The very nature of some types of class evidence (e.g., hair and fiber) and individuating evidence (e.g., DNA) lend themselves to interpretation only through statistical application. When offering an opinion based on these types of evidence, the expert, by necessity, must refer to frequency tables and offer an opinion based on statistics. Therefore, the expert's function to act as a statistician and statistics interpreter is appropriately defined. However, this arguably applies only when dealing with evidence that requires opinions to be expressed in accordance with probabilities.

Acting as Advocate

The expert's final role is to act as an advocate: not for a side, nor himself or herslef, but for his or her opinion and methods (Eggleston, 1983; Freckleton and Selby, 2002).[11] Eggleston (1983, p. 154) identifies that, in performance of this function, problems may arise due to the assumptions on which the expert may be basing his opinion. However,

[11]Also see *Clark v Ryan* (1960) 103 CLR 486.

> If he makes his assumptions clear, there is no objection to his arguing what the consequences of accepting those arguments should be; but he is not to do the jury's fact finding for it, where this depends on accepting one or other set of contradictory witnesses.

In essence, Eggleston opines that where there is any contradictory evidence to the expert's opinion, if the expert has adequately fulfilled his or her other functions, then he or she may rightly advocate his or her opinion.

It is interesting to note that Eggleston stresses the necessity for the expert to "make his assumptions" clear when he earlier states that the expert is to generalize from experience [see above]. Presumably, if the expert generalizes from experience without specifically identifying what those experiences are, then he or she undermines his or her ability to advocate for his or her opinion. Otherwise, the most dangerous situation arises: where the expert can advocate an opinion based on untestable premises and effectively, if not literally, decide the issue for the judge and/or jury. This may, even in the face of contradictory evidence, be highly persuasive to a jury and decide the outcome of the trial.

Science in the Courtroom: The Glove Doesn't Fit the Hand

Any discussion of expert evidence within the adversarial system would be deficient if it failed to identify the most common impasse between the role of the expert as a witness and the role of the expert as practitioner. Due, at least in part, to the rules which govern the reception of expert evidence in a courtroom, commonly forensic experts abound from scientific fields or, at the very least, fields which are founded on the scientific method. The scientific method, at its core, is derived from a search for scientific truth, through systematic observation and testing. However, adversarial courts are less about truth than they are about proof. The level of precision which can, and is, applied in a courtroom must be less than that applied in science: while science may be founded on facts and figures, the court process is founded on evidence and proof. The latter are, without doubt, less concrete concepts than the former.

The expert must always be mindful of the different respective bases of science and the courtroom when his or her work has a forensic aspect to it. The expert is asked, when called into the witness box, to measure his or her methods and conclusions by a different ruler to that which he or she is used to. "Scientific probability" is a different thing to "beyond reasonable doubt," and any attempt to correlate the two will almost certainly lead to conceptual, if not legal, error. Therefore, the expert must be cognizant of these divergences, and instead of trying to tailor his or her opinion to fit within the legal framework, remain faithful to his or her endeavor. Failure to do so leaves the expert vulnerable to misstatements and his or her evidence to misinterpretation. This devalues the expert's role and ultimately only confuses the court (however constituted).

AUSTRALIAN CRIMINAL PROCEDURE: AN OVERVIEW FOR EXPERTS

The foundation for any litigation is laid upon the happening of a certain event. For a criminal trial, that event is the commission and subsequent detection of a crime, or alleged crime, as the case may be. A dispute which gives rise to a *civil trial* may arise due the occurrence of event such as a contractual breach, a false advertisement, or an act of alleged negligence. It may also arise due to the perception that something actionable will occur in the future, so the court process is invoked to stop that occurrence from happening.

While the forensic criminologist's utility in the criminal trial procedure is self-evident, the role of such an expert in the civil arena may not be so readily apparent. However, depending on the subject matter of the civil litigation (also known as a *suit*) an expert forensic criminologist may be of assistance in not only giving relevant expert testimony, such evidence may ultimately be invaluable to the court in determining the dispute. An appreciation of the steps involved in, and related to, both criminal and civil litigation should enlighten.

Criminal Procedure
The Filing of Charges

In Australia, criminal litigation begins with the filing of charges, usually by some prosecuting authority appointed by the government to enforce the criminal law. [12] Depending on the subject matter and legal source of the charge, the authority will be the police or some other regulatory body (for example, the Australian Securities and Investment Commission). The charges are filed, usually after the investigation (or at least the vast majority of the investigation) has been completed by the relevant authority. Often, prior to the filing of the charges, the suspect is interviewed by police, and the nature of the allegations is put to him or her. Commonly, the interview is electronically recorded, either in audio and sometimes in video.

Upon the filing of the charges, the Suspect becomes the Defendant, and the adversarial process begins with the prosecution formally leveling the allegations against the Defendant. The case then typically proceeds through a number of preliminary or "interlocutory" steps whereby the prosecution concludes its investigation against the Defendant and provides copies of the witness statements and access to the physical exhibits (or copies if such can be provided) of the physical exhibits that it intends to rely on in proving its case against the Defendant.

Committal Hearing

After the Defendant has had the opportunity of considering the prosecution's evidence, he or she is afforded the opportunity of testing the evidence of witnesses, by cross-examination. For serious offenses (referred to as *indictable offenses*), the Defendant can do this first in the absence of the jury at a preliminary hearing, often referred to as a *committal*. While some Australian jurisdictions have done away with committal hearings altogether, other states have permitted them, but only where the Defendant shows why the cross-examination of specific witnesses is relevant and justified. [13]

The committal hearing is the first opportunity for the Defendant to hear and see the witnesses who are to give evidence against him or her. It also gives the Defendant the opportunity to test, through cross-examination (usually by his

[12]Generally prosecutions are brought by the police or the Director of Public Prosecutions representing the Crown (i.e., State or Commonwealth). However this does not mean that a private individual cannot bring a private criminal prosecution, though this is rarely done. In the state of Victoria, the Director of Public Prosecutions has the right to "take over" the prosecution of any individual under state legislation, whether or not that prosecution was commenced by the DPP or on his or her behalf: s 22 (1)(ii) of the *Public Prosecutions Act* (Vic) 1994.

[13]See, for example, Victoria where the procedure is regulated by the *Magistrates' Court Act* 1989 (Vic). Also note that due to policy reasons, some state legislatures have placed a ban on the cross-examination of child sex complainants at committal, limiting the defendant's right to cross-examine his or her accuser to the ultimate trial. Even then the cross-examination may only be permitted to be done via video-link and done at some prearranged time when the jury are not present, with the video of the cross-examination played to them sometime later.

or her counsel), the witnesses' evidence and the consistency of their account. Cross-examination is the tool that lawyers use to test a witness's evidence. It may be designed to illicit the truth or reveal a lie or show that, while the witness may be truthful, he or she is otherwise unreliable. At committal, the cross-examination is either aimed at having the charges dismissed or laying a foundation so that cross-examination of the witness at the later trial may be more successful, or even devastate the prosecution case.

There is no jury at committal.[14] The hearing is presided over by an appointed official, usually a magistrate (a judicial officer), exercising administrative rather than judicial power.[15] At the conclusion of the committal hearing, the magistrate is required to consider whether the prosecution's evidence is of sufficient weight to put the defendant on trial for any indictable (serious) offense, whether charged with that offense or not.[16]

The Trial

Should a Defendant be committed for trial, then the matter is transferred to a court of higher jurisdiction; the level of the court will be dependent on the nature of the charges on which he or she was committed. In all Australian states, homicide offenses are ultimately tried in the state Supreme Courts, whereas most other indictable offenses are heard and determined in the District Court (all states save Victoria) or County Court (Victoria only).

Unlike a committal, in all jurisdictions, a Defendant (now referred to as an *Accused* following committal) is entitled to cross-examine witnesses called by the prosecution. Unlike the committal procedure in some states which require the court's permission for cross-examination, fundamental to the adversarial principles of procedural fairness, the Accused can (usually via his or her counsel) fully engage in the adversarial process and "attack" either the credit or credibility of the witnesses. As discussed, at trial, this is usually done before a judge and jury: the judge being the judge of the law and the jury being the judges of the facts.

The trial is also the opportunity for the Accused to call witnesses (although this can be done at committal, it is extremely rare for a Defendant to call witnesses or give evidence at committal). However, just as the Accused has the right to cross-examine the prosecution witnesses, so too the prosecution may cross-examine witnesses called by the Accused upon his or her trial (including the Accused should he or she elect to give evidence).

A trial begins with opening remarks from the prosecutor where the evidence to be called is outlined. Often the defense counsel will then advise the jury of the areas of dispute, thereby focusing the jury's attention on the evidence that is to be contentious. Following the opening remarks, the prosecutor calls witnesses, who in turn may be cross-examined by the defense counsel (and re-examined

[14]Although preliminary hearing by grand jury is still available in some states, see, for example, s 354 of the *Crimes Act* 1958 (Vic).

[15]This means that it is not appealable by courts within the usual court hierarchy but may, however, be reviewable by a court of inherent (or statutory) jurisdiction as if decision were one of a government official exercising power on behalf of the executive.

[16]See for example, Queensland—*Justices Act* 1886, s 108; Tasmania—*Justices Act* 1959, ss 61 & 62.

by the prosecutor to clarify his or her evidence if necessary). After the prosecution has called all of its witnesses, the prosecution case is formally closed. It is at this juncture that the Accused gives evidence, if he or she so chooses. Other defense witnesses then follow (if they are to be called), and the process of cross-examination and re-examination occurs, but this time with the prosecutor cross-examining and the defense counsel re-examining.

When all the evidence is heard, the parties then give their closing remarks, the prosecutor usually going before defense counsel. During closing remarks the parties may engage in argument before the jury and make submissions to the jury as to which evidence they should accept, which evidence they should reject, and why. Both prosecutor and defense counsel may argue that certain evidence should apply to the issues in dispute in a way which advances their case. To this end, the closing argument is the opportunity for the lawyers to implore the jury to accept their interpretation of all the evidence and their rationalization of its meaning to the case.

Before the jury consider their verdict, the judge provides them with directions as to the law which they need to apply in reaching their decision. The judge will identify those matters of which they need to be satisfied before they may convict the Accused and the standard to which they need to be satisfied: beyond reasonable doubt. The judge will tell them how they may use certain types of evidence and, equally, how they may not use other types of evidence. What the judge tells the jury about the law is binding upon them. Unlike the prosecutor and defense counsel's closing arguments, the jury are not free to accept or reject what the judge tells them about the law. The jury cannot place less or more weight on the judge's direction of law, as they may do with parts of the evidence. The judge is the judge of the law, and the jury are bound by what he or she says about it.

The judge may, if he or she thinks it necessary, make some comment on the evidence or on some argument put to the jury by the lawyers. Unlike the judge's direction on the law, in these matters the jury are free to accept or reject the judge's comments on the evidence or argument just as they are free to accept or reject the lawyers' arguments made.

The Verdict

Armed with law they require to arrive at a decision, the evidence presented and arguments of the prosecutor and defense counsel ringing in their ears, the jury then retire to deliberate and consider their verdict. The verdict must be unanimous:[17] either all 12 are satisfied that the prosecution has proved the guilt of the Accused beyond reasonable doubt or they are not. It is significant to note at this stage that a verdict of "not guilty" (see "*not guilty*" *verdict*) is technically more akin to the phrase "not proven beyond reasonable doubt" rather than that of "innocent."

[17]Although provision is made in some jurisdictions for a "majority verdict" of 11 of the 12 jurors to be returned after a lengthy dead-locked deliberation with respect to certain offenses.

Should a jury be unable to reach a unanimous verdict, then by the stalemate the jury are said to be "hung" (see *hung jury* in key terms list). The jury is then discharged and the trial is run again before another jury.

Should the jury unanimously find that the prosecution has failed to discharge its burden of proof, then the verdict will properly be one of "not guilty." The Accused is then set free. Generally, the Accused's acquittal cannot be appealed by the prosecution, nor can he or she be tried again for the same charges nor for charges arising from the same set of circumstances.[18]

Sentencing Phase

Upon a finding of guilt (which may be achieved at any stage of the process by the Defendant/Accused pleading guilty to the offense or offenses), the jury is discharged and the matter falls to the consideration of a judge alone. The Accused again takes on another label, that of the Prisoner. That is so even if the Accused is not ultimately sentenced to imprisonment.

At this stage, the proceedings enter into the sentencing (also known as *plea*) phase whereby evidence is led and argument is made on the Prisoner's behalf with the aim of mitigating the sentence. Often the prosecution will also lead evidence, beyond that which was led at the trial to establish the effect of the Prisoner's crime and otherwise to counter the evidence and arguments led on behalf of the Prisoner. Finally, after considering the facts and circumstances of the Prisoner's offending and matters personal to the offender, the judge will pass sentence. Sentences in Australia can range from a finding of guilt without further order to life imprisonment.

Bail Application

When a Suspect is first charged, he or she may be remanded into custody pending the outcome of the matter. Whether or not this occurs will be dependent on the nature of the charges filed, the circumstances of the alleged offending, and matters personal to the specific Defendant, such as the risks posed of:

- Fleeing the jurisdiction while awaiting trial;
- Failing to appear at court when required; or
- Offending further.

An application for bail can be brought at any time prior to the conclusion of the trial and, in some circumstances, between the jury's guilty verdict and the conclusion of the sentencing phase. The application is usually brought in the court through which the case is, at that time, proceeding. However, a court of inherent jurisdiction in any state (i.e., Supreme Court) may hear and determine a bail application at any time (even pending appeal).

A bail application usually involves the court receiving evidence, either *viva voce*, or in the form of an affidavit.[19] Upon that evidence (although the laws of

[18]The rule against double jeopardy applies in practice to prohibit both prosecution appeals against an accused's acquittal and the retrying of an accused. However, this rule is not as concrete as it once was, and some common law jurisdictions, both within Australia and outside Australia, have done away with the rule by enacting statutory exceptions to the rule; for example, in New South Wales, see Part 8 of the *Crimes (Appeal and Review) Act* 2001 (NSW).

[19]Sometimes the first application for bail is made before a bail justice out of hours. This is not an example of a court process but rather the exercise of power conferred expressly by statute.

evidence do not strictly apply to an application for bail), the court will determine whether the Defendant/Accused/Prisoner is to be granted bail or whether he or she represents an unacceptable risk.

Voir Dire

Another procedure which may occur during the running of the trial is that of the *voir dire* (pronounced *vwaah—deer*). A voir dire is a trial within a trial and is reserved to be considered and determined by the trial judge only. The purpose of a voir dire is to consider a legal point which must be decided prior to the considerations of the jury. Often the admissibility of expert evidence is determined by a judge on a voir dire.

The conduct of a voir dire will be dependent on the subject matter being considered in the voir dire and the way in which the trial judge seeks for it to be conducted. It may involve the reception of evidence and cross-examination of witnesses. Alternatively, it may involve only legal argument as to an interpretation of law.

Civil Procedure

[20]The court will be determined by reference to, among other things, the nature of the remedy (including the amount of any monies claimed), the subject matter of the litigation, and the law under which the suit is brought.

Civil litigation is commenced by a party (the plaintiff or applicant) filing initiating documentation in the court in which he or she wishes to sue.[20] Depending on the court and subject matter of the suit, this documentation may be an originating motion, a summons, or a writ.

The natures of civil proceedings vary broadly depending on the claim being brought. However, in common law jurisdictions, the parties are expected to clearly identify the facts, acts, matters and things which they say, if proved, will make out their claim (or defense to the claim). Moreover, the parties are expected to provide the other side with documents in their respective possession that relate to the issues in the claim, whether they support their case or not. This is referred to as *discovery* and is fundamental to notions of procedural fairness.

Also fundamental to the principles of procedural fairness is the right to representation (and all that brings). For this reason the law recognizes that a party is not required to "discover" documents (or any communication) that are protected by "legal professional privilege." This is a wide and complex area of law; however, for the purposes of this work, the relevant test can be seen as thus: Is the dominant purpose of the documents generation either (Heydon, 2004):

1. To enable that party to obtain, or in the receiving by that party of, legal advice; or
2. With reference to litigation that is occurring, or at the time of the documents' creation, was anticipated.

The law of legal professional privilege also protects from the duty of discovery communications (and documents) to third parties, such as experts, engaged by the party as long as they fall into category (2) above. This has a direct application to the practice of the expert witness and will be discussed further later.

A civil suit, like a criminal case, usually involves two distinct considerations. However, unlike a criminal case, where the liability and penalty phases are run consecutively, in a civil case the issues are often run concurrently. The first is the question of liability; that is, is the defendant legally responsible to the plaintiff for the claim brought? The second is the question of quantum: how much does that legal responsibility amount to in terms of money? A civil suit may be fought on either or both of these bases, and each consideration is governed by its own laws and precedents.

Common law jurisdictions provide that some civil cases may be determined, at least on the question of liability, by juries. Depending on the subject matter, juries may be asked to determine the question of quantum. In the United States, juries are used much more widely than in Australia when it comes to civil cases both on issues of liability and quantum. The nature of the claim, and often the election of the parties, will determine whether a jury will determine a civil case in Australia. If a claim is to be considered without a jury, then the judge is the judge of both law and fact.

The Forensic Criminologist's Involvement
Criminal Cases
It is conceivable that an expert forensic criminologist may be involved in each and every step of the criminal process, both before the filing of the charges and after. In this sense, broadly speaking, the role of the forensic criminologist can be delineated into two categories. Either the forensic criminologist is employed to:

- Assist in the investigation or preparation of the matter for trial (investigative role); or
- Assist in the trial (evidential role).

Investigating authorities may call on the forensic criminologist to assist in understanding evidence and offender behavior with a view to identifying a suspect pool and arresting a Suspect. Similarly, the defense may engage an expert criminologist during the early stages of a matter to assist the legal team to understand the evidence or to conduct other investigations, which may ultimately assist the Defendant in challenging the case brought against him or her.

Prosecuting authorities and defense alike may later call on the forensic criminologist to testify as an expert witness. Such testimony may be given at the trial, voir dire, bail application, or sentencing phase, depending on the subject matter of the evidence and the utility sought to be made of it. When called as an expert witness, the criminologist is afforded the opportunity to explain to the court what meaning, in that expert's opinion, can be made of certain evidence. Whether the forensic criminologist engaged to perform the investigative role is called to give expert testimony upon a trial will depend largely on whether the opinion furnished upon the investigation is supportive of an argument being put forward by a particular side and is of a sufficiently probative value to justify its reception in a court. Therefore, the roles played by the forensic criminologist in the criminal process will depend not only on the timing of his or her engagement, but also on the practical and evidential utility of that opinion.

The regularity of experts' appearances in any criminal jurisdiction is largely a function of the funds made available for the defense and prosecution to engage experts. In this author's experience (practicing in several Australia federal and state jurisdictions, both in the role of prosecutor and defense counsel, as well as in international tribunals), the funds available to prosecuting authorities for engaging experts is far in excess of those available to the defense (whether privately or publicly funded). Accordingly, often courts receive expert testimony called by prosecutors, and it is for the defense to challenge that evidence without the benefit of an expert either as witness or consultant. This puts an incredibly heavy burden on the defense counsel, who is forced to challenge the bases or reasoning employed by the expert in formulating his or her opinion.

This author has often observed defense counsel concede the expert's evidence or try to diminish its value before the jury by suggesting alternative hypotheses and putting to the expert that those alternatives cannot be excluded. A careful expert will usually agree that reasonable alternative hypotheses put in cross-examination cannot be excluded and may, in doing so, destabilize the jury's confidence in his or her evidence. However, a conscientious expert will often qualify his or her response to these alternative hypotheses by explaining why he or she has excluded them and why his or her opinion should be preferred. Rash responses will come undone and may further weaken the jury's faith in the expert. But, a well-thought-out, measured response can bolster the expert's credibility and add significant weight to his or her opinion.

Other ways in which expert witnesses' evidence may be countered is to challenge the assumptions or evidence on which the opinion is based. In a recent case in which this author was involved, the cause of a serious injury was in dispute (the accused was alleged to have caused serious brain damage to a person by an assault). An expert was called by the prosecution to testify as to the likely physiological cause of the brain damage, such being the application of pressure to the carotid artery by a headlock. After several hours of cross-examination, the expert witness had excluded several other innocent hypotheses for the cause of the brain damage. He excluded these hypotheses all based on the timing of the alleged victim's display of symptoms: all eyewitnesses claimed that the victim collapsed and was mute immediately upon being released from the headlock. Following the cross-examination of the expert, closed circuit security footage was discovered which showed that the eyewitnesses' recollections were, in fact, wrong; the alleged victim was shown to be walking unaided and talking in the minutes following his being released from the headlock. Accordingly, the expert's opinion was based on false premises and his ultimate conclusion as to the cause of the brain damage was shown to be incorrect.

Civil Cases

Either party to civil litigation may have cause (and sufficient funds) to engage a forensic criminologist. The role to be played by the expert may be investigative or evidential (or both). The role may involve assisting the lawyers in framing the claim (or defense as the case may be) or in providing expert testimony going to the issues of liability and/or quantum.

Consultant Experts

A most important role that the expert forensic criminologist can play in both criminal and civil cases is that of the consultant. A *consultant expert* is one engaged by a party to litigation who provides advice and opinions behind the scenes. The consultant is not called by the party engaging him or her, but rather assists the lawyers in the presentation of their client's case. The consultant expert may be engaged to advise the lawyers on understanding the evidence of the other side's expert, or in devising a line of cross-examination designed to show flaws in that expert's evidence, reasoning, or methods.

Privilege and Waiver

Legal professional privilege (see earlier) protects communications between the expert and the side that has engaged him or her, whether in an investigative role or evidential Role. The reason is that, in all areas discussed previously, the communications between the expert and the side engaging him or her would fall under category (2) discussed earlier: the expert has been engaged (and presumably communications are made) either with reference to litigation that, at the time of the engagement (and communication), is occurring, or is anticipated. That is not the end of it, however.

Privilege is a legal right, and as such can be waived, either expressly or by the conduct of the person who enjoys the privilege (in this case, the client). The circumstances in which a waiver might occur are varied and contentious; however, distilled down to its simplest form, waiver occurs when the client acts inconsistently with the maintenance of the confidentiality protected by the privilege (Freckleton and Selby, 2002).

As it relates to the practice of expert witnesses, and communications passing between them and one party to the litigation (including that party's lawyers), privilege is most often waived knowingly and voluntarily. The reason is that the expert engaged has communicated something to that party, usually in the form of an expert report that the party seeks to rely upon.

Most Australian civil jurisdictions have rules of practice that preclude the calling of an expert witness unless the party seeking to call the expert provides the other side with a report of that expert's witness in advance. In criminal matters, in line with principles of procedural fairness, the prosecution is obliged to disclose all expert material, whether helpful or detrimental to their case, assembled in the course of the investigation (Freckleton and Selby, 2002), whether or not it is intended that the evidence will be relied on at the trial. Depending on the jurisdiction, should the Defendant intend to call an expert witness upon his or her trial, advanced disclosure as to the expected evidence of that witness is required in the form of an expert report.[21]

[21]For example, in Victoria, see s 9 of the *Crime (Criminal Trials) Act* 1999 (Vic).

Whether discovery of an expert's report is mandated by statute or the rules of court or simply by the willful calling of an expert as a witness, a party will waive the protection of privilege. The waiver, however, will not necessarily apply to all communications between that expert and the side calling him or her. The extent is determined on a case-by-case basis. As a rule of thumb, though, all communications forming the foundation (or part of the foundation) of the expert's opinion are waived when the contents of the opinion are waived. These communications may include letters passing between the expert and the party, the expert's notes, or earlier drafts of the expert's report or letters of opinion. The significance of waiver for the forensic expert is clear: any communication forming the part of the foundation of the opinion will be waived when privilege over that opinion is waived.

GENERAL PROBLEMS WITH EXPERT EVIDENCE: FALLING ON DEAF EARS?

Freckleton, Reddy, and Selby (1999, 2001) conducted two national surveys for the Australian Institute of Judicial Administration which required members of the judiciary, both judges and magistrates, at all levels to state their opinions on expert evidence. The results of these surveys were published in two separate reports, one covering magistrates' responses and the other covering the judges'. Through this survey, Freckleton et al. attempted to identify recurring problems presented by expert evidence.

The surveys were presented to 478 judges and magistrates across all Australian jurisdictions. Of the 478 survey candidates, only 244 (51.5%) responded by completing the survey. Therefore, although the results may be skewed by the reluctance on the part of some to participate, a response and sample size of 51.5% still provides a sound basis for statistical reliability.

Identified Problems

Several specific problems were identified. However, analyses of the majority of response highlighted endemic problems.

Complexity

Given the nature of expert evidence and the rule that requires the evidence of an expert to be beyond the experience and knowledge of the judge or jury, it is often quite complex. Identifying this potential problem, Freckelton focused much of his study on the difficulties in comprehending the evidence of experts. Of the Magistrates who responded, 52.28% stated that they had experienced difficulty in comprehending the evidence of expert. Similarly, 46.81% of responding judges indicated that they too had difficulty in this area. The greatest reason suggested by all respondents was the complex nature of the evidence.

Of all those who had responded positively to experiencing difficulty in comprehending the evidence of experts, 96% indicated that they occasionally had difficulty in this area, with 4% stating that this occurred frequently. The problem areas identified and ranked in order of complexity by the respondents were:

- Psychiatric evidence;
- Psychological evidence; and
- Scientific evidence.

Alarmingly, with respect to criminal trials, these are the areas that most often require expert opinion.

The obvious concern in this respect is the jurors' comprehension of the evidence, especially in criminal trials where an individual's liberty may be in the balance. If the judges and magistrates are unable to understand the evidence, and this is the type of evidence they are exposed to daily, then how can the jury be expected to comprehend, evaluate, and form their own view of the evidence?

The studies revealed that problems in comprehending the complex evidence of experts stemmed from the confusing and convoluted language used and the failure of experts to explain the bases of their opinions. Of greater concern though was the indication that poor examination in chief and cross-examination by counsel was most often a significant factor in confusing the court. This raises the issue of the role and responsibilities of the advocate where expert evidence is called (discussed later).

Field of Expertise

Around three-quarters (77.3%) of respondents indicated that experts occasionally stray out of their area of expertise and offer opinions which are beyond their capacities to make. It is concerning to further note that more than one-tenth (11.4%) of respondents were of the opinion that this occurred frequently. This suggests that there is a large amount of "opinion" evidence which is being heard in court that affronts the rules of evidence. The consequence of this is that a virtual nonexpert is purporting to give an "informed and helpful" opinion in an area which exceeds his or her field of expertise.

Bias

Due to the nature of our adversarial system of justice and the way in which experts are called by one side or another and not the court, it is implicit that the parties and their lawyers will call only experts who support their case. Moreover, it is the parties who decide (obviously limited by financial constraints and the rules of court) how many experts will be used, on what issues they will be called to testify, and the timing of disclosure of the experts' evidence. This inevitably may result in bias on the part of the experts.

[22]See *Clark v Ryan* (1960) 103 CLR 486.

The role of the expert includes acing as an advocate, not for a side, but that side's opinion.[22] However, economic ties between an expert and the lawyers who frequently call him or her the expert may result in the expert ceasing to act as an advocate of his or her opinion. The expert may then veer into the realm of becoming a witness for hire. This encourages, even if subconsciously, the expert to overassert his or her opinion, wander into areas beyond his or her expertise, and sometimes totally undermine his or her professional standards and procedures.

In a criminal case in which this author recently appeared, two "independent" experts gave evidence for different sides, each giving evidence about the way in which a complicated piece of machinery worked, and their opinions on whether such worked properly on a day in question. At the conclusion of both experts' evidence, the magistrate (sitting as judge of the law and facts) seemed equally persuaded by each expert. In turn, the judge had each expert recalled to give evidence about his respective experiences in appearing in court. The first (prosecution) expert stated that he had given evidence in hundreds of cases on behalf of the prosecution across many jurisdictions. The other expert replied that this case was the fourth in which he had given expert evidence, and only the first time he had given evidence for the defense. Contrary to expectations, but perhaps in accordance with some assessment of latent bias, the judge decided the case in favor of the defense.

Freckelton's surveys revealed that 35% of respondents cited bias as one of the major problems arising from expert evidence. Many complained about seeing the same experts appearing only for the same side in cases (i.e., only for the prosecution or only for the defense). Certainly, if this is the case, then it must be questioned just how many experts are functioning merely as advocates of their opinions and not advocates for a side, or even a paycheck.

The structure of government crime laboratories and forensic services in some jurisdictions will no doubt lead at least to the inference of "opinion for hire." The arrangement of dedicated prosecution and defense services no doubt lends itself to some perceived (if not actual) bias on behalf of experts: they are actually employed on a full-time basis by the police or the prosecuting authority or they are engaged exclusively by the defense. If justice is not only to be done but also to be seen to be done, then experts operating within such structures must, at the very least, comply with the highest principles of their profession, with ethics and transparency. Otherwise, their opinions, their evidence, and ultimately their credibility will be worthless, in court and elsewhere.

The problems arising from expert evidence are equally as vast as they are concerning. The fact that the judiciary is often confused by the testimony of experts leads one to ponder the extent to which the same perplexity affects jurors. Moreover, the underhanded inclusion of otherwise inadmissible evidence under the guise of an inappropriate expert opinion threatens to undermine not only the laws of evidence, but also the entire justice process. Contributing to this is the apparent bias of "guns for hire" who seemingly abandon their science and become some kind of testamentary mercenary for one side or the other.

Accountability of the Expert

In matters of opinion I very much distrust expert evidence, for several reasons. In the first place, although the evidence is given upon oath, in point of fact the person knows he cannot be indicted for perjury, because it is only evidence as to a matter of opinion. So that you have not the authority for legal sanction [sic]. A dishonest man, knowing he could not be punished, might be inclined to indulge in extravagant assertions on an occasion that required it.

Sir George Jessel MR in *Lord Abinger v Ashton* (1873)[23]   [23]17 LR Eq 358 at 374.

The question of whether an individual offering opinion evidence may be held criminally liable for deliberately misleading the court has been controversially discussed through a string of older common law decisions (Freckleton and Selby, 2002, p. 573).[24] Freckleton and Selby (2002, p. 573) and Hodgkinson (1990, p. 215) argue that an expert should be held liable to penalties of perjury if he or she gives sworn evidence of an opinion not truly held by him or her. Nonetheless, due to the nature of an opinion, establishing the elements of perjury to the criminal standard of proof would be most difficult.

[24]See, for example, *Adams v Canon* (1621) 73 ER 117; *Folkes v Chadd* (1782) 99 ER 589; *R v Pedley* (1784) 168 ER 265; *Lord Arbinger v Ashton* (1873) 17 LR Eq 358; *R v Schlesinger* (1847) 116 ER 255.

Civil liability of an expert's opinion is protected to the extent of any witness. Policy demands that all witnesses enjoy an unqualified immunity from civil suit in regards to things they say in the witness box even if it is false or malicious.[25] Experts also enjoy a level of immunity for work done in preparation for trial analogous to the immunity enjoyed by the advocate.[26]

[25] *Cabasi v Villa* (1940) 64 CLR 130.

[26] *Palmer v Durnford Ford* [1992] 2 WLR 407 at 412 per Tuckey J.

Distinction must be made between assertions of fact and assertions of opinion. With respect to experts, Thornton (1997) qualifies this as the difference between observation and interpretation. He differentiates between the two (p. 15): while observation may be tested, proved, and equated, interpretation is the mental process of giving meaning to an observation based on deductive processes. If the expert thoroughly executes his or her function in performance of his or her role, then the trier of fact may adequately assess his or her interpretation. Essentially, observations provide the facts on which the expert is then able to deductively produce his or her interpretation (opinion).

With respect to analyzing the liability of experts and their evidence, a clear distinction must be made between these two separate factors. In theory, just as a lay witness may be held accountable for giving false evidence of fact, so too may an expert. Should the expert say he or she has seen or done something that he or she has not seen or done, that person should feel the full weight of a perjury prosecution. However, as to his or her interpretation (or opinion), proving the expert does not actually hold a belief to which he or she attests may fall into the realm of impossibilities. Therefore, notwithstanding academic opinion, the practicalities of holding an expert criminally liable for offering a false opinion will probably only remain contentious in the minds of scholars.

Currently, the accountability of the expert and his or her conduct in relation to litigation is most adequately enforced by professional regulations. The rules of evidence require expert opinion to come from some recognized field of expertise. As stated by the U.S. Supreme Court in the leading case of *Frye v United States*:[27]

[27] (1923) 295 F 1013.

> The body of knowledge from which an expert testifies must be sufficiently established to have gained general acceptance in the particular field to which belongs.

In most circumstances this rule will have the ancillary benefit of providing some form of accountability for the expert whether through peer review, professional standing or, if some organized professional body exists in that field, through professional conduct sanction.

Courts favor expert witnesses who belong to professional regulatory bodies because the level of accountability of that expert can be viewed as higher than the nonregulated professional. The threat of professional sanction may help curb extravagant assertions and unethical conduct by the expert and assist the court to a greater degree in its pursuit of unbiased opinion.[28] Many professional bodies have codes of ethics to which all members are required to comply. Only through the aggressive enforcement of these guidelines, codes, and regulations can experts be held accountable for their actions.

THE ROLE OF COUNSEL

Experts are the most important auxiliaries … everything depends upon knowing how to make use of them. Indeed it is often less important to know who is to be questioned than to know how, upon what, and when questions must be put.

Dr. Hans Gross (1894) in System der Kriminalistik

The Freckelton et al. study (see earlier) found that experts' evidence is confusing to judges (and presumably jurors) often due to poor examination in chief and cross-examination by counsel (see earlier). Therefore, whether it be the confusion stemming from inadequate questioning or a miscarriage of justice which ensues, the role of the advocate dealing with expert evidence must be considered.

Many rules govern the conduct of advocates at trial. In Australia, both common law and the barrister's rules provide limitations and impose duties on advocates. In *R v Dick*[29] it was established that an advocate may not merely rely on textbooks in preparing and presenting his or her arguments in court. Specifically, the duty of the advocate is to know what he or she is talking about. While this in theory may extend to all matters in dispute, including the evidence of an expert, in practice this principle extends merely to advocates' knowledge of the law.

The rules governing disclosure of expert witnesses at criminal law are somewhat less stringent than those that exist in the civil realm. As observed by Lord Justice Woolf (1996), expert evidence may, and is, used as a weapon by litigators to take advantage of the other side's lack of resources or ignorance. Therefore, the use of expert evidence in this "weapon" capacity coupled with the advocate's duty to be knowledgeable about the facts in dispute place the advocate in an unenviable position.

The advocate may best serve his or her client and the court by first and foremost preparing for court thoroughly. This will include preparing the witness as well as having the witness prepare the advocate. By truly understanding the theory, procedures, and conclusions which are utilized by his or her witness, the advocate may be most effective in having the expert's opinion presented to the court. This witness preparation should include a thorough description of the expert's role, including the specific functions which he or she must execute to fulfill that role. A brief overview on the rules of expert evidence and

[28]For example, see Baeza, J. J. et al. (2000) "Academy of Behavioural Profiling: Criminal Profiling Guidelines," *Journal of Behavioural Profiling* vol. 1 (1 January) rr 2.2, 2.3, 3.0, 3.1.

[29](1982) Tas R 252.

a synopsis of the courtroom procedure may assist all in ensuring an increased cogency of the expert's evidence.

The advocate may need the expert's help in developing the order and content of questions that he or she is to ask in an attempt to determine how best to approach the evidence. Similarly, receiving expert advice in designing a cross-examination of an opposition expert may assist the advocate in gaining clarity and spotting the weaknesses of the opposition expert's evidence.

The duty to be knowledgeable that falls on the shoulder of the advocate is an onerous one. Not only must counsel be versed on the law, but he or she must also be familiar with all the facts and science of the case at hand. Realistically, the only way that counsel may duly perform this duty to both the client and the court is to ensure that he or she thoroughly prepares the case. This will most often be achieved only through consulting an expert who is not to be called as a witness. The consequences of simply accepting an opposing expert's opinion without putting it to proof may have dire consequences for the client.

A thoroughly prepared cross-examination of an expert may, however, be devastating to the side calling the expert. This author has seen skillful counsel, through clever and careful cross-examination, effectively turn the other side's expert into an expert for his or her client.

In a case involving charges related to the cultivating of a large cannabis crop, a prosecution expert gave evidence of the projected trafficable quantity of cannabis. The Accused admitted to growing the crop but denied that he had intended to grow so much: that point being the difference between two charges of differing severity.

While the sole issue for the jury's consideration was the total amount (by weight) the accused had *intended* to grow, the expert gave evidence that based on the total weight of the crop (undried and including the weight of the stems, leaves, and buds of the plants), the trafficable yield was but a fraction of the crop's overall weight. This fraction was arrived at by, among other things, reliance on empirical studies which had been conducted on the water loss (cannabis usually being smoked by its users in a dry form) in cannabis plants of a similar maturity and size. From the projected trafficable weight, the street value of the crop could be estimated based on price per weight of dried cannabis leaves and buds.

At trial, defense counsel relied on an admission that his client had made to police regarding his expected yield from the crop (which was significantly less than the expert's evidence as to the expected yield based on calculations and the studies). When the expert was called, defense counsel cross-examined the expert as to the process he employed to reach the expected trafficable yield of the crop. The defense then suggested that such methods were equally accurate when hypothetically applied in reverse (i.e., starting with the yield and working back to overall crop weight), to which the expert agreed. Using the estimated crop yield as given by the Accused in his interview to the police and asking the expert to perform the same calculations in reverse, the defense was able to use the prosecution expert to advance its case: that the Accused had not intended to grow such a big crop. The aim in doing so was to downgrade the charge from one which carried a maximum penalty of 25 years imprisonment to one which carried a maximum of 15 years.

COURT IS NOT A PLACE FOR SURPRISES: THE IMPORTANCE OF DIALOGUE

In preparing for court, the expert witness and advocate have no better friend than each other. The expert is expert in the field in which he or she is about to give his or her evidence, and the advocate is an expert in the setting in which the expert is about to give his or her evidence: the courtroom. Each can learn much from the other and make the experience one that does not necessarily have to end in tears.

The first, and often most significant, hurdle to an effective dialogue between the expert and advocate (and then, in turn, all that follows) is the fact that, professionally, both are usually from very different worlds. Each world is governed by its own protocols, rules of conduct, truisms, and jargon. Unless the advocate has some understanding of these elements, his or her ability to adequately engage in a dialogue will be severely hampered, as will the expert's. It is for this reason that, where possible, the expert should dispense with the jargon and engage in a dialogue with the advocate, in as plain language as possible. Equally, the advocate must explain his or her expectations of the expert and the function and role of the expert's evidence in plain language.

The two specialized professionals must find a common ground, such more often than not being plain language. All too often professionals of all disciplines hide behind the traditions and exclusionary language of their respective specialties, either deliberately or not, to avoid challenge. In the context of preparing for court, this is a luxury both the expert and advocate can ill afford. A challenge to the expert's rationales and conclusions should be expected, and trite defenses will come unstuck. So the first step in preparing for court must be a frank, simplified (but not overly simplified) dialogue between the expert and advocate.

For the advocate it is important to remember that the expert is a witness, and like every other witness is unlikely to be as familiar with the court setting as the advocate is. To this end, beyond the mere machinations of the evidence, it is important for the expert and advocate to discuss the impending experience. It is important to prepare, even the experienced expert witness, for what the expert can expect of the court and what the court expects of the witness. Freckelton and Selby (2002) provide 10 points of advice to the expert witness before court:

1. If unfamiliar with giving expert testimony, go and watch someone else do it first.
2. Sit or stand in the witness box and address your answers to the jury or, if there is no jury, to the judge.
3. Dress appropriately.
4. Be aware of the impressions you are making. Take care not to appear arrogant, flippant, hostile, or evasive.
5. Listen to the questions carefully and ensure you understand them before answering.
6. Be as clear, precise, and confident in your answers as the strength of your views permit.
7. If you cannot answer a question, then say so and explain why. Offer to redress the situation if possible.
8. Make sure you are aware of the factual and legal issues that invite your involvement.
9. Convey your views with whatever visual aids you believe will best assist your giving of evidence.
10. Do not misconstrue any question asked as a request to take a particular stance on an issue.

While this is a helpful checklist, there is one tenet above all else which may best encapsulate the role of the expert and ensure the expert does not waste his or her and the court's time: *do not forget your audience.*

Whether before a jury or a judge sitting alone, the expert is called upon as a witness to assist the court. The reason is that the expert has specialized knowledge accrued through years of education, training, and experience which the judge or jury do not have. The expert has been called upon by a party to explain how that knowledge can enlighten those deciding the case. It is almost axiomatic that the subject matter of the expert evidence will involve at least some concepts which are complicated for the uninitiated to grasp. Accordingly, the message must be given in a palatable form.

Advocates are often criticized for trying to dumb-down expert testimony, of reducing it to a simple string of "yes" or "no" questions. While this may be a tactic engaged to reduce the evidence of the expert to a nonsensical level, it may also be a legitimate tactic employed so that the jury may understand the complex evidence of the expert.

As can be seen by common difficulties experienced by judges and magistrates when dealing with expert evidence, so too it can be expected that juries struggle with the digestion of the expert's evidence. It is the expert's responsibility, as much as that of the advocate, to ensure that his or her opinion is understood.

The first step in ensuring that the expert's opinion (if not the basis of the opinion and methods in reaching it) is understood by the jury involves ensuring that the party calling the witness understands the opinion. One may say, well, why would a party call an expert unless he or she understood the expert's opinion? Well, it happens. Sometimes the expression of the opinion is so convoluted that the opinion itself is open to interpretation; other times the expert provides several opinions, and the party seizes on one that is favorable without fully analyzing the rest. Most frequently, when this issue arises, the expert's opinion is based, at least in part, on an assumption which later proves false and undermines the opinion, or reverses its effect entirely.

The necessity for the party calling the expert to understand the opinion has four desired effects:

1. If the expert can explain the opinion and its bases to the party calling him or her, then the expert has already turned his or her mind to and achieved a "layman's" explanation of the evidence.
2. The advocate examining the expert has a clearer understanding of the evidence he or she is eliciting and, one hopes, will not lead the jury into confusion.
3. The advocate will be better placed to cross-examine any expert called by the other side.
4. The advocate will be in a better position to argue the merits of his or her expert's opinion, why it should be utilized in determining the case, and why it should be preferred over the other side's expert.

The dialogue between the expert and the side relying on his or her professional opinion goes beyond the mere educating as to the science and logic employed. The expert has a professional and ethical obligation to be cognizant of the weaknesses in his or her theory and to convey these honestly and openly. The identification and thorough discussion of areas where the expert's evidence is most vulnerable to attack will best prepare both the advocate and the expert. Whether the expert's opinion is reached through novel methods or based on assumptions (or even assumptions drawn on assumptions), the expert should have enough professional awareness to understand from where the likely criticisms are to come. It is these areas that should be identified and justified, if possible. Only then can the advocate make an informed decision about whether to deal with them in evidence-in-chief or wait for the attack to come and redress the issue in re-examination.

Depending on the nature and number of these disclosures, the advocate may make the informed decision not to call the expert to give evidence. However, this does not mean that an expert should be professionally arrogant for fear of affecting his or her livelihood. In practice, it is the conscientious expert, the expert who can identify the weakness in his or her opinion, who will be preferred by litigators. Advocates dislike surprises in court, especially when those surprises come from their own expert for the first time under cross-examination.

Finally, like any other witness, the expert witness is a human being. Throughout our lives and careers we all make mistakes which we would prefer to forget. Sometimes these regrets have a way of cropping up when witnesses, even expert witnesses, are in the witness box. Unlike the nonexpert witness, the expert witness's regret may be a little more well known, either because it occurred professionally or because the legal community is a small one and, once revealed, the regret has a habit of resurfacing time and again.

An expert who has been discredited or caught in a lie (even if not subjected to perjury charges) while giving evidence will expose himself or herself to cross-examination on that past occurrence every time he or she steps into court. One can be assured that opposing counsel will research not only the expert's opinion, but the expert himself or herself, including past cases in which that person has given evidence and publications he or she has authored. The expert witness need not only be mindful of this, but also ensure to raise these matters with the side calling him or her to give evidence. Failure to do so may be devastating not only to the person who engaged the expert, but to the professional future of the expert witness.

SUMMARY

After one reviews this chapter, it should now be clear that expert forensic criminologists have wide and varied roles, and they have many issues to tackle in each of these roles. Forensic criminologists can work under the inquisitorial system or the adversarial system, depending on the jurisdiction. They can be called either by counsel or by the judge himself or herself.

For forensic criminologists to be useful and successful experts in court, they need to be aware of the role of the judge and the jury in both criminal and civil trials. It must also be clear to them the difference between the procedural stages that they may be involved in while working on a case, including the investigation, committal, the trial, and plea phases, as well as bail applications and voir dire hearings.

Forensic criminologists working as expert witnesses, or any expert in the adversarial system for that matter, may be called upon to perform one or more of four separate but related functions. They may generalize from their experience to educate the court, act as librarians in directing the courts attention toward relevant literature, act as statisticians, and ultimately act as advocates for their opinion. When they carry out these functions, it is crucially important that they understand how science applies in the courtroom, that their scientific goals are not necessarily in line with the courts' search for proof and evidence, and that scientific probability does not equal proof beyond a reasonable doubt. Forensic criminologists may also be involved with litigants as consultants, during the investigative phase, or during civil cases. Regardless of the specific role criminologists play, they must be keenly aware of issues related to privilege and waiver as discussed previously.

By outlining the problems with expert evidence according to those working in the court, it should become clear that criminologists giving evidence need to remember who their audience is. Complex information needs to be presented clearly in a jargon-free manner, and experts must never step over the boundaries of their expertise. Maintaining a dialogue with counsel will be of great assistance to experts, allowing them to present their opinions clearly and concisely and address any problems which may be inherent in their testimony.

The goal of this chapter was to allow forensic criminologists to be better informed as to what they should expect when entering into the court setting. Armed with the tools outlined in this chapter, each criminologist should be better equipped to assist the court in his or her area of expertise and more prepared to do so when the opportunity arises.

Review Questions

1. T/F It is the judge and jury's job to determine facts of the case in dispute.
2. T/F It is the judge's job to interpret the law relevant to the case.
3. Describe the difference between civil and criminal trials.
4. Name and explain each of the functions that an expert witness may play.
5. T/F Scientific probability is the same as determining something "beyond a reasonable doubt."
6. Name and describe each of the ways a forensic criminologist can assist the court.
7. What are the problems that commonly arise with expert evidence?
8. Name and describe each of the phases of a criminal trial.

REFERENCES

Burger, W., 1968. Adversarial and Nonadversarial Systems. Paper presented at a Conference at the Centre for the Study of Democratic Institutions, Washington, DC November.

Eggleston, R., 1983. Evidence: Proof and Probability, second ed. Weidenfeld and Nicholson, London.

Fairchild, E., Dammer, H., 2001. Comparative Criminal Justice Systems, second ed. Wadsworth Thompson Learning, Belmont, CA.

Freckelton, I., Reddy, P., Selby, H., 1999. Australian Judicial Attitudes Towards Expert Evidence. Australian Institute of Judicial Administration, Carlton, Australia.

Freckelton, I., Reddy, P., Selby, H., 2001. Australian Magistrates' Attitudes Towards Expert Evidence: A Comparative Study. Australian Institute of Judicial Administration, Carlton, Australia.

Freckleton, I., Selby, H., 2002. Expert Evidence—Law, Practice, Procedure and Advocacy, second ed. Lawbook Co., Pyrmont, New South Wales.

Gross, H., 1934. System der Kriminalistik (1894) [as adapted by Adam, J., and Adam, J. C. (1934)] Gross's Criminal Investigation, third ed. Sweet and Maxwell, London.

Gross, H., 1968. Kriminalpsychologie (1898) (H.M. Kallen, Trans. (1968) from the 4th German edition) Criminal Psychology—A Manual for Judges, Practitioners, and Students. Patterson Smith, Montclair, New Jersey.

Heydon, D., 2004. Cross on Evidence, seventh Australian ed. Butterworths, Chatswood, New South Wales.

Hodgkinson, T., 1990. Expert Evidence: Law and Practice. Sweet and Maxwell, London.

Kirk, P., Thornton, J., 1974. Crime Investigation, second ed. John Wiley and Sons, New York.

Lord Woolf, M.R., 1996. Access to Justice: Final Report to the Lord Chancellor on the Civil Justice System in England and Wales. Her Majesty's Stationery Office, London.

Murphy, P., 2002. Murphy on Evidence, eighth ed. Oxford University Press.

Ranson, D.L., 1996. Forensic Medicine and the Law. Melbourne University Press, Melbourne.

Saferstein, R., 2001. Criminalistics—An Introduction to Forensic Science, seventh ed. Prentice Hall, New Jersey.

Thornton, J.I., 1997. The General Assumptions and Rationale of Forensic Identification. In: Faigman, D.L., et al. (Eds.), Modern Scientific Evidence—The Law and Science of Expert Testimony, vol. 2. West Publishing Co., St. Paul, MN.

Turvey, B.E., 2002. Criminal Profiling, second ed. Academic Press, London.

CHAPTER 3

Cognitive Ethos of the Forensic Examiner

Wayne Petherick and Brent E. Turvey

The appropriate response to complexity should not be to call in the witch doctor for a magic spell, but rather to demand the best science available and remain aware of its limitations.

Faigman, Kaye, Saks, and Sanders (2004, p. 69)

KEY TERMS

Admissibility: "[A]s applied to evidence…means that the evidence introduced is of such character that the court or judge is bound to receive it; that is, allow it to be introduced at trial" (Black, 1990).

Cherry Picking: Selectively reporting and thereby emphasizing only desired results or information rather than the entirety of examinations performed and results achieved.

Cognitive Dissonance: The mental discomfort or anguish that occurs when scientific integrity meets cultural, financial, and moral consequences.

Cognitive Ethos: A person's peculiar nature of acquiring knowledge and understanding.

Due Process: Essentially a fairness requirement in the U.S. Constitution. Any condition or treatment that tends to bias a judge, jury, or the process as a whole in favor of the state is considered in violation of it.

Evidence: "[T]estimony, writing, material objects, or other things presented to the senses that are offered to prove the existence or non-existence of a fact" (Black, 1990).

Experimentation: The act of testing hypotheses with an eye toward disproving or falsifying them.

Expert: Someone deemed an expert by virtue of his or her knowledge, skill, experience, training, or education. A legal classification.

CONTENTS

Hypothesis: An educated estimate regarding the possible answer to a question or problem.

Legal Truth: Information and events that have been established by a court ruling based on a narrow factual record—either at the discretion of a judge or jury.

Metacognition: "[t]he ability to know how well one is performing, when one is likely to be accurate in judgment and when one is likely to be in error" (Kruger and Dunning, 1999, p. 1121).

Observation: The action of observing something regarding some event, fact, or object.

Observer Effects: The outcomes present when the results of a forensic examination are distorted by the context and mental state of the forensic examiner to include the examiner's subconscious expectations and desires.

Role Strain: The difficulties or strain caused by contradictions inherent in one's role.

Scientific Fact: Information and events that have been established based on a broad factual record to a reasonable degree of scientific certainty by scientists using the scientific method.

Scientific Method: A way to investigate how or why something works, or how something happened through the development of hypotheses and subsequent attempts at falsification through testing and other accepted means.

Scientific Principles: The scientific theories which have stood the test of time and independent study.

Scientific Theory: A premise which may be stated or presented with a reasonable degree of scientific certainty.

Ultimate Facts: The facts that allege the substance of a cause of a legal action, distinct from those that merely describe events related to the action.

Ultimate Issue: The legal question before the trier of fact; it relates to legal findings of guilt, innocence, or, in a civil matter, liability.

Ultimate Issue Doctrine: A principle which holds that witnesses are prohibited from giving an opinion on the ultimate issue of a case.

The forensic criminologist is a scientific forensic examiner charged with analyzing and interpreting case-related evidence or applying criminological theory to case-related issues, within the objective constraints of the scientific method. After obtaining findings or results, forensic criminologists are segregated from the many other kinds of scientists, and even criminologists in general, as servants to the justice system. They fully expect their work to be used in the education of investigators, attorneys, judges, and jurors—commonly in that order. As explained in Thornton and Peterson (2002, p. 148):

> What then, of the forensic scientist? The single feature that distinguishes forensic scientists from any other scientist is the expectation that they will appear in court and testify to their findings and offer an opinion as to the significance of those findings. The forensic scientist will, or should, testify not only to what things *are*, but to what things *mean*. Forensic science is science exercised on behalf of the law in the just resolution of conflict. It is therefore expected to be the handmaiden of the law, but at the same time this expectation may very well be the marina from which is launched the tension that exists between the two disciplines.

Unlike the research criminologist whose findings are bound for publication in a professional journal, or the university lecturer who speaks before students and colleagues from an arrangement of PowerPoint slides, the forensic criminologist ultimately renders expert opinions and interpretations in reports, affidavits, declarations, depositions, and expert testimony before the court. This is almost always under the penalty of perjury. In this context, the consequences for society, and the penalties to the forensic criminologist, for falsity, incompetence, and inaccuracy are more than academic.

Before we embark on that part of our journey in subsequent chapters, however, we need to consider how actual forensic scientists are meant to think. Forensic criminologists unfamiliar with their own *cognitive ethos*—their peculiar nature of acquiring knowledge and understanding—are mentally lost. They cannot know if they are unbiased, rational, or even competent. Consequently, they cannot know whether they are practicing good science, let alone whether they are practicing science at all. This calls to mind the wise assertion that "[i]f there is no science, there can be no forensic science" (Thornton and Peterson, 2002, p. 162).

The purpose of this chapter is to help readers acquire both knowledge and understanding in the manner that every kind of forensic criminologist must—to help develop their cognitive character. It is about mapping out how to best meet the analytical needs of forensic practice, but also how we commonly fail in the effort. First, we will define the essential components and directives of good scientific practice. Then we must provide some of the basic rules and expectations in the forensic realm, as this is likely to be foreign territory. Finally, we will chart a course through the realm of failed reasoning, applying these concepts to forensic criminology.

To begin with, let us attend to the scientific method.

THE SCIENTIFIC METHOD

…[M]any, perhaps even most, forensic scientists are not just inattentive to the scientific method, but ignorant.

Dr. John I. Thornton[1] (1994, p. 485)

[1] John Thornton was mentioned in Chapter 1 as a "modern architect" of forensic criminology.

A full embrace of the scientific method and its underlying philosophy is the best way to ensure competent methodology, findings, reasoning, and interpretations. This requires a forensic criminologist who "objectively and skeptically employs the scientific method" (Kennedy and Kennedy, 1972, p. 5). Unfortunately, the criminal justice community as a whole, to include forensic criminologists, remains uninformed regarding what the scientific method is and what it intends. Faigman et al. (1997, p. 47) are rather unforgiving, but honest, when observing:

> The subject of the scientific method … has been described innumerable times, in a multitude of works on manifold subjects, from elementary school textbooks to post-graduate treatises. And yet it remains a subject that is foreign to most lawyers and judges.

Thornton and Peterson (2002, p. 159) go further, including the majority of forensic practitioners in the mix of those who do not understand what the scientific method is or how to apply it correctly:

> But those individuals engaged in "scientific" work rarely study the scientific method. To be sure, those engaged in research are expected to pick up the scientific method somewhere along the way; for the most part scientists don't study the implementation of the scientific method. Philosophers of science think about the scientific method. Basic research scientists use it to generate new knowledge. Applied scientists typically study the knowledge that the scientific method has managed to accumulate. For example, the chemist studies the hydrogen bond, and the biologist studies the double helix of DNA, but rarely does either receive instruction concerning the scientific method per se. It is not only possible, but indeed is generally the case, that a person with a Bachelor's Degree in chemistry, geology, biology, or other scientific discipline, has not had a single college lecture on precisely how the scientific method works.

> This ultimately works against the best interests of the forensic scientist, who ordinarily does not learn much about how undiscovered information is brought to light…

> The failure of scientists in general, and of forensic scientists in particular, to understand how knowledge is acquired and applied, leads to abuse.

As a consequence of these conditions, we are barred from assuming that everyone is working from the same page in a discussion of what science is and how the scientific method is meant to be employed. Even scientists may be clueless on these questions. Some further, basic explanations are necessary.

Step by Step: Science as Falsification

As explained in the first chapter, the *scientific method* is a way to investigate how or why something works, or how something happened, through the development of hypotheses and subsequent attempts at falsification through testing and other accepted means. It is a structured process designed to build scientific knowledge by way of answering specific questions about observations through careful analysis and *critical thinking*. Observations are used to form testable hypotheses, and with sufficient testing, hypotheses can become scientific theories. Eventually, over much time, with precise testing marked by a failure to falsify, scientific theories can become scientific principles. An excellent discussion is provided in Edwards and Gotsonis (2009, pp. 4–11):

> The methods and culture of scientific research enable it to be a self-correcting enterprise. Because researchers are, by definition, creating new understanding, they must be as cautious as possible before asserting a new "truth." Also, because researchers are working at a frontier, few others may have the knowledge to catch and correct any errors they make. Thus, science has had to develop means of revisiting provisional results and revealing errors before they are widely used. The processes of peer review, publication, collegial interactions (e.g., sharing at conferences), and the involvement of graduate students (who are expected to question as they learn) all support this need. Science is characterized also by a culture that encourages and rewards critical questioning of past results and of colleagues. Most technologies benefit from a solid research foundation in academia and ample opportunity for peer-to-peer stimulation and critical assessment, review and critique through conferences, seminars, publishing, and more. These elements provide a rich set of paths through which new ideas and skepticism can travel and opportunities for scientists to step away from their day-to-day work and take a longer-term view. The scientific culture encourages cautious, precise statements and discourages statements that go beyond established facts; it is acceptable for colleagues to challenge one another, even if the challenger is more junior. The forensic science disciplines will profit enormously by full adoption of this scientific culture.

The scientific method is, ultimately, the particular approach to knowledge building and problem solving employed by scientists of every kind.

The first step in the scientific method is *observation*. An observation is made regarding some event, fact, or object. This observation then leads to a specific question regarding the event, fact, or object, such as where or when an object originated or how an object came to possess certain traits.

The second step in the scientific method is attempting to answer the question that has been asked by forming a *hypothesis*, or an educated estimate, regarding the possible answer. Often, there is more than one possible answer. These answers must be investigated and developed, considering all possible alternatives.

The third step in the scientific method is *experimentation*. Of all the steps in the scientific method, this is the one that separates scientific inquiry from other forms of investigation. Scientists must design experiments intended to *disprove* their hypotheses. Once again, they must design experiments intended to *disprove* their hypotheses—not to prove them. Any research study or laboratory experiment designed to prove a hypothesis or theory suffers from *confirmation bias*, and is not, by definition, scientific.[2]

If one calls oneself a scientist yet fails to follow these basic steps, then something other than science is being practiced.

The absolute cornerstone of the scientific method is *falsification*, as described by Sir Karl Popper (1902–1994), the Austrian-British scientific philosopher.

[2]In the science of cognitive psychology, confirmation bias (a.k.a. confirmatory bias) is the tendency to search for or interpret information in a way that confirms one's preconceptions. It involves actively seeking out and assigning more weight to evidence that confirms a hypothesis or theory, and ignoring or undervaluing evidence that could disconfirm a hypothesis or theory.

SCIENCE AS FALSIFICATION

These considerations led me in the winter of 1919–20 to conclusions which I may now reformulate as follows.

1. It is easy to obtain confirmations, or verifications, for nearly every theory—if we look for confirmations.

2. Confirmations should count only if they are the result of risky predictions; that is to say, if, unenlightened by the theory in question, we should have expected an event which was incompatible with the theory—an event which would have refuted the theory.

3. Every "good" scientific theory is a prohibition: It forbids certain things to happen. The more a theory forbids, the better it is.

4. A theory which is not refutable by any conceivable event is nonscientific. Irrefutability is not a virtue of a theory (as people often think) but a vice.

5. Every genuine test of a theory is an attempt to falsify it, or to refute it. Testability is falsifiability; but there are degrees of testability: Some theories are more testable, more exposed to refutation, than others; they take, as it were, greater risks.

6. Confirming evidence should not count except when it is the result of a genuine test of the theory; and this means that it can be presented as a serious but unsuccessful attempt to falsify the theory. (I now speak in such cases of "corroborating evidence.")

7. Some genuinely testable theories, when found to be false, are still upheld by their admirers—for example by introducing ad hoc some auxiliary assumption, or by reinterpreting the theory ad hoc in such a way that it escapes refutation. Such a procedure is always possible, but it rescues the theory from refutation only at the price of destroying, or at least lowering, its scientific status. (I later described such a rescuing operation as a "conventionalist twist" or a "conventionalist stratagem.")

One can sum up all this by saying that the criterion of the scientific status of a theory is its falsifiability, or refutability, or testability.

—**Sir Karl R. Popper, 1963, pp. 33–39**

If a hypothesis remains standing after a succession of tests or experiments fail to disprove it, then it may become a *scientific theory*. As such, it may be stated or presented with a reasonable degree of scientific certainty. Scientific theories that withstand the test of time and independent study eventually become *scientific principles*. There is no universal agreement as to whether and when a scientific theory crosses the threshold to become a scientific principle. It is, however, accepted that a scientific theory, necessarily developed with the assistance of the scientific method, has a greater degree of reliability and validity than mere observation, intuition, or speculation.

Science requires doubt and skepticism at all junctions. It is not about making friends or impressing colleagues. Useful instructions for the forensic criminologist are found in Kennedy and Kennedy (1972, p. 4):

> To be objective, an inquirer should be prepared to accept and record whatever facts he may encounter. He must not let personal feelings affect what he sees or hears. Although he does not need to like the nature of the information, he must be willing to investigate it. When such an investigation is begun, it must be carried through with a degree of skepticism. Skepticism does not imply cynicism or a distrust of the world. It only suggests that the [forensic criminologist] must be prepared to distinguish truth from the opinion or inclinations of others.

The authors have noted that the lesson of science as skeptical falsification is all but lost in modern classrooms. The rare student who has been exposed to the scientific method will routinely believe, for lack of informed instruction or general inattentiveness, that scientists are meant to prove given theories with their various methods and research efforts. This is reflected in exams, in classroom discussions, in thesis papers, and ultimately in published research.

Science does not seek confirmation; science seeks eradication. The failure to remove an idea or theory with the direct application of facts supporting every skeptical postulation available proves its strength. Conversely, the failure to apply skeptical postulations to a theory proves the doubts of those who fear its eradication.

Observer Effects

The majority of criminal justice and criminology education is oriented toward government, corrections, and law enforcement employment. When applied subjects are offered, they are taught by government-employed practitioners to give the program an affiliation that will smooth the way for student internships and future student employment. Subsequently, most forensic practitioners learn of, and go to work for, the police, the prosecution, or the prisons. At least at the beginning of their career, this tends to be true. The nature of this educational pathway creates a pro-prosecution bias in philosophy and practice that is very difficult to unseat, or even to perceive as harmful.

As cognitive psychologists have repeatedly documented, tested, and proven, "[t]he scientific observer [is] an imperfectly calibrated instrument" (Rosenthal, 1966, p. 3). The imperfections of such observers stem from the fact that subtle forms of bias, whether conscious or unconscious, can easily contaminate their seemingly objective undertakings. *Observer effects* are present when the results of a forensic examination are distorted by the context and mental state of the forensic examiner, to include the examiner's subconscious expectations and desires.

Identifying and curtailing this kind of bias is a considerable task when one takes into account the forensic community's aforementioned affiliation with both law enforcement and the prosecution. Specifically, this association has fashioned an atmosphere in which an unsettling number of forensic professionals have all but abandoned objectivity and have become completely partial to the prosecution's objectives, goals, and philosophies [Giannelli (1997) discusses how the forensic community's structural configuration has created many pro-prosecution forensic scientists]. They may even go so far as to regard this association as virtuous and heroic, and believe any alternative philosophy to be a manifestation of something that is morally bankrupt, as previously discussed. So strong is the influence of this association between forensic science and law enforcement that some forensic examiners have even deliberately fabricated evidence, or testified falsely, so that the prosecution might prove its case; however, this is the extreme end of the spectrum.[3]

[3]See, generally, the Forensic Fraud Archive, which is a database of more than a hundred cases involving forensic and law enforcement experts who have provided sworn testimony, documents, or reports intended for the court that contain deceptive or misleading information, findings, opinions, or conclusions. Located online at http://www.corpus-delicti.com/forensic_fraud.html.

As Professor D. Michael Risinger and colleagues (2002, p. 9) e~ groundbreaking law review article on observer effects in forens different forms of observer effects exist: "At the most gener effects are errors of apprehension, recording, recall, comput; tation that result from some trait or state of the observer." T are more concerning than deliberate fraud and misconduc often misperceived, or even thought of as beneficial, and go undetected. Consequently, to blunt their impact, scient must be aware that these influences exist and can indeed ence their analyses. Once conceded, they can be studied a understood, they can be addressed and even mitigated. The v~ entific disciplines accept the need to blunt examiner bias and observer eneuo as a given, and it is reflected in their published research. Put simply, "[s]ensitivity to the problems of observer effects has become integral to the modern scientific method" (Risinger et al., 2002, p. 6).

THE FORENSIC PERSPECTIVE

To be a good scientist, one must embrace and execute the scientific method until it is second nature. One's approach to problem solving must be objective and skeptical. One must also seek to recognize and blunt observer effects. Such practice and traits must be an inseparable part of one's professional identity—known to all and doubted by none. This is also necessary to the sound practice of forensic criminology. However, it is only part of the equation. Being a good scientist in no way ensures forensic knowledge or ability.

Each year, many competent scientists are hired into forensic service. Most are enlisted directly from university. They may enter the forensic realm as a freshly minted graduate to be employed at entry level in a government agency, or as a seasoned professor to be employed as a forensic consultant.

Unless these individuals have had specific education in the forensic sciences by someone who is practicing it, whether in the area of criminology or not, they will arrive for their first court appearance with little knowledge of what is happening—even as it happens. Despite being given a forensic role or job title, they will not understand their function, their responsibilities, or even the very laws that govern their conduct—sometimes belligerently so, depending on their professional and intellectual character. The purpose of this section is to help alleviate that condition with some basic instruction.

It is important for readers to understand that the intersection of scientific and criminal justice ambition is problematic at best—whether you are practicing in Australia, Canada, the United Kingdom, or the United States. The mandates of science are frequently in direct conflict with the needs of investigators, the desires of attorneys, and even the rule of law as decided by various courts. The criminal justice system is like a great flowing river. Each mile of the river has its own tides and currents, or laws and rules; and each requires very different things. Consequently, scientists are at a terrific disadvantage when they practice within the justice system. This must be conceded at the outset of any forensic endeavor. As explained in Thornton (1983, pp. 86–88):

> Basic conflicts that influence the practice of forensic science become apparent at the interface of law and science. Law and science on occasion have conflicting goals, each having developed in response to different social and attitudes and intellectual needs. The goal of law is the just resolution of human conflict, while the goal of science traditionally has been cast, although perhaps too smugly, as the search for "truth." Certainly there is nothing intrinsically dichotomous in the pursuit of these goals; the court or jury strive in good faith to determine the truth in a given situation as a way to resolve conflicts. But proof is viewed somewhat differently by law and science, as is the application of logic and the perception of societal values.

> Numerous writers have commented on these differences, including Glanville Williams in his *Proof of Guilt* (1958): "The principles of [the legal system] are not the product of scientific observation, but embody a system of values. These values do not necessarily have to be changed with the march of knowledge of the material world... The rule conferring upon an accused the right not to be questioned... may be a good or a bad rule, [but it] has certainly not been made better or worse by the invention of printing or the aeroplane."...

> How, then, do these differences between law and science lead to abuse of forensic science? They do simply because all the players want to win and are likely to use any ethical means at their disposal to do so. The attorneys in a case are aligned with only one side, and it is entirely appropriate under the adversary system for them to advocate a particular point of view, even without full and fair disclosure of all relevant facts. Subject only to the rules of evidence, the rules of procedure, and the Code of Professional Responsibility, attorneys are free to manipulate scientific evidence to maximize the opportunity for their side to prevail. Not only is behavior of this sort countenanced by the law, it is the ethical responsibility of counsel to attempt to do so.

[4]Barton L. Ingraham is a former Harvard-educated lawyer with a doctorate in criminology from Berkeley. After practicing law in 10 different states for more than a decade, he retired to academia and is currently an Associate Professor at the Institute of Criminal Justice and Criminology at the University of Maryland in College Park.

In fact, the domains of science and law are so divergent and so foreign to each other's purpose that one legal authority argues against academic and research criminologists testifying in adversarial proceedings at all (Ingraham[4], 1987, p. 179):

The adversary "game" is not a procedure whose underlying purpose is to communicate facts or determine truth but rather to communicate position statements about reality, and ultimately the expert witness is forced into the role of a coadvocate selling a partisan position to the trier-of-fact rather than an impartial source of information.

He subsequently argues that "criminologists are not ethically justified" in testifying as expert witnesses because (p. 179):

in the final analysis, the expert witness from the social sciences participates in a process which cannot, by reason of its structure and the people who operate it (lawyers and judges), lead to an objective understanding of scientific knowledge. Therefore, because of the ethical principles to which most academicians subscribe... a social scientist, such as a criminologist, cannot ethically participate in what amounts to a circus of illusion and deception.

The authors of this text do not share this view in its entirety. It is true that in the negotiation of justice, science may be selectively employed, wholly ignored, and terribly abused by those managing the justice system. The virtues of scientific fact and subsequent expert inferences can be easily muddied by skilled counsel or quelled by a cautious or ignorant judge. With this in mind, forensic practitioners must free themselves to not just anticipate but also assume that their findings and related testimony will be, at best, misrepresented by attorneys making arguments on both sides of the courtroom once they have left the witness stand. And that it may be misunderstood by the court. It is consequently their duty to report findings and testify in such a manner as to prevent this from happening whenever possible.

The authors of this text would argue that it is not unethical to participate in the adversarial process for fear that science and facts will not carry the day; rather, it is unethical for scientists to withhold their knowledge, skills, and ability from a process that so desperately needs it. They have a duty to make a faithful scientific record for honest agents within the criminal justice system to find and set to use. Criminologists who refuse to educate the criminal justice process on moral grounds lose their moral authority to criticize its outcomes as a consequence. So while the legal system is not necessarily concerned with science or truth, this makes the participation of scientists all the more necessary.

However, it's not at all easy. In fact, the less one knows about the criminal justice system, the simpler it likely seems. To assist readers with navigating this professional cloverleaf, we would offer the following points of regular concern—without which scientists may find their standards and conduct easily misled. It should be noted that while the rules and laws mentioned are specific to the United States, the scientific philosophy and sentiment are universal.

1. The Federal Rules of Evidence.

The Federal Rules of Evidence (FRE) govern the admissibility of facts as evidence in the United States Federal Court. Many states have adopted these rules, or a close variation, to govern the admissibility of facts as evidence at the state court level. Moreover, they are taught in law, criminal justice, and even some forensic science programs across the United States. It is fair to argue that they are a regularly updated legal touchstone.

The section on Opinions and Expert Testimony are particularly relevant to the forensic criminologist (FRE, 2006, pp. 13–15):

ARTICLE VII. OPINIONS AND EXPERT TESTIMONY

Rule 701. Opinion Testimony by Lay Witnesses

If the witness is not testifying as an expert, the witness' testimony in the form of opinions or inferences is limited to those opinions or inferences which are (a) rationally based on the perception of the witness, and (b) helpful to a clear understanding of the witness' testimony or the determination of a fact in issue, and (c) not based on scientific, technical, or other specialized knowledge within the scope of Rule 702.

(As amended Mar. 2, 1987, eff. Oct. 1, 1987; Apr. 17, 2000, eff. Dec. 1, 2000.)

Rule 702. Testimony by Experts

If scientific, technical, or other specialized knowledge will assist the trier of fact to understand the evidence or to determine a fact in issue, a witness qualified as an expert by knowledge, skill, experience, training, or education, may testify thereto in the form of an opinion or otherwise, if (1) the testimony is based upon sufficient facts or data, (2) the testimony is the product of reliable principles and methods, and (3) the witness has applied the principles and methods reliably to the facts of the case.

(As amended Apr. 17, 2000, eff. Dec. 1, 2000.)

Rule 703. Bases of Opinion Testimony by Experts

The facts or data in the particular case upon which an expert bases an opinion or inference may be those perceived by or made known to the expert at or before the hearing. If of a type reasonably relied upon by experts in the particular field in forming opinions or inferences upon the subject, the facts or data need not be admissible in evidence in order for the opinion or inference to be admitted. Facts or data that are otherwise inadmissible shall not be disclosed to the jury by the proponent of the opinion or inference unless the court determines that their probative value in assisting the jury to evaluate the expert's opinion substantially outweighs their prejudicial effect.

(As amended Mar. 2, 1987, eff. Oct. 1, 1987; Apr. 17, 2000, eff. Dec. 1, 2000.)

Rule 704. Opinion on Ultimate Issue

(a) Except as provided in subdivision (b), testimony in the form of an opinion or inference otherwise admissible is not objectionable because it embraces an ultimate issue to be decided by the trier of fact.

(b) No expert witness testifying with respect to the mental state or condition of a defendant in a criminal case may state an opinion or inference as to whether the defendant did or did not have the mental state or condition constituting an element of the crime charged or of a defense thereto. Such ultimate issues are matters for the trier of fact alone.

(As amended Oct. 12, 1984.)

Rule 705. Disclosure of Facts or Data Underlying Expert Opinion

The expert may testify in terms of opinion or inference and give reasons therefor without first testifying to the underlying facts or data, unless the court requires otherwise. The expert may in any event be required to disclose the underlying facts or data on crossexamination.

(As amended Mar. 2, 1987, eff. Oct. 1, 1987; Apr. 22, 1993, eff. Dec. 1, 1993.)

Rule 706. Court Appointed Experts

(a) Appointment—The court may on its own motion or on the motion of any party enter an order to show cause why expert witnesses should not be appointed, and may request the parties to submit nominations. The court may appoint any expert witnesses agreed upon by the parties, and may appoint expert witnesses of its own selection. An expert witness shall not be appointed by the court unless the witness consents to act. A witness so appointed shall be informed of the witness' duties by the court in writing, a copy of which shall be filed with the clerk, or at a conference in which the parties shall have opportunity to participate. A witness so appointed shall advise the parties of the witness' findings, if any; the witness' deposition may be taken by any party; and the witness may be called to testify by the court or any party. The witness shall be subject to cross-examination by each party, including a party calling the witness.

(b) Compensation—Expert witnesses so appointed are entitled to reasonable compensation in whatever sum the court may allow. The compensation thus fixed is payable from funds which may be provided by law in criminal cases and civil actions and proceedings involving just compensation under the fifth amendment. In other civil actions and proceedings the compensation shall be paid by the parties in such proportion and at such time as the court directs, and thereafter charged in like manner as other costs.

(c) Disclosure of appointment—In the exercise of its discretion, the court may authorize disclosure to the jury of the fact that the court appointed the expert witness.

(d) Parties' experts of own selection—Nothing in this rule limits the parties in calling expert witnesses of their own selection.

(As amended Mar. 2, 1987, eff. Oct. 1, 1987.)

Forensic criminologists are admonished to learn these rules, or their variations, in jurisdictions of anticipated testimony. Suffice to say that they exist in some form everywhere.

2. The rules for the defense and the prosecution are different. And they must be.

It comes as an unhappy surprise to many forensic practitioners that the prosecution, and their agents, must follow different rules of conduct than the accused and theirs. This is owing to the fact that we have an adversarial system and not an inquisitorial one, as discussed in Chapter 2. A fundamental virtue of our criminal justice system is that all defendants are presumed innocent. Consequently, all aspects of a criminal trial are loaded with this ideal. As explained in Nelson (2008, p. 713):

> Unlike the inquisitorial systems of Continental Europe, our adversarial system erects numerous protections for the accused. Indeed, "[n]o principle is more firmly established in our system of criminal justice than the presumption of innocence that is accorded to the defendant in every criminal trial."

This echoes Hardaway (2008, p. 271), which provides more historical background:

> The presumption of innocence in favor of the accused is firmly ingrained in American jurisprudence. This fundamental principle has been traced to biblical origins and has been shown to be substantially embodied in Roman and Canon law. Early English legal scholars, as well as esteemed members of the court, have acknowledged this

principle in varied recitations of the maxim that it is better to acquit ten guilty people than to convict one innocent person.

The presumption of innocence places the burden of proving criminal guilt entirely on the government. In theory, the state must prove a defendant's guilt *beyond a reasonable doubt* in order to obtain a conviction. As explained in Hardaway (2008, pp. 271–272):

> The presumption of innocence does not automatically establish the burden of proof required to determine an accused's guilt or innocence. The presumption is an instrument of proof created by the law in favor of one accused, whereby his innocence is established until sufficient evidence is introduced to overcome the proof which the law has created. The degree of proof required to overcome the presumption of innocence is defined by the prevailing burden of persuasion.

Conversely, the defense has an entirely lower evidentiary threshold. Ideally, they must only prove the existence of a *reasonable doubt* to obtain an acquittal. Hardaway (2008) explains that although there are some clear interpretations regarding this standard, there has also been ongoing disagreement between courts regarding both the definition of reasonable doubt, and whether it must actually be explained to the jury (pp. 272–273):

> In the American criminal justice system, the accused must be proven guilty beyond a reasonable doubt.
>
> …
>
> *Commonwealth v. Webster* [1850] is representative of the time when American courts began applying the beyond a reasonable doubt standard "in its modern form in criminal cases." Writing for the majority, Chief Justice Shaw defined reasonable doubt as:
>
>> [N]ot a mere possible doubt; because everything relating to human affairs, and depending on moral evidence, is open to some possible or imaginary doubt. It is that state of the case, which, after the entire comparison and consideration of all the evidence, leaves the minds of jurors in that condition that they cannot say they feel an abiding conviction, to a moral certainty, of the truth of the charge … but the evidence must establish the truth of the fact to a reasonable and moral certainty; a certainty that convinces and directs the understanding, and satisfies the reason and judgment, of those who are bound to act conscientiously upon it.

Many courts adopted Justice Shaw's definition of reasonable doubt in the nineteenth century, with one court characterizing the instruction as "probably the most satisfactory definition ever given to the words

'reasonable doubt' in any case known to criminal jurisprudence."
[*People v. Strong*, 30 Cal. 151, 155 (1866)] However, while the Supreme
Court has held that proof beyond a reasonable doubt is a constitutional
requirement in every criminal trial and juries shall be instructed on the
necessity of such proof, the Constitution does not require a definition
of reasonable doubt as part of this instruction (*Jackson v. Virginia*, 443
U.S. 307, 320 n.14 (1979) (explaining that "failure to instruct a jury on
the necessity of proof of guilt beyond a reasonable doubt can never be
harmless error"); *Sullivan v. Louisiana*, 508 U.S. 275, 278 (1993) ("[T]he
Fifth Amendment requirement of proof beyond a reasonable doubt and
the Sixth Amendment requirement of a jury verdict are interrelated ....
[T]he jury verdict required by the Sixth Amendment is a jury verdict
of guilty beyond a reasonable doubt."). The Supreme Court's lack of
guidance on the instruction of the reasonable doubt standard has given
rise to confusion and a wide lack of uniformity in the treatment of its
definition among federal and state courts. Not only does the definition
of reasonable doubt vary between courts, but the jurisdictions also
diverge on whether or not a jury is to be instructed on the definition.

This issue provides an excellent reminder to scientists that the law is not a
series of unequivocal "if-then" statements that are clearly understood, rationally interpreted, and consistently applied. Each judge in each courtroom in
every country interprets and applies the law in his or her own way. On this
particular matter, some believe in providing helpful definitions of key terms to
juries; some believe in a "hands-off" policy to let jurors decide for themselves;
and some can be found in-between. The result is a wide diversity with respect
to understanding and application of the law by differing judges and courts,
and frequent jury confusion.

For their part, scientists in forensic practice are bound to accept these rules and
circumstances in their approach, analyses, and interpretations—so long as they
do not interfere with good scientific practice. For instance, they must not generally assume the guilt of a defendant as part of their analysis as this is the very
issue to be decided at trial. Even in postconviction work, where guilt is a legal
reality, this may be an issue under review. In some cases, however, guilt will
have been conceded by the defense, and such an assumption may be appropriate or even required by the court.

Moreover, scientists employed by the prosecution have a very specific burden
with respect to their findings and what is referred to as *due process*. The 5th
and 14th Amendments to the United States Constitution provide that the government may not deprive its citizens of "life, liberty, or property without due
process of law." This provision is essentially a fairness requirement. Ideally,
citizens may only be tried and punished for crimes alleged by the state under

the most impartial and unprejudiced conditions. Any condition or treatment that tends to bias a judge, jury, or the process as a whole in favor of the state is considered a violation of due process. Common examples include things like inadequate defense, access to legal counsel or private experts, and failure to disclose exculpatory evidence or witnesses. In reality, the government has more money, more resources to draw from, and often benefits from a presumption of guilt held by ignorant and even partial jurors. Under these conditions, due process is an ideal rather than a reality.

To abide the mandates of due process, scientists employed by the government must conduct forensic examinations in such a way as to be transparent in their methods and findings. As explained in Edwards and Gotsonis (2009, pp. 6–3):

> As a general matter, laboratory reports generated as the result of a scientific analysis should be complete and thorough. They should describe, at a minimum, methods and materials, procedures, results, and conclusions, and they should identify, as appropriate, the sources of uncertainty in the procedures and conclusions along with estimates of their scale (to indicate the level of confidence in the results). Although it is not appropriate and practicable to provide as much detail as might be expected in a research paper, sufficient content should be provided to allow the nonscientist reader to understand what has been done and permit informed, unbiased scrutiny of the conclusion.
>
> Some forensic laboratory reports meet this standard of reporting, but most do not. Some reports contain only identifying and agency information, a brief description of the evidence being submitted, a brief description of the types of analysis requested, and a short statement of the results (e.g., "The green, brown plant material in item #1 was identified as marijuana"). The norm is to have no description of the methods or procedures used, and most reports do not discuss measurement uncertainties or confidence limits. Many disciplines outside the forensic science disciplines have standards, templates, and protocols for data reporting. Although some of the Scientific Working Groups have a scoring system for reporting findings, they are not uniformly or consistently used.
>
> Forensic science reports, and any courtroom testimony stemming from them, must include clear characterizations of the limitations of the analyses, including associated probabilities where possible. Courtroom testimony should be given in lay terms so that all trial participants can understand how to weight and interpret the testimony. In order to enable this, research must be undertaken to evaluate the reliability of the steps of the various identification methods and the confidence intervals associated with the overall conclusions.

In other words, notes and reports must be discovered to the defense in a timely fashion prior to trial. Scientists must willingly make themselves available to the defense for pretrial interviews about their methods and findings. They must not withhold, conceal, or distort their methods and findings—especially if their findings tend to exculpate or exonerate the defendant. And generally they must treat the prosecution and the defense equally—even if the police department or prosecutor's office signs their paycheck.

In the United States, this is done to comply with a well-known and often-ignored legal standard passed down from the U.S. Supreme Court regarding evidence and its discovery to the defense in *Brady v. Maryland* (1963).[5] In so doing, scientists are meant to help create equal access to the government's findings, prevent what is generally referred to as "trial by ambush," and seek to avoid miscarriages of justice. As explained in Gershman (2006, pp. 685–686):

> Brady's holding is familiar to virtually every practitioner of criminal law: "[T]he suppression by the prosecution of evidence favorable to an accused upon request violates due process where the evidence is material either to guilt or to punishment, irrespective of the good faith or bad faith of the prosecution."

> This principle, according to the Brady Court, reflects our nation's abiding commitment to adversarial justice and fair play toward those persons accused of crimes. As the Court observed: "Society wins not only when the guilty are convicted but when criminal trials are fair; our system of the administration of justice suffers when any accused is treated unfairly." Indeed, by explicitly commanding prosecutors to disclose to defendants facing a criminal trial any favorable evidence that is material to their guilt or punishment, Brady launched the modern development of constitutional disclosure requirements.

As experienced forensic practitioners are well aware, the high-minded language offered in *Brady* requiring timely disclosure of potentially exculpatory evidence stands in contrast to its interpretation and application. It was intended as a clear standard set forth for reasonable minds to appreciate and follow. However, the adversarial nature of the criminal justice system, and the general lack of accountability for even blatant prosecutorial misconduct, has left *Brady* without the teeth it needs. This was in fact the conclusion offered in Gershman (2006, pp. 727–728):

> Reflecting on the evolution of *Brady v. Maryland*, one is struck by the stark dissonance between the grand expectations of Brady, that the adversary system henceforth would be transformed from a "sporting contest" to a genuine search for truth, and the grim reality that criminal litigation continues to operate as a "trial by ambush." The development

[5]Variations of this rule exist in most adversarial legal systems. In Australia, for example, there is the Queensland Criminal Code Act of 1899, Chapter 62, Division 3, Subdivision C on "Disclosure" which is very similar. The UK criminal code is generally the same, with respect to legal disclosure of expert evidence and its foundation pretrial.

of the Brady rule by the judiciary depicts a gradual erosion of Brady: from a prospective obligation on prosecutors to make timely disclosure, to the defense of materially favorable evidence, to a retrospective review by an appellate court into whether the prosecutor's suppression was unduly prejudicial. The erosion of Brady has been accompanied by increasing prosecutorial gamesmanship in gambling that violations will not be discovered or, if discovered, will be allowed, and tactics that abet and hide violations. Finally, the absence of any legal or ethical sanctions to make prosecutors accountable for violations produces a system marked by willful abuse of law, cynicism, and the real possibility that innocent persons may be wrongfully convicted because of the prosecutor's misconduct. Indeed, more than any other rule of criminal procedure, the Brady rule has been the most fertile and widespread source of misconduct by prosecutors; and, more than any other rule of constitutional criminal procedure, has exposed the deficiencies in the truth-serving function of the criminal trial.

The original language in *Brady* has been expanded by the Supreme Court to cover any and all potentially exculpatory information in control of the prosecution, the police, and their agents. This includes government-operated crime labs, as well as private labs and private experts contracted into government service. Unfortunately, ignorance regarding *Brady* remains even in these informed circles, as explained in Giannelli and McMunigal (2007, pp. 1517–1518):

> The U.S. Supreme Court has extended Brady to cover exculpatory information in the control of the police. Some courts have explicitly included crime labs within the reach of Brady. In one case, the Supreme Court of California noted that a laboratory examiner "worked closely" with prosecutors and was part of the investigative team. The court concluded that the "prosecutor thus had the obligation to determine if the lab's files contained any exculpatory evidence, such as the worksheet, and disclose it to petitioner." [In re Brown, 952 p. 2d 715, 719 (Cal. 1998)]

> In another case, a court wrote that an experienced crime lab technician "must have known of his legal obligation to disclose exculpatory evidence to the prosecutors, their obligation to pass it along to the defense, and his obligation not to cover up a Brady violation by perjuring himself." [Charles v. City of Boston, 365 F. Supp. 2d 82, 89 (D. Mass. 2005)] While the expert should have been on notice about perjury, it is less clear that the Brady obligation would be known to lab personnel—without the prosecutor tutoring the lab. How often do prosecutors discharge this duty? Many lab examiners have never heard of Brady.

One common *Brady* violation, often committed out of nothing more than ignorance, is related to the forensic practice of labeling a finding or report "inconclusive." There are forensic practitioners employed by the government, from fingerprint analysts to DNA technicians, who erroneously believe that inconclusive or indeterminate findings are not an actual result. Therefore, they feel comfortable withholding the existence of such tests and related findings by virtue of failing to write them up in a report, or failing to disclose those kinds of reports to the defense. Consider the discussion and examples provided in Giannelli and McMunigal (2007, pp. 1515–1516):

a. Timing of Disclosure

Brady is a trial right, not a pretrial disclosure rule. Nevertheless, exculpatory evidence must be disclosed in time for defense counsel to make use of it. Here, as with the discovery rules discussed above, delayed disclosure may place a defendant in an untenable position. In Ex parte Mowbray, [943 S.W.2d 461 (Tex. Crim. App. 1996)] a murder case, the prosecutor used a blood spatter expert to refute the defense suicide theory. According to the prosecutor, his case "depended upon" this evidence. Prior to trial, the prosecution retained another expert, Herbert MacDonell, considered the premier expert in the field. After reviewing the crime scene, the physical evidence and the photographs, MacDonell concluded months before trial that "it was more probable than not that the deceased died from a suicide rather than a homicide." Yet the defense did not receive his written report until ten days before trial and then only after the trial judge threatened sanctions. MacDonell never testified. The court wrote,

> … State's counsel early on recognized the potential lethal effect of MacDonell's testimony on their theory of the case, and beginning in November and continuing until May they engaged in a deliberate course of conduct to keep MacDonell's findings and opinions from Applicant's counsel until the last days before trial. Even then they caused Applicant's counsel to believe MacDonell would be a witness and available for cross-examination.

b. "Exculpatory" Requirement

Brady does not apply unless the evidence is exculpatory. Consequently, labeling a laboratory report as inconclusive may relieve the prosecution of the disclosure requirement. For example, in one case an inconclusive handwriting report "was not exculpatory, but merely not inculpatory." [United States v. Hauff, 473 F.2d 1350, 1354 (7th Cir. 1973)] Similarly, a report showing that hair from a rape defendant was not found at the scene of the crime was deemed a "neutral" report. [Norris v. Slayton,

540 F.2d 1241, 1243–44 (4th Cir. 1976)] However, as one court correctly understood,

> [S]uch a characterization [as neutral] often has little meaning; evidence such as this may, because of its neutrality, tend to be favorable to the accused. While it does not by any means establish his absence from the scene of the crime, it does demonstrate that a number of factors which could link the defendant to the crime do not. [Patler v. Slayton, 503 F.2d 472, 479 (4th Cir. 1974)]

Similarly, in Bell v. Coughlin, [820 F. Supp. 780, 786–87 (S.D.N.Y. 1993)] the prosecution failed to turn over FBI ballistics test results to the defense.

> The lab positively matched a cartridge shell (B3) to the .45 caliber pistol but reported that no conclusion could be reached with respect to the two bullets (J/R2 and J/R4) in its possession. Thus, although the results of the FBI tests may be characterized as mixed, they clearly contained exculpatory material.

In a research facility, it may very well be standard procedure to discard undesirable or unhelpful results—though it would be scientifically dishonest to conceal such a practice when publishing related research. However, in a forensic context, this practice is referred to as *cherry picking*: selectively reporting (and thereby emphasizing) only desired results or information rather than the entirety of examinations performed and results achieved. Specifically, this practice violates due process because:

1. The concealment of any examination performed on any item of evidence represents a break in the *chain of custody* for that item to those third parties involved in reviewing subsequent reports (i.e., judges, juries, attorneys, and independent forensic examiners). The defense in particular has a right to know of every individual who handled an item of evidence, what he or she did with it or to it and where, and in what order.

2. The execution of any examination on an item of evidence has a potential impact on its volume and quality (destruction, consumption, contamination, etc.). The nature of any impact on the evidence must be made clear to the police, court, and all of the attorneys involved in a case.

3. The failure to notify the police, court, or attorneys involved in a case regarding the existence of inconclusive examinations assists with concealing the causes behind such results. This can include errors in examination procedure, problems with the evidence itself, or individual examiner proficiency. Unless the cause of an inconclusive

result has been unequivocally established, the impact on the interpretation of any subsequent or related results is unknown and potentially limiting.

4. The failure to investigate and report the cause of inconclusive results potentially conceals the error rate and/or the individual examiner proficiency rate related to a particular test. If these are unknown, then the scientific reliability of that test is not known. This may in turn create a false illusion of competence and proficiency in the mind of forensic examiners, their superiors, and the court.

Inconclusive findings are clearly relevant to the reconstruction of a crime, the nature and extent of examinations performed, the evidence they were performed on, the quality of any testing, the competency of the examiner, and the legal proceedings that hinge upon the weight the court places on evidence of every kind. They are a result, just not one that is expected or even desired. Consequently, the failure to disclose such results is a violation of due process, and could foreseeably be conceived as an obstruction to justice—which is in fact a criminal charge. This is, however, unlikely, as the police and prosecutors very rarely sanction their own experts for conduct it generally encourages. Thus, such misconduct by government-employed scientists often goes unrecognized or uninvestigated.

Consider the following case example of *Brady* in action, which highlights disparities between the agendas of law enforcement and science. Note that police investigators in particular want to clear and prosecute suspects in their cases. To accomplish these goals, they can lie to suspects about the existence of evidence or witnesses during initial interviews. In some states they are allowed to fabricate false reports and produce false evidence without fear of sanction; in others it is a crime. The laws and policies governing police conduct vary from agency to agency, and also with respect to jurisdiction.

Matthew Christian is, as of this writing, a detective with the San Jose Police Department in California. He fabricated a report from the district attorney's crime lab with a phony lab analyst's name that "confirmed" the presence of semen on a blanket related to an alleged sex crime.[6] He then used this fabricated report during a suspect interview to gain an inculpatory statement. Unfortunately, he forgot about his deception and put the "ruse report" into his case file alongside a real lab report that contradicted it. The district attorney proceeded to trial thinking she had hard physical evidence—denying several defense requests about the contradictory lab results. When asked about it on the stand during a preliminary hearing, Detective Christian falsely testified as though the fake lab report and analyst were real and the findings had been inculpatory. The fake lab analyst was even put on the district attorney's witness list. Only when the defense was finally able to speak with the lab did they

[6]In San Jose, the crime lab is a division of the district attorney's office. It is in fact called "Santa Clara County District Attorney's Criminalistics Laboratory." Detective Christianson used the district attorney's seal and official documents in making his phony report.

discover the confirmatory report was a fake. This information was forwarded to the district attorney, who had not verified the report.[7]

In December of 2006, all charges were dropped against the accused (Griffy, 2007a). Detective Christianson remains on active duty with San Jose Police Department. The use of ruse reports remains standard practice.

Without the cover of *Brady* and the tenacity of alert defense counsel, the detective's error and his related misconduct might not have been revealed until during trial—after the damage had already done by forcing the accused to appear in front of a jury.

Currently, *Brady* is only as good as the investigators and prosecutors who follow it, the judges who enforce it, and the defense counsel who understand and raise it as an issue. The general absence of prosecutorial sanctions for *Brady* violations has put the criminal justice system on the honor system in this regard. Scientific experts in their employ, therefore, have a tremendous responsibility to self-govern with respect to their evidence and its discovery. Their failure to comply, despite the cheers of the prosecution and the indifference of some trial courts, has repeatedly been the cause of reversal at the appellate level.

While scientists employed by the government are admonished to comply with *Brady*, scientists employed by the defense are admonished to work within the restrictions of the *attorney-client privilege*. This legal entitlement is intended to facilitate truthful communication and fully informed advocacy by a defendant's counselors. It protects the confidentiality of dealings between lawyers and their clients, but also extends to their agents, which includes expert consultants. If a scientific consultant renders a finding that is useful to the defense, he or she may be asked to write a report or declaration that will be discoverable to the prosecution under the rules of evidence, and even to give subsequent expert testimony before the court. If the consultant renders findings that are harmful to defense theories of the case, the forensic consultant may be kept within the privilege and expected to abide by it, that is, unless concealing findings presents an ethical conflict or facilitates a crime—as will be discussed in the next chapter.

The rules for the accused and the rules for the prosecution are very different. In an adversarial system with the presumption of innocence and right to due process, they must be. And these rules will have nothing to do with the mandates of good science, but rather due process and its interpretation by a given court or government agency. Forensic criminologists must understand, expect, and conform to the nature of this imbalance to serve their role effectively and without prejudice. If they do not believe in these rules and their underlying assumptions regarding the rights of the accused, then they should not seek to serve in a forensic capacity.

[7] In 1990, the same police department had been warned by the judiciary to cease the practice of creating phony lab reports. However, in 2002, "detective Juan Serrano [of the San Jose Police Department] described the use of ruse crime lab reports as 'standard procedure' at that time" (Griffy, 2007b).

3. *Every defendant is entitled to objective scientific expert assistance.*

In the United States, forensic criminologists, regardless of their employer, must accept the legal principle that every defendant is entitled to an adequate defense, which includes reasonable access to scientific expert assistance should the need arise. This stems from the right of the accused to due process. Without adequate access to independent scientific assistance in the examination of evidence, or even interpreting the government's findings, and set against the overwhelming resources of the government, due process cannot prevail. As explained in Giannelli (2005, p. 539):

> In many criminal cases, securing the services of experts to examine evidence, to advise counsel, and to testify at trial is critical. As the commentary to the American Bar Association (ABA) Standards notes: "The quality of representation at trial … may be excellent and yet unhelpful to the defendant if the defense requires the assistance of a psychiatrist or handwriting expert and no such services are available." As early as 1929, Justice Cardozo commented: "[U]pon the trial of certain issues, such as insanity or forgery, experts are often necessary both for the prosecution and for defense …. [A] defendant may be at an unfair disadvantage, if he is unable because of poverty to parry by his own witnesses the thrusts of those against him." Similarly, Judge Jerome Frank observed in a 1956 opinion: "The best lawyer in the world cannot competently defend an accused person if the lawyer cannot obtain existing evidence crucial to the defense, e.g., if the defendant cannot pay the fee of an investigator to find a pivotal missing witness or a necessary document, or that of an expert accountant or mining engineer or chemist." He went on to observe: "In such circumstances, if the government does not supply the funds, justice is denied the poor—and represents but an upper-bracket privilege."

> The ABA Standards require adequate access to experts for both the defense and prosecution, and there are some statutory provisions for defense experts. For example, the Criminal Justice Act provides for expert assistance for indigent defendants in federal trials. The Act, however, limits expenses for experts to $1,000.00 unless the court certifies that a greater amount is "necessary to provide fair compensation for services of an unusual character or duration." But, as Judge Weinstein has noted, "The Act's $1,000 limit for defense experts is far too low … and must be increased if due process is to be afforded defendants." Many states have comparable provisions, but the monetary limits are often incredibly low—until recently $250 maximum in capital cases in Illinois.

In Ake v. Oklahoma, [470 U.S. 68 (1985)] the Supreme Court recognized a due process right to a defense expert. The Court wrote: "[W]hen a State brings its judicial power to bear on an indigent in a criminal proceeding, it must take steps to assure that the defendant has a fair opportunity to present his defense." This fair opportunity mandates that an accused be provided with the "basic tools of an adequate defense." Nevertheless, some courts have attempted to limit this right to capital cases or to psychiatric experts. This narrow application fits the facts in Ake but not its rationale. Other courts have imposed demanding threshold standards for the appointment of defense experts. If the threshold standard is too high, the defendant faces a "catch-22" situation, in which the standard "demand[s] that the defendant possess already the expertise of the witness sought."

A number of sources indicate that the lack of defense experts continues to be a problem for indigent defendants.

We mentioned the importance of *Ake* to the development of forensic criminology in the United States in Chapter 1. The legal entitlement to expert assistance provides a professional mandate to forensic experts wherein they fail the intentions of the criminal justice system should they select clients solely based on their alignment for or against a particular side. That is to say, the objective forensic criminologist has an obligation to perform examinations for whichever side approaches him or her first. If one is truly an impartial scientist, then one has no stake in the outcome and sides are a nonissue. If one's examinations are truly scientific, and the results are insusceptible to biasing influences, then it cannot matter to the scientist which side of a legal conflict asks that they be performed. The scientific facts must out for justice to be served. Refusal to work for either side based simply on the politics of alignment with one over the other, for fear of personal or professional sanction or out of a misplaced moral imperative, accurately telegraphs examiner bias.

This also demonstrates that the objective scientific expert is one who is able and willing to work for either side in a legal dispute, offering precisely the same interpretations under like fact patterns and circumstances regardless. The authors sympathize with government-employed forensic practitioners who may, by policy, be barred from practice outside their place of employment. The issue of examiner bias associated with such isolated forensic engagement will be discussed later in this chapter.

However, we take note that many government forensic analysts enjoy a jurisdictional exception, where they may provide forensic services on private cases beyond the borders of their employer's influence to maintain an impartial practice while also avoiding obvious conflicts of interest. Employees of a county crime lab may privately consult on cases in other counties or in other states, for example. The same may also be true for those employed by police agencies. Similarly, forensic psychologists may work for a state hospital but may consult privately on matters out of state. Again, this is a matter of internal agency policy, not of law.

Often, the refusal of forensic practitioners to work private cases for the defense is the result of the very real fear of being "blacklisted" by their prosecution-oriented friends and colleagues (to keep experts in line and forensic expertise aligned with the prosecution), or out of the belief that their work might help a guilty party go free. This second line of reasoning arrogantly assumes the ultimate issue of legal guilt, which will be discussed shortly. It also suggests a diminished view in the abilities of the prosecution, and an underlying belief that cases should not be tried with the full force of good science on the side of the accused. It suggests that the prosecution may not have a good case, or good evidence, and that subsequently its way should be smoothed by the absence of competent analysis and testimony. These are not the holdings characteristic of a true scientist, let alone a forensic one.

4. The objective scientist is a not a member of the adversarial "team."

While the criminal justice system necessarily sets two legal sides against each other—the prosecution and the defense—we have already explained that objective scientists do not take up the banner of either. In fact their only value to the legal process is with respect to their objectivity. These scientists are there to advocate for evidence and its dispassionate interpretation—nothing more. They can have no emotional, professional, or financial stake in the outcome. In other words, they cannot be paid to guarantee findings or testimony favorable to their employer, nor can their advancement be connected to the success of one party over another. This is, of course, separate from being compensated for time spent performing analysis and giving testimony. The second author (Petherick) is reminded of a discussion with a private forensic consultant who was, without discussing the specifics of the case, citing his involvement in a civil case. While outlining his involvement, the private consultant made the somewhat bold claim that "we are going to win this one." When asked what he meant, the private consultant referred specifically to himself and the legal "team" that had sought his assistance, as though there was some right and wrong side of the legal argument. Such alignment is inappropriate and telegraphs a biased mindset.

The division of investigative, legal, and scientific spheres exists to allow forensic practitioners to act as an objective foil to those who hire them—whether they are attorneys or law enforcement investigators. As previously discussed, investigators and lawyers have different goals and ethical considerations than do scientists. Each is admonished to act within the scope afforded his or her role, and not intrude upon that of the others. For example, lawyers at trial are interested in the facts and evidence that assist their case. The rest they are content to distort or simply ignore. This is discussed in Ingraham (1987, p. 183):

> [O]ne often hears the following specious argument that the adversarial system has a built-in protection against the partial, partisan, and one-sided presentation of the evidence: "Not to worry. What is left uncovered by one side of the dispute will surely be brought out and highlighted by the other side. Before the case is over, the jury will have these facts in it possession. Moreover, it will have all the facts critically evaluated, their having passed through a searing test of rigorous cross-examination."
>
> …[I]t rarely works out this way. It is not always in the best interest of the other side to bring out evidence that has been omitted or obfuscated by opposing counsel; that evidence may be just as damaging to the "version" that the other side is pressing. Thus, quite frequently, both sides will obscure or omit facts essential for a just and impartial assessment of the event for tactical reasons, with the result that the jury never gets the full story.

When scientists step outside their objective role, to withhold or distort relevant findings and in essence take sides, justice is perverted. Consider the example of then Sgt. Tom Bevel, a well-known bloodstain pattern analyst from Oklahoma. In *Oklahoma v. Smith* (1987), while employed by the police, serving as a senior officer for the International Association of Bloodstain Pattern Analysts, and holding no scientific qualifications, he testified for the prosecution that he was a "blood expert" (p. 30). This is a statement that he clearly believed despite how ridiculous such testimony would appear to an actual *serologist* (a scientist specializing in the scientific study of blood). This characterization would allow Sgt. Bevel to testify before the court as an expert not only in bloodstain patterns, but as an expert with respect to the chemistry underlying tests for the presence of blood—namely *Luminol*.

Sgt. Bevel admitted under oath to performing Luminol tests on an item of clothing evidence (the defendant's jeans) with negative findings that he made *no* record of in his one and only written police report. These findings documented the absence of blood that should have been present for the prosecution's theory of the case against the accused to be true. Concealing these negative findings by failing to report them could only assist the prosecution and hamper the defense in the preparation of their respective cases.

The existence of Sgt. Bevel's Luminol examination of the jeans findings did not come to light until mid-trial during the cross-examination of a forensic scientist from the police crime lab—Janice Davis. Ms. Davis went out of her way to volunteer the existence of Luminol testing performed by Sgt. Bevel when responding to a general question about Luminol from defense counsel. The prosecution objected and informed the court that this was in fact the first time they were hearing about any such testing.

Negative Luminol results strongly support the conclusion that the defendant's jeans had not been stained with blood at any time (Gaensslen, 1983). This chemical finding contradicted witness statements that the defendant had blood on his jeans that needed cleaning. As such, the results of the Luminol test that Sgt. Bevel administered were exculpatory evidence, which he conceded under cross-examination in the following exchange and sidebar involving M. L. Cantrell, attorney for Richard Smith and Michael Gahan, Asst. District Attorney for El Reno, Oklahoma (*Oklahoma v. Smith*, 1987, pp. 30–31):

> **Q.** Well, Sergeant, would it be fair to characterize you, in effect, as a blood expert?
>
> **A.** I believe that's correct, yes, sir.
>
> **Q.** If you were the blood expert in this case and, as you say, you conducted tests for splatters on the car and, I assume, tested chips and scrapings or supervised their testing, and tested with the luminol, why did you not include that in your report?
>
> **A.** Well, at that particular time, I didn't see that it had any relevance. I discussed it with the detective on the case and really did not want to perform the examination in the first place, given what he had described as the condition the jeans were found in. In other words, we did it simply from his request. I certainly did not expect to find anything at all. And, of course, that was the case.
>
> **Q.** Well you, of course, are an experienced officer and you understand that that is what is referred to as exculpatory evidence?
>
> **MR. GAHAN:** Objection, Your Honor. The question calls for the witness to make a legal conclusion.
>
> **MR. CANTRELL:** It calls for him to make a conclusion about evidence of a sort in which he is an expert at.
>
> **THE COURT:** I'll allow inquiry into that area.
>
> **A.** I'm sorry. Would you —
>
> **Q.** Yes. You understand, of course, that that evidence which, of course, as you know, a negative test result is, in and of itself, a type of evidence, was of an exculpatory nature, do you not?
>
> **A.** I would have to say at this point that I can agree with what you're saying, yes, sir.

According to the trial transcript, Sgt. Bevel admitted under oath that he understood the Luminol findings to be exculpatory, but saw no need to make a record of the test or the result. Just to be clear, since it did not help the prosecution, the Luminol test performed on the defendant's jeans was not reported or documented at all, and the findings were almost lost. In light of *Brady*, the bankruptcy of this sort of biased practice from those employed by the government should be evident to the objective forensic practitioner.

Forensic practitioners must be judged solely based on how well they understand and apply the scientific method in their analysis, and the objectivity and transparency of their findings. This is a fundamental divide between investigators and lawyers on the one hand, and scientists on the other, that cannot be violated. Taking up an adversarial mission successfully violates that divide at the cost of due process. Just as forensic practitioners cannot lie without losing their scientific credibility, they cannot administer their practice in a partisan fashion without losing their impartiality. Unambiguous separation of the forensic practitioner from the legal team is necessary to maintain that objectivity, as well as clarity of purpose for both. The partisan practitioner serves only vanity, and ultimately serves neither justice nor the law.

5. Scientific fact and legal truth are not the same.

As we have already demonstrated, scientific fact and legal truth are very different propositions. Not only are they established by entirely different means, they are also sought for what can be incompatible ends. Forensic criminologists need to learn the difference to be able to maintain their scientific identity.

Science seeks to find out what happened and why; the law seeks just resolution of legal conflict. These are not necessarily mutually exclusives ends, but they can be, as explained in Thornton and Peterson (2002, p. 148):

> The courts are interested in forensic science only from the standpoint of how science may be used by the trier of fact to resolve technical issues.
>
> But there is a fundamental conflict here. The classical goal of science is the production of truth, while the goal of law is the achievement of justice.
>
> Few forensic scientists harbor serious misgivings about the expectation of good science on the part of their clients, be they the police, the prosecution, or the defense bar; indeed, most forensic scientists are rather cynical on this point. The clients want good science and the truth if it will help their case. If good science and the truth will not help their case, they will willingly settle for poor science and something less than the absolute truth.

> Most forensic scientists accept the reality that while truthful evidence derived from scientific testing is useful for establishing justice, justice may nevertheless be negotiated.

Investigators gather facts for use in legal proceedings. Scientists use the scientific method to examine, establish, and interpret the facts and evidence available in a given case. The decisions reached by judges and juries, referred to as the *triers of fact*, are legal determinations based on a narrow picture of that evidence for the sake of justice.

This disparity of roles and goals creates tension between the scientist and the court—and can result in an unfortunate amount of misunderstanding and even hostility between the two. It is interesting to note that this situation can also create tension between the forensic criminologist and the public, should they hold themselves out improperly—or should the public confuse scientific fact and legal truth without being corrected.

Scientific fact refers to information and events that have been established based on a broad factual record to a reasonable degree of scientific certainty by scientists using the scientific method. *Legal truth* refers to information and events that have been established by a court ruling based on a narrow factual record—either at the discretion of a judge or jury. Scientific fact is the result of objective and analytical deliberation; legal truth is the result of something else entirely, as explained in Thornton and Peterson (2002, p. 149):

> Scientific "truths" are established when the validity of a proposition is proven to the satisfaction of a prudent and rational mind. Legal "truths" are not established by the exercise of the scientific method, but by the processes of the adversary system.

> The role of physical evidence in the administration of justice may reasonably be described as follows: Science offers a window through which the law may view the technological advances of our age. Science spreads out a smorgasbord of (hopefully) valid facts and, having proudly displayed its wares, stands back. The law now picks out those morsels that appear most attractive to it, applying selection criteria that may or may not have anything to do with science. These selection criteria may appear sensible, even obligatory to the law, but may appear illogical or even whimsical to science.

By undertaking forensic practice, forensic criminologists accept this disparity and recognize their role as educators to the legal process. They are not final arbiters of legal outcomes. This distinction must be made clear at every opportunity to help avoid confusion and improper expectations.

Conversely, despite the holdings of some misled jurists, the superior court (a.k.a. the trial court) is not the final arbiter of scientific fact. Rather, it determines the admissibility of evidence and legal outcomes until the next legal cycle, such as a postconviction hearing or appeal. Any position to the contrary ignores the reality of the appellate process, in which state or federal appellate and supreme courts can reverse lower court decisions. It also ignores the advent and impact of DNA exonerations and even false confessions. These provide recurring scientific proof that many in the United States are found legally guilty in court while being factually innocent of their alleged crimes. As explained in Uphoff (2006, p. 838):

> The growing number of DNA exonerations and the attendant publicity surrounding these cases and other wrongful convictions sound an increasingly loud [and] discordant note in the normal chorus of praise for the American criminal justice system.

The ever-increasing number of exoneration cases has altered the way judges, lawyers, legislators, the public, and scholars perceive and ultimately portray the criminal justice system's accuracy. That is to say, its fallibility is becoming more and more apparent. Legal truth, then, is most accurately perceived as a function of the prevailing judgments in a given court at a given moment—all susceptible to the scrutiny of appellate review, revision, and reversal.

Given these considerations, students must be disciplined in, and alert to the need for, cleaving established scientific facts and interpretations from legal truth. They should work carefully to disallow one from clouding or intruding upon the other. They must also remain confident that scientific facts and interpretations are determined by means of the scientific method and are meant to exist in a sphere independent of the court. No legal finding can change or intrude upon a scientific fact or interpretation; it can only rule on its admissibility. Ironically, scientific facts and interpretations change legal findings almost daily. Should this perspective be lost, the student may grow into a practitioner who cannot tell one from the other or worse—one who considers them to be the same thing.

6. The "ultimate issue" is the province of trier of fact.

The *ultimate issue* is the legal question before the trier of fact (a.k.a. the judge or the jury). As explained in *Black's Law Dictionary* (Black, 1990), the ultimate issue is "That question which must finally be answered as, for example, the defendant's negligence is the ultimate issue in a personal injury action." That is to say, the ultimate issue relates to legal findings of guilt, innocence, or, in civil matters, liability. The ultimate issue is meant to be determined by the trier of fact based on consideration of the *ultimate facts*, defined in Black (1990) as "facts which are necessary to determine issues in cases, as distinguished from evidentiary facts supporting them." The judge decides what the ultimate facts of a case are, based on his or her deductions and good judgment as they relate to the evidentiary facts. This will be discussed further in the next section.

The history of case law that prohibits forensic experts from intruding on the ultimate issue by directly answering these kinds of questions for the judge or jury is referred to as the *Ultimate Issue Doctrine*. This holds that witnesses are prohibited "from giving an opinion on the ultimate issue is the case. The rationale underpinning the ultimate issue rule is that expert opinion should not be permitted to invade the province of the jury" (Moenssens, Starrs, Henderson, and Inbau, 1995, p. 75).

Careful readers will note that FRE 704, provided in a previous section, all but abandons the Ultimate Issue Doctrine, explaining that testimony "in the form of an opinion or inference otherwise admissible is not objectionable because it embraces the ultimate issue to be decided by the trier of fact." Rather, the FRE require that expert opinions be "helpful." However much subsequent case law retains the prohibition, with courts all across the United States unwilling to allow experts to give this kind of testimony, though there are exceptions (Moenssens et al., 1995).

The rules of evidence and related case law are essentially conflicted on the question of ultimate issue testimony from forensic experts. This pretty much guarantees that experts will be asked to violate it by zealous advocates. In fact, it is customary in some courts. Forensic criminologists must take notice of whether and how their findings intrude on the ultimate issues before writing reports, let alone taking the witness stand.

Forensic practitioners routinely hold scientific findings or inferences within their respective fields that bear closely or directly on the ultimate issue. As explained in Moenssens et al. (1995, p. 76):

> The problem regarding the ultimate issue limitation is simply that in complex cases involving issues beyond the abilities of a layman, a jury may need an expert's opinion on the ultimate issue in order to reach a fair verdict. Opinion on the issues of identity [i.e., DNA, fingerprint comparison, etc.], value, insanity, and intoxication, for instance, all border on what would be considered ultimate fact issues, yet they are generally held admissible.

Forensic practitioners should, of course, be able and willing to educate the court as to scientific opinions related to and bordering on the ultimate issue, but they must fully acknowledge their limitations.

Because scientific fact and legal truth do not abide by the same standards, forensic practitioners are necessarily barred from intruding on the ultimate issue when it involves a purely legal determination or subject matter that is beyond their area of expertise. The reasons for this are fairly straightforward: forensic practitioners are not generally experts at rendering legal conclusions within the complex considerations of regional statutes and case law that binds the average jurist; and, while they may hold opinions on many issues, not all of these are necessarily expert opinions. If the ultimate issue relates to a question that is within the practitioner's area of expertise, then it is disingenuous for the court to bar the forensic practitioner from giving related testimony. However, this assumes that both the court and the practitioner are being careful to delineate the nature and scope of that expertise. This is not always the case.

Some examples may be useful:

- A psychiatrist may be asked to give an opinion on the ultimate issue of competency or sanity in a pretrial hearing. As the interpretation of either is a question of mental character, this is properly within certain kinds of psychiatric and even psychological expertise. In such cases the ultimate issue of guilt is either conceded or irrelevant to the proceedings.

- A DNA criminalist may be asked to give testimony regarding the nature and probability of a particular DNA "match" at trial. He or she may then be asked a follow-up question regarding the identity of the contributor of a particular DNA sample. These are properly within their area of expertise—assuming that the criminalist has sufficient education and training in probabilities and statistics. However, asking him or her to opine regarding the guilt or innocence of a particular person based on these findings would intrude on the ultimate issue in an improper fashion.

- An expert on rape or rape investigation may be asked to give testimony on the existence of injuries related to sexual assault, or false reports of sexual assault, and related indicia. Then he or she may be asked whether or not the case at hand involves a rape or false report. If the expert has expertise and evidentiary findings that bear directly on this issue, as well as a related expert opinion, then there is no reason for the court to exclude it. Rather, the expert has a duty to refrain from delving into issues of ultimate legal guilt or innocence. He or she must stick with the scientific facts and make clear that he or she is not drawing any legal conclusions. This is analogous to a forensic pathologist testifying as to cause and manner of death and determining cause as a gunshot wound and manner as homicide (which is a crime, and subsequently an ultimate issue)—without naming the person responsible.

Suffice it to say that forensic criminologists should be ever mindful of the ultimate issue, and approach the question of whether and when they may violate it with great care. Sometimes they will be barred from doing so when it is clearly within their scope; sometimes they will be invited to do so when it is not. In either instance they must abide the rulings of the court—even when they disagree.

This brings us to our final point of major concern.

7. *The judge is always right.*

The forensic realm is one of laws, not science. Science is merely an occasional guest. The forensic realm is generally presided over by judges. Barring misconduct, a judge's authority over his or her cases must be respected and his or her will conformed to. The judge decides who the experts are, what evidence is admissible, and how and when court will proceed. If one seeks to engage in forensic practice, one must accept this reality and the many disappointments that will necessarily follow.

Consider the issues of *evidence* and *experts*.

Evidence, as explained in Black (1990), is "testimony, writing, material objects, or other things presented to the senses that are offered to prove the existence or non-existence of a fact." This is consistent with Lilly (1987, p. 2), which provides that evidence is "any matter, verbal or physical, that can be used to support the existence of a factual proposition." Evidence in a forensic context is not a scientific designation; rather, it is a legal construct.

Consider that any fact or finding gathered in relation to a legal proceeding is considered evidence until a judge says it is not. For example, documentation of a factual event may exist, such as a taped interview or a written confession or an exclusionary test result. However, a judge may determine that it is not admissible, for whatever reason, and that fact and related documentation may not be considered as evidence at trial.

As direct result of this legal reality, the sum total of evidentiary facts under consideration by a judge or jury in a given case generally does not represent the entire picture of known facts or findings; rather, it is the court's interpretation and reduction of the evidence based on its determination of what is and is not admissible. According to Black (1990) *admissibility* "as applied to evidence... means that the evidence introduced is of such character that the court or judge is bound to receive it; that is, allow it to be introduced at trial." Trial judges have broad discretionary authority with respect to deciding the admissibility of any proposed evidence. It is in reality a complex and inconsistently applied legal heuristic whereby a judge determines which facts and circumstances may actually be introduced as evidence based on "material relevance." Such determinations may be standardized for certain kinds of proposed evidence, or they may require an evidentiary hearing.

A forensic *expert*, according to FRE 702, is qualified by virtue of "knowledge, skill, experience, training, or education," at the discretion of the judge. The entire concept of forensic expertise is a legal one, unrelated to scientific practice. That is to say, in the domain of science there are those who use the scientific method and those who do not. It is a question of objectivity, methodology, and competence. Everyone's work should be transparent and replicable. In the forensic realm, the court designates or "qualifies" experts: those with knowledge beyond that of the average layman. Some have misinterpreted this to suggest that being designated a forensic expert by the court is akin to recognition of mastery of a given subject. This is not the case: "expert" is a legal classification and not a scientific or professional one.

Judges are meant to invoke standards for the admissibility of experts, such as *Frye*, *Daubert*, or *Kumho*,[8] to screen out junk science or unproven methods of analysis. However, these are guidelines only and not requirements, as judges have, again, broad discretion with respect to admissibility of all things—to include experts and expert testimony. In reality, judicial rulings on expert admissibility are partial to say the least, as discussed in Moreno (2004):

> Judges routinely admit expert testimony offered by prosecutors, but frequently exclude expert testimony offered by the defense. A review of federal criminal court cases reveals that 92% of prosecution experts survive defense challenges while only 33% of defense experts survive challenges by federal prosecutors. A recent study of federal appellate criminal cases found that more than 95% of prosecutors' experts are admitted at trial, while fewer than 8% of defense experts are allowed to testify. Why do judges consistently fail to scrutinize prosecution experts? Maybe it is the uniform. The most common prosecution expert witness is a police officer or a federal agent. In state and federal criminal trials, law enforcement experts are routinely permitted to testify to opinions and conclusions derived from their on-the-job experience and personal observations. Prosecutors rely on police officer experts most frequently in narcotics cases. In drug cases, law enforcement experts are often asked to interpret ambiguous words or phrases used by the defendant and/or his coconspirators. The purpose of, and problem with, this expert testimony is that it tells jurors precisely which inculpatory inferences they should draw from the factual evidence.

[8] *Frye v. United States* (293 F. 1013, D.C. Cir. 1923) requires that expert testimony be generally accepted by the relevant scientific community; in *Daubert v. Merrell Dow Pharmaceuticals, Inc.* (509 U.S. 579, 1993), the Supreme Court held that Rule 702 superceded *Frye*, requiring scientific testimony to be "not only relevant, but reliable"; In *Kumho Tire Co. v. Carmichael* (526 U.S. 137, 1999), the Supreme Court held that Daubert "applies not only to testimony based on 'scientific' knowledge, but also to testimony based on 'technical' and 'other specialized' knowledge."

At this point, our discussion must necessarily double back to the ground covered in the previous section regarding the distinctions between scientific fact and legal truth. The habits found in the assignment of expert status by the courts paints the very clear picture that scientific prowess and forensic expertise are not the same thing, as employment by the prosecution is far and above a more significant consideration in the forensic realm.

These are just some of the rules of the court that forensic criminologists and other forensic practitioners must learn and abide.

Readers should, in general, take notice that few of the terms or definitions provided in this section has anything to do with the practice of science, the use of the scientific method, the establishment of scientific fact, or the inference of scientific opinion. The notion of experts, evidence, ultimate facts, admissibility, relevance, and even the ultimate issue exist purely as legal constructs. This additional set of terms, definitions, and rules can create role strain and lead to cognitive dissonance among even the most seasoned forensic practitioners.

ROLE STRAIN AND COGNITIVE DISSONANCE

Forensic criminologists work within the convergence of science, investigations, and the law—and often academia. They may, within the hours of a single day, find themselves working with students, consulting with police officers, advising lawyers, testifying before judges, and even seeking advice from other forensic practitioners. Their circumstances are constantly changing, and each realm has its own set of values, rules, and expectations. With each transition, be it in thought or physical surroundings, they must consciously shift their mission gears. However, realms often collide.

Role Strain

The constant shifting of roles and the collision of multiple-role expectations can cause what sociologists refer to as *role strain*. As explained in Kennedy and Kennedy (1972, p. 16), role strain is a reference to the "difficulties and contradictions inherent in one's role." In private practice, forensic criminologists must abide by the often-incompatible principles of both science and law. This is compounded by the expectations of judges and lawyers. If the government employs them, agency policy and politics will ensure further tension. In some government bureaus "the culture of group loyalty and protection is powerful" and attitudes develop where "loyalty to [coworkers]—even corrupt ones—exceeds loyalty to the [agency] and to the law," (Mollen, 1994, p. 5). As these conflicting rules, values, and circumstances compound, strain draws and weakens even the most honorable practitioners.

When roles and expectations are in direct and irrefutable conflict, forensic criminologists must decide which duty is primary and which set of rules they are going to follow. Theoretically, science should win out: objectivity and skepticism are what give them value to the criminal justice system at all. In reality, however, acting objectively and skeptically comes at a cost. It can end friendships, it can earn one the derision of colleagues or supervisors, it can hamper promotions and pay raises, it can bring unwanted attention to individual errors and failings, and it can even get one fired. Role strain blurs matters further, and weakens the resolve to conduct oneself impartially.

Cognitive Dissonance

The mental discomfort or anguish that occurs when scientific integrity meets cultural, financial, and moral consequences is a form of *cognitive dissonance*. A useful explanation is offered in Seaman (2006, pp. 1109–1110):

> The theory of cognitive dissonance... posits that people feel discomfort when they hold two discrepant cognitions in mind at once. As a result, they are driven to reconcile these cognitions by somehow bringing them closer to consonance. A paradigmatic instance of dissonance is presented when one's beliefs conflict with one's behavior or experience. And a paradigmatic response to such conflict, as predicted by dissonance theory, is rationalization. By rationalizing—constructing reasonable justifications that appear to bring the attitude and experience into consonance—the person satisfies the psychological drive for coherence and reduces the discomfort of dissonance.

> Humans are exceptionally adept at rationalization. Indeed, recent research suggests that at least some attitude change occurs automatically and without conscious processing.

As dictated by *self-affirmation theory*, "thought and action are guided by a strong motivation to maintain an overall self-image of moral and adaptive adequacy" (Aronson, Cohen, and Nail, 1999, p. 128). If a fact or circumstance comes to bear which suggests or demonstrates that we are not good, capable, intelligent, or in control, we feel pressure to act. Reducing dissonance (a.k.a. disagreement, lack of harmony, etc.) helps restore a cohesive self-view. We do this by rationalizing and by seeking out confirmations of our beliefs while at the same time developing habits that keep us safe from contradictory materials, environments, and even individuals. We look for validation, and we scorn everything else. When scientists do this, they actually become part of the problem they are meant to help solve.

Forensic criminologists experience cognitive dissonance in many ways, but commonly it involves confrontations with and violations of their scientific role: when they are compelled to disguise or conceal unfavorable findings, to veil error and ineptitude, and to generally take the side of one adversary over another. Others experience cognitive dissonance when they uncover and loathe reporting the misconduct of others. Too many of those employed by government agencies reconcile their cognitive dissonance by conforming to the real or perceived cultural values of their peers and employers, embracing the belief that the ends justify the means. Sometimes the ends are a paycheck and a pension; sometimes the ends involve cultural approval rather than abandonment; and sometimes it means choosing what is believed to be morally right.

In a discussion that again highlights the differences between scientific and law enforcement culture, McClurg (1999, pp. 412–413) provides the following:

> Police officers rarely lie to intentionally convict innocent persons. They lie to convict those whom they believe to be guilty. And, in fact, the vast majority of criminal suspects are guilty. This is undeniably true in Fourth Amendment matters, the arena where most police lying occurs. In search and seizure litigation, incriminating evidence has been found in the possession of the suspect. The lying concerns not the factual guilt or innocence of the defendant. Rather, it usually involves the post hoc manufacturing of probable cause intended to justify the seizure of the incriminating evidence.

The findings of the Mollen Commission Report [Mollen, 1994] bear out the conclusion that police falsification in such matters occurs principally because of an end-means rationalization:

> What breeds this tolerance (to falsification) is a deep-rooted perception among many officers of all ranks within the Department that nothing is really wrong with compromising facts to fight crime in the real world. Simply put, despite the devastating consequences of police falsifications, there is a persistent belief among many officers that it is necessary and justified, even if unlawful. As one dedicated officer put it, police officers often view falsification as, to use his words, "doing God's work"—doing whatever it takes to get a suspected criminal off the streets. This attitude is so entrenched, especially in high-crime precincts, that when investigators confronted one recently arrested officer with evidence of perjury, he asked in disbelief, "What's wrong with that? They're guilty."

> By elevating the importance of factual guilt in an individual case above their moral and ethical responsibilities to themselves and to the public they serve, many police officers have become conditioned to believe they are not acting wrongly when they lie to convict criminals. So deeply ingrained is this "end justifies the means" mentality that 29% of the respondents in the Orfield Study did not equate falsification of testimony at a suppression hearing with the crime of perjury. [Orfield, 1992]

This rationalization becomes a huge problem when forensic criminologists working for or within a police agency are expected to go along with it. Or at least, it should. For some, the need to conform to peers and authority is simply too great an influence. As explained in Oleson (2007, p. 686):

Most people are familiar with peer pressure, and understand the instinct to fit in, but most of us do not understand how insidious the need to conform truly is. Researchers have found that even when there was no extrinsic reward whatsoever, subjects would provide obviously incorrect answers to easy questions, simply to belong. Far more terrifying than mere conformity, though, is our obedience to authority. More dangerous than garden-variety conformity, obedience implies acquiescence to an authoritative command.

This position created by pressure from peers can be seen in a variety of situations from the first days of schooling to the early—and in some cases the latter—stages of one's career and may manifest itself in a variety of ways and circumstances.

Rather than hold fast their scientific perspective and principles, it is undoubtedly easier for "embedded" forensic criminologists to follow the path of least resistance and adapt beliefs, attitudes, and behaviors that are rewarded, or at the very least not punishable, within a foreign culture such as those found in law enforcement or the courtroom.

Knowing about cognitive dissonance and self-affirmation tendencies is a big step toward alleviating their harmful effects. Mental discipline is the next. Forensic criminologists have a scientific duty to hold their objective mandates as primary and remain alert of their own cognitive dissonance.

METACOGNITION AND COGNITIVE FAILURE

Not all falsity and incompetence are deliberate or subconsciously influenced by cognitive dissonance or observer effects. Many practitioners in the forensic community use incompetent methods and weak or flawed logic simply because they do not know any better. At the most basic level, these individuals are unaware that what they are doing is inept because they lack the cognitive ability to recognize their own incompetence. This relates to an area of cognitive psychology known as metacognition. *Metacognition* (a.k.a. metamemory, meta-comprehension, and self-monitoring) refers to "the ability to know how well one is performing, when one is likely to be accurate in judgment, and when one is likely to be in error" (Kruger and Dunning, 1999, p. 1121). At a fundamental level, metacognition can be conceived of as thinking about thinking. For metacognitive ability to engage, there must first be a level of self-awareness. This entails explicit knowledge that one exists separately from other people in full recognition of one's capabilities, strengths, weaknesses, likes, and dislikes. Then forensic practitioners must possess the requisite knowledge relating to their particular field to be able to perform competently; they must know the basic principles and practice standards that they should employ and be able to explain why. Finally, they must have the cognitive capacity to stop or pause during the performance of a task or examination, reflect on their work and results, apply critical thinking skills, and critique their own performance to that point.

It has been demonstrated that, with respect to the nature of expertise, novice practitioners tend to possess poorer metacognitive skills than do expert practitioners, for lack of experience confronting their own errors or with problem solving particular to the geography of their domain. Moreover, Kruger and Dunning (1999, p. 1122) have suggested that, based on these findings, "unaccomplished individuals do not possess the degree of metacognitive skills necessary for accurate self-assessment that their more accomplished counterparts possess." As Kruger and Dunning (1999, p. 1121) explain:

> [W]hen people are incompetent in the strategies they adopt
> to achieve success and satisfaction, they suffer a dual burden:
> Not only do they reach erroneous conclusions and make unfortunate
> choices,but their incompetence robs them of the ability to realize it.
> Instead … they are left with the mistaken impression that they are
> doing just fine.

We refer to this particular phenomenon as *metacognitive dissonance*—believing oneself capable of recognizing one's own errors in thinking, reasoning, and learning, despite either a lack of evidence or overwhelming evidence to the contrary. General examples include believing oneself to be knowledgeable despite a demonstrable lack of knowledge; believing oneself to be incapable of error despite the human condition; believing oneself to be logical in one's reasoning despite regular entrapment by logical fallacies; and believing oneself to be completely objective despite the persistence of observer effects. Miller (1993, p. 4) explains: "It is one of the essential features of such incompetence that the person so afflicted is incapable of knowing that he is incompetent. To have such knowledge would already be to remedy a good portion of the offense."

By our making clear the nature of the scientific method, in combination with observer effects, role strain, and cognitive dissonance, which are compounded by working under the strains of the forensic realm, we hope that the remedy of awareness has at the very least been successfully provided.

CASE EXAMPLE

Consider the case of the late Dr. Baldev Sharma (tragically murdered in 2007, at the age of 72, during a carjacking). He was hired into the forensic profession by an inept fraud, and lacked the ability to grasp, let alone accept, just how incapable he was as a forensic scientist. Indeed, Dr. Sharma held a doctorate in organic chemistry from Delhi University in India. He started his career at a pharmacology lab in Delhi, and after moving to the United States, he took a job for the City of Houston Department of Public Works where he tested drinking water. From there, and without any forensic qualifications or training, he was recruited to work for the Houston Police Department Crime Laboratory in 1989. As explained in Patterson (2008):

> What happened inside Houston's crime lab remained largely unknown until reporters began showing up and Houston City Council, in March 2005, was obligated to authorize a comprehensive, independent investigation. Michael Bromwich, a former inspector general for the U.S. Department of Justice, spent two years at his task and last year posted his 400-page final report on the Web. The failure of the crime lab, he concluded, was mainly caused by inept leadership and a lack of financial support.
>
> "Starved for resources," the lab couldn't offer competitive pay for its jobs. Less-than-qualified people tended to apply, and those who were hired discovered that money to educate them was scarce. The staff, as a result, was "woefully undertrained," and perhaps the most deficient among them was the man who hired Baldev Sharma, Ph.D.
>
> James Bolding sometimes boasted of holding a doctorate, but the investigator found that he had none, nor any training in serology when, years earlier, he had come to work in the serology department. Within Bolding's first year, his supervisor died, leaving Bolding in charge. Over the many years that Bolding remained in charge, the serology department became marked, according to Bromwich, by a "disregard for scientific integrity." Analysts beneath Bolding often neglected to test evidence that was presented to them; the tests they did perform were "generally unreliable." They misinterpreted, misrecorded, misreported the results. The investigator even found a case in which Bolding seemed to have committed "outright scientific fraud and perjury."
>
> And yet, as indifferent as he was to the mission of his unit, Bolding enjoyed supervising it and was apparently trying to enlarge his kingdom when, in the late 1980s, he requested permission to add to his section the capability of examining DNA. DNA analysis was then assuming importance in forensic-science circles around the country, but in Houston's crime lab, only Bolding was interested. No one in the police department noticed anything awry with him, and no one objected to his plan, as long as he secured funding through grants.

Sharma was among the first DNA analysts Bolding employed, and you can imagine the sense of triumph that greeted Sharma's arrival in 1989—and the air of authority as the highly educated man sat down to his work. Perhaps you can also imagine the surprise of his colleagues as Sharma began struggling with even the most basic functions of the job. Restriction fragment length polymorphism seemed to baffle him; his bands were weak and diffuse. He could not even begin to perform polymerase chain reaction testing; he had never learned how. As Bromwich later discovered, Sharma was indeed highly educated, but he had the wrong education for the job—"no experience in forensic science and only a basic theoretical knowledge of molecular biology." The investigator could only conclude that Baldev Sharma was "technically incompetent."

Another man might have sensed his shortcomings and quit, but Sharma seems to have been inoculated against feelings of inadequacy by his degree. And certainly there was no one to fire him. Bolding "almost surely lacked the competence" to recognize problems in the DNA section, according to the investigator. Indeed, Bolding's point of view was much like Sharma's: any education is better than none. Thus, in 1993, when Bolding was elevated to oversee a larger portion of the lab, he chose Sharma to replace him as DNA director, unable to think of anyone more "appropriately credentialed."

Those who would be directed by Sharma were less blind to his faults, however. Because of his advanced degree, Sharma had initially been hired as a senior DNA analyst; among more junior analysts, he had quickly developed a reputation, according to the investigator, for an inability to perform the tests. His willingness to ask others to do the tests for him was also well known, as was his comfort in supervising these people from his more advanced position.

Once Sharma was officially named supervisor, it became only more natural to ask less-educated subordinates to perform work that was beneath him. Sharma liked the job. No aspect pleased him more than being called to court, on which days he got to wear a suit. Sharma enjoyed wearing suits and could never understand why members of his staff seemed not to enjoy testifying. He thought maybe they didn't like wearing suits.

Many expressed doubts to him, though, about the quality of their work. When one staff member remarked that the practice of transferring each case through numerous analysts might lead to the loss of information, "Dr. Sharma dismissed these concerns," Bromwich reported. Sharma merely informed his subordinate that the cases were transferred "according to the SOP." Some complained about standard operating procedures, but Sharma ultimately let them know that if it was SOP, it must be right.

He became a "widely disliked supervisor." His own superiors did not attempt to intervene until May 1995. Without any formal serology training himself, Sharma was training a new serologist when he "made a serious error." Trying to determine the presence of semen in a dried fluid stain, Sharma conducted no chemical test, as was SOP, but instead simply glanced through a microscope. No semen, he reported. Later, a fiber analyst noticed that the cloth had not been chemically tested and alerted Bolding, who had no choice but to order a new test. The results proved Sharma's conclusion to be utterly wrong—but only after the prosecutor had cut a deal with the accused based on the first result.

Bolding again had no choice but to lower Sharma's evaluation rating and to resume direct control of the DNA section. At least, this is what Bolding tried to do. Sharma, for his part, wouldn't stand for it. Soon after the promotion, Sharma had refused to recognize the authority of his less-educated boss and now resisted Bolding's attempts either to reprimand or supervise him. "Open and prolonged feuding" broke out between them, Bromwich reported. Donald Krueger, the "isolated and detached" director of the crime lab, stood by.

Another scandal was meanwhile growing within the DNA section, and eventually the media started quacking about a man who waited nine months in the Harris County jail before someone got around to testing his DNA. After the man was cleared, police chief Sam Nuchia ordered an investigation into how the DNA/serology section managed its cases, which internal audit found that there was little management oversight at all. Sharma, in short, was found incompetent, again, and it was just before this official conclusion was released that Krueger finally reached down, in August 1996, plucked Sharma out of DNA and put him in a new position.

Now, here's the most incredible part: After Sharma was ousted from the DNA section, after the police department's top brass undeniably knew how bad it was in there, *everything got worse*. The news cameras went away. Funding never improved. And Krueger began to think that maybe the DNA/serology section didn't really need a direct supervisor.

Thus, as DNA analysis became all the rage in other crime labs around the country, the DNA/serology section in Houston rotted into a sort of Dickensian sweatshop: undertrained, unsupervised analysts generating their "mistake-ridden and poorly documented casework" as rain poured in through a leaky roof, the "bloody water dripping out of the boxes containing the evidence and pooling on the floor."

With only Bolding to look in on the section from time to time, the same problems that plagued the serology department now took over the analysis of DNA. Bromwich found that analysts examined only evidence associated with a known suspect. Of this evidence, they tended to report "only those results that, from their perspective, were 'safe' in the sense that they were consistent with other evidence in the case or with the investigators' expectations." This was "accepted practice" within the section, Bromwich reported, and "when such selective reporting was coupled with the Crime Lab's systematic exaggeration of the statistical significance of [test] results," he went on, "a very significant risk of injustice was created."

Everything changed with the discovery of an actual injustice. In December 2002, reporters from KHOU began looking into the case of a man convicted of aggravated sexual assault. They discovered that a DNA analyst had both misinterpreted the results of her test and overstated their significance to a jury by about five orders of magnitude. As a result of their reports, Josiah Sutton was released after four years in prison, the DNA section was shut down and, ultimately, Bromwich was brought in.

The investigator seems to have been surprised when he arrived to find Baldev Sharma still on the premises. Krueger had named Sharma the lab's director of quality assurance/quality control, a decision that Bromwich had difficulty comprehending. "Because of Dr. Sharma's laziness and lack of professionalism, he was extremely unlikely to succeed in establishing an effective QA/QC program for the Crime Lab," the investigator wrote. Indeed, many Crime Lab employees reported seeing Sharma asleep on the job, "and they joked about videotaping him." In Bromwich's view, Sharma proved even less effective in quality control than he had been in the DNA/serology section. Even Sharma admitted that he only did about a year's worth of work in four-plus years on the job. And yet when Krueger demoted him from director of quality assurance, Sharma seems not to have understood. He appears to have thought job performance irrelevant, as long as you are a man of credentials.

From his new position as analyst of marijuana cases, Sharma felt justified in seeking a promotion. The job he sought was equivalent to Bolding's—the supervisor of numerous departments. When it was given to a man with less education, Sharma told his wife the "department politics" were unbearable. Sometime in 2005, he decided to retire.

This report is consistent with the findings in Bromwich (2005a), and the subsequent findings in Bromwich (2005b), which explains that (p. 17):

> Dr. Sharma received a Ph.D. in Chemistry from Delhi University's All India Institute for Medical Sciences in 1966. Prior to joining the Crime Lab, Dr. Sharma had no experience in forensic science and only a basic theoretical knowledge of molecular biology. From November 26, 1989 through December 20, 1989, Mr. Bolding and Dr. Sharma attended the FBI Academy's Laboratory Application of DNA Typing Methods School, which covered RFLP analysis. Upon returning from the FBI Academy, Mr. Bolding and Dr. Sharma adopted the training manuals they had received from the FBI into the standard operating procedures ("SOPs") for the DNA Section.

Earlier reports regarding Dr. Sharma also provide that (Olsen and Khanna, 2003):

> Baldev Sharma, former DNA section supervisor and current head of quality control, has master's and Ph.D.-equivalent degrees in chemistry. Though his college transcripts are not in city files, an internal HPD memo said he had failed proficiency tests and therefore did not qualify for his position as quality-control supervisor.

> He was suspended for five days in 1997 for mismanagement of the DNA section, but earned a promotion to quality control and was put in charge of getting the lab accredited.

Regarding the incompetence and fraud of James Bolding, it is further explained in Olsen and Khanna (2003): "The founder and former head of the DNA section, James Bolding, retired in June after the police chief recommended he be fired. Bolding himself did not meet the standards for the job. Among other things, he failed both algebra and geometry in college, though he later passed both, and he never took statistics." This is consistent with the characterization of Mr. Bolding in Bromwich (2005b) which provides that (p. 16):

> James R. Bolding joined the Crime Lab in October 1979 and worked as a drug chemist for approximately 18 months. In the spring of 1981, the Crime Lab's head serologist invited Mr. Bolding to train in serology in order to replace recent departures from the Lab. Mr. Bolding has described his serology training as consisting of less than five months of on-the-job training under the supervision of the head of serology. Within a year after Mr. Bolding began training in serology, his supervisor died. Mr. Bolding was the only remaining serologist in the

Crime Lab. He had not yet received any formal training in fundamental serological techniques, including ABO blood typing. Mr. Bolding told us that he "took books home and did the best he could." On November 14, 1981, Mr. Bolding was promoted to Criminalist II.

In July 1982, Mr. Bolding successfully completed an intensive course in bloodstain analysis at the Serological Research Institute ("SERI") in Emeryville, California. That same month, and less than a year after his promotion to Criminalist II, Mr. McDonald recommended that Mr. Bolding be promoted to Criminalist III "as soon as possible" because he "is the only Criminalist II we have who is a qualified and experienced Forensic Serologist and he has recently completed the SERI course in Forensic Serology." In the fall of 1982, he was promoted to Criminalist III, despite his minimal experience in serology.

Among the many lessons that can be learned from this narrow extrusion of the ongoing HPD Crime Lab scandal[9] is one of forensic humility: research laboratory science and forensic laboratory science are not the same. Having a Ph.D. in chemistry or genetics or biology, taking an FBI short course in DNA, and believing oneself to be an expert—these are not sufficient forensic credentials to start working in, let alone running, a forensic lab. No matter how much experience one accumulates under such circumstances, and without the proper forensic education and outlook, the quality of that experience is necessarily substandard.

[9]The HPD Crime Lab remains, as of this writing, one of the most scandal-ridden crime labs in the United States. This is in no small part owing to the fact that it suffered a second series of scandals and a second shutdown in early 2008, caused, again, by those brought in to fix the problems identified in the first.

Science has a very specific mandate, and forensic examiners are meant to satisfy a very particular role. Their participation in the justice system is often painful and thankless while also being vital to fairness. To do more good than harm, forensic examiners must be objective, mitigate bias when necessary, employ the scientific method scrupulously, and engage in their practice with the utmost humility.

SUMMARY

Forensic criminologists are first and foremost scientific forensic examiners. They must therefore utilize the scientific method to not seek confirmation of their hypotheses, rather eradication. In their analysis and interpretation of related case evidence, forensic criminologists must keep several points of concern in mind. These are the federal rules of evidence; that the defense and prosecution have different rules; that every defendant is entitled to objective scientific expert assistance regardless of his or her circumstances; that as scientists they are not members of either adversarial "team"; that scientific fact and legal truth are not one in the same; that the ultimate issue is for the trier of fact to decide, not the expert witness; and that no matter what, the judge is always right.

To maintain objectivity and the resolve to conduct themselves impartially, it is crucially important that forensic criminologists also understand the issues of role strain, peer pressure, and cognitive dissonance, as well as metacognition and cognitive failure. Once these issues have been adequately acknowledged, they can be understood, addressed, and, one hopes, mitigated to some degree in each practitioner's work product.

Review Questions

1. T/F The majority of forensic practitioners do not understand what the scientific method is or how to apply it correctly.
2. Explain what observer effects are and how they may impact forensic examinations.
3. What are the Federal Rules of Evidence? Why are they so important for forensic criminologists?
4. According to Edwards and Gotsonis (2009), what elements are necessary in reports provided by a forensic criminologist for legal purposes?
5. What was so important about the *Brady v. Maryland* ruling? What is a Brady violation?
6. T/F Inconclusive or indeterminate forensic findings are not an actual result and may therefore be omitted.
7. Describe how cherry picking evidence violates due process.
8. Describe the differences between the goals of science and those of the law, as well as the difference between scientific fact and legal truth.
9. T/F The sum total of evidentiary facts under consideration by a judge or jury in a given case generally does not represent the entire picture of known facts or findings.
10. How do forensic criminologists experience cognitive dissonance?
11. Why do novice practitioners have poorer metacognitive skills?

REFERENCES

Aronson, J., Cohen, G., Nail, P., 1999. Sel-Affirmation Theory: An Update and Appraisal. In: Harmon-Jones, E., Mills, J. (Eds.), Cognitive Dissonance. The American Psychological Association, Washington D.C.

Brady v. Maryland, 1963. 373 U.S. 83.

Bromwich, M., 2005a. Second Report of the Independent Investigator for the Houston Police Department Crime Laboratory and Property Room, Fried, Frank, Harris, Shriver & Jacobson LLP, Washington D.C., May 31; url: http://www.hpdlabinvestigation.org

Bromwich, M., 2005b. Third Report of the Independent Investigator for the Houston Police Department Crime Laboratory and Property Room, Fried, Frank, Harris, Shriver & Jacobson LLP, Washington D.C., June 30; url: http://www.hpdlabinvestigation.org

Edwards, H., Gotsonis, C., 2009. Strengthening Forensic Science in the United States: A Path Forward. National Academies Press, Washington D.C.

Faigman, D.L., Kaye, D.H., Saks, M.J., Sanders, J., 1997. Modern Scientific Evidence: The Law and Science of Expert Testimony, vol. 2. West Publishing Co., St. Paul, MN.

Faigman, D.L., Kaye, D.H., Saks, M.J., Sanders, J., 2004. Admissibility of Scientific Evidence. In: Faigman, D.L., Kaye, D.H., Saks, M.J., Sanders, J. (Eds.), Annotated Scientific Evidence Reference Manual. West Publishing Co., St. Paul, MN.

Federal Rules of Evidence, 2006. U.S. Government Printing Office, Washington D.C: December 1; url: http://www.uscourts.gov/rules/Evidence_Rules_2007.pdf

Gaennslen, R.E., 1983. Sourcebook in Forensic Serology, Immunology, and Biochemistry. National Institute of Justice Publication, USDOJ.

Gershman, B., 2006. Reflections on Brady v. Maryland. South Texas Law Review 47 (Summer), 685–728.

Giannelli, P., 1997. The Abuse of Scientific Evidence in Criminal Cases: The Need for Independent Crime Laboratories. Virginia Journal of Social Policy & Law 4 (Spring), 439–470.

Giannelli, P., 2005. Forensic Science. J. Law Med. Ethics 33 (Fall), 535–543.

Giannelli, P., McMunigal, K., 2007. Prosecutors, Ethics, and Expert Witnesses. Fordham Law Rev. 76 (December), 1493–1537.

Griffy, L., 2007a. Sex Case Hinged on Phony Lab Report: S. J. Officer's Ruse Became Evidence. San Jose Mercury News December 16.

Griffy, L., 2007b. Fake Lab Reports Were Common: Judge Warned Cops About Using Ruses. San Jose Mercury News December 23.

Hardaway, R., 2008. Beyond a Conceivable Doubt: The Quest for a Fair and Constitutional Standard of Proof in Death Penalty Cases. New England Journal on Criminal and Civil Confinement 34 (2), 221–289.

Ingraham, B., 1987. The Ethics of Testimony: Conflicting Views on the Role of the Criminologist as Expert Witness. In: Anderson, P., Winfree, L. (Eds.), Expert Witnesses: Criminologists in the Courtroom. State University on New York Press, Albany, NY.

Kennedy, D.B., Kennedy, B., 1972. Applied Sociology for Police, Charles C. Thomas, Springield, IL.

Kruger, J., Dunning, D., 1999. Unskilled and Unaware of It: How Difficulties in Recognizing One's Own Incompetence Lead to Inflated Self-Assessments. J. Pers. Soc. Psychol. 77 (6), 121–1134.

Lilly, G., 1987. An Introduction to the Law of Evidence, second ed. West Publishing Co., St. Paul, MN.

Miller, W.I., 1993. Humiliation. Cornell University Press, Ithaca, NY.

Moenssens, A., Starrs, J., Henderson, C., Inbau, F. (Eds.), 1995. Scientific Evidence in Civil and Criminal Cases, fourth ed. The Foundation Press, New York.

Mollen, M., 1994. Commission Report, The City of New York. Commission to Investigate Allegations of Police Corruption and the Anti-Corruption Procedures of the Police Department, published July 7.

Moreno, J., 2004. What Happens When Dirty Harry Becomes an (Expert) Witness for the Prosecution? Tulane Law Review 79 (November), 1–54.

Nelson, J., 2008. Facing Up to Wrongful Convictions: Broadly Defining 'New' Evidence at the Actual Innocence Gateway. Hastings Law Journal 59 (3), 711–729.

Oklahoma v. Richard T. Smith, 1987. Case No. CRF-86-394, March 12; trial transcript.

Oleson, J., 2007. The Antigone Dilemma: When the Paths of Law and Morality Diverge. Cardozo Law Review 29 (November), 669–702.

Olsen, L., Khanna, R., 2003. DNA Lab Analysts Unqualified: Review Finds Education, Training Lacking. Houston Chronicle, September 7.

Orfield, M., 1992. Deterrence, Perjury, and the Heater Factor: An Exclusionary Rule in the Chicago Criminal Courts. University of Colorado Law Review 63, 75–107.

Patterson, R., 2008. A Deadly Twist at Houston's Crime Lab: When DNA Is the Only Evidence, a Good Analyst Is Especially Important, Houston Press, November 27; url: http://www.houstonpress.com/content/printVersion/1011657

Popper, K., 1963. Conjectures and Refutations. Routledge and Keagan Paul, London.

Risinger, D.M., Saks, M.J., Thompson, W.C., Rosenthal, R., 2002. The Daubert/Kumho Implications of Observer Effects in Forensic Science: Hidden Problems of Expectation and Suggestion. California Law Review, 90 (1), 1–56.

Rosenthal, R., 1966. Experimenter Effects in Behavioral Research. Appleton-Century-Crofts, New York, NY.

Seaman, J., 2006. Cognitive Dissonance in the Classroom: Rationale and Rationalization in the Law of Evidence. Saint Louis University Law Journal 50 (Summer), 1097–1114.

Thornton, J., 1997. The General Assumptions and Rationale of Forensic Identification. In: Faigman, D.L., Kaye, D.H., Saks, M.J., Sanders, J. (Eds.), Modern Scientific Evidence: The Law and Science of Expert Testimony, vol. 2. West Publishing Co, St. Paul, MN.

Thornton, J., Peterson, J., 2002. The General Assumptions and Rationale of Forensic Identification. In: Faigman, D. L., Kaye, D. H., Saks, M. J., Sanders, J. (Eds.), Modern Scientific Evidence: The Law and Science of Expert Testimony, vol. 3. West Publishing Co, St. Paul, MN.

Thornton, J.I., 1983. Uses and Abuses of Forensic Science. In: Thomas, W. (Ed.), Science and Law: An Essential Alliance. Westview Press, Boulder, CO.

Thornton, J.I., 1994. Courts of Law v. Courts of Science: A Forensic Scientist's Reaction to Daubert. Shepard's Expert Scientific Evidence Quarterly 1 (3), 475–485.

Uphoff, R., 2006. Convicting the Innocent: Aberration or Systemic Problem? Wisconsin Law Review 739–842.

Vollmer, A., 1949. The Criminal. Brooklyn: Foundation Press.

Williams, G., 1958. The Proof of Guilt: A Study of the English Criminal Trial. Stevens & Sons, Ltd, London.

PART

2

Forensic Examinations

CHAPTER 4

Forensic Criminological Assessments

Wayne Petherick and Brent E. Turvey

The problem is not teaching the inferrer to think: the problem is the examination of how inferences have been made by another and what value his inferences may have for our own conclusions.

—Dr. Hans Gross, 1924, p. 16

KEY TERMS

Beyond a Reasonable Doubt: The burden of proof for the prosecution in criminal cases; this is very high, akin to a 98% or 99% certainty on the part of the trier of fact.

Burden of Proof: The responsibility of demonstrating the truth and validity of disputed charges or allegations; this rests with the prosecution in criminal cases.

Case Linkage: (a.k.a. *linkage analysis*) The process of determining whether there are discrete connections between two or more previously unrelated cases through crime scene analysis.

Common Law: (a.k.a. *case law*) A system in which crimes and punishments are dictated by a contemporary interpretation of prior court decisions passed down through history.

Defendant: The person accused of committing a crime in criminal cases and/or the person accused of causing harm in civil cases.

Equivocal: Anything that can be interpreted in more than one way or to any interpretation that is questionable.

Equivocal Death Psychological Autopsy (EDPA): A form of death investigation that must investigate alternative manners of death in an attempt to provide new information about the circumstances surrounding the death that can then be further investigated by the appropriate authorities (Spellman and Heyne, 1989).

Felonies: Serious criminal offenses that involve extended prison sentences.

CONTENTS

133

Liability: In civil disputes, the measure of responsibility that a group or individual incurs for any harm that has been caused.

Misdemeanors: Lesser criminal offenses involving little if any actual jail time.

Motive: The emotional, psychological, and material needs that impel and are satisfied by behavior.

Plaintiff: (a.k.a. *claimant* or *pursuer*) The party that initiates a lawsuit; the party claiming to have been wronged and/or injured in civil cases.

Premises Liability: A landowner's duty to protect individuals from harm, including third-party assaults (La Fetra, 2006).

Prosecution: The attorney or attorneys representing the state who are responsible for bringing criminal charges against defendants based on the investigations of complaints conducted by law enforcement agencies.

Psychological Autopsy: An evaluation of a decedent's mental state prior to death.

Suicide Psychological Autopsy (SPA):   An examination with the purpose of understanding which psychosocial factors have contributed to a suicide.

Torts: Wrongful acts that cause or lead to the infringement of an individual's rights and result in legal liability.

Victim Exposure: The amount of exposure to harmful elements experienced by a victim. A function of lifestyle and incident exposure.

Forensic criminologists perform criminological assessments for the purpose of addressing investigative and legal questions. *Criminological assessments* are, simply put, those types of inquiries and examinations traditionally performed by a criminologist. This admittedly circular definition actually encompasses a wide variety of analyses that are beyond the general understanding of most jurors, let alone many nonforensic criminologists. As will be made clear, they are also a regular feature of both criminal and civil proceedings.

This chapter is aimed at providing the common guise and context for examinations and expert testimony that tend to fall within the aegis of forensic criminology. It is not meant to be all-inclusive; rather, it will give readers a sense of the major assessments provided by criminologists to law enforcement agencies, private clients, and before the court. For reference purposes, we also make an effort to delineate the investigative and forensic value of each. Case examples are also provided.

CRIMINAL VERSUS CIVIL COURTS

Owing perhaps to the cultural popularity and subsequent proliferation of violent crime dramas involving police investigators, prosecutors, and criminal defense attorneys, the vast majority of the public seems to believe that they have good idea of what goes on in court. Moreover, they tend to apply what they have learned about criminal law, often from inaccurate fictionalized depictions related through film or television, to the civil arena. This has created a situation in which even the best of our criminology and criminal justice students do not understand the major differences between criminal and civil proceedings, let alone that differences exist at all.

The following sections seek to ameliorate the problem by offering limited discussions regarding the major distinctions between criminal and civil courts. It is important to understand that forensic criminology is practiced in both.

Jurisdiction

The first area to consider when distinguishing between criminal and civil proceedings is related to jurisdiction, or authority.

Criminal courts have jurisdiction over crimes committed against the state as set forth in a criminal code, to include misdemeanors and felonies. *Misdemeanors* are lesser criminal offenses involving little if any actual jail time. *Felonies* are serious criminal offenses that involve imprisonment. There are no uniform definitions for these terms beyond the basic distinctions provided here, as every jurisdiction handles them differently. What may be a felony in one country or state may be a lesser felony or a misdemeanor in another (if it is a crime at all). Most jurisdictions have their own unique criminal code in which laws detailing the nature of criminal offenses, and any subsequent penalties, are outlined. This is true within both Australia and the United States, where there are separate criminal codes for federal crimes and individual states or territories.

In the United Kingdom, however, England and Wales do not have a precise criminal code. Rather, they have a common law system without the benefit of specific legal statutes. In a *common law* (a.k.a. case law) system, crimes and punishments are dictated by a contemporary interpretation of prior court decisions passed down through history. In the UK, common law decisions are monitored by *The Law Commission*, an independent government agency created by the Law Commissions Act of 1965 to keep common law under review and recommend reforms as needed.[1]

Civil courts, on the other hand, have jurisdiction over statutes set forth in a code of civil procedure. They handle noncriminal disputes between the state, private corporations, and individuals. This can include disagreements

[1] See: http://www.lawcom.gov.uk/

within the confines of family law (e.g., marriage, civil unions, divorce, spousal abuse, child custody and visitation, alimony, child support, and adoption), property law, contract law, and tort law. *Torts* are wrongful acts that cause or lead to the infringement of an individual's rights and result in legal *liability*; they feature prominently in the assessments section of this chapter.

Legal Parties

The legal parties involved in criminal disputes are different from those involved in civil disputes.

Criminal court cases are brought by the state against an individual. The state is also referred to as the *prosecution*. The prosecution, helmed by a prosecutor or a district attorney, brings criminal charges based on the investigations of complaints conducted by law enforcement agencies. In criminal cases, the person accused of committing a crime is referred to as the *defendant*.

Civil court cases are brought against governments, corporations, and individuals against each other. The *plaintiff* (a.k.a. the claimant or the pursuer) is the party that initiates the lawsuit; it is the party claiming to have been wronged and/or injured. In civil cases, the person accused of causing harm is also referred to as the *defendant* (a.k.a. the defender). The plaintiff is required to set forth and prove the wrongs committed by the defendant, as well the nature of any relief, or damages, being sought.

The Burden of Proof

The *burden of proof* is the major difference between criminal and civil cases. This refers to the responsibility of demonstrating the truth and validity of disputed charges or allegations. In criminal cases, the prosecution holds the burden of proof. They must prove their case *beyond a reasonable doubt*. This means that the trier of fact must be "fully satisfied, entirely convinced, satisfied to a moral certainty" (Black, 1990, p. 161). This is a very high standard, akin to a 98% or 99% certainty on the part of the trier of fact. In civil cases, the burden of proof is on the plaintiff; however, the plaintiff needs only prove his or her case to a "preponderance of evidence" or a "clear and convincing evidence" standard. This is akin to a certainty greater than 50%, or "more probable than not" (Black, 1990, p. 1183). This lowered standard also effectively shifts a burden of proof onto the defendant. In criminal trials the prosecution must prove guilt to more than 98% certainty; in civil trials one side must prove that it is at least 51% in the right.

It must be noted that these evidence standards are highly subjective in application, and in many courts they are also poorly explained.

Rights

Criminal defendants enjoy far more legal protection than do defendants in civil actions. For example, criminal defendants in the United States have the right not to testify against themselves, the right to a speedy trial, and the right to competent legal representation. Civil defendants do not. Moreover, criminal defendants may not be tried twice for the same crime, or a similar lesser crime, for the same offense (double jeopardy). For civil defendants, this is a distinct possibility. And criminal prosecutors are barred from appealing a verdict of "not guilty," while plaintiffs in civil actions commonly exercise their right to appeal judgments of nonliability as soon as it is rendered.

Legal Consequences

Perhaps the greatest difference between criminal and civil disputes resides in the nature of legal consequences.

In criminal cases, the court system seeks to determine who is culpable with respect to a crime. It is about assigning blame and demonstrating that a defendant acted "purposefully, knowingly, recklessly, or negligently" (Black, 1990, p. 379). Those found criminally culpable may suffer financial penalties, but generally risk losing their liberty and even their life under extreme circumstances. When a defendant is charged with a felony, prison looms as a very real consequence at the close of a criminal trial. Conversely, there are generally no criminal sanctions for prosecutors who fail to make their case, unless extreme prosecutorial malfeasance can be proved.

In civil cases, however, the court system seeks to determine who is legally *liable*. That is to say, civil proceedings are meant to determine the nature and extent of any harm, who caused it, and the extent of any responsibility to compensate for damages incurred. Those parties found civilly liable can suffer financial penalties, as well as the loss of rights, property, and other assets. Furthermore, prison does not exist as a penalty in civil cases. However, if a plaintiff fails to make his or her case to a judge or jury, he or she may be required to repay all or some of the legal costs incurred by the defense.

DUTIES OF THE EXPERT

Whenever a court requires scientific or knowledgeable opinions to assist with establishing the likelihood or plausibility of a theory, or to support an argument being made by counsel, forensic experts are employed (Anderson, 1987). As explained in Van der Hoven (2006, p. 152):

> Expert testimony in criminal courts has a long history. The necessity
> for expert witnesses who are more qualified than the court to express
> their opinion regarding certain matters, has been acknowledged since

the 14th century (Schmidt & Rademeyer 2000:463; Pretorius 1997:334). According to Anderson (1987:12) social science research was formally introduced into the judicial system in 1908 by Louis Brandeis in *Muller v Oregon*. Since the 1950s social scientists in the United States have played a pivotal role as expert witnesses in litigation regarding school desegregation. Behavioural and social scientists with criminological and criminal justice expertise have increasingly been requested to appear as expert witnesses.

It has been said that it is not unreasonable to ask that "expert witnesses who are called upon to testify, either against the defendant or in his behalf, know what they are doing," given everything at stake in a trial (Thornton, 1974, pp. v–vi). In other words, the expert has a responsibility to be knowledgeable, adept, and to generally refrain from the vice that is ignorance of their subject matter. Otherwise, they are essentially unworthy of offering expert opinions and testimony of any kind.

Specific duties of the forensic expert are set forth in Dwyer (2008, pp. 96–97):

> The concept of an expert's duty was developed further by Cresswell J in *The Ikarian Reefer* in 1993.[*] These principles, which to varying degrees had already emerged elsewhere at common law, are of sufficient significance in the development of the concept of an expert's duties to warrant full quotation:
>
> 1. Expert evidence presented to the court should be, and should be seen to be, the independent product of the expert uninfluenced as to form or content by the exigencies of litigation ... (*Whitehouse v Jordan* [1981] 1 W.L.R. 246 at 256, *per* Lord Wilberforce).
>
> 2. An expert witness should provide independent assistance to the court by way of objective unbiased opinion in relation to matters within his expertise (see *Polivitte Ltd v Commercial Union Assurance Co plc* [1987] 1 Lloyd's Rep. 379 at 386, *per* Garland J. and *In re J* [1990] F.C.R. 193, *per* Cazalet J.). An expert witness in the High Court should never assume the role of an advocate.
>
> 3. An expert witness should state the facts or assumptions upon which his opinion is based. He should not omit to consider material facts which could detract from his concluded opinion (*In re J*).
>
> 4. An expert witness should make it clear when a particular question or issue falls outside his expertise.
>
> 5. If an expert's opinion is not properly researched because he considers that insufficient data is available, then this must be stated with an indication that the opinion is no more than a provisional one

(*In re J*). In cases where an expert witness who has prepared a report could not assert that the report contained the truth, the whole truth and nothing but the truth without some qualification, that qualification should be stated in the report (*Derby & Co Ltd v Weldon, The Times,* 9 November 1990, *per* Staughton LJ).

6. If, after exchange of reports, an expert witness changes his view on a material matter having read the other side's expert's report or for any other reason, such change of view should be communicated (through legal representatives) to the other side without delay and when appropriate to the court.

7. Where expert evidence refers to photographs, plans, calculations, analyses, measurements, survey reports or other similar documents, these must be provided to the opposite party at the same time as the exchange of reports.

[*] National Justice Compania v Prudential Assurance [1993] 2 Lloyd's Rep 68, Comm. Ct ('The Ikarian Reefer').

[**] Approved by Otton LJ in Stanton v Callaghan [2000] QB 75, [1999] 2 WLR 745, CA.

These specific duties, provided from within a British context, are applicable on an international scale. They are useful as a guide whether one works as an expert witness in Los Angeles, South Africa, Sydney, or London. They are also relevant to and consistent with other practice standards discussed throughout this text.

It is in the context of criminal and legal proceedings, and within the scope of the duties defined here, that forensic criminological assessments are performed.

FORENSIC CRIMINOLOGICAL ASSESSMENTS

Forensic criminologists are both scholars and practitioners. They are therefore required to work comfortably in academic, investigative, and legal realms. Rather than being a product of "occupational affinity" (Morn, 1995, p. 79), they are the result of scientific education and training, tempered by mentoring, peer review, and case experience. Their profession is a conscious choice rather than an incidental civil service job title. This will be reflected in their ability to competently and scientifically perform criminological assessments with a high degree of functional literacy.

There are essentially three kinds of criminological evidence presented at trial: *theory presentation, the results of research/surveys,* and *evidence examination/ assessment.*

Theory Presentation: This involves the presentation of any criminology theory to the court, to be used as a building block for arguments to be made by attorneys, or in consideration by the jury when dealing with questions related to the ultimate issue. For example, a well-trained criminologist is the best expert to present evidence regarding *Routine Activity Theory* and its application within a specific case. Routine Activity Theory explains crime by consideration of three converging elements: likely offenders, suitable targets, and the absence of capable guardians (Reid, 2006). The forensic criminologist could either explain this theory to a judge or jury in general terms, so that they could consider it in their deliberations on a related matter; or they could take this theory into consideration as an applied part of any related analysis. The forensic criminologist could also provide testimony to rebut that of any would-be criminologist offering related opinions without its consideration. This is just one example from many.

The Results of Research Surveys: Criminologists are known for conducting and publishing scholarly research. The results of that research may have a direct bearing on questions that arise in criminal and civil proceedings. For example, one of the authors has published research in the area of staged crime scenes (Turvey, 2000; Turvey, 2004; Turvey, 2008a), as well as false reporting (Baeza and Turvey, 2000; Savino and Turvey, 2004; Turvey, 2008a). As a regular feature of testimony in homicide and sex crime trials, in both criminal and civil arenas, the author has been asked to explain that crime scene staging and false reporting exist as actual phenomena, and to define the limits of these terms as they are used in case examination. Additionally, the author has been asked to explain whether research findings tend to lend credibility to the theory that a crime scene was indeed staged, or whether adequate consideration and due diligence were afforded by investigators to the possibility that a complaint of a rape may be false.

With respect to both crime theory and criminology research presentation in court, consider the following discussion from Van der Hoven (2006, pp. 155–156):

> The study field of criminology involves the social sciences as well as elements of criminal law. Bartol (1999:3) considers criminology as the multidisciplinary study of crime. Reid (2003:G3) defines the term criminology as the scientific study of crime, criminals, criminal behaviour and efforts to regulate crime. According to Dantzker (Hunter & Dantzker 2002:24), criminology is the scientific approach to the study of crime as a social phenomenon, that is, a theoretical application involving the study of the nature and extent of criminal behaviour.
>
> Terblanche (1999:10) describes the field of study of criminology as follows: "Criminology, broadly speaking, studies crime, criminals,

victims, punishment and the prevention and control of crime. The most important role of a criminologist is to study crime, and to interpret and explain crime." In the past, the emphasis was on explaining the behaviour of the offender, but the emphasis has recently shifted to include analysis of the consequences of imposed sentences. This makes it all the more important for judicial officers to take note of the research done by criminologists.

Criminologists such as Reid (2003:xvii–xx), Siegel (2004:xv–xvi) and Bartol (1999:v–viii) identify the following main areas of criminology:

- Criminal statistics (measuring crime patterns and trends)
- Distribution of criminal behaviour amongst gender, age and ethnic groups
- Detailed studies of specific types of crime (economic crimes, crimes of violence, etc.)
- Causes of crime and criminality (biological, psychological, social factors)
- Theoretical explanations of crime (various perspectives)
- Impact of crime on individuals and communities
- Social origin of the criminal law, development of laws and the role of law in society, as well as the function of legislation
- Societal reaction to crime
- Criminal Justice Administration, including the police and legal professions
- Correctional programmes
- Victimology (the nature and cause of victimisation as well as aiding crime victims).

Briefly, it can be stated that criminologists are trained in the social sciences and focus mainly on the causes, explanation and prevention of criminal behaviour. The study field includes the profiling of offenders as well as of victims of crime. The main emphasis is therefore on the *individuals* involved in the criminal act.

Dr Irma Labuschagne (2003:5) rightly points out that criminology not only focuses on individual criminal behaviour, but also on all environmental circumstances, as well as the context within which the criminal was functioning when the crime was committed.

Criminologists specifically study the criminal in all his facets, such as causal factors contributing to the criminal event, predisposition (e.g. personality make-up, genetic factors), precipitating factors, triggering factors, the interaction between the offender and the victim, victim vulnerability, victim rights, role of the victim in the criminal justice process, the criminal justice process, the prevention of crime and victim support, et cetera. Criminological studies involve personality and sexual deviations, for example the antisocial personality, paedophilia, violent offenders, rapists, and phenomena such as domestic violence, school violence and workplace violence.

Criminologists focus on the causes, dynamics, theoretical explanation and prevention of violent behaviour. They also study the offender's patterns of criminal behaviour in the past to predict his or her behaviour in future.

This discussion is useful as it defines the role of criminologist not only as a scholar who understands criminological research, crime theory, and crime-victim psychodynamics, but also as a practitioner who can apply this understanding to assessing the facts and circumstances of a given case.

Evidence Examination/Assessment: Criminologists of every kind may be asked to perform examinations and assessments of the evidence gathered in relation to a particular case. The following are some common examples.

Custom, Practice, and Guidelines

Criminologists who are familiar with cultural customs, standards of professional practice, or professional guidelines may be allowed testify in court regarding (1) their existence; (2) what they are and what they mean; and (3) whether they were followed by actors in the case at hand. The trier of fact is then left to sort out what that means with respect to the ultimate issue.

Consider the following relevant findings provided by one of the authors (Turvey) in a Forensic Examination Report prepared for criminal defense attorney Jim Gray in anticipation of trial testimony for *Mississippi v. Robert Grant* (2006) (Turvey, 2006):

> **Conclusion #1:** Law enforcement efforts to secure and process the crime scene were almost non-existent, and consequently did not meet the minimum national standards for competent forensic practice with respect to adhering to the "fundamental principles of investigating a crime scene and preserving evidence that should be practiced in every case." (TWGCSI, 2000, pp. 1–2)

> **Conclusion #2:** Because of the failure to meet minimum crime scene practice standards, many key items of potentially exculpatory physical evidence were not documented, collected, preserved, or tested.

The report went on to explain which standards of practice were violated and how, and also which items of evidence were not collected and subsequently tested.

As evidenced by this example, taken from among many, findings related to adherence with guidelines and practice standards may be useful in a forensic context to establish a line of questioning for opposing counsel, and to educate the trier of fact regarding whether a reasonable standard of care was met by those subordinate to him or her. They may also be used to confirm or refute the strength of arguments based on the solvency of evidence collected in and out of compliance with those standards. Equally important, the trier of fact may use ignorance of basic national protocols to gauge the solvency of other law enforcement efforts and case theories.

Offender Classification

Criminologists create and employ various classification schemes and typologies to describe offenders, their offenses, and their victims. Rather than being treatment oriented, these schemes are designed for investigative and research purposes, to develop a deeper understanding of the relationships between crime, criminals, and their victims. There are behavioral-motivational typologies, serial murder typologies, stalker typologies—the list is endless. Forensic criminologists are best suited to apply these classification systems within a given case during either the investigation or to interpret their meaning during expert testimony at trial when there is a dispute regarding appropriate usage.

Moreover, such classifications and typologies are not treatment oriented, so they are also not diagnostic in nature and therefore not the purview of mental health professionals without the appropriate criminological background.

Additionally, the court and attorneys have been known to use or develop offender classifications that are well within the expertise of forensic criminologists to decipher. Consider the following examples.

Example #1: "Thrill Kill"

Reports were as follows (Turvey, 2006b):

> On Monday, January 27, 1992, the body of Victor Esparza was found in a cubicle at the main office of Sam & Libby's in a secured building at 1123 Industrial Road, San Carlos, California. He was the night janitor under contract to clean the premises. Cause of death was a penetrating gunshot wound to the head fired at a distance of 6 to 12 inches. His wallet had been stolen.

> On Thursday, March 12, 1992, the body of Caroline Gleason was found in the copy room of Sophia Systems at 777 California Ave, Palo Alto, California. She was the office manager of that business. Cause of death was a near contact perforating gunshot wound to the head. Her keys, purse, and car were subsequently stolen.

On Monday, March 16, 1992, Dr. Allan Marks, a pediatrician, was attacked by a black female intruder in the front doorway of his office at 801 Brewster #250 in Redwood City, California, a few minutes subsequent to concluding an after hours appointment with a patient and his parents. A struggle ensued when the female intruder tried to enter the office, and Dr. Marks suffered three gunshot wounds before managing to push her out into the hallway: one in the left shoulder, one in the right forearm, and one in the left thumb (the thumb wound may have been received in conjunction with one of the other injuries, as only two projectiles were recovered). He subsequently called 911.

Celeste S. Carrington, an unemployed black female janitor, was connected to the case by virtue of her previous employment for janitorial services contracted to the locations involved, and by virtue of her physical description as provided by eyewitness accounts. On March 20, 1992, she was arrested. After initially denying involvement in these crimes, she ultimately made a full taped confession to investigators to these and other related offenses. These confessions were rendered over the course of a single evening—Carrington met with multiple investigators from multiple law enforcement agencies.

In May and June of 1994, Carrington was tried for these crimes, convicted, and sentenced to death. She appealed that sentence.

During closing arguments at trial, the prosecution referred to the defendant as a "thrill killer." During the appeal, the defense asked one of the authors (Turvey) to, among other tasks, assess the appropriateness of this inflammatory offender classification. Taken from the expert declaration in that case is the following conclusion and its basis (Turvey, 2006):

34. Given these facts and circumstances, it is my expert opinion that there is no definitive support for the theory that Gleason was kneeling when she was shot.

The Facts And Circumstances Are Inconsistent With A "Thrill Kill"

35. The facts and circumstances in the Esparza, Gleason, and Marks cases are entirely inconsistent with a "Thrill Kill" or Thrill-Oriented motivation.

36. Throughout the state's closing arguments at both guilt and sentencing phases of the trial, the prosecutor repeatedly asserts that Celeste Carrington was motivated by the thrill she received from her enjoyment of killing. See, e.g., page 5047 ("we have a thrill killer on our hands..."); page 6671 ("This is a death penalty case because of her brutality, her thrill, her enjoyment in killing. It sets it apart from

a whole class of crimes because of the circumstances attending the crime."); page 6678 ("These weren't just murders during the course of robberies and burglaries. There were more serious things going on, and we'll talk about that, being on their knees, being shot at close range. Cold blooded, and the thrill of it all in her statement, enjoying it."); page 6691 (a predator like Celeste Simone Carrington, who slaughters innocent human beings for the thrill of it..."); page 6692 ("a predator who enjoyed slaughtering human beings.").

37. The concept of the "Thrill Killer" originated as a feature of the popular media, used to sell newspapers and true crime novels. By the late 1980s, the concept of the "thrill killer" had been incorporated into the professional serial murder literature in the textbook Serial Murder (1988). This seminal text provides dominant motives for murder patterns, including the "Thrill-Oriented" murder.

38. Of the Thrill-Oriented type, DeBurger & Holmes (1988, p. 76–77) write the following: "The central motive in this type of serial murder typically reflects a quest for 'highs,' thrills, or excitement. In the asocial logic of the thrill killer's sociopathic mind-set, the excitement connected with the kill overrides any concern or sympathy for the victim. This type of perpetrator tends to focus on the process of killing instead of simply carrying out a quick act of murder... the thrill-oriented murderer is primarily impelled to kill not by sexual motives, but by a craving for excitement or bizarre experience. In short, the act or process of killing is enjoyable for this kind of serial murderer."

39. In my expert opinion, Thrill-Oriented motivation is eliminated as a possibility in all three cases I have reviewed based primarily on the following considerations:

a) Carrington selected locations where she had worked in the past, because she knew the security, knew the work schedules, knew how to gain entry, knew the layouts, knew the specific types of valuables that could be found, and often had retained a key.

b) Carrington specifically chose to enter buildings at times when there was little or no chance of encountering anyone. This was to facilitate protracted, uninterrupted searches for valuables.

c) In none of the cases could Carrington have planned to encounter anyone. At Sam & Libby's, her entry was detected because the security procedures had changed; at Marcus & Millichap, she was encountered by an employee who had chanced to come in after hours; and she encountered Dr. Allan Marks in his office only because he had an atypical, after-hours appointment. These encounters could not have been anticipated, and the shootings are much more suggestive of a reactive response to unexpected circumstances.

d) In each case, Carrington was focused on entering the place of business in search of specific types of valuables to steal. At Sam & Libby's she was searching for cash in desks; at Marcus & Millichap she was searching for cash and money order blanks; at Dr. Marks's building she was searching for drugs in the emergency medical kit. Moreover, in both homicide cases, she took valuables from the victims.

e) In each homicide case, Carrington engaged a "con" to dissuade the victim from considering her a threat, in order to avoid suspicion. She told Esparza that she worked for Sam & Libby's, and she told Gleason that she worked in the building as a janitor.

f) These crimes all were committed in a manner to lower the risk of detection and avoid people. This directly contradicts the primary motive of the Thrill Killer, who tends to impulsively commit murder with low skill, and high risk of detection, with the explicit intent of direct contact with victims.

g) Carrington used a stolen gun, happened upon in the course of a burglary, to commit the shootings. She apparently used only the limited rounds of ammunition that she originally stole with the gun. A Thrill Killer would have shown excitement, arousal, or enthusiasm towards this instrument of killing in some fashion (buying lots of ammunition; excessive cleaning; stealing more firearms; flashing the firearm to others, etc.).

h) After an exhaustive review of the taped interviews of Carrington by law enforcement, I detected no verbal excitement, arousal, or interest in describing or reliving the murders with investigators. Rather, Carrington demonstrated a flat affect (i.e., no emotion, detachment) throughout the confessions. Everything was delivered in a matter of fact fashion. This is in stark contrast to those offenders who could be labeled Thrill Killers, who discuss their crimes with passion, interest, and excitement. They enjoy reliving their crimes for others, and would not be characterized by a flat affect.

Example #2: "Sexually Violent Predator"

Consider the court's ruling in *Commonwealth v. Conklin* (2006), described in Takah (2006), which provides that to meet the burden of proving that a sex offender is a "sexually violent predator" (a.k.a. SVP), the state need not provide a clinical diagnosis by a licensed psychiatrist or psychologist. Rather the opinion of a qualified criminal justice expert is sufficient (pp. 129–132):

Appellant, Donald Robert Conklin, was accused of sexually abusing his daughter for a period of nearly three years. Conklin was found guilty in the Wayne County Court of Common Pleas of various offenses in connection with the abuse after his daughter testified that he began assaulting her when she was six years old and that his assaults included acts of forced intercourse. Thereafter, the Commonwealth determined that Conklin qualified as a sexually violent predator (SVP) subject to provisions contained in Megan's Law II. The Pennsylvania Supreme Court granted Conklin's petition for review to ascertain whether the Commonwealth had carried its burden of introducing the testimony of a "licensed psychiatrist, psychologist or criminal justice expert" when it offered the testimony of a social worker.

In March 2002, Conklin's daughter informed her mother that Conklin had been sexually abusing her for approximately three years. Subsequently, Conklin was arrested and charged with a number of sexual offenses.

At trial, a jury convicted Conklin of numerous charges relating to the sexual abuse of his daughter. As a result, Conklin was required by Megan's Law II to undergo an evaluation by the State Sexual Offender Assessment Board (the "Board") to determine whether he was a sexually violent predator.

The assessment was completed by a licensed clinical social worker, David Humphreys, who was also a member of the Board. With his findings, Humphreys determined that Conklin's mental condition increased the likelihood of recidivism. Following Humphreys' assessment, the trial court conducted an SVP hearing, at which Humphreys proffered expert testimony for the state. After considering Humphreys' testimony, the trial court concluded that Conklin should be classified as an SVP.

Conklin appealed to the Pennsylvania Superior Court, challenging Humphreys' qualifications as an expert. In an unpublished decision, the superior court affirmed both the Board and the trial court's determination that Conklin was an SVP. The superior court predicated its decision that Humphreys was qualified to perform SVP assessments and to testify to that effect on the undisputed fact that Humphreys was a criminal justice expert.

Conklin then appealed to the Pennsylvania Supreme Court, reprising his argument that only licensed psychiatrists or psychologists qualify to provide expert testimony as to mental abnormalities or personality disorders. Arguing that the terms "mental abnormality" and "personality disorder" constituted psychological terms of art, Conklin theorized that such terms could be used only by those parties licensed to practice psychiatry or psychology.

Responding to Conklin's contentions, the supreme court examined the qualifications of experts in the context of sexually violent crime. Specifically, the court questioned whether, in order to prove that a sex offender is an SVP, the Commonwealth must provide a clinical diagnosis by a licensed psychiatrist or psychologist, or whether the opinion of a qualified criminal justice expert suffices. Unmoved by Conklin's position, the court held that the opinion of a qualified criminal justice expert suffices to prove that a sex offender is an SVP and that the Commonwealth need not provide a clinical diagnosis by a licensed psychiatrist or psychologist.

While the authors do not necessarily disagree with this specific practice in its entirety, and each jurisdiction will have or create its own laws in relation to the issue, this case signals the recognition of a distinction between offender classifications and clinical diagnoses. It provides for expert testimony from criminologists in areas where the courts essentially invent or adopt terminology that requires definition and assessment by qualified professionals. And when treatment is not the goal, forensic mental health experts may not be the only behavioral scientists qualified to perform such assessments.

Equivocal Forensic Analysis

The word *equivocal* refers to anything that can be interpreted in more than one way or to any interpretation that is questionable. As described in Turvey (2008a, p. 190), an *"equivocal forensic analysis* refers to a review of the entire body of evidence in a given case, questioning all related assumptions and conclusions." This critical assessment of all case facts and evidence helps insulate the forensic analyst from investment in prior case theories.

Equivocal forensic analysis is a necessary and useful tool in both investigative and forensic realms, especially in those cases in which the facts lend themselves to multiple conclusions. If the case at hand is referred to as rape, the forensic examiner critically reviews the evidence which is meant to establish rape, such as the crime scene evidence, the medical report, the sexual assault kit, and any victim statements; if the crime at hand is referred to as a homicide, the forensic examiner critically reviews the evidence which is meant to establish homicide, such as the crime scene, the crime scene documentation, the autopsy report, and the autopsy photos. When the evidence supports initial conclusions, the forensic examiner may move forward with additional assessments; whenever there is a doubt, it must be noted and case theories stemming from such conclusions must be amended.

Engaging in this sort of assessment at the outset of any case in which conclusions are predicated on the quality of the work that has been done prior is necessary to avoid bias and to identify weak or nonexistent evidence.

One of the authors (Petherick) was involved in a case of alleged stalking and harassment involving former domestic partners, one of whom was a male police officer. The female half of the dispute hired Dr. Petherick, as she was at the time a defendant facing serious criminal charges. She protested her innocence. Prior to Dr. Petherick's involvement in the case, there had been no attempt to investigate the charges against her; rather, the word of the alleged victim—in this case, the police officer—was being taken essentially at face value as proof, along with that of a fellow officer for corroboration. Upon creating a basic timeline and a simple reconstruction of activities using the available record of events from witness statements, cell phone records, text messages, and emails, Dr. Petherick was able to establish the impossibility of the officer's claims. The officer had not only given false statements, but also had induced others to do so as well to back up his claims. This assessment was sent up through the police chain of command through the defendant's attorney, all criminal charges were dropped, and the officer was investigated for falsifying evidence and witness tampering.

Crime Reconstruction/Staged Crime Scene Determination

Crime reconstruction is the determination of the actions and events surrounding a crime (Chisum and Turvey, 2007). A simulated or staged crime scene is one in which the physical evidence has been purposefully altered by the offender to mislead authorities and misdirect any investigation (Turvey, 2008a). Establishing whether a crime scene has been staged requires expertise in crime reconstruction, which is a subspecialty of the forensic sciences.

Staging is a possibility in every case. Therefore, in every case, this explanation must be considered and excluded before being entirely abandoned. When staging is found, it tends to strongly suggest an offender who would be considered a likely suspect; the motive (precautionary crime concealment) is to deflect or hamper law enforcement investigations.

Consider the following excerpt related to crime reconstruction and crime scene staging from the Forensic Examination Report prepared by one of the authors (Turvey) in the criminal matter of *Mississippi v. Robert Grant* (2006) (Turvey, 2006):

> **Conclusion #3:** The *simulated*, or *staged*, crime scene is that in which evidence has been purposefully altered by an offender to mislead authorities and/or redirect the investigation (Turvey, 2002, p. 249). Often, it is the owners or occupants of a residence that stage

crime scenes, in order to move investigators away from the obvious conclusion that they were in some manner responsible for the crime that was committed there.

The crime scene in this case was *staged* to appear as though the shooting death of Arthur Joshua occurred outside the residence. This is based on a careful consideration of the following inconsistencies in the evidence:

A. According to the report by Det. Kramer, he "discovered that the back porch light had been removed." The light bulb was subsequently located near the back yard door by Capt. Rocker.

- The removal of a porch light bulb by an offender is time-consuming and impractical. It is seen in movies and television but it is uncommon in actual break-ins, especially when the residents are known to be home.

- The light bulb that was collected (Exhibit 8) is pictured in photo #337, covered by the grass. This would require someone placing the bulb into the grass and perhaps even combing grass over it. This is inconsistent with the bulb being dropped, tossed, or thrown. Again, this is time consuming, impractical, difficult to do in the dark, and serves no purpose to a potential home invader aside from increasing their risk of discovery by occupants.

- The back porch light is clearly visible in place, in photo #339. This is inconsistent with the light having been removed in the first place and requires reconcilement with Det. Kramer's statement in his report.

B. According to the statement by Terry Adams, the attacker with the gun "started to try to tie up my hand and that's when my girlfriend and Skipper arrived back home and he broke out." He does not indicate that he was fully tied up, or that his hands were behind his back, or that he was on the floor at any time. According to his girlfriend, Tishma Peralta, she found Adams "on the floor with his hands tied behind his back." She does not indicate what kind of material he was tied with or how he was able to get free.

- There is no documentation of any binding materials found at the scene to confirm that Mr. Adams was tied up.
- There is no documentation of any ligature marks or other injuries to Mr. Adams' wrists that would be present if his hands had indeed been bound behind his back.
- According to the Trace Evidence reports by the Mississippi Crime Laboratory dated June 13, 2005, Terry Adams is the only person in the residence who tested positive for gunshot residue, on his left palm.

C. Tishma Peralta claims to have seen two men invading the home. She states that one of them was wearing a white mask with big eyeholes through which she could see his black skin. Ultimately, she states that she sees "the other dude" "run out" after "busting out the back door." This was accomplished, according to her statement, with some force and difficulty. This is when she claims to hear the final gunshot. It is unclear where the shooter is standing in her version of events (inside or outside the residence). Notably:

- She does not describe the exit of the man wearing the white mask (Arthur Joshua).

- If an assailant had to "bust out" or break out of the back door once he had already gained entry into the residence, this would indicate that it was closed and locked. It would certainly not be necessary to "bust out" of a door that one had used to gain entry. This statement by Ms. Peralta precludes the use of the back door as a point of entry.

- There is no documentation or indication that heavy force was used to break or "bust" the back door open from the inside. Upon close examination of photograph #53, the door appears to be undamaged from the inside.

D. Wesley Jerome Williams alleges that someone entered through the front door and then struck him twice in the head with a wooden 2 × 4, telling him to get down on the floor. Only one injury was documented related to the attack on Mr. Williams—a minor reddening of the scalp in a single linear pattern consistent with at least one of the edges of the 2 × 4 (see photo # 56). The following inconsistencies are noted:

- There is only one minor injury to Mr. Williams' forehead, and no other reported injuries to his body.
- There is an absence of swelling in the area of the injury, which would be expected with a heavy blow to the head using a 2 × 4, and the passage of time. At least an hour, if not more, had passed before this photograph could have been taken.
- There is an absence of hemorrhage beneath the skin, which would be expected with a heavy blow to the head using a wooden 2 × 4.
- On close inspection of the photograph, there is an absence of splinters transferred to Mr. Williams' scalp, or injuries from splinters, which would be expected given the condition of the 2 × 4 and the severity of the blow.

E. Two bloody white masks were recovered from the scene. Tishma Peralta did not report seeing an assailant that wore two masks. She reported the intruder that she saw, up close, was wearing a white mask with big eyeholes. Only one assailant is known to have been injured in this case, and consequently only one mask should have been found with blood on it. This inconsistent finding begs further examination and investigation.

F. Only some of the items allegedly taken from the safe and placed into the blue pillowcase have value to a thief (the cash, the marijuana, perhaps the pipe/papers, the coins, the wallet, and the GPS). However, the personal note, two drink coasters, a Crown Royale bag, a film container, and the set of glasses w/glass tray have no value on the street. Taking these items makes little or no sense from the perspective of profit.

- It should be noted that the content of the Crown Royale bag is not documented.
- It should be noted that the content of the film container is not documented.
- It should be noted that there was apparently a white container recovered from the blue pillowcase with the contents undocumented.

G. The glass contents of the blue pillowcase were carefully wrapped with newspaper prior to being placed inside. The advertisements on the newspaper used to wrap these items are consistent with the advertisements on the newspaper from the table in the living room at the crime scene (see photo #54). This supports the conclusion that the items were carefully wrapped at the scene. This activity was not described by any of the witnesses interviewed in this case.

H. Tishma Peralta, Skipper, and Wesley Jerome Williams would have to be in the living room when the shot that killed Arthur Joshua was fired, ricocheted off the front door, and landed on the couch (detailed in *Conclusion #4*). There is no documentation that any one of these three individuals suggested this event to investigators. This omission is a logical break in the known sequence of events and must be resolved.

I. The victim was shot through the lungs and trachea. His lungs would have collapsed and he would be spitting blood on the inside of his mask, making it difficult to stand, walk, or see. This makes an unassisted exit from the residence unlikely. His body would have to be carried or dragged from the inside of the residence to where it was ultimately found outside.

In this case, after being confronted with the evidence from the Forensic Examination Report under cross-examination, Terry Wayne Adams confessed on the witness stand to staging numerous aspects of the crime scene. However, and despite an absence of direct physical evidence, Robert Barnes was convicted for an undisclosed and undefined role in the crime.

As is clear from this example, staging has both investigative and forensic applications. It can help narrow the suspect pool early on, limiting it to those who would be considered immediate suspects in the crime, and it may be admissible as a point of reconstruction in criminal and civil trials. This point will be expounded upon further in the case example at the end of the chapter.

Victim Risk/Exposure Assessment

As explained in Turvey (2008a, p. 378): "One of the many lenses that may be used to examine the victim-offender relationship is in terms of the *exposure* involved. *Victim exposure* is the amount of exposure to harmful elements experienced by the victim. It is determined by examining *lifestyle exposure* and *situational exposure*." The forensic criminologist may conduct this type of assessment during investigations to help define and then narrow the suspect pool. In a criminal or civil proceeding, the forensic criminologist may testify regarding victim exposure as part of a critique related to best investigative practices and suspect viability, or as part of an assessment related to premises liability issues. This issue will be discussed further in Chapter 6.

Psychological Autopsy

A *psychological autopsy* involves the evaluation of a decedent's mental state prior to death. When suicide is determined to be the manner of death, this assessment helps to clarify the factors that lead to the victim's taking his or her own life. When the manner of death is unclear, this assessment helps to weigh out existing evidence to determine which theories it favors, if any. As explained in LaFon (2008, p. 420):

> There are two basic applications of the psychological autopsy: the suicide psychological autopsy (SPA) and the equivocal death psychological autopsy (EDPA) (La Fon, 1999). These applications both use a similar psychological autopsy procedure; however, each application's purpose or goal is very different. The first type of PA, the SPA, is conducted when the manner of death is unequivocally a suicide. The Centers for Disease Control (CDC) provides clear guidelines that establish suicide as the appropriate mode of death (Jobes et al., 1987). These guidelines classify a death as suicide based on the presence of self-inflicted injury evidence and an explicit/implicit intent to die.
>
> The purpose of the *suicide psychological autopsy* (SPA) is to understand which psychosocial factors have contributed to the suicide. Suicidologists collect and database information from the SPA to better understand suicide causation for the purposes of intervention and prevention. There is no extended legal or forensic investigation following an SPA.

The second type of psychological autopsy application is the *equivocal death psychological autopsy* (EDPA). An equivocal death is any death in which the *manner/mode of death*—that is, the reason why the death occurred—is not immediately clear. Shneidman (1981) estimates that between 5% and 20% of all deaths are equivocal. The EDPA is a form of death investigation that must investigate alternative manners of death in an attempt to provide new information about the circumstances surrounding the death that can then be further investigated by the appropriate authorities (Spellman and Heyne, 1989).

A psychological autopsy is performed during the investigative phase, ideally, to inform medicolegal determinations and help establish whether a crime has been committed. However, it is also useful in legal proceedings, to help the trier of fact determine whether a crime has been committed (if a defendant is on trial for a homicide that may actually be a suicide), whether there may have been negligent care issues related to the victim's mental health (if he or she killed himself or herself while under the care of a mental health provider), or whether the death was accidental (as occurs in civil cases brought against insurance companies by plaintiffs who are denied death benefits from those who suffer autoerotic death).

A psychological autopsy does not involve diagnostic or treatment goals. Rather the goals are solely investigative and forensic. As a consequence, one need not be a psychologist to render opinions related to the issue. However, one must have a strong psychology background and be fully educated as a behavioral scientist. Any criminologist performing a psychological autopsy without this background is often doing so from a place of ignorance regarding the intersection of criminological theory, human behavior, and psychodynamics.

Motivational Analysis

As explained in Turvey (2008a), *motive* is a function of the emotional, psychological, and material needs that impel and are satisfied by behavior. Intent, on the other hand, is the end aim that guides behavior. Motive is objectively established by examining known offender behavior and choice patterns before, during, and after the commission of a crime. The determination of motive helps with the following investigative and forensic ends (Turvey, 2008a, p. 274):

- It reduces the suspect pool to those individuals with a particular motive.
- It assists with the investigative linkage of unsolved crime with a similar motive.
- Along with other class evidence (i.e., means, opportunity, associative evidence), motive can provide circumstantial bearing on offender identity.

- Along with other contextual evidence, motive can provide circumstantial bearing on offender state of mind.
- Along with circumstantial evidence, motive can provide circumstantial bearing on whether a crime has actually occurred.

This topic will be discussed further in Chapter 5.

Determination of Torture

Forensic criminologists with education and training in crime reconstruction, wound pattern analysis, and psychodynamics can examine a case to determine whether torture is evident. That is to say, whether the offender intentionally inflicted pain on the victim for the sake of pleasure, or revenge, or to gain information. This has investigative applications in that torture might be a part of an offender's modus operandi or offense signature, and therefore it may be useful for case linkage purposes. However, in a criminal trial, the presence of torture may be an aggravating factor that a jury may consider when deliberating regarding the death penalty.

Consider the following excerpt from a Forensic Examination Report by one of the authors (Turvey) in *California v. Jack Lewis* (2008), a death penalty case involving allegations of torture (Turvey, 2008c):

> **Conclusion 5:** The crime scene behavior in this case is consistent with an anger motivation, and not consistent with torture.
>
> According to Turvey (2002, p. 307) motives are the "emotional, psychological, and material needs that impel and are satisfied by behavior."
>
> As described previously in this report, there are multiple behavioral indicators that are inconsistent with torture, such as the presence of lubrication, the consensual anal sex video, and the potentially short duration required to effect behaviors necessarily associated with the homicide. There is also evidence of mutual consensual anal penetration with the "Mag-Lite." This includes a lack of evidence of physical bindings; both victim and defendant excrement being present at the scene; and the mutual use of methamphetamine that intensifies the sex drive and lowers sexual inhibitions.
>
> There is also no profit motivation evident in this case; the victim has no valuables and is essentially indigent. In point of fact, the victim is the primary source of money for the defendant (via her job and her family), but only so long as she remains alive.
>
> Intense, directed rage is evidenced in this case by the combination of brutal force, lethal force, and overkill.

- *Brutal and lethal force* are evidenced in this case by the onset of multiple injuries that inflict tremendous damage until death results: this includes the cumulative blunt force trauma, the hair pulling, and the manual strangulation as previously described.

- *Overkill* is injury beyond that needed to cause victim death. The volume of blunt force trauma and injury associated with the manual strangulation evidences overkill in this case. As previously stated, the number of these injuries exceeds 100.

- Unexplained behavior in this case includes the fact that at some point, the defendant or the victim smeared excrement on the floor and walls. This may be related to the anger motivation, or it may have been transferred incidentally. In any case, the presence of excrement is consistent with mutual anal penetration, as both victim and defendant DNA is present.

It is important to note that it is not generally possible to discriminate whether this level of rage is caused by real or perceived wrongs. In other words, the offender may have been agitated by an accumulation of actual events, a misinterpretation of actual events, or by imagined events. Consequently, crime scenes involving the following can be difficult to distinguish: *domestic/intimate* homicide; *drug/alcohol related* homicide; homicide committed by the *mentally ill*.

In this particular case, the author was not allowed to offer a specific opinion regarding the presence of torture. However, the author was allowed to testify regarding other opinions, as well as the facts and circumstances that formed the basis for the opinion that torture was not clearly evident. Ultimately, 39-year-old Jack Henry Lewis was found guilty of the murder of 48-year-old Jan Hasegawa (his longtime girlfriend) along with the special circumstance allegation that the murder involved torture. He had indeed killed her while both were high on methamphetamine, and this was never in dispute; their mutual addiction to the drug as well as its involvement in their sexual activity had an extensive history. However, the jury also found against the death penalty: Lewis received life in prison.

Criminal Profiling

Criminal profiling involves the inference of offender characteristics (Turvey, 2008a). There are more than a few ways to make these inferences—though not always with a high degree of reliability. Forensic criminologists, or profilers, can predict offender characteristics based on statistical models, prior research, or experience; they can use hard physical evidence to make deductions about physical characteristics; or they can use analytical logic, critical thinking, and the scientific method to make deductions about offender relational and psychological characteristics based on an analysis of crime scene behavior (Turvey, 2008a).

Criminal profiling has utility during criminal investigations if it can reliably define and reduce the suspect pool. It also has some value at trial, as explained in Turvey (2008a, p. 558):

> Criminal profiling and related techniques were developed as tools to be used in the investigative process to assist in the identification of *suspects*. There are also a number of useful forensic ends that they can serve that are not necessarily related to establishing offender identity. These include focusing the suspect pool, explaining behavioral evidence, case linkage, and assisting in the development of investigative strategies.
>
> There is something further to be said for the potential use of criminal profiles as an ingredient to assist in educating the trier of fact as to the general type of offender that may be responsible for a particular crime. Criminal profiles may be a reasonable aid to the trier of fact, given two very important caveats. First, the court must understand, and be explicit in its instructions to the jury about, the limits of behavioral evidence as described in this work. Second, criminal profilers must not disregard these limits and intrude on the issue of guilt by giving opinions as to whether or not the accused fits a particular profile.

As this suggests, for criminal profiling to be of use at trial, there must be no doubt about the profiler's knowledge and expertise, beyond merely working for a law enforcement agency and having a civil service job title. Moreover, profilers themselves must have a high capacity for ethical self-governance, a clear understanding of what the ultimate issues are, and a propensity for avoiding their violation.

Criminal profiling will be discussed further in Chapter 5.

Case Linkage

Case linkage, or linkage analysis, is the process of determining whether there are discrete connections between two or more previously unrelated cases through crime scene analysis. This is accomplished through a careful examination of offender *modus operandi*[2] and *signature aspects*[3] (Turvey, 2008a). Case linkage has investigative applications with respect to identifying the existence of potential serial offenders, as well as a possible suspect pool, and then allocating investigative resources appropriately. It also has forensic relevance because the court may allow testimony on case linkage issues for the purpose of demonstrating a common plan, scheme, or design in actual or alleged serial offenses, if the offenses are sufficiently similar.

[2] Refers to "the manner in which a crime has been committed" (Turvey, 2008a, p. 310).

[3] Refers to "general emotional or psychological themes that the offender satisfies when committing an offense" (Turvey, 2008a, p. 310).

Consider the following excerpt from a report by one of the authors (Turvey) in a criminal case in which linkage analysis was initially at issue. It involves the comparison of M.O. and signature behaviors in a child sexual homicide to a sexual assault on a teen, highlighting gross dissimilarities, in the case of *California v. Joseph Cordova* (Turvey, 2006b):

> It is the opinion of this examiner that there is no behavioral evidence to support the conclusion that there is behavioral commonality or similarity between the 1979 sexual murder of [8-year-old] Cannie Bullock and the sexual assault of 12-year-old Nina Sharp in Lakewood, Colorado in 1992.
>
> The basis for this opinion is the consideration of numerous significant behavioral dissimilarities, to include at least the following:
>
> 1. The 1992 sexual assault of Nina Sharp involved opportunity created by a position of trust—the defendant was babysitting the victim at the time of the incident.
> 2. The 1992 sexual assault of Nina Sharp involved fondling only; it did not involve sexual penetration of any kind.
> 3. The 1992 sexual assault of Nina Sharp did not involve strangulation.
> 4. The 1992 sexual assault of Nina Sharp did not involve blunt force trauma or other forms of physical violence.
> 5. The 1992 sexual assault of Nina Sharp involved bargaining behavior with the victim as opposed to the use of any force.
> 6. The 1992 sexual assault of Nina Sharp involved primarily *reassurance oriented* behaviors and motives—that is to say that the sexual contact involved behaviors that are intended to restore self-confidence or self-worth. This low aggression and pseudo-foreplay oriented behavior often suggests a lack of confidence and a sense of personal inadequacy (Turvey, 2002).
> 7. The 1992 sexual assault of Nina Sharp did not result in a homicide.

While case linkage efforts are primarily of value in criminal trials, they may also be a component of civil actions. One of the authors has worked many serial rape cases, and at least three in civil actions involving case linkage issues: the first involved multiple former employers suing an employer that they argued was a sexual predator, requiring a comparison of case similarities to determine if they had occurred and whether they were actually related; the second involved a single victim from many suing the property where her particular attack occurred, requiring an analysis of all cases to establish whether a common scheme or plan existed and what that meant; the last involved a civil commitment in which a man convicted of a rape was argued to have committed many more, requiring an analysis of all suspected cases to determine whether these could be introduced as evidence in a civil commitment hearing.

Presentence Investigations, Evaluations, and Mitigation

In criminal trials, the prosecution and the defense employ forensic criminologists to help investigate, establish, and make recommendations regarding sentencing. This aids in helping to make a decision about punishment
that is specific to the circumstances of the individual, as prescribed by law.
Such investigations and evaluations are conducted at any time prior to sentencing, and may include what is referred to as mitigating evidence (evidence
that tends to explain, contextualize, limit the culpability of, or even justify
certain offense behavior). According to the Guidelines of the American Bar
Association (2003):

> Mitigation evidence includes, but is not limited to, compassionate
> factors stemming from the diverse frailties of humankind, the
> ability to make a positive adjustment to incarceration, the realities
> of incarceration and the actual meaning of a life sentence, capacity
> for redemption, remorse, execution impact, vulnerabilities related
> to mental health, explanations of patterns of behavior, negation of
> aggravating evidence regardless of its designation as an aggravating
> factor, positive acts or qualities, responsible conduct in other areas of
> life (e.g. employment, education, military service, as a family member),
> any evidence bearing on the degree of moral culpability, and any other
> reason for a sentence less than death.

The concept of mitigation in death penalty cases as a constitutional requirement and its origins will be discussed in Chapter 12.

Of the Presentence Investigation report in non-death penalty cases, however,
U.S. Federal Judge Helen G. Berrigan explains that they are a vital part of determining an appropriate sentence when conducted by a qualified professional
(2008, pp. 819–821):

> In noncapital cases, the jury determines guilt or innocence, and if
> the defendant is found guilty, the judge has the task of deciding
> the appropriate sentence. A judge does not, however, decide the
> penalty in a vacuum. In the federal system, a detailed Pre-Sentence
> Investigation report ("PSI") is prepared in virtually all cases,
> including misdemeanors. The report is typically twenty or more
> pages long, single-spaced, and contains a comprehensive account
> of the defendant's life history. Along with details of the offense
> and the defendant's prior criminal record, it includes personal and
> family data, which discuss parents, siblings, their occupations and
> health, and their interactions with the defendant. The PSI recites the
> circumstances of the defendant's upbringing, family support or lack
> thereof, and updated information from family members interviewed.
> It incorporates the defendant's own marital and parental history

and interviews with his or her spouse or former spouse and children. The report includes a section on the defendant's physical condition, which recites everything from childhood and adult illnesses and accidents to even current tattoos. It contains a section on mental and emotional health, setting forth any commitments, psychological treatments, or difficulties the defendant has had and a separate section on substance abuse, including what drugs the defendant has sampled or is addicted to, and what treatment programs, if any, he or she attended. After that, a section on education and vocational skills details school and college attendance, where and for how long, how successful, and occupational training, if any.

The employment record follows, with job descriptions, how long each job lasted, the pay, and the reason for leaving the employment. This is followed by a financial condition section, which sets forth the defendant's assets and liabilities, including a credit report.

Finally, the report includes several pages of sentencing options, setting out the statutory ranges of imprisonment, supervised release, and fines, the availability of probation, the appropriateness of restitution, and the sentencing guideline ranges and possible reasons for departure upward or downward from those ranges. The report even includes a confidential and detailed sentencing recommendation from the probation officer.

The probation officers who prepare these reports are highly educated and trained. A minimum of a bachelor's degree is required with one year of experience in such fields as investigation, counseling and guidance of offenders in community corrections, or the equivalent in a related field such as social work or psychology. The officers frequently have master's degrees in one of the related fields or a law degree. For example, in the Eastern District of Louisiana, the Chief Probation Officer has a law degree and worked for a child protection agency prior to becoming a federal probation officer and PSI writer. The Deputy Chief has a Master of Social Work degree and worked in a District Attorney's Office prior to coming to U.S. Probation, also working in the Pre-Sentence Report division.

According to Van der Hoven (2006), the forensic criminologist is uniquely qualified to assist with the preparation of presentencing reports, offering the following discussion in which the behavioral sciences of criminology and psychology/psychiatry are distinguished (pp. 156–157):

When compiling pre-sentence reports and testifying in court, there are certain limitations that should be taken into consideration. Criminologists are not trained to diagnose mental illnesses or personality deviations. They neither apply or interpret personality tests, nor intelligence tests unless specifically trained as psychometrists. Diagnosis, as well as applying and interpreting psychometric tests, is the highly specialised and exclusive field of the psychiatrist and the clinical psychologist. Although personality deviations are the study field of criminologists, they are not trained to diagnose a person for instance as an Antisocial Personality or Psychopath, but they can describe the characteristics of such a person and indicate that the accused shows similar characteristics. Should a criminologist suspect that the accused may be suffering from a mental illness or personality disorder, it should be brought to the attention of the accused's legal representative, and a psychiatric or psychological report requested before the commencement of the court hearing.

When the criminologist is required to write a pre-sentence report for the court regarding a dangerous criminal, the criminologist can indicate risk factors pointing to future violent behaviour. Criminologists cannot perform personality tests, but they can develop their own scales and models to identify risk factors which may indicate the individual's level of dangerousness. Criminologists should have sufficient knowledge to evaluate the offender and, on the basis of certain specific risk factors, to indicate whether the person poses a danger to society or not. The criminologist's prediction of dangerousness should be supported by an evaluation report from a psychiatrist or clinical psychologist.

While criminologists cannot give an opinion in court regarding the accused's mental capacity or accountability, they can give an opinion concerning the accused's blameworthiness based on mitigating and aggravating factors. When compiling a pre-sentence report, criminologists follow a holistic approach, taking all relevant factors into consideration which could have influenced the personality make-up of the individual and the development of violent tendencies. In order to obtain a complete picture, their reports should be complemented and supported by psychiatric and psychological reports. Ideally, a psychiatrist, a clinical psychologist, a criminologist and a social worker should work together as a team in high-profile cases when violent offenders who committed serious crimes, are on trial. Owing to their divergent and specialised training, each expert will approach the case from a different perspective as determined by their specific discipline. The psychologist focuses on the psychological aspects of an individual, whereas the forensic criminologist has a holistic view and approaches the offender in his or her totality (Labuschagne 2003:5). The psychiatrist's main role is determining the criminal capacity of the accused before judgment. The forensic criminologist, in turn, can only consider the offender's moral blameworthiness after conviction, but before sentencing (Labuschagne 2003:5).

Pre-sentence reports compiled by all the above-mentioned experts can contribute to a complete and clearer picture of the offender as a person and the most appropriate sentence and treatment programme for rehabilitation purposes.

As provided in Berrigan (2008), when forensic criminologists act as mitigation specialists, the criminal justice system benefits dramatically because they are better trained in the area than lawyers, they are generally less expensive than lawyers with a lower hourly rate, and they increase the speed at which information about the defendant is gathered and distributed by virtue of their insight into what to look for and how to best summarize it.

Police Liability and Use of Deadly Force

Every time a police or corrections officer attempts to deal with a perceived threat, especially when deadly force is involved, there is the possibility of criminal and civil litigation. The officer may have violated the law; subsequently, criminal charges may be involved. The officer may have, through negligence and failure to follow established policies, wrongfully caused a death; subsequently a civil lawsuit may be filed by the decedent's estate. As explained in Anderson (1987, p. 14), specific to the issue of deadly force: "Several thousand cases are filed annually under the Civil Rights Act, which allege that units of local government acted negligently in selection, training, or supervision of personnel or in the establishment of policies related to the use of deadly force."

Forensic criminologists who have conducted research in the area of law enforcement or corrections policies and procedures are well suited to the task of performing assessments on the issues of negligent training and supervision, negligent failure to investigate, negligent employment and retention, wrongful termination, false arrest, conditions of confinement, assault and battery, excessive force, and the appropriate use of deadly force. This is especially true for those without direct ties to law enforcement, and no residual loyalty to law enforcement culture as a whole, because bias is less of a factor. Unfortunately, it is the tendency of the prosecution to use law-enforcement-friendly experts whenever possible in relation to such questions. The court should be unwilling to let such testimony into the record without an external review from an unaffiliated expert, but unfortunately this is not always possible.

Premises Liability

Premises liability refers to a landowner's duty to protect individuals from harm, including third-party assaults (La Fetra, 2006). When there is a negligent failure to prevent this kind of harm, by virtue of the fact that the property owner knew or should have known that danger was a possibility and did not take sufficient precautions against it, there is the potential for civil action. As explained in Kennedy (2006, p. 120):

> Among the myriad duties of the modern security manager is the responsibility to limit an organization's exposure to premises liability for negligent security. As a result of the evolution of case law in the US and Commonwealth countries over the past three decades, landowners and landlords of all stripes may be legally liable should a passenger, customer, client, tenant, guest, or other category of visitor to the premises be assaulted while on property under their control. For example, merchants may be sued by a customer attacked in a store's restroom or car park. A hotel guest sexually assaulted in her room by a nighttime intruder may have a cause of action against hotel management. Students at a university, visitors to a corporate headquarters, and passengers of common carriers are increasingly looking to the courts to order compensation from the owners and managers of the property whereupon their injures were sustained (Michael and Ellis, 2003). The actual perpetrators of these acts are unlikely targets of such lawsuits since their identities often remain unknown or they themselves are simply uncollectible. This leaves, of course, the third-party corporate entity which is often looked upon as a 'deep pockets' defendant.

When there is a dispute regarding whether danger was either foreseeable or preventable by the property owner, forensic criminologists may be asked to perform assessments regarding the deterrability of the offender, or the security of the premises. These concepts will be discussed thoroughly in Chapter 7.

SUMMARY

CASE EXAMPLE: MANHEIMER v. MORRISETT

ATTEMPTED HOMICIDE OF LINDA MORRISET

Report by:

Brent E. Turvey, MS Forensic Science
Forensic Scientist & Criminal Profiler

[P.O. Box 2175]
Sitka, AK 99835
Ph#: [xxx-xxx-xxxx]
Email: bturvey@corpus-delicti.com

For:

Beach, Proctor, McCarthy, & Slaughter, LLP
789 South Victoria Ave, Suite 305
Ventura, CA 93003
Ph#: xxx-xxx-xxxx
Fx#: xxx-xxx-xxxx

Re: *Mannheimer v. Morrisset*, Case No. CIV 195861

Jill Heybl, an attorney representing Linda Morrisset in this matter, asked this examiner, Brent E. Turvey, MS, to examine the investigation, crime scene evidence, and forensic documentation relating to the assault of Linda Morrisset.

In order to complete this task, this examiner was provided with and examined the following case material relating to the assault of Linda Morrisset:

- Ventura County Sheriff's Department crime scene and investigative reports
- Available hospital and crime scene photos
- Crime scene diagrams
- Available medical and related reports
- Available forensic reports
- Available witness and suspect interviews
- Available media accounts (LA Times, etc.)
- Available correspondence of Linda Morrisset with Lee Mannheimer and Family members
- Available court filings and correspondence of Lee Mannheimer
- Available personal and financial records of Linda Morrisset and Lee Mannheimer

Additionally, this examiner was provided with and examined the following case material relating to the conspiracy to commit murder/ solicitation of murder investigation into the actions of Lee Mannheimer and others:

- Various FBI interview and investigative reports
- Various California Department of Justice interview and investigative reports

- Various Sacramento County Sheriff's Department interview and investigative reports
- Various media accounts

This examiner also visited the crime scene on May 8th, 2002.

BACKGROUND

On the morning of Sept. 12, 1999, 48-year-old Linda Morrisset (a Certified Public Accountant) was found unconscious in her Camarillo, California home. Her childcare provider and concerned neighbors discovered her in the hallway leading to her bedroom, after repeated attempts to get someone at the front door failed. She had suffered multiple blows to the head with a blunt force object and had bruises on her biceps. By some reports, she also had brain material oozing from her head and nose.

According to the victim, she was home with her 22-month-old son, Robbie, and her 9-year-old son, Max, at the time of the assault. Robbie was found sleeping in his crib, in his own room, when the victim was discovered.

Because of history and factual circumstances, law enforcement immediately focused their investigative attention on Linda Morrisset's ex-husband, Lee Mannheimer. Mr. Mannheimer is suing Linda Morrisset for her inculpatory statements to the police and media. Linda Morrisset has filed a counter suit for damages relating to her injuries sustained in the above-described attack.

CONCLUSIONS

After a careful examination of the case material described above, this examiner has reached the following conclusions:

Conclusion #1—The victim, Linda Morrisset, was at a low overall lifestyle and incident risk of being the victim of a violent stranger crime.

Conclusion #2—The crime scene in this case appears *staged* to lead investigators to believe that a stranger entered the victim's house through the sliding glass door in her bedroom, and then assaulted the victim during the course of a burglary. This suggests that the offender would be an obvious, immediate, and/or logical suspect to investigators.

Conclusion #3—The physical and behavioral crime scene evidence is most consistent with an anger/revenge motivation.

Conclusion #4—Consideration of Lee Mannheimer's involvement in the assault on Linda Morrisset is more than reasonable. Failure to consider and investigate Lee Mannheimer's involvement in the assault to the point of exclusion would represent a serious investigative shortcoming.

REASONING FOR CONCLUSION #1

After examining the available victimology, it is the opinion of this examiner that the victim, Linda Morrisset, was at a low overall lifestyle and incident risk of being the victim of a violent stranger crime.

Victimology is the study of victims. Establishing the victimology in a particular case is a necessary part of determining the context of some crimes (Baeza and Turvey, 2000). Furthermore, it is generally accepted that a victim's social, medical and mental health history can provide insight into the behavior/state of mind of an individual, focus further investigation, and produce clues that will aid in establishing the cause, manner, and circumstances of their demise (NMRP, 1999).

As discussed in Turvey (2002):

> Victimology is first and foremost an investigative tool, providing context, connections, and investigative direction. In an unsolved case, where the offender is unknown, a thorough victimology defines the suspect pool. Their lifestyle in general and their activities in particular must be scrutinized in order to determine who had access to them, what they had access to, how and when they gained and maintained access, and where the access occurred.

> If we can understand how and why an offender has selected known victims, then we may also be able to establish a relational link of some kind between the victim(s) and that offender. These links may be geographical, work related, schedule oriented, school related, hobby related, or they may be otherwise acquainted. These links provide a suspect pool that includes those with knowledge of or access to the linked areas.

Lifestyle risk—This term refers to the overall risk present by virtue of an individual's personality, and their personal, professional, and social environments. The belief is that certain circumstances, habits, or activities tend to increase the likelihood that an individual will suffer harm or loss (Turvey, 1999). By all accounts, Linda Morrisset was at a low overall lifestyle risk of being the victim of a violent stranger crime. This is given the following circumstances:

- The available material does not suggest that the victim engaged in criminal activity.
- The available material does not suggest that the victim was routinely exposed to crime or those engaged in criminal activity.
- The available material does not suggest that the victim lived in a high crime area.
- The available material suggests that the victim lived in an area that could be described as rural.
- The available material does not suggest that the victim has a history of addiction to illegal or controlled mood altering substances.
- The available material does not suggest that the victim has a history of mental disorder.
- The available material does not suggest that the victim is prone to anger or aggressiveness.
- The available material does not suggest that the victim is prone to impulsivity.

Incident risk—This term is used to refer to the risk present at the time of the victim's assault by virtue of her state of mind and hazards in her immediate environment. By all accounts, Linda Morrisset was at a low overall incident risk of being the victim of a violent stranger crime at the time of the assault. This given the following circumstances:

- The victim was in her home at the time of the assault.
- The available material does not suggest that the victim lived in a high crime area.
- The available material suggests that the victim lived in an area that could be described as rural.
- The available investigative material does not suggest that there was a string of unsolved burglaries, burglary/rapes, burglary/assaults, burglary/homicides, or burglary/rape-homicides occurring in the victim's neighborhood at the time of the assault.
- The victim was not known to be using alcohol or medications at the time of the assault.
- As suggested by the witness statements, the victim was not known to be particularly agitated or distressed on the evening prior to the assault.

REASONING FOR CONCLUSION #2

The term *crime scene staging* refers to the alteration or simulation of physical evidence at a location where a crime has occurred, or where a crime is alleged to have occurred, in order to mislead authorities and/or redirect their investigation by attempting to simulate an offense, or event, that did not actually take place (Turvey, 2000).

After reviewing the available evidence, it is the opinion of this examiner that the crime scene in this case appears *staged* to lead investigators to believe that a stranger entered the victim's house through the sliding glass door in her bedroom, and then attacked the victim during the course of a burglary. This suggests that the offender would be an obvious, immediate, and/or logical suspect to investigators.

The basis for this opinion resides in the consideration of the following facts:

- The available evidence indicates that there was no sign of forced entry.

- The victim's front door was reportedly locked when childcare provider Thelma Meeks arrived on the morning after the assault. Meeks noted that this was not a usual circumstance, as the door was usually unlocked when she arrived. This suggests the possibility that the offender locked the door prior to leaving the residence, after assaulting the victim. This possibility is further strengthened by the discovery of small amounts of blood transfer evidence in the entryway, inside of the front door area, suggesting the offender's presence there after the assault.

- A locked front door at a crime scene could cause investigators to search for an alternate point of entry that was either forced or left open, thus ignoring potential transfer evidence at the true point of entry.

- The initial crime scene presentation suggests that the apparent point of entry may have been the sliding glass door in the victim's master bedroom. The sliding glass door was reportedly open approximately two feet when first discovered by Thelma Meeks and concerned neighbors. However, this may not be the true point of entry. A door or window intentionally left open by the offender open is a common feature of the staged crime scene (Turvey, 2000).

- By all indications (state of dress; lay pattern on top of bed; evidence of reading material and glasses in victim's possession at time of assault) the victim was apparently laying on her unmade bed, fully clothed and reading prior to the assault. The available evidence provides that victim's glasses and reading material were discovered in or near the hallway area, near the area where the victim was found. It is not likely that the victim bothered to carry these items from the bed with her into the hallway once the assault began. However, it is more likely that the victim would have carried them with her to answer the front door, or during some other normal, non-life threatening activity.

- By all evidentiary indications (blood evidence; damage to the hallway floor; the final resting place of the victim; the absence of blood spatter elsewhere in the home; the absence of disturbed items elsewhere in the home) the assault started and ended in the hallway. It is possible that the victim answered the front door and was assaulted while retreating to the bedroom from perceived danger. It is not likely that the offender entered the lit master bedroom with a waking victim through the glass sliding door given the risk involved. However, if the offender had entered through the bedroom, the attack would most likely have occurred there. Moreover, if the victim were quick enough to elude an offender entering through the sliding glass door and succumbed to an attack in the hallway, she would most likely have left her glasses and reading material behind.

- The available evidence indicates that 5 necklaces were taken from the jewelry cabinet in the victim's bedroom. The jewelry cabinet was left open, most likely to direct investigators to note the missing jewelry and infer a stranger burglary gone awry. However, many other jewelry items were left behind, and there is no evidence to suggest that any other items of value were removed from the residence (including TVs, computers, and the victim's purse, which was in plain view in the kitchen area).

- By all accounts, it was the impression of investigators at the crime scene that it appeared to have been staged.

It should be noted that as this crime scene is consistent with having been staged, this suggests an offender who is concerned about concealing their relationship with the victim. In this examiner's study of staged crime scenes, all of the cases studied involved an offender and a victim with a prior family/intimate relationship (Turvey, 2000).

REASONING FOR CONCLUSION #3

In an anger-retaliatory crime, a main goal of offense behavior is to service cumulative rage and aggression. The offender is retaliating against the victim for real or perceived wrongs, and their aggression can manifest itself in a wide range, from verbally abusive language to hyper-aggressed homicide with multiple collateral victims (Turvey, 2002). After reviewing the available evidence, it is the opinion of this examiner that the physical and behavioral crime scene evidence is most consistent with an anger-retaliatory motivation.

The basis for this opinion resides in the consideration of the following facts:

- Multiple blows to the victim's head with a blunt object. These were repeated, powerful blows that crushed through the skull to the brain. These were not intended merely to incapacitate, but to kill. This is inconsistent with an offender whose primary goal is to burglarize a residence for profit, barring a victim that is violently fighting back (the available evidence does not provide indications that the victim fought back or was hostile towards the offender to any great measure, though defensive injuries on her forearms indicate that she protected herself during the attack).

- The available evidence indicates that the assault was immediate, overwhelming, and short lived. This is consistent with an anger-retaliatory motivation.

- The available evidence indicates that no sexual activity or assault occurred in relation to the physical assault. This is inconsistent with an offender whose primary goal is sexually assault.

- The available evidence indicates an overall absence of a profit motive in relation to the entry of the residence and the assault (many items of value in clear view left untouched—TVs, computers, victim's purse, victim's jewelry, VCRs, etc.; residence not apparently ransacked for valuables; victim's vehicle Ford truck apparently untouched, left behind; victim's garage not breached— tools and other items of value left behind; victim's office building on property found locked and untouched—numerous items of value not taken).

- The available evidence indicates that the offender left almost immediately after the assault. From this we may infer that the offender left because their object had been achieved—if they had other objects to achieve, there would certainly have been plenty of time. This is consistent with an anger-retaliatory motivation.

- The investigators at the crime scene believed that this was an attempted homicide, as indicated by the charges listed on even their initial investigative reports.

REASONING FOR CONCLUSION #4

After reviewing the available evidence, it is the opinion of this examiner that consideration of Lee Mannheimer's involvement in the assault on Linda Morrisset is more than reasonable. Failure to consider and investigate Lee Mannheimer's involvement in the assault to the point of exclusion would represent a serious investigative shortcoming.

The basis for this opinion resides in the consideration of the following facts:

- The victim was at a low overall lifestyle and incident risk of being the victim of a violent stranger crime. This suggests that the most fruitful avenues of investigative effort would be an examination of suspects known to the victim.

- The physical and behavioral crime scene evidence is most consistent with an anger-retaliatory motivation. The consideration of current and ex-spouse involvement in such crimes is all but dictated by anger-retaliatory motivated offenses.

- The crime scene is consistent with having been staged, suggesting an offender intent on misdirecting the investigation because they would be an obvious, immediate, and/or logical suspect. Moreover, in this examiner's study of staged crime scenes, all of the cases studied involved at least one offender and at least one victim with a prior family/intimate relationship which the staging activity was meant to conceal (Turvey, 2000).

- In 1993, there was a well-documented murder-for-hire plot to kill Linda Morrisset, which by all accounts was investigated and confirmed by the FBI and the Sacramento County Sheriff's Office. Those directly involved, including a business associate of Lee Mannheimer, claimed that Mr. Mannheimer paid them, and implicated Mr. Mannheimer as the chief instigator of the murder plot. This occurred just prior to the couple's divorce.

- The circumstances of the victim's assault resemble the circumstances prescribed in the previously described murder-for-hire plot. Lee Mannheimer was reported to have given instructions that the victim was to be killed when she was at home, alone, when the kids were not present, and injuries were to be delivered to her head.

- Law enforcement maintains a "hazard file" on Lee Mannheimer in relation to the above-mentioned 1993 murder-for-hire plot.

- Linda Morrisset and Lee Mannheimer share custody of a then 9 year old son, Max, over whom there have been continuous, intense and bitter disputes.

- As laid out by the material provided to this examiner, the relationship between Linda Morrisset and Lee Mannheimer has been one of cumulative dissatisfaction and antagonism. This has continued since their divorce both interpersonally, and through issues relating to the joint custody of their son, Max.

- Lee Mannheimer has admitted to previous incidents of physical violence towards Linda Morrisset.

- Family members have stated that the 5 necklaces removed from the victim's residence in association with the assault were gifts from Lee Mannheimer.

- The available material does not indicate that Linda Morrisset ever had significant trouble, antagonism, or disputes with anyone in her life other than Lee Mannheimer.

- The available material does not suggest that there is any definitive evidence excluding Lee Mannheimer as a suspect in this case.

Brent E. Turvey, MS

When it comes to addressing investigative and legal questions, criminologists can perform many different tasks. They work with both criminal and civil cases in various jurisdictions with various goals. First and foremost, then, it is crucial for forensic criminologists to understand the issues inherent in being involved in these systems, such as the differences between criminal and civil cases, the legal parties involved, reasonable doubt and the burden of proof, as well as the rights of those involved and the legal consequences.

CONCLUSION

Once these elements are understood, forensic criminologists can perform any number of different analyses for investigators and the court. Criminologists may advise on issues relating to custom, practice, and guidelines; offender classification; equivocal forensic analyses; determination of staging and crime reconstruction; victim risk and exposure; psychological autopsies; analysis of the motives involved; determination of whether torture was involved; criminal profiling; case linkage; presentence investigations, evaluations, and mitigation; police liability and the use of deadly force; and premises liability. Each of these roles (and any combination of them) requires a distinct skill set and constant consideration of the issues present. On the whole, forensic criminologists are charged with remaining objective and knowing their limits regardless of the role they may play.

Review Questions

1. Discuss the distinction between criminal and civil cases in relation to jurisdiction, legal parties, rights, and legal consequences.
2. Describe in detail three of the specific duties of the expert as outlined by Dwyer (2008).
3. Describe the three types of criminological expert evidence which can be given to the court.
4. T/F Criminology is both theoretical and practical.
5. What is the difference between a suicide psychological autopsy and an equivocal death psychological autopsy?
6. T/F A psychological autopsy has investigative, forensic, and treatment goals.
7. Why is it important to establish motive? How does it help?
8. Why is it so important to establish whether torture was involved in any given case?

REFERENCES

American Bar Association, 2003. Guidelines for the Appointment and Performance of Defense Counsel in Death Penalty Cases, Revised Edition. Hofstra Law Review 31 (4). Summer.

Anderson, P.R., 1987. Scholarship in the Courtroom: The Criminologist as Expert Witness. In: Anderson, P.R., Winfree, L.T. (Eds.), Expert Witnesses: Criminologists in the Courtroom. State University of New York Press, New York.

Baeza, J., Turvey, B., 2000. False Reports in Cases of Sexual Assault: Literature Review and Investigative Suggestions. Journal of Behavioral Profiling, December, 1 (3).

Bartol, C.R., 1999. Criminal Behavior. A Psychosocial Approach, fifth ed. Prentice Hall, Upper Saddle River, NJ.

Berrigan, H., 2008. The Indispensable Role of the Mitigation Specialist in a Capital Case: A View from the Federal Bench. Hofstra Law Review 36 (Spring), 819–833.

Black, H.C., 1990. Black's Law Dictionary, sixth ed. West Publishing Co., St. Paul, MN.

Chisum, W.J. and Turvey, B., 2007. Crime Reconstruction. Elsevier Science, Boston.

Commonwealth v. Conklin, 2006. 897 A. 2d 1168.

Dwyer, D., 2008. Legal Remedies for the Negligent Expert. The International Journal of Evidence and Proof Edition 12, 93–115.

Gross, H., 1924. Criminal Investigation. Sweet & Maxwell, London.

Holmes, R. and De Burger, J., 1988. Serial Murder. Sage Publications, Newbury Park.

Hunter, R.D., Dantzker, M.L., 2002. Crime and Criminality. Causes and Consequences. Prentice Hall, Upper Saddle River, NJ.

Jobes, D.A., Berman, A.L. and Josselson, A.R., 1987. Improving the Validity and Reliability of Medical-Legal Certifications of Suicide. Suicide and Life-Threatening Behaviors, 17(14), 310–325.

Kennedy, D., 2006. Forensic Security and the Law.In: Gill, M. (Ed.), The Handbook of Security. Palgrave Macmillan, New York.

La Fetra, D., 2006. A Moving Target: Property Owners' Duty to Prevent Criminal Acts on the Premises. Whittier Law Review, 28 (Fall), 409–462.

La Fon, D.S., 1999. Psychological Autopsies for Equivocal Deaths. International Journal of Emergency Mental Health, 3, 183–188.

La Fon, D., 2008. The Psychological Autopsy. In Turvey, B. (Ed) Criminal Profiling, third ed. Elsevier Science, San Diego.

Labuschagne, I.L., 2003. The Role of the Criminologist as Expert Witness in Court, in Comparison with Those of Other Specialists, such as Psychologists, Psychiatrists or Social Workers. Paper presented at a symposium: "Expert Evidence in Court: Requirements and Expectations," held at the Sunnyside Campus, UNISA on 30 May 2003.

Labuschagne, J.J., 2003. The Necessity for Establishing a Professional Board for Criminologists: Purpose, Requirements and Compilation of a Constitution. Paper presented at a symposium: "Expert Evidence in Court: Requirements and Expectations," held at the Sunnyside Campus, UNISA on 30 May 2003.

Michael, K. and Ellis, Z., 2003. Avoiding Liability in Premises Security, fifth ed. Strafford Publications, Atlanta.

Morn, F., 1995. Academic Politics and the History of Criminal Justice Education. Greenwood Press, Wesport, CT.

NMRP (National Medicolegal Review Panel), 1999. Death Investigation: A Guide for the Scene Investigator. National Institute of Justice, Washington, DC.

Pretorius, J.P., 1997. Cross-examination in South African Law. Butterworths, Durban.

Reid, S., 2003. Crime and Criminology, tenth ed. McGraw-Hill, New York.

Savino, J., Turvey, B., 2004. Rape Investigation Handbook. Academic Press, San Diego.

Schmidt, C.W.H., Rademeyer, H., 2000. Bewysreg, fourth ed. Butterworths, Uitgawe, Durban.

Shneidman, E.S., 1981. The Psychological Autopsy. Suicide and Life Threatening Behaviors, 11(4), 325–340.

Siegel, L.J., 2004. Criminology: Theories, Patterns and Typologies, eighth ed. Thomson/ Wadsworth, Belmont, Canada.

Spellman, A., and Heyne, B., 1989. Suicide? Accident? Predictable? Avoidable?: The Psychological Autopsy in Jail Suicides. Psychiatric Quarterly, 60(2), 173–183.

Takah, J., 2006. A Social Worker Qualifies as a Criminal Justice Expert for the Purposes of Classifying a Sex Offender as a Sexually Violent Predator: Commonwealth v. Conklin. Duquesne Law Review, Fall, 45,129–145.

Technical Working Group on Crime Scene Investigation (TWGCSI), 2000. Crime Scene Investigation: A Guide for Law Enforcement. National Institute of Justice January.

Terblanche, S.S., 1999. The Guide to Sentencing in South Africa. Butterworths, Durban.

Thornton, J.I. (Ed.), (1974). Preface. In: Kirk, P. (Ed.), Crime Investigation. John Wiley and Sons, Inc, New York.

Turvey, B.,1999. Criminal Profiling: An Introduction to Behavioral Evidence Analysis, 1st Ed. Academic Press, London.

Turvey, B., 2000. Staged Crime Scenes: A Preliminary Study of 25 Cases. Journal of Behavioral Profiling, December, 1 (3).

Turvey, B., 2002. Forensic Examination Report. Mannheimer v. Morrisset May 9.

Turvey, B., 2004. Staged Burglary: Technical Note and Civics Lesson. Journal of Behavioral Profiling, December, 5 (1).

Turvey, B., 2006a. Forensic Examination Report. Mississippi v. Robert Grant February 3.

Turvey, B., 2006b. Linkage Analysis Report, *California v. Joseph S. Cordova*, October 17.

Turvey, B., 2008a. Criminal Profiling: An Introduction to Behavioral Evidence Analysis. Academic Press, San Diego.

Turvey, B., 2008b. Expert declaration. *California v. Celeste S. Carrington*, March 10.

Turvey, B., 2008c. Forensic Examination Report. *California v. Jack Lewis* May 22.

Van der Hoven, A.E., 2006. The Criminologist as an Expert Witness in Court. Acta Criminologica 19 (2), 152–171.

Criminal Profiling

Wayne A. Petherick and Claire E. Ferguson

KEY TERMS

Crime Reconstruction: "The determination of the actions surrounding the commission of a crime" (Chisum, 2002, p. 81).

Criminal Profiling: An investigative tool that infers offender characteristics from the analysis of offenders' behavior, their interaction with the crime scene and victim, and their choices during the crime.

Deductive Argument: An argument in which the conclusion is implicitly contained within the premise, where offender characteristics are a direct extension of the available physical and behavioral evidence.

Evidence Dynamics: Influences that change, relocate, obscure, or obliterate physical evidence regardless of the person or circumstance that brought about the change.

Inductive Argument: An argument that provides a conclusion which is made likely, or a matter of probability, by offering supporting documentation.

Inter-rater Reliablity: Consistency between different individuals rating the same offender.

Investigate Phase: A stage of criminal profiling that involves discerning features of the unknown offender for the known crime.

Psychological Autopsy: (a.k.a. equivocal death analysis) An evaluation of a decedent's mental state prior to death.

Short Course: Any truncated pathway to education or information that is offered in an intensive mode, often without the enforcement of educational standards or assessment.

Socratic Method: An approach to knowledge building and problem solving based on discussion and debate.

CONTENTS

Trial Phase: A stage of criminal profiling that involves providing information about a crime or series of crimes for which there is a suspected offender.

Victim Exposure: The amount of exposure to harmful elements experienced by a victim.

Victimology: An examination of all aspects of a victim's life, including lifestyle, hobbies, habits, friends, enemies, and demographic features.

One of the more widely recognized and practiced subspecialities within forensic criminology is that of criminal profiling. It has a long history, as detailed in Turvey (2008a). It also boasts a small library of distinct literature, with different methods and subspecialities all its own.

Criminal profiling is a practice that has seen increasing popular and media attention over the past several decades. It has been depicted in popular fiction such as films like *Silence of the Lambs* (1991) and television programs like *Criminal Minds* (2005–present). It has also been applied in a number of high profile cases, including the "Washington Snipers" (see Turvey and McGrath, 2005, for an extended discussion of profiling and the media in the D.C. Sniper case). As a result, students of criminology commonly express an interest in studying criminal profiling with a view to becoming profilers themselves.

At the same time, many professionals, including criminologists and psychologists, have rather abruptly entered the field by hanging out shingles proclaiming related areas of expertise. The resulting student push and practitioner pull have made it a subject of keen interest, but confusion remains among many. So while advances have been made in the field and interest is high, there is still much debate about the efficacy of profiling and even fundamental educational standards.

It is the purpose of this chapter to present an overview of criminal profiling and what it involves in relation to the forensic criminologist. First, we will examine what criminal profiling is, what its goals are, what is necessary to complete a profile, as well as the ways in which a profile may assist with investigations. Second, we will discuss the logic and reasoning utilized by profilers, including the basic theories behind practical approaches to profiling, the differences between inductive and deductive logic, and the methods that use them. Next, we will address the main types of profiling, discuss their strengths and criticisms, and touch on the background knowledge required by the profiler to use each of these methods. Finally, we will address the educational requirements of the profiler and comment on the appropriate pathways necessary within university, the importance of the Socratic method as it relates to studying specific cases, and issues with undertaking short courses. We will also discuss those areas in which the criminologist may be able to provide profiling advice, as well as the perils and pitfalls doing so may present. First, we turn to a broad introduction of profiling, examining definitional issues, goals, and the like.

WHAT IS CRIMINAL PROFILING?

Although the practice of criminal profiling has been documented for centuries in different forms (Turvey, 2008a), the term *offender profiling* was first put into regular use by a small group of FBI analysts. They used it to describe the process of making inferences about offenders' characteristics from their actions during a crime (Canter, 1995). In its most basic form, criminal profiling is an investigative tool that discerns offender characteristics from the crime scene and the behavior of the offenders. It is an inferential process that involves the analysis of offender behavior, their interactions with the crime scene and the victim, and their choices during the crime (Petherick, 2003).

Despite its appearing in many of the early works on profiling, the FBI no longer uses the term *criminal profiling*. This term and others like it, such as *criminal personality profiling* and *psychological profiling*, have been deliberately replaced by the general term *criminal investigative analysis (CIA)*.[1] This newer term covers profiling and a number of other services: indirect personality assessments; equivocal death analysis (otherwise known as *psychological autopsy*, meaning determining from information and evidence gathered whether a death was accidental, natural, suicide, or homicide); and trial strategy. Regardless of the change in labeling, the FBI's methods in this regard remains unchanged. The process of *criminal investigative analysis* will be discussed in more detail in the inductive methods section later.

Goals of Criminal Profiling

Irrespective of the nomenclature used to describe it, or the actual processes utilized, all methods of profiling have a similar goal. Throughout its application across time, profiling has been designed to help law enforcement develop a viable suspect pool in unsolved crimes, either by narrowing an extensive list of suspects to a small and more manageable group, or by providing new areas of inquiry (Homant and Kennedy, 1998). As noted by Napier and Baker (2005, p. 615), "the purpose of offender profiling is to supply offender characteristics to help investigators narrow the field of suspects based on the characteristics of the crime scene and initial investigative information." It is not the goal of profiling to identify a particular person or to give his or her identity (Douglas, Ressler, Burgess, and Hartman, 1986), and Muller (2000) notes that the profile will rarely be so accurate as to suggest a certain individual as being responsible.

[1] It has been demonstrated that the newer term was developed to distinguish FBI "profilers" from psychologists with actual education in the behavioral sciences, as well as to facilitate courtroom admissibility of profiling conclusions (Turvey, 2008a).

Nor should it, as determining guilt or innocence of any individual is the task of the trier of fact, not the profiler.

Petherick and Turvey (2008a) identify two main phases of profiling, divided by their goals and priorities. The first is the *investigative phase*, which involves discerning features of the unknown offender for the known crime. It is this phase that will be most aligned to stereotypical notions of profiling. In the investigative phase, there are seven primary goals (p. 138):

1. Evaluate the nature and value of forensic and behavioral evidence to a particular crime or series of related crimes
2. Reduce the viable suspect pool in a criminal investigation
3. Prioritize the investigation into remaining suspects
4. Link potentially related crimes by identifying crime scene indicators and behavior patterns (i.e., *modus operandi* [MO] and signature)
5. Assess the potential for escalation of nuisance criminal behavior to more serious or more violent crimes (i.e., harassment, stalking, voyeurism)
6. Provide investigators with investigatively relevant leads and strategies
7. Help keep the overall investigation on track and undistracted by offering fresh insights

The second phase identified is the *trial phase*, which involves providing information about a crime or series of crimes for which there is a suspected offender. A profile can be useful at this stage of an investigation because it can assist in developing proper interview and interrogation strategies among other things; further, a profile may be used in court as expert evidence to argue for aggravating circumstances and the like, sometimes meaning the difference between life-imprisonment and death penalty cases. Therefore, during the trial phase of an investigation, a profiler's goals are to (Petherick and Turvey, 2008a, p. 138):

1. Evaluate the nature and value of forensic and behavioral evidence to a particular crime or series of related crimes
2. Develop interview or interrogation strategies
3. Help develop insight into offender fantasy and motivations
4. Develop insight into offender motive and intent before, during, and after the commission of a crime (i.e., levels of planning, evidence of remorse, precautionary acts, etc.)
5. Link potentially related crimes by identifying crime scene indicators and behavior patterns (i.e., MO and signature)

The goals of profiling may also be dictated in part by the type of crime being profiled and by the needs of the investigative team requesting help.

Also, some crimes are more suited to profiling than others. Therefore, it is also necessary to consider the types of crimes that profiling might assist in and whether a case requires the use of what may be an expensive and time-consuming tool.

Generally, it is noted that profiling is most suited to crimes involving psychopathology, or where there is some evidence of psychological dysfunction (McCann, 1992; Pinizzotto, 1984), or in crimes of a sexual nature because they involve more interaction between the offender and the victim (Nowikowski, 1995). Such crimes typically involve murder, rape, arson, and bombing but may also include anonymous letter writing (Davis, 1999; Homant, 1999; Strano, 2004) and other crimes of an unusual, bizarre, violent, sexual or repetitive in nature (Cook and Hinman, 1999; Geberth, 1981; Palermo, 2002; Royal Canadian Mounted Police, 2005; Strano, 2004). It has also been used in hostage negotiations and threats (Davis, 1999; Douglas and Hazelwood, 1986) and assessing suicidality (see Canter, 1999; Homant and Kennedy, 1998; La Fon, 2002). Teten (1989, pp. 366–367) provides this poignant commentary, summing up the issue nicely:

> Therefore, while it is theoretically possible to prepare an accurate profile of the perpetrator in any type of crime, it is not feasible. Psychological profiling should be utilised only in those types of crimes where the crime-scene investigation is as complete and thorough as possible.
>
> As a practical matter, this procedure can be expected to provide usable data in only a few highly specific types of crimes. Even then, it is totally dependent upon the psychological value of the evidence collected. Most of the offences, to be appropriate for profiling, must feature some form of overt sexual activity or a loss of contact with reality. Generally speaking, the types of crimes in which profiling has been most successful include:
>
>> Homicides that involve sexual activity, or appear to be sex related
>> Forcible rapes
>> Sexual molestations
>> Indecent exposures
>> Some forms of arson
>> Homicides involving the parents, children or a majority of the members of a family
>> Deaths by hanging

These are not the limits of the application of profiling, however, and it has also been applied to more esoteric areas, such as intrusion management in computer security (see Schlarman, 1999), threat management in stalking (see Petherick, 2008), and premises liability in civil actions (see Kennedy and Homant, 1997; explained further in Chapter 8). Regardless of the fact that profiling can be and has been used to understand a broad range of criminal behaviors, it should be noted that the goals of profiling remain consistent—to narrow the suspect pool, provide new areas of inquiry, keep the investigation on track and undistracted, and understand the behaviors more completely.

Inputs and Outputs of Criminal Profiling

To successfully complete a profile in a given case, a variety of information may be required, depending on the method used. This ranges from statistical data regarding past crimes, to physical evidence and witness statements, to the reconstruction and interpretation of offender behavior. Ostensibly, the more complete this information, the more accurate profiling inferences can be. If the information is incomplete or incorrect, depending on the profiling method used, certain characteristics may be impossible to determine; at the very least it may seriously undermine the veracity of the conclusions. Therefore, it is generally true that more information is better.

For example, the first stage of the FBI method is profiling inputs, and describes those elements necessary to compile the assessment (see Douglas, Ressler, Burgess, and Hartman, 1986). These elements include a complete synopsis of the crime, location, weather conditions, and complete victim information including domestic setting, employment, reputation, and criminal history. Forensic information relevant to the crime is also necessary; autopsy reports, photographs and toxicology, as well as crime scene photographs of the area and crime scene sketches to help provide an overall picture.

However, it may not be said that a limited amount of evidence will produce a limited profile in every case. Some profilers show constraint with the information or outputs they provide in their profiles, whereas others are considerably more liberal in their estimates. This liberalism is typical of inductive methods which focus more on offense generalizations, and not necessarily on the available evidence, resulting in a broader range of characteristics offered. Inductive methods will be discussed thoroughly later.

Turvey (2008b) is an example of someone who is more conservative in his approach. He argues that in most cases, during the investigative phase only about four relevant offender characteristics can be deductively inferred from crime scene behavior. These are Criminal Skill, Knowledge of the Victim, Knowledge of the Crime Scene, and Knowledge of Methods and Materials. Although other characteristics are potentially inferable, they are considered less relevant to investigative needs by virtue of failing to narrow the suspect pool or failing to discriminate from the general public, thus not allowing for new avenues of inquiry to be proposed. However, Turvey (2008b) notes that although only four characteristics are relevant to determining a suspect, after that person is located (during the trial phase), there will be additional questions of forensic interest regarding the crime scene and offender that may be of further value to the court.

At the other end of the spectrum is Geberth (1996), who provides an exhaustive list of those things he believes can be determined from the crime, including:

1. Name
2. Age
3. Sex
4. Race
5. Height and weight
6. Marital status
   a. Children, ages and sex
   b. Wife, pregnant and recent birth
7. Education level
8. Socioeconomic status
9. History of, and type of, sexual problems
10. Physical abnormalities and/or defects such as
    a. Acne, speech impediment, obese, walks with a limp, etc.
11. Residence, condition of, etc.
12. Automobile, condition of, etc.
13. Behavior including any noticeable change recently and describe
14. Mannerisms and personality
15. Employment, recently laid off? Skills associated with job?
16. Day or night person?
17. Users of drugs or alcohol, recent increase?
18. Dress, sloppy or neat? Type of clothing?
19. Known to carry, collect, or display weapons? What type?
20. Rigid versus flexible personality

This list is consistent with Ault and Reese (1980) and O'Toole (2004), who provide exhaustive lists of inferable offender traits and emotional states, covering almost every facet of their past, present, and future. It should be noted, however, that the means for inferring these broader and less investigatively relevant traits is typically through comparison to past offenders who committed similar crimes, and not through a process of case-based deduction. The problems inherent in this process will become clear in the following section discussing how profilers may render their findings.

LOGIC AND REASONING IN THE METHODS OF CRIMINAL PROFILING

The following sections will briefly introduce readers to the logic and reasoning used within profiling before covering the major approaches to profiling that are available. Far from being an in-depth exposition, these sections seek to provide readers the necessary and relevant points of each. For a more in-depth treatment of these matters, readers should consult Petherick (2003), Petherick (2005), and Petherick and Turvey (2008b).

Logic and Reasoning

Before considering the different methods of criminal profiling, we need to canvass some fundamental issues related to logic and reasoning. The reason is that, regardless of profiling method used, they differ most according to the way in which the final conclusion is rendered. It could be said that there are predominantly two types of logic used: the first is inductive and the second is deductive. Inductive methods are those relying on statistical or correlational reasoning, and these methods will be discussed forthwith. The final method, Behavioral Evidence Analysis, is deductively oriented and will be discussed in "Deduction: The Suggested Approach" section later.

The science of logic is variously defined, and in the broadest sense it is the process of argumentation. As Farber (1942, p. 41) argues, logic is "a unified discipline which investigates the structure and validity of ordered knowledge." According to Bhattacharyya (1958, p. 326):

> Logic is usually defined as the science of valid thought. But as thought may mean either the act of thinking or the object of thought, we get two definitions of logic: logic as the science (1) of the act of valid thinking, or (2) of the objects of valid thinking.

Stock (2004, p. 8) suggests:

> Logic may be declared to be both the science and the art of thinking. It is the art of thinking in the same sense in which grammar is the art of speaking. Grammar is not in itself the right use of words, but a knowledge of it enables men to use words correctly. In the same way a knowledge of logic enables men to think correctly or at least to avoid incorrect thoughts. As an art, logic may be called the navigation of the sea of thought.

It is the purpose of logic to analyze the methods by which valid judgements are obtained in any science or discourse, which is met by the formulation of general laws that dictate the validity of judgements (Farber, 1942). Without a solid foundation in logic and reasoning, the criminologist cannot proceed competently.

Inductive Criminal Profiling

An *inductive argument* provides a conclusion (or offender characteristic) that is made likely, or a matter of probability, by offering supporting argumentation. In profiling, this support often includes things like physical and behavioral evidence, research findings, or even profiler experience and expertise. A good inductive argument will provide strong support for the conclusion offered, but this still does not make the argument necessarily correct. In reality, even the best inductive argument is a generalization, hypothesis, or theory awaiting verification through testing (Turvey, 2008a). Although inductive generalizations may be true in some—even many—cases, there is no way to guarantee that they will apply to the case being profiled.

A key identifying feature of inductive profiles is the use of qualifiers, such as *probably*, *may be*, or *typically*, among others, highlighting the probabilistic nature of the assessment. For example, crime figures from the United States (Federal Bureau of Investigation, 2002) provide that approximately 90% of offenders who committed murder in that year were male. Even though this relationship is relatively strong, it still does not mean that a male will have committed every homicide in that year. As it stands, this statistic could be used to make the inductive argument that an offender in a given case is *more likely*, or even *probably*, a male, all else being equal. That is, a profiler using an inductive method may state "the offender in this case is most likely male." However this argument based on nationwide statistics could very easily be wrong. This happens because in the examination of individual cases, all things are not equal. The likelihood of an offender being male changes based on a variety of factors, including the type of offense, the type of weapon used, and the sex of the victim, to name but a few, and even taking these things into account does not guarantee the accuracy of the predicted characteristic (in this case, the sex). Therefore, looking narrowly at just the issue of male versus female homicide offenders doesn't accurately reflect the complexity that will exist in the context of a real case.

Apart from context, two of the issues which may seriously impact on the generalizability of any statistical data used to generate inductive theories are sample size and research methodology. This is perhaps best illustrated by a specific FBI study (Burgess and Ressler, 1985) that originally set the stage for the subsequently developed method of profiling. The study, which was the basis for the FBI's entire profiling method, involved only 36 offenders (not all of whom were serial offenders). Furthermore, the methodology of the study was heavily criticized by the peer reviewers who noted, among other things, small sample size (Burgess, 2003) and a lack of *inter-rater reliability* (consistency between different individuals rating the offender) (Fox, 2004). Others have been critical of this study as well, with Canter (2004, p. 6) noting that "the FBI agents conducting the study did not select random or even a large sample of all offenders."

The FBI, being very much aware of the limitations of its inductive profiling methods, provides more than a qualifier with its criminal investigative analysis reports (profiles). It actually goes so far as to provide a broad disclaimer at the beginning of each investigative profile. While the wording may vary, the theme is consistent, with the following example being representative (Vorpagel and Harrington, 1998, p. 62):

> It should be noted that the attached analysis is not a substitute for a thorough and well-planned investigation and should not be considered all inclusive. The information provided is based upon reviewing, analysing, and researching criminal cases similar to the case submitted by the requesting agency. The final analysis is based upon the probabilities, noting, however, that no two criminal personalities are exactly alike, and therefore the offender at times may not always fit the profile in every category.

This standard FBI disclaimer signals the weakness of purely inductive profiling methodologies.

Deductive Criminal Profiling

Deductive profiling relies on a more scientific and systematic process whereby offender characteristics are a direct extension of the available physical and behavioral evidence (Turvey, 2008a). If the premises are true, then the conclusions must also be true (Bevel and Gardiner, 1997) (recall in inductive arguments if the premises are true, the conclusion is possible but not necessarily true). Neblett (1985, p. 114) goes further, stating, "if the conclusion is false, then at least one of the premises must be false." For this reason, it is incumbent on the profiler to establish the veracity and validity of each and every premise before attempting to draw conclusions from them.

Because a *deductive argument* is structured so that the conclusion is implicitly contained within the premise, and unless the reasoning is invalid, the conclusion follows as a matter of course. A deductive argument is designed so that it takes us from truth to truth. That is, a deductive argument is valid if (Alexandra, Matthews, and Miller, 2002, p. 65):

- It is not logically possible for its conclusion to be false if its premises are true.
- Its conclusions must be true if its premises are true.
- It would be contradictory to assert its premises yet deny its conclusions.

In profiling, deduction draws on the scientific method which is a "reasoned step by step procedure involving observations and experimentation in problem solving" (Bevel, 2001, p. 154). Unlike induction, then, deduction takes the possible hypotheses garnered from statistics and research (the inductive conclusions) and tests them against the physical evidence present in each case. This is undertaken with a view not to prove the hypothesis, but rather to disprove it. That is, each possible characteristic of the offender is tested against the evidence with the goal of falsifying it or proving it to be untrue. If falsified, the inductive hypothesis is dropped or restructured, while those hypotheses that consistently and repeatedly fail to be disproved survive. It is only after this rigorous testing that we can be certain an analysis is complete and truths are arrived at. Once a hypothesis has consistently withstood falsification, it can be presented in a deductive fashion. It is under this strict procedure of testing and retesting that deductive profiling operates. From an analysis of case inputs, theories are formed inductively and tested against the evidence. After numerous and repeated attempts to disprove the theories, a deductive conclusion can be put forth.

However, the profile that results from this process is by no means static and may be updated in light of new information. New physical evidence may be incorporated into the decision process to update the conclusion. Also, new advances in science and understanding may challenge long-held assumptions and question the current hypothesis. Although it may appear as such, this is not a problem with the process because a deduction can operate only within the realm of established laws and principles. This tenet of argumentation is made clear by Farber (1948, p. 48):

> Every "logical system" is governed by principles of structure and meaning. A system that claims to be a "logic," i.e., which operates formally with one of the various definitions of implication, possibility, etc., is subject to the laws of construction of ordered thought, namely, to the fundamental principles of logic. This requirement imposed on all systems cannot amount to a law that there shall be law. The specific application is provided by the rules in each system.

When these laws or principles change because of new knowledge, so too must the nature of the deduction made.

Armed with an understanding of logic, let us now turn to the inductive methods.

Inductive Methods of Criminal Profiling

The following is a basic primer on the major forms of inductive profiling methodology.

Criminal Investigative Analysis

Without doubt, the best known method of criminal profiling is that of the FBI, known variously as criminal investigative analysis (CIA) and crime scene analysis. This approach arose primarily from the study mentioned previously, which was conducted between 1979 and 1983, with the research focus on the development of typologies from an examination of various features of crimes perpetrated by incarcerated sexual murderers (see Burgess and Ressler, 1985). The goal was to determine whether there are any consistent features across offenses that may be useful in classifying future offenders (Petherick, 2005). A number of publications have arisen from this original research, including Burgess, Hartman, Ressler, Douglas, and McCormack (1986); Ressler and Burgess (1985); Ressler, Burgess, and Douglas (1988); Ressler, Burgess, Douglas, Hartman, and D'Agostino (1986); and Ressler, Burgess, Hartman, Douglas, and McCormack (1986).

The study resulted in an organized/disorganized dichotomy, which became the FBI profiling method. This dichotomy classifies offenders by virtue of the level of sophistication, planning, and competence evident in the crime scene. An organized crime scene is one with evidence of planning, where the victim is a targeted stranger, the crime scene reflects overall control, there are restraints used, and aggressive acts occur prior to death. This suggests that these offenders are organized in their daily life with the crime scene being a reflection of their personality, meaning they will be average to above average in intelligence, be socially competent, prefer skilled work, have a high birth order, have a controlled mood during the crime, and may also use alcohol during the crime. A disorganized crime scene shows spontaneity, where the victim or location is known to the offender, the crime scene is random and sloppy, there is sudden violence, minimal restraints are used, and there are sexual acts after death. These characteristics are again suggestive of the personality of these offenders, with disorganized offenders being below average in intelligence, being socially inadequate, having a low birth order, having an anxious mood during the crime, and involving the minimal use of alcohol during the offense. Despite having these mutually exclusive classifications, it is generally held that no offender will fit neatly into either category, with most offenders being somewhere between the two; these offenders are called "mixed."

Despite suggestions that the organized and disorganized terminology was an outgrowth of the study conducted in the late 1970s and early 1980s and published in 1985, it had actually been in use for some time. The terminology first appeared in its original form of *organized nonsocial* and *disorganized asocial* in "The Lust Murderer" in 1980 (see Hazelwood and Douglas, 1980). As such, the study is best thought of as further developing an existing concept rather than generating a new one.

Like virtually all the profiling methods, CIA is composed of a number of steps or stages in which information about the offense is gathered, and determinations are made about its relevance and meaning. Despite the fact that an articulated methodology is available, there is much anecdotal evidence to suggest that protagonists of the FBI method do not adhere strictly to all steps or stages. Furthermore, many FBI employed and trained "profilers" are generally not qualified to perform certain analyses proposed as part of the method (for example, crime scene reconstruction; see Chisum, 2000; Superior Court of California, 1999).

In theory, CIA is a six-step method, though in reality it is five steps with the sixth step involving the arrest of an offender if one is identified. These first five steps are profiling inputs, decision process models, crime assessment, criminal profile, and investigation. The final phase (ostensibly the sixth) is apprehension.

Douglas and Burgess (1986, p. 9) suggest a seven-step process that is "quite similar to that used by clinicians to make a diagnosis and treatment plan." These seven steps are:

- Evaluation of the criminal act itself
- Comprehensive evaluation of the specifics of the crime scene(s)
- Comprehensive analysis of the victim
- Evaluation of preliminary police reports
- Evaluation of the medical examiner's autopsy protocol
- Development of profile with critical offender characteristics; and
- Investigative suggestions predicated on the construction of the profile

The FBI method is one of the most prevalent today; however, despite (or perhaps owing to) its widespread use, this method of profiling has suffered the most criticisms, including:

- The mythology of the FBI profiling unit has led some to suggest the hype is ill deserved (Jenkins, 1994) and enjoys little in the way of a scientific framework or scrutiny (Canter, Alison, Alison, and Wentink, 2004).

- Its popularity may be a function of simplicity in that it requires little or no training or knowledge to apply the prefabricated offender templates to current cases (Petherick, 2005; Turvey, 2008a).

- A number of case dynamics might influence the level of organization or disorganization evident in a case. This includes evidence dynamics, an offender under the influence of controlled substances, an interrupted offense, anger-motivated offenses, or staged crimes (Turvey, 2008a).

- The method simply reduces offender behavior to a few observable parameters (Turvey, 2008a).

- The original study on 36 offenders was considerably flawed and criticized heavily by the peer reviewers (Fox, 2004).

- The classifications were seemingly made on the basis of information about the offenders and the crime scene involved (Homant and Kennedy, 1998) according to the offenders themselves.

- Most offenders will be neither organized nor disorganized, but will fall somewhere between the two extremes (Ressler and Schachtman, 1992) although this "mixed" category is less helpful to investigators because this decreases discrimination between types of offenders (Baker, 2001) and presents a problem because the two categories are supposedly discrete.

- The casework of FBI profilers has been heavily criticized in individual cases (see Darkes, Otto, Poythress, and Starr, 1993; Fox and Levin, 1996; Investigations Subcommittee and Defense Policy Panel of the Committee on Armed Services, 1990; Kopel and Blackman, 1997; Thompson, 1999; Turvey, 2008a).

As a conclusion to criminal investigative analysis, let us consider the skills required in various domains to be able to apply this model. The following chart outlines possible background knowledge and experience which may be necessary to profiling, and whether it is required for this method specifically. A similar chart will be used to describe the background knowledge necessary to apply each method, to assist in conceptualizing and comparing the abilities and strengths of profilers using various types of profiling:

Background	Requirement
Research	Unnecessary
Law enforcement affiliation	Helpful
Psychology	Helpful
Investigative	Helpful
Forensic knowledge	Helpful
Analytical logic	Unnecessary

Diagnostic Evaluations

Diagnostic evaluations (DEs) do not represent a single profiling method or approach, but instead are generic descriptions of the services offered by psychologists and psychiatrists relying on clinical judgment in profiling offenders (Bradley, 2003). These evaluations are done on an as-needed basis (Wilson, Lincoln, and Kocsis, 1997) usually as one part of a broad range of psychological services offered by that individual. Historically, some of the earliest examples of profiling available are diagnostic evaluations, and prior to the formation of the FBI's Behavioral Sciences Unit, police sought the advice of psychologists and psychiatrists on particular crimes with varying results (Towl and Crighton, 1996). In modern terms, the contribution of mental health experts to investigations took shape when various police forces asked if clinical interpretations of unknown offenders might help in identification and apprehension (Canter, 1989).

Even though other profiling methods have come to the fore, Copson (1995) claims that over half of the profiling done in the United Kingdom is conducted by psychologists and psychiatrists using a clinical approach. In a study of the range of services offered by police psychologists, Bartol (1996) found that, on average, 2% of the total monthly workload of in-house psychologists was spent profiling, and that 3.4% of the monthly workload of part-time consultants was spent criminal profiling. It is not these results that are of particular interest, however, but that 70% of those surveyed did not feel comfortable giving this advice and felt that the practice was extremely questionable. Furthermore (Bartol, 1996, p. 79),

> One well-known police psychologist, with more than 20 years of experience in the field, considered criminal profiling "virtually useless and potentially dangerous." Many of the respondents wrote that much more research needs to be done before the process becomes a useful tool.

Without a clear and identifiable process, these evaluations are a little more idiosyncratic and rely to a large degree on the background of the individual compiling them. One's education, training, and experience dictate the approach taken at a given point in time, with the profile being an outgrowth of the clinician's understanding of criminals and criminal behavior, personality, and mental illness (Gudjonsson and Copson, 1997). Developmental and clinical issues play a considerable role in DE profiles, and Jackson and Bekerian (1997) dedicate a discussion in their work to these areas, focusing heavily on the application of personality theory to profiling.

Boon (1997) describes how psychoanalytic/psychodynamic, learning, dispositional/trait, humanist/cognitive, and alternative/Eastern philosophies affect case assessment. To illustrate how personality theories apply to profile compilation, Boon supplies several cases of extortion to which specific personality characteristics are applied. He concludes that the feedback given in the profile will always be reflective of the psychological framework employed by the clinician, with those employing a psychoanalytic background offering advice typical of the Freudian paradigm and so on.

Badcock (1997, p. 10) similarly discusses some of the background issues to offender development (i.e., developmental issues) and clinical issues (such as the prevalence of mental illness in offending populations):

> Where developmental issues are great enough and begin early enough they can change the entire concept of what is "normal" for an individual. Everyone tends to assume that what they are used to must be normal and some people grow up with what most others would consider abnormal ideas of the meaning of normality. People who have been seriously abused from an early age, for example, can grow up believing that abuse is the basis of normal relationships. They may have great difficulties in relating to others in ways that do not include abuse and some of them will become abusers themselves.

The implication is that, as these issues have the potential to impact on later behavior by the individual, it is necessary for profilers to have the capacity to understand how these manifest in behavior. Specific issues cited include jealousy, envy, control, power, sadomasochism, fantasy, and paraphilias.

Turco (1990), in a widely cited article, provides his own adaptation of the diagnostic approach through psychodynamic theory. Turco is critical of anyone without clinical experience (p. 151):

> The experienced clinician has an underlying inherent understanding of psychopathology, experience with predictability, a capacity to get into the mind of the perpetrator and a scientific approach without moral judgement or prejudice....The most productive circumstance likely to arise is when the profiler has both *clinical* (as opposed to academic) training and law enforcement experience. One cannot expect to obtain a graduate degree and make accurate predictions in the absence of a sound theoretical basis or clinical experience.

In examining the role of forensic psychiatrists, McGrath (2000, p. 321) provides the following reasons why they may be particularly suited to providing profiles:

- Their background in the behavioral sciences and their training in psychopathology place them in an enviable position to deduce personality characteristics from crime scene information.

- The forensic psychiatrist is in a good position to infer the meaning behind signature behaviors

- Given their training, education, and focus on critical and analytical thinking, the forensic psychiatrist is in a good position to "channel" their training into a new field.

Although these may seem obvious areas in which forensic mental health specialists can apply their skills, McGrath also notes that any involvement in the profiling process should not revolve around, or focus on, treatment issues. It is here that we shall turn to the criticisms of diagnostic evaluations:

■ Mental health officials must not fall prey to "role confusion" (McGrath, 2000; Petherick, 2006, p. 45) and give treatment advice while attempting to derive the characteristics of the offender.

■ While learning and personality theories may play a role, it is difficult, if not impossible, to determine the degree to which they apply in a given case until a structured clinical assessment with the perpetrator is undertaken by a mental health professional.

■ Many clinicians have no investigative experience and so there may be a disconnect between the perceived and actual requirements of an investigation (see Ainsworth, 2001; Canter, 1989; Dietz, 1985; West, 2000; Wilson, Lincoln, and Kocsis, 1997).

■ There is a reliance on indirect methods of assessment, including intuition, psychodynamic theories, and statistical reasoning (Gudjonsson and Copson, 1997).

■ Without a unified approach, theory, or process, diagnostic evaluations may be hit-and-miss, and any attempts to study the underlying reasoning or logic behind these profiles may be hampered by the inability to reproduce the train of thought that led to profile characteristics.

The following chart provides a list of the necessary background knowledge and experience required to perform a diagnostic evaluation.

Background	Requirement
Research	Helpful
Law enforcement affiliation	Unnecessary
Psychology	Required
Investigative	Unnecessary
Forensic knowledge	Unnecessary
Analytical logic	Unnecessary

Investigative Psychology

The main advocate of investigative psychology (IP) is David Canter, a British psychologist who promotes a scientific-research-based approach to the study of offender behavior. Investigative psychology is an inductive approach and is dependent on the amount of data collected (McGrath, 2000). Although sample size is a problem for some inductive methods, Canter is constantly carrying out research to improve the samples on which conclusions are based, and rigorous social scientific methods to expand knowledge are employed (Egger, 1998; Petherick, 2003). As a result, the conclusions are still inductive but based on more empirically robust evaluations.

As with the FBI approach, investigative psychology identifies profiling as only one part of an overall methodology. This is explained in Canter (2000, p. 1091):

> The domain of investigative psychology covers all aspects of psychology that are relevant to the conduct of criminal and civil investigations. Its focus is on the ways in which criminal activities may be examined and understood in order for the detection of crime to be effective and legal proceedings to be appropriate. As such, investigative psychology is concerned with psychological input to the full range of issues that relate to the management, investigation and prosecution of crime.

It is further explained in Canter (2004, p. 7):

> The broadening and deepening of the contributions that psychology can make to police investigations, beyond serial killers and personality profiles, to include the effective utilisation of police information, through interviews and from police records, as well the study of police investigations and decision support systems has lead to the identification of a previously unnamed domain of applied psychology... called...Investigative Psychology.

According to the program's Web site, investigative psychology provides the following:

> [A] scientific and systematic basis to previously subjective approaches to all aspects of the detection, investigation and prosecution of crimes. This behavioral science contribution can be thought of as operating at different stages of any investigation, from that of the crime itself, through the gathering of information and on to the actions of police officers working to identify the criminal then on to the preparation of a case for court.

Canter (1998, p. 11) has also gone to great pains to differentiate IP from "every-day" profiling:

> So should psychologists be kept out of the investigation of crimes? Clearly as the Director of the Institute of Investigative Psychology I do think that psychologists have much to offer to criminal and other investigations. My central point is to make a distinction between "profiling" and Investigative Psychology.

Further, to distinguish between IP and those idiosyncratic profiling approaches, the following is noted (Canter, 1998, p. 11):

> Investigative psychology is a much more prosaic activity. It consists of the painstaking examination of patterns of criminal behavior and the

testing out of those patterns of trends that may be of value to police investigators.... Investigative psychologists also accept that there are areas of criminal behavior that may be fundamentally enigmatic.

This method, commonly referred to as the five-factor model, has five main components that reflect an offender's past and present. These are interpersonal coherence, significance of time and place, criminal characteristics, criminal career, and forensic awareness. These components will be addressed in turn.

Interpersonal coherence refers to the way people adopt a style of interaction when dealing with others, where crime is an interpersonal transaction involving characteristic ways of dealing with other people (Canter, 1995). Canter believes that offenders treat their victims in a similar way to that in which they treat people in their daily lives; that is, criminals carry out actions that are a direct extension of the transactions they have with other people (Wilson and Soothill, 1996). For example, a rapist who exhibits selfishness with friends, family, and colleagues in daily life will also exhibit selfishness with victims. Similarly, an offender may select victims who possess characteristics of people important to him or her (Muller, 2000). This belief is not unique to IP, and most profiling approaches rely on the notion of interpersonal coherence in developing offender characteristics (Petherick, 2003).

As "interpersonal processes gain much of their psychological nuance from the time and place in which they occur" (Canter, 1989, p. 14), time and space considerations should also be reflective of some aspects of the offender. That is, the time and place may be specifically chosen by the offender and so provide further insight into his or her actions in the form of mental maps. The implication is that "an offender will feel more comfortable and in control in areas which he knows well" (Ainsworth, 2001, p. 199). Two considerations are important: the first being the specific location, and the second being the general spatial behavior which is a function of specific crime sites (Canter, 1989). Canter (2003) dedicated a whole work to these aspects that are largely based on the foundational theory of environmental criminology.

Next, criminal characteristics provide investigators with some idea about the type of crime they are dealing with. The idea is to determine "whether the nature of the crime and the way it is committed can lead to some classifications of what is characteristic...based upon interviews with criminals and empirical studies" (Canter, 1989, p. 14). This is an inductive component of the approach and, as it stands, is similar to attempts made by the FBI in applying an organized/disorganized typology.

Studying a criminal career provides an understanding of the way offenders may modify behavior in light of experience (Nowikowski, 1995). There is room for adaptation and change, with many criminals responding to victim, police, or location dynamics owing to learning and experience. This adaptation and change may be reflective of past experiences while offending. For example, a criminal may bind and gag a current victim, based on the screams and resistance of a past victim (Canter, 1989). This may reflect the evolution of MO displayed by many offenders who learn through subsequent offenses and continue to refine their behavior. Additionally, the nature and types of precautionary behaviors may provide some insight into whether the offender has experience with or exposure to investigative practices.

Finally, forensic awareness may show an increase in learning based on past experience with the criminal justice system. Perpetrators may be sophisticated in that they will use techniques that hinder police investigations, such as wearing a mask or gloves or through attempts to destroy other evidence (Ainsworth, 2000). A rapist may also turn to using condoms to prevent the transfer of biological fluids for DNA analysis.

Further, five characteristics utilized in the IP method may be instructive to investigators. They are self-explanatory and include residential location, criminal biography, domestic/social characteristics, personal characteristics, and occupation/education history (Ainsworth, 2000). While there is not necessarily any greater weighting placed on any of these profile features, Boon and Davies (2003) suggest that research from the United Kingdom identifies residential location and criminal history as the most beneficial, whereas domestic, social, occupational, and educational characteristics are of least value (again highlighting the emphasis IP places on crime geography).

The following criticisms could be made of investigative psychology:

- The rigorous reconstruction of offender behavior is not undertaken, so the meaning of behavior may be questionable.
- The generalization of past cases to the current case is dangerous and potentially misleading.
- Offender characteristics are only a possibility, and nothing concrete or specific about the current case is offered.
- IP assumes that the research on a particular crime type is valid to the crime type (general research on murder versus specific research on domestic homicide) and to the crime under consideration (that the probabilities within the research apply to the extant case).

The following chart provides the background requirements necessary for those practicing investigative psychology.

Background	Requirement
Research	Required
Law enforcement affiliation	Helpful
Psychology	Helpful
Investigative	Unnecessary
Forensic knowledge	Unnecessary
Analytical logic	Unnecessary

DEDUCTION: THE SUGGESTED APPROACH

In profiling terms, Behavioral Evidence Analysis (BEA) is the most recent of the individual profiling methods. The method was developed by Brent Turvey in the late 1990s. It is based on forensic science and the collection and interpretation of physical evidence, and by extension what this means about an offender. BEA is primarily a deductive method and, as a result, will not make a conclusion about an offender unless specific physical evidence exists that suggests the characteristic. This means that, instead of relying on averaged offender types, BEA profilers conduct a detailed examination of the scene and related behaviors and argue from this what offender characteristics are evidenced in the behavior and scene.

The strength of BEA lies in the fact that the profiler works only with what is known; nothing is assumed or surmised (Petherick, 2003), and a great deal of time is spent determining the veracity of the physical evidence and its relationship to the criminal event. In this way, evidence that is irrelevant or unrelated has little evidentiary value and is not given weight in the final analysis. This assists in maintaining objectivity and leads to a more accurate and useful end product.

Like its inductive counterparts, BEA involves a number of steps, with each building on previous stages to provide an overall picture.

The first stage of BEA is referred to as the *forensic analysis* and "must be performed on the physical evidence to establish the corresponding behavioral evidence in a case before a BEA profile can be attempted" (Petherick and Turvey, 2008b, p. 135). In this stage all the physical evidence surrounding a case is examined to assess its relevance and determine its overall nature and quality. This step also ensures the probative quality of the evidence should the case end up in court. Ultimately, the forensic analysis informs the profilers what evidence they have to base a profile on, what evidence may be missing, what evidence may have been misinterpreted, and what value that evidence has in the subsequent analyses. Thornton (2006, p. 37) contextualizes the importance of physical evidence:

> We are interested in physical evidence because it may tell a story. Physical evidence—properly collected, properly analysed, and properly interpreted—may establish the factual circumstances at the time the crime occurred. In short, the crime may be reconstructed. Our principal interest is ultimately in the reconstruction, not the evidence per se.... Also, along with the ethos is an ethic—a moral obligation to maintain the integrity of the processes by means of which the reconstruction is accomplished. In short, the ethics of crime reconstruction represents an imperative to "get it right." "Getting it right" involves more than guessing correctly. It necessitates a systematic process. It involves the proper recognition of the evidence, the winnowing of the relevant wheat from the irrelevant chaff, and the precise application of logic, both inductive and deductive. The process is not trivial.

Because this stage relates to the examination of physical evidence, profilers who are not familiar with or qualified to interpret physical evidence should not undertake this task. Instead, they should work with trained professionals whom they trust to examine the evidence on which they are basing their conclusions. The importance of establishing a set of given facts from information given during an investigation should be apparent, but this information is all too often assumed as correct without question. Two cases that exemplify the pitfalls of working with information that has been gathered and interpreted by others are the investigation of the explosion aboard the USS Iowa and the homicide of Joel Andrew Shanbrom, for which brief explanations are provided next.

USS Iowa

Early one morning in 1989, Turret Two on board the USS Iowa exploded, killing 47 of the ship's crew (Thompson, 1999). The explosion sent shockwaves throughout the U.S. Navy, with the subsequent investigation revealing dangerous practices, incompetence, cover-ups, and investigative failures, only some of which were related to the explosion and deaths. Given the magnitude of the disaster, the Navy consulted agents from the FBI's Behavioral Sciences Unit to provide some insight into what they felt were the actions of a suicidal homosexual by the name of Clayton Hartwig stationed on the ship.

In an attempt to provide this insight, the FBI agents used a technique known as Equivocal Death Analysis (EDA) to examine Hartwig. While the EDA was not responsible for first bringing attention to him as the person responsible, it was most certainly responsible for cementing this opinion in the minds of investigators and the naval executive. What followed was a series of events that perpetuated bad judgment and showed just how dangerous it can be to accept at face value information that has not been observed or collected first hand: investigators from the Naval Investigative Service (NIS) started by assuming Hartwig's guilt and then provided this information to the FBI profilers, whose assessment fed this line of thinking back to the NIS and the Navy.

With regards to their analysis, a report of the Investigations Subcommittee of the Committee on Armed Services House of Representatives noted two important issues with the FBI's analysis (pp. 6–7):

- The procedures the FBI used in preparing the EDA were inadequate and unprofessional. As a matter of policy, the analysts do not state the speculative nature of their analyses. Moreover, the parameters that the FBI agents used, either provided to them or chosen by them, biased their results toward only one of three deleterious conclusions. Further biasing their conclusions, the agents relied on insufficient and sometimes suspect evidence. The FBI agents' EDA was invalidated by 10 of 14 professional psychologists and psychiatrists, heavily criticized even by those professionals who found the Hartwig possibility plausible.

- The FBI analysis gave the Navy false confidence in the validity of the FBI's work. If the Navy had relied solely on the work of the NIS's own staff psychologist—which emphasized that such psychological autopsies are by definition "speculative"—the Navy would likely not have found itself so committed to the Hartwig thesis.

Despite the questionable nature of the EDA process and its methodology, there were more fundamental concerns about the material on which the analysis was based. The following concerns were also raised by the Investigations Subcommittee about the process and results:

- Richard Ault (working for the FBI) admitted that the Navy had only provided him with fragments of the evidence assembled against Hartwig.

- Ault was asked who wrote the poem "Disposable Heroes," a key piece of information on which Hartwig's alleged homosexuality hinged, and he didn't know.

- Asked whether the agents were aware that another gunner's mate told Admiral Milligan that another sailor had written the poem, Hazelwood stated that this was immaterial because Hartwig had the potential to see it.

- The agents were asked if they were aware that David Smith had recanted the testimony used in their EDA, and they claimed they weren't sure what he had recanted.

- The agents had relied entirely on the information provided to them by the NIS and had not done any interviews themselves.

There were further concerns about the veracity of the information on which the profile was based (Investigations Subcommittee and Defense Policy Panel of the Committee on Armed Services, 1990, p. 42):

> The preponderance of material came from interviews conducted and provided to the FBI by the NIS. As the subcommittee found earlier, serious questions were raised about the leading nature or bias introduced in the interviews by the NIS interviewing agents. Some witnesses denied making statements to NIS that are significant to the profile...in at least one instance, the witness recanted several portions of his testimony, but was still considered a valuable witness.

Joel Andrew Shanbrom

Another example stressing the importance of not only establishing a set of facts for oneself, but also in assessing evidence dynamics, is the homicide of Joel Andrew Shanbrom, a school district police officer in California. Shanbrom's wife, Jennifer, claimed that she was upstairs bathing their son when she heard an altercation downstairs between her husband and some [black] men. A profile of the alleged offender was compiled by Mark Safarik of the FBI's Behavioral Analysis Unit.

Safariks's assessment gave considerable weight to the apparent ransacking of certain rooms in the house, including that of the son Jacob:

> The dressers and night stands in the master bedroom, Gisondi's room, and Jacob's bedroom had been disturbed.... In Jacob's bedroom, a room clearly identified as a child's bedroom, the dresser drawers were pulled out to give the appearance they were searched. Such a room would not be expected to contain any valuables and this would have been passed over by offender(s) looking for valuables.

While police had trouble with Jennifer Fletcher's story from the outset, particularly after discovering significant life insurance policies on her husband, the profile remained steadfast to its assessment of someone ransacking the bedroom in an attempt to stage a burglary. It wasn't until later that an expert profiler, in providing trial assistance to the defense, was able to establish through consideration of evidence dynamics that the scene had in fact been altered by a police officer in her search for clothing for Jacob Shanbrom, who was naked and cold from hiding in a bedroom closet with his mother since the alleged homicide. In a postscript to this case, Jennifer and her new husband, Matthew Fletcher, were both charged with the 1998 murder of Shanbrom after facing counts of fraud and conspiracy (Associated Press, 2002; Blankstein, 2002).

It is also necessary to establish the accuracy and quality of the information which serves as the basis of the profile because of *evidence dynamics*. This refers to influences that change, relocate, obscure, or obliterate physical evidence, regardless of the intent of the person or circumstance that bring about the change (Chisum and Turvey, 2008). So, evidence dynamics may be the result of the offender moving from one room to another during an offense, a bleeding but not yet deceased victim crawling down a hallway, paramedics attending the scene of a violent crime, or firefighters attending a fire scene. However, evidence dynamics is important in the case far beyond the extant circumstances of the crime scene, playing a role from the time the evidence is deposited until the final adjudication of the case (Chisum and Turvey, 2000). To provide some context to the way that evidence dynamics may alter the physical presentation of crime scene actions, consider the following example from Chisum and Turvey (2000, p. 9):

> A youth was stabbed several times by rival gang members. He ran for a home but collapsed in the walkway. A photo of the scene taken prior to the arrival of the EMT team shows a blood trail and that the victim was lying face down. Subsequent photos show the 5 EMT's working on the body on his back. He had been rolled over onto the blood pool. It became impossible for bloodstain patterns interpretation to be used to reconstruct the events leading to the death of the youth.

Given these examples, the importance of the forensic analysis and establishing a set of facts for oneself should be clear. Although only three cases have been used as examples, there are numerous others with a similar lack of critical appraisal of the presenting evidence (see also Superior Court of California, 1999). The other aspect of the forensic analysis that is important and factors in evidence dynamics is *crime reconstruction*, which is "the determination of the actions surrounding the commission of a crime" (Chisum, 2002, p. 81). Popular conceptions of crime reconstruction abound, with some believing the process involves the physical rebuilding of the crime scene in another location. Saferstein (2004) suggests that "reconstruction supports a likely sequence of events by the observation and evaluation of physical evidence, as well as statements made by witnesses and those involved with the incident." Rynearson (2002) incorporates "common sense reasoning" and its use with forensic science to interpret evidence as it resides at the crime scene. Cooley (1999, p. 1), in an excellent paper written while a graduate student at the University of New Haven, suggests that crime scene reconstruction is the foundation of the BEA method:

> Deductive reasoning, via crime scene reconstruction, can and will provide the profiler with the appropriate information allowing him or her to construct the most logical profile of an unknown offender. This will enable the profiler to supply the requesting agency with investigatively relevant information.

The second stage of the BEA process, *victimology*, examines all aspects of the victim including lifestyle, hobbies, habits, friends, enemies, and demographic features. The information derived through the victimology can help to determine the existence or extent of any relationship between the victim and the offender. Two other related components of the victimology are victim exposure and offender exposure. *Victim exposure* refers to the possibility of suffering harm or loss by virtue of an individual's personal, professional, and social life (Petherick and Turvey, 2008c). This risk is further partitioned into overall exposure (lifestyle exposure) and the exposure present at the moment of victimization (incident exposure). As a general rule, exposure can be low, medium, or high, indicating that a person is at a low exposure by virtue of personal, professional, and social life and so forth. In BEA just as much time should be spent examining the victim's personality and behavioral characteristics as would be spent assessing the offender.

In the third stage, crime scene analysis, the profiler determines such factors as the method of approach and attack, method of control, location type, nature and sequence of any sexual acts, materials used, type of verbal activity, and any precautionary acts the offender engaged in (Petherick and Turvey, 2008b), such as wearing gloves or a balaclava, altering one's voice, or wearing a condom. This stage also sets out to determine what types of crime scenes are involved in a criminal event. They include the point of contact; primary, secondary, and tertiary scenes; and the dump or disposal site. For example, a victim with extensive wounds that would have produced a substantial amount of bleeding is found in an area devoid of bloodstains. This suggests the victim was killed elsewhere (a primary crime scene) and then moved to the scene where the body was found (the dump or disposal site).

The final stage is the actual offender profile, known as offender characteristics. All the information from the previous stages is integrated and assessed through deductive reasoning to determine what the physical evidence, victimology, and crime scene characteristics collectively argue about the offender. Turvey (2008b) argues against offering the profile characteristics of age, sex, race, and intelligence because these are typically assessed inductively and not based on physical evidence. As mentioned in the "Inputs and Outputs of Criminal Profiling" section earlier, it is argued that the following four conclusions can be offered deductively and posited with a high degree of confidence:

- Knowledge of the victim
- Knowledge of the crime scene
- Knowledge of methods and materials
- Criminal skill

While BEA is a method relying on deductive logic, it could not, however, be characterized as purely deductive. The reason is that the process of deduction relies in part on induction, which produces theories that may be tested against the evidence. This is confirmed by Stock (2004, p. 5), who writes, "in the natural order of treatment inductive logic precedes deductive, since it is induction which supplies us with the general truths, from which we reason down in our deductive inferences."

Because of the reliance on physical evidence and the reconstruction of the behavior involved in the criminal event, many inductive generalizations will be employed. Wound patterns and victimology are two such examples in which inductions may be used to form the basis of a later deduction. The type of knife used, its width, the length of the blade, and other characteristics of edged weapons have typically been determined through a study of known weapons and their features. However, the application of this knowledge to the particular features of a set of wounds present on a victim's body involves the deductive application of this knowledge. Petherick (2003, p. 186) presents another example of the application of the reasoning:

> If a prostitute is murdered, a principally inductive approach suggests that because of her profession she was at high risk of victimisation. However, a more in depth deductive approach may determine that she had a small select clientele, was naturally cautious, had taken self defense training, and worked only in established premises. All of these factors work to reduce her risk.

There are no direct criticisms of BEA in the literature, though there is some minor discussion of deductive approaches in general. Most seem to be quite confused by the application of the reasoning (Canter, 2004; Godwin, 1999), whereas others provide some cursory discussion of it but seem unsure of how the overall process operates. Holmes and Holmes (2002, p. 7) note that "much care is taken from the examination of forensic reports, victimology, and so forth and the report will take much longer to develop using only this approach." These authors seem largely unaware of the finer points of logic, such as induction being a component of and important to the overall process of deduction. Readers are also left with the distinct impression that the thoroughness of the approach (and the subsequent time involved) is pejorative. A final deductively rendered opinion will rely on inductively derived knowledge, though Holmes and his colleague tend to treat both processes as being dichotomous and largely exclusive. This suggests a fundamental lack of overall knowledge of the processes involved in reasoning.

McGrath (2000) has however identified one critical observation of this method, and that is if the initial premises on which conclusions are based are wrong, then the subsequent conclusions will also be wrong. Given that one of the primary purposes of the EFA is to establish the veracity of the premises, this is not necessarily a problem as long as profilers are aware that it is incumbent on them to establish the basic information on which their decisions are based. If the basis of the premises cannot be established, then this may limit the number of characteristics that can be offered (because deductive approaches will derive conclusions only on what has been unequivocally established). Beyond these observations, there has been little criticism of this approach.[2]

[2]While it is noted that BEA is a largely deductive method and does not rely on research in developing the final conclusion, research is employed to generate hypotheses that are then tested against the physical evidence which subsequently informs the deductive decision-making process.

The following chart breaks down the background knowledge necessary to use a deductive approach to profiling.

Background	Requirement
Research	Helpful
Law enforcement affiliation	Unnecessary
Psychology	Required
Investigative	Required
Forensic knowledge	Required
Analytical logic	Required

CRIMINAL PROFILING EDUCATION

The issue of profiler education has not been touched upon in any significant way in the literature on profiling, with most discussions revolving around the theoretical paradigm offered by respective authors. That is, those psychologists engaged in the process argue for an educational experience including advanced study in psychology; law enforcement officers engaged in profiling (mostly the FBI and those they train) argue that law enforcement experience is a necessity; those who approach profiling from the perspective of physical evidence argue that a broad-based understanding of physical evidence, its relevance, and meaning is important. The following sections of this chapter will discuss the issues relevant to profiler education, what is required, and where to get it.

Tertiary Education

A tertiary education typically involves formal and structured classes in a variety of areas as dictated by the degree program students enroll in. Those taking psychology will be educated in aspects of human behavior and cognition, from introductory courses on the history of psychology through to abnormal psychology, the neuropsychological basis of behavior, and treatment and assessment. Those taking criminology or criminal justice programs will be exposed to the role, structure, and function of the police, courts, and prisons. Depending on the program, they may also get extensive training in the behavioral sciences in areas that have traditionally been the province of psychology (human behavior and psychological disorders, among others). For those taking accounting or business, students will be taught business administration, entrepreneurship, account and book-keeping, and other business-related activities.

The point is this: not all educational experiences are equal, and the degree of instruction one receives in any area related to profiling differs based on a variety of factors. This may be owing to the educational institution or degree program at a broad level, there being critical differences not only among the institutions, but also between two programs even of the same name. Consider the following example: Two universities in the same general location both offer Criminology and Criminal Justice degrees. One is housed within a social science faculty, and the other is located within a law school. In the first program, there is a degree of overlap between criminological offerings and psychological offerings, exposing students to a range of issues relating to human behavior and cognition. The students in this program will develop a healthy understanding of behavioral science and how this applies to the profiling endeavor. In the latter program, students are taught primarily by legal professionals and theoretical sociologists in such a way that they develop a healthy understanding of policy and procedure as it relates to the legal system. It should be clear that students in the first program would be better placed to consider a career in profiling than students in the second.

Staffing may also dictate the quality of a given program, with those staff undertaking research or casework in a given area perhaps being more equipped to provide a holistic education than those approaching any given topic from a purely theoretical point of view. The reason is that they will be better able to understand and subsequently explain the nuances of casework, evidence examination, and report writing.

Interested students should seek out a program that not only has a sufficient level of education in the behavioral sciences, but also one that is taught by staff who understand the theory of what they are teaching, why it is important, and how it applies.

With regards to specific areas of study, the following discrete areas of study are suggested:

- Criminology
- Psychology
- Forensic Science
- Law

The areas of criminology and psychology should be self-explanatory and have been covered elsewhere within the chapter. Forensic science is suggested because it will provide a fundamental understanding of the nature of physical evidence, its identification, limitations, benefits, and interpretation. Because profiling is based on an assessment of behavior, and the behavior is often determined through the lens of the physical evidence, students seeking work in the area would be left wanting in an education that did not encompass some aspect of forensic science. Law, or at least some understanding of the criminal justice system, expert evidence, and procedure, will be required because profilers, whether private or government employed, are forensic examiners. As such, there is an expectation that they may have to provide evidence in a court of law before a trier of fact.

It should also be noted that the subject area under which one decides to study is not the only thing to think about when preparing for work in profiling. Similar to the issues of institutions and programs, all things are not created equal when it comes to studying criminal profiling. Unlike many courses in the criminology field, such as theories of crime courses which have an fairly predictable and consistent curriculum across teachers and universities, not all courses related to profiling are created equal. That is, depending on what school the profiling course is run from, and who teaches it, which aspects of profiling are important, which methods should be utilized, and which issues are most salient will differ. Students should seek out those courses that compare and contrast different methods; that study actual profiles and real cases; and that endorse the scientific method, analytical logic, and critical thinking.

As an adjunct to these forms of tertiary study, it is also suggested that profilers engage in short courses. However, there are a number of perils and pitfalls evident in such a practice, as outlined next.

Bricks, Mortar, and the Socratic Method

For those who are already working in the criminal justice system or outside it, there is often a desire to return to university to acquire a new or round out an existing education. It has been the authors' experience over the years that there are a variety of reasons why students may return to university, including change of a career, promotion or advancement, interest, or simply to increase their knowledge base.

Aside from choosing the right university, program, and staff, students are further presented with a number of other options in terms of full-time or part-time degrees, on-campus, and external programs. Which option to take will be dictated largely by the requirements of the prospective student, availability and commitments to work and family, motivation, and financial means. However, students should not choose a university simply because it meets their time commitments or is affordable; doing so may mean that, in the grand scheme of things, the quality of the program is sacrificed for expedience of completion or because it doesn't unduly stretch the purse strings. The net result is that they spend a given amount of time and energy on a program that means little if anything in terms of their vocational prospects or the quality of the information they receive and bring to bear at a later time.

For busy professionals, their choices may be limited to those programs that offer classes at night or via an external-only option where students are sent class materials, furnished with deadlines in which to submit their work, and contact their instructors through a variety of electronic means. Some distance programs also employ an on-campus option during the semester, often titled a "residential school," where students attend the university for lectures and tutorials and face time with teaching staff.

While this is true in some instances, it does not apply to all distance programs. Unfortunately, in today's competitive educational market, some institutions have watered down their approach to education such that students are never seen, feedback on assessment is scarce, and they are not given the opportunity to engage in any meaningful way with their peers. The most significant aspect of this would be the lack of ability to engage in a question-and-answer environment so as to have the basis of their beliefs questioned, to highlight the flaws in thinking, and to shape their critical thinking skills. This is the province of the *Socratic Method*.

According to Goldberg (2007, p. 18):

> The Socratic Method, which takes its name from the process Socrates used to ascertain philosophical truths, exposes the weakness of arguments through a process of relentless inquiry.
>
> ...
>
> While the Socratic Method forces students to think on their feet, it also replicates the tension of standing before a judge in court, knowing he or she can humble you at any moment. "The tension is a necessary part of the learning experience," says University of Chicago law professor Richard Epstein, a proponent of the Socratic Method, who is thought to be one of its most skilled practitioners.

The Socratic Method is "an approach to knowledge building and problem solving based on discussion and debate" (Chisum and Turvey, 2007, p. 100). It is process oriented in that it seeks to identify weak assumptions in an argument and, through repeatedly interrogating these assumptions, arriving at a more valid conclusion or answer. It is what the first author refers to as "intellectual Darwinism"—a reference to Darwin's theory of evolution whereby weak theories are systematically culled.

As a pedagogical tool, the Socratic Method involves interaction between two or more people where one (usually a lecturer or instructor) asks a question of another (a student or participant). The responses are then queried within a general or specific theoretical framework and any flaws identified. Further questions are then tailored to incorporate the new arguments, and the process goes on. This step-wise procedure for the Socratic Method is identified by Pedersen (2006, p. 1) as it applies to legal reasoning:

Students study cases before class.

In class, the professor calls on a student, with no advance notice.

The student gives a recitation of the facts and the procedural history.

The professor questions the student, probing underlying legal issues, thus forcing the student to identify relevant facts, question assumptions, take a position and argue its defence.

Meanwhile the rest of the class remains attentive by answering the professor's questions in their own mind.

The same process may be applied to the process of profiling and crime analysis in the following way regarding motive (the following is hypothetical, but follows general discussions that take place in both authors' classes regarding Criminal Profiling and Behavioral Evidence Analysis):

Q: With regards to the case study, let's discuss the motive or motives that are evident in the offender's behavior.
A: I think that the motive for the crime was murder.
Q: But murder is a term that describes a behavior or penal classification. A motive is a physical or psychological need. So what would you suggest the motive would be?
A: (Another student) The motive might be profit, as the offender didn't do anything sexual with the victim.
Q: So what evidence do we have that the motive was profit? What would you expect to find in a profit offense?
A: You would expect to see something stolen: money, jewelry, computers, or something of value. There is no evidence that anything has been stolen.
Q: So if nothing has been stolen, is it likely the motive was profit?
A: It might be possible that the offense was interrupted, and that the offender didn't have the chance to actually take anything....

[3]During the Behavioral Evidence Analysis class taught by the first author, the students spend 12 weeks working on an actual case file including autopsy reports, crime scene photographs, police brief of evidence, and other material. Each week, the Socratic Method is employed, beginning with basic questions before moving onto more advanced issues, culminating in the students' writing a report on the case outlining their conclusions and reasoning.

If an acceptable answer is reached, then a new question is developed and the process begins again. For a more detailed or complex problem, the process may take minutes or hours, or may even span multiple sessions.[3]

It should be noted that the process follows along similar lines to the use of the scientific method as a form of inquiry, which is a "way to investigate how something works, or how something happened, through the development of hypotheses and subsequent attempts at falsification through testing and other accepted means" (Petherick and Turvey, 2008b, p. 47). Furthermore, the process works in much the same way as dissecting a case for which a criminologist's opinion has been sought. In this way, by utilizing the scientific method, we are essentially teaching students how to pull a case apart, put it back together, and infer conclusions from it.

With both authors working in the tertiary education environment, our recommendation to students is that they seek out a relevant education that will better equip them to understand the range of issues they will face in the analysis of crime and criminal behavior. They should seek out instructors who are actively working, researching, or publishing in the areas they teach; and they should seek this out in an actual institution, with staff who can mentor and challenge them, students with whom they can engage, and educational requirements that will provide them with the theory and practice that will enable them to become tomorrow's practitioners.

Short Courses: Perils and Pitfalls

There is an inherent attraction in that which requires the least effort; anything that demands less of our time and attention is seen as being of greater significance regardless of that fact that whatever it is may be of lesser value. Because of this tendency toward the path of least resistance, *short courses* offer a significant attraction for many.

A short course is any truncated pathway to education or information that is offered in an intensive mode, often without the enforcement of educational standards or assessment. Before going any further, we need to point out that both authors are advocates of short courses, given the right context and framework.

Perhaps one of the best discussions of short courses comes from Chisum (2007, pp. 314–317). While this discussion relates specifically to short courses in bloodstain pattern analysis, the juxtaposition to general criminology should be easy to see:

> In addition to reading the recommended publications, it is advised that anyone interested in crime reconstruction take a course in bloodstain analysis from a qualified forensic scientist. These courses can be useful for providing certain basic overviews of fundamental concepts. However, depending on the scientific background of the instructor, they may be lacking in certain crucial areas. A true scientist will find that a majority of the short bloodstain classes are lacking with regard to a discussion of accuracy, precision, and significant numbers. Appreciating these deficiencies is the difference between the technician's pedantic understanding of bloodstains and the forensic scientist's interpretive role in the reconstruction of the crime.

The preceding passage is useful and captures both the benefit and dangers of short courses; they are useful in providing overviews of certain basic concepts, but many such courses are not taught by qualified instructors, and they are by no means a holistic approach to education in any given domain.

But don't get us wrong. Many authors in this volume run short courses in many different countries around the world, and these courses do have value. It is the authors' opinion that short courses are useful for a variety of reasons, including the following:

- They provide an overview of certain fundamental concepts.
- They keep students and professionals abreast of new theories and techniques.
- They give potential students an insight into a discrete area so they can make informed choices about future streams of study.
- Short courses can be invaluable for teaching process-oriented tasks.
- Students and professionals can learn a variety of valuable skills through a case study approach that is not always practical in formal tertiary environments.

The main point is that a short course, while offering a number of benefits, should be considered only one small part of an overall educational approach; they should not be taken as a standalone. That is, taking one short course on profiling does not qualify a person to represent himself or herself as a profiler, or to actively profile ongoing cases; this would be considered dangerous, irresponsible, and dishonest.

CRIMINAL PROFILING AND THE CRIMINOLOGIST

The argument for the involvement of criminologists in profiling is relatively straightforward on its face. Criminologists are those who, by definition, are involved in the study of crime, so it would seem a natural extension of their other responsibilities. However, the reality is far from this clear. Some criminologists are involved only in research activities, an endeavor that may leave them ill equipped to understand the foibles of human behavior in a practical sense. Some criminologists are involved in other discrete areas, such as crime prevention, victimology, policy and procedure, or purely theoretical areas that will similarly leave them ill equipped in the evaluation of specific criminal acts. Recall from the first chapter, criminologists by their nature come from an array of similarly vast and diverse backgrounds including sociology, anthropology, psychology, psychiatry, law enforcement, or medicine, among others. Some will be able to lay legitimate claim to a stake in the profiling community; some would never even make the attempt; whereas others still will lack the acumen but jump on the bandwagon, so to speak, of an area that is popular among the media, other professionals, and students. Given this, it is necessary to explore a more concrete foundation for education and background requirements for criminologists who want to "try their hand" at profiling.

The main suggestion we would offer for criminologists involved in profiling is to ensure that their knowledge is as well rounded and holistic as possible. Just because one is an "expert" in "crime" does not mean that one is an expert in all areas of crime, regardless of what he or she thinks. As such, the criminologist-profiler should make every effort to educate himself or herself in the areas of behavioral science, physical evidence, and the law.

Criminologists should have as detailed knowledge as possible in the different areas in which they will analyze evidence as profilers. This means acknowledging that different kinds of analysis require different experience, education, and training. It also means knowing their own limits and where their work stops and that of another should start. It means not going beyond their own qualifications and abilities, and knowing when to raise their hands for help. It means being cognitively aware enough to understand the limits of what they can— and can't—do.

As suggested by the discussion on profiling inputs earlier, the range of material criminologists-profilers may be expected to deal with is considerable. From autopsy reports, to first response police reports, to crime reconstructions, to witness statements and crime scene photographs, criminologists-profilers needs to know what they are looking at, what they are looking for, how to interpret it, and what it means within the global context of the crime. Lacking in any of these areas will result in nothing less than an incomplete examination of the facts, which will lead to a dangerously incomplete assessment and possible flawed conclusions.

So what does all this mean? The answer is simple, but lost on a few overzealous individuals who fail to appreciate what and where their limits are. This doesn't mean that one has to be a forensic pathologist to read an autopsy report, but it does mean that one should know the difference between cause, mechanism, and manner of death. It doesn't mean that one has to be a bloodstain pattern analyst, but it does mean one knows what an angle of impact is, the difference between high and low velocity spatter, and how the surface of an object will effect the bloodstain pattern. It doesn't mean one has to be a forensic scientist, but it does mean one needs to understand the difference between a positive result, a negative result, and an inconclusive result.

So, based on this, criminologists-profilers should work with other professionals they know can be trusted and who produce valid work. They need to know enough of the language to ask educated questions and to understand what a response means in both a theoretical sense and an applied one (that is, how the answer to their questions impacts their analysis and conclusions).

If nothing else, this highlights the multidisciplinary and often team-based approach that profilers should take. It also warns us that short course education is not enough and that every person has limits—even though we don't often like to admit them.

SUMMARY

Criminologists may be well suited to the practice of criminal profiling, provided their education is complete in the sense that it has equipped them to understand the intricacies of offender behavior, including an assessment of the physical evidence that creates the record of it. They may be further suited to profiling because their training and education often involved instruction not only in social sciences, but also in law, so that they understand the limits of expert witnesses and reports. Furthermore, they may be suited to the task of profiling by virtue of the analytical processes they employ in other aspects of their work.

This chapter provided students and practicing criminologists with an overview of criminal profiling, the "inputs" and "outputs" of the process, the nature of logic and reasoning, and the major paradigms involved in profiling. These have included the inductive methods of criminal investigative analysis, investigative psychology, and diagnostic evaluations. The authors have also suggested a preferred theoretical/practical approach in Behavioral Evidence Analysis, a predominantly deductive method of profiling involving the detailed analysis and reconstruction of physical evidence, victimology, and crime analysis.

As criminologists, we have also been warned not to be carried away with our own abilities, but to know the limits of our own analysis and when to seek help. In this way, criminologists-profilers will be able to provide more accurate and forensically oriented assessments of crime and criminal behavior and to assist the police in their investigative decision processes and the trier of fact in their determinations of culpability.

Review Questions

1. Describe the goals of criminal profiling and how they differ between the investigative and trial phases.
2. What are profile inputs? Why are they crucial to any profiling effort?
3. Name and explain the two types of logic used to produce profiles.
4. T/F Deductive profiles are static.

5. Describe the organized/disorganized dichotomy which makes up the FBI method of profiling. What are some of criticisms leveled at this dichotomy?
6. T/F Diagnostic evaluations may be doubly helpful in investigations because they can also provide treatment advice.
7. T/F Forensic knowledge is not necessary to practice investigative psychology.
8. Describe Behavioral Evidence Analysis and how it differs from the other three profiling methods.

REFERENCES

Ainsworth, P.B., 2000. Psychology and Crime: Myths and Reality. Longman, Essex.

Ainsworth, P.B., 2001. Offender Profiling and Crime Analysis. Willan Publishing, Devon.

Alexandra, A., Matthews, S., Miller, M., 2002. Reasons, Values and Institutions. Tertiary Press, Croydor, VA.

Associated Press, 2002. Wife of Slain Man Charged. Las Vegas Review Journal. http://www.reviewjournal.com/lvrj_home/2002/Mar-02–Sat-2002/news/18218577.html (accessed 14.11.05).

Ault, R., Reese, J.T., 1980. A Psychological Assessment of Crime Profiling. FBI Law Enforcement Bulletin 49 (3), 22–25.

Badcock, R., 1997. Developmental and Clinical Issues in Relation to Offender Profiling. In: Jackson, J., Bekerian, D. (Eds.), Offender Profiling: Theory, Research and Practice. Wiley, Chichester.

Baker, T.E., 2001. Understanding and Apprehending America's most Dangerous Criminals. Law and Order 49 (5), 43–48.

Bartol, C.R., 1996. Police Psychology: Then, Now and Beyond. Criminal Justice and Behaviour 23 (1), 70–89.

Bevel, T., 2001. Applying the Scientific Method to Crime Scene Reconstruction. Journal of Forensic Identification 51 (2), 150–165.

Bevel, T., Gardiner, R., 1997. Bloodstain Pattern Analysis: With an Introduction to Crime Scene Reconstruction. CRC Press, Boca Raton.

Bhattacharyya, S., 1958. The Concept of Logic. Philosophy and Phenomenological Research 18 (3), 326–340.

Blankstein, A., 2002. Couple Charged in Man's Shooting: Jennifer and Matthew Fletcher Are Accused of Murder in the 1998 Death of Her Former Husband, Joel Shanbrom. http://www.xwma.org/mattfletcher.html (accessed 15.11.05).

Boon, J., 1997. The Contribution of Personality Theories to Psychological Profiling. In: Jackson, J., & Berkerian, D. (Eds.), Offender Profiling: Theory, Research and Practice. Wiley, Chichester.

Boon, J., Davies, G., 2003. Criminal Profiling: Investigators Are Making Increased Use of a Science Which Can Identify the Type of Offender for Whom They Should Be Looking. Policing 9, 218–227.

Bradley, P., 2003. Criminal Profiling: What's It All About? Inpsych August, pp. 19–21.

Burgess, A.W., 2003. Personal Communication, July 17.

Burgess, A. W., Ressler, R. K. (1985). Sexual Homicides: Crime Scene and Pattern of Criminal Behaviour. National Institute of Justice Grant 82–IJ-CX-0065.

Burgess, A.W., Hartman, C.R., Ressler, R.K., Douglas, J.E., McCormack, A., 1986. Sexual Homicide: A Motivational Model. J. Interpers. Violence 1 (3), 251–272.

Canter, D., 1989. Offender Profiles. The Psychologist 2 (1), 12–16.

Canter, D., 1995. Psychology of Offender Profiling. In: Bull, R., Carson, D. (Eds.), Handbook of Psychology in Legal Contexts. John Wiley and Sons, New York.

Canter, D., 1998. Profiling as Poison. Inter alia 2 (1), 10–11.

Canter, D., 1999. Equivocal Death. Profiling in Policy and Practice. In: Canter, D., & Alison, L. (Eds.), Profiling in Policy and Practice. Ashgate Publishing, Aldershot.

Canter D., 2000. Investigative Psychology. In: Siegel, J., Knupfer, G., Saukko, P. (Eds.), Encyclopedia of Forensic Science. Academic Press, Boston.

Canter, D., 2003. Mapping Murder: The Secrets of Geographical Profiling. Virgin Books, London.

Canter, D., 2004. Offender Profiling and Investigative Psychology. Journal of Investigative Psychology and Offender Profiling 1, 1–15.

Canter, D., Alison, L.J., Alison, E., Wentink, N., 2004. The Organised/Disorganized Typology of Serial Murder. Myth or Model? Psychology, Public Policy and Law 10, 293–320.

Chisum, W.J., 2000. A Commentary on Bloodstain Analyses in the Sam Sheppard Case. Journal of Behavioural Profiling 1 (3).

Chisum, W.J., 2002. An Introduction to Crime Reconstruction. In: Turvey, B.E. (Ed.), Criminal Profiling: An Introduction to Behavioural Evidence Analysis, second ed. Academic Press, London.

Chisum, W.J., 2007. Reconstruction Using Bloodstain Evidence. In: Chisum, W.J., Turvey, B.E. (Eds.), Crime Reconstruction. Academic Press, Boston, pp. 313–360.

Chisum, W.J., Turvey, B.E., 2000. Evidence Dynamics: Locard's Exchange Principle and Crime Reconstruction. Journal of Behavioural Profiling 1 (1).

Chisum, W.J., Turvey, B.E., 2007. Practice Standards for the Reconstruction of Crime. In: Chisum, W.J., Turvey, B.E. (Eds.), Crime Reconstruction. Academic Press, Boston, pp. 85–126.

Chisum, W.J., Turvey, B.E., 2008. An Introduction to Crime Reconstruction. In: Turvey, B.E. (2002). (Eds.), Criminal Profiling: An Introduction to Behavioural Evidence Analysis, third ed. Academic Press, London, pp. 155–186.

Cook, P.E., Hinman, D.L., 1999. Criminal Profiling. Journal of Contemporary Criminal Justice 15 (3), 230–241.

Cooley, C., 1999. Crime Scene Reconstruction: The Foundation of Behavioural Evidence Analysis. Paper presented in the Master of Forensic Science Degree, University of New Haven. http://www.law-forensic.com/crime scene reconstruction_the foundation of behavioural evidence analysis.doc.(accessed 27.10.05).

Copson, G., 1995. Coals to Newcastle? Part 1: A Study of Offender Profiling. Police Research Group Special Interest Series Paper 7. Home Office, London.

Darkes, J., Otto, R.K., Poythress, N., Starr, L., 1993. APA's Expert Panel in the Congressional Review of the USS Iowa Incident. American Psychologist January, 8–15.

Davis, J.A., 1999. Criminal Personality Profiling and Crime Scene Assessment: A Contemporary Investigative Tool to Assist Law Enforcement Public Safety. Journal of Contemporary Criminal Justice 15 (3), 291–301.

Dietz, P.E., 1985. Sex Offender Profiling by the FBI: Preliminary Conceptual Model. In: Ben-Aron, M.H., Hucher, S.J., Webster, C.D. (Eds.), Clinical Criminology. M and M Graphics, Toronto.

Douglas, J.E., Burgess, A.E., 1986. Criminal Profiling: A Viable Investigative Tool against Violent Crime. FBI Law Enforcement Bulletin 55 (12), 9–13.

Douglas, J.E., Ressler, R.K., Burgess, A.W., Hartman, C.R., 1986. Criminal Profiling from Crime Scene Analysis. Behav. Sci. Law 4 (4), 401–421.

Egger, S., 1998. The Killer Among Us: An Examination of Serial Murder and Its Investigation. Prentice Hall, New Jersey.

Farber, M., 1942. Logical Systems and the Principles of Logic. Philosophy of Science 9 (1), 40–54.

Federal Bureau of Investigation (FBI), 2002. Uniform Crime Report. http://www.fbi.gov/ucr/cius_02/html/web/index.html (accessed 23.09.04).

Fox, J., 2004. Personal communication, 16 March.

Fox, J.A., Levin, J., 1996. Killer on Campus. Avon Books, New York.

Geberth, V.J., 1981. Psychological Profiling. Law and Order September, 46–52.

Geberth, V.J., 1996. Practical Homicide Investigation: Tactics, Procedures and Forensic Techniques, third ed. CRC Press, Boca Raton.

Godwin, G.M., 1999. Hunting Serial Predators: A Multivariate Approach to Profiling Violent Behaviour. CRC Press, Boca Raton.

Goldberg, S.B., 2007. Beyond the Socratic Method: Law Schools Are Discovering That How You're Taught Matters as Much as What You're Taught. Student Lawyer 36 (2), 18–22.

Gudjonsson, G., Copson, G., 1997. The Role of the Expert in Criminal Investigation. In: Jackson, J., Bekerian, D. (Eds.), Offender Profiling: Theory, Research and Practice. Wiley, Chichester, pp. 61–76.

Hazelwood, R.R., Douglas, J.E., 1980. The Lust Murderer. FBI Law Enforcement Bulletin 49 (4), 1–5.

Holmes, R.M., Holmes, S.T., 2002. Profiling Violent Crimes: An Investigative Tool, third ed. Sage Publications, Thousand Oaks.

Homant, R., 1999. Crime Scene Profiling in Premises Security Litigation. Security Journal 12 (4), 7–15.

Homant, R., Kennedy, D., 1998. Psychological Aspects of Crime Scene Profiling: Validity Research. Criminal Justice and Behaviour 25 (3), 319–344.

Investigations Subcommittee and Defense Policy Panel of the Committee on Armed Services, 1990. USS Iowa Tragedy: An Investigative Failure. U.S. Government Printing Office, Washington, DC.

Jackson, J., Bekerian, D., 1997. Offender Profiling: Theory, Research and Practice. Wiley, Chichester.

Jenkins, P., 1994. Using Murder: The Social Construction of Serial Homicide. Aldine de Gruyter, New York.

Kennedy, D.B., Homant, R.J., 1997. Problems with the Use of Criminal Profiling in Premises Security Litigation. Trial Diplomacy Journal 20, 223–229.

Kopel, D.B., Blackman, P.H., 1997. No More Wacos: What's Wrong With Federal Law Enforcement and How to Fix It. Plenum Press, New York.

La Fon, D.S., 2002. The Psychological Autopsy. In: Turvey, B.E. (Ed.), Criminal Profiling: An Introduction to Behavioural Evidence Analysis. Academic Press, London, pp. 157–168.

McCann, J., 1992. Criminal Personality Profiling in the Investigation of Violent Crime: Recent Advances and Future Directions. Behav. Sci. Law 10 (14), 475–481.

McGrath, M.G., 2000. Criminal Profiling: Is there a Role for the Forensic Psychiatrist? Journal of the American Academy of Forensic Psychiatry and the Law 28 (3), 315–324.

Muller, D., 2000. Criminal Profiling: Real Science of Just Wishful Thinking? Homicide Studies 4 (3), 234–264.

Napier, M.R., Baker, K.P., 2005. Criminal Personality Profiling. In: James, S.H., Nordby, J.J. (Eds.), Forensic Science: An Introduction to Scientific and Investigative Techniques, second ed. Taylor and Francis, Boca Raton.

Neblett, W., 1985. Sherlock's Logic: Learn to Reason Like a Master Detective. Barnes and Noble Books, New York.

Nowikowski, F., 1995. Psychological Offender Profiling: An Overview. The Criminologist 19 (4), 225–251.

O'Toole, M.E., 2004. Criminal Profiling: The FBI Uses Criminal Investigative Analysis to Solve Crimes. In: Campbell, J.H., DeNevi, D. (Eds.), Profilers: Leading Investigators Take You Inside the Criminal Mind. Prometheus Books, Amherst, pp. 223–228.

Palermo, G.B., 2002. Criminal Profiling: The Uniqueness of the Killer. Int. J. Offender Ther. 46 (4), 383–385.

Pedersen, A.M., 2006. In Defense of the Oft-Maligned Socratic Method. The National Law Journal, September.

Petherick, W.A., 2003. What's in a Name? Comparing Applied Profiling Methodologies. Journal of Law and Social Challenges June, 173–188.

Petherick, W.A., 2005. Serial Crime: Theoretical and Practical Issues in Behavioral Profiling, Academic Press, Boston.

Petherick, W.A., 2006. Criminal Profiling Methods. In: Petherick, W.A. (Ed.), Serial Crime: Theoretical and Practical Issues in Behavioural Profiling. Academic Press, Boston.

Petherick, W.A., Turvey, B.E., 2008a. Behavioral Evidence Analysis: Ideo-Deductive Method of Criminal Profiling. In: Turvey, B.E. (Ed.), Criminal Profiling: An Introduction to Behavioral Evidence Analysis, third ed. Academic Press, San Diego.

Petherick, W.A., Turvey, B.E., 2008b. Criminal Profiling, the Scientific Method, and Logic. In: Turvey, B. E. (Ed.), Criminal Profiling: An Introduction to Behavioral Evidence Analysis, third ed. Academic Press, Boston.

Petherick, W.A., Turvey, B.E., 2008c. Victimology. In: Turvey, B.E. (Ed.), Criminal Profiling: An Introduction to Behavioral Evidence Analysis, third ed. Academic Press, Boston.

Pinizotto, A.J., 1984. Forensic Psychology: Criminal Personality Profiling. Journal of Police Science and Administration 12 (1), 32–40.

Ressler, R.K., Burgess, A.W., 1985. Crime Scene and Profile Characteristics of Organized and Disorganized Serial Murderers. FBI Law Enforcement Bulletin 54 (8), 18–25.

Ressler, R.K., Shachtman, T., 1992. Whoever Fights Monsters. Pocket Books, New York.

Ressler, R.K., Burgess, A.W., Douglas, J.E., 1988. Sexual Homicides: Patterns and Motives. Lexington Books, New York.

Ressler, R.K., Burgess, A.W., Douglas, J.E., Hartman, C.R., D'Agostino, R.B., 1986. Sexual Killers and Their Victims: Identifying Patterns Through Crime Scene Analysis. J. Interpers. Violence 1 (3), 288–308.

Ressler, R.K., Burgess, A.W., Hartman, C.R., Douglas, J.E., McCormack, C.R., 1986. Murderers Who Rape and Mutilate. J. Interpers. Violence 1 (3), 273–287.

Royal Canadian Mounted Police, 2005. Criminal Investigative Analysis. Available from: http://www.rcmp.ca/techops/crim_prof_e.htm

Rynearson, J., 2002. Evidence and Crime Scene Reconstruction: A Guide for Field Investigations, sixth ed. National Crime Investigation and Training, Redding, CA.

Saferstein, R., 2004. Criminalistics: An Introduction to Forensic Science, eighth ed. Prentice Hall, New Jersey.

Schlarman, S., 1999. Meet Your Cracker: Intrusion Management Using Criminal Profiling. Information Systems Security 8 (3), 21–26.

Stock, G.W.J., 2004. Deductive Logic. Project Gutenberg Press, Oxford.

Strano, M., 2004. A Neural Network Applied to Criminal Psychological Profiling: An Italian Initiative. Int. J. Offender Ther. Comp. Criminol. 48 (4), 495–503.

Superior Court of California, 1999. The People of the State of California v Douglas Scott Mouser. Available from: http://www.corpus-delicti.com/mouser_101999_pro-dan_direct.html (accessed 11.11.2005).

Teten, H., 1989. Offender Profiling. In: Bailey, W. (Ed.), Encyclopedia of Police Science. Garland Publishing, New York, pp. 475–477.

Thompson, C.C., 1999. A Glimpse of Hell: The Explosion aboard the USS Iowa and Its Cover Up. W. W. Norton and Co., New York.

Thornton, J., 2006. Crime Reconstruction–Ethos and Ethics. In: Chisum, J., Turvey, B.E. (Eds.), Crime Reconstruction. Academic Press, San Diego, pp. 37–50.

Towl, G.J., Crighton, D.A., 1996. Handbook of Psychology for Forensic Practitioners. Routledge, London.

Turco, R.N., 1990. Psychological Profiling. Int. J. Offender Ther. Comp. Criminol. 34, 147–154.

Turvey, B.E., 2008a. Criminal Profiling: An Introduction to Behavioral Evidence Analysis, third ed. Academic Press, Boston.

Turvey, B.E., 2008b. Offender Characteristics: Rendering the Profile. In: Turvey, B.E. (Ed.), Criminal Profiling: An introduction to Behavioral Evidence Analysis, third ed. Academic Press, Boston.

Turvey, B.E., McGrath, M., 2005. Criminal Profiling and the Media: Profiling the Beltway Snipers. In: Petherick, W.A. (Ed.), Serial Crime: Theoretical and Practical Issues In Behavioural Profiling. Academic Press, Boston, pp. 113–136.

Vorpagel, R., Harrington, J., 1998. Profiles in Murder: An FBI Legend Dissects Killers and Their Crimes. De Capo Press, New York.

West, A., 2000. Clinical Assessment of Homicide Offenders: The Significance of Crime Scene in Offense and Offender Analysis. Homicide Studies 4 (3), 219–233.

Wilson, P., Soothill, K., 1996. Psychological Profiling: Red, Green or Amber? The Police Journal July, 349–357.

Wilson, P., Lincoln, R., Kocsis, R.N., 1997. Validity, Utility and Ethics of Profiling for Serial Violent and Sexual Offenders. Psychiatry, Psychology and Law 4 (1), 1–12.

CHAPTER 6

Forensic Victimology

Claire E. Ferguson, Wayne A. Petherick, and Brent E. Turvey[1]

[1]This chapter is adapted from material published in Petherick and Turvey (2008).

KEY WORDS

Critical Victimology: The study that questions how criminality and victimity are established, tolerated, and even sanctioned.

Forensic Victimology: The scientific study of victims for the purposes of addressing investigative and forensic issues.

General Victimology: The study of all the individuals or groups who have suffered harm or loss, whether they are victims of a specific crime, general oppression, or a natural disaster.

Interactionist Victimology (a.k.a. *penal victimology*): The study of the dynamics between victims and their offenders.

Lifestyle Exposure: The potentially harmful elements that exist in a victim's everyday life as a consequence of biological and environmental factors, as well as past choices.

Situational Exposure: The amount of actual exposure or vulnerability experienced by a victim to harm, resulting from his or her environment and personal traits at the time of victimization.

CONTENTS

Forensic victimology, a subdiscipline of forensic criminology, is the scientific study of victims for the purposes of addressing investigative and forensic issues. Forensic victimology is intended to serve the justice system by educating it. This area of study is aimed at helping to provide for informed investigations, to require scientific examinations of victim evidence to be presented in court, and to result in more informed legal outcomes.

The purpose of this chapter is to provide a discussion regarding the nature and scope of forensic victimology, its investigative implications, and its impact on court proceedings. We will begin with a brief section outlining the more

219

traditional forms of victimology because readers may have encountered them previously. Then we will discuss the purpose of forensic victimology, its investigative utility, and the forensic context. We will conclude with a discussion regarding who forensic victimologists are and what they actually do.

TRADITIONAL VICTIMOLOGY

Victimology is intended to be the scientific study of victims (Drapkin and Viano, 1974). Victimologists tend to find themselves operating within one of three main subgroups: general victimology, penal/interactionist victimology, and critical victimology.

General victimology is the study of all those individuals or groups who have suffered harm or loss, whether they are victims of a specific crime, general oppression, or a natural disaster. According to Mendelsohn (1976), this vast landscape includes victims of criminal offenders, the social-political environment, the natural environment, technology, and even those who victimize themselves. General victimologists are concerned with identifying or developing preventative measures as well as tools for victim assistance. They not only want to study the characteristics and causes of victimization, but also want to determine remedies.

Interactionist victimology, or penal victimology, is the study of the dynamics between victims and their offenders. It is limited, however, to those who have been the victims of a specific crime. Interactionist victimologists study a victim's participation in crime causation through his or her interaction with the offender, the interaction between the victim and society, and the victim's subsequent role in the criminal justice system. Like the general victimologist, the interactionist intends to examine causes to develop remedies that favor the victim.

Critical victimology has developed in reaction to the way that victimology is defined and studied by the first two subgroups. It seeks to question how criminality and victimity are established, tolerated, and even sanctioned. The basic premise is that any mainstream view of victims perpetuates existing yet inadequate definitions of crime and victimization. This may be observed in the overemphasis in research and policy on certain types of crime and crime victims, because they are clearly defined and easier to grasp. This in turn results in a failure to study—let alone recognize—a host of both victim populations and their related social issues. It may also be observed in the way that a given justice system penalizes those who would elsewhere be viewed as victims, such as prostitutes who are selectively punished in some Western cultures, and victims of rape who may be punished in some Islamic cultures.

These victimology subgroups are alike in that they are ultimately oriented toward helping victims, in studying ways of "speeding up a victim's emotional recovery, overcoming adversity, reimbursing financial damages, promoting reconciliation between the injured party and the wrongdoer, and restoring harmony to a strife-torn community" (Karmen, 2004, p. 24). In other words, the professional compass in these subgroups points toward victim betterment. While this is an admirable goal and one well worth serving, it does not always promote an environment where scientific study is welcome.

Contemporary victimologists can be found in many professions, including those associated with academia, the justice system, victim treatment, victim's advocacy, and politics. They routinely have a mandate to help victims above all other considerations, or for political reasons they may need to be perceived as having such a mandate. However, satisfying this ideological imperative often requires uncritical and unconditional regard for those who present themselves, or are presented contextually, as victims. When this political or functional need clashes with the reality of victim imperfection, the results to any given professional can be chilling. The pendulum of bias can swing widely for and against.

It is important to recall that victimology is meant to be a scientific study. However, bias that develops for or against victims because of routine contact with them can act as a wall to the mandates of scientific inquiry, namely the requirements of doubt and skepticism.[2] This is a problem because some witnesses lie, some victims lie, and some people lie about being victims. Blind faith in a victim shields them from scientific inquiry; overt mistrust of victims shields others. This is where forensic victimology comes in.

[2]For further discussion on the need for doubt and skepticism in science, see Popper (1963); Kennedy and Kennedy (1972); and Turvey (2008).

DISTINGUISHING FORENSIC VICTIMOLOGY

Forensic victimology is related to interactionist victimology, in which victims are defined by having suffered harm or loss due to a breach of law. This study involves the accurate, critical, and objective outlining of victim lifestyles and circumstances, the events leading up to their injury, and the precise nature of any harm or loss suffered.

Forensic victimology does not seek to assist with victim advocacy or promote victim sympathy. Nor is the forensic victimologist invested in restoring victims and making them whole. However, there is awareness that the victim evidence gathered, as well as subsequent interpretations, may be used by others for these purposes at a later time.

INVESTIGATIVE UTILITY

As detailed in Turvey (2006), for more than a century the investigative and forensic science literature has acknowledged the importance of establishing the relationships between the primary components of a crime in order to solve it. These supporting pillars relate directly to evidence that establishes the relationships between *the victim, the suspect,* and *the crime scene.* This expansive body of work has given more than a small share of its pages to explaining the necessity of carefully investigating and documenting evidence as it relates to each, and determining the connections that can be reliably demonstrated. Establishing these pillars and the details of their relationships is in fact a threshold goal of all criminal investigation, so that criminal investigators and subsequent forensic examiners may adequately provide the foundation for any related court action.

When these pillars are not investigated, examined, and firmly established, the theories of a case are essentially unsupported. They are at best a weak guess, and at worst, the erroneous result of biasing influences such as politics, emotion, ignorant beliefs, and personal interest. In this context, the application of *forensic victimology* is a necessary safeguard.

As described in Dienstein (2005, p. 160) *criminal investigation* is the process of gathering facts to be used as evidence of proof in a court of law. Without an investigation, the facts will be absent and proofs will be impossible to attain. Schultz (2005, p. 122) explains that prior to being tested in the courtroom, a competent investigation will gather or prepare evidence of the following: "knowledge or proof that a crime has been committed; the existence of a victim(s) … an approved report of the investigation answering the questions of who, what, where, when, why and how; and evidence that has been identified and preserved for the prosecutor." Only then may investigators proceed with their case to the district attorney for prosecutorial consideration.

In the investigative realm, forensic victimology provides for the consistent recognition, collection, preservation, and documentation of victim evidence by investigators. Questions are asked, context is established, and history is documented. Each piece of victim evidence is scrutinized by investigators and then acted upon again and again until it is an exhausted possibility. This informs the nature, scope, and depth of the investigation. It can also lead to the discovery of additional relevant or dispositive evidence. Ultimately, forensic victimology assists with answering the question of whether and how criminal charges may be levied and civil liabilities may have been incurred, all of which is going to be decided in court.

FORENSIC CONTEXT

It is understood that investigative and forensic venues are quite different in scope, structure, and function. The questions they need answered are particular to their unique geographical variations. They also represent very different standards of evidence. What may be investigatively useful speculation or theory at one point may lack the sufficiency for subsequent court-worthy opinions. Given the capacity for investigative work to find its way into court, this distinction must be ever-present and crystal clear.

In the forensic realm (which continuously considers the courtroom), forensic victimology is a form of evidence that informs the nature, scope, and depth of any legal proceedings to be decided by the trier of fact (a judge or jury). When presented by a forensic expert, it involves the scientific interpretation of various kinds of victim evidence gathered during the investigation and any subsequent analysis. Ultimately, it assists with demonstrating the actual limits of victim evidence—which criminal or civil theories it supports and which it refutes.

FORENSIC VICTIMOLOGISTS IN PRACTICE

Forensic victimology is an applied discipline as opposed to a theoretical one. Forensic victimologists seek to examine, consider, and interpret particular victim evidence found in a particular case, or series of cases, in a scientific fashion. Their numbers include anyone who uses their knowledge of victimology to serve investigative or forensic ends. The social scientist researching victim-offender relationships, the investigator going though a victim's garbage or cell phone records, the criminal profiler reading a victim's diary or making a "friends and family" list, the forensic nurse taking a victim history or looking for evidence of injury, the reconstructionist examining a victim's toxicology or making a timeline of activities leading up to his or her demise, the psychiatrist or psychologist performing a mental health assessment, the medical examiner establishing a victim's place of employment or last meal—each collects, examines, and interprets evidence related to forensic victimology. Their work serves criminal investigation and anticipates courtroom testimony. Their findings and interpretations bear directly on determining whether there is a victim, precisely who the victim is, and the potential consequences for those who caused that person harm.

Commonly, forensic victimologists serve investigations and eventual court proceedings with reports and testimony by endeavoring to:

1. Assist with contextualizing allegations of victimization;
2. Help support or refute allegations of victimization;
3. Help establish the nature of victim exposure to harm or loss;
4. Assist with the development of offender modus operandi and motive;
5. Help establish an investigative suspect pool;
6. Assist with the investigative linkage of unsolved cases.

GENERAL GUIDELINES

In terms of what is required for a thorough victimology, the national guidelines for *Death Investigation* of the National Institute of Justice (NIJ), Section E: "Establishing and Recording Decedent Profile Information," is a good place to start. However, we do not recommend that readers confine themselves to any single victimology checklist. Rather, examiners should treat nothing about a victim as trivial.

Examiners therefore need to analyze each characteristic that presents itself until it is an exhausted possibility, to see how it relates to the rest of the victim information. Weston and Wells (1974, p. 97) provide a quick checklist of preliminary victimological queries that have proven to be most useful in eliciting investigative information. This is the kind of information that should be gathered immediately, ideally before the investigator arrives at a given crime scene:

1. Did the victim know the perpetrator?
2. Does the victim suspect any person? Why?
3. Has the victim a history of crime? A history of reporting crimes?
4. Did the victim have a weapon?
5. Has the victim an aggressive personality?
6. Has the victim been the subject of any field [police] reports?

The following are some basic victimological inquiries that we have found useful when applied to actual casework. Gathering this information, along with the careful examination of physical evidence, provides the starting point for investigative activity. This list is inclusive of items found in the National Institute of Justice (1999):

1. Determine the victim's hard physical characteristics (race, weight, height, hair color, eye color, etc.).
2. Determine the victim's occupation or place of work and shift schedule.
3. Compile the victim's criminal history.
4. Compile a list of the victim's daily routines, habits, and activities.
5. Compile a complete list of the victim's family members with contact information. Interview each of them.
6. Compile a complete list of the victim's friends with contact information. Interview each of them.
7. Compile a complete list of the victim's coworkers with contact information. Interview each of them.
8. Compile the victim's medical history.
9. Compile the victim's psychiatric history. Interview all of the victim's mental health care providers.
10. Compile a list of the victim's medications. Compare this with known victim toxicology.
11. Compile the victim's financial history (credit card usage, tax returns, insurance policies, etc.).
12. Compile the victim's educational history.

13. Compile a residence history of the victim (where he or she has lived, when, and with whom, etc.).

14. Spend time, when possible, with the victim's personal items, in the personal environments (hangouts, work, school, home/bedroom, etc.). Examine any available photo albums, diaries, or journals. Make note of music and literature preferences. Do this to find out who victims seemed to believe they were, what they wanted everyone to perceive, and how they seemed to feel about their life in general.

15. Compile all available information regarding the victim's mobile phone, computer, and Internet usage. When available, at least attempt to do the following:

   - Determine the victim's service providers.
   - Determine the victim's email addresses.
   - Examine the victim's address books or contact databases.
   - Examine the victim's incoming and outgoing email.
   - Examine all documents on the victim's computer.
   - Determine the last known usage of the victim's computer and various software applications.

16. Create a timeline of the victim's last known activities, factoring in all witness statements and physical evidence.

17. Travel the last known route taken by the victim in whatever manner the victim used. Try to see that route from the victim's perspective and then from the potential perspectives of the offender. Keep these perspectives separate.

18. Look for security video cameras along the victim's route, or potential route, that may have documented the victim's activities or even the actual crime.

Once this has been accomplished, the forensic victimologist can set to the task of determining victim lifestyle and situational exposure.

VICTIM LIFESTYLE EXPOSURE

Victim *lifestyle exposure* is concerned with studying the potentially harmful elements that exist in a victim's everyday life as a consequence of biological and environmental factors, as well as past choices. As defined in Petherick and Turvey (2008, p. 383), victim *lifestyle exposure* is "the amount of exposure to harmful elements experienced by the victim and resulting from the victim's usual environment and personal traits."

This study requires an investigation and assessment of the victim's personality, and his or her personal, professional, and social environment (Turvey, 2008).

The causal link between a victim's lifestyle and his or her victimization is not always clear. The reason is that it is difficult to reconcile just how much influence any one lifestyle factor has on the criminal situation. Generally, lifestyle factors can influence harm to the victim in three ways: by creating a perceived conflict with an offender, by increasing the victim's presence around offenders or those predisposed toward criminality, or by enhancing an offender's perception of victim vulnerability.

A victim's general *lifestyle exposure* to harm or loss should not be confused with *situational exposure,* which refers to harmful elements experienced by the victim resulting from his or her environment and personal traits at the time of victimization. One analogy to differentiate these concepts is to consider lifestyle exposure as a "weather forecast," anticipating what harmful elements may be present by virtue of what has been present in the past under similar conditions and given various indicators; incident exposure can then be considered the "daily weather report," identifying the actual cloud coverage, temperature, and precipitation on a given day.

The interpretation of a particular victim's lifestyle exposure is not just a function of compiling abstract group statistics for application to nonexistent victim stereotypes, though this is an unfortunate victimological tradition. Much more is required to achieve a concrete and actual understanding.

To accurately determine a specific victim's lifestyle exposure, one needs to assess the victim's harm in the context of his or her specific lifestyle and personality traits. For investigative purposes, lifestyle factors must be questioned as to how, specifically, they contributed to harm. By utilizing the concept of victim *risk,* one may infer a conclusion based on statistical analyses of the potential to be harmed as being part of a demographic group. These conclusions ignore the specific characteristics of the victim and how they uniquely interacted with the offender given their situation. For example, statistics indicate that college students are at higher risk of victimization (Fisher et al., 1998). One might assume that the mere situation of being a college student increases exposure to harm. This assumption is not necessarily correct; not all college students are identical. Some expose themselves to more harm than others through their drug and alcohol use, routine, sexual activity, and a number of other factors. Making conclusions about the victim's level of harm based on statistical analyses or probability estimates of risk do not accurately reflect how a specific victim's lifestyle contributed to his or her harm, nor does it necessarily provide investigative relevance.

In contrast, the concept of *victim exposure* examines how a lifestyle factor specifically increased a victim's contact with harm. Taking the example of Fisher et al. (1998) again, an investigator can discover that the victim was a college student and acknowledge that college students are at an increased exposure to harm; however, the specific interaction of *this* college student with her environment will dictate the *actual* level of potential for harm. One particular student who does not consume alcohol or drugs, lives at home with her parents, does not engage in high-risk sexual activity, and takes self-defense classes will represent a very different level of exposure than the student who does consume alcohol and drugs, lives in a bad part of town, engages in high-risk sexual practices, and does not take self-defense classes. Certain lifestyle traits such as interacting with potential offenders, drug use, and a high frequency of casual sex with strangers may also increase a victim's exposure to harm. Only by looking at the specific interactions of the variables can one sufficiently argue that a victim was exposed to harm.

It should also be noted that, generally speaking, not all lifestyle factors can be said to have the potential to increase harm to a victim. It cannot be reasonably argued that the habit of collecting baseball cards played a significant role in the sexual assault of a male at a nightclub. Nor can it be easily argued that a victim's depression solely increased her exposure to gang-related homicide. Thus, for one to argue that a lifestyle factor influenced victim-offender dynamics, it needs to be both potentially harmful, in the sense that its presence could be argued to influence opportunity for harm to occur, and also relevant, within the context of who the particular victim was and the criminal behavior that occurred.

VICTIM SITUATIONAL EXPOSURE

Victim situational exposure is the amount of actual exposure or vulnerability experienced by the victim to harm, resulting from his or her environment and personal traits, *at the time of victimization* (Petherick and Turvey, 2008).

Consider the issue of alcohol. Being a person who routinely becomes intoxicated increases one's lifestyle exposure to the many harmful effects of alcohol, which will be mentioned shortly. However, unless a victim is actually intoxicated at the time of victimization, it does not necessarily raise her situational exposure. It is possible to have a high lifestyle exposure related to alcohol abuse, but a low situational exposure from lack of alcohol use or abuse at the time of victimization. The opposite is also true.

Consider also the issue of firearms. Being a person who does not own a firearm, use a firearm, have one in one's home, or live with or interact with those that do decreases one's overall lifestyle exposure to the harmful effects of firearms. However, if a victim is at a shooting range for the first time with a new friend or romantic interest and is accidentally shot, it must be recognized that his incident exposure to harm from firearms was quite high at the time of victimization. This is true even if he was not participating or holding a gun, given his situational proximity to multiple loaded firearms being discharged by multiple persons of varying skill levels.

However, not all immediately harmful exposure is as transparent and easy to recognize from the victim's perspective as these basic examples might suggest. Harmful exposure may not even be apparent to investigators, owing to investigative apathy, or the reliance on false investigative assumptions about who and what were present during the crime. The situational harm coming from persons, environments, and circumstances relating to a particular crime must be thoroughly investigated, carefully established, and never assumed.

The interpretation of a particular victim's situational exposure is not just a function of compiling crime stats, comparing them to the victim's presumed state of being when attacked, and making a general risk assessment. Much more is required to achieve a concrete and actual understanding. The nature, depth, and character of each victim's harm must be investigated, examined, and explained in its context. This means scrupulous examination of the information gathered regarding associated persons and locations. Barring this level of information and effort, the forensic victimologist must have the scientific courage to admit what is known and what is not. He or she must understand the scope and limits of the evidence. This is not too much to ask of any competent forensic examiner.

FORENSIC VICTIMOLOGY AT TRIAL

In cases in which victims' actions, history, or demeanor are relevant to legal proceedings, a victimologist may be asked to examine victim-oriented behavioral evidence and contextualize it before the trier of fact. This is the *forensic* aspect of forensic victimology. As has been discussed, the rules of admissibility vary from state to state, court to court, and judge to judge, as admissibility of victimology evidence is made by the court on an individual basis and based on a sometimes-unique interpretation of the law.

The question arises, then, as to the role of victimology—and the victimologist—in this venue. In general, forensic victimologists should conduct themselves as both scientists and educators. It is their role to provide a cooling effect to the often-heated issues surrounding victim-oriented behavioral evidence. They must examine the evidence impartially, through the lens of the scientific method, and render conclusions related to victimology in accordance with their findings. When necessary, they must be able to explain their findings to the court and show how they achieved them.

For the small percentage of cases that do go to trial, there is an unavoidable vulnerability to the culmination of errors, improper motivations, and the zeal of advocates on either side of the courtroom. This is particularly true of information related to the victim. As described in previous chapters, victimological information can be compiled ineptly, reported inaccurately, or provided in a biased manner—and that is when it is collected at all. The misinformation that follows may combine during court proceedings to have a tremendous impact. Bad information can create a snowball effect: errors and omissions in the original information provided to the police can lead to errors in the investigation; these can lead to problems in the case assembled against the accused; which can lead to mistakes in the charges handed down and how the case is brought by the prosecution; leading to false perceptions by the judge, jury, and media. All these factors can have influence over whether or not a defendant is convicted and how he or she is sentenced.

Generally speaking, one purpose of forensic victimology is to help prevent this snowball effect from happening. Victimological information should be gathered objectively and consistently, and then used to describe or evaluate victims and their circumstances so that judges and juries are privy to information that may be relevant to their decisions. In this context, direct questions must be asked: Was the victim using drugs? Does the victim have a history of falsely reporting crime? What was the extent of the victim's physical injuries? Was the victim conscious during the attack? Does the victim have a history of taking rides from strangers or letting strangers into his or her home? Does the victim lock the door at night? The judge, who determines what is legally admissible, decides the issue of relevance for these and similarly themed questions. Then, as already discussed, the judge makes a ruling: sometimes everything about a victim is admissible, sometimes nothing, and sometimes the court "splits the baby" by admitting a percentage of victim information.

The more accurate and complete the victim information provided, the clearer the context of the crime. This is an investigative axiom. During an investigation, everything about the victim must be learned and documented, with nothing treated as trivial. Unfortunately, there is a tendency on the part of some investigators to avoid gathering some or all of the victimology, to deprive the court of contextual information that might sway the findings against prevailing case theories. The court should view this practice with dismay, as informed decisions about what to admit and what to keep out cannot be made in the absence of a complete investigative effort and record.

As already discussed, presenting victimological information in court involves a different standard from the investigative effort. Investigative victimology gathers everything; the court decides admissibility based on that record in the context of the collective issues in a case. Typically, victimological evidence must serve a particular purpose related to a legal issue to be admissible.

For example, victimological information may demonstrate that a crime has actually occurred, or that the elements of this case meet the definition of the charges brought against the accused. Information about the victim will undoubtedly contextualize the crime and help to reconstruct exactly what took place and in what order. Information about the victim may also allow the judge and jury to better understand who the victim is or was, why he or she was targeted, how he or she was acquired and harmed, and most importantly by whom. On the other hand, if there is a specific reason to doubt the victim's credibility or the accuracy of particular statements, victimology may be introduced at trial to bring this to light. These are just some of the many possible scenarios, but the theme remains clear: to be admissible in court, victimology must be relevant to a factual matter or legal question, and not simply part of a smear campaign.

CASE EXAMPLE: CANNIE BULLOCK

Joseph S. Cordova was accused of the sexual murder of 8-year-old Cannie M. Bullock, whose nude body was discovered in her backyard, covered with a blanket, on Saturday, August 25, 1979, during the early morning hours. Mr. Cordova was eventually identified as a suspect in her murder after a "cold hit" in 2002 matched his DNA to sperm found in the victim's vagina. In 2007, he was convicted of capital murder in relation to her death.

Consider the timeline and victimology information provided in the following example, excerpted from the Crime Analysis report prepared in this case by one of the authors (Turvey) in preparation for subsequent expert testimony on behalf of the defense. It is representative of the type of information that is considered when investigating and interpreting victim exposure (a.k.a. victim risk).

SUMMARY

Background / Timeline

The following background and timeline information is rendered from police reports, including the statements of Linda Bullock (29 y.o.) (the victim's mother), Debra Fisher (19 y.o.), and Mary Magdeline Sequeira (31 y.o.). It should be noted that during this period of time, Linda Bullock has admitted to frequently abusing both alcohol and methamphetamine. She also stated to police that she and Cannie (8 y.o.) had lived at 2628 ½ Dover Ave for approximately 3 months prior to Cannie's murder. She explained to police they moved there from Richmond where she had lived with her ex-boyfriend, Larry Buholzer, a member of a biker gang. They had recently broken up. While living with Buholzer, she admitted to frequently having different male visitors over to have sex and do drugs in her bedroom. Police directly asked her whether she had prostituted herself or her daughter Cannie for drugs or money, though Linda Bullock denied doing either (this issue is revisited in the *victimology* section of this report).

1. 8/24/79 just prior to 2300hrs – According to Debra Fisher, Cannie Bullock got in the shower and then Linda Bullock, who also wanted to take a shower, kicked her out. Cannie got out and dressed in her white bathrobe. According to Debra Fisher, who lived with Linda and Cannie at the time, it is unlikely that Cannie was wearing anything beneath the bathrobe.

2. 8/24/79, between 2300 and 2330hrs – Linda Bullock and Debra Fisher left the Bullock residence, 2628 ½ Dover Ave, San Pablo, for Oscar's Bar in Richmond, to play pool. Cannie was left home alone with instructions not to open the door for strangers. Linda Bullock claimed to have the only key to the residence, and locked Cannie inside as she left. She also made certain to latch the front gate on her way out. Starting out on foot, Linda and Debra ultimately hitched a ride to Oscar's with a man they knew named Bobby. It should be noted that the precise nature of the relationship between Bullock and Fisher (friends, lovers, etc....) has not been made clear. This issue should be investigated further.

3. 8/25/79, 0200hrs – Debra Fisher and Mary Magdeline Sequeira (a bartender at Oscars, aka "Bobby") left Oscars Bar for Cleo's Corner to play pool. Linda Bullock stayed at Oscar's Bar to play pool with a man named Dennis (also a bartender at Oscar's).

4. Between 2330 and 0300 – While at Oscar's Bar, Linda Bullock got into a fight with "Pam" over a previous altercation that had occurred at a house party at Bullock's residence. That evening, Linda Bullock threw a drink in Pam's face, while Pam threw a cigarette in Linda Bullock's face.

5. 8/25/79, between 0245 and 0300hrs – Linda Bullock got a ride home with Dennis the bartender. She explained to police that she was afraid of retaliation by Pam, and Dennis was escorting her. Dennis entered the house with her. Linda found the front gate unlatched, the front door ajar, the porch light off and non-functioning, and Cannie missing. She searched the residence and found the sofa bed where Cannie sleeps in disarray, and Cannie's bathrobe at the foot of the sofa bed with red stains on it. She subsequently asked Dennis to leave.

6. 8/25/79, 0245hrs to 0330hrs – Linda Bullock searched for Cannie, during which she found the gate ajar in the backyard. However, she did not report seeing the blanket or finding the body in the backyard.

7. 8/25/79, 0300hrs – Debra Fisher and Mary Magdeline Sequeira left Cleo's Corner for Linda Bullock's residence, where Fisher planned to spend the night. They found Linda Bullock yelling for Cannie and further assisted with the search. Mary Sequeira observed torn bedding on the sofa, and Cannie's bathrobe stuffed between the mattress and the sofa bed. They still do not report seeing the blanket or finding the body in the backyard.

8. Note: CSI Bentley found the victim's robe on the floor near the doorway to the kitchen area where he understands Linda Bullock dropped it. He takes time in his report to explain that persons entering the residence would likely have stepped on the robe. This issue is revisited in the *investigative suggestions* section of this report.

9. 8/25/79, after 0300hrs – Linda Bullock reportedly contacted her landlady, Rose Azevedo, at 2628 Dover (the house in front of hers). In the past, Azevedo has taken Cannie into her home when her mother has been out late. There is some hostility between them. On this occasion, Azevedo reportedly refused to let Linda Bullock into her home to search for Cannie, or to use the phone to call authorities. Linda Bullock does not have a phone.

10. 8/25/79, prior to 0330hrs – Cannie Bullock is reported missing to San Pablo Police Department by Debra Fisher, who uses Linda Bullock's name. Debra Fisher reportedly got Azevedo to agree to let her use the phone. At this point, no one has reported seeing the blanket or finding the body in the backyard.

11. 8/25/79, prior to 0330hrs – Lt. Burke and Officer Vaughan searched the interior and exterior of Bullock's residence at 2628 ½ Dover, finding Cannie's body in the backyard.

12. 8/25/79, approx. 0451hrs – Police inform Linda Bullock that her daughter Cannie is dead. She subsequently becomes hysterical, sits on the floor, starts crying, and then passes out. Police are unable to get any further information from her at this point.

13. 8/27/79, approx. 1400hrs – During a police initiated interview at her home in Pinole, Debra Fisher presents Det. Bennet with a Sear's sewing machine catalog and a small charm resembling the zodiac sign of Sagittarius (the Archer). Fisher explained that she and Linda Bullock had found these items on the coffee table of Bullock's living room. She explained that they did not know where they came from, and that neither owned a sewing machine.

Victimology

Victimology is the study of available victim information for the purposes of assessing their risk of becoming the victim of a particular type of crime. There are two kinds of victim risk to assess: *lifestyle risk* and *incident risk*. *Lifestyle risk* is a term that refers to the overall risk present by virtue of an individual's personality, and their personal, professional, and social environments. *Incident risk* is a more specific term that refers to the risk present at the moment an offender initially acquires a victim, by virtue of the victim's state of mind, and the hazards of the immediate environment (Burgess & Hazelwood, 1995; Turvey, 2002).

Each type of victim risk may be generally characterized in one of three ways: low, medium, or high. The term *low-risk victim* refers to an individual whose personal, professional, and social lives do not normally expose them to a possibility of suffering harm or loss. The term *medium-risk victim* refers to an individual whose personal, professional, and social lives can expose them to a possibility of suffering harm or loss. The term *high-risk victim* refers to an individual whose personal, professional, and social lives continuously expose them to the danger of suffering harm or loss (Burgess & Hazelwood, 1995; Turvey, 2002).

In this case, we have a victim (Cannie Bullock) with a high lifestyle risk, and a high incident risk. Cannie Bullock would be classified as having a high lifestyle risk because of at least the following lifestyle influences:

1. Cannie Bullock was an 8-year-old child that spent much of her time without monitoring or parental supervision.
2. Cannie Bullock and her mother lived in a home in a secluded area behind their landlady's house where it is extremely difficult to observe activity from the street.
3. Cannie Bullock's only true caregiver (her mother, Linda Bullock) abused both alcohol and methamphetamine prior to and up until the time of her death.
4. Cannie Bullock was left without care or supervision until the early hours of the morning on a regular basis.
5. Cannie Bullock's mother was known to have an angry temper.
6. Cannie Bullock's mother was known to frequently have different male visitors in their home to have sex and consume drugs.
7. Cannie Bullock's mother had just recently ended a long-term relationship with a male in a biker gang.

Note: It is unknown whether or not Cannie Bullock suffered from chronic physical or sexual abuse prior to her death. These issues were not addressed sufficiently at autopsy. It is strongly recommended that an investigation be conducted into whether or not Child Protective Services, or some similar child welfare organization, had a file on Cannie Bullock, or this home. In cases such as this, it is common for investigators to fail with respect to investigating or establishing these circumstances, for fear of alienating a parent as a witness.

Cannie Bullock would be classified as having a **high incident risk** because of at least the following circumstances present on the evening of her death:

1. Cannie Bullock's home is a nexus for high-risk activity (drug abuse, alcohol abuse, partying, sexual activity with an increasing number of different men, etc....). Simply being at that specific location increased her risk of harm.
2. Cannie Bullock had been left at home alone.
3. Cannie Bullock was an 8-year-old child; she would be less able to physically defend herself from any form of danger that presented itself that evening.
4. Cannie Bullock had been left at home after 11pm on a Friday night. Because of the time of day, the darkness, and the fact that it was the beginning of the weekend in conjunction with the activities regularly associated with the home, Cannie was essentially left alone to confront anyone who came looking for any of the above mentioned high risk activities.
5. Cannie Bullock's mother had gone to the bar that night to drink, leaving Cannie at home alone.
6. Cannie Bullock's mother had gotten into a fight that night before coming home.

It should be noted that the police specifically asked Linda Bullock whether she had prostituted herself or her daughter Cannie for drugs or money. This means they had specific reasons to suspect that this activity was going on, as these are not questions to be asked lightly. Indications of both exist in the material provided to this examiner, though there is no definitive evidence. If either circumstance were the case, the very highest level of lifestyle and incident risks would be in play.

Given the lifestyle and incident risk in this case, this examiner concludes that the number of potential suspects for the homicide in this case is quite high. At the same time, this victimology also strongly suggests that Cannie Bullock would not have opened the door for a complete stranger.

Victimology refers to the scientific study of victimization, including the relationships between victims and offenders, investigators, courts, corrections, media, and social movements (Karmen, 2004). *Forensic victimology* is the idiographic and nomothetic study of violent crime victims for the purposes of addressing investigative and forensic issues (Petherick and Turvey, 2008). This type of victimology differs from traditional forms of penal victimology, in that it is the objective study of victims with a focus on impartially and completely describing all aspects of their life and lifestyle in order to gain a better understanding of how they came to become victimized and their relationship to the offender and the crime scene.

The goal of the forensic victimologist is not one of advocacy or rehabilitation; it is accurately, critically, and objectively describing the victim to better understand victims, crime, and criminals to assist the court. Forensic victimology seeks to study victims as they are in a critical and scientific manner, disregarding stereotypical views to better understand the dynamics of the criminal act as well as the victims themselves.

In terms of what is necessary to compile a victimology, the answer is dependent on the case as well as the victim. No one checklist will encompass everything that should be examined about a victim. Nothing should be treated as trivial. This information can then be used for a number of purposes, including supporting or refuting allegations of victimization, establishing a suspect pool, and so on.

Importantly, victimologists need to make note of any factors which influence the victim's lifestyle and situational exposure. Determining these levels of exposure will assist with the development of the offender's modus operandi and signature, assist with linkage of unsolved cases, narrow suspect pools, and assist with contextualizing the case.

When it comes to a trial setting, victimologists may help the court determine that a crime has occurred; help the court determine that elements of the case meet the definition of the charges brought against the accused; reconstruct and contextualize what occurred; and demonstrate who the victim is/was, why he or she was targeted, how he or she was acquired, and most importantly by whom.

Review Questions

1. Describe the differences between forensic victimology and more traditional types of victimology.
2. Why is it necessary to determine the relationships between the primary components of a crime to solve it? What are these primary components?
3. Why is it necessary for forensic victimologists to understand the difference between investigatively useful speculation and court-worthy opinions?
4. T/F Forensic victimology assists with demonstrating the actual limits of victim evidence.

5. T/F Forensic victimology is a theoretical discipline.
6. Name and describe four ways forensic victimologists assist with investigations and court proceedings.
7. Name and describe five general victimological inquiries which are often made.
8. Describe the difference between victim lifestyle exposure and situational exposure.

REFERENCES

Burgess, A., Hazelwood, R., 1995. Practical Aspects of Rape Investigation, 2nd ed. CRC Press, Boca Raton, FL.

Dienstein, W., 2005. Criminal Investigation. In: Bailey, W. (Ed.), The Encyclopedia of Police Science, second ed. Garland Publishing, New York, pp. 160–162.

Drapkin, I., Viano, E., 1974. Victimology: A New Focus. Lexington Books, Lexington, MA.

Fisher, B., Sloan, J., Cullen, F., Lu, C., 1998. Crime in the Ivory Tower: The Level and Sources of Student Victimization. Criminology 36, 671–710.

Karmen, A., 2004. Crime Victims: An Introduction to Victimology, fifth ed. Thompson/Wadsworth, Belmont, CA.

Kennedy, D., Kennedy, B., 1972. Applied Sociology for Police. Charles C. Thomas Publishers, Springfield, IL.

Mendelsohn, B., 1976. Victimology and Contemporary Society's Trends. Victimology 1 (1), 8–28.

National Institute of Justice (NIJ), 1999. Death Investigation: A Guide for the Scene Investigator. Research Report NCJ 167568. NIJ, Washington, DC.

Petherick, W., Turvey, B., 2008. Forensic Victimology. Elsevier Science, San Diego.

Popper, K., 1963. Conjectures and Refutations. Routledge and Keagan Paul, London.

Schultz, D., 2005. Courtroom Testimony. In: Bailey, W. (Ed.), The Encyclopedia of Police Science. Garland Publishing, New York, pp. 122–124.

Turvey, B., 2002. Criminal Profiling: An Introduction to Behavioral Evidence Analysis, 2nd ed. Elsevier Science, Boston.

Turvey, B.E., 2006. Beneath the Numbers: Rape and Homicide Clearance Rates in the United States. Journal of Behavioral Profiling 6 (1).

Turvey, B.E., 2008. Criminal Profiling: An Introduction to Behavioral Evidence Analysis, third ed. Elsevier Science, San Diego.

Weston, P., Wells, K., 1974. Criminal Investigation: Basic Perspectives, second ed. Prentice Hall, Englewood Cliffs, NJ.

CHAPTER 7

Premises Liability

Wayne Petherick and Brent E. Turvey

Lawsuits are a vital complement to the criminal justice system because civil litigation offers more options for redress, lower standards of proof, and greater opportunities for survivors to steer their litigation. Even the U.S. Department of Justice—hardly a shill for the plaintiffs' bar—distributes a publication that "encourages victim consideration of civil remedies."

> —Tom Lininger, Associate Professor of Law, University of Oregon
> (2008, p. 1560)

KEY TERMS

Balancing Test: A legal test which provides that property owners need to scale their security efforts to meet known threats based on the potential for harm, and within reason.

Deterrent: "[A]nything which impedes or has a tendency to prevent" (Black, 1990, p. 450).

Expressive Offender: An offender who is defined by heightened emotional state; his or her motive is personal, being associated with jealousy, anger, power, or even sexual desire.

Foreseeability: "[T]he ability to see or know in advance; e.g. the reasonable anticipation that harm or injury is a likely result from certain acts or omissions" (Black, 1990, p. 649).

Imminent Harm Test: (a.k.a. *specific harm test*) A test which "requires the plaintiff to show that a landlord was aware that a specific individual was acting in such a manner as to pose a clear threat to the safety of an identifiable target" (Kennedy, 2006, p. 124).

Instrumental Offender: An offender who is defined by the desire to achieve a specific end, usually financial or materially oriented. Such offenders are deliberate, planful, and engage in acts of precaution to limit their exposure to being apprehended and identified.

CONTENTS

237

Premises Liability: The civil responsibility incurred by property owners
  who fail to provide reasonable and adequate security to their lessees,
  customers, and other invited patrons or guests while on their property, to
  include the structures within.
Prior Similar Acts Test: A test which is based on the premise that the past
  is in fact the best indication of the future.
Reasonableness: In legal terms, a reference to what a rationally thinking
  layperson would think or do under a particular set of circumstances.
  Highly subjective.
Totality of the Circumstances Test: The determination of foreseeability
  by virtue of examining the social and environmental factors related to a
  particular type of crime.

As should be clear by now, the role of forensic criminologists is not confined to assistance with criminal trials, despite their crime-oriented expertise. This is a result of ever increasing civil litigation initiated by victim-plaintiffs related to liability for the harm caused during criminal acts (Voigt and Thornton, 1996). Kennedy (2006, p. 122) provides a useful explanation:

> Generally speaking, negligent security constitutes a tort at English
> common law. A tort is a civil wrong for which the plaintiff hopes
> to receive compensation. In order to prove his or her case, the
> plaintiff must establish by a preponderance of the evidence that the
> defendant (1) owed the plaintiff a *duty* to act in a certain way, that (2)
> the defendant *breached* his or her duty by failing to act as the duty
> required, and that this (3) *caused* some (4) *harm* to the plaintiff.

Negligence lawsuits are not necessarily a function of victim litigiousness and greed, as explained in Lininger (2008), because the criminal justice system serves only to punish the criminal and not to make the victim whole. Though he was referencing sex crimes in specific, we will learn that Lininger's comments may be generalized to just about any type of violent crime (pp. 1559–1560):

> The last few years have seen a tremendous increase in lawsuits
> alleging rape or sexual assault. Not only has the number of plaintiffs
> grown, but claimants are recovering larger awards. In particular, 2007
> was a record year for such suits. According to one scholar, the recent
> success of civil claims for sexual abuse proves the symbiosis of tort law
> and criminal law.
>
> There are many reasons for this burgeoning civil litigation. Broader
> insurance coverage, better organization among the plaintiffs' bar,
> innovative theories of third-party liability, feminist support for civil

remedies, the success of civil claimants in high-profile cases—all have played a role in expanding civil litigation by survivors of rape.

One important change in the last decade is the government's endorsement of civil litigation as a remedy for rape victims. At both the federal and local level, agencies are urging survivors of rape to consider civil recourse. These agencies recognize that criminal prosecutions cannot make victims whole.

When civil litigation involves a violent crime, forensic criminologists are among the more common and useful examiners to employ. Civil attorneys, often outside their usual realm in these cases, need an able guide to the investigative and forensic practices and opinions they will encounter, as well as independent analyses to find any weaknesses in the opposition's theories. For forensic criminologists, the various types of assessments performed are the same or similar to those utilized in investigative and criminal proceedings; however, there will be different questions to answer and radically different admissibility issues (see Chapter 4).

This chapter is aimed at educating forensic criminologists regarding the nature and scope of premises liability, the criminological issues that need to be assessed, and specific analytical recommendations that will assist in the task. Their knowledge of and proficiency with these issues and assessments will separate them from security experts without a scholarly background, as well as those who simply testify for a paycheck (Kennedy, 2006). While this chapter will set forensic criminologists on the right path, it will not make them experts in premises liability issues or assessments on its own. Case examples will be provided as needed.

PREMISES LIABILITY AND EXPERT TESTIMONY

Premises liability is the civil responsibility incurred by property owners who fail to provide reasonable and adequate security to their lessees, customers, and other invited patrons or guests while on their property, to include the structures within. This includes harm caused by third parties engaged in the commission of criminal acts. As explained in Voigt and Thornton (1996, p. 167):

> When a property owner fails to provide a reasonably safe environment to patrons and, as a result, an invited individual suffers a criminal victimization such as a rape, armed robbery, or assault by a third party, the property owner may be liable under civil jurisdiction for losses the patron incurs. Relatives of patrons who are murdered on premises are, likewise, subject to civil remedy associated with the loss of a loved one. Losses may include costs associated with physical injury, psychological trauma leading to inability to enjoy life or earn a living, and future income foregone as a result of victimization.

Kennedy (2006, p. 120) offers further elucidation of those crimes and circumstances that commonly result in premises-liability-related negligence suits:

> ...[L]andowners and landlords of all stripes may be legally liable should a passenger, customer, client, tenant, guest, or other category of visitor to the premises be assaulted while on property under their control. For example, merchants may be sued by a customer attacked in a store's restroom or car park. A hotel guest sexually assaulted in her room by a nighttime intruder may have a cause of action against hotel management. Students at a university, visitors to a corporate headquarters, and passengers of common carriers are increasingly looking to the courts to order compensation from the owners and managers of the property whereupon their injures were sustained (Michael and Ellis, 2003). The actual perpetrators of these acts are unlikely targets of such lawsuits since their identities often remain unknown or they themselves are simply uncollectible. This leaves, of course, the third-party corporate entity which is often looked upon as a 'deep pockets' defendant.

> Not only might a commercial enterprise be sued for a criminal act occurring on its property, a lawsuit might arise out of the actions of its own employees. Should a salesperson assault a customer, or a contract security officer wrongfully detain a suspected shoplifter, liability may attach. In addition to crimes by employees, modern organizations must be concerned about crimes *against* employees. Traditionally, business entities had been relatively immune from lawsuits instituted against them by their own employees for injuries sustained while at work because in many jurisdictions workers' compensation was their exclusive remedy. Even this barrier, however, is beginning to erode as more and more courts are carving out exceptions to workers' compensation laws and allowing increasing numbers of employees or their heirs to successfully sue employers for crime-related injuries sustained while on the job (Sakis and Kennedy, 2002).

Premises liability and security experts of all backgrounds have been thrown into the civil realm to provide assessments in these cases. Few have the education, training, or experience to do so at the same level as criminologists (Voigt and Thornton, 1996), though many incorrectly believe otherwise. Rather than being a matter of second-guessing, 20/20 hindsight, or Monday morning quarterbacking, as is often suggested (and even practiced by some), the criminological assessment of premises liability cases must be rooted in deliberately constructed analysis of objective case features by qualified forensic examiners.

Consider the following examples, both for and against the admission of experts in what is essentially forensic criminology, provided by Britt (2001, pp. 34–36):

In Lincoln Property Co. v. DeShazo, the plaintiff was attacked in a shopping center parking lot that was leased by several commercial tenants. The owner of the shopping center had one security guard on duty the night of the attack. One shopping center tenant was a bar that occasionally hosted events known as "college nights." The plaintiff attended one of these events and was attacked in the parking area near the bar's entrance.

The plaintiff sued the company that owned the shopping center, claiming it knew that customers of the bar were often assaulted in its parking lot during college nights. A jury awarded the plaintiff compensatory and punitive damages. The owner appealed, arguing, among other things, that the trial court should have excluded the plaintiff's expert testimony about the standard of care, proximate cause, and gross negligence.

The expert had 10 years of experience as a police officer and had "moonlighted" as a security officer for a department store and a hospital. He had been the head of security for a mall. He was later the agent in charge of the federal Drug Enforcement Administration office in Lubbock, Texas, where his duties included analyzing commercial properties to assess the risks associated with enforcing federal laws against drug-related crimes that might occur on those premises.

The expert testified that a reasonably prudent property owner would have employed at least five or six security officers to control the college-night crowd and that the plaintiff's injuries would not have occurred if the shopping center had provided the extra guards. The shopping center owner argued that the expert's security experience was too remote and superficial. The appellate court held that the shopping center's objection "addresse[d] the credibility or weight of [the expert's] testimony, not its admissibility."

Although an expert with experience in security is preferable, and the best expert is someone who actually does security work (not a professional expert witness), a witness does not necessarily have to possess this experience to be qualified as a security expert. Under Kumho, this person's conclusions must be based on the same standards he or she uses in everyday work in the field.

In Warmack & Co. v. Beltz, a plaintiff who was attacked by a robber while shopping sued the mall for negligence. Defense counsel challenged the qualifications of a witness who testified at trial that additional security was needed and that it would have reduced the likelihood of the injury.

The witness had a college degree and 30 years of experience with the police department, the last 10 of which he spent as a lieutenant of detectives in the special thefts unit. The witness testified that during his tenure as a detective, he was in charge of several groups that helped shopping malls with their security arrangements during the Christmas season. He had also set up the security arrangements for a major manufacturer in the area. He testified that because of his experience, he was qualified to assess the security arrangements at shopping malls.

Defense counsel argued that the witness was not qualified as an expert under Daubert because, although he had experience in law enforcement, he did not have particular expertise in shopping mall security.

The trial court allowed his testimony, and the court of appeals affirmed, holding: Based on the testimony of Bradley's background and his experience in security matters (both generally and specifically relating to shopping malls), his experience and understanding of the working of the criminal mind, and his background in law enforcement, the court's decision to admit him as an expert witness was within its discretionary authority.

As Warmack shows, some courts will consider a witness's general experience and understanding of the "working of the criminal mind" when determining whether he or she is qualified to serve as a security expert.

However, in 1998's Shah v. Pan American World Services, the appellate court upheld a district court's refusal to allow expert testimony in a case brought by passengers and representatives of those injured or killed by hijackers on board an aircraft in Pakistan. The trial court refused to allow the expert to testify because he "had never been a security officer with an American commercial airport or American airline, had never performed a threat assessment of an airport, had performed no recent consulting work, and had received no training with respect to airport or airline security."

Although the court did not discuss the witness's education or training, it appears to have focused on his lack of experience in disqualifying him.

In Kerlec v. E-Z Serve Convenience Stores, Inc., a district court considered the defendant's motion to exclude testimony of the plaintiff's security expert. The plaintiff was robbed and shot by two assailants outside an E-Z Serve. The plaintiff retained a forensic criminologist who specialized in crime analysis, crime prevention, and security assessment to evaluate the adequacy of security at the store and its relation to the attack on the plaintiff.

E-Z Serve argued that the expert's opinions were unreliable speculation and not relevant because they were matters of common knowledge.

In a straightforward Daubert analysis, the district court held that the witness's opinions were reliable because he had a doctorate in sociology with a specialty in criminology, had extensive experience in security analysis and consulting, was widely published in the area of crime prevention, and provided an analysis of the location that included references to crime prevention guidelines.

The court also concluded that his opinions were relevant, finding that they were not within the common knowledge of the average person. The court recognized that the witness's report analyzed various conditions at the store in light of security guidelines, risk factors, and crime prevention recommendations.

Relying more on the witness's experience than on the substance of his testimony, the court concluded that his "knowledge of social science, his reliance on industry standards, and his experience in security assessment is outside of the common knowledge of laypersons and... his testimony will assist the jury to determine facts in issue."

As these cases demonstrate, there is no universal or set standard for showing expertise in premises liability issues. Every court has its own sense of who is and is not qualified as an expert on related matters, and such standards are often case specific. However, the general tendency favors those with advanced education in criminology, along with assessment experience and publications related to the type of crime at hand; or extensive law enforcement experience with the crimes and circumstance involved.

THE DUTY TO PROTECT

In a negligence case, the court will rule on whether the defendant owes the alleged victim a duty of care—from a legal standpoint. This determination will likely happen without the input of forensic criminologists, so that by the time they are involved, the issue may already be resolved. This is one of the many legal determinations that forensic criminologists will need to accept as being within the explicit purview of the court.

Kennedy (2006, p. 122) describes the two cases in the United States which are regarded as the "forerunners of third-party litigation against landlords, businesses, and corporate entities": *Kline v. 1500 Massachusetts Avenue Apartment Corporation* and *Garzilli v. Howard Johnson's Motor Lodges, Inc.*:

> In the 1970 case of *Kline v. 1500 Massachusetts Avenue Apartment Corporation*, a tenant sued her landlord for allowing the apartment building's security to deteriorate after she had moved in. Ms Kline was subsequently assaulted and robbed. Ultimately, the appeals court ruled the landlord had a duty to take steps to protect Ms. Kline since only the landlord had sufficient control of the premises to do so. The court ruled the landlord-tenant contract required the landlord to provide those protective measures which are within his reasonable capacity. It also noted that the relationship of the modern apartment house dweller to a landlord is akin to that of innkeeper and guest, and, therefore, a duty similar to that imposed on innkeepers would apply (Carrington and Rapp, 1991).

> The Garzilli case, also known as the 'Connie Francis' case, has given great impetus to victims' rights litigation. In *Garzilli v. Howard Johnson's Motor Lodges, Inc.*, the internationally known recording artist was assaulted in 1974 while in her motel suite. The unit's sliding glass doors gave the appearance of being locked, but the faulty latches were easily defeated by an intruder. The property manager had known the locks were defective but had not yet provided for secondary-locking devices. The notoriety of the Connie Francis case came because of her star status and because the jury initially awarded her over two million dollars in compensatory damages (Carrington and Rapp, 1991). Thereafter, crime victims were more inclined to pursue redress through the civil courts and soon found their pleas resonating with plaintiffs' attorneys, juries, and the judiciary as well.

Both cases involve clearly defined circumstances where there is a special relationship binding the plaintiff (the victim) to the defendant (the property owner).

Generally speaking, there is no duty of care owed any victim "unless there is a special relationship between the two parties such as that of merchant–invitee, landlord–tenant, innkeeper–guest, public carrier–passenger or the like" (Kennedy, 2006, p. 122). As explained in Driscoll (2006, p. 883), those who are invited onto a property (a.k.a. invitees), or have some other right to be there, are ostensibly under the supervision and guardianship of those holding ownership:

> The owner owes the highest duty of care to the invitee. There is some disagreement in the literature about what exactly defines an invitee: some argue that if the land has been held open to the public in such

a way as to imply an invitation, then anyone entering becomes an invitee; whereas others argue that the concept of an invitee only encompasses business relationships. This ambiguity is reflected in the Restatement (Second) of Torts which defines an invitee as not only one who enters the land "for a purpose for which the land is held open to the public," but also as a "business visitor" who comes upon the land for a purpose connected in some way with "business dealings with the possessor of the land." Since the invitee has been invited onto the land by the landowner, whether implicitly or explicitly, the landowner has a duty of "reasonable care for his safety." Thus, he must not only warn the invitee of conditions which may exist and cause harm, but also protect him against those dangers of which the invitee "knows or has reason to know, where it may reasonably be expected that he will fail to protect himself notwithstanding his knowledge."

Conversely, trespassers enter a property with no rights and no special relationship, accepting the risk of whatever they encounter. There are exceptions to this, including "situations in which the landowner knows or has reason to know that members of the public constantly trespass, knows or has reason to know of a specific trespasser on the land, or with trespassers who are children" (Driscoll, p. 885). Barring these exceptions, owners need only refrain from intentional and unprovoked acts against trespassers to avoid this kind of premises liability. Despite what is often seen in films and on television, property owners may not set traps for, or deliberately shoot at, those who are simply trespassing on their land or in their structures.

Once a duty of care is established by virtue of a special relationship, the question will arise as to what precisely that duty is, and whether the defendant breached it. This is where the forensic criminologist comes in. As explained in Kennedy (2006, p. 129):

> ...[L]itigants will often introduce evidence purporting to establish certain standards of care against which a defendant's conduct is to be compared. Theoretically, a jury's job would be much easier if it could simply assess a defendant's behavior and then compare it to a known, descriptive standard specifying what the behavior should have been. The problem, of course, is identifying just what the standard of care is for a given set of circumstances. Not only will knowledgeable people disagree as to the nature of the appropriate standard, debates over the meaning of related concepts such as 'guidelines' or 'best practices' are likely to ensue. In order for the forensic security specialist to navigate in the legal arena, it is important for him or her to understand the sources of various standards of care pertaining to security.

As this suggests, standards of care vary from cases to case, depending on the region, community, and professionals involved. The standards of care at a hospital, for example, are radically different from the standards of care that govern hotels or even schools.

Kennedy (2008, p. 5) suggests that best practice, or the community standard of care, may be determined by referencing the following sources:

1. Statutes and ordinances
2. National consensus standards
3. Community practices
4. Organizational policies and procedures
5. Learned treatises, association literature, and expert opinions
6. Reasonableness

Reasonableness is the most subjective of these, referring to what a reasonable person would do. However, this is intended to be distinct from personal standards of care offered *ipse dixit*.[1] This is warned against as being essentially self-interested and contrary to those adopted by a community or a group of professionals. The absence of a consensus regarding practice standards in a particular professional community or discipline may therefore be used to argue negligence—because those involved may not have pulled it together enough to bother defining best professional practice. In such cases, those with a duty of care may be acting without an informed and appraisable professional compass despite the need for one.

[1]Latin phrase meaning "he himself said it." This refers generally to statements that are asserted solely on the basis of faith in an expert or authority, without proofs or critiques.

FORESEEABILITY

Foreseeability refers to "the ability to see or know in advance; e.g. the reasonable anticipation that harm or injury is a likely result from certain acts or omissions" (Black, 1990, p. 649). As explained in Huber (1988, p. 58): "Foreseeing the future depends largely on remembering the past. This means that an accident involving bizarre behavior becomes foreseeable as soon as it has happened." Easily confused with concrete prediction, assessing foreseeability is actually about determining whether the occurrence of a particular crime was more likely than not. This is done by examining the current case and its circumstances in light of the past.

To determine the foreseeability of a particular crime and subsequent harm within the facts of a given case, Voigt and Thornton (1996, p. 171) suggest the employment of an overall "crime foreseeability model." This mandates an in-depth analysis of prior similar and other interpersonal crimes; incident reports and supplemental crime data related to the offense; other types of crime at the location (e.g., property crimes, burglaries); the level of physical security at the location, including the security plan and philosophy (if any); relevant and applicable industry standards as set forth by related professional organizations; the social, economic, and demographic characteristics of the area surrounding the location; the nature and profile of the offender; and the nature and profile of the victim. The presence of synergistic factors from this evidence and material can be used to effectively argue the likelihood of a particular crime and the harm it caused, so long as the forensic criminologist is familiar with the data and published research related to each.

Kennedy (2006, p. 123), on the other hand, provides that "foreseeability should be assessed on a continuum from not foreseeable to highly foreseeable," explaining that there are at least four tests being used in different legal jurisdictions: the imminent or specific harm test, the prior similar acts test, the totality of the circumstances test, and the balancing test. These should, in some fashion, incorporate the analyses didactically suggested in Voigt and Thornton (1996).

The *imminent harm test*, a.k.a. the specific harm test, "requires the plaintiff to show that a landlord was aware that a specific individual was acting in such a manner as to pose a clear threat to the safety of an identifiable target. Given the large size of much commercial property open for business to the public, it is unlikely that landlords or their agents will be physically present at many emergent situations, thus effectively absolving them of liability" (Kennedy, p. 124).

The *prior similar acts test* is based on the premise that the past is in fact the best indication of the future. As explained in Kennedy (2006, p. 124): "It is almost axiomatic in forensic criminology and psychology that the best predictor of future behavior is past behavior." Contrary to the adage that lightning doesn't strike twice in the same place, it is an empirical reality that once a particular crime has occurred at a given location, its reoccurrence becomes more likely as "hot spots" develop. Moreover, the same is true of offenders; once they have committed a particular type of crime, the likelihood that they will commit it again goes up (p. 124):

> Empirical research involving the course of crime at 'hot spots' has shown, for example, that in one major city, each location had initially only an 8 percent chance of suffering a predatory offense. Once such an offense occurred, however, the chance of a second increased to 26 percent. After a third offense, the risk of a fourth within the year exceeded 50 percent (Sherman, Gartin, and Buerger, 1989). Should a burglary take place at a residential location, the likelihood it will be reburglarized may increase up to fourfold (Weisel, 2002). Similar patterns may be applied to individuals. Criminal recidivism rates often reach 60 to 70 percent (Austin and Irwin, 2001). The more crimes an individual has committed in the past, the more crimes he is likely to commit in the future. This is particularly true of early-onset delinquents and psychopaths (Lykken, 1995; Piquero and Mazerolle, 2001). Given

the importance of past history in attempting to forecast future events, the forensic security expert should immediately acquaint himself with the history of a property either to be protected or which has already become the subject of litigation. Jurisdictions will vary as to whether prior crime must be substantially similar to the litigated crime or whether, for example, as in Georgia, crimes against property may also make crimes against persons foreseeable (Gorby, 1998).

This makes clear the need for not only educating oneself regarding the recidivism literature related to offenses in particular regions as they bear on specific types of crime, but also the need for staying current as crime trends evolve. What may have been true for one type of crime in a particular region five years ago may not hold true today.

The *totality of the circumstances test* refers to the determination of foreseeability by virtue of examining the social and environmental factors related to a particular type of crime (Kennedy, 2006). Certain demographic characteristics are associated with increased crime in urban areas, such as proximity to criminal activities, criminal populations, the poverty level and population mobility. Additionally, certain locations are known to attract or generate criminal activity. These are explained in Kennedy (2006, p. 127):

> Further related to land use, an interesting distinction can be made between properties described as crime 'attractors' and those described as crime 'generators' (Brantingham and Brantingham, 1995). The former tend to experience more crime than other locations simply because there are more potential victims from which criminals may choose although the level of risk per individual may not be heightened. Crime generators, on the other hand, foretell more crime because of the illicit nature of activities on the premises, such as illegal gambling, prostitution, and drug trafficking. Since the association between drug use, drug trafficking, and crime is so well established (Goldstein, 1985), security managers must take action to both prevent and aggressively respond to any such activities occurring on the properties for which they are responsible.

Forensic criminologists are charged with the analysis of as much contextual information as is available when using this particular test because less information about social and demographic characteristics is not better.

The *balancing test* is a compromise used in legal jurisdictions where the prior similar incidents test is seen to overly favor the landowner, and the totality of circumstances test is seen to overly favor the victim. It provides that property owners need to scale their security efforts to meet known threats based on the potential for harm, and within reason. That is to say, they need not engage in the extravagant security efforts. Moreover, as "the gravity of the possible harm increases, the likelihood of its occurrence needs to be correspondingly less in order to trigger the implementation of appropriate security measures" (Kennedy, 2006, p. 127). A specific recommendation regarding the prongs of this test to be employed by forensic criminologists is provided in Kennedy (p. 127):

> The three prongs of this test are: (1) the level of crime foreseeability, (2) the likelihood a given combination of security measures will prevent future harm, and (3) the burden of taking such precautions.

As a consequence of jurisdictional inconsistency regarding legal standards of proof on the issue of foreseeability, forensic criminologists must take care to learn those in use by the presiding court when accepting a premises liability case. This will dictate the nature, scope, and admissibility of their expert opinions. However, they should still fall back on the recommended "crime foreseeability model" as a basis for any findings because criminological assessments are to be conducted outside the influence of the court. Recall that the court may rule on what is admissible, but they may not dictate the limits of good science or best criminological practice.

As pointed out by Kennedy (2006), unless the foreseeability of harm can first be established, there is no duty to protect. If a forensic criminologist determines that a crime was not foreseeable, then this may be used by defense to argue that no duty existed in the case at hand. Consequently, while the court may determine that a defendant has a clear duty of care, the issue of foreseeability can be used to remove it. This makes the findings of the forensic criminologist on this particular issue highly relevant to such proceedings.

OFFENSE AND OFFENDER DETERRABILITY

Once the issue of foreseeability has been assessed, forensic criminologists may examine the same evidence to determine whether the offense would have been preventable and the offender deterrable.

In this context, a *deterrent* is "anything which impedes or has a tendency to prevent" (Black, 1990, p. 450). This refers to specific security measures that may be taken by property owners to impede different types of crime. Some work, and some don't. As explained in Kennedy (2006, p. 134):

> ...[L]ighting is not the automatic crime deterrent it is thought to be by so many laymen (Farrington and Welsh, 2002; Marchant, 2004) nor does CCTV function universally to deter crimes against the person (Gill and Loveday, 2003; Painter and Tilley, 1999; Welsh and Farrington, 2003; Welsh and Farrington, 2004). Just as random police patrol is

losing ground to directed patrol, security managers may need to rethink standard security officer deployment practices based on the best empirical evidence available (e.g. Sherman, Gottfredson, MacKenzie, Eck, Reuter and Bushway, 1997).

The forensic implications of these critical evaluations are obvious: improved lighting may not have prevented an attack in a parking lot so there may be no obvious causal relationship between a defendant's lighting levels and the crime. If CCTV does not prevent violent crimes in convenience stores, how can failure to install CCTV at a given location be the cause of a clerk's attack? On the other hand, lighting and CCTV may manifest preventive benefits in certain circumstances involving certain perpetrators. Lighting, for example, seems to be the catalyst which provides for the synergy of several security measures working together to more effectively harden a target. Hence, the liability implications of conventional security measures still need to be sorted out on a case-by-case basis. Lighting, CCTV, and preventive patrol are mentioned only as examples of popular security practices which need to be evaluated for the purposes of each particular property. Other security measures should also be realistically assessed before implementation so that a false sense of security is not generated.

This is simply to say that every security measure has an appropriate aim and context; some are capable of deterring only certain offenders from specific offenses, while others may actually encourage them by recording it. And not every security measure seeks to deter but rather may only provide for the later identification of suspects, as with CCTV cameras, providing they are of sufficient quality and actually turned on (the authors have worked cases in which such cameras are only for show, without connection to a power source or a recording device).

However, Voigt and Thornton (1996, p. 186) argue that certain offenses cannot be predicted, and certain offenders cannot be deterred:

> Certain types of particularly heinous or dangerous offenders who have severe character disorders or mental illnesses (e.g. antisocial personality, conduct disorders, or psychoses) or who otherwise commit bizarre, one-of-a-kind types of offenses (e.g. rampage or mass murders) present threats to public or private establishments that cannot be reasonably predicted or deterred by usual security methods.

While this may be true in specific cases, the authors would disagree with the generalization that all offenders with mental health issues or illnesses are necessarily undeterrable, or that all rampages and mass murders are unpredictable. Each case must be assessed on its own merits. For example, prior threats of mass murder by an employee or a student make the anticipation of a shooting spree fairly reasonable in the right context; and certain mental disorders can make offenders very predictable with respect to their propensity for irrationality and level of violence, depending on their individual affliction. So while we agree with the spirit of Voigt and Thornton (1996), that there are some offenders and offenses that cannot be predicted or deterred, we also agree that this must be assessed on a case-by-case basis and without blanket generalizations.

Of concern are those offenders with distorted perceptions of reality owing to specific types of mental illness or substance abuse. They are unpredictable and often unaffected by traditional security measures for failure to perceive them at all, let alone perceive them as a threat to safety, identification, and capture. Particularly of interest are those with psychopathic traits. Psychopathic offenders are impulsive, unpredictable, and do not experience fear as the rest of us do (Hare, 1993). They are therefore more apt to be undeterred by security measures that might cause more deliberate offenders to rethink their plans.

Another useful measure is whether offenders are instrumental or expressive in the commission of their crimes. *Instrumental offenders* are defined by their desire to achieve a specific end, usually financial or materially oriented. They are deliberate, planful, and engage in acts of precaution to limit their exposure of being discovered, identified, and apprehended. *Expressive offenders* are defined by their heightened emotional state; their motive is personal, being associated with jealousy, anger, power, or even sexual desire. As discussed in Kennedy (2006, p. 135):

> As a practical matter, criminologists have generally found the criminal who acts instrumentally to be more deterrable (or displaceable) than one whose crimes tend to be expressive in nature (cf. Nettler, 1989). Thus, a professional criminal who tends to choose a lucrative target carefully might be more sensitive to security measures than a morbidly jealous man who charges into his girlfriend's place of work and shoots her in front of many witnesses because he had recently heard rumors of her infidelity.

The highly variable nature of offense and offender deterrability, again, speaks to the need for the forensic criminologist to make a deliberate assessment of the facts and circumstances on a case-by-case basis, not blanket generalizations about security efforts and offender types. For specific methodology on ideographic (case based) offender profiling as an assessment technique, see Chapter 5.

THE IMPORTANCE OF VICTIMOLOGY

Equally important to the criminological assessment of the offender in a premises liability case are similar assessments that must be conducted of the victim. It is accepted in civil litigation that the victim may have engaged in contributory negligence with respect to the harm that has befallen him or her. In other words, the victim may be partially, if not completely, responsible for his or her own suffering or loss. In civil actions arising out of criminal acts, this is far less likely, but it can be a legitimate defense against all or part of the property owner's liability.

The victim may be in a vulnerable state: whether intoxicated, using a controlled substance, or in an agitated mental state (e.g., angry or excited). Or the victim may possess personal or lifestyle traits that increase his or her vulnerability, such as old age, mental illness, or mental or physical disability. Whatever the circumstance, the forensic criminologist must conduct a victimology to determine whether and how enduring victim traits and temporary circumstances played a role in their victimity. As discussed in Voigt and Thornton (1996), the questions to resolve when assessing a victim revolve around establishing his or her responsibility for the crime, and the nature of the victim's vulnerability to crime (p. 187):

> Using these two variables (responsibility and risk), criminologists attempt to explain the dynamic and varied relationship between the criminal and the victim....

> Complete innocence is the most commonly accepted category of victimization. It includes people who did nothing that conceivably could have elicited criminal action. They have no culpability for the crime. Unintentional facilitation is unwittingly, carelessly, or negligently making it easier for a crime to occur, such as leaving car keys in the ignition of a car or leaving a door to an apartment unlocked....

> Victim precipitation, on the other hand, occurs when a person willfully initiates the encounter with the eventual offender, directly enticing, challenging, insulting, provoking, or even initially assaulting the person.

It should be noted that victim responsibility and risk are not either/or propositions as this passage might tend to suggest; victim responsibility is not a binary state in which one is either completely innocent or completely precipitant. Rather, responsibility and risk exist on a continuum that must be assessed on a case-by-case basis. Most victims are not going to be completely innocent, but that does not necessarily remove or even diminish the liability of property owners. The degree to which this holds true will be determined by the trier of fact. It is the place of the forensic criminologist to ensure that, when making these determinations, the trier is given the most complete and accurate picture of related events.

For specific methodology related to ideographic (case-based) victimology as an assessment technique in forensic work, particularly with respect to incident and lifestyle exposure, see Chapter 6.

ASSESSMENT RECOMMENDATIONS

Beyond the assessment recommendations already provided, the authors strongly encourage forensic criminologists to consider the following additional measures:

1. Before setting to the task of assessing the crime, victim, or offender, forensic criminologists should attempt to exclude the possibility of a false report with an equivocal forensic analysis of the underlying case facts (see Chapter 4).

2. Forensic criminologists should not be afraid to consider and assess the strengths and weaknesses of opposing counsel's theory of liability as it relates to criminological issues. This is useful both for reasons of objectivity and full disclosure. An attorney-client will be glad to know from where the swords may fall, and forensic criminologists may identify facts and information that would otherwise be left without consideration.

3. If opposing counsel appoints an expert with an alternate view, forensic criminologists should make certain to study that expert's notes and reports carefully to determine whether and how findings differ and why.

4. On the same note, forensic criminologists should take care to scrutinize any opposing experts by diligently checking out their resumes for errors, omissions, exaggerations, and falsifications. Forensic criminologists should be certain that all qualifications ring true, and that they are actually related to the area of expertise being proffered.

5. Interviewing the offender is optional because that task is more aligned with psychological assessments than criminological ones. Moreover, any interview conducted at this stage is not going to be proximate to the offense. Reading offender interviews or statements from the police file and examining case facts closer in time to events will provide better insight in motive and intent. That is, unless there are specific questions that may benefit from an answer despite the passage of time.

Consider the following case example.

CASE EXAMPLE

Estate of Elizabeth Garcia v. Allsup's Convenience Stores, Inc. (2008)

This case involves the abduction, rape, and murder of 26-year-old Elizabeth Ann Garcia, in the early morning hours of January 16, 2002, from her place of work at Allsup's Convenience Store located at 5312 N. Lovington Hwy, Hobbs, New Mexico. She was working alone when she was abducted, and her body was found later that day in a field, with evidence of sexual assault and having suffered 57 stab wounds. The cause of death was provided as "multiple stab wounds of head, neck and torso." Paul Lovett was arrested for Elizabeth Garcia's murder in 2003, after he was first connected to the murder of another woman almost a year later (35-year-old Patty Simon). He has been convicted of both homicides.

The family of Elizabeth Garcia filed a lawsuit against the convenience store chain that she had worked for, alleging its negligence contributed to her death. The defense hired retired FBI Profiler Gregg O. McCrary as a security expert to evaluate the offender behavior, and the offense, in the light of those claims.

Mr. McCrary testified pretrial that Elizabeth Garcia was preselected as a target by Paul Lovett, and therefore undeterrable by any security measures—this despite the fact that they did not know each other, had never met, and did not have a pre-existing relationship. In his deposition, McCrary also strayed wildly into profiling-related areas while claiming that he wasn't, and claimed expertise that he does not actually possess.

Mr. McCrary also failed to give his clients damaging impeachment information regarding prior cases in which his testimony had been excluded; fabricated a degree on his resume (not for the first time); and generally misrepresented his education, training, and experience under oath. The plaintiff in this case retained the services of one of the authors (Turvey), and these facts were brought to light in a subsequent expert declaration. As provided in an excerpt from that declaration (Turvey, 2008b):

> 8. I [Brent E. Turvey] have been asked by Allegra C. Carpenter, an attorney for The Estate of Elizabeth Garcia, to examine the deposition testimony of Gregg O. McCrary in *Estate of Elizabeth Garcia v. Allsup's Convenience Stores, Inc.* I was asked to evaluate soundness of his methodology and findings with respect to the current state of forensic practice and literature.
>
> 9. This case involves the abduction, rape, and murder of 26-year-old Elizabeth Ann Garcia, in the early morning hours of January 16, 2002, from her place of work at Allsup's Convenience Store located at 5312 N. Lovington Hwy, Hobbs, NM. She was working alone when she

was abducted, and her body was found later that day in a field, with evidence of sexual assault and having suffered 57 stab wounds. Cause of death was provided as "multiple stab wounds of head, neck and torso." Paul Lovett was arrested for Garcia's murder in 2003, after he was first connected to the murder of another woman almost a year later, 35-year-old Patty Simon. He has been convicted of both homicides.

10. In rendering my opinions, I have examined the transcript of Mr. McCrary's deposition (Second Judicial District Court, County of Santa Fe, State of New Mexico, No. D-0101–CV-2005–00045, December 12, 2007), and reviewed CV that he provided in this case. I have also examined the autopsy report of Elizabeth Garcia by Ross Zumwalt, MD (Feb. 12, 2002) and related reports documentation, to include trauma-grams, notes, toxicology report, and investigative notes and reports.

FINDINGS

11. Mr. McCrary has provided false information on his CV in this case. The undated McCrary CV provided to this examiner, which appears to have been updated through at least July 2006, provides on page 1 under EDUCATION "Master of Arts in Psychology, Marymount University Arlington, VA 1992." This would suggest that Mr. McCrary holds a graduate degree in psychology from Marymount University through their school of psychology, received in 1992. This is false information. As provided to Ms. Carpenter, this examiner has examined this issue with respect to Mr. McCrary on a previous occasion, as a consultant to the defense in *U.S. v. O.C. Smith* (2005). Consistent with a previous version of Mr. McCrary's CV obtained by this examiner when consulting on the *Estate of Sam Sheppard v. Ohio* (2000), Mr. McCrary actually a holds Master of Arts in Professional Psychological Services from Marymount University—obtained through their school of education. In *U.S. v. O.C. Smith*, Mr. McCrary provided a similar false CV to the court and was removed as an expert witness from the case by the prosecution when this information was disclosed to them. That Mr. McCrary has continued to provide this same false information on his CV subsequent to the Smith case removes the possibility of it being a typo, or similar error.

12. Mr. McCrary has offered himself as an expert in behavioral science without demonstrable behavioral science qualifications (e.g. deposition testimony at p. 7 "deterrability occurs in only one place, and that is in the mind of a would-be offender"). His undergraduate degrees are in music and criminal justice, and his graduate degree is related to guidance counseling. One could argue that as an FBI agent he accrued knowledge in the behavioral sciences, but there is no evidence of

this. His experience and training appears to be that of an analyst or investigator preparing investigative findings—not forensic ones—without completing formal education in any of the behavioral sciences (psychology, sociology, criminology or even anthropology). Moreover, his CV provides no peer reviewed research or publications in this subject area. On his CV, there are three publications listed. The first involves his contributor status to the Crime Classification Manual—as one of more than a hundred law enforcement contributors with no specific showing of his contribution to the text; the second involves a five page paper on stalking (Journal of Interpersonal Violence, Vol. 11, No. 4, pp. 487–502, 1996) with five other contributors; and the final publication is a co-authored, true crime, trade oriented, memoir style book of no professional merit or value. This lack of demonstrable expertise in the behavioral sciences may explain why false information is provided on the CV.

13. Mr. McCrary did not prepare written findings in this case. As provided in Chisum and Turvey's Crime Reconstruction (2007, pp. 120–121), the employment of verbal opinions alone is a substandard practice:

> Hans Gross referred to the critical role that exact, deliberate, and patient efforts at crime reconstruction can play in the investigation and resolution of crime. Specifically, he stated that just looking at a crime scene is not enough. He argued that there is utility in reducing one's opinions regarding the reconstruction to the form of a report in order to identify problems in the logic of one's theories (Gross, 1924, p. 439):
>
> > So long as one only looks on the scene, it is impossible, whatever the care, time, and attention bestowed, to detect all the details, and especially note the incongruities: but these strike us at once when we set ourselves to describe the picture on paper as exactly and clearly as possible... The "defects of the situation" are just those contradictions, those improbabilities, which occur when one desires to represent the situation as something quite different from what it really is, and this with the very best intentions and the purest belief that one has worked with all of the forethought, craft, and consideration imaginable.
>
> Moreover, the reconstructionist, not the recipient of the reconstructionist's opinions (i.e., investigators, attorneys, and the court), bears the burden of ensuring that her conclusions are

effectively communicated. This means writing them down. This means that the reconstructionist must be competent at intelligible writing, and her reports must be comprehensive with regard to examinations performed, findings, and conclusions.

Verbal conclusions should be viewed as a form of substandard work product. They are susceptible to conversions, alterations, and misrepresentations. They may also become lost to time. Written conclusions are fixed in time, easy to reproduce, and are less susceptible to accidental or intentional conversion, alteration, and misrepresentation. An analyst who prefers verbal conclusions as opposed to written conclusions reveals his preference for conclusive mobility.

Though speaking of reconstructionists specifically in this section, the authors were referring to forensic examiners in general when rendering these practice standards from the available literature.

14. On p. 56 of his deposition, Mr. McCrary testifies regarding deterrability: "That is the humbling reality of violent crime, is that, like I say, not all crime is evenly distributed by place—type of crime or place of occurrence. And we don't really know why that is. There are lots of theories about this. Criminologists have a lot of theories. Law enforcement has theories. We try different things. Some things seem to work better than other things. In the long run, sometimes we find out, well, it was just a coincidence that that worked. It really didn't have any—you know, it was a correlation rather than a causation, so bottom line is, we really don't know why that is." This position would seem to preclude offering opinions about what may or may not deter any criminal from committing any given offense. However, Mr. McCrary has given the opinion that Mr. Lovett was not deterrable because he went to the convenience store for the specific purpose of killing the victim, making the crime "target-oriented."

15. Mr. McCrary has provided no research or authority, other than his own unqualified experience, that "target-oriented" offenders are any more or less deterrable than other offenders. When asked directly he evades the issue and argues experience—of which he has none as it relates to convenience store crime. Experience is not meant to be a shield. As explained by Dr. John I. Thornton, the dishonest forensic examiner exploits the ignorance of their audience by citing experience rather than demonstrating knowledge. Taken from Thornton, John I. (1997) "The General Assumptions and Rationale of Forensic Identification," In David L. Faigman, David H. Kaye, Michael J. Saks, &

Joseph Sanders, (Eds.), *Modern Scientific Evidence: The Law And Science Of Expert Testimony*, Volume 2):

> Experience is neither a liability nor an enemy of the truth; it is a valuable commodity, but it should not be used as a mask to deflect legitimate scientific scrutiny, the sort of scrutiny that customarily is leveled at scientific evidence of all sorts. To do so is professionally bankrupt and devoid of scientific legitimacy, and courts would do well to disallow testimony of this sort. Experience ought to be used to enable the expert to remember the when and the how, why, who, and what. Experience should not make the expert less responsible, but rather more responsible for justifying an opinion with defensible scientific facts.

Equally important are the words of Dr. Paul L. Kirk from his text *Crime Investigation* (1953, pp. 17–18):

> The question of what constitutes adequate experience for the expert witness is a critical one in court procedures, and appears to be poorly understood in many quarters. It is quite common for the witness to be interrogated as to the number of years during which he has worked in a field, and the number of cases he has handled, the number of pieces of evidence he has examined, and similar quantitative matters. It must be apparent that the amount of his experience is not important beside the question of what he has learned from it.

The summoning of experience in this context is a red herring that moves attention away from matters of science, objectivity, and sound methodology. This is not a legitimate forensic practice.

16. When pressed, Mr. McCrary concedes his opinion that the offender is "target-oriented" is actually based on one of several possible scenarios—none of which he has investigated or reliably established. As shown in the exchange on p. 158 "A: Well, he certainly could have stumbled into her. He could have wanted to kill her and then just stumbled into her. That is a possibility. But I think it's more likely that he went there with the intention of killing her and did. Q: Even though you have no evidence that he knew she was working there? A: That never came out. That wasn't an issue in the criminal trial that I could see." See also p. 185 "I have no evidence that she knew him. I have no evidence that she did not know him. I have no evidence one way or the other." This testimony suggests that Mr. McCrary has assumed knowledge of the victim by the offender for the purpose of his analysis. This is not a legitimate forensic practice.

17. On p. 112 of his deposition, Mr. McCrary testifies that part of his opinion regarding the Paul Lovett's individual deterrability is that "there is profound pathology here." Presumably, this refers to some disease on the part of Mr. Lovett. Mr. McCrary is not a mental health professional, nor a behavioral scientist, nor has he interviewed and evaluated Mr. Lovett. Furthermore, I could find no evidence that Mr. Lovett had been examined in a forensic context, or diagnosed with any mental disorders. This inference by Mr. McCrary seems to overstep his expertise by a wide margin, as well as not being based on any known mental health evidence.

18. Based on his deposition, Mr. McCrary's opinions in this case are not based on the necessary victimological information required to make assessments about victim-offender interactions, and whether or not the offense could have been planned (e.g. p. 157–159; McCrary concedes not gathering information relating to victim's work habits, schedule, and other related information—he did not know which stores she worked at, when, who had knowledge of this schedule, or if the offender actually knew the victim or her schedule). As explained in Mr. McCrary's own text on the subject (*Crime Classification Manual*, Burgess et al, 1992, p. 7) "Victimology is often one of the most beneficial investigative tools in classifying and solving violent crime. It is also a crucial part of crime analysis. Through it, the investigator tries to evaluate why this particular person was targeted for a violent crime." Failure to perform a complete victimology before offering an opinion about whether or not the victim was targeted is not a legitimate forensic practice.

19. Mr. McCrary testified that he is an expert in general security, and therefore to a degree in convenience store security, despite no experience working or researching cases involving convenience stores. (See p. 56 "Q: You're not an expert in convenience store security, are you? A: I think security, in general, and to the degree it carries over to a convenience store, I would say, yes. Q: Yes, you are an expert in convenience store security? A: Security, in general. And, certainly, security at a convenience store would be the same security issue you face in any workplace. Q: Yes, sir. You have never done an analysis of any convenience store chain? A: No.") Suggesting that general knowledge is equal to specialized knowledge is a non-sequitor. Moreover, that Mr. McCrary believes convenience store security involves the same issues as any workplace belies his expertise on this subject. That he does not know enough to know that he is inexpert on this issue, given the facts and circumstances of this particular case, is problematic at best.

20. Mr. McCrary came to his opinions in this case without having read the whole law enforcement investigative file. (See p. 61 "A: Well, again, I don't know exactly what the police did. I have some idea from reading the trial transcript of what the investigation was, but, you know, I haven't seen the whole investigative file.") The investigative file often contains victimological detail, forensic information, and behavioral indicators about the crime that are not available elsewhere. Failing to avail oneself to this prior to rendering court-worthy behaviorally oriented conclusions is not a legitimate forensic practice.

21. P.188–194 of Mr. McCrary's deposition involves an exchange regarding Mr. McCrary's known error rates. He testifies that he and other FBI profilers were routinely "tested" while at the FBI, and that he is or has been in charge of testing analysts for the IACIAF. However, paradoxically, he claims to be unaware of his error rate, and then claims that there is no way to really know whether or not conclusions are truly accurate. This testimony does not seem consistent.

22. Mr. McCrary's testimony in this case regarding his error rates may be at odds with his previous testimony in *Estate of Sam Sheppard v. Ohio* (2000). As reported in McKnight, K., "Expert's Opinion Challenged," *Ohio Beacon Journal*, April 1, 2000:

> An ex-FBI agent who said he hasn't been wrong yet in his analyses of crime scenes, was prepared to testify for the state yesterday that the long-debated 1954 bludgeoning death of Marilyn Sheppard was the result of a "staged domestic homicide."

> But ready or not, Gregg O. McCrary—like many of the state's witnesses in the Dr. Sam Sheppard wrongful imprisonment civil trial—spent the bulk of the day being challenged by Sheppard attorney Terry Gilbert over whether he was enough of an expert to make such a determination.

Though I have not read the transcript, my information from counsel Terry Gilbert is this characterization of his testimony is accurate.

23. One test of FBI profiling methods that may cast some light on the error rate issue is provided by Howard Teten (the very first FBI profiler). In an FBI study of 192 cases where profiling was performed, 88 cases were solved. Of those 88 cases, the profile helped with the identification of the suspect only 17% of the time (15 cases). So the known efficacy rate for FBI profilers (using criminal investigative analysis) is 15 out 192. Taken from Teten, H. "Offender Profiling" in Bailey, W. (Ed.) (1995) *The Encyclopedia of Police Science*, p. 475.

Subsequent to the disclosure of findings by the author, the plaintiffs in this case filed a motion to exclude the testimony of Mr. McCrary. Upon consideration of these findings, incorporated into the motion and cross-examination of Mr. McCrary at a hearing, the judge issued the following order (*Garcia et al v. Allsup's Convenience Stores Inc.,* 2008):

ORDER

THIS MATTER having come before the Court on the Plaintiffs Daubert/Alberico Motion to Exclude Defense Expert Gregg McCrary and the Court having reviewed the briefing, heard the arguments of counsel and the testimony of Mr. McCrary and Dr. Ross Zumwalt on February 13, 2007,

FINDS, as follows:

1. Crime scene analysis and criminal profiling related to the motives of a killer do not meet the standards for expert testimony in Daubert v. Merrell Dow Pharmaceuticals or State v. Alberico;

2. The methodology used by Mr. McCrary is:
   a. Not able to be tested by experiments, research or otherwise;
   b. Not based upon or is not capable of scientific analysis;
   c. Not reproducible;
   d. Not reviewable for any rate of error.

3. The opinions of Mr. McCrary related to the motives of Paul Lovett, whether described as "victim-targeted" behavior, deterrability or foreseeability, are not reliable;

   ...

4. The opinions of Mr. McCrary related to "crime scene analysis" whether described as "victim-targeted" behavior, deterrability or foreseeability, do not comply with New Mexico Rule of Evidence 11–702 in that they will not materially assist the trier of fact to determine facts in issue in this case.

IT IS ORDERED:

1. The testimony of Gregg McCrary on crime scene analysis and any issue related to the motives of Paul Lovett, whether described as "victim-targeted" behavior, deterrability, foreseeability or some other heading, is excluded at trial;

2. Based on his law enforcement background, Mr. McCrary may testify about the best practices to prevent crime and the adequacy of security at this Allsup's store, provided he does the following:
   a. Within 10 days of the date of the hearing (by February 23, 2009), Mr. McCrary produces to the plaintiff all documents, studies,

training materials, guidelines and other materials he has used or uses when providing security advice to other companies; and

b. Mr. McCrary makes himself available for deposition at least 20 days before trial.

RAYMOND Z. ORTIZ
DISTRICT JUDGE RAYMOND Z. ORTIZ

Approved as to Form:

Randi McGinn
MCML, P.A.
Attorneys for the Plaintiff
Approved Telephonically 2/19/08
Tom Outler
RODEY, DICKASON, SLOAN, AKTN & ROBB, P.A.
Phil Krehbiel
Chris Key
Attorneys for the Defendant

Subsequent to this decision by Judge Ortiz, Mr. McCrary was not called to testify when the case went to trial. Instead, the defense relied on the testimony of Dr. Merlyn Moore.[2] Dr. Moore is a former naval intelligence officer with a strong academic background and a professor in the College of Criminal Justice at Sam Houston State University. As reported in Sharpe (2008b):

> The defense called security expert Merlyn Moore, who said having two clerks on duty could increase the potential for an injury because the clerks might confront a robber. Bullet-proof enclosures, he said, suggest a high-crime area, inhibit communication between clerks and customers, and even cause criminals to turn on customers. Moore said alarms can endanger clerks if a robber sees them activating one. "It might be valuable as a last resort if someone is forcing you out of the store," he added. He said video surveillance can assist police after the fact, but "I don't know if it would have deterred Paul Lovett."

The jury did not agree with Dr. Moore's assertions. The case ultimately settled for an undisclosed amount during jury deliberations, just as a verdict was about to be returned. As reported in (Sharpe, 2008a):

> Lawyers in the case of an Allsup's clerk murdered during her graveyard shift settled her estate's wrongful-death lawsuit Tuesday, minutes before a Santa Fe jury was to return a $51.2 million verdict.
>
> Jury forewoman Jean Lehman said jurors had decided to assess Allsup's Enterprises $21.2 million in compensatory damages and $30 million in punitive damages.

[2]Dr. Moore holds a Ph.D. from Michigan State University in Criminal Justice and Criminology; an M.S. in Criminal Justice; and a B.A. in Police Administration.

But when they told the bailiff they were ready to deliver a verdict about 4:30 p.m., she said, the bailiff told them they were to return to court, where state District Judge Raymond Ortiz informed them the case had been settled.

Allegra Carpenter, one of three Albuquerque lawyers representing the three minor children of Elizabeth Garcia, 26—who was abducted from an Allsup's in Hobbs, raped and stabbed to death Jan. 16, 2002, on just her fourth day on the job—said she could not reveal the amount of the monetary settlement. During closing arguments Monday, plaintiffs' lawyers suggested jurors award the estate $60 million.

Carpenter said the settlement includes a promise from Allsup's that it will never again challenge state regulations requiring convenience stores open between 11 p.m. and 7 a.m. to put at least two clerks on duty, station a guard with one clerk or put clerks in bulletproof enclosures.

Garcia's death spurred efforts to boost security at convenience stores, and Carpenter said Allsup's lobbyists or the Petroleum Marketers Association, to which Allsup's belongs, have challenged the rules every year since they were passed. A jury verdict could not have included such an assurance, and the settlement would not have been possible if not for the pressure of the lawsuit, she said.

"There was a little bit of talk (with lawyers for Allsup's) back and forth, but none of it was very serious until today," Carpenter said.

Lehman, a real-estate agent, said jurors were heavily influenced toward the plaintiff when they learned Allsup's successfully sued its previous insurance company over how to make its stores safer, yet never implemented any of the suggestions. "That was a huge inconsistency," she said.

Lehman said jurors also were curious why so little information was provided about Paul Lovett, the man convicted of abducting, raping and killing Garcia. Last year, Lovett was sentenced to life in prison for murdering Garcia and another woman. Although defense attorneys called Lovett's ex-wife and her father, they did not call Lovett or present a deposition from him during the two-week trial. Lehman and another juror, Elaine Lucero, said it seemed Allsup's provided little information on past crimes at its stores. Attorneys for Garcia's estate said they had to do much of their own research to prove, for example, that 12 Allsup's clerks have been murdered in 30 years, making the near-minimum-wage jobs the most dangerous in the state.

This case illustrates not only the seriousness of premises liability lawsuits and the types of violent crimes they can encompass, but also the tremendous stakes involved for both sides. Additionally, it demonstrates the fact that such lawsuits are not always merely about seeking and receiving financial gain—though this can be an effective lesson for the negligent. Liability actions of all kinds can also be about leveraging much-needed reform, confirming their value to the justice system.

SUMMARY

As a result of ever-increasing civil litigation initiated by victim-plaintiffs related to liability for the harm caused during criminal acts, forensic criminologists may now be heavily involved with educating the court on issues of standards of care, foreseeability, deterrability, and the like.

Each of these issues varies from cases to case, depending on the region, community, and professionals involved. For example, the standards of care at a hospital are radically different from the standards of care that govern hotels or even schools.

Foreseeability is perhaps the most important issue for criminologists because unless the foreseeability of harm can first be established, there is no duty to protect. If a forensic criminologist determines that a crime was not foreseeable, then this may be used by defense to argue that no duty existed in the case at hand. Consequently, while the court may determine that a defendant has a clear duty of care, the issue of foreseeability can be used to remove it. Once the issue of foreseeability has been assessed, the forensic criminologist may examine the same evidence to determine whether the offense would have been preventable and the offender deterrable.

The highly variable nature of offense and offender deterrability, again, speaks to the need for forensic criminologists to make a deliberate assessment of the facts and circumstances on a case-by-case basis, not blanket generalizations about security efforts and offender types. It is only when all of this is considered that forensic criminologists are able to advise the court on these pertinent issues which often involve settlements worth millions of dollars.

Review Questions

1. Explain the universal standard for expertise in premise liability cases.
2. T/F Landowners may not set traps for trespassers.
3. What is a crime foreseeability model? Why is it important?
4. Explain the four tests under which foreseeability can be assessed.
5. What is deterrability? How does it relate to premises liability?
6. Describe the importance of a thorough victimology in premises liability cases.
7. How should forensic criminologists go about assessing premises liability cases?
8. Describe the difference between instrumental and expressive offenders.

REFERENCES

Austin, J., Irwin, J., 2001. It's About Time, third ed. Wadsworth, Belmont, CA.

Black, H.C., 1990. Black's Law Dictionary, sixth ed. West Publishing Co, St. Paul, MN.

Brantingham, P., 1995. Criminality of Place: Crime Generators and Crime Attractors. European Journal on Criminal Policy and Research 3 (1), 5–26.

Britt, C., 2001. Premises Liability: Getting Your Security Expert over the Daubert Hurdle. Trial 37, December, 31–37.

Burgess, A.N., Burgess, A.W., Douglas, J., Ressler, R. (Eds.), 1992. Crime Classification Manual. Lexington Books, New York.

Carrington, F., Rapp, J., 1991. Victims' Rights: Law and Litigation. Matthew Bender, New York.

Chisum, W.J., Turvey, B., 2007. Crime Reconstruction. Elsevier Science, Boston.

Driscoll, R., 2006. The Law of Premises Liability in America: Its Past, Present, and Some Considerations for Its Future. Notre Dame Law Review 82, December, 881–909.

Estate of Elizabeth Garcia et al., Plaintiffs v. Allsup's Convenience Stores Inc., Defendant, 2008. Case no. D-010 1–CV-20050 0045, First Judicial District Court, County of Santa Fe, State of New Mexico, Order dated February 22.

Farrington, D., Welsh, B., 2002. Improved Street Lighting and Crime Prevention. Justice Quarterly 19 (2), 313–342.

Gill, M., Loveday, K., 2003. What Do Offenders Think about CCTV? Crime Prevention and Community Safety 5 (3), 17–25.

Goldstein, P., 1985. The Drugs/Violence Nexus: A Tripartite Conceptual Approach. Journal of Drug Issues 15 (1), 493–506.

Gorby, M., 1998. Premises Liability in Georgia, The Harrison Company, Norcross, GA.

Gross, H., 1924. Criminal Investigation. Sweet & Maxwell, London.

Hare, R., 1993. Without Conscience: The Disturbing World of the Psychopaths Among Us. The Guilford Press, New York.

Huber, P., 1988. Liability: The Legal Revolution and Its Consequences. Basic Books, Inc, New York.

Kennedy, D., 2006. Forensic Security and the Law. In: Gill, M. (Ed.), The Handbook of Security. Palgrave MacMillan, New York.

Kennedy, D., 2008. Colloquium: Criminologists in the Courtroom: Consulting and Forensic Criminology. School of Criminal Justice, Michigan State University, February 25.

Kirk, P., 1953. Crime Investigation. Interscience, New York.

Lininger, T., 2008. Is It Wrong to Sue for Rape? Duke Law J 57, April, 1557–1640.

Lykken, D., 1995. The Antisocial Personalities. Lawrence Erlbaum, Hillsdale, NJ.

Marchant, P., 2004. A Demonstration That the Claim That Brighter Lighting Reduces Crime Is Unfounded. British Journal of Criminology 44 (3), 441–447.

McKnight, K. (2000). Expert's Opinion Challenged. Ohio Beacon Journal April 1.

Michael, K., Ellis, Z., 2003. Avoiding Liability in Premises Security, fifth ed. Strafford Publications, Atlanta.

Nettler, G., 1989. Criminology Lessons. Anderson, Cincinnati.

Painter, K., Tilley, N. (Eds.), 1999. Surveillance of Public Space: CCTV, Street Lighting and Crime Prevention. Criminal Justice Press, Monsey, NY.

Piquero, A., Mazerolle, P. (Eds.), 2001. Life-Course Criminology: Contemporary and Classic Readings. Wadsworth, Belmont, CA.

Sakis, J., Kennedy, D., 2002. Violence at Work. Trial 38 (12), 32–36.

Sharpe, T., 2008a. Allsup's Settles with Family of Slain Clerk: Jurors Say They Were Ready to Award Estate $51.2 Million. The New Mexican April 8.

Sharpe, T., 2008b. S.F. Jurors Weighing Allsup's Culpability in Worker's Rape, Slaying. The New Mexican April 7.

Sherman, L., Gartin, P., Buerger, M., 1989. Hot Spots of Predatory Crime: Routine Activities and the Criminology of Place. Criminology 27 (1), 27–55.

Sherman, L., Gottfredson, D., MacKenzie, D., Eck, J., Reuter, P., Bushway, S., 1997. Preventing Crime: What Works, What Doesn't and What's Promising. U.S. Department of Justice, Washington, DC.

Teten, H., 1995. Offender Profiling. In: Bailey, W. (Ed.), The Encyclopedia of Police Science. Garland Publishing, New York, pp. 475–477.

Thornton, J.I., 1997. The General Assumptions and Rationale of Forensic Identification. In: Faigman, D., Kaye, D., Saks, M., Sanders, J. (Eds.), Modern Scientific Evidence: The Law and Science of Expert Testimony, vol. 2, West, St. Paul, MN.

Turvey, B., 2008a. Criminal Profiling: An Introduction to Behavioral Evidence Analysis. Academic Press, San Diego.

Turvey, B., 2008b. Expert declaration. Estate of Elizabeth Garcia v. Allsup's Convenience Stores, Inc., January 9.

Voigt, L., Thornton, W., 1996. Sociology and Negligent Security: Premises Liability and Crime Prevention. In: Jenkins, P.J., Kroll-Smith, S. (Eds.), Witnessing for Sociology: Sociologists in Court. Praeger, Westport, CT.

Weisel, D., 2002. Burglary of Single Family Houses. U.S. Department of Justice, Washington, DC.

Welsh, B., Farrington, D., 2003. Effects of Closed-Circuit Television on Crime. Ann. Am. Acad. Pol. Soc. Sci. 587, May, 110–135.

Welsh, B., Farrington, D., 2004. Surveillance for Crime Prevention in Public Space: Results and Policy Choices in Britain and America. Criminology and Public Policy 3 (3), 497–525.

CHAPTER 8

Forensic Criminology in Correctional Settings

Brent E. Turvey and Angela N. Torres

KEY TERMS

Community Corrections: The placement of offenders back into the community at various levels of housing, employment, accountability, and even treatment when mental health or substance abuse issues are involved.

Correctional Officers: Those persons who maintain security and order within a prison.

Corrections: The branch of the criminal justice system that deals with the probation, incarceration, management, rehabilitation, treatment, parole, and execution of convicted criminals.

Duty of Care: The state's responsibility for what happens to inmates while in its custody.

Federal Prisons: The facilities where those convicted of felonies that violate federal law will be sentenced to serve time; they are operated by the Federal Bureau of Prisons, which is an agency in the U.S. Department of Justice.

Jails: The facilities used to hold those who have been recently arrested prior to any court proceedings in law enforcement custody or for the short-term incarceration of offenders convicted of nonfelonies.

Prisons: The facilities where convicted felons serve long-term sentences.

State Prisons: The facilities where defendants convicted of felonies against the state will be sentenced to serve time; they are operated by the state government usually through a Department of Corrections.

CONTENTS

Corrections is the branch of the criminal justice system that deals with the probation, incarceration, management, rehabilitation, treatment, parole, and sometimes execution of convicted criminals. The purpose of this chapter is to provide a basic outline of corrections and its role with an eye to the kinds of civil liability that correctional institutions regularly incur. Forensic criminologists are involved in the assessment of institutional liability at every level. We

267

will therefore discuss their role in this regard, while also providing information about the range of employment opportunities available in corrections.

It bears noting, again, that the United States, the United Kingdom, and Australia are very much alike from a legal standpoint. Each country has similar legal and penal systems, sharing democratic conventions based on English Common Law (Turner, 2008). Additionally, they are each fragmented in the same general fashion, being composed of individual states and territories with even smaller jurisdictional regions (such as counties, boroughs, cities, and townships), all possessing their own distinct sets of criminal statutes and codes. Relevant to the purposes of this chapter, the corrections systems in the United States, the United Kingdom, and Australia are also similarly vulnerable to civil liability for the harms caused by negligence. Therefore, while this chapter will focus primarily on correctional settings in the United States, the issues discussed as they relate to security, negligence, liability, and forensic criminologists transcend borders despite the particular laws and institutions involved.

INCARCERATED POPULATIONS

By far, more people are incarcerated in the United States than any other country in the world. And that number is currently at its highest rate in U.S. history. As described in Aizenman (2008, p. A1):

> More than one in 100 adults in the United States is in jail or prison, an all-time high that is costing state governments nearly $50 billion a year and the federal government $5 billion more....

> With more than 2.3 million people behind bars, the United States leads the world in both the number and percentage of residents it incarcerates, leaving far-more-populous China a distant second, according to a study by the nonpartisan Pew Center on the States.

> The growth in prison population is largely because of tougher state and federal sentencing imposed since the mid-1980s. Minorities have been particularly affected: One in nine black men ages 20 to 34 is behind bars. For black women ages 35 to 39, the figure is one in 100, compared with one in 355 for white women in the same age group.

Comparatively, the U.K. prison population is at approximately 79,861, which translates to 148 per 100,000; and the prison population of Australia is approximately 25,353, which translates to 126 per 100,000 (Turner, 2008).

The situation in the United States is particularly troubling. It has not only put a tremendous strain on state budgets, but has also become an undeniable racial issue. As discussed in Jones (2008, pp. 179–180):

Prisons and jails in the United States are overcrowded and many strain to handle the vast number of inmates they detain. In fact, the increase in the rate of imprisonment in America far exceeds the rate of increase in the general population. Additionally, the majority of inmates are black or Hispanic. The impact of the growth of imprisonment has been most severe on black men. Almost three in ten black males will be incarcerated at some point in their lives. That figure is three in twenty for Hispanic men and less than one in twenty-five for white men.

And similarly in Aizenman (2008, p. A1):

About 91 percent of incarcerated adults are under state or local jurisdiction. And [there are] tradeoffs state [that] governments have faced as they devote larger shares of their budgets to house them. For instance, over the past two decades, state spending on corrections (adjusted for inflation) increased 127 percent; spending on higher education rose 21 percent....

Despite reaching its latest milestone, the nation's incarcerated population has been growing more slowly since 2000 than it did during the 1990s, when harsher sentencing laws began to take effect. These included a 1986 federal law (since revised) mandating prison terms for crack cocaine offenses that were up to eight times as long as for those involving powder cocaine. In the 1990s, many states adopted "three-strikes-you're-out" laws and curtailed the powers of parole boards.

Many state systems also send offenders back to prison for technical violations of their parole or probation, such as failing a drug test or missing an appointment with a supervisory officer. A 2005 study of California's system, for example, found that more than two-thirds of parolees were being returned to prison within three years of release, 40 percent for technical infractions.

Because of these policy shifts, the nationwide prison population swelled by about 80 percent from 1990 to 2000, increasing by as much as 86,000 a year. By contrast, from 2007 to 2008, that population increased by 25,000, a 2 percent rise.

Many criminologists and criminal justice practitioners view the prison population issues in the United States differently. Some have come to perceive the corrections system in general as a "penal archipelago" that is easy to become trapped and lost in. This in turn creates a class of discarded ex-citizens with few rights and little representation in a society that they no longer have a stake in supporting or protecting. Some are also frustrated by what they see as offenders going through ever-revolving penal doors with inadequate supervision. As quoted in Aizenman (2008, p. A1):

"We're just stuck in this carousel that people get off of, then get right back on again," said Los Angeles Police Chief William J. Bratton, who as New York City police commissioner in the 1990s oversaw a significant reduction in crime.

Still, others see ever-increasing prison populations as a necessary step toward a safer society. As further quoted in Aizenman (2008, p. A1):

Sociologist James Q. Wilson, who in the 1980s helped develop the "broken windows" theory that smaller crimes must be punished to deter more serious ones, agreed that sentences for some drug crimes were too long. However, Wilson disagreed that the rise in the U.S. prison population should be considered a cause for alarm: "The fact that we have a large prison population by itself is not a central problem because it has contributed to the extraordinary increase in public safety we have had in this country."

No matter how one views the circumstance, whether as a warning sign of a broken system or as a necessary protective measure in the face of existing crime, there can be no denying that the penal system is filled well beyond the capacity of federal, state, or local governments to budget it acceptably. And as the years roll forward and prison populations increase, more funding will be required.

THE ROLE OF CORRECTIONS

Ideally, the role of corrections is to securely detain those convicted of crimes, to protect them from themselves and others detained in the same facility, and to provide basic medical and mental healthcare. This can include treatment for drug and alcohol addictions. It can also include treatment for various personality disorders.

With respect to society, the role of corrections is to provide protection. Historically, this has meant protection in the immediate sense by virtue of separating dangerous felons from regular citizens. But it also requires a role in inmate rehabilitation—to ensure that what comes out is not worse than what went in.

As society has become less tolerant of crime and criminality, legislators and courts have felt the push to deliver sometimes appropriate but sometimes inflated "tough on crime" sentences. Additionally, they have felt great pressure from voters to cut prison costs and amenities, so as not to "coddle" inmates and reward their crimes with above-standard living conditions. However, the current economic crisis has forced many of those involved with the criminal justice system to rethink political motivations for tougher sentencing in favor of financial ones, as explained in Johnson (2009):

> ...[A]cross the nation, the deepening financial crisis is forcing dramatic changes in the hard-line, punishment-based philosophy that has dominated the USA's criminal justice system for nearly two decades.
>
> As 31 states report budget gaps that the National Governor's Association says totaled nearly $30 billion last year, criminal justice officials and lawmakers are proposing and enacting cost-cutting changes across the public safety spectrum, with uncertain ramifications for the public.
>
> There is no dispute that the fiscal crisis is driving the changes, but the potential risks of pursuing such policies is the subject of growing debate. While some analysts believe the philosophical shift is long overdue, others fear it could undermine public safety.
>
> Ryan King of The Sentencing Project, a group that advocates for alternatives to incarceration, says the financial crisis has created enough "political cover" to fuel a new look at the realities of incarcerating more than 2 million people and supervising 5 million others on probation and parole.
>
> "It's clear that locking up hundreds of thousands of people does not guarantee public safety," he says.
>
> Joshua Marquis, a past vice president of the National District Attorneys Association, agrees the economy is prompting an overhaul of justice policy but reaches a very different conclusion about its impact on public safety.
>
> "State after state after state appears to be waiting for the opportunity to wind back some of the most intelligent sentencing policy we have," Marquis says. "If we do this, we will pay a price. No question."
>
> Among recent state actions:
>
> - Kansas officials closed two detention facilities last month to save about $3.5 million. A third will be shuttered by April 1, says Roger Werholtz, chief of the state prison system. Inmates housed in the closed units will be moved to other facilities in the state.
>
> - A California panel of federal judges recommended last month that the cash-strapped state release up to 57,000 non-violent inmates from the overcrowded system to help save $800 million.
>
> - Kentucky officials last year allowed for the early release of non-violent offenders up to six months before their sentences end to serve the balance of their time at home.

- New Mexico and Colorado are among seven states where some lawmakers are calling for an end to the death penalty, arguing capital cases have become too costly to prosecute, reports the Death Penalty Information Center, which tracks death penalty law and supports abolition of the death penalty.

"State governments operated on the principle that if you built it, they would come," King says of prison construction during the economic boom. Since 1990, corrections spending has increased by an average of 7.5% annually, reports the National Association of State Budget Officers.

"As soon as they built those prisons, they filled them," King says. "They were never able to keep up with it. There is certainly a different atmosphere now."

Despite economic hardships and the need for fiscal belt-tightening, the government retains a dual duty to both society and the inmates they take into custody. The reason is that the mission of corrections is not just to incarcerate, but also to rehabilitate. To meet the minimum requirements of these mandates, to be discussed shortly, hardliners who support more costly initiatives, such as the death penalty, may find themselves unable to keep their moral imperatives.

Punishment vs. Rehabilitation

Often the question arises as to whether the role of incarceration is to punish offenders or rehabilitate them. Initially, prisons were established in the United States to contain and to punish; the term *penitentiary* comes from being penitent, or having to atone for one's misdeeds. Classical schools of criminology posit that confining and punishing individuals acts not only as a specific deterrent to those individuals, in that they are incarcerated and cannot commit crimes in the community, but also more a general deterrence to others in the community not wanting to commit crimes to avoid the prisoners' fate. The Positive school of criminology, in contrast, offers that rehabilitation should take place in prisons to avoid future recidivism. In the United States, the United Kingdom, and Australia, corrections are intended to be administered by the state in such a fashion as to accomplish both. Consider the following correctional mission statements.

U.S.—State of California Department of Corrections and Rehabilitation:[1]

We enhance public safety through safe and secure incarceration of offenders, effective parole supervision, and rehabilitative strategies to successfully reintegrate offenders into our communities.

[1]Taken from http://www.cdcr.ca.gov/About_CDCR/docs/mission.pdf

U.S.—State of Illinois Department of Corrections:[2]

The mission of the Department of Corrections is to protect the public from criminal offenders through a system of incarceration and supervision which securely segregates offenders from society, assures offenders of their constitutional rights and maintains programs to enhance the success of offenders' reentry into society.

[2]Taken from http://www.idoc.state.il.us/mission_statement.shtml

UK—Her Majesty's Prison Service:[3]

Her Majesty's Prison Service serves the public by keeping in custody those committed by the courts. Our duty is to look after them with humanity and help them lead law-abiding and useful lives in custody and after release.

[3]Taken from http://www.hmprisonservice.gov.uk/abouttheservice/statementofpurpose/

Our Vision

- To provide the very best prison services so that we are the provider of choice
- To work towards this vision by securing the following key objectives.

Objectives

To protect the public and provide what commissioners want to purchase by:

- Holding prisoners securely
- Reducing the risk of prisoners re-offending
- Providing safe and well-ordered establishments in which we treat prisoners humanely, decently and lawfully.

Australia—Queensland Corrective Services:[4]

Queensland Corrective Services (QCS) in partnership with other key criminal justice agencies, is committed to the critical role of "community safety and crime prevention through the humane containment, supervision and rehabilitation of offenders."

[4]Taken from http://www.correctiveservices.qld.gov.au/About_Us/The_Department/index.shtml

The similarity of these mission statements is fairly straightforward, and explicitly repeated themes are those of public safety, "secure confinement" of inmates, the reduction of recidivism, and rehabilitation. The examples demonstrate that, ideologically, current corrections are intended to join these goals in a single venture. As we will learn, this is a difficult task given that these ambitions are often in conflict.

The Role of Correctional Officers

Correctional officers are primarily tasked with maintaining security and order within prisons. They are also required to enforce the rules while modeling appropriate behavior to inmates. Far from being mere guards, they are required to help support and even facilitate rehabilitation efforts being made by other prison staff. It is an odd balance because providing security and maintaining order can require corrective behavior that should not be tolerated from inmates and also may hinder offender vocational initiatives or treatment. It is a tough and often thankless job.

Further complicating matters are the conditions under which correctional officers must work, as explained in Appelbaum, Hickey, and Packer (2001, p. 1345):

> Correctional officers face significant job-related pressure. In many states they must cope with understaffing, mandatory overtime, rotating shift work, and low pay. However, correctional officers identify the threat of violence by inmates as their most frequent source of stress.

Many criminal justice and criminology students go on to become correctional officers because an undergraduate degree is preferred by many agencies. However, college education is by no means a firm requirement. The lack of educational standards, poor employment screening, and low pay can be a problem in corrections, as correctional officers account for much of the contraband that ends up in a given facility—to include drugs and other forbidden material. Unfortunately, the smuggling of contraband by prison staff is not always a terminal offense, as reported in a study conducted by Sandberg and Stiles (2009):

> Knives and drugs, cell phones and smokeless tobacco. Even McDonald's hamburgers.
>
> Texas prisons are a virtual bazaar of prohibited and illicit goods smuggled in by guards and correctional employees who have rarely faced harsh punishment when caught, according to a Houston Chronicle review.
>
> Nearly 300 employees, many lowly paid correctional officers, were reprimanded for possessing prohibited items at 20 prison units with the most pervasive contraband problem between 2003 and 2008, records show.
>
> Of the 263 employees disciplined solely for contraband, about three-fourths were given probation, where they were placed under special scrutiny for specified periods. Thirty-five were fired; 26 received no punishment at all. One of the 263 was criminally prosecuted for the contraband, but served no prison time.
>
> Contraband trafficking gained national attention ... when a Texas death row inmate used a smuggled cell phone to threaten a prominent

lawmaker. The phone was used by fellow death row inmates to place 3,000 other calls.

John Moriarty, the prison system's inspector general, called contraband "the biggest security problem the prisons face."

Until recently, guards found introducing contraband into the system were more likely to be handed minimal penalties rather than be fired, and the punishment varied widely, a newspaper review of five years of disciplinary records shows. In 47 cases in which an employee attempted to deliver contraband to an offender, only seven cases resulted in dismissals, according to the analysis.

Firing not automatic

Top prison officials have called for zero tolerance in stamping out prison contraband, though it "doesn't mean someone is terminated," said the prison system's spokeswoman, Michelle Lyons.

"It means it's addressed and is dealt with accordingly. In some cases, depending on the contraband, the fitting punishment is probation or suspension," she said. "In more serious cases, where the facts support that the person intended to introduce contraband to an offender, then it's dealt with possibly by termination."

But in 2003 a correctional officer at the Estelle Unit was given 10 months probation and suspended for four days without pay after his backpack turned up an assortment of knives, prescription drugs, a cell phone, two electric razors, a box blade, a lighter, a set of portable radios, cigarettes and cigars.

Another correctional officer with an otherwise clean record at the Beto Unit got six months' probation, simply for walking through a metal detector with an unopened can of chewing tobacco.

A retired Estelle Unit prison guard said getting cigarettes into the prisons was never a problem. "I used to walk behind the cellblocks every night and would find cigarette ashes out there behind maybe a third of the cellblocks," said the former guard, who was once placed on probation for being found on prison grounds with a bag containing a paring knife, a spoon, scissors, an alarm clock, a deck of playing cards and an ashtray.

Not all contraband is intended for inmates. "A lot of it is personal use stuff," Moriarty said. Officials must try to figure out whether a guard simply forgot to unload his cell phone before entering a prison, or intended to deliver it to an inmate, and pocket as much as $2,000 for one destined for death row, he said.

Lyons said changes made after the death row cell phone scandal, such as pat-downs of everyone entering the prisons, have made it harder for contraband to get in.

Still, more than 200 cell phones have been confiscated systemwide since a lockdown for illicit items ended ..., including eight seized from death row.

...

Whitmire said ... that few inside the system would acknowledge the problem until he found himself on the line with a death row prisoner. Now, the lawmaker is calling for a no-tolerance policy regarding contraband.

He said staffing shortages have forced prison administrators to compromise in both discipline and hiring practices, adding, "There are instances where they are hiring people with matters in their background who normally wouldn't be hired."

He said rank-and-file officers' salaries—their base pay is capped at $34,000 annually—contribute to the problem. "The low pay certainly would make those who are susceptible to being dishonest cross the line."

One legislative proposal would give correctional officers as much as a 20 percent raise—at a two-year cost of at least $400 million.

Brian Olsen, executive director of the Texas branch of the American Federation of State, County and Municipal Employees, a union that represents prison workers, said the contraband problem could persist unless guards receive professional wages.

Still, he said most officers follow the rules, and others get into trouble for "trafficking" in seemingly harmless items, such as candy and soft drinks. "There are going to be bad officers," Olsen said. "I don't think it's as rampant a problem as everyone says."

This line of argumentation is important to note, as low pay is repeatedly used throughout the criminal justice system as the reason for hiring and retaining the unqualified or even criminal in law enforcement and corrections (see Chapter 10 of this text).

TYPES OF FACILITIES

Depending on the nature of their offense and where it took place, convicted offenders may be incarcerated in a *jail* or one of several different types of *prisons*. Defendants convicted of felonies against the state will be sentenced to serve time in *state prisons*. Those convicted of felonies that violate federal law will be sentenced to serve time in *federal prisons*.

Jails

Most local (county and municipal) law enforcement agencies and courthouses have on-site jail facilities. *Jails* are used to hold those who have been recently arrested prior to any court proceedings, such as an arraignment, in law enforcement custody. They are also available for the short-term incarceration of offenders convicted of non-felonies. Further still, they are used to accommodate the local court appointments of felons "visiting" from other jails and correctional institutions.

Jail is vastly different from prison. Jails tend to have fewer amenities because incarceration is meant to be brief, and they are in a constant state of turnover with respect to population. Also, those in jail are more likely to be in custody while severely intoxicated or under the influence of controlled substances than those in prison. It is in fact violent and/or criminal behavior associated with substance abuse that lands many in jail to begin with. This makes jail a strained and often explosive environment with respect to the ever-present danger of violence.

Prisons

Federal and state penitentiaries are designed to facilitate the long-term sentences of convicted felons. Generally speaking, state prisons are operated by the state government, usually through a Department of Corrections. Federal prisons, on the other hand, are operated by the Federal Bureau of Prisons, which is an agency in the U.S. Department of Justice.

Prisons tend to have more amenities than jails because they accommodate longer sentences, but also suffer from less inmate population turnover.

State Prisons

According to the most recently published data, the vast majority of felony convictions in the United States occur in state courts (94%), while the remainder occur in federal courts. The conviction rate in state court is about 31%, and about one-third of those received no jail time, as detailed in Durose and Langan (2007, p. 1):

> In 2004 State courts convicted an estimated 1,079,000 adults of a felony, a number about 24% higher than the 872,000 adults convicted in 1994. About a third of convicted felons were drug offenders, and about 1 in 5 were violent offenders....

> During this 10-year period, the conviction rate for violent crimes also rose. For every 100 persons arrested for a violent felony in 1994,

an estimated 23 were convicted. In 2004, the rate was 31 persons convicted for every 100 persons arrested.

Persons convicted of a felony were most likely to receive an incarceration sentence in 2004. Forty percent were sentenced to a period of confinement in State prison and 30% in local jail. An estimated 28% of convicted felons were sentenced to probation with no jail or prison time.

Moreover, Durose and Langan explain that most but not all of those convicted of felonies in state court were actually incarcerated (2007, p. 2):

In 2004, 70% of all persons convicted of a felony in State courts were sentenced to a period of confinement—40% to State prison and 30% to local jail. In some cases the incarceration sentences also included a term of probation supervision. Persons convicted of a violent felony (78%) were most likely to receive an incarceration sentence in 2004. An estimated 28% of convicted felons were sentenced to probation with no jail or prison time. Two percent of felons were not sentenced to any incarceration or probation but received a sentence that included fines, restitution, treatment, community service, or some other penalty (for example, house arrest or periodic drug testing).

As of 2004, charges related to drugs were the most prevalent state offenses that suspects were being arrested for (34%). This was followed by property offenses (29%) and violent offenses (18%) such as murder, rape, and robbery.

Federal Prisons

In the United States, the Federal Bureau of Prisons manages incarceration for federal offenses. As explained in Roberts (1997, p. 53):

The Federal Bureau of Prisons (BOP), a component of the U.S. Department of Justice, has primary responsibility for housing sentenced federal offenders and shares responsibility with the U.S. Marshals Service for housing inmates awaiting trial or sentencing in federal courts. It works closely with the U.S. probation and pretrial services system in such areas as providing community corrections and pretrial detention bedspace, offering alternative sanctions for supervised release violators and probation violators, determining the prison to which an inmate will be designated, and coordinating certain case management operations and other program activities.

In federal prisons, arrest and incarceration are driven by the nature of the offense (e.g., kidnapping across state lines) in addition to locality (e.g., reservations, national parks). The particulars of whether a crime is classified as federal is often a function of popular sentiment. Generally speaking, it is "public outcry," or the perception of one, that causes legislators to write a bill into law in order to make the crime *du jour* a federal offense (as happened with crack in 1980s, and as is currently happening with methamphetamine abuse). This has tremendous ramifications to the penal system in the United States because the conviction rate for federal crimes is 90%. This is significantly higher than the conviction rate in state court. As detailed in Motivans (2008, p. 1):

> The likelihood of being prosecuted, convicted, and sentenced to prison increased from 1995 to 2005. Sixty percent of all suspects in 2005 were prosecuted, up from 54% in 1995. In 2005, 9 in 10 (90%) defendants charged with a federal violation were convicted, up from 84% in 1995 and 79% of defendants convicted were sentenced to prison, up from 67% in 1995. Of the defendants convicted in 2005, 13% were sentenced to probation, down from 24% in 1995.

> The number of persons sentenced to federal prison nearly doubled from 1995 to 2005. At yearend 2005, 375,600 persons were under some form of federal supervision—62% in secure confinement and 38% in the community.

According to information from the Federal Bureau of Prisons Web site, there are many federal prison facilities around the United States, each operating at one of five different security levels (http://www.bop.gov/locations/institutions):

> The Bureau operates institutions at five different security levels in order to confine offenders in an appropriate manner. Security levels are based on such features as the presence of external patrols, towers, security barriers, or detection devices; the type of housing within the institution; internal security features; and the staff-to-inmate ratio. Each facility is designated as either minimum, low, medium, high, or administrative.

Minimum Security

Minimum security institutions, also known as Federal Prison Camps (FPCs), have dormitory housing, a relatively low staff-to-inmate ratio, and limited or no perimeter fencing. These institutions are work- and program-oriented; and many are located adjacent to larger institutions or on military bases, where inmates help serve the labor needs of the larger institution or base.

Low Security

Low security Federal Correctional Institutions (FCIs) have double-fenced perimeters, mostly dormitory or cubicle housing, and strong work and program components. The staff-to-inmate ratio in these institutions is higher than in minimum security facilities.

Medium Security

Medium security FCIs (and USPs designated to house medium security inmates) have strengthened perimeters (often double fences with electronic detection systems), mostly cell-type housing, a wide variety of work and treatment programs, an even higher staff-to-inmate ratio than low security FCIs, and even greater internal controls.

High Security

High security institutions, also known as United States Penitentiaries (USPs), have highly-secured perimeters (featuring walls or reinforced fences), multiple- and single-occupant cell housing, the highest staff-to-inmate ratio, and close control of inmate movement.

Correctional Complexes

A number of BOP institutions belong to Federal Correctional Complexes (FCCs). At FCCs, institutions with different missions and security levels are located in close proximity to one another. FCCs increase efficiency through the sharing of services, enable staff to gain experience at institutions of many security levels, and enhance emergency preparedness by having additional resources within close proximity.

Administrative

Administrative facilities are institutions with special missions, such as the detention of pretrial offenders; the treatment of inmates with serious or chronic medical problems; or the containment of extremely dangerous, violent, or escape-prone inmates. Administrative facilities include Metropolitan Correctional Centers (MCCs), Metropolitan Detention Centers (MDCs), Federal Detention Centers (FDCs), and Federal Medical Centers (FMCs), as well as the Federal Transfer Center (FTC), the Medical Center for Federal Prisoners (MCFP), and the Administrative-Maximum (ADX) U.S. Penitentiary. Administrative facilities are capable of holding inmates in all security categories.

As of 2005, charges related to immigration were the most prevalent federal offenses that suspects were being arrested for (27%). This was followed closely by drug (24%) and supervision violations (17%) (Motivans, 2008).

Private Correctional Facilities

Throughout the United States, the United Kingdom, and Australia, it has become common for the government to contract out the administration responsibilities of its correctional facilities. This is done because of increased inmate populations and escalating costs, to streamline the budgets and management of often-declined state prison systems, and to reduce the overall size of government in response to taxpayer demands. It is also done with the idea that private companies competing for government contracts may achieve a higher quality of service, and a greater responsiveness to changing circumstances, than a state bureaucracy is capable of. As explained in Harding (1992, p. 2):

> 'Privatisation' of prisons is something of a misnomer. The concept refers not to private ownership and control of an enterprise but to contract management, that is private sector (or non-government) management of institutions which remain a public sector responsibility.

> There may be lesser degrees of privatization—for example, contracting out particular services to the private sector, such as the supply of meals or building maintenance. Conversely, there may be greater degrees— such as private sector design, construction, and financing of a new institution, followed by leasing back to the state.

Pozen (2003) offers further explanation (p. 254):

> Privatization of prisons can take a variety of forms, spanning from no facility ownership and partial operational administration to total facility ownership and total operational administration by the private contractor. In all existing privatization schemes, the state retains full responsibility for allocating punishment in the sentencing phase, but it delegates the responsibility for delivering imprisonment services to a nongovernmental entity. In theory, "private prisons" could encompass those run by private nonprofit organizations as well as private for-profit ones, but in both the United States and the United Kingdom there are at present no secure correctional facilities for adults run by nonprofits.

This means that privatization is not an all-or-nothing proposition—there are all different levels. It also means that the state is still responsible for inmates, even when privatization is at its most unqualified.

Despite the proliferation of privately run correctional facilities, there is little research to suggest that they are necessarily better or more cost effective than the institutions they are meant to replace. The available research is in fact mixed on the issue. However, we are unlikely to abandon the privatized prison model, given the state of affairs rendered in Pozen (2003, pp. 255–256):

> It has been quite a debate: since their beginnings in the mid-1980s and the early 1990s, respectively, the prison privatization movements of the United States and the United Kingdom have provoked several rounds of congressional and parliamentary hearings and hundreds of articles discussing their philosophical, organizational, economic, and legal implications. Yet while there remains a contingent of vocal critics

of private prisons in both countries today, the debate over privatization has lost much of its early ardor and prominence as the industry has reached a level of maturity over the course of the past decade. After the initial flurry of academic and popular commentary on American private prisons in the 1980s, public discussion had largely died down by 1990. Pushed back seven years or so, the literature in Britain experienced a similar recession of interest in the topic. As the number and variety of privately operated prisons have steadily increased, they have come to be seen by many in the United States and the United Kingdom as a natural part of the correctional system....

However, even as prison privatization has entered the criminological mainstream and the controversy has largely faded from the public eye, nothing resembling consensus has emerged regarding the desirability or even the performance of private prisons.

Given current contractual obligations which would need to extend well into the future, and the logistical reality of finding alternative facilities, there seems to be little incentive for pulling out of the privatized prison approach. That is to say, we are so heavily entrenched in it, with so many stakeholders, that change will not come unless there is some catastrophic failure which forces it.

At this point, it is useful to note that while the courts provide sentencing, any decisions about inmate security, housing, and privileges are made by prison staff at various points during their stay at a given facility.

Community Corrections

Common to the penal systems in both Australia and the United States, *community corrections* involves the placement of offenders back into the community at various levels of housing, employment, accountability, and even treatment when mental health or substance abuse issues are involved. It is an alternative to incarceration, meant to defer the rising cost of full-time imprisonment or assist offenders with the often-difficult process of re-entry into society. As explained in Palmer (2009):

Kathy Waters, director of Adult Probations Services Division of the Arizona Administrative Office of the Courts, said community corrections programs have proven to lower costs, reduce recidivism and, if necessary, avoid costly incarcerations. Still, she declined to say whether she thinks Arizona is sending more offenders to prison than necessary.

Waters said she has revoked more than her "fair share" of probationary sentences during her 20-year career, but she is convinced the programs are worthwhile.

"I'm a strong advocate for community corrections," she said. "I think locking people up is the easy way."

Offenders can benefit from tailored probationary programs of varying severities that help change lifestyle factors, including thought processing, anger management, substance abuse, choice of associates and preferred leisure activities, she said.

In many cases, intensive probation for low-level offenders has been proven to increase recidivism rates, she said.

Sentencing alternatives related to community corrections efforts are detailed in *Community Corrections* (1998, pp. 2–3):

Community corrections offers viable alternatives to incarceration for offenders at various stages of the criminal justice process. The following is a brief description of many of the alternatives which may be available to offenders:

1) Bail Supervision Programs: While awaiting trial, the accused, rather than being held in custody, is supervised by a member of the community.

2) Alternative Measures Programs: The offender is diverted from the criminal justice system before or after a charge is laid. The offender enters into a kind of contractual agreement to answer for his/her crime. The agreement can include performing community service work, personal service to the victim, charitable donation, participating in counseling or any other reasonable task or condition.

3) Restitution Programs: The offender must pay back the victim for damages or loss.

4) Fine Options Programs: The offender may work off a fine by performing approved community work for a set hourly rate of pay. The rate varies among provinces but in Alberta it is currently $5 per hour.

5) Community Service Order: A condition on a probation order, or a separate disposition in the case of young offenders, which requires the offender to perform work in the community.

6) Probation: The offender is supervised in the community and must follow the set of conditions (rules) set out in his/her probation order. Conditions of probation include keeping the peace, being of good behaviour and obeying the law and reporting regularly to a probation officer and may include a range of other, optional conditions.

7) Intensive Supervision Probation: An alternative to incarceration in the United States which is similar to probation but involves more frequent surveillance and greater controls.

8) Conditional Sentence of Imprisonment: A prison sentence of less than two years which the judge allows the offender to serve in the community. Offenders serving conditional sentences are more closely supervised than probation clients and must abide by certain conditions, similar to the conditions of a probation order.

9) Attendance Centre Programs: A non-residential, community facility to which some offenders on temporary absence from correctional institutions report frequently for supervision or programs.

10) Electronic Monitoring: The offender is fitted with an anklet or bracelet that transmits signals of his or her whereabouts to a correctional officer, allowing the offender to continue with employment or education commitments in the community.

11) Community-Based Centres: Community-based residential facilities are privately operated, while community correctional centres are operated by the government. Inmates are often released to community-based centres as part of their gradual re-integration into the community. The residents of these centres are usually in the process of returning to school or looking for employment.

12) Temporary Absence Programs: An inmate is released into the community for a specified amount of time for reasons such as seeking employment, medical treatment or family visitation.

13) Parole: A form of conditional release available to offenders who are incarcerated. It is similar to probation but the offender is in the community while still serving some of the prison sentence.

Critics of community corrections efforts argue that the liability to the state in the current environment is tremendous because supervision is minimal to nonexistent. The reason is that probation officers often have far too many parolees to watch, and some halfway houses provide almost no supervision at all. Since many individuals are concerned about having a halfway house in their neighborhood, these placements are often located in areas that are saturated with drugs and crimes, making it additionally difficult for residents to avoid re-offending. Consider that it is common for offenders to be convicted of a violent or sexually motivated crime and then get sentenced to a form of community corrections that involves no direct supervision of their daily activities.

On the other side of the corrections coin, probation and community corrections officers wield tremendous authority over the offenders under their supervision. They hold in their arsenal a unique ability to send offenders back to prison based on a single report or infraction. In this role, probation officers act as gatekeepers who decide, based on their personal discretion and values, who re-enters the jails or prisons. It is a powerful discretionary tool that some argue facilitates corruption and abuse. For offenders, having such arbitrary boundaries can be difficult to navigate, leading to confusion about which behaviors will cause a violation with their current supervisor.

Confounding these circumstances is research that suggests parole and community corrections officers with higher education levels tend to be more sympathetic to offenders, more open to the idea of rehabilitation, and more willing to listen to offender grievances. While conversely offenders tend to have low education, bad credit, poor finances, and a high incidence of addiction and mental illness. This creates mistrust, or "*social distance* as the differences in education, income, lifestyle, and background characteristics between [offenders] and their community corrections officers [who] believed that officers who came from backgrounds of higher social class, education, and prosocial lifestyle have too little in common with most offenders to be able to understand, appreciate, and help them meet their needs" (Helfgott and Gunnison, 2008, p. 4).

Parolee Lovelle Mixon killed three police officers and injured a fourth in a stand-off on March 21, 2009, with SWAT before being killed by officers at the scene.

CASE EXAMPLE: LOVELLE MIXON

Consider the case of Lovelle Mixon, a 26-year-old parolee in Oakland, California, who had been released into the community after serving time for assault with a deadly weapon. The tragic details of March 21, 2009, highlight the problems with community corrections efforts and the extreme consequences when things go wrong. Taken from Wohlsen (2009):

> The parolee who killed three Oakland police officers and left a fourth brain-dead over the weekend had been tentatively linked by DNA evidence to a rape the day before the shootings, authorities said.
>
> Oakland police spokesman Jeff Thomason confirmed a report on the San Francisco Chronicle's Web site on Monday night that DNA from an unsolved rape in Oakland in February was a probable match to that of 26-year-old Lovelle Mixon.

Investigators got that information Friday, the day before Mixon opened fire on the officers following a routine traffic stop. Mixon is the primary suspect in the rape and is being investigated to see if there are any connections to other rapes, Thomason said.

…

Earlier Monday, state Attorney General Jerry Brown said he will examine how 26-year-old Lovelle Mixon was monitored following his release from prison in November on a conviction for assault with a deadly weapon. Mixon also was a suspect in a murder last year but was never charged, according to state prison officials.

"Mixon was certainly a character that needed more supervision," said Brown, the former mayor of Oakland. "In Oakland, the highway patrol has an office there, sheriff and police. And all those agencies should have a list of the more dangerous, threatening parolees so they can keep a watch on them."

Problems involving parolees from California's overcrowded prison system have long beset state officials who must monitor them, local officials who try to keep streets safe and federal authorities who enforce firearms and other laws.

Mixon was one of 164 Oakland parolees in mid-March who had outstanding arrest warrants for parole violations, state prison records show.

The city of 400,000 had more than 1,900 total parolees at the time, including nearly 300 who had been returned to custody or whose parole was about to be revoked.

Statewide, almost 17,000 of the nearly 125,000 parolees were wanted for violating their parole requirements, state records show.

Mixon's family members said he was upset that he was unable to find work, felt his parole officer was not helping him and feared he would be arrested for a parole violation.

Mixon was wanted for missing an appointment with his parole supervisor.

State prison officials said Mixon's parole officer was responsible for 70 parolees.

A caseload of that size is nearly unmanageable, and also not unusual, said Lance Corcoran, spokesman for California's prison guard union, which includes parole officers.

Too many parolees prevents officers from effectively monitoring or guiding them back into society, Corcoran said. "There is no control," he said. "It's simply supervision, and supervision at distance."

Mixon was driving a 1995 Buick when motorcycle patrolmen Sgt. Mark Dunakin, 40, and Officer John Hege, 41, stopped him around 1 p.m. Saturday, police said. Dunakin was shot dead at the scene. Hege was declared brain-dead over the weekend but remained on life support Monday.

...

Police have not said why Mixon was pulled over, but relatives who talked to him on his cell phone just before the traffic stop said he was looking for a parking space.

After the first two officers were shot, Mixon fled to what his family said was a younger sister's apartment around the corner. A SWAT team stormed the apartment around 3 p.m. Sgt. Ervin Romans, 43, and Sgt. Daniel Sakai, 35, were gunned down before officers fatally shot Mixon.

The SWAT team had little choice but to try to take the suspect by force, experts said.

"They knew this was a killer who hadn't hesitated to kill uniformed police officers," said Joseph McNamara, retired San Jose police chief and a research fellow at Stanford University's Hoover Institution.

"The normal SWAT strategy of surrounding, containing, negotiating, trying to resolve the situation without violence has to change once the killing has begun," McNamara said. "Police strategy then changes to, they must go in."

...

California prison records show that authorities issued a warrant for Mixon's arrest after he failed to make a mandatory meeting with his parole officer on Feb. 19. Parole violators typically face five to nine months in prison, said Gordon Hinkle, a spokesman for the state Department of Corrections.

PRISON LIABILITY

When the state takes someone's liberty and confines that person to a prison, it also takes on the responsibility for his or her health, safety, and general welfare. That is to say, the state has a *duty of care*; the state cannot simply lock up inmates and forget about them. It is responsible for what happens to the inmate while in its custody. This is discussed in Tartaro (2005, p. 113):

When police or corrections personnel take custody of an alleged offender, the government becomes responsible for that person's safety and general well-being (*Estelle v. Gamble*, 1976).

When the state or one of its agents breaches its duty of care, the state is civilly liable for any harm that is suffered. Precisely what constitutes an acceptable standard of care for inmates is a matter of much debate and continuous litigation.

Civil Rights: Section 1983

An adjunct to the basic duty of care that exists between prisons and inmates is the provision that the state must refrain from violating the inmate's civil rights. In the United States, all citizens are guaranteed protection of their rights by Title 42, Section 1983 of the United States Code titled "Civil action for deprivation of rights." It provides in whole that:

> Every person who, under color of any statute, ordinance, regulation, custom, or usage, of any State or Territory or the District of Columbia, subjects, or causes to be subjected, any citizen of the United States or other person within the jurisdiction thereof to the deprivation of any rights, privileges, or immunities secured by the Constitution and laws, shall be liable to the party injured in an action at law, suit in equity, or other proper proceeding for redress, except that in any action brought against a judicial officer for an act or omission taken in such officer's judicial capacity, injunctive relief shall not be granted unless a declaratory decree was violated or declaratory relief was unavailable. For the purposes of this section, any Act of Congress applicable exclusively to the District of Columbia shall be considered to be a statute of the District of Columbia.

The nature, intent, and usage of Section 1983 protections are explained in Rigby (2008, p. 419):

> Title 42, Section 1983 of the United States Code prohibits public officials from violating individuals' civil rights and liberties guaranteed by the Constitution and federal law. The Act seeks to accomplish its objective by providing a civil cause of action for plaintiffs whose civil rights and liberties are infringed by government actors. Section 1983 is frequently employed to sue state and local law enforcement and corrections officers. Although the legal elements of Section 1983 apply equally throughout the United States, the effect of Section 1983 may vary depending on each jurisdiction studied. For instance, individuals in some areas of the nation seem to be particularly at risk of having their individual constitutional rights violated. In other jurisdictions, however,

the government appears to be burdened by an unusual amount of frivolous Section 1983 claims.

Section 1983 is meant to provide citizens, even incarcerated ones, with the ability to hold the government civilly accountable for violations of their civil rights. It is one of the only safeguards that citizens have against abuses by law enforcement and corrections officers because of its power to hold them accountable, as well as its deterrent effect. It also serves the important role of reminding government agents that they are subordinate to the law just like everyone else.

Ironically, Section 1983 lawsuits are often filed by prison inmates without the benefit of legal counsel, many of which are successful. Access to the prison's legal library, after all, is considered a right.

Health Care

One of the key duties of care held by the state with respect to prison inmates involves providing adequate health care. As provided in *Estelle v. Gamble* (1976):

> An inmate must rely on prison authorities to treat his medical needs; if the authorities fail to do so, those needs will not be met. In the worst cases, such a failure may actually produce physical "torture or a lingering death," ... The infliction of such unnecessary suffering is inconsistent with contemporary standards of decency as manifested in modern legislation codifying the common law view that "it is but just that the public be required to care for the prisoner, who cannot, by reason of the deprivation of his liberty, care for himself." We therefore conclude that deliberate indifference to serious medical needs of prisoners constitutes the "unnecessary and wanton infliction of pain," *Gregg v. Georgia, supra,* at 173 (joint opinion), proscribed by the Eighth Amendment. This is true whether the indifference is manifested by prison doctors in their response to the prisoner's needs or by prison guards in intentionally denying or delaying access to medical [p105] care or intentionally interfering with the treatment once prescribed. Regardless of how evidenced, deliberate indifference to a prisoner's serious illness or injury states a cause of action under § 1983.

This duty is significant because inmate populations are on the rise and rates of inmate illness are much higher than those found on the outside. The situation is described in Jones (2008, p. 181):

> The prison population in America is not only vast and rapidly expanding, but also "the prevalence of chronic illness, communicable diseases, and severe mental disorders among people in jail and prison is far greater than among other people of comparable ages."

> Specifically, the "[s]ignificant illnesses afflicting corrections populations include coronary artery disease, hypertension, diabetes, asthma, chronic lung diseases, HIV infection, hepatitis B and C, other sexually transmitted diseases, tuberculosis, chronic renal failure, physical disabilities and many types of cancer."

While physical illness is prevalent in inmate populations, so too is mental illness.

Appelbaum, Hickey, and Packer (2001) provide a useful discussion that explains how to approach the problem to achieve some success (p. 1343):

> Prisons have become the homes of thousands of inmates who have mental disorders. The stress of incarceration can cause morbidity among these individuals, resulting in more severe symptoms and more disruptive behavior. Effective treatment for such inmates often involves services provided by a multidisciplinary treatment team that includes correctional officers. Correctional officers can assist in observations and interventions, and they play a unique role on specialized housing units. Successful collaboration between correctional officers and treatment teams requires a foundation of mutual respect, shared training, and ongoing communication and cooperation. With these elements in place, correctional officers can assist the treatment team and make important and constructive contributions to the assessment and management of offenders who have mental disorders.

This discussion suggests one standard of care that involves all prison staff working together for the betterment of the inmate. However required standards of care vary widely. For example, in U.S. federal institutions, prisoners have a right to the standard of care that exists in the community where the facility is located. As a result, inmates at the Federal Medical Clinic in Rochester, Minnesota, are entitled to treatment at the Mayo Clinic because this is the local standard of care. In communities with less access to quality medical care, the prison's standard of care is lower.

When prison staff or administrators are aware of medical conditions that go untreated, or of treatment conditions that are beneath the ascribed standard of care, both the state and the individual may be held responsible. This is explained in a discussion regarding the dangers of outsourcing prison health care to private for-profit corporations in Jones (2008, pp. 201–202):

> The practice of outsourcing health care in prisons and jails to for-profit corporations is fundamentally broken. The level of care these corporations provide inmates is dangerously inadequate and considering the race to the bottom that occurs when several of these

corporations compete for the same contract, the level of care can only get worse. Because prison officials know of the substantial risk to inmate health that outsourcing prison health care can cause, when a prison official chooses to implement a prison health care system that is outsourced to a for-profit corporation, that prison official is deliberately indifferent to the health care rights of inmates. Therefore, that prison official could be held liable for violating the Constitutional rights of inmates by implementing a prison health care system that is the equivalent of cruel and unusual punishment.

As an example of what administrators are and are not aware of with respect to offender treatment, consider the following: to cut down on the high costs of prisoner mental health care, many facilities no longer have a psychiatrist on staff. In such cases, consultations may be performed through tele-psychiatry rather than by an on-site psychiatrist. Furthermore, many inmate psychological services are also currently being provided for by master's degree-level counselors or practicum students who are supervised by a few doctoral-level psychologists.

THE ROLE OF THE FORENSIC CRIMINOLOGIST

Forensic criminologists have a long-established tradition of participation in civil trials where issues related to prison negligence and liability are concerned. They may be hired by either side of a legal dispute to determine whether a standard of care was met; whether harm to an inmate or staff was foreseeable; or whether harm to an inmate or staff was in any way preventable. In their role as forensic consultants or experts, they can determine and evaluate the circumstances surrounding these issues and render findings to assist with legal proceedings.

TYPES OF LIABILITY

In Chapter 7 we discussed the concept of premises liability. The types of liability incurred by prisons may be viewed as, essentially, a specialized subset of premises liability. Having touched on other areas of liability already in this chapter, in the following sections we will discuss liability issues related to conditions of confinement, assault, rape, in-custody deaths, and negligent supervision and release.

Conditions of Confinement

Inmates are able to bring suit against correctional facilities for a broad spectrum of issues related to the circumstances of their incarceration. Common

[5]Unless otherwise noted, these are adapted from *Williams v. Ozmint* (2008).

problems raised in inmate lawsuits include complaints regarding conditions of confinement such as the following:[5]

- *Cruel and unusual punishment:* This requires demonstrating that the deprivation of a basic human need was sufficiently serious and that prison staff acted with a "sufficiently culpable state of mind."

- *Excessive use of force by prison staff:* This requires establishing whether the force applied was "in a good faith effort to maintain or restore discipline, or maliciously and sadistically to cause harm."

- *Inadequate medical care:* This requires establishing whether prison staff were deliberately indifferent to the inmate's serious medical needs. As explained in *Miltier v. Beorn*, 896 F.2d 848, 851 (4th Cir.1990) "To establish that a health care provider's actions constitute deliberate indifference to a serious medical need, the treatment must be so grossly incompetent, inadequate, or excessive as to shock the conscience or to be intolerable to fundamental fairness."

- *Access to courts:* Inmates have a right to fair access to the courts, and must be provided with the means to present appeals and complaints. According to *Bounds v. Smith*, 430 U.S. 817, 825, 97 S.Ct. 1491, 52 L.Ed.2d 72 (1977), inmate access must be "adequate, effective and meaningful." This means that the prison must either provide inmates with access to a law library, or with some form of legal counsel. To prove such claims, the inmates must demonstrate that their right to access has been interfered with in some way, if not entirely infringed upon.

Consider the issues related to conditions of confinement raised in a suit filed on behalf of 40 female inmates against New Jersey State Prison (Hepp, 2008):

A judge [has] denied the state's request to toss out a civil-rights lawsuit filed by female inmates held in "lock-down conditions" at New Jersey's maximum-security prison, finding that their claims "if later found to be true, constitutes cruel and unusual punishment."

The American Civil Liberties Union filed the lawsuit in December on behalf of 40 women who were sent to New Jersey State Prison in Trenton in March 2007 to alleviate overcrowding at the Edna Mahan Correctional Facility for Women.

The women claim they have been kept in their cells for up to 22 hours a day because prison officials must separate them from the facility's 1,800 male inmates. As a result, the women allege they do not have access to the prison's law library and school, they receive medical attention in an open area of their unit as prison guards watch and they are barred from the men's prison yard.

"Plaintiffs raise a number of significant genuine issues of material fact as to the general conditions of confinement, and specific actions or inaction on the part of the defendants, which if later found to be true, constitutes cruel and unusual punishment," wrote Superior Court Judge Maria Sypek. "A fact-finding record is necessary in order to analyze all of these allegations and reach a conclusion as to what, if any constitutional and civil rights are being violated."

While sometimes frivolous, the ability of inmates to make these kinds of legal complaints is an important part of acknowledging their civil rights, as well as providing a check against abuse.

Assault

Assault is common in prison, whether it is staff-on-inmate, inmate-on-staff, or inmate-on-inmate. Some assaults may be both foreseeable and preventable. As mentioned previously in this chapter, it is incumbent on prison staff to provide a safe environment for people in their custody. However, there are documented instances when prison staff have openly encouraged inmates to harm each other for their own amusement. Consider the following case, in which Daniel Zabuski, a convicted rapist, alleged that guards tipped off other inmates regarding the nature of his crime. As reported in Krikorian (2003):

A convicted rapist sentenced to 80 years to life in prison has been awarded $17,500 by Los Angeles County to settle a lawsuit that claimed he was assaulted by other inmates while in the custody of the Sheriff's Department in 2001....

Daniel Zabuski of Canoga Park, who was sentenced last August to state prison for the rape and assault of three women he met through the Internet, sued the county and the Sheriff's Department in December 2001.

Zabuski, 43, alleged in the suit that he was "beaten beyond recognition" by inmates on various occasions between Jan. 3 and Feb. 13, 2001, while at the Peter J. Pitchess Detention Center in Castaic.

He said three sheriff's deputies implied to other inmates that he had been charged with sexually assaulting a minor, which led to the beatings. He also alleged negligence by the deputies for doing nothing to stop the attacks.

Los Angeles County Deputy Counsel Johanna Fontenot called the settlement a matter of "cost benefit."

"We were confident we would have prevailed, but this was just one of those cases where we really look at the cost benefit," Fontenot said. "We think we would have had a good chance at winning at trial, but it didn't seem worth going to trial."

Although Zabuski had requested placement in a segregated housing unit because of the nature of the charges against him, at the time of the alleged beatings he was in the jail's general population.

Although the preceding example would not be included in what is often called a "frivolous lawsuit," jail and prison administrators may be confronted with these types of lawsuits. For example, inmates have sued over receiving soggy sandwiches (*Brittaker v. Rowland*), finding gristle on their turkey leg (*Attwood v. Bowers*), and for having to watch network television rather than satellite television (*Jackson v. Barton*).[6] While it is certainly true that it is important to perform a cost-benefit analysis when deciding whether to settle inmate lawsuits, a policy of favoring settlement would seem to encourage the very type of frivolous suits that the state should want to discourage.

[6]See http://www.lectlaw.com/files/fun30.htm

Rape

Conservative estimates from a number of different studies suggest that between 13% and 25% of prison inmates have been raped while incarcerated (Peretti, 2007). As with instances of assault, rape in prison can occur staff-on-inmate or inmate-on-inmate. Ironically, this act is committed for a variety of motives shared by staff and inmates alike, such as the assertion of power and control, as a form of punishment, or as an extension of entitlement. Moreover, it has become less difficult for inmates to hold prison staff accountable for rapes that they commit or allow by virtue of a failure to protect, as reported in Egelko (2009):

The state Supreme Court allowed a transgender former prison inmate … to proceed with a lawsuit accusing prison guards of failing to protect her from being raped and beaten by her cellmates.

In her suit, Alexis Giraldo said she was being held at Folsom State Prison for shoplifting and a parole violation in January 2006 when a cellmate began assaulting and raping her on a daily basis. She said prison staff ignored her complaints until March 2006, when she was transferred to segregated housing after a second cellmate attacked her with a box-cutter. She was paroled in July 2007.

Prison officials denied failing to protect Giraldo, who was housed at the all-male prison because she had not undergone surgery. A San

Francisco jury rejected her emotional-distress claim against six prison employees in August 2007 after the trial judge dismissed her claim of negligence, ruling that guards have no legal duty to protect inmates from harm.

The First District Court of Appeal in San Francisco overturned the judge's ruling last November, saying a jailer who takes a prisoner into custody must take reasonable steps to protect that prisoner from foreseeable injuries. California's high court denied review of the state's appeal …, allowing Giraldo to pursue her claim that negligence by prison employees was a cause of the assaults.

There are certain characteristics which are known to increase inmate risk of being the victim of rape, discussed thoroughly in Peretti (2007, pp. 762–763):

From the day he sets foot in the penitentiary, the male inmate faces the possibility of sexual assault at the hands of another inmate or group of inmates. There are certain inmates, however, who have a higher probability of being attacked. Sexual predators look for vulnerable inmates upon whom to prey. The most vulnerable inmates usually are "young, nonviolent, first-time offenders who are small, weak, shy, gay or effeminate, and inexperienced in the ways of prison life." The classic example of an obvious sexual assault target is Dee Farmer, the inmate whose litigation led to the current Supreme Court's definition of the "deliberate indifference" standard. Farmer was a preoperative transsexual with breast implants who looked young and had many feminine characteristics. Within two weeks of arriving at a maximum-security federal prison, Farmer was savagely beaten and raped in his own cell by another inmate.

Often an inmate's physical characteristics immediately indicate to a predator that an inmate is particularly vulnerable. As in Farmer's case, inmates who have feminine characteristics are at a severe risk of sexual assault. An inmate's "aura of femininity," which may include a high-pitched voice, youthful look, small build, feminine clothing or hairstyle, or open homosexuality, suggests to a predator prisoner that the inmate is available for sex. Younger prisoners also face a greater risk. Because these inmates' youthful features may correlate with femininity, physical weakness, or inexperience with respect to prison life, they are extremely vulnerable to sexual assault. Physically smaller inmates are also in great danger of being victimized in prison, as they are less able to defend themselves against any physical attack.

An inmate's prior prison experience and personal history are also strong factors in determining whether he will be the target of a sexual assault. New "fish" entering prison for the first time might not know the system and are often unaware of the unwritten "rules of the game." A sexual predator may give a new inmate some cigarettes or candy with the expectation of sexual favors in the future. The new inmate, unaware that there is nothing free in prison, may unsuspectingly take the "gift." Or, lacking friends and allies for protection, a new inmate may be threatened with physical violence if he does not submit to sexual acts. Describing what life is like for a new inmate, an Arkansas prisoner told Human Rights Watch that "[u]nless the new arrival is strong, ugly, and efficient at violence, they are subject to get seduced, coerced, or raped." Additionally, inmates who come from middle- or upper-class backgrounds usually are not "street-wise," do not possess personal combat skills, and are unfamiliar with life in confinement, making them even more vulnerable.

Prisoners who possess any one of these physical characteristics or personal histories are generally more likely than other inmates to be subject to prison rape. Inmates who possess multiple characteristics are significantly more likely to be targeted by sexual predators. Prison officials who witness prison life daily understand these inmate dynamics, as well as the reality that there are some prisoners who are more susceptible to rape than others. Based on the common victim profile, prison officials—and even outside observers with minimal understanding of life behind bars—can predict with a high degree of accuracy which inmates will be victims of sexual assault.

In describing the nature and impact of prison rape on inmates, Corlew (2006, pp. 160–161) offers the following, which is consistent with concerns raised throughout this chapter regarding the strain of prison environment, the compounded mental anguish, and the high risk of contracting or spreading disease:

The impact of prison rape upon its victims can be debilitating and overwhelming. Sexual victimization has profound physical, social, and psychological effects—effects that are magnified in confinement settings. Victims often endure great physical pain and sustain various injuries. Moreover, any episode of sexual assault could ultimately prove deadly since incarcerated victims are at an increased risk of contracting sexually transmitted and other communicable diseases such as HIV, AIDS, tuberculosis, and hepatitis B and C. For instance, the rate of HIV in prison is ten times higher than in the population at large. Consequently, a misdemeanor offender could go into prison with only a short sentence, but end up being dealt—in effect—a death sentence.

Like victims of sexual assault generally, incarcerated victims experience
a host of psychological problems, including anger, anxiety, depression,
shame, Post Traumatic Stress disorder, and Rape Trauma Syndrome.
These emotional hurts often cause victims to attempt suicide.
Furthermore, if a prisoner is raped once, it is likely that he or she
will be targeted again: repeated victimization is common in prisons.
Targeted prisoners are stigmatized (derogatorily called "punks,"
"bitches," "turnouts," or "queens"); they live in fear and hopelessness.
Not only do the victims themselves suffer, but the victims' families
experience feelings of desperation and helplessness as well, and are
afraid for their loved one's physical and emotional well-being.

Exasperating the situation, incarcerated victims often feel continuously
vulnerable—an escape from the torture is impossible and victimization
is inevitable. They can neither run nor can they hide from their
attackers. They cannot choose their cellmates. Many have found
grievance and investigation procedures inadequate. Pleas for help are
frequently unnoticed, ignored, or disbelieved. Prisoner grievances are
often denied for lack of evidence. While studies of corrections officers
generally show that they are willing to protect inmates from sexual
assault, many victims are still told they have two choices: in prison
vernacular, "fight or fuck;" or in other words, fend for yourself. An
inmate-victim in a Texas prison endured severe sexual abuse at the
hands of incarcerated gang members. Considering him its "property,"
the gang threatened and beat the victim, and forced him to engage in
oral and anal sex. The victim filed many grievances and reported the
abuse to prison guards, but for over nine months, his pleas for help
were ignored. Prison staff members told him that he was lying about
being sexually abused, that he "must be gay," and that he should "be a
man [and] take care of [his] business."

Inmates who break the "code of silence" by reporting an incident
may be subjected to increased violence if corrections officials do not
adequately protect them. Because victimized inmates fear such a result,
many incidents go unreported. Those who do come forward to report
incidents of rape may be stigmatized even more than they were before,
and other inmates may ridicule them in the prison yard. To protect
prison rape victims, prison officials often separate them from the
general population, but this solution could mean the victim is isolated,
a situation that carries with it its own negative emotional baggage.
Thus, victimized inmates experience difficulty in reporting sexual
abuse, which contributes to the lack of definitive statistics concerning
prison sexual assault. Another factor contributing to the problem
of prison rape is that prison officials may find it hard to distinguish

consensual relationships from coercive ones. At first, victims may fight to defend themselves, but repeated beatings from stronger (or multiple) attackers often cause once-strong fighting spirits to break. Many victims eventually submit to a "protective pairing relationship" (called "hooking up"), where one inmate allows another inmate to control his or her body in exchange for protection from other inmates. Although these relationships are by their nature coercive—maintained by threats and intimidation—prison officials may look the other way, finding it hard to distinguish protective-pairing sexual relationships from truly consensual ones.

What this suggests is that liability from prison rape is not just about the harm caused to the victim in the immediate sense, but also the ongoing and collateral damage that ensues in the prison environment. Moreover, the inmate characteristics that increase the risk of rape are not unknown to those in the prison system. So despite being a long-standing part of prison culture, prison rape represents a tremendous health and safety issue that requires acknowledgment and remedy—not tacit approval or open encouragement, as has been historically the case.

Prison rape is in fact a serious enough problem in the United States that it has required presidential intervention to define what it is and how prisons must respond to its occurrence. As explained in Corlew (2006, p. 158):

> On September 4, 2003, President Bush signed into law the Prison Rape Elimination Act of 2003 ("PREA" or "Act"). Although many Americans treat the issue of sexual assault in prisons as the topic of jokes, Congress decided it was no laughing matter and unanimously passed PREA—a bipartisan effort to reduce and eliminate prison rape in an effective and comprehensive manner. Through the Act, Congress intends "[t]o provide for the analysis of the incidence and effects of prison rape in Federal, State, and local institutions and to provide information, resources, recommendations, and funding to protect individuals from prison rape." The Act defines "prison rape" broadly to encompass various coercive sexual acts (including penetration of any sort, oral sodomy, sexual assault with an object, and sexual fondling) accomplished through physical force or intimidation and occurring in any federal, state, or local confinement facility. To be eligible for federal funding for prisons, a state must cooperate with prison rape studies and implement minimal national standards for preventing, investigating, and prosecuting incidents of prison rape. Through this legislation, the federal government hopes to confront, eradicate, and prevent sexual assault in the nation's prisons and jails—a problem that, until now, had largely been ignored by government officials.

The message sent to prisons by the federal government is clear: rape is not a joke and must not be tolerated—so start taking it seriously or risk losing federal dollars. However, while its intentions are good and useful, the extent to which this Act may be enforced is debatable, although it does provide a useful yardstick for duty of care during litigation.

An inmate is a protected person because he or she is in the custody of the government. Therefore, the very nature of the power differential between staff and inmate make even "consensual" sex nonconsensual. It is similar to statutory rape when a teenager may "consent" to sex with an adult but is incapable of legally offering that consent due to legal status. Unfortunately, there are many cases of staff, both correctional officers and support staff, being "walked out" of institutions after engaging in sexual acts with inmates. Sometimes these "consensual" relationships are initiated by staff, but often inmates will target vulnerable staff and court them. Inmate-initiated romantic relationships with staff are sometimes used as a means to garner special privileges, to have contraband smuggled in for them, or even to aid in escapes. Once any rule violation is made by the staff member, the inmate essentially has leverage for future requests to violate protocol. When the staff member is no longer useful to that inmate, he or she may report the sexual relationship to authorities. These staff people are then open to criminal prosecution for rape or abuse in addition to various other criminal charges.

In-Custody Deaths

When an inmate dies in the custody of a jail or a prison, that death must be investigated. This holds true whether the death is a suicide or not, and even when suicide is believed to be "obvious." As provided in Tartaro (2005, p. 113):

> Officers are responsible for not only keeping inmates safe from each other, but they are obligated to keep inmates safe from themselves (Collins, 1995; Hanser, 2002). Officers and civilian staff in prisons, jails and police lock-ups have to deal with the possibility that inmates under their supervision might attempt to take their own lives.

In-custody death investigations are typically massive and involve far-reaching interviews of prison staff, inmates, and reviews of collateral information such as the inmate's property, medical charts, and institutional paperwork. Investigators must determine whether the event was foreseeable and whether all staff members involved with the inmate's care were performing their work in accordance with policy during the time frame in question.

In-Custody Suicide

Consider the case of 18-year-old Angela Enoch, incarcerated at the Taycheedah Correctional Institution in Wisconsin. She was mentally ill and had been in and out of institutions and out of foster care her entire life. It was reported that (Diedrich, 2008):

> The State of Wisconsin has agreed to pay $635,000 to the family of a woman who committed suicide while in the Taycheedah Correctional Institution, according to federal court documents.
>
> Angela Enoch, 18, killed herself in 2005 after reportedly pleading for psychiatric help for days. She used ripped pieces of her pillow to strangle herself.
>
> The two sides entered into settlement talks, which broke down without an agreement, said James Gende, an attorney representing Enoch's estate and two of her sisters.
>
> Then the state filed a pleading, offering to pay $635,000, he said. The plaintiffs decided to take that offer rather than go to trial, Gende said. The state did not admit liability in the case, he said.
>
> "Our goal is the care of the family. Of course, we could have held out for more money. It is a substantial sum of money for the family," he said....
>
> That lawsuit, filed in May 2006, alleged the health care system at Taycheedah was "grossly deficient," leaving women vulnerable to contagious diseases and subjecting them to medical mistakes that resulted in suicide or painful disabilities.
>
> ...
>
> Separately, the U.S. Department of Justice reported in 2006 that Taycheedah's mental health system was unacceptable and threatened to sue.
>
> John Dipko, spokesman for the Wisconsin Department of Corrections, said state officials continue to work with federal officials on those issues. He said 33 positions have been added and care programs expanded, and that plans are under way for a new health facility at the prison.

Further details are reported in Harris (2009):

> Enoch entered Wisconsin's juvenile court system at age 12 and was charged with her first adult crime at 14. She had a history of assaults, as well as self-destructive and suicidal behavior.
>
> She had been diagnosed with bipolar disorder, personality disorder, mood disorder and attention deficit hyperactivity disorder. Despite a court order to give Enoch her prescription medications, Taycheedah staff "failed to take the necessary action in administering (her)

prescribed medications in the days immediately preceding her death of June 19, 2005," the lawsuit alleges.

The suit also alleges it took staff six to eight minutes to enter Enoch's cell after observing her strangling herself.

"(Taycheedah) staff's reaction to Enoch's self-strangulation was unreasonably delayed and in violation of their standard operating procedures for response to an emergency situation, which was a substantial cause of Enoch's death," the suit reads.

Among the violations of law, the suit alleges wrongful death, cruel and unusual punishment, violation of equal protection, and violations of the federal Rehabilitation Act and the Americans with Disabilities Act.

The suit also alleges gender-based disparities. Female prisoners are not afforded the same level of psychiatric care available to male offenders at the Wisconsin Resource Center, a specialized mental health facility administered by the state Department of Health and Family Services through a partnership with the Department of Corrections.

While the state concedes no wrong in this case, it is useful to note that the head of the prison cited that improvements were being made at the prison with respect to more and better educated staff.

In-Custody Homicide

Consider the case of Brian Thomas Edwards, serving time in a maximum-security prison in Victoria, Australia. It was reported that (Murdered inmate 'failed' by prison, 2007):

The son of an inmate fatally stabbed in a maximum security Victorian prison nine years ago says prison authorities failed in their duty of care to protect his father.

Brian Thomas Edwards was murdered by two inmates in Barwon Prison, south-west of Melbourne, on March 2, 1998. The 48-year-old was attacked from behind, suffering six stab wounds to the chest with a stolen knife, and died in an ambulance soon after, the Victorian Coroner's Court heard today.

Edwards' son, Mark Edwards, told coroner Jane Hendtlass that his father was "in care" at Barwon, which he believed was negligent over his father's "barbaric death."

"I certainly think they failed in their duty of care (to my father)," Mr Edwards said.

Dr Hendtlass told Mr Edwards it was not under her jurisdiction to determine whether the prison had failed in its duty of care over his father's death.

The inquest into Edwards' death follows a cold-case investigation in which conclusive DNA evidence led to the arrest of Stephen Matthew Wenitong and Nathan Daniel Berry.

Wenitong, 35, and Berry, 29, were arrested in St Kilda in January 2004 by homicide squad detectives.

They were found guilty of murdering Edwards in the Victorian Supreme Court in November 2005.

Wenitong was sentenced to a non-parole period of 20 years and Berry, a non-parole period of 17 years.

Homicide squad Detective Sergeant Anthony Thatcher told the inquest a "code black" or a total prison lockdown was called after Edwards was found in his cell, covered in blood and bleeding from his chest.

"Ambulance officers attempted to revive him... he died in the rear of the ambulance," Det Sgt Thatcher said.

After forensic testing, the sports shoes belonging to Wenitong and Berry had DNA evidence traced to Edwards, Det Sgt Thatcher said.

Edwards' family asked through coroner's assistant Senior Constable Greg McFarlane about the motive of the murder, to which Det Sgt Thatcher replied: "There was a misconception that Mr Edwards was a police informer... but that was totally untrue."

Det Sgt Thatcher also said an associate of Berry had harboured "ill-feeling" towards Edwards.

Edwards was found guilty of drug-related offences in February 1998 and was sentenced to 27 months.

He was due to be released from prison on May 4, 2000.

Edwards was described as an "experienced prisoner who was a gentle giant with a passive demeanour."

While the precise liability of the prison in this case is unclear, it does present a fact pattern that requires investigation. The placement of a nonviolent offender in a maximum-security prison; the histories of those he was placed with; the supervision required at the time of his death. All these questions and more beg answering to establish whether or not the prison or the state is liable.

Negligent Housing, Release, and Supervision

Individuals who work in corrections and in community supervision should be aware of the potential liability they may incur as individuals or for the institution they are working for at the time. People who work in corrections must make many tough decisions regarding inmate housing, access to treatment, and how to address grievances in a timely and judicial manner. When an incident occurs that brings these decisions under scrutiny by authorities and a forensic criminologist, the correctional worker will have to justify his or her decision and above all have these decisions well documented.

Regarding inmate housing, an inmate has to be placed in the least restrictive environment given his or her crime and behavioral history. Those with less serious crimes and with no history of violence should be housed with similar risk level inmates and not with the most violent offenders. In addition to placing an inmate in the least restrictive yet appropriate security level, correctional staff must decide whether to grant an inmate protective custody status or segregation status. Protective custody (PC) is often requested (e.g., "P-C up") by vulnerable inmates who wish to be housed separately from the general population. Depending on the size of the institution, these individuals will be housed either on their own unit or in individual segregation housing. Some PC inmates may make grievances about the level of restriction they may have as a result of their protective status, or allege that staff treat them in a derogatory manner because PC inmates can be perceived by some as weak or lacking integrity since some have sex offense charges or are informants.

Access to treatment, as mentioned previously, is a right of inmates in the custody of the government. Most requests for treatment are done through some kind of formal process, often a written request to medical or to psychology staff. Many institutions have time frames in which these requests should be addressed, and it is imperative that the workers address these concerns in a timely fashion. If an incident does occur involving this inmate and the staff member has not addressed the request in a timely fashion, the institution might be liable. Documentation of when requests were received, when the worker responded to that request, and the resolution of that request is all important when reviewed by an outside investigator.

When a person is given probation or an inmate is released on parole (in the few states that still grant parole), those who supervise the individual might come under scrutiny by various professionals. Keeping clear notes of times the person met with the parolee/probationer as well as documentation of times they have spoken on the phone or attempted to make contact is important when reducing liability. Essentially, when a case is reviewed, an action occurred only if it was documented. If a supervisee commits a crime while under supervision, a probation and parole officer must then demonstrate that he or she did everything according to the standards of that profession and to prove that through documentation.

SUMMARY

Far more people are incarcerated in the United States than in any other country in the world, whether they are housed in jails, state or federal prisons, and regardless of the security level. This has become a tremendous strain on state budgets, as well as an undeniable racial issue. Ideally, the role of corrections is to securely detain those convicted of crimes, to protect them from themselves and others detained in the same facility, to provide basic medical and mental health care, and to separate dangerous felons from regular citizens.

The role of correctional officers is to maintain security and order in prisons. These individuals often work under difficult conditions. Although charged with this important job, there is often a lack of educational standards, poor employment screening, and low pay among correctional officers. This unfortunately leads to the smuggling of contraband by prison staff.

Community corrections is an alternative to incarceration meant to defer the rising cost of full-time imprisonment or assist offenders with the process of re-entry into society. These sentencing alternatives involve Bail Supervision Programs, Alternative Measures Programs, Restitution Programs, Fine Options Programs, Community Service Orders, Probation, Intensive Supervision Probation, Conditional Sentence of Imprisonment, Attendance Center Programs, Electronic Monitoring, Community-Based Centers, Temporary Absence Programs, and Parole.

When inmates are incarcerated, they cannot simply be locked up and forgotten about. That is, the staff as well as the state have a duty of care when it comes to inmates. The state therefore must provide adequate health care as well as mental health interventions. Moreover, prisons may also be liable for issues related to conditions of confinement, such as excessive use of force by prison staff, inadequate medical care, and access to courts; assault; rape; in-custody deaths, including suicide and homicide; and negligent housing, supervision, and release. Forensic criminologists may play a role in facilitating the civil trials where these issues of prison negligence and liability are concerned.

Review Questions

1. T/F There are more people incarcerated in the United States than in any other country.
2. What is the role of corrections?
3. What is the role of correctional officers?

4. T/F In most jurisdictions correctional officers caught smuggling contraband into the prison are fired on the spot.

5. What is the difference between a federal and a state court conviction?

6. Name and describe five different community corrections options.

7. Why is a policy favoring settlement for inmate lawsuits detrimental to the state?

8. What is the state and staff's duty of care? How does this relate to their civil liability?

REFERENCES

Aizenman, N.C., 2008. New High in U.S. Prison Numbers: Growth Attributed to More Stringent Sentencing Laws. Washington Post Friday, February 29, p. A1.

Appelbaum, K., Hickey, J., Packer, I., 2001. The Role of Correctional Officers in Multidisciplinary Mental Health Care in Prisons. Psychiatric Services 52, October, 1343–1347.

Collins, W. C., 1995. The Court's Role in Shaping Prison Suicide Policy. In: L. M. Hayes (Ed.), Prison Suicide: An Overview and Guide to Prevention. Department of Justice, National Issue of Corrections, Washington, DC, pp. 58–67.

Community Corrections, 1998. Publication C29. John Howard Society of Alberta, Alberta. url: http://www.johnhoward.ab.ca/PUB/C29.htm

Corlew, K., 2006. Congress Attempts to Shine a Light on a Dark Problem: An In-Depth Look at the Prison Rape Elimination Act of 2003. American Journal of Criminal Law 33 (Spring), 157–190.

Diedrich, J., 2008. State Settles Prison Suicide Case; $635,000 Payment to Go to Inmate's Family. Milwaukee-Wisconsin Journal Sentinel August 19.

Durose, M., Langan, P., 2007. Felony Sentences in State Courts, 2004 Bureau of Justice Statistics Bulletin, July, NCJ 215646. U.S. Department of Justice, Washington, DC.

Egelko, B., 2009. Inmate Raped by Cellmates Can Sue Prison Guards. San Francisco Chronicle Thursday, February 12; url: http://www.sfgate.com/cgi-bin/article.cgi?f=/c/a/2009/02/11/BA7C15SKL5.DTL

Estelle v. Gamble, 1976. 429 U.S. 97, Case No. No. 75–929, November 30.

Hanser, R. D., 2002. Inmate Suicide in Prisons: An Analysis of Legal Liability Under 42 USC Section 1983. The Prison Journal 82, 459–477.

Harding, R., 1992. Private Prisons in Australia, Trends and Issues in Crime and Criminal Justice, no. 36, May. Australian Institute of Criminology, Canberra.

Harris, W., 2009. Lawsuit Filed in Taycheedah Inmate's Death; Treatment Used Alleged to Worsen Mental State. Post-Crescent, March 25; url: http://www.postcrescent.com/article/99999999/APC0101/704250628

Helfgott, J., Gunnison, E., 2008. The Influence of Social Distance on Community Corrections Officer Perceptions of Offender Reentry Needs. Federal Probation 9, June, 2–9.

Hepp, R., 2008. Judge Rules Female Inmates' Lawsuit May Proceed. The Star-Ledger Thursday, July 24; url: http://www.nj.com/news/index.ssf/2008/07/judge_rules_female_inmates_law.html

Johnson, K., 2009. To Save Money on Prisons, States Take a Softer Stance. USA Today March 17; url: http://www.usatoday.com/news/nation/2009–03–17–prison-economy_N.htm

Jones, D., 2008. A Cruel and Unusual System: The Inherent Problems of the Practice of Outsourcing Health Care of Prisons and Jails. Chicana/o-Latina/o Law Review 27, 179–202.

Krikorian, M., 2002. L.A. County Reaches Settlement in Assault Lawsuit Filed by Inmate. Los Angeles Times, July 19; url: http://articles. latimes.com/2003/jul/19/local/me-zabuski19

Motivans, M., 2008. Federal Justice Statistics, 2005 Bureau of Justice Statistics Bulletin, September, NCJ 220383. U.S. Department of Justice, Washington, DC.

Murdered Inmate 'Failed' by Prison, 2007. The Age, November 28; url: http://www.theage.com.au/news/national/murdered-inmate-failed-by-prison/2007/11/27/ 1196036865489.html

Palmer, C., 2009. Locking 'em Up—At What Cost? Arizona Capital Times, March 20; url: http://www.azcapitoltimes.com/story.cfm?id = 10750

Peretti, C., 2007. Aligning the Eighth Amendment with International Norms to Develop a Stronger Standard for Challenging the Prison Rape Epidemic. Emory International Law Review 21 (Fall), 759–788.

Pozen, D., 2003. Managing a Correctional Marketplace: Prison Privatization in the United States and the United Kingdom. Journal of Law and Politics 19 (Summer), 253–284.

Rigby, J., 2008. Section 1983 Actions in North Dakota: An Empirical Study of Agency Policies and Law Enforcement and Correctional Officers. North Dakota Law Review 84, 419–451.

Roberts, J., 1997. The Federal Bureau of Prisons: Its Mission, Its History, and Its Partnership with Probation and Pretrial Services. Federal Probation 61, March, 53–57.

Sandberg, L., Stiles, M., 2009. Illicit Goods Keep Flowing into Prisons: Workers Caught with Contraband Rarely Get Fired. Houston Chronicle March 15.

Tartaro, C., 2005. Section 1983 Liability and Custodial Suicide: A Look at What Plaintiffs Face in Court. Californian Journal of Health Promotion 3 (2), 113–124.

Turner, K., 2008. Raising the Bars: A Comparative Look at Treatment Standards for Mentally Ill Prisoners in the United States, United Kingdom, and Australia. Cardozo Journal of International and Comparative Law 16 (Summer), 409–456.

Williams v. Ozmint, 2008. United States District Court, D. South Carolina, Charleston Division, C/A No. 6:07–2409–DCN-WMC, September 22.

Wohlsen, M., 2009. Parolee in Police Shootings Linked to Rape. Associated Press, March 23; url: http://www.mercurynews.com/breakingnews/ci_11975841

CHAPTER 9

Miscarriages of Justice: Causes and Suggested Reforms

Craig M. Cooley

KEY TERMS

Drylabbing: Testifying to forensic tests that were never conducted.

Exculpatory Evidence: Evidence that tends to show that a defendant is not guilty or had no criminal intent.

Forensic Fraud: Cases in which forensic science and law enforcement experts have provided sworn testimony, documents, or reports intended for the court that contain deceptive or misleading information, findings, opinions, or conclusions.

Innocence Network: An association of organizations dedicated to providing free legal and/or investigative services to prisoners for whom evidence discovered post conviction can provide conclusive proof of evidence.

Pro Bono: Work undertaken voluntarily or without payment for the public good.

Prosecutorial Misconduct: Improper or illegal behavior by any prosecutor that violates his or her sworn duty to follow the law and act on behalf of the public good when attempting to secure a conviction (e.g., failure to disclose exculpatory evidence or witnesses; subornation of perjury; and tainting the jury pool with false or misleading public statements).

CONTENTS

We may be hardened to the idea of criminals harming innocent people, but everyone cringes at the notion that innocent people may be mistakenly punished for a crime (or crimes) they did not commit. Indeed, English common law and the United States criminal justice system are premised on the maxim that it "is far worse to convict an innocent man than to let a guilty man go free."[1] Consequently, "concern about the injustice that results from the

---

[1] In re *Winship*, 397 U.S. 358, 372 (1970) (Harlan, J. concurring); accord T. STARKIE, EVIDENCE 756 (1824) ("The maxim of the law is… that it is better that ninety-nine… offenders should escape, than that one innocent man should be condemned").

307

conviction of an innocent person has long been at the core of our criminal justice system."[2] Simply put, then, "the central purpose of any system of criminal justice is to convict the guilty and free the innocent."[3]

To achieve this objective, the Drafters of the Federal Constitution incorporated several "constitutional provisions" that "have the effect of ensuring against the risk of convicting an innocent person."[4] For instance, the 6th Amendment affords criminal defendants the right to confront witnesses,[5] the right to a jury trial,[6] the right to compulsory process,[7] and the right to effective assistance of counsel.[8] Similarly, pursuant to the 14th Amendment's Due Process Clause, a criminal defendant is entitled to the presumption of innocence, and may insist that the State prove his guilt beyond a reasonable doubt.[9] The Due Process Clause also mandates that the government disclose evidence that exculpates the defendant or mitigates his or her sentence.[10] Moreover, in capital cases, because "death is different," the U.S. Supreme Court "has imposed a series of unique substantive and procedural restrictions designed to ensure that capital punishment is not imposed without the serious and calm reflection that ought to precede any decision of such gravity and finality."[11]

Thus, as Justice O'Connor proclaimed before the DNA revolution, "Our society has a high degree of confidence in its criminal trials, in no small part because the Constitution offers unparalleled protections against convicting the innocent."[12] As a result, before DNA testing exposed the justice system's unexpected error rate, Justice Stevens intimated that wrongful convictions "and 'substantial claims of innocence' were 'extremely rare.'"[13] Eighty-five years ago, Judge Learned Hand offered a similar sentiment when he observed that "[o]ur

---

[2]*Schlup v. Delo*, 513 U.S. 298, 325 (1995).

[3]*United States v. Nobles*, 422 U.S. 225, 230 (1975).

[4]*Herrera v. Collins*, 506 U.S. 390, 398–99 (1993).

[5]*Crawford v. Washington*, 541 U.S. 36 (2004); *Coy v. Iowa*, 487 U.S. 1012 (1988).

[6]*Duncan v. Louisiana*, 391 U.S. 145 (1968).

[7]*Taylor v. Illinois*, 484 U.S. 400 (1988).

[8]*Strickland v. Washington*, 466 U.S. 668 (1984); *Gideon v. Wainwright*, 372 U.S. 335 (1963).

[9]In re *Winship*, 397 U.S. 358 (1970).

[10]*Kyles v. Whitley*, 514 U.S. 419 (1995); *Brady v. Maryland*, 373 U.S. 83 (1963).

[11]*Thompson v. Oklahoma*, 487 U.S. 815, 856 (1988) (O'Connor, J., concurring); *see also Baze v. Rees*, 128 S.Ct. 1520, 1550 (2008) (Stevens, J., concurring in judgment) (noting that the Supreme Court has "relied on the premise that 'death is different' from every other form of punishment to justify rules minimizing the risk of error in capital cases."); *Gardner v. Florida*, 430 U.S. 349, 357–58 (1977) (plurality opinion).

[12]*Herrera v. Collins*, 506 U.S. 390, 420 (1993) (O'Connor, concurring).

[13]*Schlup v. Delo*, 513 U.S. 298, 321 (1995).

procedure has been always haunted by the ghost of the innocent man convicted," but posited, optimistically, that "[i]t is an unreal dream."[14]

Thanks to the advent of DNA technology, dogged defense attorneys, and ethical prosecutors, however, we have learned that despite all the protections afforded by the Federal Constitution, innocent people are wrongfully convicted at a rate much higher than ever thought imaginable, particularly in death penalty cases. The U.S. Supreme Court recently took notice of this unpleasant reality when it stated "we cannot ignore the fact that in recent years a disturbing number of inmates on death row have been exonerated."[15] As Justice Stevens explained, "the risk of error in capital cases may be greater than in other cases because the facts are often so disturbing that the interest in making sure the crime does not go unpunished may overcome residual doubt concerning the identity of the offender." Consequently, "[w]hether or not any innocent defendants have actually been executed, abundant evidence accumulated in recent years has resulted in the exoneration of an unacceptable number of defendants found guilty of capital offenses."[16] The same can be said in noncapital cases, but with greater force because, as will be discussed, the vast majority of DNA exonerations are noncapital cases.

The reasons for such an unprecedented number of wrongful convictions are multifaceted and complicated. For instance, while the U.S. Constitution bestows upon the criminal defendant many procedural and substantive safeguards, the Supreme Court has made clear that "due process does not require that every conceivable step be taken, at whatever cost, to eliminate the possibility of convicting an innocent person."[17] As Chief Justice Rehnquist explained, "To conclude otherwise would all but paralyze our system for enforcement of the criminal law."[18] Another reason may be the simple fact that the criminal justice system is administered by fallible human beings. The Supreme Court conceded this very point in *Herrera v. Collins* when it wrote: "It is an unalterable fact that our judicial system, like the human beings who administer it, is fallible."[19] Justices Thomas and Scalia reinforced this point in *Kansas v. Marsh*. In light of the DNA exonerations, Justice Thomas acknowledged that our justice system was in fact "imperfect,"[20] while Justice Scalia went further

---

[14]*United States v. Garsson*, 291 F. 646, 649 (S.D.N.Y.1923).

[15]*Atkins v. Virginia*, 536 U.S. 304, 320 n.25 (2002); *accord Kansas v. Marsh*, 548 U.S. 163, 207–211 (2006) (Souter, J., dissenting) (commenting on the "repeated exonerations of convicts under death sentences").

[16]*Baze v. Rees*, 128 S.Ct. at 1550 (Stevens, J. concurring in judgment). Justice Marshall made a similar observation 35 years earlier. *See Furman v. Georgia*, 408 U.S. 238, 366 (1972) (Marshall, J., concurring) ("Our 'beyond a reasonable doubt' burden of proof in criminal cases is intended to protect the innocent, but we know it is not foolproof. Various studies have shown that people whose innocence is later convincingly established are convicted and sentenced to death.").

[17]*Patterson v. New York*, 432 U.S. 197, 208 (1977).

[18]*Herrera v. Collins*, 506 U.S. 390, 399 (1993).

[19]*Herrera v. Collins*, 506 U.S. 390, 415 (1993).

[20]*Kansas v. Marsh*, 548 U.S. 163, 181 (2006).

and stated: "Like other human institutions, courts and juries are not perfect. One cannot have a system of criminal punishment without accepting the possibility that someone will be punished mistakenly. That is a truism, not a revelation."[21]

Chief Justice Rehnquist and Justices Thomas and Scalia are each right—the criminal justice will always, unfortunately, represent a "fallible" or "imperfect" system that produces errors. For instance, the criminal process must rely predominantly on eyewitnesses when investigating and prosecuting crimes. Eyewitnesses, however, are prone to error when certain factors are present. Likewise, the criminal process must also depend heavily on experts and forensic evidence in order to solve and prosecute crimes. For a variety of reasons, which are discussed later, forensic experts have unnervingly high error rates. Lastly, like any other human institution, rogue actors or agents will undermine the institution's accuracy and call into question its integrity by engaging in unethical or unprincipled behavior. For example, rogue and corrupt investigators have elicited countless false confessions, from wholly innocent people, through physical and psychological coercion. Similarly, many amoral investigators have turned to unreliable jailhouse informants to fabricate evidence against a wholly innocent defendant.

The fact that some degree of error will always permeate the criminal justice system does not mean they cannot be minimized to the greatest extent possible. To the contrary, social scientists and criminal justice reformers have identified and articulated a plethora of simplistic and innovative reforms that are aimed at minimizing the likelihood of a wrongful conviction without reducing the probability of accurate convictions. These reforms cover all problem areas such as eyewitness identification, forensic science, police interrogations, jailhouse informants, and lawyering.

HISTORICAL CONCERN

Concern for the innocent and wrongly convicted is not a recent phenomenon.

Edwin M. Borchard, known for his governmental liability research,[22] is credited for being the father of wrongful conviction research. Borchard's interest for the wrongly convicted dates back, at least, to 1913 when he published an

---

[21] *Kansas v. Marsh*, 126 S.Ct. 2516, 2539 (2006) (Scalia, J., concurring).

[22] *See* Edwin M. Borchard, "European Systems of State Indemnity for Errors of Criminal Justice," 3 J. *Crim. L. & Criminology* 684 (1913); Edwin M. Borchard, "Governmental Liability [Responsibility] in Tort," 34 *Yale L. J.* 1, 129, 229 (1924), 36 *Yale L. J.* 1, 757, 1039 (1926), 28 *Colum. L. Rev.* 577, 734 (1928) (this was Borchard's eight-part treatise); Edwin M. Borchard, "State Indemnity for Errors in Criminal Justice," 21 *B.U. L. Rev.* 201 (1941).

article in the *Journal of Criminal Law and Criminology*.[23] According to Borchard, "No attempt whatever seems to have been made in the United States to indemnify [the wrongly convicted]… although cases of shocking injustices are not infrequent occurrences."[24] Over the next two decades, Borchard researched the erroneously convicted's plight. Borchard's research culminated in his groundbreaking work, *Convicting the Innocent*,[25] in which he detailed the stories of 65 wrongly convicted individuals. From Borchard's perspective:

> Among the most shocking… [and] glaring of injustices are erroneous convictions of innocent persons. The State must necessarily prosecute persons legitimately suspected of crime; but when it is discovered after conviction that the wrong man was condemned, the least the State can do to right his essentially irreparable injury is to reimburse the innocent victim, by an appropriate indemnity, for the loss and damage suffered.[26]

Borchard's data indicated that wrongful convictions were not unique to a specific jurisdiction.[27] Moreover, while wrongful convictions occurred most often in murder cases (29 out of 65), erroneous convictions were also documented in robbery cases (23); forgery cases (5), criminal assault cases (4); obscenity cases (2); bribery cases (1), and prostitution cases (1).[28] The primary causes of wrongful convictions included:

> [M]isidentification, circumstantial evidence, frame-ups, overzealous police or prosecutors, prior convictions or unsavory records, community opinion demanding a conviction, and unreliability of expert evidence. In addition, erroneous convictions result[ed] from guilty pleas and confessions by innocent persons, or from the use of a false alibi by an innocent accused.[29]

---

[23] *See* Edwin M. Borchard, "European Systems of State Indemnity for Errors of Criminal Justice," 3 *J. Crim. L. & Criminology* 684 (1913).

[24] *Id.* at 684.

[25] *See* Edwin M. Borchard, *Convicting the Innocent* (1932).

[26] *Id.* at v.

[27] For instance, California (8); New York (8); Massachusetts (7); Illinois (4); Alabama (3); Minnesota (3); Mississippi (3); Missouri (2); New Jersey (2); Ohio (2); West Virginia (2); Arkansas (1); District of Colombia (1); Florida (1); Indiana (1); Iowa (1); Kentucky (1); Maine (1); Maryland (1); Oklahoma (1); Pennsylvania (1); Texas (1); Vermont (1); Virginia (1); and Wisconsin (1). *Id* at vi.

[28] *Id.*

[29] Joseph H. King, Jr., "Compensation of Persons Erroneously Confined by the State," 118 *U. Pa. L. Rev.* 1091, 1094 (1970) [referring to Edwin M. Borchard, *Convicting the Innocent* (1932)]. *See also* Edwin M. Borchard, "State Indemnity for Errors in Criminal Justice," 21 *B.U. L. Rev.* 201 (1941) ("The accidents … of the criminal law happen either through an unfortunate concurrence of circumstances or perjured testimony or are the result of mistaken identity, the conviction having been obtained by zealous prosecuting attorneys on circumstantial evidence.").

Not surprisingly, many of these causes are prevalent in criminal justice systems around the world, including the United States, Canada, the United Kingdom, and Australia. While Borchard identified 65 wrongful convictions, his book was for the most part descriptive rather than analytical: he described how the error occurred, how it was ultimately uncovered, and how the case against the innocent defendant subsequently unraveled. He did not quantify, tabulate, or systematically analyze the causes of error in the cases he studied.

Legal scholars and capital punishment opponents have also written extensively on the topic of executing the innocent. The earliest attempt to identify such cases took place in 1912 by the American Prison Congress.[30] According to the Prison Congress, it "carefully investigate[d] every reported case of unjust conviction and [tried] to discover if the death penalty [had] ever been inflicted upon an innocent man."[31] After reviewing these cases for a year, the Congress concluded that no innocent people had ever been put to death.

Over the next 70 years, few social scientists or law professors pursued the subject with great vigor. However, this changed with Hugo Bedau and Michael Radelet's 1987 landmark study, "Miscarriages of Justice in Potentially Capital Cases," published in the *Stanford Law Review*.[32] Bedau and Radelet identified 350 wrongful convictions in potentially capital cases in the United States from 1900–1987 and methodically analyzed the causes of error, the sources of discovery of the error, and the number of innocent people who had been executed.[33] Bedau and Radelet identified 23 presumably innocent people who were executed.[34] In 1992, Bedau, Radelet, and Constance Putnam, published *In Spite of Innocence*,[35] which identified 66 more wrongful murder convictions, raising the total to 416.[36] They were unable, however, to identify more cases in which a presumably innocent person was executed. Following this monograph, Bedau, Radelet, and William S. Lofquist, conducted further studies on the fallibility of capital convictions.[37] Their investigation identified

---

[30]Gault, R.H. "Find No Unjust Hangings," 3 J. *Am. Inst. Crim. L. & Criminology* 131 (1912–1913).

[31]*See* Hugo Adam Bedau and Michael L. Radelet, "Miscarriages of Justice in Potentially Capital Cases," 40 *Stan. L. Rev.* 21, 56–64 (1987).

[32]*See* Hugo Adam Bedau and Michael L. Radelet, "Miscarriages of Justice in Potentially Capital Cases," 40 *Stan. L. Rev.* 21, 56–64 (1987).

[33]*Id.* at 56–64.

[34]*Id.* at 72.

[35]*See* Michael L. Radelet, Hugo Adam Bedau, and Constance E. Putnam, *Spite of Innocence: Erroneous Convictions in Capital Cases* (1992).

[36]*Id.* at 360.

[37]*See* Michael Radelet, William S. Loftquist, and Hugo Adam Bedau, "Prisoners Released from Death Rows Since 1970 Because of Doubts about Their Guilt," 13 *T.M. Cooley L. Rev.* 907 (1996) (chronicling the experiences of wrongfully convicted prisoners); *see also* Michael Radelet and Hugo Bedau, "The Execution of the Innocent," *Law & Contemp. Probs.* 105, 110–16 (1998) (analyzing data on wrongful convictions).

70 cases in which death row inmates were later released because of doubts about their guilt.[38]

While death penalty opponents have yet to definitively identify an innocent person who has been executed, since 1973 they have identified 133 who have been freed from death row because newly discovered evidence—like DNA results—proved their innocence or so undermined confidence in the State's case that a reviewing court vacated the individual's conviction and death sentence and the State refused to re-prosecute them.[39] This remarkable number has caused many states to reconsider their position on capital punishment. For instance, the Governor of Illinois imposed a moratorium on capital punishment in January 2000.[40] In May 2002, the Governor of Maryland also placed a moratorium on all executions until, at least, the end of his term.[41] In 2007, the Governor of New Jersey entirely abolished capital punishment in New Jersey.[42]

THE DNA REVOLUTION

For much of the twentieth century, few people believed that innocent people could be wrongly convicted. Even if an appellate court vacated a conviction due to newly discovered evidence of innocence, many lay people interpreted the reversal as another guilty criminal who got off on a mere technicality. Put simply, identifying the innocent and the wrongly convicted, and convincing courts and the public that these people were actually innocent, was nearly impossible because much of the newly discovered evidence prior to DNA testing consisted of recanted statements or new witnesses who, for various reasons, were not discovered or did not come forward with their exculpatory statements until years after a defendant's trial and conviction. Courts and lay people, however, viewed this evidence with much skepticism.[43] For instance,

---

[38]*Id.* at 916.

[39]*See* http://www.deathpenaltyinfo.org/article.php?scid = 6&did = 110.

[40]*See* http://www.state.il.us/gov/press/00/Jan/morat.htm for Governor Ryan's January 31, 2000, press released statement. *See also Illinois Commission on Capital Punishment Report* 1 (2002) ("The moratorium was prompted by serious questions about the operation of the capital punishment system in Illinois…").

[41]Libit, H. "Death Penalty Issue No. 1; Impact of Moratorium to Be Felt in Races for Governor," *Balt. Sun,* May 12, 2002, *available at,* 2002 WL 6958264. For Governor Glendening's May 9, 2002 press release, *see* http://www.gov.state.md.us/gov/press/2002/may/html/baker.html.

[42]N.J. Stat. Ann. § 2C:11–3 (West 2008); *see also* "Death Penalty Banned in N.J.: First State in 43 Years to Abolish Capital Punishment," *Chi. Trib.,* Dec. 18, 2007, at 3 ("N.J. Gov. Jon Corzine signed into law… a measure that abolishes the death penalty, making New Jersey the first state in more than four decades to reject capital punishment. The bill… replaces the death sentence with life in prison without parole…. The measure spares eight men on the state's death row.").

[43]*See Byrd v. Collins,* 209 F.3d 486, 508 n.16 (6th Cir. 2000) (noting that recantations "are viewed with extreme suspicion by the courts.").

Justice Brennan, the Supreme Court's liberal crusader and pro-defendant Justice for so many years, said this about recantations:

> Recantation testimony is properly viewed with great suspicion. It upsets society's interest in the finality of convictions, is very often unreliable and given for suspect motives, and most often serves merely to impeach cumulative evidence rather than to undermine confidence in the accuracy of the conviction.[44]

DNA evidence, however, offered the type of evidence that could conclusively establish, with a level of certainty never witnessed before in the criminal justice system, not only a defendant's guilt, but also his or her innocence. As one judge proclaimed in 1988: "DNA Fingerprinting… constitute[s] the single greatest advance in the 'search for truth', and the goal of convicting the guilty and acquitting the innocent, since the advent of cross-examination."[45] More importantly, DNA evidence has provided lay persons and the public with concrete proof that innocent people are in fact convicted for crimes they did not commit. As we will see, while the DNA innocence movement started slowly, it has reached a level no one could have imagined back in 1989 when Gary Dotson became the first person to be exonerated with DNA evidence. In short, as the U.S. Supreme Court recently observed, DNA evidence has been of "central importance" to many postconviction claims of innocence and exonerations.[46]

The First DNA Exoneration: Gary Dotson

On July 9, 1977, Cathleen Crowell Webb told Chicago police officers that she had been kidnapped by three men and raped in their car. Her story gained credibility when a doctor examined her at a local hospital and found vaginal trauma and carvings on her abdomen. After she described the attack in great detail and looked through hundreds of mug shots, she identified her attacker as Gary Dotson, a high school dropout with a criminal record. Although Dotson steadfastly proclaimed his innocence, a Cook County jury convicted in 1979 and the trial judge sentenced him to 25 to 50 years in prison.[47]

After his conviction, Dotson fought to prove his innocence, while Webb ultimately moved to New Hampshire, married, and became a born-again Christian. Her conversion ultimately led her to repudiate her testimony, admitting that

---

[44] *Dobbert v. Wainwright*, 468 U.S. 1231, 1233–34 (1984) (Brennan, J., dissenting from denial of certiorari).

[45] *People v. Weasley*, 533 N.Y.S.2d 643, 644 (Albany Co. Ct. 1988).

[46] *House v. Bell*, 547 U.S. 518, 540 (2006).

[47] *See People v. Dotson*, 516 N.E.2d 718, 719 (Ill. App. Ct. 1987); Scott Kraft, "Nation Debates Jailed Man's Innocence: Recantation Puts Rape Case in Spotlight," *L.A. Times*, Apr. 21, 1985, at 1; David Remnick, "Making Right Her Wrong: Cathy Webb's Public Mission after Recanting the Rape Tale," *Wash. Post*, Apr. 16, 1985, at B1.

she fabricated the entire rape story to hide a legitimate sexual encounter with her boyfriend, which she thought resulted in a pregnancy.[48] Dotson filed an immediate appeal requesting a new trial and received an evidentiary hearing regarding Webb's recantation. The trial judge, however, ruled that Webb's trial testimony was more credible than her recantation and denied Dotson's request for a new trial.[49] Dotson's inability to obtain a new trial, despite credible new evidence from the victim herself, prompted an intense media storm, with newspapers, magazines, and morning television shows profiling the case and engaging in a national debate on the way courts treat recantation evidence.[50]

The Illinois governor accepted authority for the case and held a session of the Illinois Prison Review Board to consider Dotson's request for a pardon. The governor said he disbelieved Webb's recantation and refused to pardon Dotson. On May 12, 1985, however, he commuted Dotson's sentence to the six years he had already served, pending good behavior. In 1987, he revoked Dotson's parole after his wife accused him of assault. On Christmas Eve 1987, the governor granted Dotson a "last chance parole." Two days later, police arrested Dotson for his involvement in a barroom fight, and his parole was revoked.[51]

In 1988, Dotson's new attorney requested that a new scientific technique—one that was not available in 1977 when Dotson was prosecuted—be used to analyze the biological evidence collected from Webb's rape examination. The new scientific technique was DNA testing. Prosecutors and the defense attorney sent a semen sample from Webb's underwear to Dr. Alec Jeffreys in England for RFLP analysis. The sample was badly degraded, however, and Dr. Jeffreys's results proved inconclusive. Semen samples were then sent to Forensic Science Associates (FSA) in Richmond, California. FSA employed a newer, more sensitive DNA test, PCR DQ Alpha, which proved that the semen on Webb's underwear could not have come from Dotson but could have come from Webb's boyfriend.[52]

---

[48]Scott Kraft, "Nation Debates Jailed Man's Innocence: Recantation Puts Rape Case in Spotlight," *L.A. Times,* Apr. 21, 1985, § 1, at 1.

[49]*People v. Dotson*, 516 N.E.2d 718, 718–19, 721,-22 (Ill. App. Ct. 1987) (affirming trial court's finding that Webb's 1979 trial testimony was more credible than her 1985 evidentiary hearing testimony).

[50]*See* Laurent Belsie, "Recanted Testimony: Issue Tests Criminal-Justice Credibility," *Christian Sci. Monitor,* Apr. 19, 1985, at 5; Peter W. Kaplan, "NBC, at No. 1, Snaps 10-Year Ratings Decline," *N.Y. Times,* June 1, 1985, at 46 (explaining that CBS interrupted its live coverage of the Claus von Bülow trial to show the Dotson rape hearings); Janice J. Repka, Comment, "Rethinking the Standard for New Trial Motions Based upon Recantations as Newly Discovered Evidence," 134 *U. Pa. L. Rev.* 1433, 1454–58 (1986).

[51]Nat'l Inst. of Justice, U.S. Dep't of Justice, *Convicted by Juries, Exonerated by Science: Case Studies in the Use of DNA Evidence to Establish Innocence After Trial* 51–52 (1996).

[52]*Id.* at 52.

On August 14, 1989, the chief judge of the Cook County Criminal Court vacated Dotson's conviction, after he served a total of eight years in prison for a rape that never happened. Prosecutors ultimately decided not to reprosecute Dotson based on Webb's recantation and the DNA results.

The Innocence Project

Even before Gary Dotson's DNA exoneration, two veteran New York City Legal Aid attorneys named Barry Scheck and Peter Neufeld foresaw DNA evidence's exonerative capabilities when they pursued DNA testing in 1987 to prove that Marion Coakley was wrongly convicted for an October 1983 rape. Although the DNA tests failed to produce an interpretable DNA profile and were thus unable to exonerate Coakley,[53] Scheck and Neufeld knew that DNA evidence could be a revolutionary tool that could free the innocent and provide a more accurate assessment of the criminal justice system's error rate.

After litigating several high profile DNA cases during the late 1980s and early 1990s, Scheck and Neufeld started the Innocence Project (Project) in 1992.[54] While the Project's objective was simple—to identify cases where DNA evidence can prove a convicted defendant's innocence—identifying these cases, locating the physical evidence, and litigating these cases presented several obstacles. In terms of resources and manpower, because Scheck was a law professor at Cardozo School of Law in New York City, he and Neufeld enlisted the help of several Cardozo law students. Thus, the Project was originally a law clinic at Cardozo School of Law.

Once up and running, Scheck, Neufeld, and the Project's law students scoured the country for potential cases in which DNA evidence could conclusively prove a defendant's innocence or so undermine the State's case that the defendant should be awarded a new trial or set free. Once the Project identified a case and agreed to represent the defendant, the Project's law students conducted exhaustive evidence searches in order to locate the most probative items of physical evidence collected from the victim or the crime scene. If the law students located the physical evidence, they then worked in conjunction with Scheck or Neufeld in reaching out to the local district attorney to inquire whether he or

[53] *See* Barry Scheck, Peter Neufeld, and Jim Dwyer, *Actual Innocence: When Justice Goes Wrong and How to Make it Right,* Ch. 1 (2003). Additional serology tests, performed shortly after the inconclusive DNA tests, ultimately exonerated Coakley. *Id.*

[54] With all due respect to the Innocence Project, while the Innocence Project may be the most well-known nonprofit agency for investigating potential claims of wrongful convictions, the Innocence Project was not the first nonprofit agency specifically created to investigate potential cases of wrongful convictions. Innocence projects have existed in the United States since the establishment of Centurion Ministries in 1983. *See* http://www.centurionministries.org/aboutus.html. The innocence movement, however, did not get truly kick-started until the late 1990s, when the Center for Wrongful Convictions at Northwestern School of Law held the first National Conference on Wrongful Convictions and the Death Penalty in 1998.

she would consent to DNA testing. If the district attorney refused to consent, which was not uncommon during the Project's formative years (and still not usual),[55] the law students then assisted Scheck and Neufeld in drafting legal arguments to access the physical evidence so the Project could have it subjected to DNA testing. If consent was obtained or a court granted access to the evidence, the physical evidence was generally sent to a DNA laboratory mutually agreed upon by the Project and the prosecutor and the evidence was tested.

As the Project identified and accepted more and more cases, the number of DNA exonerations slowly increased for two reasons. Not only did the Project identify and exonerate several innocent prisoners, the Project's influence encouraged other defense attorneys to pursue DNA testing to prove their client's innocence. This in turn resulted in additional DNA exonerations. Thus, by 1996 there were 28 DNA exonerations; by 2001 there were 100 DNA exonerations; and by 2007 there were 200 DNA exonerations. As noted later, while the Project cannot not lay claim to all these DNA exonerations, it ultimately led to the creation of the *Innocence Network*, which has served as counsel in the majority of these cases. The Project also played a significant role in the National Institute of Justice's 1996 and 1999 reports pertaining to DNA exonerations and postconviction DNA testing. As noted later, these reports had a tremendous impact in state and federal courts and in state and federal legislative sessions.

The 1996 National Institute of Justice (NIJ) Report

By the mid-1990s, DNA testing's ability to incriminate or exonerate was now well known to the American public thanks to the O. J. Simpson trial and the ever-increasing number of DNA exonerations. While researchers and policy analysts exhaustively studied its law enforcement and incriminatory potential, there were few research or policy discussions regarding its exonerative capabilities and how identifying wrongful convictions can actually improve the criminal justice system's accuracy. In June 1995, however, (then) Attorney General

---

[55] *See* Daniel S. Medwed, " The Zeal Deal: Prosecutorial Resistance to Post-Conviction Claims of Innocence," 84 *B.U. L. Rev.* 125 (2004); Bruce Green, "Why Should Prosecutors 'Seek Justice'?," 26 *Fordham Urb. L.J.* 607, 638 n.133 (1999) (noting that the typical prosecutorial response to postconviction innocence claims is to deny that the newly discovered proof is legitimate and that the prisoner is innocent). District attorneys frequently oppose DNA testing on the grounds that it cannot prove the prisoner's innocence and is a waste of time and money. For instance, Pennsylvania prosecutors spent seven years fighting Bruce Godschalk's request for DNA tests on physical evidence related to his two rape convictions. *See,* for example, Michael Rubinkam, "DNA Evidence Frees Man Jailed Since '87 in Rape of 2 Women; Prosecutor to Seek Dismissal of Charges," *Pitt. Post-Gazette,* Feb. 15, 2002, at B2. Ultimately, Godschalk sued in federal court to force the release of the evidence that was uncovered during the criminal investigation, and DNA tests eventually exonerated him. *See id.* Godschalk's case prompted *The Washington Post* to publish an editorial arguing that "[e]ven in the absence of more permissive rules, prosecutors need to be more open to testing that could undermine a verdict. You just never know when a seemingly airtight case will melt on close inspection." Editorial, "Yet Another DNA Exoneration," *Wash. Post,* Feb. 18, 2002, at A22.

Janet Reno commissioned the National Institute of Justice (NIJ) to study and profile all the DNA exonerations to date. As Attorney General Reno explained:

> The development of DNA technology furthers the search for truth by helping police and prosecutors in the fight against violent crime. Through the use of DNA evidence, prosecutors are often able to conclusively establish the guilt of the defendant... *At the same time, DNA aids in the search for truth by exonerating the innocent.*"[56]

The purpose of the NIJ study "was to identify and review cases in which convicted persons were released from prison as a result of post-trial DNA testing of evidence."[57] By early 1996, the NIJ researchers identified 28 such cases: "DNA tests results obtained subsequent to trial proved that, on the basis of DNA evidence, the convicted persons could not have committed the crimes for which they were incarcerated."[58]

In 1996, the NIJ researchers published their findings in a report titled *Convicted by Juries, Exonerated by Science: Case Studies in the Use of DNA Evidence to Establish Innocence After Trial*. The report chronicled the stories of the 28 men who had been wrongly convicted and exonerated by DNA testing. The 28 cases were tried in 14 different states and the District of Columbia. Likewise, most of the cases involved convictions from the mid- to late-1980s, a period when DNA testing was not readily accessible to many crime laboratories. Similarly, all 28 cases involved some form of sexual assault. Lastly, the prisoners served, on average, seven years in prison for a crime they did not commit. More importantly, the 28 cases identified three reoccurring factors that played significant roles in the wrongful convictions: eyewitness misidentification, use of rudimentary or misleading forensic evidence, and government or *prosecutorial misconduct*. Each of these issues will be discussed further in subsequent sections.

The 1999 National Institute of Justice Report

In response to the NIJ's report, Attorney General Reno requested that the NIJ establish a National Commission on the Future of DNA Evidence (Commission) "to identify ways to maximize the value of DNA in our criminal justice system."[59] The NIJ established the Commission in 1998, which included representatives from the bench, the prosecution, the defense bar, law enforcement, the scientific community, the medical examiner community, academia, and victims'

---

[56]Nat'l Inst. of Justice, U.S. Dep't of Justice, *Convicted by Juries, Exonerated by Science: Case Studies in the Use of DNA Evidence to Establish Innocence After Trial* iii (1996).

[57]*Id.* at 2.

[58]*Id.*

[59]Nat'l Comm'n on the Future of DNA Testing, *Post Conviction DNA Testing: Recommendations for Handling Requests* iii (1999).

rights organizations. The Commission was charged with identifying and suggesting "recommendations to the Attorney General that [would] help ensure more effective use of DNA as a crime-fighting tool and foster its use throughout the entire criminal justice system."[60] One of the five working groups of the Commission—the Postconviction Issues Working Group—focused exclusively on postconviction DNA testing issues. In 1999, the Postconviction Working Group published its report titled *Postconviction DNA Testing: Recommendations for Handling Requests*. By the time the Commission released the Report in 1999, the total number of DNA exonerations had reached approximately 70.[61]

The report did several important things for criminal justice actors. First, it categorized the types of cases in which postconviction DNA is generally pursued and recommended which types of cases warranted DNA testing. The report's category of cases has played an important role for prisoners trying to convince a prosecutor or trial judge to grant them access to the physical evidence so they can have it subjected to DNA testing. Second, it identified and discussed the "thorny legal issues" relating to postconviction DNA testing. When the Commission issued its report, very few states had postconviction DNA testing statutes that gave prisoners a state law right to access the physical evidence for DNA testing purposes. Thus, prior to the enactment of these types of statutes, the legal landscape was "tricky" because requests for postconviction DNA testing did "not fit well into existing procedural schemes or established constitutional doctrine."[62] And third, the report identified and discussed recommendations for prosecutors, defense attorneys, the judiciary, and victims' rights advocates. These recommendations, like the categories of cases, have been instrumental in numerous DNA exonerations, particularly those in which prosecutors assisted defense counsel in locating the physical evidence or in which a trial judge disagreed with the prosecutor and granted a prisoner's DNA motion because it qualified for testing under the report's guidelines and recommendations.

The 2000 Release of Actual Innocence

While the NIJ's 1996 and 1999 reports on DNA exonerations and postconviction DNA testing affected the relevant criminal justice actors (i.e., judges, prosecutors, and defense counsel), these reports had little impact on the public in general simply because most lay persons do not read government reports. Thus, while criminal justice professionals were well aware of the DNA innocence movement, the general public was not. This all changed, however, when Barry Scheck and Peter Neufeld, the Innocence Project's Co-Directors, teamed

---

[60] *Id.* at v.

[61] *Id.* at iii ("Since the publication of [the 1996] report, more than 40 other similar cases have been identified.").

[62] *Id.* at xiv.

up with award-winning *New York Times* journalist Jim Dwyer to write about their experiences litigating DNA cases and what these cases taught them about America's criminal justice system. Scheck, Neufeld, and Dwyer released their book, *Actual Innocence*, in 2000. *Actual Innocence* chronicled 67 DNA exonerations and identified the primary causes of wrongful convictions by using numerous case illustrations. Scheck, Neufeld, and Dwyer identified the following factors as the leading causes of wrongful convictions: eyewitness misidentification, forensic fraud, unreliable forensic science, jailhouse informants (or snitches), prosecutorial misconduct, and poor lawyering. It not only had an immediate impact on the criminal justice system, it had an equally impressive impact on the general public because it was written in a simplistic, easy-to-read format that lay persons could easily understand. The general public could no longer claim ignorance regarding wrongful convictions or that they did not occur, as *Actual Innocence* did a masterful job weaving the wrongful conviction issue into the fabric of America's consciousness.

The Innocence Network

Thanks to the Innocence Project's remarkable success, several legal clinics and organizations came together and formed the Innocence Network in 2003. The Innocence Network (Network) is an association of organizations dedicated to providing *pro bono* legal and/or investigative services to prisoners for whom evidence discovered postconviction can provide conclusive proof of innocence. The 52 current members of the Network represent hundreds of prisoners with innocence claims in all 50 states and the District of Columbia, as well as Canada, the United Kingdom, and Australia.[63] The Network and its members are also dedicated to improving the accuracy and reliability of the criminal justice system in future cases. Drawing on the lessons from cases in which the

---

[63]The member organizations include the Alaska Innocence Project, Arizona Justice Project, Association in the Defence of the Wrongly Convicted (Canada), California & Hawaii Innocence Project, Center on Wrongful Convictions, Connecticut Innocence Project, Cooley Innocence Project (Michigan), Delaware Office of the Public Defender, Downstate Illinois Innocence Project, Georgia Innocence Project, Griffith University Innocence Project (Australia), Idaho Innocence Project (Idaho, Montana, Eastern Washington), Indiana University School of Law Wrongful Convictions Component, Innocence Network UK, The Innocence Project, Innocence Project Arkansas, Innocence Project New Orleans (Louisiana and Mississippi), Innocence Project New Zealand, Innocence Project Northwest Clinic (Washington), Innocence Project of Florida, Innocence Project of Iowa, Innocence Project of Minnesota, Innocence Project of Texas, Kentucky Innocence Project, Maryland Office of the Public Defender, Medill Innocence Project (all states), Mid-Atlantic Innocence Project (Washington, D.C., Maryland, Virginia), Midwestern Innocence Project (Missouri, Kansas, Iowa), Mississippi Innocence Project, Nebraska Innocence Project, New England Innocence Project (Connecticut, Maine, Massachusetts, New Hampshire, Rhode Island, Vermont), North Carolina Center on Actual Innocence, Northern Arizona Justice Project, Northern California Innocence Project, Ohio Innocence Project, Pace Post Conviction Project (New York), Rocky Mountain Innocence Project, Schuster Institute for Investigative Journalism at Brandeis University—Justice Brandeis Innocence Project (Massachusetts), Texas Center for Actual Innocence, Texas Innocence Network, The Reinvestigation Project of the NY Office of the Appellate Defender, University of British Columbia Law Innocence Project (Canada), University of Leeds Innocence Project (Great Britain), and the Wisconsin Innocence Project.

system convicted innocent persons, the Network advocates study and reform designed to enhance the criminal justice system's truth-seeking functions to ensure that future wrongful convictions are prevented. The Network pioneered the postconviction DNA model that has to date exonerated over 200 innocent people, and has served as counsel in the majority of these cases.

THE PRESENT STATE OF AFFAIRS

DNA Exonerations

To date, there have been 240 DNA exonerations in the United States alone.[64] The ever-increasing number has impacted the public's perception of the criminal justice system like no other event in our nation's history. More importantly, the DNA exonerations have laid to rest, once and for all, the notion that wrongful convictions are an "unreal dream" or that they are "extremely rare." The American Bar Association even commented that the escalating number of DNA exonerations "undermines the assumption that the criminal justice system our nation has so proudly developed sufficiently protects the innocent."[65] These exonerations have convincingly established that much of the evidence frequently introduced by prosecutors to prove a defendant's guilt—such as informant testimony, accomplice testimony, eyewitness testimony, forensic evidence, and confessions—is more unreliable than anyone ever realized. Moreover, the DNA exonerations has led to tremendous reforms all over the country, such as the improvement of eyewitness identification procedures,[66] the videotaping of police interrogations,[67] crime lab reform,[68] and the creation of innocence commissions that recommend reforms in individual states.[69] Additionally, as of January 1, 2009, 46 states have enacted postconviction DNA testing statutes,[70] while the federal government enacted the

---

[64] *See* http://www.innocenceproject.org (last visited February 5, 2009).

[65] ABA Criminal Justice Section's Ad Hoc Innocence Committee to Ensure the Integrity of the Criminal Process, *Achieving Justice: Freeing the Innocent, Convicting the Guilty*, at xv (Jack Hanna ed., 2006).

[66] *See* Innocence Project, Fix the System: Priority Issues: Eyewitness Identification, http://www.innocenceproject.org/fix/Eyewitness-Identification.php (last visited July 6, 2008) (providing a list of jurisdictions that have implemented eyewitness identification reforms, either through the legislature, the courts, or other means).

[67] *See* Thomas P. Sullivan, "Electronic Recording of Custodial Interrogations: Everybody Wins," 95 *J. Crim. L. & Criminology* 1127, 1131 (2005) (listing the jurisdictions that require the recordation of custodial interrogations as a means of safeguarding against false confessions).

[68] *See* S.B. 351, 423d Gen. Assem., Reg. Sess. (Md. 2007) (providing for the regulation of state crime labs).

[69] *See* Innocence Project, http://www.innocenceproject.org/Content/415.php (last visited July 6, 2008) (listing North Carolina, Wisconsin, California, Connecticut, Illinois, and Pennsylvania as states that have each created commissions to study the problem of wrongful convictions and recommend state reforms).

[70] *See* Innocence Project, Fix the System: Priority Issues: DNA Testing Access, www.innocenceproject.org/fix/DNA-Testing-Access.php (last visited June 25, 2009).

Innocence Protection Act (IPA) in 2004, which provides federal prisoners access to postconviction DNA testing.[71]

Michigan University 2005 Study

In 2005, researchers from the University of Michigan published a report that examined 340 DNA and non-DNA exonerations between 1989 and 2003.[72] In terms of statistics, of the 340 exonerations, 327 men and 13 women; 144 were cleared by DNA evidence, 196 by other means. More than half served prison terms of 10 years or more, while 80% had been in prison for at least 5 years. As a group, they spent more than 3,400 years in prison for crimes they did not commit—an average of more than 10 years each.[73]

The researchers defined the term *exoneration* as an "official act declaring a defendant not guilty of a crime for which he or she had previously been convicted."[74] This occurred in four ways: (1) In 42 cases governors (or other appropriate executive officers) issued pardons based on evidence of the prisoners' innocence; (2) in 263 cases, courts dismissed criminal charges after new evidence of innocence emerged, such as DNA; (3) in 31 cases the defendants were acquitted at a retrial on the basis of evidence that they had no role in the crimes for which they were originally convicted; and (4) in 4 cases, states posthumously acknowledged the innocence of defendants who had already died in prison.[75]

In terms of what types of cases have spawned exonerations, the researchers found that 96% of the 340 exonerations occurred in murder—60% (205/340)—or rape/sexual assault—36% (121/340)—cases. Most of the remaining 14 cases were crimes of violence—six robberies, two attempted murders, a kidnapping, and an assault—plus a larceny, a gun possession case, and two drug cases.[76] In terms of geographic distribution of wrongful convictions, the 340 exonerations occurred in 38 states and the District of Columbia. However, the top four states—Illinois, New York, Texas, and California—accounted for more than 40% of the total (144 of 340), and the top 10 (those four plus Florida, Massachusetts, Louisiana, Pennsylvania, Oklahoma, and Missouri) include two-thirds (226/340).[77] Finally, the

---

[71]Pub. L. No. 108–405, 118 Stat. 2260.

[72]*See* Samuel R. Gross et al., "Exonerations in the United States: 1989 Through 2003," 95 *J. Crim. L. & Criminology* 523 (2005).

[73]*Id.* at 524.

[74]*Id.*

[75]*Id.*

[76]*Id.* at 528–29, Table 1.

[77]*Id.* at 541, Table 2.

researchers identified different forms of evidence and factors that played significant roles in these 340 exonerations, these were eyewitness misidentification, false confessions, and the race of the offender. These will be elaborated on in summary later.

How Many People in Prison Are Innocent?

Now that the DNA exonerations have incorporated the term *wrongful conviction* into our everyday lexicon, the question that countless people ask is how many people in our nation's prisons are actually innocent. Indeed, the issue has even captured the U.S. Supreme Court's attention. For instance, in *Kansas v. Marsh*, Justice Scalia had this to say about Professor Gross's study and its claim that there are thousands of innocent people languishing in America's prisons:

> [L]et's give the professor the benefit of the doubt: let's assume that he understated the number of innocents by roughly a factor of 10, that instead of 340 there were 4,000 people in prison who weren't involved in the crime in any way. During that same 15 years, there were more than 15 million felony convictions across the country. That would make the error rate .027 percent—or, to put it another way, a success rate of 99.973 percent.[78]

As intimated by the divergent views of Justice Scalia and individuals like Professor Gross and his colleagues, accurately answering the question of how many innocent people are in prison is notoriously difficult. Perhaps the most obvious reason is that the United States' criminal justice system is extremely fragmented; it is administered by 50 separate states and commonwealths that are composed of more than 3,000 different counties that have thousands of separate trial courts and prosecuting authorities. Moreover, there is no national database of exonerations, or straightforward manner to glean from official court documents which dismissals, pardons, or overturned convictions are based on a prisoner's actual innocence. As a result, social scientists and law professors usually learn about exonerations from media reports or word of mouth.

Considering the fragmented nature of our criminal justice system, there has yet to be a comprehensive study aimed at trying to quantify—as accurately as possible—the number of people in prison who may be innocent. Thus, when social scientists, law professors, prosecutors, defense attorneys, and U.S. Supreme Court Justices identify a "success rate" or an "error rate" (depending on speaker's context), this number must be viewed through a cautious lens because it is most likely not premised on empirical research. Consequently, due to the dearth of research and the difficulties involved in conducting such research, the author cannot and will not opine on how many people in American prisons

---

[78]*Id.* at 197–98 (quoting "The Innocent and the Shammed," *N.Y. Times*, Jan. 26, 2006, at A23).

are actually innocent. Instead, all that can be said—at least at this point—is that there are more innocent people in prison than we ever imagined.

CAUSES OF WRONGFUL CONVICTIONS

Wrongful convictions occur for a variety of reasons. As mentioned, the wrongful conviction research has identified the following factors as the primary causes of wrongful convictions: (1) eyewitness misidentification, (2) erroneous forensic science, (3) fabricated forensic evidence, (4) false confessions and guilty pleas, (5) jail house informants, (6) government misconduct, and (7) bad lawyering.

What needs to be emphasized is that wrongful convictions do not normally occur because one individual made a single error. When a wrongful conviction is exposed, blame is usually directed at a particular witness, item of evidence, or state actor (e.g., prosecutor, investigator, or crime lab analyst). For instance, a rape victim misidentified a suspect in a line-up, a fingerprint examiner mistakenly attributed a crime scene fingerprint to the innocent defendant, a detective wrongly believed that the suspect knew something that only the real killer would know, a prosecutor failed to disclose an exculpatory lab report, and the list of reasons can go on and on. While these factors play significant roles in wrongful convictions, they are rarely the only errors that produce a wrongful conviction. Instead, what generally happens is that once an error is incorporated into an investigation, this error contaminates (i.e., cross-contamination) other items of evidence.

For example, consider William Harris's wrongful rape conviction.[79] In December 1984, a young woman was sexually assaulted in Rand, West Virginia, Harris's hometown. On March 4, 1985, the victim viewed a line-up that included Harris; the victim said she knew Harris and that he was not the assailant. However, when Fred Zain (of the West Virginia State Police Crime Laboratory) examined the semen evidence, he informed investigators that only a small percentage of the population had the same genetic markers identified in the semen and that Harris was included in this small percentage. Remarkably, once the victim learned of Zain's results, she reconsidered her previous statement where she said that Harris was not the assailant. By the time Harris went to trial, she was certain that Harris was her assailant. Indeed, at trial she testified that she had "no doubt" that Harris was her assailant. Due in large part to the victim's identification and Zain's testimony, Harris was convicted and sentenced to 10 to 20 years in the West Virginia Penitentiary.

[79]The description of Harris's case is taken from George Castelle and Elizabeth Loftus, "Misinformation and Wrongful Convictions," in *Wrongly Convicted: Perspectives on Failed Justice* 17–35 (Saundra D. Westervelt and John A. Humphrey eds. 2001).

In 1993, an audit of the West Virginia State Police Crime Laboratory's serology unit revealed that Zain fabricated serology results in numerous cases. This finding allowed Harris's defense attorneys to request DNA testing—testing that did not exist at the time of his 1987 trial. The DNA results conclusively demonstrated that Harris could not have been the assailant. The DNA results, more importantly, establish how easy it is for one error to contaminate another item of evidence. In Harris's case, Zain's erroneous serology results mistakenly led the victim to reconsider her initial conclusion that Harris was not her assailant. These two errors, however, were not the only factors that led to Harris's wrongful conviction. Indeed, another significant contributing factor was that the prosecution failed to disclose the victim's initial statement wherein she said she knew Harris and that Harris was not her assailant. Indeed, the State of West Virginia finally disclosed the victim's initial report during the civil litigation that followed Williams's release.

Eyewitness Identification

The most consistent factor in wrongful convictions is eyewitness misidentification. This is by no means a novel discovery; Borchard made the same conclusion more than 70 years ago when he wrote: "Perhaps the major source of these tragic errors is an identification of the accused by the victim of a crime of violence."[80] Likewise, Justice Brennan emphasized the unreliability of eyewitness testimony when he wrote that the "vagaries of eyewitness identification are well-known; the annals of criminal law are rife with instances of mistaken identification."[81] Of the 240 DNA exonerations to date, misidentifications played a role in nearly 80%.[82] This statistic is unsurprising when one considers that "eyewitness identification evidence has a powerful impact on juries. Juries seem most receptive to, and not inclined to discredit, testimony of a witness who states that he saw the defendant commit the crime."[83] Again, as Justice Brennan succinctly explained:

> [E]yewitness testimony is likely to be believed by jurors, especially when it is offered with a high level of confidence, even though the accuracy of an eyewitness and the confidence of that witness may not

---

[80]Borchard, *supra* note 25, at 376.

[81]*United States v. Wade*, 388 U.S. 218, 228 (1967). Justice Brennan echoed this sentiment years later. *See Watkins v. Sowders*, 449 U.S. 341, 350 (1981) (Brennan, J., dissenting) ("eyewitness identification evidence is notoriously unreliable."); *see also Jackson v. Fogg*, 589 F.2d 108, 112 (2d Cir. 1978) ("Centuries of experience in the administration of criminal justice have shown that convictions based solely on testimony that identifies a defendant previously unknown to the witness is highly suspect. Of the various kinds of evidence it is the least reliable, especially where unsupported by corroborating evidence.").

[82]*See* http://www.innocenceproject.org (last visited January 3, 2009).

[83]*Watkins v. Sowders*, 449 U.S. 341, 352 (1981) (Brennan, J., dissenting).

be related to one another at all. All the evidence points rather strikingly to the conclusion that there is almost nothing more convincing than a live human being who takes the stand, points a finger at the defendant, and says "That's the one!"[84]

The social science research on what variables can often lead to misidentifications is voluminous and will not be comprehensively summarized in this section. Instead, the author will briefly discuss some of these variables.

Stress Effect
Social scientists have routinely established a correlation between an individual's stress level and the individual's ability to remember certain events, items, or places. Indeed, as an individual's stress level increases, his or her ability to remember events, objects, or places decreases.[85] This is significant because most victims of violent crimes experience an incredible amount of stress as they are being assaulted, stabbed, shot at, or raped. Quite often, the victim's main priority during these life-threatening situations is self-preservation, rather than trying to capture an adequate description of his or her assailant(s). As a result, the victim's ability to accurately describe and subsequently identify his or her assailant is significantly hindered.

Weapons Effect
Many violent crimes are perpetrated with a weapon—be it a knife, firearm, baseball bat, etc. This is important because social scientists have repeatedly demonstrated that when a weapon is involved, the victim's attention is very often directed toward the weapon rather than the assailant. Again, this detracts from the victim's ability to accurately describe and subsequently identify his or her assailant.[86]

Manner in Which Line-up Is Conducted
The manner in which law enforcement officers conduct photo or physical line-ups can increase or minimize the likelihood that an innocent suspect will be erroneously identified.

Nonsequential Line-ups
For years, law enforcement officers used nonsequential line-ups or line-ups where victims are asked to view more than one suspect at one time. In this simultaneous format, eyewitnesses compare line-up members using a process called *relative judgment* to determine which one most closely resembles the

---

[84]*Id.* (citation omitted).

[85]*See* "Memory Fails You After Severe Stress," *New Scientist*, June 14, 2004, available at http://www.newscientist.com/news /news.jsp?id = ns99995089.

[86]*See* Kerri L. Pickel, "Unusualness and Threat as Possible Causes of 'Weapon Focus,'" 6 *Memory* 277 (1998); Nancy Mehrkens Steblay, "A Meta-Analytical Review of the Weapon Focus Effect," 16 *Law & Hum. Behav.* 413 (1992).

eyewitness's memory of the perpetrator. Even when the true perpetrator is absent from the lineup, it is likely one of the fillers will provide a better relative match to the witness's memory than the others. This process increases the risk of a misidentification. The Innocence Project, the National Institute of Justice, and many reputable social scientists have urged law enforcement agencies to use sequential line-ups, in which the witness is shown a series of suspects–*one at a time*–and asked to make a decision about each one individually.[87]

Confirmation Bias

Another practice that increases the risk of misidentification during a line-up is confirmation bias. For instance, in several DNA exonerations where misidentifications played a role, the law enforcement officer who arrested the innocent suspect was the same law enforcement officer who conducted the line-up. In situations such as this, it is likely that the officer consciously or unconsciously directed the victim's attention toward the (innocent) arrested suspect. To combat this problem, law enforcement should have employed a "double-blind" lineup, in which the officer conducting the identification does not know which person is the suspect.[88]

Other Procedural Problems

Other procedural problems witnessed during line-ups include the following:

- When the officer conducting the line-up informs the eyewitness that the suspect is in the line-up.
- Failing to use "fillers" who look like the suspect.
- Having two or more eyewitnesses view the line-up simultaneously.
- Informing the eyewitness that he or she correctly identified the suspect.

Additional Reading Material

For more information regarding eyewitness identification procedures see NIJ (1999) *Eyewitness Evidence: A Guide for Law Enforcement*, Washington, D.C.: U.S. Department of Justice.

Forensic Science Errors

Forensic science errors can be broken down into two types: (1) erroneous (or honest human) errors, and (2) purposeful errors and fabrications. As noted later, forensic science errors represent the second most commonly witnessed variable in wrongful convictions. Due in large part to these errors and

---

[87] *See* Gary L. Wells and Eric P. Seelau, "Eyewitness Identification: Psychological Research and Legal Policy on Line-ups," 1 *Psychol. Pub. Pol'y & L.* 765, 775–78 (1995); Gary L. Wells et al., "Eyewitness Identification Procedures: Recommendations for Line-ups and Photospreads," 22 *Law & Hum. Behav.* 603, 639 (1998).

[88] *See* Gary L. Wells and Elizabeth A. Olson, "Eyewitness Testimony," 54 *Ann. Rev. Psychol.* 277, 289 (2003); Gary L. Wells et al., "Eyewitness Identification Procedures: Recommendations for Line-ups and Photospreads," 22 *Law & Hum. Behav.* 603, 639 (1998).

fabrications, courts have started questioning the forensic science system's accuracy and reliability.[89] For instance, Sixth Circuit Court of Appeals Judge Boyce Martin has called crime labs "unreliable."[90] Elsewhere, Federal District Court Judge Jed Rakoff wrote: "False positives—that is, inaccurate incriminating test results—are endemic to much of what passes for 'forensic science.'"[91] Public officials have even acknowledged the issues connected with unreliable and fraudulent forensic science. For instance, according to former Massachusetts Governor Mitt Romney's Council on Capital Punishment:

> Serious problems, including both inadvertent errors… as well as deliberate and conscious acts of wrongdoing, have arisen in crime laboratories, medical-examiner offices, and forensic-service providers around the country. This not only undermines the public trust in the criminal justice system, but can contribute significantly to erroneous verdicts in death penalty cases.[92]

Likewise, Illinois Governor George H. Ryan noted in his 2002 capital punishment commission report that:

> The quality and professionalism of the forensic work being performed by scientists in crime labs across the country has been the subject of increasing debate. Recently, in some high-publicized cases, it has been alleged that incompetence or even intentional misconduct has resulted in defendants being accused or convicted of crimes they did not commit.[93]

Erroneous Forensic Science

When Professors Michael J. Saks and his colleague Jonathan J. Koehler reviewed 86 DNA exonerations, they concluded that nearly 65% of these cases involved

---

[89]See *United States v. Crisp*, 324 F.3d 261, 273 (4th Cir. 2003) (Michael, J., dissenting); *Ramirez v. State*, 810 So. 2d 836, 853 (Fla. 2001) ("In order to preserve the integrity of the criminal justice system… particularly in the face of rising nationwide criticism of forensic evidence in general… state courts… must… cull scientific fiction and junk science from fact."); *People v. Saxon*, 871 N.E.2d 244, 256 (Ill. App. 2007) (McDade, J., dissenting) (noting that "1/3 of the wrongful convictions" have been "linked to the misapplication of forensic disciplines" which is defined as where "forensic scientists and prosecutors presented fraudulent, exaggerated, or otherwise tainted evidence to the judge or jury which led to the wrongful conviction") (citing http://www.innocenceproject.org); *State v. Clifford*, 121 P.3d 489, 503 (Mont. 2005) (Nelson, J., concurring) (noting how "long-accepted forensic science evidence has recently received greater public scrutiny not only because the "experts' proffering the evidence were either astonishingly inept or downright corrupt, but also because of recent scientific developments such as DNA tests which have revealed the limitations of forensic techniques such as hair identification analysis….") (citation omitted); *State v. Quintana*, 103 P.3d 168, 170 (Utah App. 2004) (Thorne, J., concurring) ("Most evidence points to a lack of consistent training of [fingerprint] examiners and an absence of any nationally recognized standard to ensure that examiners are equipped to perform the tasks expected of them.").

[90]Moore v. Parker, 425 F. 3d 250, 269 (6th Cir. 2005) (Boyce, J., dissenting).

[91]United States v. Bentham, 414 F. Supp. 2d 472, 473 (S.D.N.Y. 2006).

[92]Report on the Governor's Council on Capital Punishment, 80 Ind. L.J. 1, 23 (2005).

[93]George Ryan (2002) "Report of the Commission on Capital Punishment," Office of the Governor, State of Illinois, April; url: http://www.idoc.state.il.us/ccp/ccp/reports/commission_report/index.html.

erroneous forensic science.[94] In many of these cases, forensic examiners offered opinions that DNA tests later proved wrong. Besides hair misidentifications, convictions have been vacated or overturned due to misidentified fingerprints, misinterpreted firearms evidence, miscalculated DNA statistics, misinterpreted drug evidence, misidentified bite marks, faulty blood testing, misinterpreted burn patterns, misidentified ear prints, misidentified handwriting, and erroneous autopsy conclusions.

Fabricated Evidence and Improper Forensic Testimony

When the Innocence Project's Barry Scheck and Peter Neufeld examined 62 of the first 67 DNA exonerations, they concluded that one-third of them involved "tainted or fraudulent science."[95] Professors Saks and Koehler identified a similar percentage (27%) when they reviewed the first 86 DNA exonerations.[96] Moreover, of the 340 (DNA and non-DNA) exonerations that Professor Samuel Gross and his University of Michigan colleagues examined, 24 involved perjured testimony from forensic scientists.[97] Finally, in the first study to explore forensic science testimony by prosecution experts in the trials of innocent people, University of Virginia Law Professor Brandon Garrett and Innocence Project Co-Director Peter Neufeld found that in 139 trials where forensic evidence supported the exoneree's conviction, 61% involved improper testimony by the prosecution's forensic expert.[98]

Instances of *forensic fraud* include fabricating fingerprints, falsifying the results of DNA tests, testifying to autopsies which were never performed, knowingly excluding or removing information from a report that is unmistakably exculpatory, knowingly providing false testimony, failing to report potentially exculpatory results, purposely concealing the fact one has previously committed an error in practice, deliberately drafting deceptive forensic reports, fabricating one's academic credentials, testifying to forensic tests which were never conducted (i.e., *drylabbing*), falsifying reports to hide the fact an examiner contaminated an evidence sample, stealing evidence from the evidence vault, describing and reporting "presumptive" positive tests as absolutely confiring the existence of a certain substance (e.g., blood, controlled substance),

[94] *See* Michael J. Saks and Jonathan J. Koehler, "The Coming Paradigm Shift in Forensic Identification Science," 309 *Sci.* 892, 892 fig. 1 (2005).

[95] *See* Barry Scheck et al., *Actual Innocence: Five Days to Execution and Other Dispatches from the Wrongly Convicted* 246 (Signet 2000).

[96] *See* Michael J. Saks and Jonathan J. Koehler, "The Coming Paradigm Shift in Forensic Identification Science," 309 *Sci.* 892, 892 fig. 1 (2005).

[97] *See* Samuel R. Gross et al., "Exonerations in the United States 1989 through 2003," 95 J. *Crim. L. & Criminology* 523 (2005).

[98] *See* Brandon L. Garrett and Peter J. Neufeld, "Invalid Forensic Science Testimony and Wrongful Convictions," 95 *VA. L. Rev.* 1 (2009).

testifying beyond the realm of science or one's expertise, falsifying lab reports to hide the destruction of potentially *exculpatory evidence* during the testing, and presenting testimony based on unsubstantiated techniques. Several other cases could possibly be incorporated into this discussion, but it is more difficult to discern whether fraud or gross incompetence produced the errors in these cases.[99]

Reasons for Errors and Misconduct

Forensic science errors and misconduct occur for a variety of reasons. To provide criminologists with an applied perspective of the issue, the following sections discuss some of the more common causes of error and misconduct in forensic science.

Poor Funding

Forensic science is poorly funded. Poor funding prevents crime labs from hiring an adequate number of analysts to process cases, and it prevents crime labs from purchasing newer and more efficient technology. Poor funding also leads to high turnover in publicly funded crime labs, as analysts take higher paying positions at private DNA or forensic science labs. High turnover, not surprisingly, leads to understaffing and increased case loads for analysts. The higher the analyst's case load, the more likely the analyst will make an honest human error or will pursue shortcuts that undermine the accuracy of his or her conclusions.[100]

Little or No Science

Forensic science, remarkably, is composed of very little science. Outside forensic toxicology and forensic DNA testing, the many fields that make up the forensic science community—for example, fingerprinting, toolmark identification, firearm identification, bitemark identification, hair and fiber identification—are not premised on verifiable scientific principles. All of these identification fields are premised on the notion of individuality. Stated differently, examiners in these fields claim that they can examine an impression (e.g., fingerprint or footprint) or a mark (toolmark) left at a crime scene and determine, with 100% accuracy, what object (e.g., boot, tool, etc.) or body part (e.g., a suspect's fingerprints or bite pattern) created that impression or mark to the exclusion of all other objects or body parts in the world. Unfortunately, the three premises that underlie the notion of individuality are not valid.[101]

---

[99]*See* Craig M. Cooley, "Forensic Science and Capital Punishment Reform: An 'Intellectually Honest' Assessment," 17 *Geo. Mason U. Civ. Rts. L.J.* 299, 390–95 (2007) (listing cases).

[100]*Id.* at 307–17.

[101]*Id.* at 340–45.

As of this writing, the author, along with the entire criminal justice community, eagerly awaits the publication of a report on the state of forensic science in the United States by the National Academy of Sciences (NAS). Reviews of draft copies of the report suggest that it will give particular insight into this and related issues discussed in this section. As explained in the *New York Times*:

> Forensic evidence that has helped convict thousands of defendants for nearly a century is often the product of shoddy scientific practices that should be upgraded and standardized, according to accounts of draft report by the nation's pre-eminent scientific research group.
>
> The report by the National Academy of Sciences is to be released this month. People who have seen it say it is a sweeping critique of many forensic methods that the police and prosecutors rely on, including fingerprinting, firearms identification and analysis of bite marks, blood spatter, hair and handwriting.
>
> The report says such analyses are often handled by poorly trained technicians who then exaggerate the accuracy of their methods in court. It concludes that Congress should create a federal agency to guarantee the independence of the field, which has been dominated by law enforcement agencies, say forensic professionals, scholars and scientists who have seen review copies of the study. Early reviewers said the report was still subject to change.
>
> …
>
> In 2005, Congress asked the National Academy to assess the state of the forensic techniques used in court proceedings. The report's findings are not binding, but they are expected to be highly influential.
>
> …
>
> Forensics, which developed within law enforcement institutions — and have been mythologized on television shows from "Quincy, M. E." to "CSI: Miami" — suffers from a lack of independence, the report found.
>
> The report's most controversial recommendation is the establishment of a federal agency to finance research and training and promote universal standards in forensic science, a discipline that spans anthropology, biology, chemistry, physics, medicine and law. The report also calls for tougher regulation of crime laboratories.
>
> In an effort to mitigate law enforcement opposition to the report, which has already delayed its publication, the draft focuses on scientific shortcomings and policy changes that could improve forensics. It is largely silent on strictly legal issues to avoid overstepping its bounds.

Perhaps the most powerful example of the National Academy's prior influence on forensic science was a 2004 report discrediting the F.B.I. technique of matching the chemical signatures of lead in bullets at a crime scene to similar bullets possessed by a suspect. As a result, the agency had to notify hundreds of people who potentially had been wrongfully convicted.

In its current draft report, the National Academy wrote that the field suffered from a reliance on outmoded and untested theories by analysts who often have no background in science, statistics or other empirical disciplines.

...

Donald Kennedy, a Stanford scientist who helped select the report's authors, said federal law enforcement agencies resented "intervention" of mainstream science — especially the National Academy — in the courts.

He said the National Institute of Justice, a research arm of the Justice Department, tried to derail the forensic study by refusing to finance it and demanding to review the findings before publication. A bipartisan vote in Congress in 2005 broke the impasse with a $1.5 million appropriation.

Mr. Shelby also accused the National Institute of Justice of trying to infiltrate the forensic study panel with lobbyists for private DNA analysis companies, who were seeking to limit the research to DNA studies.

The National Institute of Justice said it would not comment until the report was released. But a preview of potential turf wars played out in the presentations to the National Academy in December 2007. A forensic expert from the Secret Service blasted the F.B.I. for developing questionable techniques "on an ad-hoc basis, without proper research."

He said the Secret Service wanted the National Academy "to send a message to the entire forensic science community that this type of method development is not acceptable practice."

Everyone interviewed for this article agreed that the report would be a force of change in the forensics field.

One person who has reviewed the draft and who asked not to be identified because of promises to keep the contents confidential said: "I'm sure that every defense attorney in the country is waiting for this report to come out. There are going to be challenges to fingerprints and firearms evidence and the general lack of empirical grounding. It's going to be big."[102]

The author agrees that the NAS report will have a tremendous impact on both the criminal justice system in general and the forensic science community in specific.

Little to No Standards

Developing and implementing standards are vital in science because science is premised on replication. Standards must be clearly articulated and represent the consensus of opinion among a profession's members. Forensic science, unfortunately, has yet to develop standards for a variety of forensic techniques. Forensic examiners have been content with nebulous or improvised standards because they permit the greatest flexibility and discretion. Unfettered discretion, however, increases the chances that forensic examiners will fail to embrace the most accurate and discriminatory test(s) available. Moreover, when standards have been developed, the forensic science community has generally failed to ensure that examiners are actually adhering to these standards.[103]

No Independence

Scientists need to be independent and objective. However, the independence and objectivity of forensic examiners are frequently threatened or minimized because most crime labs are annexed to and controlled by federal, state, county, or local law enforcement or prosecutorial agencies. This configuration creates ethical challenges that can easily impact how a forensic analyst approaches a case. For instance, there is a natural tension between the perspectives and objectives of law enforcement officers and scientists. Law enforcement officers approach their jobs with a confirmatory mindset—that is, they try to prove or confirm that a particular person committed a certain offense or series of offenses. Scientists, on the other hand, approach their tasks with a cynical or disconfirmatory perspective—that is, they are trained to try to disprove a hypothesis before they can offer an opinion as to whether the hypothesis is plausible. If the scientist cannot disprove the hypothesis, the scientist has only supported the hypothesis—he or she has not proved the hypothesis.[104]

---

[102]S. Moore (2009) "Science Found Wanting in Nation's Crime Labs," *N.Y. Times*, February 4.

[103]*Id.* at 353–55.

[104]Craig M. Cooley, "Forensic Science and Capital Punishment Reform: An 'Intellectually Honest' Assessment," 17 Geo. Mason U. Civ. Rts. L.J. 299, 353–55 (2007).

Additional Reading Material

For more information regarding forensic science and wrongful convictions, see the following articles and publications:

- Craig M. Cooley and Gabriel S. Oberfield, "Increasing Forensic Evidence's Reliability and Minimizing Wrongful Convictions: Applying Daubert Isn't the Only Problem," 43 *Tulsa L. Rev.* 285 (2007)
- Craig M. Cooley, "Forensic Science and Capital Punishment Reform: An 'Intellectually Honest' Assessment," 17 *Geo. Mason U. Civ. Rts. L.J.* 299 (2007)
- Craig M. Cooley, "Reforming the Forensic Science Community to Avert the Ultimate Injustice," 15 *Stan. L. & Pol'y Rev.* 381 (2004)
- Michael J. Saks and Jonathan J. Koehler, "The Coming Paradigm Shift in Forensic Identification Science," 309 *Science* 892 (2005)
- Keith A. Findley, "Innocents at Risk: Adversary Imbalance, Forensic Science, and the Search for Truth," 38 *Seton Hall L. Rev.* 893 (2008)

False Confessions

Confessions are among the "the most probative and damaging evidence that can be admitted against [a defendant],"[105] even when they conflict with the crime scene evidence and contain blatant mistakes. The reason is that the critical actors in the criminal justice system—that is, judge, jurors, prosecutors, and police—all view confessions as self-validating and see them as quintessential evidence of guilt.[106] More importantly, the notion that an individual would falsely confess to a crime or series of crimes that he or she did not commit is alien to most jurors and the general public. Not only are false confessions viewed as contrary to common sense, illogical, and self-destructive, most law-enforcement-induced false confessions are believable because police interrogators make certain that the confessor includes "elective statements" such as crime scene details, expressions of remorse, the confessor's alleged motives, and acknowledgments of voluntariness.[107]

False confessions, unfortunately, are more common than jurors and the general public would dare to imagine. As Justice Souter recently acknowledged, a significant number of wrongful convictions have "resulted from… false

---

[105] *See Arizona v. Fulminante*, 499 U.S. 279, 292 (1991).

[106] *See* Saul Kassin and Gisli Gudjonsson, "The Psychology of Confessions: A Review of the Literature and Issues," 5 *PSYCHOL. SCI. PUB. INT.* 33 (2004); *Cruz v. New York*, 481 U.S. 186, 195 (1987) (White, J., dissenting) ("Confessions… have profound impact on juries.").

[107] *See* Saul Kassin, "On the Psychology of Confessions: Does Innocence Put Innocents at Risk?," 60 *Am. Psychol.* 215, 223 (2005), available at http://www.unc.edu/~kome/inls201/kassinPsychologyConfessions.pdf.

confession[s][.]"[108] Several recent studies support Justice Souter's claim. For instance, of the 240 DNA exonerations, 25% involved cases in which innocent defendants made incriminating statements, delivered outright confessions, or pled guilty.[109] Another group of researchers concluded that "[i]n fifty-one of the 340 exonerations between 1989 and 2004—15%—the defendants confessed to crimes they had not committed."[110] Two other researchers "identified false confession as the leading or primary cause of wrongful conviction in anywhere from 14–25% of the sample cases studied."[111] Similarly, a more recent study found that of the first 200 DNA exonerations, 31 (or 16%) involved false confessions which prosecutors introduced at trial.[112] Finally, the Innocence Project's most recent report, which analyzed 23 wrongful convictions from New York State, revealed that in 10 of the 23 cases, "innocent people falsely confessed or admitted to crimes that DNA later proved they did not commit."[113] So problematic are false confessions that several states have enacted criminal justice commissions to study the problem; several of these commissions issued studies regarding their findings and recommendations for minimizing or preventing false confessions.[114]

The causes of false confessions are manifold and too numerous to discuss in this chapter. The reader is encouraged to review the articles and publications

---

[108]*Kansas v. Marsh*, 126 S.Ct. at 2545 (Souter, J., dissenting). History is replete with examples in which persons, when faced with incurring capital punishment, confess to criminal offenses now recognized as impossible. *See* Mary Smith, 2 How. St. Tr. 1049; Three Devon Witches, 8 How. St. Tr. 1017; Bury St. Edmond's Witches, 6 How. St. Tr. 647; and Essex Witches, 4 How. St. Tr. 817. For example, consider the witchcraft trials in which individuals freely confessed to imaginary offenses, in minute detail, to serious and heinous crimes. *See* T.B. Howell, "Proceedings Against the Essex Witches," in *State Trials* 818, 856–57 (1816) (the examination of Anne Cate); *Id.* at 840–14 (the confession of Rebecca West); *Id.* at 852–53 (the examination of Rose Hallybread); *Id.* at 853 (the examination of Joyce Boanes); *Id.* at 854–55 (the examination of Rebecca Jones). Time has not changed the human psyche; today's social scientists have identified various forms of false confessions and a plethora of reasons of how and why they are produced. *E.g.*, Richard A. Leo and Richard J. Ofshe, "The Consequences of False Confessions: Deprivations of Liberty and Miscarriages of Justice in the Age of Psychological Interrogation," 88 *J. Crim. L. & Criminology* 429 (1998).

[109]*See* http://www.innocenceproject.org (last visited January 17, 2009).

[110]Samuel R. Gross et al., "Exonerations in the United States 1989 through 2003," 95 *J. Crim. L. & Criminology* 523 (2005).

[111]*See* Steven A. Drizin and Richard A. Leo, "The Problem of False Confessions in the Post-DNA World," *N.C. L. Rev.* 891, 902 (2004).

[112]*See* Brandon L. Garrett, "Judging Innocence," 108 *Colum. L. Rev.* 55 (2008); *accord* Saul M. Kassin and Gisli H. Gudjonsson, "True Crimes, False Confessions," *Scientific American Mind*, June 2005, at 26 ("Typically 20 to 25 percent of DNA exonerations had false confessions in evidence.").

[113]The Innocence Project, *Lessons Not Learned*, Exc. Summary, at 4 (Oct. 2007).

[114]*E.g.*, Wisconsin Criminal Justice Study Commission, *Position Paper on False Confessions* (2007) (Wisconsin Report); *California Commission on the Fair Administration of Justice: Report and Recommendations Regarding False Confessions* (2006) (California Report); *Illinois Capital Punishment Commission*, Ch. 2 (2002) (Illinois Report).

on false confessions listed at the end of this section. Nonetheless, while the causes may be too numerous to discuss here, the most important remedy for minimizing false confessions can be summed up with two simple words: videotaped interrogations. Many people who were wrongly convicted thanks in part to a false confession have claimed that they confessed only because the police had lied to them, physically abused them, or tortured them. Thus, the theory goes, if police interrogations are recorded—visually and with sound—from the moment they began, this would decrease the likelihood of police misconduct during interrogations.

For more information regarding false confessions and wrongful convictions, see the following articles and publications:

- Steven A. Drizin & Richard A. Leo, "The Problem of False Confessions in the Post-DNA World," *N.C. L. Rev.* 891 (2004)
- Richard A. Leo & Richard J. Ofshe, "The Consequences of False Confessions: Deprivations of Liberty and Miscarriages of Justice in the Age of Psychological Interrogation," 88 *J. Crim. L. & Criminology* 429 (1998)
- Richard A. Leo, "Inside the Interrogation Room," 86 *J. Crim. L. & Criminology* 266 (1996)

IDENTIFYING, STUDYING, AND LEARNING FROM WRONGFUL CONVICTIONS

Our greatest expansion of knowledge occurs when we identify our mistakes and we study them from several different perspectives to decipher what went wrong and why it went wrong. For many professions, mistakes can be identified quickly and easily. For instance, U.S. Airways and the flight crew on flight 1549 knew immediately, as did the entire world, that something had gone terribly wrong when Capt. Chesley B. Sullenberger had to make an emergency landing in the Hudson River in January 2009. Similarly, consider the March 2004 harbor boat tragedy in Baltimore, Maryland. The entire country, along with the harbor pilot community, immediately knew that something went drastically wrong.[115] Furthermore, in the National Football League, if a wide receiver is wide open, with no one within 10 yards of him, the opposing team will immediately know that one or more of its defensive players made a mistake because no wide receiver should be that wide open. Lastly, if a doctor prescribes a certain medication to an ill patient and the patient's symptoms do not disappear within a reasonable time, the doctor immediately recognizes that

---

[115]*See* Rex Bowman, "3 from Virginia Remain Missing: Baltimore Harbor Boat with 25 People Aboard Flipped Over Saturday," *Rich. Times-Dispatch*, Mar. 9, 2004, at A1.

he may have misdiagnosed his patient and that he may need to reevaluate the patient so he can prescribe the right medication. By identifying errors quickly, these professionals can instantly study their mistakes and identify workable solutions or reforms as soon as possible, thereby minimizing the likelihood that future errors will occur. In many professions, these solutions or reforms can and will save lives, money, time, or a football game.

What separates these professions from the criminal justice system is that they have built-in feedback mechanisms that allow their professionals to identify mistakes and errors immediately. The criminal justice system does not have a parallel feedback mechanism that can immediately notify criminal justice actors when a factually innocent person has been wrongly accused or convicted. Moreover, if a factually innocent person is convicted, there is a strong possibility that the prisoner's innocence may never be exposed, especially if a prisoner is unable to utilize DNA testing. Furthermore, even if a prisoner's innocence is revealed, it is usually years after the prisoner's conviction, and it is generally premised on luck rather than an inherent component of the criminal justice system. For instance, the majority of the DNA exonerees could seek DNA testing only because critical items of evidence from their case where not destroyed; there are many prisoners, however, who have not been as fortunate; indeed, the author is currently litigating or has litigated several postconviction DNA cases in which evidence was destroyed or has yet to be located after years of investigation and searching.

In the criminal justice system, figuring out how and why an innocent person was wrongly convicted poses a double imperative—a justice imperative and a public safety imperative. As Professor Keith Findley explained:

> Justice to the accused and victims alike demands that every reasonable measure be taken to ensure that no innocent person is wrongly convicted. By the same token, public safety demands such truthfinding accuracy, for when we convict an innocent person, the true perpetrator usually goes unpunished, free to commit other crimes that might have been prevented had the system not misfired.[116]

Despite these imperatives, in most jurisdictions there is no governmental body tasked with the responsibility of studying wrongful convictions, determining what might have caused them, and articulating suggested reforms aimed at minimizing the likelihood of future wrongful convictions, while not minimizing the likelihood of an accurate conviction. As Barry Scheck, Peter Neufeld, and Jim Dwyer explained in their book *Actual Innocence*:

---

[116]Keith A. Findley, "Learning from Our Mistakes: A Criminal Justice Commission to Study Wrongful Convictions," 38 *Cal. W. L. Rev.* 333, 337–38 (2002).

> In the United States, there are grave consequences when an airplane falls from the sky; an automobile has a defective part; a patient is the victim of malpractice, a bad drug, or an erroneous lab report. Serious inquiries are made: What went wrong? Was it systemic breakdown? An individual's mistake? Was there official misconduct? Can anything be done to correct the problem and prevent it from happening again?[117]

Instead, many criminal justice actors, government officials, and even Supreme Court Justices view wrongful convictions as anomalies, which are inevitable by-products of any criminal justice system.[118] Consequently, in the vast majority of jurisdictions across the United States, "the criminal justice system exempts itself from self-examination. Wrongful convictions are seen not as catastrophes but topics to be avoided."[119]

Given the criminal justice system's obvious shortcomings with respect to identifying wrongful convictions, studying wrongful convictions, and instituting or adopting new policies or reforms to minimize wrongful convictions, it is imperative that the criminal justice system take the necessary steps to address these shortcomings and to develop mechanisms that can adequately and quickly review questionable convictions to determine whether a person may have been wrongly convicted. Three mechanisms or institutions that can achieve these objectives are Innocence Projects, Innocence Commissions, and Prosecutorial Innocence Units.

Innocence Projects

As mentioned, the initial success of the Innocence Project at Cardozo School of Law led to the creation of more than 40 similarly situated projects aimed at reviewing questionable convictions to identify those prisoners who have been wrongly convicted. These projects quite often have different organizational structures. For instance, some are aligned with law schools and operated as clinical programs for law students; law clinic projects usually investigate and litigate a prisoner's innocence claim in court. Other innocence projects are annexed with journalism schools, which generally focus on exposing and publicizing a prisoner's innocence claim via the media rather than litigating the claim in court. And finally, some innocence projects operate as independent, public-interest, nonprofit law firms. For instance, while the Innocence Project

---

[117] *Actual Innocence, supra* note 53, at 246.

[118] *Actual Innocence, supra* note 53, at 246.

[119] *Id.*

is still associated with Cardozo School of Law, it became an official nonprofit, public-interest law firm in 2005.[120]

While all innocence projects have a singular goal in mind—that is, freeing the innocent—each project goes about achieving this goal in slightly different ways. For instance, some projects, like the Innocence Project, focus exclusively on cases in which DNA testing can prove a prisoner's innocence. Other projects, like the Michigan Innocence Clinic (which is associated with the University of Michigan School of Law), focus on innocence cases "where there is no biological evidence to be tested."[121] The Midwestern Innocence Project (which is associated with the University of Missouri-Kansas City School of Law) reviews and litigates cases only from the following six states: Arkansas, Oklahoma, Missouri, Kansas, Iowa and Nebraska.[122] Lastly, many projects, like the Innocence Project and the Northern California Innocence Project, work tirelessly with local, state, and federal lawmakers to enact new policies, procedures, or statutes aimed at enhancing the criminal justice system's truth-seeking function and minimizing the likelihood of wrongful convictions. For instance, the Innocence Project's Policy Department has played an instrumental role in lobbying for state and federal statutes that provide prisoners access to DNA testing; to date, 46 states and the federal government have enacted postconviction DNA testing statutes.[123]

Again, the universal connection between these projects is a shared commitment to advocating for innocent prisoners, to establishing their innocence, and to obtaining their release from prison. The creation of the Innocence Network in 2003, as mentioned, has only strengthened this commitment to identifying the innocence. The 45 current members of the Network work cooperatively to pool resources, to coordinate legislative proposals, and to share knowledge and strategies about litigating innocence claims in state and federal court.

Innocence Commissions

Some United States jurisdictions, as well as certain countries, have made it a priority to study wrongful convictions by creating so-called Innocence Commissions. For instance, the United Kingdom empowers its Criminal Cases Revision Commission (CCRC) to investigate wrongful convictions.[124]

---

[120]For the various descriptions of innocence projects, *see* Daniel S. Medwed, "Actual Innocents: Considerations in Selecting Cases for a New Innocence Project," 81 *Neb. L. Rev.* 1097, 1103–04 (2003).

[121]*See* http://www.law.umich.edu/centersandprograms/clinical/Pages/InnocenceClinic.aspx (last visited February 6, 2009).

[122]*See* http://www.innocenceprojectmidwest.org/index.php/our-vision (last visited February 6, 2009).

[123]*See* http://www.innocenceproject.org/Content/304.php (last visited February 6, 2009).

[124]*See* Lissa Griffin, "The Correction of Wrongful Convictions: A Comparative Perspective," 16 *Am. U. Int'l L. Rev.* 1241, 1277 (2001); see also David Horan, "The Innocence Commission: An Independent Review Board for Wrongful Convictions," 20 *N. Ill. U.L. Rev.* 91 (2000).

The CCRC is authorized to function as an independent executive agency with complete subpoena power to evaluate allegedly questionable convictions. The CCRC cannot overturn convictions but can submit cases to appellate courts.[125] Similarly, in Canada a person can request that the Minister of Justice assemble a Criminal Conviction Review Group (CCRG) to review questionable cases and make recommendations to the Minister. The Minister can then order a new trial, hearing, or refer a case to a court.[126]

With respect to American jurisdictions, Illinois was the first state to convene an independent body to review exonerations and a state's criminal justice system to determine whether systemic changes could be identified and suggested. In 2000, Governor George Ryan halted all executions once he learned that Illinois had exonerated more death row inmates (13) than it had executed (12) since 1977. After announcing his moratorium, Governor Ryan appointed a multidisciplinary, blue ribbon Commission on Capital Punishment, to review the 13 death row exonerations and Illinois's death penalty system. After two years of public hearings and research, the Commission submitted its final report in April 2002. The Commission put forth 85 recommendations that, "if implemented… [would] enhance significantly the fairness, justice and accuracy of capital punishment in Illinois."[127] The 14-chapter report discussed reforms ranging from police and pretrial investigations, to DNA and forensic testing, to death-eligibility, to prosecutorial functions in capital cases, to the role of defense counsel and the trial judge, to pretrial proceedings, to the guilt-innocence phase, to the sentencing phase, to imposing a death sentence, to postconviction proceedings, and to funding.

The first state in the United States to develop an "Innocence Commission" was North Carolina in the aftermath of several high-profile DNA exonerations.[128] The Chief Justice's Commission was established to "provide a forum for education and dialog between representatives from the different perspectives of the criminal justice system regarding prevention and rectification of wrongful convictions."[129] The Chief Justice's Commission studied and reviewed the postconviction review process in North Carolina and

[125]*Id.* at 1277.

[126]See Kathryn Campbell, "Policy Responses to Wrongful Convictions in Canada," 41 *Crim. Law Bulletin* 4 (2005).

[127]*Comm. on Capital Punishment, supra* note 91, at i.

[128]*See* Christine C. Mumma, "The North Carolina Actual Innocence Commission: Uncommon Perspectives Joined by a Common Cause," 52 *Drake L. Rev.* 647, 648 (2004) ("Because of the recent number of irrefutable DNA exonerations, a common ground now exists on which law enforcement, prosecution, and defense can stand together and agree that if there are ways to decrease the possibility of a wrongful conviction without risking conviction of the guilty, they should be pursued.").

[129]*See* http://www.innocencecommission-nc.gov/ABOUTUS.htm.

the United States for nearly two years and drafted and presented the North Carolina General Assembly a bill establishing the North Carolina Innocence Inquiry Commission. Signed into law in August 2006, the Innocence Inquiry Commission is an eight-member panel that is "charged with providing an independent and balanced truth-seeking forum for credible claims of innocence in North Carolina."[130]

During the past decade, 11 other states, besides North Carolina, have formed innocence commissions.[131] The majority of these commissions are bipartisan associations of law enforcement experts, academics, retired judges, politicians, and community activists charged with conducting retrospective reviews of wrongful convictions, identifying the root causes of these wrongful convictions, and recommending systemic reforms.

Prosecutorial "Innocence" Units

Similar to Innocence Projects and Innocence Commissions, the prosecutor's office represents another agency that can review cases in which viable claims of innocence are presented. By reviewing such cases, prosecutorial offices can identify wrongful convictions. More importantly, once these cases are identified, prosecutors can systemically study them to determine whether any prosecutorial policies or decisions may have contributed to an innocent person being wrongly convicted and to adopt adequate reforms if such reforms are needed to minimize—to the greatest possible extent—the likelihood of wrongful convictions. This form of prosecutorial review or self-regulation can (and most likely will) have a tremendous impact on the criminal justice system because prosecutors represent the most powerful repeat players in the criminal justice system.

Prosecutors in Boston, for instance, instituted several new reforms, particularly eyewitness identification reforms, after DNA testing and other newly discovered evidence exposed several high-profile exonerations.[132] Likewise, Los Angeles County prosecutors spear-headed the review of nearly 100 convictions in the Ramparts Division police corruption scandal.[133] Additionally, over the past 5 to 10 years, several prosecutorial offices have created "innocence" units or "conviction integrity" units to review prior convictions to

---

[130] Id.

[131] See Robert C. Schehr, "The Criminal Cases Review Commission as a State Strategic Selection Mechanism," 42 Am. Crim. L. Rev. 1289, 1299 (2005) (listing the 12 states).

[132] See Brandon L. Garrett, "Innocence, Harmless Error, and Federal Wrongful Conviction Law," 2005 Wis. L. Rev. 35, 87–88 (2005).

[133] See Beth Barrett and Greg Gittrich, "Attorneys Confront D.A.; Flurries of Defense Motions Fly in Attempt to Open Files on Rogue Cop," Daily News, Mar. 20, 2000; Rick Orlov, "Truth of 234 More Cases in Question," Daily News, May 5, 2000.

determine whether there are any cases with legitimate claims of innocence.[134] In 2002, for instance, the Ramsey County District Attorney's Office in St. Paul, Minnesota, proactively tested biological evidence from a 1985 rape case; the DNA results proved that the man convicted for the rape could not have perpetrated the rape. Upon learning of the results, the Ramsey County District Attorney's Office asked the state trial judge to vacate the man's conviction; the trial judge granted the request, which in turn created the first prosecutor-initiated exoneration in the United States.[135] Prosecutors in New York City and Houston have also sought DNA testing—on their own initiative—which have resulted in several exonerations.[136] Perhaps the most successful and comprehensive prosecutorial "innocence" unit in the United States is Dallas County's Conviction Integrity Unit (CIU). Created in 2007 by Craig Watkins, the first African-American District Attorney in Texas, the CIU has reviewed (and continues to review) hundreds of old cases and convictions to determine whether DNA testing could prove a prisoner's innocence. For instance, in September 2007, Watkins directed the CIU to review nearly 40 death row cases to ensure the accuracy of those convictions and death sentences.[137] Moreover, the CIU has cleared seven men of rape, murder, or robbery due to its proactive DNA testing approach.[138] To date, 21 prisoners have been exonerated with DNA testing—12 of which occurred before Watkins created the CIU.[139]

THE CRIMINOLOGIST AND WRONGFUL CONVICTIONS

Criminologists, as both behavioral and social scientists, can serve the justice system relative to miscarriages of justice in multiple ways and at multiple

---

[134]See Judith A. Goldberg and David M. Siegel, "The Ethical Obligations of Prosecutors in Cases Involving Postconviction Claims of Innocence," 38 *Cal. W. L. Rev.* 389, 394 n.21 (2002) (mentioning sources listing prosecutor-initiated reviews); Seth F. Kreimer and David Rudovsky, "Double Helix, Double Bind: Factual Innocence and Postconviction DNA Testing," 151 *U. Pa. L. Rev.* 547, 557–60 (2002) (noting prosecutor reviews in Minnesota as well as San Diego and Orange County, California); Daniel S. Medwed, "The Zeal Deal: Prosecutorial Resistance to Post-Conviction Claims of Innocence," 84 *B.U. L. Rev.* 125, 125–26 & n.3 (2004).

[135]See Paul Gustafson, "DNA Exonerates Man Convicted of '85 Rape," *Star Trib.* (Minneapolis), Nov. 14, 2002, at 1A; Jodi Wilgoren, "Prosecutors Use DNA Test to Clear Man in '85 Rape," *N.Y. Times,* Nov. 14, 2002, at A22.

[136]See Adam Liptak, "Houston DNA Review Clears Convicted Rapist, and Ripples in Texas Could Be Vast," *N.Y. Times,* Mar. 11, 2003, at A14 (discussing a Houston exoneration); Nick Madigan, "Houston's Troubled DNA Crime Lab Faces Growing Scrutiny," *N.Y. Times,* Feb. 9, 2003, at A20 (same); Robert D. McFadden, "DNA Clears Rape Convict After 12 Years," *N.Y. Times,* May 20, 2003, at B1 (discussing a New York exoneration).

[137]See Jennifer Emily and Steve McGonigle, "Watkins Seeks Review of Nearly 40 Death Row Cases," *Dallas Morning News,* September 16, 2008, at 1A.

[138]See Jennifer S. Forsyth, "The Exonerator," *Wall. St. J.,* Nov. 11, 2008, at A1.

[139]See Jennifer Emily, "Photo Lineup Study Dropped," *Dallas Morning News,* Jan. 16, 2009, at 1B.

junctures. Two primary contributions come immediately to mind: case examination and research.

With respect to case examination, forensic criminologists, whether they are generalists or specialists, may be called at any time in the postconviction interval. During the appeals process, they may be asked to review evidence, investigations, and court proceedings to help determine whether there has been missed evidence (which would be newly found evidence), adequate investigative practice, or ineffective defense counsel. In one case an independent criminal profiler may be asked to determine if proper methodology and accurate testimony was provided by a criminal profiler for the state; in another case, a reconstructionist may be asked to evaluate the statements of a jailhouse snitch against physical evidence that was not originally examined or reconstructed.

With respect to research, criminologists, for the most part, not only try to identify and understand the social, psychological, economic, and biological forces that produce crime, but also study how society and government respond to crime—that is, what regulations or sanctions are created to deter or minimize future criminal behavior or what social, mental health, or medical services are created to assist those individuals most susceptible to succumb to criminal behavior. By studying crime from multiple perspectives, criminologists can identify previously undetected correlations between two or more variables, which in turn can be used by state and federal governments to pursue new economic, medical, or social policies and laws aimed at reducing crime and helping crime victims and those most vulnerable to becoming victims or future criminals.

Given what criminologists do on a daily basis, it should come as no surprise that criminologists are uniquely situated—and suitably trained—to advance and develop the wrongful conviction knowledge base. Rather than study the social, psychological, economic, and biological causes of crime and the citizenry's response to crime, criminologists have the resources, know-how, and research background to study wrongful convictions from these divergent perspectives in order to better understand how and why wrongful convictions occur (i.e., causes of wrongful convictions) and what policies or laws can be enacted to minimize the risk of wrongful convictions (i.e., society's and government's reaction to wrongful convictions).

In terms of causes of wrongful convictions, criminologists can study the following variables: (1) the *roles* of criminal justice actors such as police, prosecutors, judges, defense counsel, crime lab personnel, and crime victims; (2) the *relationships* between different criminal justice actors such as police and prosecutors, prosecutors and judges, crime lab personnel and police, victim(s) and prosecutor, and defense counsel and judge; (3) the *funding* of different criminal justice agencies such as the prosecutor's office, the public defender's office, the crime lab, and the police; (4) the *organizational structure* of criminal justice agencies; and (5) the *race* of those wrongly convicted. It must be emphasized that this does not represent an exhaustive list of variables that criminologists can study; indeed, countless other variables can be studied to paint a clearer and more poignant picture of how and why wrongful convictions occur. The four identified in this section merely represent multiple brush strokes of this picture.

With respect to the *roles* of criminal justice actors, criminologists can study whether there are intrinsic social, psychological, political, or economic forces regarding certain roles—such as a prosecutor or lead detective—that cause these actors to act unethically or to overlook the actual offender and instead focus on a wholly innocent person. For instance, what motivates a detective to coerce a confession from an innocent person or an ethical prosecutor to turn a blind eye to exculpatory evidence?

In regards to *relationships*, criminologists can study how certain relationships between criminal justice agencies and actors can ultimately play to an innocent person's detriment. For instance, because the police and prosecutors work so intimately together on most serious felonies, such as rape and murder, prosecutors are influenced when the police engage in tunnel vision regarding a particular suspect. Likewise, because crime lab personnel work closely with the police and prosecutors, can the attitudes or beliefs of the police and prosecutors taint the crime lab analyst's ultimate conclusions? The same can be said with judge and prosecutors, because so many criminal court judges are former prosecutors, are criminal court judges more prone to favor the prosecution rather than the defense?

Regarding the *funding* issue, criminologists can study how funding can increase or minimize the likelihood of wrongful convictions. For instance, several crime labs across the country have been mired in scandals over the past decade due to inaccurate or fraudulent work that played a role in several wrongful convictions. Criminologists could study whether inadequate funding played a role in these errors or fraudulent behaviors. For instance, if the lab received inadequate funding, analysts may have been encouraged to take shortcuts to save money. Similarly, a large percentage of the DNA exonerees received poor representation from their court-appointed trial attorneys. Their court-appointed attorneys, however, often times worked for scantily funded public defender agencies. These are just two critical agencies that comprise the criminal justice system; there are many other criminal justice agencies that can be affected by inadequate funding. Such research can lead to new funding sources for certain agencies or a redistribution of monies to impoverished agencies.

Criminologists can also study the *organizational structure* of criminal justice agencies to determine whether their structure or hierarchy can impact their decision making. For instance, a fertile area of study in this respect is the crime lab system; publicly funded crime labs, for the most part, are annexed with either a prosecutorial or law enforcement agency. As a result, it is not uncommon for a crime lab director to take direction from the Chief of Police or the district attorney. Criminologists could study—in great depth—the consequences of this hierarchy and whether it would be more beneficial to make crime labs independent of any state agency.

Finally, criminologists can also study how *social economic status* and *race* play a role in wrongful convictions. Indeed, many of the 240 DNA exonerees are not only minorities, but are mostly poor and uneducated.

SUMMARY

The American criminal justice system has three laudable objectives: to convict the guilty, to seek justice for the victims and, perhaps most importantly, to protect the innocent from wrongful imprisonment. Indeed, "concern about the injustice that results from the conviction of an innocent person has long been at the core of our criminal justice system."[140] This concern emanates from the common law when William Blackstone wrote that it was "better that ten guilty persons escape, than that one suffer."[141] Due to this "core" concern of the criminal justice system, the Framers of the United States Constitution incorporated several protections into the Bill of Rights aimed at preventing wrongful convictions. For instance, criminal defendants have the right to remain silent, the right to confront their accusers, the right to have their peers determine their guilt or innocence, the right to have effective representation, and the right to compulsory process.

For many years (if not centuries), criminal justice actors and the lay public believed that these constitutional protections wholly eliminated the possibility that an innocent person could be wrongly convicted. Indeed, nearly 90 years ago Judge Learned Hand observed that "[o]ur procedure has been always haunted by the ghost of the innocent man convicted," but posited, sanguinely, that "[i]t is an unreal dream."[142] Today, however, thanks in large part to advancements in science—particularly DNA technology—our desire to join Learned Hand's optimism, must give way to the unfortunate reality that innocent people are convicted of crimes they did not commit.

---

[140]*Schlup v. Delo*, 513 U.S. 298, 325 (1995).

[141]William Blackstone, *4 Commentaries* *352.

[142]*United States v. Garsson*, 291 F. 646, 649 (S.D.N.Y. 1923).

Wrongful convictions occur for a variety of reasons such as honest eyewitness misidentifications, misidentification premised on highly suggestive police line-up techniques, erroneous forensic science, fraudulent forensic science, coercive police interrogation techniques that lead to false confessions, prosecutorial misconduct, lousy lawyering, and jail house informants. More importantly, wrongful convictions are generally caused by a combination of these factors—not just one. For instance, a faulty eyewitness identification can cause the police to develop tunnel vision on a particular rape suspect; this in turn can lead the police to channel domain-irrelevant information to the fingerprint examiner assigned to the case (i.e., informing the analyst that the victim already identified the suspect); this information can taint the fingerprint examiner's subjective examination of the fingerprint evidence—ultimately leading to a misidentified fingerprint that incriminates the suspect; the misidentified fingerprint can then be used to elicit a false confession from the indigent suspect because he now thinks the victim identified him and his fingerprints were recovered from critical items of evidence.

To prevent wrongful convictions, we need to identify and comprehensively study them so we can determine how and why an innocent person was convicted of a crime he or she did not commit. To achieve these objectives, we need to develop three institutions: (1) Innocence Projects; (2) Innocence Commissions; and (3) Prosecutorial Innocence Units. As our knowledge of wrongful convictions increase, so too will our ability to create and institute new procedures and policies to minimize—to the greatest possible extent—the likelihood of wrongful convictions.

Finally, criminologists and wrongful convictions go hand-in-hand. Instead of studying the social, psychological, economic, and biological forces that produce crime, criminologists have the wherewithal, expertise, and research background to study wrongful convictions from these divergent perspectives to better understand how and why wrongful convictions occur (i.e., causes of wrongful convictions) and what policies or laws can be enacted to minimize the risk of wrongful convictions (i.e., society and government's reaction to wrongful convictions).

Review Questions

1. Name and describe the problems with police line-ups.
2. What is forensic fraud, and how does it relate to wrongful convictions?
3. Why are false confessions a problem for those involved in the criminal justice system? How are they generally gained?
4. Discuss the number of people that are currently incarcerated even though they are innocent.
5. T/F The first DNA exoneration occurred in 1977.

6. What were the major findings of *The Innocence Project*? Why was this project so important?

7. As of February 2009, how many DNA exonerations have there been?

8. Discuss how jail house informants lead to wrongful convictions?

9. In what two ways can criminologists add to the discussion of wrongful convictions?

REFERENCES

ABA Criminal Justice Section's Ad Hoc Innocence Committee to Ensure the Integrity of the Criminal Process, 2006. Achieving Justice: Freeing the Innocent, Convicting the Guilty (J. Hanna, Ed.).

Barrett, B., Gittrich, G., 2000. Attorneys Confront D.A.; Flurries of Defense Motions Fly in Attempt to Open Files on Rogue Cop. Daily News.

Bedau, H.A., Radelet, M.L., 1987. Radelet, Miscarriages of Justice in Potentially Capital Cases. Stan. L. Rev. 21, 56–64.

Belsie, L., 1985. Recanted Testimony: Issue Tests Criminal-Justice Credibility. Christian Sci. Monitor 5.

Borchard, E.M., 1913. European Systems of State Indemnity for Errors of Criminal Justice. J. Crim. L. & Criminology 3, 684.

Borchard, E.M., Governmental Liability [Responsibility] in Tort. Yale L. J. 34 (1), 129, 229 (1924), Yale L. J. 36 (1), 757, 1039 (1926), Colum. L. Rev. 28, 577, 734 (1928).

Borchard, E.M., 1941. State Indemnity for Errors in Criminal Justice. B.U. L. Rev. 21, 201.

Borchard, E.M., 1932. Convicting the Innocent: Errors of Criminal Justice. Yale University Press, New Haven.

Bowman, R., 2004. 3 from Virginia Remain Missing: Baltimore Harbor Boat with 25 People Aboard Flipped Over Saturday. Rich. Times-Dispatch A1.

Campbell, K., 2005. Policy Responses to Wrongful Convictions in Canada. Crim. Law Bulletin 41, 4.

Castelle, G., Loftus, E., 2001. Misinformation and Wrongful Convictions. In: Westervelt, S.D., Humphrey, J.A. (Eds.), Wrongly Convicted: Perspectives on Failed Justice. pp. 17–35.

Cooley, C.M., 2007. Forensic Science and Capital Punishment Reform: An Intellectually Honest Assessment. Geo. Mason U. Civ. Rts. L.J 17, 299, 307–317, 390–395.

Cooley, C.M., 2004. Reforming the Forensic Science Community to Avert the Ultimate Injustice. Stan. L. & Pol'y Rev. 15, 381.

Death Penalty Banned in N.J.: First State in 43 Years to Abolish Capital Punishment, 2007. Chi. Trib. 3.

Drizin, S.A., Leo, R.A., 2004. The Problem of False Confessions in the Post-DNA World. N.C. L. Rev. 891, 902.

Emily, J., 2009. Photo Lineup Study Dropped. Dallas Morning News 1B.

Emily, J., McGonigle, S., 2008. Watkins Seeks Review of Nearly 40 Death Row Cases. Dallas Morning News 1A.

Findley, K.A., 2002. Learning from Our Mistakes: A Criminal Justice Commission to Study Wrongful Convictions. Cal. W. L. Rev. 38, 333, 337–338.

Forsyth, J.S., 2008. The Exonerator. Wall. St. J. A1.

Garrett, B.L., 2005. Innocence, Harmless Error, and Federal Wrongful Conviction Law. Wis. L. Rev. 35, 87–88.

Garrett, B.L., 2008. Judging Innocence. Colum. L. Rev. 108, 55.

Garrett, B.L., Neufeld, P.J., forthcoming 2009. Improper Forensic Science and Wrongful Convictions. VA. L. Rev. 95.

Gault, R.H., 1912–1913. Find No Unjust Hangings. J. Am. Institute Crim. L. & Criminology 3, 131.

Giannelli, P.C., 2007. Wrongful Convictions and Forensic Science: The Need to Regulate Crime Labs. N.C. L. Rev. 86, 163.

Goldberg, J.A., Siegel, D.M., 2002. The Ethical Obligations of Prosecutors in Cases Involving Postconviction Claims of Innocence. Cal. W. L. Rev. 38 (21), 389, 394.

Green, B., 1999. Why Should Prosecutors Seek Justice? Fordham Urb. L.J 26 (133), 607, 638.

Griffin, L., 2001. The Correction of Wrongful Convictions: A Comparative Perspective. Am. U. Int'l L. Rev. 16, 1241, 1277.

Gross, S.R., et al., 2005. Exonerations in the United States: 1989 Through 2003. J. Crim. L. & Criminology 95, 523.

Gustafson, P., 2002. DNA Exonerates Man Convicted of '85 Rape. Star Trib. (Minneapolis), 1A.

Horan, D., 2000. The Innocence Commission: An Independent Review Board for Wrongful Convictions. N. Ill. U.L. Rev. 20, 91.

Howell, T.B., 1816. Proceedings Against the Essex Witches. State Trials 818, 840–857.

Kaplan, P.W., 1985. NBC, at No. 1, Snaps 10-Year Ratings Decline. N.Y. Times 46.

Kassin, S., 2005. On the Psychology of Confessions: Does Innocence Put Innocents at Risk? Am. Psychol. 60, 215, 223, available at http://www.unc.edu/~kome/inls201/kassinPsychologyConfessions.pdf

Kassin, S., Gudjonsson, G., 2004. The Psychology of Confessions: A Review of the Literature and Issues. Psychol. Sci. Pub. Int. 5, 33; Cruz v. New York, 481 U.S. 186, 195 (1987).

Kassin, S.M., Gudjonsson, G.H., 2005. True Crimes, False Confessions. Scientific American Mind 26.

King Jr., J.H., 1970. Compensation of Persons Erroneously Confined by the State. U. Pa. L. Rev. 118, 1091, 1094.

Kraft, S., 1985. Nation Debates Jailed Man's Innocence: Recantation Puts Rape Case in Spotlight. L.A. Times 1.

Kreimer, S.F., Rudovsky, D., 2002. Double Helix, Double Bind: Factual Innocence and Postconviction DNA Testing. U. Pa. L. Rev 151, 547, 557–560.

Leo, R.A., Richard, J., 1998. Ofshe, The Consequences of False Confessions: Deprivations of Liberty and Miscarriages of Justice in the Age of Psychological Interrogation. J. Crim. L. & Criminology 88, 429.

Libit, H., 2002. Death Penalty Issue No. 1; Impact of Moratorium to Be Felt in Races for Governor. Balt. Sun, available at, 2002 WL 6958264.

Liptak, A., 2003. Houston DNA Review Clears Convicted Rapist, and Ripples in Texas Could Be Vast. N.Y. Times A14.

Madigan, N., 2003. Houston's Troubled DNA Crime Lab Faces Growing Scrutiny. N.Y. Times A20.

McFadden, R.D., 2003. DNA Clears Rape Convict After 12 Years. N.Y. Times B1.

Medwed, D.S., 2003. Actual Innocents: Considerations in Selecting Cases for a New Innocence Project. Neb. L. Rev. 81, 1097, 1103–1104.

Medwed, D.S., 2004. The Zeal Deal: Prosecutorial Resistance to Post-Conviction Claims of Innocence. B.U. L. Rev. 84 (3), 125, 125–126.

Memory Fails You After Severe Stress, 2004. New Scientist available at www.newscientist.com/news /news.jsp?id = ns99995089

Moore, S., 2009. Science Found Wanting in Nation's Crime Labs. N.Y. Times.

Mumma, C.C., 2004. The North Carolina Actual Innocence Commission: Uncommon Perspectives Joined by a Common Cause. Drake L. Rev. 52, 647, 648.

National Commission on the Future of DNA Testing, 1999. Post Conviction DNA Testing: Recommendations for Handling Requests iii.

National Institute of Justice, U.S. Department of Justice, 1996. Convicted by Juries, Exonerated by Science: Case Studies in the Use of DNA Evidence to Establish Innocence After Trial 51–52.

National Institute of Justice, U.S. Department of Justice, 1996. Convicted by Juries, Exonerated by Science: Case Studies in the Use of DNA Evidence to Establish Innocence After Trial iii.

Orlov, R., 2000. Truth of 234 More Cases in Question. Daily News.

Pickel, K.L., 1998. Unusualness and Threat as Possible Causes of Weapon Focus. Memory 6, 277.

Radelet, M.L., Bedau, H.A., Putnam, C.E., 1992. Spite of Innocence: Erroneous Convictions in Capital Cases.

Radelet, M., Loftquist, W.S., Bedau, H.A., 1996. Prisoners Released from Death Rows Since 1970 Because of Doubts about Their Guilt. T.M. Cooley L. Rev. 13, 907.

Remnick, D., 1985. Making Right Her Wrong: Cathy Webb's Public Mission after Recanting the Rape Tale. Wash. Post B1.

Repka, J.J., 1986. Comment, "Rethinking the Standard for New Trial Motions Based upon Recantations as Newly Discovered Evidence". U. Pa. L. Rev. 134, 1433, 1454–1458.

Rubinkam, M., 2002. DNA Evidence Frees Man Jailed Since '87 in Rape of 2 Women; Prosecutor to Seek Dismissal of Charges. Pitt. Post-Gazette B2.

Ryan, G., 2002. Report of the Commission on Capital Punishment. Office of the Governor, State of Illinois; url: http://www.idoc.state.il.us/ccp/ccp/reports/commission_report/index.html

Saks, M.J., Koehler, J.J., 2005. The Coming Paradigm Shift in Forensic Identification Science. Sci. 309, 892, 892 fig. 1.

Scheck, B., et al., Signet 2000. Actual Innocence: Five Days to Execution and Other Dispatches from the Wrongly Convicted 246.

Scheck, B., Neufeld, P., Dwyer, J., 2003. Actual Innocence: When Justice Goes Wrong and How to Make it Right, Ch. 1.

Schehr, R.C., 2005. The Criminal Cases Review Commission as a State Strategic Selection Mechanism. Am. Crim. L. Rev 42, 1289, 1299 (listing the 12 states).

Steblay, N.M., 1992. A Meta-Analytical Review of the Weapon Focus Effect. Law Hum. Behav. 16, 413.

Sullivan, T.P., 2005. Electronic Recording of Custodial Interrogations: Everybody Wins. J. Crim. L. & Criminology 95, 1127, 1131.

The Innocent and the Shammed, 2006. N.Y. Times A23.

Wells, G.L., Olson, E.A., 2003. Eyewitness Testimony. Ann. Rev. Psychol. 54, 277, 289.

Wells, G.L., Seelau, E.P., 1995. Eyewitness Identification: Psychological Research and Legal Policy on Line-ups. Psychol. Pub. Pol'y & L. 1, 765, 775–778.

Wells, G.L., et al., 1998. Eyewitness Identification Procedures: Recommendations for Line-ups and Photospreads. Law Hum. Behav. 22, 603, 639.

Wilgoren, J., 2002. Prosecutors Use DNA Test to Clear Man in '85 Rape. N.Y. Times A22.

Yet Another DNA Exoneration, 2002. Wash. Post A22.

3 PART

Working with Investigators and Forensic Specialists

CHAPTER 10

Law Enforcement Investigations: Essential Considerations

Stan Crowder

Nobody is going to take your views seriously if you cannot support them.

Robert K. Miller (1992, p. 3)

KEY TERMS

Administrative Investigations: Fact-finding inquiries conducted by an agency or government regarding its own management and performance.

Assessment (of Intelligence): Determining the significance of information.

Criminal Intelligence: Information compiled, analyzed, and/or disseminated in an effort to anticipate, prevent, or monitor criminal activity.

Criminal Investigations: Inquiries conducted when there is a suspected violation of criminal codes or statutes to determine whether a crime has been committed, to gather evidence related to the identity of suspects, to locate and facilitate arrest, to recover property, and to prepare a case for criminal prosecution.

Deduction (of Intelligence): Determining the useful conclusions which may be drawn from the assessment and integration of intelligence.

Employment Tribunals: Independent judicial bodies who determine disputes between employers and employees over employment rights, usually involving cases of discrimination and wrongful terminations (Dodd, 2009).

Garrity Rule: A legal protection which provides that during an administrative investigation, a police officer or other public employee may be compelled to provide statements under threat of discipline or discharge, but those statements cannot be used to prosecute the officer criminally.

High Intensity Drug Trafficking Area (HIDTA): A program that designates areas within the United States that face drug trafficking threats affecting other areas and develops and implements a strategy

CONTENTS

353

to address the drug threat there through partnerships with local, state, and federal agencies.

Information: Knowledge gathered from other people.

Instrumentation: The application of instruments and the methods of physical sciences to the detection of crime.

Integration (of Intelligence):   Combining the elements of an analysis to produce a picture of activities.

Intelligence: The gathering and analyzing of information that does not involve complaints or events but is in anticipation of them.

Interrogation: The skillful questioning of witnesses and suspects.

Investigation: Any systematic inquiry to determine the facts surrounding an event or situation (Ortmeier, 2006).

Law Enforcement (LE):   Sworn officers or agents of government agencies chartered to enforce criminal laws within their jurisdiction and to investigate related infractions.

Link Analysis Charting: Using a graphical visual design (e.g., flow charts) to show the relationships between individuals and organizations.

Local Law Enforcement: Campus and city police departments, as well as county sheriffs' offices.

Lucubration: Long, hard study, often at night, sometimes resulting in a written, scholarly work.

Ratiocination: Clear thinking, putting forth a logical argument.

Regional Information Sharing Systems (RISS):   A U.S.-wide law enforcement information sharing program, offering secure communication, access to intelligence databases, and investigative resources and services.

Vice Squads: Units or teams that are in charge of investigating crimes which involve someone profiting from another person's pleasure (i.e., crimes relating to drugs, prostitution, gambling, alcohol, cigarettes, and so on).

Dr. P. J. Ortmeier (2006, p. 320) explains that an *investigation* is "any systematic inquiry to determine the facts surrounding an event or situation." Careful readers will note that this definition does not assume criminality, it does not assume victimity, and it does not assume a particular outcome. It suggests, rather, that the facts are not known. It is used to describe a situation in which the facts must be gathered, verified, and organized so that meaningful inferences may be drawn from them. On that same line of reasoning, the need for an investigation suggests that conclusions about persons or events are unwarranted until the necessary inquiry has been conducted.

Law enforcement investigators of every kind are charged, within the scope of their inquiries, to answer the time-honored questions of *who*, *what*, *where*, *when*, *how*, and *why*. The results of an investigation, once assembled, may be used as proofs—that someone did or did not do something, that something did or did not happen, that patterns or motives are present or absent. The contexts for developing investigative proofs vary widely but tend to involve administrative or legal proceedings.

Law enforcement agency policies and the criminal codes that law enforcement agents are meant to enforce vary from agency to agency, from city to city, from state to state, and from country to country. However, investigative goals and best investigative practice standards are universal. It is fair to say that, in general terms, all investigators are after the same thing: the facts about what happened. In narrower terms, however, every investigator has different rules to follow while getting there. Whether one is a homicide detective in Australia, a sex crimes detective in New York City, an Inspector working for Scotland Yard, a vice detective in Los Angeles, or a detective/constable in Barbados—no one law enforcement agency is the same as any other, even within the same country. For the uninitiated, this can be disorienting and frustrating.

The purpose of this chapter is to help orient forensic criminologists with a general but applied understanding of what law enforcement investigations involve, who performs them, and to what end. It will discuss the two major types of investigations, the roles of agencies charged with performing them, the problem of jurisdiction, and educational requirements and recommendations. It will conclude with a discussion regarding the use of outside experts, such as forensic criminologists, and some friendly advice.

LOCAL, STATE, AND FEDERAL LAW ENFORCEMENT IN THE UNITED STATES

The term *law enforcement* refers to sworn officers or agents of government agencies chartered to enforce criminal laws within their jurisdiction and to investigate related infractions.

In the United States, *local law enforcement* refers to campus and city police departments, as well as county sheriffs' offices. Most law enforcement occurs at the local level (Ortmeier, 2006, p. 17) because just about every U.S. city has its own police department of varying size and capability. Ortmeier further reveals, "the majority of police agencies employ less than ten full-time sworn police officers and approximately one-third employ less than five full-time officers" (p. 17). Most counties have an elected sheriff who leads his or her respective office, and a few have a police department as well. In the counties where there is both a sheriff's office and police department, the duties of the sheriff are somewhat limited, depending on which tasks of law enforcement are delegated to the police department by the elected officials. The bottom line is that it is done a little differently everywhere, and broad generalizations about roles and responsibilities will not always apply.

State agencies that conduct criminal investigations are varied and encompass numerous enforcement tasks. Generally, state law enforcement agencies have an investigative arm or subdivision (i.e., a State Bureau of Investigation). However, many other state agencies have investigators and agents who perform criminal investigations. They include, but are certainly not limited to, the State Medical Board, the Department of Health, the Attorney General's Office, Child and Family Welfare (a.k.a. Child Protective Services), Department of Human Services, gaming commissions, the Department of Indian Affairs—the list goes on and on. With all these agencies, one can easily become confused.

As a general example, it is a criminal violation to commit welfare fraud; yet, the investigation will often be conducted by investigators in the Department of Human Resources, not the "State Bureau of Investigations," state law enforcement, or state police.

In Georgia, as a more specific example, the Georgia Bureau of Investigations (GBI) has statewide jurisdiction and is independent of other criminal justice agencies. The GBI provides assistance to local and state agencies through the Investigations Division, the State Crime Laboratory, and the Georgia Crime Information Center. The largest division is the Investigations Division, and GBI Agents assist local agencies with violent crime investigations.

Federal agencies (often called the "letter agencies" by street cops), on the other hand, are organized and tasked with specific and limited enforcement challenges by law, executive order, or design. As noted by Ortmeier (2006, p. 15) "Federal law enforcement agencies do not have general police powers because the U.S. Constitution limits the authority of the national government." Ortmeier (2006) further notes the existence of law enforcement and investigative duty within the following U.S. departments: Labor, Agriculture, Defense, Interior, Postal Service, Treasury, and Transportation. The smallest federal law enforcement agency is the U.S. Fish and Wildlife Agency with approximately 261 special agents and 122 wildlife inspectors. Additionally, each branch of the military has its own investigative division.

The U.S. Department of Homeland Security (DHS) encompasses 22 federal agencies with varied law enforcement and intelligence-gathering tasks. By examining the Border and Transportation Security Directorate, one can find the following agencies and tasks: Transportation Security Administration (TSA)—tasked to protect the transportation systems and security at airports; Customs and Border Protection (CBP)—tasked to manage, control, and protect the nation's borders; Immigration and Customs Enforcement (ICE)—tasked to identify and counter vulnerabilities in the nations border, economic, transportation, and infrastructure security; U.S. Secret Service (USSS)—tasked to protect the president and national leaders and financial and critical infrastructure. Other agencies in DHS include United States Park Police, the law enforcement branch of the National Park Service—tasked to protect national parks and monuments and Food and Drug Administration (FDA)—tasked to protect food, the blood supply, and drug tampering.

Among the most well known federal agencies, the Federal Bureau of Investigation has charter over 200 categories of federal law, including counterterrorism, counterintelligence, cybercrime, public corruption, civil rights, organized crime, white collar crime, and major thefts/violent crime (see http://www.fbi.gov for a complete list). It also has its own crime lab. However, it does not have charter over sex crimes or homicides unless they occur on federal property. This is infrequent, to say the least, and quite a contrast to their portrayal in film and television.

TYPES OF INVESTIGATIONS

Generally speaking, two types of investigations are performed by government (a.k.a. public) and law enforcement agencies: *administrative* and *criminal*.

Administrative Investigations

Administrative investigations are fact-finding inquiries conducted by an agency or government regarding its own management and performance. Such investigations are authorized as a routine matter, by suspected infractions of policies, or by the concerns of a person in authority. They involve an investigation into an event or circumstance involving one or more of the following (examples only):

- Employee background;
- Employee character and fitness;
- Promotions and pay raises;
- Employee or departmental performance reviews;
- Employee or departmental audits;
- Employee safety;
- Officer-involved shootings;
- Violations of agency policies, rules, or protocols;
- Professional misconduct;
- Harassment or discrimination;
- Property misuse/damage/theft;
- Threatening, intimidating, or violent behavior;
- Potential criminal activity involving agency personnel or resources.

These circumstances and related violations are generally noncriminal and may result in disciplinary action such as suspension, demotion, financial sanctions, and even dismissal. However, the circumstances can also be procedural—in relation to promotions, pay raises, transfers, or in response to a particular yet general concern. In such cases, administrative investigations can result in favorable outcomes, like changes to existing agency policies, rules, and protocols.

Force of Effect

Administrative investigations have the weight of the investigating agency behind them—but not necessarily the weight of the law. If those in the agency are forward thinking and reform oriented, then the findings of these inquiries are given a priority and action is taken. If not, then there may be little or no agency response at all, resulting in diminished internal accountability. Under these circumstances, it is possible that even when a clear violation has occurred, the penalties may be misunderstood, misapplied, or ignored altogether. Agency response is entirely up to those in charge of the agency.

In Atlanta, Georgia, for example, police hiring policies related to pre-employment background investigations are well-guarded secrets, but the results are not. As explained in Eberly (2008):

> Keovongsa Siharath was arrested in Henry County on charges he punched his stepfather.

> Jeffrey Churchill was charged with assault in an altercation with a woman in a mall parking lot.

> Calvin Thomas was taken into custody in DeKalb County on a concealed weapons charge.

> All three are now officers with the Atlanta Police Department.

> More than one-third of recent Atlanta Police Academy graduates have been arrested or cited for a crime, according to a review of their job applications. The arrests ranged from minor offenses such as shoplifting to violent charges including assault. More than one-third of the officers had been rejected by other law enforcement agencies, and more than half of the recruits admitted using marijuana.

> "On its face, it's troubling and disturbing," said Vincent Fort, a state senator from Atlanta. "It would be very troubling that people might be hitting the streets to serve and protect and they have histories that have made them unqualified to serve on other departments."

> But Atlanta police say it's not so simple. Officials have been trying without success for more than a decade to grow the department

to 2,000 officers, an effort hurt by this year's budget crisis. With competition for recruits intense among law enforcement agencies, Atlanta has had to make concessions.

"We would like, in an ideal world, to see every applicant with a clean record, but obviously that's not reality," said Atlanta police Lt. Elder Dancy, who runs the department's recruitment unit. "I don't think you'll find any departments who hire only applicants with squeaky-clean records."

Three decades ago, a police officer with a criminal record was much less common than it is now, said Robert Friedmann, a criminal justice professor at Georgia State University. But times have changed and many agencies have had to relax their hiring policies, Friedmann said.

Other local police agencies have hiring guidelines similar to Atlanta's. Police departments for Cobb, DeKalb and Gwinnett counties don't hire recruits with felony convictions but do hire those with misdemeanor arrests, on a case-by-case basis.

Dancy would not divulge all of Atlanta's restrictions but said the department won't hire anyone with felony convictions, or those with convictions for obstruction of justice, sex or domestic crimes.

Even so, police documents show that many of their recruits have blemishes on their records.

The Atlanta Journal-Constitution, through an Open Records Act request, asked in mid-August for the job applications of the Atlanta Police Department's two most recent graduating classes. The department provided 36 applications for police recruits who graduated June 10 and Aug. 4. All the graduates are currently Atlanta police officers.

Some departments have a zero tolerance policy for pre-employment criminal conduct; whereas, others do not. However, having a policy and following it are two different things.

In the United Kingdom, guidelines provided by the Home Office and the Association of Chief Police Officers offer the following with regards to driving under the influence (Cobain, 2008):

An officer convicted by a court of a drink driving offence can expect to face a formal misconduct hearing.

The usual sanction to be applied or, in the case of a senior officer, recommended by the tribunal and applied by the police authority, is either dismissal or a requirement to resign to reflect the serious view which is taken both inside the service and by society generally.

However, despite having faced internal administrative misconduct hearings, many officers have been allowed to stay on the job. Cobain (2008) describes the following reality, not entirely dissimilar to the results in Atlanta, where those charged and convicted of a crime are allowed to continue serving in law enforcement:

Scores of police officers across the UK are avoiding dismissal after being convicted of drink-driving, despite Home Office guidelines that say they should usually be sacked or forced to resign because of the seriousness of the offence. The Guardian has learned that at least 170 officers have been allowed to remain serving—or to retire at taxpayers' expense—after being convicted of drunk-driving since the guidelines were issued six years ago.

A series of requests for information made under the Freedom of Information Act have revealed wide differences in the manner in which forces deal with officers convicted of drink-driving, or related offences such as failing to provide a breath or blood specimen.

Some, such as Nottinghamshire, Thames Valley and Essex, demand the resignation of every officer convicted of the offence if they do not volunteer their resignations, while others, such as West Midlands, demand the resignation of the overwhelming majority of those caught drink-driving.

Within other forces, such as the Police Service of Northern Ireland and Northumbria police, the majority of officers convicted of the offence have been allowed to continue serving or to retire.

This passage brings us back to the reality that many government and law enforcement agencies perform administrative investigations but are essentially free to decide what the results mean even when the law has been violated. Under these conditions, there are agencies that act with impunity until compelled by government intervention, public outcry, or civil litigation to enact reform.

Who Performs Administrative Investigations?

Administrative investigations may be conducted by a supervisor, by a particular department or unit within the affected agency, or by an independent agency, investigator, or tribunal. Most procedural investigations or minor infractions relating to individual officers are conducted in house and kept relatively quiet. There may even be a unit dedicated to handling these kinds of inquiries, such as an Internal Affairs Division or an Audit Department. The more severe, systemic, or public the administrative concern, the more there is a need for the appearance of action and objectivity, and the more likely an independent inquiry will be involved.

Historically, independent investigations and audits of law enforcement agencies have been reactive—a response to highly publicized incidents of failure or malfeasance. Quasi-independent investigations involve outside agencies, like bringing in the state or federal authorities to investigate a local department. Fully independent investigations have involved various specialists and specialist panels drawn from forensic criminology disciplines. Two major examples include New York City's Commission to Investigate Allegations of Police Corruption and the Anti-Corruption Procedure of the Police Department headed by retired judge Milton Mollen (1994) and the independent investigation of the Houston Police Department Crime Lab from 2004–2007 headed by attorney Michael Bromwich, formerly of the United States Department of Justice, Office of the Inspector General.[1]

It is common for law enforcement agencies to prefer independent investigators with some kind of prior law enforcement experience or connection. This preference is inherently problematic: while such investigators may have the required knowledge and expertise to perform an investigation, past alignment with law enforcement may facilitate bias or its appearance. Consequently, bringing in an ex-commissioner of police or an ex-police detective to perform an investigation or audit of any kind is ill advised unless his or her reputation outside law enforcement is impeccable and his or her findings are made available for public scrutiny.

Administrative investigations related to employment issues have their own rules. As mentioned in the previous section, the United Kingdom has *Employment Tribunals,* which "are independent judicial bodies who determine disputes between employers and employees over employment rights."[2] They hear cases involving discrimination and wrongful termination for all public employees, including police officers (Dodd, 2009). In Australia, there is a similar government agency called the Australian Industrial Relations Commission (AIRC).[3]

In the United States, the only comparable national agency is the Equal Employment Opportunity Commission (EEOC),[4] which operates at the federal level. However, each individual state has its own peculiar employment laws and investigating agencies. When law enforcement officers are involved in administrative investigations, especially those that might result in their termination, the Garrity Rule applies.

[1]See http://www.hpdlabinvestigation.org

[2]See http://www.employmenttribunals.gov.uk

[3]See http://www.airc.gov.au

[4]See http://www.eeoc.gov

The Garrity Rule

As demonstrated in the previous sections, it is entirely foreseeable that noncriminal inquiries may uncover criminal activity. If an administrative investigation confirms the likelihood or the existence of criminal activity, then a separate criminal investigation must be requested by the appropriate law enforcement agency. However, if this occurs within a law enforcement agency in the United States, a controversial protection is engaged, referred to as the *Garrity Rule*.

The Garrity Rule refers to the U.S. Supreme Court's decision in *Garrity v. New Jersey* (1967). It provides that during an administrative investigation, a police officer or other public employee may be compelled to provide statements under threat of discipline or discharge, but those statements may not be used to prosecute him or her criminally. As explained in Clymer (2001, pp. 1314–1321):

> Police departments routinely conduct noncriminal, administrative investigations into allegations of police misconduct to determine whether discipline is warranted. As part of those investigations, investigators often interview the suspect officer or officers along with witness officers. In cases in which alleged misconduct may result in criminal charges, suspect officers have a valid basis for asserting their Fifth Amendment privilege and refusing to answer questions on the ground that their statements may incriminate them. To promote thorough investigations, and perhaps to avoid the unseemly spectacle of officers refusing to cooperate with their own departments, regulations, state statutes, and departmental policies often require that police officers, whether suspects or witnesses, answer questions that investigators pose. Refusal to do so can result in discipline, including job loss.

> In a series of cases decided from 1967 to 1977, the Supreme Court confronted states' use of economic sanctions—job termination, loss of pension benefits or political office, disbarment from legal practice, and ineligibility for state contracts—to compel cooperation in criminal and noncriminal investigations. In all but one of these "so-called 'penalty' cases," public employees and officials, contractors, and others refused to waive immunity or answer questions and later contested the resulting economic sanctions. Garrity v. New Jersey arrived in the Supreme Court in a different posture. In Garrity, the employees, most of whom were police officers, answered the questions, thus avoiding the threatened economic sanctions, and challenged the state's subsequent use of their answers in criminal prosecutions. Garrity, unlike the other penalty cases, presented the question whether compelled statements were admissible in criminal prosecutions.

Edward Garrity, the Chief of Police for the New Jersey Borough of Bellmawr, other police officers, and a court clerk were suspected of fixing traffic tickets. The Supreme Court of New Jersey ordered the state Attorney General to conduct an investigation into the alleged misconduct and report his findings. A deputy attorney general questioned the suspects. A state statute required that they answer questions or lose their jobs and pensions. Before conducting the interrogation, the deputy attorney general told each interviewee that his answers could be used in state criminal proceedings and that "if he refused to answer he would be subject to removal from office." The interviewees answered the questions posed to them. Later, local prosecutors brought criminal charges and introduced into evidence at trial the statements that the defendants had made to the deputy attorney general. After their convictions, the defendants appealed, claiming that the use of their compelled statements violated their constitutional rights. New Jersey courts rejected those claims. But, in a five-to-four decision, the United States Supreme Court reversed, holding the admission of the compelled statements unconstitutional. The Court offered two explanations: The statements were inadmissible under the Due Process Clause as coerced confessions, and the state's threat to fire the police officers unless they gave statements was an unconstitutional condition.

In a later case, the Court offered a different rationale for the result in Garrity: The police officers' compelled statements were analogous to immunized testimony and thus inadmissible under the Fifth Amendment privilege. Many lower courts have followed suit, describing Garrity as a case involving the privilege and compelled statements as "immunized."

The compelled statements in Garrity resembled formally immunized testimony. When a witness before a court or a grand jury asserts the privilege against self-incrimination, the prosecution can compel her testimony by securing an immunity grant. In Kastigar v. United States, the Court held that "use and derivative use" immunity (often simply called "use immunity") is sufficient to require a witness to testify despite an assertion of the privilege. If an immunized witness persists in her refusal to testify, she can be held in contempt. The immunized testimony is thus compelled by the contempt threat.

Use immunity does not foreclose later criminal charges against the witness for matters described in the immunized testimony. Rather, it prevents the prosecution from making use of the testimony and any evidence derived there from against the witness in a criminal trial. The

Kastigar Court reasoned that a grant of such immunity is coextensive with the Fifth Amendment because it leaves the witness-turned-defendant "in substantially the same position as if the witness had claimed the Fifth Amendment privilege" and remained silent.

The Garrity protection operates in a similar manner—it enables states to compel statements from public employees by threatening job termination but bars use of the statements in later criminal prosecutions. Accordingly, when the deputy attorney general threatened Garrity and the others with loss of their jobs, he granted them de facto use immunity in exchange for their answers. Although Garrity and the others did not first assert the privilege, an action typically required to trigger its protection, the Court since has concluded that when assertion itself would be penalized, as was the case in Garrity, the protection is self-executing.

Opponents of the Garrity Rule argue that it essentially immunizes corrupt law enforcement officers by operating "as a trap for investigators and prosecutors who fail either to take steps to minimize exposure to compelled statements or to prepare to disprove taint." Further, the rule "can serve as a tool for unscrupulous internal affairs investigators who seek to undermine criminal prosecutions by disseminating compelled statements and treacherous police witnesses who allege that they are tainted in order to avoid giving prosecution testimony" (Clymer, 2001, p. 1382).

Consider the recent case of Police Officer Sam Streater, 45, from New Haven, Connecticut. He was arrested in 2008 for soliciting a known prostitute, Vanessa DiVerniero, by paying her $20 to have sex with him in his car. As explained in Kaempffer (2009):

A Superior Court judge last month approved an application from Officer Sam Streater, a 17-year veteran, for accelerated rehabilitation, a program reserved for first-time, nonviolent offenders. The probation will last a year and, if he stays out of trouble, the charges would be dismissed.

Supervisory State's Attorney David Strollo said Monday Streater was treated like any other defendant. It's common for defendants in similar circumstances to receive AR, he said, so his office did not oppose Streater's application.

"Given that he was not on duty as a police officer (when the misconduct occurred), we thought it would be fair to treat him like any other citizen on this case," Strollo said, describing the resolution as "consistent" with similar cases.

Streater was caught with a suspected prostitute last September in Fair Haven, not long after members of the department's gun unit finished up a prostitution sting in the neighborhood. After the sting was over, officers went looking for a woman they had seen earlier in the night, for whom they believed they had an active warrant. They saw her in Streater's car and pulled it over.

During an internal affairs investigation, Streater admitted under Garrity protection that he had solicited the woman for sex. Under the Garrity rule, a department can order a police officer to give a statement about alleged misconduct but can't use that information in a criminal prosecution. The criminal charges against Streater—soliciting a prostitute and soliciting a prostitute from a motor vehicle—relied on statements made by the woman.

Streater was suspended without pay for two weeks in late November. The suspension was still in effect when IA served the arrest warrant, which police at the time indicated was pursued at the urging of the State's Attorney's office.

…

The department has indicated it plans no other discipline as a result of the arrest.

Further details are reported in Kaempffer (2008):

During the internal affairs probe, Streater allegedly admitted he had solicited the prostitute. But because he was ordered to give the statement and did not do so voluntarily, a legal ruling called the Garrity protection was triggered. The protection, which is similar in concept to invoking the Fifth Amendment right against self-incrimination, means nothing he said could be used against him criminally.

The state's charges, however, appear to be based on statements made by the woman, who acknowledged to police that she engaged in a sexual act with Streater in his car for $20, according to an arrest warrant affidavit.

The warrant states that the police department's drug unit was conducting a prostitution sting the night of Sept. 23 in Fair Haven, and officers observed a woman, Vanessa DiVerniero, walking in the area. Police described her as a known prostitute who had an arrest warrant pending, but the squad supervisor told them not to serve the warrant until after the sting was completed.

> Once the operation was done, the officers went looking for DiVerniero, and observed her in a white Dodge Intrepid.
>
> DiVerniero later told the internal affairs unit that when officers stopped the car and approached, the driver, who was Streater, told them, "Yeah, it's me.... I got a C-I." C-I is police jargon for confidential informant.
>
> DiVerniero said she initially denied to police that anything happened, but told IA in a subsequent interview that Streater had picked her up and paid her for sex.

In this case, the Garrity Rule offered little protection to the officer against the statements of the prostitute. However, it does appear to have shielded the officer from being held accountable for false statements he made at the scene—namely that the prostitute was his confidential informant (a.k.a., C.I.). In any case, as of this writing, the officer's department will continue to employ him despite his conviction for a crime. As has been made clear in previous sections, this scenario is not unique to law enforcement in New Haven or even the United States.

Criminal Investigations

Criminal investigations are conducted when there is a suspected violation of criminal codes or statutes (Lyman, 2008). Gilbert (2004, p. 37) notes, "Criminal investigation is a logical, objective, legal inquiry involving a possible criminal activity." In the United States, suspected criminal violations are investigated by local, state, and federal law enforcement agencies based on jurisdictional authority as provided by law.

It is generally the purpose of a criminal investigation to determine whether a crime has been committed, to gather evidence and information related to the identity of suspects, to locate and facilitate the arrest of suspects, to recover lost or stolen property, and to prepare a case fit for criminal prosecution. These fundamentals have not changed in centuries, but the means to achieve them, including the technology used, has certainly evolved (see generally Gross, 1906; O'Connell and Soderman, 1936; O'Hara, 1970; and Savino and Turvey, 2004; Turvey, 2008). Fundamentals change as does the concept of crime and criminality, given that criminal statutes and their enforcement evolve from year to year, and are only as firm as those who write and rewrite them.

O'Hara (1970, p. 1) provides an important touchstone regarding investigative basics:

> The tools of the investigator are, for the sake of simplicity, referred to as the three "I's", namely Information, Interrogation, and Instrumentation. By the application of the three "I's" in varying proportions the

investigator gathers the facts which are necessary to establish the guilt of the accused in a criminal trial.

O'Hara goes on to explain that *Information* is "knowledge which the investigator gathers from other persons" (p. 7)—including records and statements provided by witnesses, informants, and other individuals. O'Hara further explains that *Interrogation* refers to "the skillful questioning of witnesses as well as suspects" (p. 9)—including interviews with the impartial who have no reason to withhold facts, and the confrontational questioning of suspects or others who might have a reason to be deceptive in their answers. Finally, O'Hara offers that *Instrumentation* refers to "the application of instruments and the methods of physical sciences to the detection of crime" (p. 11). The term is used to suggest analyses performed both in the crime lab by scientists and in the police station by investigators (p. 11):

> Instrumentation, however, is taken here to mean rather more than criminalistics. It includes also all the technical methods by which the fugitive is traced and examined and, in general, the investigation is advanced. Thus, fingerprint systems, modus operandi files, the lie detector, communication systems, surveillance equipment such as telephoto lens and detective dyes, searching apparatus such as the x-ray unit and the metal detector, and other investigative tools are contained within the scope of the term.

Using Information, Interrogation, and Instrumentation, the fact that a crime was committed is proved or refuted. Once the elements of the crime, or the corpus delicti, have been established, the person responsible must be identified. Offenders are identified by means of a confession, an eyewitness, or circumstantial evidence such as motive, means, opportunity, and associative evidence.

O'Hara (1970, p. 19) makes it clear that, while the investigator is "basically a collector of facts," he or she must use logic and reasoning to develop case theories and draw conclusions about the crime. Though crimes can be complex, the investigator is admonished to take no shortcuts in the search for information. He or she must be scrupulous in his or her methods and objective in rationale. This suggests a duty to be intellectually and temperamentally prepared to do so.

Criminal investigators have an onus beyond that of mere "fact collector" because of the consequences that will arise from their work. Unlike many administrative investigations, the results of criminal investigations carry with them the weight of the courts and the law. As result, investigations can lead to criminal charges, criminal convictions, fines, jail time, and even the death penalty under certain circumstances. On the facts and conclusions drawn from a solid investigation, a criminal is arrested and the innocent remain free. And the opposite is also true.

In smaller agencies with fewer resources, there may be only a couple of detectives catching cases full time who are required to work everything that comes through the door. In the smallest agencies, with fewer than 10 sworn officers, there may be no dedicated investigators at all. The smaller the agency, the more reliant it is on assistance from neighboring agencies or those higher up the food chain with larger budgets, more manpower, and better investigative "toys" (county, state, and federal agencies).

Most local law enforcement agencies have dedicated investigators assigned to the investigation of violent crime, such as robbery, sexual crimes, and homicide. In larger agencies there will be investigative subunits, broken down by crime type per the needs within a given jurisdiction (e.g., homicide unit, robbery unit, sex crimes unit, vice unit, organized crime unit, etc.). In larger law enforcement agencies, or those with sufficient budgets, there may even be intelligence units.

Investigation vs. Intelligence Gathering

There is an important distinction between an active investigation and the gathering of what is referred to as *intelligence*. Investigations are reactive—based on a complaint or an event. Intelligence gathering and analysis is proactive—it occurs separate from complaints and events in anticipation of them. Dr. David Carter (2004, p. 7) explains that with respect to law enforcement:

> Intelligence is the product of an analytic process that evaluates information collected from diverse sources, integrates the relevant information into a cohesive package, and produces a conclusion or estimate about a criminal phenomenon by using the scientific approach to problem solving (i.e., analysis). Intelligence, therefore, is a synergistic product intended to provide meaningful and trustworthy direction to law enforcement decision makers about complex criminality, criminal enterprises, criminal extremists, and terrorist.

Criminal intelligence is a related term used in American law enforcement and is defined as "information complied, analyzed, and/or disseminated in an effort to anticipate, prevent, or monitor criminal activity" (Peterson, 2005, p. 39).

Many law enforcement agencies have a Criminal Intelligence Unit, or a division with a similar designation, which is essentially a team of investigators charged with collecting and analyzing information for decision-making and crime prevention strategies. Through the process of informed analysis, information collected from a variety of streams becomes intelligence (FM 34–3, p. 1–1). By "connecting the dots," analyzing patterns and establishing connections, the bits and pieces of information gathered from multiple sources can provide a bridge to a path for the investigator. A path that leads to the recognition that something has happened, may happen, or may happen again.

What Is Intelligence?

What are intelligence analysts examining? The answer depends. Carter (2004) provides that the information examined can be any unanalyzed data, evidence, events, or processes that reveal a crime or witness. "Analysis is the determination of the significance of the information relative to information and intelligence already known and drawing deductions about the probable meaning of the evaluated information" (FM 34–3, p. 2–1).

RISS

One example of successful intelligence gathering and dissemination within the law enforcement community would be the *Regional Information Sharing Systems (RISS)* program, which has been in existence since the 1980s with an emphasis on organized crime control (Lyman, 2008, p. 180). RISS is a nationwide law enforcement information-sharing program, offering secure communication, access to intelligence databases, and investigative resources and services. As explained at http://www.riss.net:

> The mission of RISS is to support law enforcement efforts nationwide to combat illegal drug trafficking, identity theft, human trafficking, violent crime, terrorist activity, and to promote officer safety. Traditional support services provided to law enforcement member agencies are:
>
> - Information sharing resources
> - Analytical services
> - Loan of specialized investigative equipment
> - Confidential funds
> - Training conferences
> - Technical assistance
>
> RISS operates a secure intranet, known as RISSNET™, to facilitate law enforcement communications and information sharing nationwide. RISS local, state, federal, and tribal law enforcement member agency personnel have online access to share intelligence and coordinate efforts against criminal networks that operate in many locations across jurisdictional lines. The RISS Program is a federally funded program administered by the U.S. Department of Justice (DOJ), Bureau of Justice Assistance (BJA).

RISS provides a means by which regional law enforcement agencies can share intelligence though a centralized database, analysis of intelligence and investigative data, specialized and technical equipment, training, and funds (Lyman, 2008, pp. 180–181). Working with these systems during the 2005 G-8 Summit at Sea Island, Georgia, those of us in the U.S. military police community were impressed by the sharing of information as law enforcement prepared for the security mission for President Bush and numerous world leaders.

HIDTA

Another example of successful intelligence gathering would be the efforts of *High Intensity Drug Trafficking Area (HIDTA)* analysts. As explained at http://www.hidta.org:

> The High Intensity Drug Trafficking Area (HIDTA) Program was created by the Anti-Drug Abuse Act of 1988. This act authorized the Director of the Office of National Drug Control Policy (ONDCP) to designate regions within the United States that face drug trafficking threats affecting other areas of the nation as HIDTAs.
>
> The HIDTA Program provides resources to assist each HIDTA in developing and implementing a strategy to address its regional drug threat. Each HIDTA strives to create partnerships between federal, state and local law enforcement agencies and promote a coordinated, intelligence driven response to its drug trafficking problems.

For example, HIDTA analysts can, upon receiving a written request from any law enforcement agency inquiring about a person or a location, set to work. Accessing multiple civilian and law enforcement databases by hand (because these databases are not cross-searchable), they accumulate every related public document and record. The caveat being that the search must be germane to a homicide or drug-related crime to get analyst priority. This program is a valuable tool for helping to locate suspects, develop lists of known associates, and determine connections across residences, vehicles, and other assets.

The author was part of a team that developed a deconfliction initiative in the Atlanta (Georgia) HIDTA office in 2000. The program replicated, in part, successful programs in Baltimore and Miami HIDTA offices. The deconfliction mission was developed to ensure that when multiple jurisdictions are involved in drug investigations in many areas of the city or state, law enforcement agencies share intelligence to prevent law enforcement officers from interfering with or even facing each other in drug arrests. The Law Enforcement Assistance and Deconfliction (LEAD) program remains active and ensures jurisdictional challenges are examined in high-risk investigations.

There are many other kinds of intelligence and intelligence-gathering tools; however, these have been among the most useful to the author in terms of providing an informed nexus within and across the law enforcement community.

They are provided as examples of more successful efforts. As already suggested, each agency will have its own peculiar streams of intelligence as dictated by where it is, what it does, and what crime occurs in its jurisdiction.

Analyzing Intelligence

Analysis of intelligence consists of three subtasks: assessment, integration, and deduction (FM 34–3, p. 2–12).

Assessment is the determination of the significance of information. To evaluate information it must be scrutinized to determine the pertinence of the information, the reliability of the source, and the creditability of the information (FM 34–3, p. 2–10). Is the information pertinent to the investigation, and what value does it have to whom? Is the information coming from known sources that provided accurate or corroborated data in past cases? Can a comparison with other data sources be conducted? These questions provide direction for an intelligence analysis.

Integration is the combination of the elements from an analysis to produce a picture of activities (FM 34–3, p. 2–13). Integration may be accomplished by *link analysis charting*, which refers to "a technique designed to show relationships between individuals and organization using a graphical visual design. It is used to show graphically transactions or relationships that are too large and confusing for one to assimilate through the reading of reports." This flow-charting may track events, commodities, people, places, and times (Lyman, 2008, p. 177–179).

Deduction of valid intelligence should be the result of integration efforts. Is there a useful conclusion derived from the assessment and integration? What is the probable meaning of the work completed? Using critical thinking skills, can we draw a conclusion or make a prediction about future events? These are the questions asked by investigators.

JURISDICTION AND POLITICS

Criminal investigations are conducted by law enforcement agencies within their respective geographical and statutory jurisdictions. As already described, within the United States there are local, state, and federal agencies investigating all manner of criminal violations. Local law enforcement has jurisdiction over most major crimes such as robbery, sex crimes, and homicides. State and federal authorities may provide support with these types of cases upon request, but unlike film and television, it is not generally their show if they do. Additionally, there is tribal law enforcement on Native American reservations and military law enforcement on military bases and installations.

Complicating matters is the harsh reality that there is often little communication between any of the aforementioned entities. In some cases there is open rivalry within jurisdictions and across multiple agencies and multiple levels of local, state, and federal law enforcement characterized by repeated turf wars. Every agency, it seems, wants its share of the spoils of good investigative efforts—from good press, to seized vehicles for departmental use or sale, to better clearance statistics.

With multiple levels and types of law enforcement, who is responsible and who is in charge at any given moment on any given case? Authorization to conduct criminal investigations, as well as territorial geographical boundaries, reflects the jurisdiction of U.S. law enforcement. Agency jurisdiction is addressed by statute for federal agencies. State and local agencies that are accredited by the Commission on Accreditation for Law Enforcement Agencies, Incorporated (CALEA) are required to develop written directives addressing the geographical boundaries, responsibilities on concurrent jurisdiction, and procedures for requesting federal law enforcement assistance (CALEA standards 2.1–2.1.4). However, multiple agencies at multiple levels may have jurisdiction over particular crimes. In illegal drug investigations, a local agency, a state agency, and federal agencies might all be involved.

Yet other investigative tasks, such as property crime or homicide, have failed to raise the level of communication across jurisdictional boundaries, except when task forces are formed. Multijurisdictional drug task forces paved the way for the development of other types of task forces to address specific issues, such as serial crime, fugitives, and arson. Task forces or major case squads are formed when political pressure, media scrutiny, or management dictates the resolution of crime though a combined team effort. Agency leadership must provide labor (investigators) and resources to participate in task force operations. However, forming a task force is not a simple answer to complex problems. With multiple levels of political influence and pressure, the personality differences of agency leadership and vastly different policies and procedures, the task force is hard pressed to run effectively and efficiently from the first day. However, the formation of a task force can work. Good leadership is the key to success in any task force.

At the local and state level, a memorandum of agreement between agencies appears to guide investigative efforts. Simply putting the jurisdictional issue in writing with written directives or agreements, often developed by middle managers and signed by agency executives, has been successful. Deputy Chief of Police, David Beam, Marietta (Georgia) Police Department noted to the author that (2009), "We have clear cut jurisdictional lines so this is rarely an issue; if however, a problem develops, the Chief of Police usually irons it out with the head of the other agency."

How are day-to-day issues of jurisdiction handled? It is the experience of the author that the lowest ranking persons involved can work through these issues when given a chance. If management gives investigators the authority to work with their peers in jurisdictional issues, the investigators can work it out. There will always be territorial turf protecting by those higher in the chain of command; however, the investigators on the ground seem to have the tenacity to work through issues with other agency investigators. Supervisors should be encouraged to let them.

While the creation of a task force is not a silver bullet for interagency communication, especially when run by a poor leader, the good ones are a start in the right direction. In any given case there are going to be jurisdictional conflicts, potential and actual alike. On a good day, this conflict can provide checks and balances and give agencies the ability to cooperate and share resources. On a bad day, it can make an investigator's worst fears come to life.

INVESTIGATOR QUALIFICATIONS

This chapter has provided only a glimpse of the greater picture that is the world of investigations, and only from a law enforcement perspective. That is to say, these are only some of the jobs that exist, and certainly this chapter does not include all the investigative work conducted in the private or defense sector. Nonetheless, it is fairly representative of what law enforcement investigative efforts are meant to involve and accomplish, if only in the most general sense.

It is important to understand that investigations are not a surreal or even unusual task undertaken only by those with special knowledge or abilities. They are everyday occurrences involving methods and skills that can be taught and learned by individuals of varying educational backgrounds. Soderman and O'Connell explain (1935, p. 1):

> Natural Science began to develop by leaps and bounds in the middle of the nineteenth century. This introduced exactness and a widespread knowledge of things. The obscure mysticism which had prevailed concerning everything disappeared as the clear, cold light of science clarified matters, and the change quickly became apparent in criminal investigation. Justice, which had been for centuries to solve problems and search for the truth, turned to science.

We must, therefore, acknowledge that many outside the investigative community possess more than adequate investigative skills. Conversely, we must accept that many within the investigative community do not. The reason is that, for some, being an investigator is merely a job title; for others, it is a political appointment; for even fewer, it is a profession; and for the smallest number, it is a true calling. As warned in Dienstein (1995, p. 160):

> The adequacy of an investigation and the skill of the investigator can result in a successful prosecution and conviction of the offender or the exoneration of a person unjustly accused. An inadequate investigation can result in a failure of the prosecution or the conviction of the wrong person.

Given the consequences for substandard investigations that are beneath best practices, investigations must be conducted thoroughly and only by those who have taken the time to get the proper education and training. Experience is less of an issue as it is a problem that time will solve.

Investigator Education Requirements

Not all law enforcement agencies have equal access to manpower and resources. Larger departments have larger budgets. The more crime within their jurisdiction, the more of their budget is spent responding to crime with less available funding for training and qualified personnel. Conversely, smaller departments with less crime in well-off areas may have more funding available for training and luring in good applicants. This eventuality can create a gap between the best-trained and most-experienced investigators. It also shapes the quality of applicants, the results of which can vary widely, as we have seen.

Detectives and inspectors are almost exclusively drawn from the ranks of patrol officers. That is to say, they are grown from successful applicant/graduates of a local police academy who get hired by a local department, get assigned a car and a patrol, and stay with a particular agency for a predetermined period of time. Some departments allow officers to take a shortcut to their detective's shield by working in the *vice squad* as an undercover. Eventually, these officers apply to work in investigations from that experience base. If accepted, perhaps based on passing some kind of detective's exam or perhaps based on more subjective criteria, generally they learn their trade on the job from senior investigators.

It should also be noted that truly experienced law enforcement investigators are not as common as depicted in film or on television. In fact, for most police officers, a homicide is a rare event that they may see once in a career if at all. And serial murder cases are almost unheard of (serial rape, robbery, and burglary cases are all too common, however). This is especially true for investigators working outside the United States, where rapes and homicides are much less frequent.

With respect to pre-employment education, most federal law enforcement agencies in the United States require a four-year college degree and/or varying amounts of experience depending on the agency. State and local agencies may require a four-year degree, though many do not. Assignment to specialized squads may also require specific internal or external certifications.

For example, assignment as an arson investigator in a local jurisdiction required the following (Cloer, 2009):

1. High school diploma or General Educational Development (GED) supplemented by five or more years knowledge and skills developed by work experience within the agency, with a minimum of one year experience as a Fire Investigator Technician
2. State of Georgia Firefighter Certification
3. State of Georgia Fire Investigator Certification
4. State of Georgia Peace Officer Certification

Marietta (Georgia) Police Department (MPD) leadership recommends officers attend various Peace Officer Standards and Training Counsel courses, such as interviews and interrogations, basic criminal investigations courses, and search warrants and affidavits, in preparation for a detective assignment. Upon selection as a detective, an officer attends specialized courses in homicide investigations, blood splatter interpretation, and others. Although a degree is not required at MPD for selection as a detective, if two applicants have the same qualifications, the degreed applicants will usually be selected (Beam, 2009).

College degree programs that most benefit investigators range from traditional criminology and criminal justice programs to specifically designed concentrations within these programs. At Kennesaw State University in Georgia, for example, the criminal justice major includes three concentrations; the Forensic Behavioral Sciences concentration offers students courses in Criminal Investigations, Profile of the Serial Offender, and Criminal Profiling and Analysis. It is the concentrations available within a criminology or criminal justice program that make a degree opportunity more focused and useful.

The author would argue, based on his years of performing investigations and educating future generations, that the ability to complete any four-year degree program should be a basic requirement for applicants pursuing investigatively oriented careers. The more focused on the specialty area of investigations, the better. Being able to complete such a program says that these applicants can commit to a course of study and achieve its completion, that they know how to work with equals (other students) and superiors (professors and administrators) in a constructive fashion, and that they have been given the basics of a liberal arts education—meaning that they know the world is bigger than themselves and their own experience. Likely, it also means they have tasted success and failure. All these are valuable experiences and invaluable raw material for future investigators. Unfortunately, this is not yet a requirement, and while many fine investigators lack a formal college education, it is still a very useful tool for discriminating qualified applicants at any point prior to and during a law enforcement career.

THE "OUTSIDE" EXPERT

As we have seen in this chapter, forensic criminologists of just about every kind may be asked to provide advice or opinions during administrative and criminal investigations by law enforcement. Often it is late in the investigation when leads and clues seem to be exhausted or after there has been a massive public failure or conflict of some kind and outside eyes are "requested." Investigators in law enforcement agencies may welcome another "set of eyes" examining their case, that is, if the outside expert is truly an expert. As explained by Chief David Beam of the MPD (2009): "They must be credentialed and have the background to testify as an expert witness in court in regard to whatever we are using them for." However, this cuts both ways, as those at the Ph.D. level have a tradition of simply rubbing law enforcement the wrong way—for being too theoretical or too uninformed.

The author offers the following advice to consulting forensic criminologists who may be unfamiliar with law enforcement practice and culture:

1. Ensure that agency personnel have a clear picture of what you can and will do. Do not lead them to think you will solve the case; rather, lead them to the thought that you may offer some ideas and direction.

2. Ensure that agency personnel know your qualifications, education, and experience. Although a curriculum vitae may provide insight, that alone will not impress the street-level investigator.

3. Remember that law enforcement is a rather closed society, and you may be viewed as an interloper. Do not expect to be welcomed with open arms by everyone in the agency.

4. Do not be hyper critical! Many agency leaders have a phobia about "airing their dirty laundry" or the perception that "they could not solve the case." If you find policies and procedures that need improvements, that issue should be addressed but is usually not the focus of the invitation to examine an investigation. If you find something wrong, help the agency find the fix to the imbroglio.

5. When investigators have performed well and done the right thing, kudos are in order.

6. Be truthful, do not embellish, do not exceed your area of expertise, and provide a bridge to a path for improving the resolution of the case.

7. Be prepared for the heinous cases to stay locked away in the recesses of your mind. They will not go away. Remember that at the end of the day, it is all about justice, not about you.

RATIOCINATION AND LUCUBRATION

The purpose of this chapter is to assist forensic criminologists' understanding of what law enforcement investigations involve, the various types of investigations, the roles of agencies, the problem of jurisdiction, educational requirements for investigators, and some advice if asked to opine on an investigation. We hope that this information will help with your ratiocination and lucubration.

Ratiocination is clear thinking; it is putting forth a logical argument. *Lucubration* is long, hard study, often at night, sometimes resulting in a written scholarly work. Both of these are considered required traits and tasks for forensic criminologists. In all things we do to ensure the scales of justice are balanced, we must be the epitome of critical thinking experts. "Critical thinkers prize truth and so are constantly on the lookout for inconsistencies, both in their own thinking and in the arguments and assertions of others" (Bassham, Irwin, Nardone, and Wallace, 2008, p. 5).

SUMMARY

To be effective forensic criminologists, we need to understand the logistics of how law enforcement operates. Although various jurisdictional issues are present everywhere, the fundamental goals and practices behind investigative efforts remain consistent across time and space. All investigators, whether they are carrying out an administrative or criminal investigation and regardless of whether they are local, state, or federal, have similar aims. That is, they seek to determine whether a crime or violation has been committed, to gather evidence and information related to the identity of the person suspected of carrying out this behavior, to locate and facilitate the arrest or discipline of the person, to recover property, and to prepare a case fit for criminal prosecution or disciplinary action. One of the over-arching differences between administrative and criminal investigations, then, is that many agencies are free to decide what to do with the results of administrative investigations. Administrative investigations are used to determine such things as demotions, suspensions, dismissals, promotions, changes to policy or protocol, and the like; whereas, criminal investigations often involve much more dire consequences in light of more serious violations. Unlike administrative investigations, then, criminal investigations carry with them the weight of the court and the law.

Apart from having serious consequences, criminal investigations also involve intelligence gathering, assessment, integration, and deduction. That is, information which has been gathered before a crime has occurred—in fact, in anticipation of it—can be very useful to law enforcement on many different levels and across jurisdictions.

It should also be noted that in law enforcement communities there are often jurisdictional and political considerations that need to be made known to forensic criminologists. Despite some good intelligence programs designed for information sharing, there is often little communication between agencies or even an open rivalry. This conflict may provide checks and balances to the agencies involved or have much more negative effects. In light of this, it is crucially important that forensic criminologists involved with these agencies, and the agencies themselves for that matter, maintain open lines of communication, an ability to think critically about themselves and others, and the initiative and motivation to get past any bumps in the road.

Review Questions

1. T/F Investigative goals and best practices change depending on the jurisdiction.
2. Explain the difference between administrative and criminal investigations in terms of who performs them, their goals, and the consequences of related violations.
3. T/F Police agencies have a zero-tolerance policy for pre-employment criminal conduct.
4. Why is it problematic to have an independent investigator with a prior law enforcement connection to carry out an administrative investigation?
5. What is the Garrity Rule? Why is it important for law enforcement?
6. Name and explain the three I's proposed by O'Hara (1970).
7. T/F The investigator is simply a fact collector. Why or why not?
8. When are forensic criminologists generally called in to assist with ongoing investigations?

REFERENCES

Bassham, C., Irwin, W., Nardone, H., Wallace, J.M., 2008. Critical Thinking: A Student's Introduction, third ed. McGraw-Hill, New York.

Beam, D., 2009. Deputy Chief, Marietta Police Department personal communication, January 18, 2009.

Carter, D.L., 2004. Law Enforcement Intelligence: A Guide for State, Local, and Tribal Law Enforcement Agencies. U.S. Department of Justice, Washington, DC.

Cloer, G., 2009. Investigator, Cobb County Fire Investigations Unit, personal communication, January 22, 2009.

Cobain, I., 2008. POLICE failing to Sack Drink-Drive Officers, UK. The Guardian, Monday, April 21.

Clymer, S., 2001. Compelled Statements from Police Officers and Garrity Immunity. N. Y. Univ. Law Rev. 76, 1309–1382.

Dienstein, W., 1995. Criminal Investigation. In: Bailey, W. (Ed.), The Encyclopedia of Police Science, second ed. Garland Publishing, New York.

Dodd, V., 2009. Police Played 'Spot the Black Officer in the Dark', Tribunal Hears UK. The Guardian March 2.

Eberly, T., 2008. One in Three Recent Atlanta Police Academy Graduates Have Criminal Records. The Atlanta Journal-Constitution October 12.

Field Manual Number 34–3, 1986. Intelligence Analysis. Headquarters, Department of the Army, Washington, DC.

Garrity v. New Jersey, 1967. U.S. Supreme Court, No. 13, 385 U.S. 493, January 16, 1967.

Georgia Bureau of Investigations, n.d. Retrieved January 19, 2009, from the Georgia Bureau of Investigations Web site: http://gbi.georgia.gov/02/gbi/home/0,2615,67862954,00.html

Gilbert, J.N., 2004. Criminal Investigations, sixth ed. Pearson Prentice Hall, Upper Saddle River, NJ.

Gross, H., 1906. Criminal Investigation. Ramasawmy Chetty, Madras, India.

Kaempffer, W., 2008. State Files Charges against Veteran Cop in Prostitution Case. New Haven Register December 4.

Kaempffer, W., 2009. Sullied City Cop Given Special Probation. New Haven Register February 3.

Lyman, M.D., 2008. Criminal Investigations: The Art and the Science, fifth ed. Pearson Prentice Hall, Upper Saddle River, NJ.

Miller, K., 1992. The Informed Argument: A Multidisciplinary Reader and Guide, third ed. Harcourt Brace Jovanovich, Inc, Orlando, FL.

Mollen, M., 1994. Commission Report. Commission to Investigate Allegations of Police Corruption and the Anti-Corruption Procedure of the Police Department, The City of New York, July 7.

O'Hara, C., 1970. Fundamentals of Criminal Investigation, second ed. Charles C. Thomas, Springfield, IL.

O'Connell, J., Soderman, H., 1936. Modern Criminal Investigation. Funk and Wagnalls Co., New York.

Ortmeier, P.J., 2006. Introduction to Law Enforcement and Criminal Justice, second ed. Pearson Prentice Hall, Upper Saddle River, NJ.

Peterson, M., 2005. Intelligence-Led Policing: The New Intelligence Architecture. U.S. Department of Justice, Washington, DC.

Savino, J., Turvey, B., 2004. Rape Investigation Handbook. Elsevier Science, Boston.

Soderman, H., O'Connell, J., 1935. Modern Criminal Investigation. Funk and Wagnalls Co., New York.

Turvey, B.E., 2008. Criminal Profiling: An Introduction to Behavioral Evidence Analysis, third ed. Elsevier Science, San Diego.

CHAPTER 11

The Criminal Investigator

Terry Goldsworthy

One should always look for a possible alternative and provide against it. It is the first rule of criminal investigation. It is of the highest importance in the art of detection to be able to recognize out of a number of facts, which are incidental and which vital. Otherwise your energy and attention must be dissipated instead of being concentrated.

("Sherlock Holmes" in *The Black Peter* by Sir Arthur Conan Doyle)

KEY TERMS

Investigation: The process of discovering, collecting, preparing, identifying, and presenting evidence to determine what happened and who is responsible.

Investigative Relevance: The significance of information to an investigation if it assists in the identification/apprehension of an offender.

Modus Operandi: An offender's mode of operating, which includes those acts that needed to be carried out for the crime to be completed.

Signature Behavior: Those acts committed by an offender that are not necessary to complete the offense.

Victimology: A victim profile which includes but is not limited to the victim's history, associates, criminal links, family, and financial records.

CONTENTS

The words of Sherlock Holmes illustrate that very often it is the small details which make for a successful investigation. The criminal investigator is in many regards a storyteller—the person charged with telling the story of the victim to the court in such a way that the story is impervious to criticism or doubt. Many cogs make up the machinery of the justice system, yet without doubt the most important is that of the criminal investigator. Without a competent investigator and a thorough investigation, many crimes would go unsolved and never proceed to the further stages of the justice system.

381

It is the detective who, as the investigator, arrests the offender and begins the judicial process that ultimately will see the offender punished for his or her crimes. The investigator brings the threads of evidence together and combines them into a legally presentable and compelling brief of evidence that will prove the guilt of the accused beyond a reasonable doubt. So what does an investigation involve and what does the investigator do?

WHAT IS AN INVESTIGATION?

When any crime has been committed, investigators are usually faced with the task of determining who is responsible for the crime, as in many cases the identity of the perpetrator is unknown. Law enforcement agencies, specifically detectives within such organizations, are called upon to investigate the crime with a view to bringing the offender to justice by successfully identifying and prosecuting him or her. The investigator becomes a collector of evidence, as well as a central figure in giving the investigation direction, which ultimately will determine the success or otherwise of the investigation. Bennett and Hess (2000, p. 3) state that an *investigation* is "the process of discovering, collecting, preparing, identifying and presenting evidence to determine what happened and who is responsible."

Swanson, Chamelin, and Territo (2000) and Bennett and Hess (2000) suggest that when a crime is committed, the investigator is charged with responsibilities. These responsibilities are to establish that a crime has been committed, to identify and apprehend the suspect, and to assist in prosecuting the suspect. In addition, the investigator needs to consider the following basic investigative principles during the course of the investigation:

- Determining whether a crime has been committed (e.g., is the death a murder or an accidental death as the result of some sexual behavior?). While this question may seem simple, it is often the most crucial question facing an investigator when arriving at the scene of an incident.
- Identifying the offender.
- Locating the offender.
- Identifying and showing a nexus between the offender and the victim and the crime. (This can be achieved in a number of ways, such as physical evidence, admissions, witness statements, etc.)

The initial notification of a crime is a crucial period. It is in this time period that evidence can be lost or destroyed by a failure of investigative agencies to take action to protect the crime scene. It is for this reason that the best policy is one of treating all potential scenes as crimes until proven otherwise. This is especially so in cases of serious assault or death in which the victim may not be able to provide a version of events and investigators need to rely on evidence at the scene to provide details of what occurred. No criticism can be leveled at investigators who are overcautious and treat a noncriminal event as a crime scene; however, failure to secure and process a crime scene due to inaction will be sure to draw criticism.

THE TRAITS OF A CRIMINAL INVESTIGATOR

Swanson et al. (2000) argue that much of the success of an investigation depends on the investigator being self-disciplined, professional, and attentive to detail. Peak et al. (1998, p. 165) put forward the following thoughts on what makes a good investigator:

> In addition to performing the usual investigative functions, investigators must be able to think logically, comprehend and understand complex masses of data, communicate and relate well with other members of the agency, and understand the concepts of organised crime, intelligence collecting and civil liberties. They must also have self-discipline, patience, attention to detail, knowledge of the law and some understanding of scientific techniques. Deductive and inductive reasoning and decision making abilities are also assets.

In Australia, the training of detectives has been standardized to some extent. Most state police services require detectives to have minimum lengths of service, usually three years, before being allowed to move to plain-clothes duties. Upon taking a position in a plain-clothes unit (which can include the Criminal Investigation Branch, Child Protection Units, or specialist units such as the Armed Robbery, Drug and Fraud Squads, etc.), officers are required to undertake specific training in relation to criminal investigation duties. In Queensland, this takes the form of three phases of detective training that total 10 weeks of intensive study in both the theory and practical aspects of criminal investigations. At the successful conclusion of such training, officers are able to apply for detective status if they can produce sufficient practical work examples and have a minimum of three years' worth of plain-clothes duties. If successful in this application, officers are given the designation of Detective and also awarded an Advanced Diploma in Investigative Practice.

Most police services have a generic Criminal Investigation Branch (CIB) or the like in regional areas. Specialist units will exist for specialized crimes such as sex offenses and murders in commands separate from the regions. These crimes require more expertise and by their very nature are usually more complex and protracted. The specialist units act as support to the general CIB units, which still undertake the majority of the investigation in most jurisdictions in Australia.

THE INVESTIGATIVE PROCESS: A MODEL

How should an investigator approach a crime? Is there a model or process the investigator can undertake to bring an investigation to a successful conclusion? At this point there is no definitive or standardized investigative model in use within most Australian police services. Certainly, it is basic knowledge and practical experience that dictates how investigations are usually approached. An investigation can be likened to a series of gates, at each of which certain evaluations and judgments must be made before proceeding to the next gate (Swanson et al., 2000, p. 23). But what if an officer does not possess sufficient experience to know how to approach an investigation? In that case an investigative model would clearly be of use to show how an investigation should be approached. In the model shown in Figure 11.1, it was decided to adopt

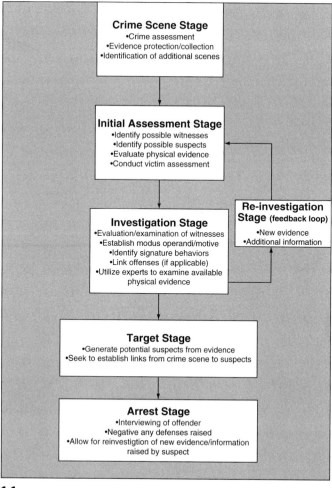

FIGURE 11.1

A model of the investigative process.

a generic form. The main reason for this is that in generic form the model is organic and can adapt to meet the differing requirements of various investigations (e.g., there will be elements in a rape investigation that do not apply to a burglary investigation, such as a medical examination of the victim and possible locations of evidentiary specimens).

Using such a model allows the investigator to follow a clear and logical series of steps or stages that can assist him or her in bringing the investigation to a successful conclusion. Bennett and Hess (2000) argue that it is essential that an investigation be conducted in a logical sequence and that all actions undertaken are legally defensible. The importance of this tenet cannot be underestimated because one legal flaw in the early stages can lead to a total disintegration of the case later. The saying "fruit from the poison vine" holds true in this respect. All evidence stemming from an earlier unlawful act can be subject to findings of inadmissibility at trial later.

Bowker (1999) states that an investigative plan can be used to focus the investigation to ensure all offense elements are addressed. It can also assist by ensuring investigators avoid duplication, coordinate activities, provide stability and communication, and finally it can also be a training aid to inexperienced staff. The use of this model allows investigators to focus on the overall goals of the investigation by clearly setting out the path they should follow to achieve these goals. Bennett and Hess (2000) and Swanson et al. (2000) support the idea of a preliminary investigation and a subsequent follow-up investigation. In the model in Figure 11.1, the preliminary investigation would include the crime scene stage and initial assessment stage. The follow-up investigation would consist of the investigation stage, target stage, and arrest stage.

To produce a model which allows for and deals with any eventuality would make the model too cumbersome. The model is designed to be simple to use and to provide investigators with an easy-to-understand series of stages that can easily be adapted to the crime under investigation. All the stages described in the following sections can be applied to any investigation.

Crime Scene Stage

The crime scene stage deals with the initial response of police to the report of an alleged crime. Rossmo (1997) states that the focus of any police investigation is the crime scene and its evidentiary contents. Often the first few minutes or hours will be crucial in ensuring that the scene is protected or evidence collected and in determining the success or otherwise of the investigation. In many cases the first officers to the scene will not be trained investigators but rather general duty officers with limited exposure to serious crimes and their associated crime scenes. Saferstein (1998, p. 38) argues, "It is the responsibility of the first officer arriving on the scene of a crime to take steps to preserve and protect the area to the greatest extent possible." Turco (1990) suggests that the final outcome of an investigation rests on thorough police work being conducted at the crime scene.

It is incumbent upon investigators, after being notified of a crime and its associated crime scene, to take steps to ensure that the scene is protected. This should be done by issuing clear commands to those officers on site until trained investigators can physically arrive at the scene. The scene needs to be cordoned of both from the public and perhaps more importantly from curious police officers who may wish to attend and enter the scene for no valid investigative purpose. Contamination of the scene after police have arrived is both preventable and unacceptable. The investigator should maintain command and control of the scene because he or she will be taking the matter to court in the event of an arrest; as such, the investigator is answerable for all actions taken in relation to the crime scene. While some forensic services or crime scene officers may argue they have control of the scene, in reality this is not the case; the forensic service personnel process the scene at the direction of the investigator.

Upon arrival, trained investigators need to make an initial assessment. Does the situation need to be treated as a crime scene or is it a noncriminal event (e.g., suicide versus homicide)? After having decided that the event should be treated as a crime scene, investigators should conduct a thorough examination of the crime scene and ensure that all evidence is protected and collected. The initial preservation, collection, and recording of physical evidence are important to the success of any investigation. This does not always happen. For example, in Sydney, New South Wales, police were called upon to investigate the serial murders of elderly women; these murders came to be called the "Granny Murders" (Hagan, 1992, p. 136):

> One of the problems experienced by the homicide investigators in the "Granny Murders" was the interference with crime scenes...persons acting in good faith, washed blood and other forensic material away from crime scenes prior to notification and arrival of police, so as to alleviate the anxiety that could be caused to other elderly people.

Particular attention should be given to determining if this is the only crime scene or whether there are secondary crime scenes that need to be located, according to Saferstein (1998, p. 38):

> Investigators will have only a limited amount of time to work a crime site in its untouched state. The opportunity to permanently record the scene in its original state must not be lost. Such records will not only prove useful during an investigation but are also required for presentation at trial....

Geberth (1996) states that it is important that, upon arrival at the scene, investigators implement crime scene procedures, supervise uniform personnel, and provide direction to the investigation. To facilitate this, an investigative team should be nominated; this team should consist of an arresting officer, a corroborating officer, and an exhibit officer. This procedure is standard in most police services for any major crime. The exhibit officer is responsible for protection and collection of exhibits, through to the examination of exhibits and their final production in court cases. The arresting officer and corroborating officer are responsible for interactions with suspects and have final responsibility prosecuting the matter to trial. This team should be overseen by a senior detective who has a broad management role in ensuring that the investigation progresses in an orderly fashion and maintains focus and direction. Part of this role is also ensuring that a Major Incident Room (MIR) or command post is established to support and manage investigative functions both at the crime scene and also the later stages of the investigation.

Initial Assessment Stage

By the initial assessment stage, trained investigators should have control of the investigation and begin to identify possible witnesses and suspects. They should begin this stage by evaluating physical evidence located with a view to assisting with suspect generation by prioritizing the most important evidence (e.g., DNA located at a scene is powerful evidence as compared to an unidentified item of clothing).

It is also at this point that the investigators should familiarize themselves with the victim by performing interviews with the victim, if still alive, or alternatively by conducting a *victimology* (or profile) if the victim is deceased. The profile should include the history of the victim, associates, criminal links, family, and financial records. This step is important because the characteristics of a victim can provide links to possible suspects; in particular, investigators may be able to be draw inferences about the offender's motive, modus operandi, and signature behaviors (Turvey, 1999). Having done this, the investigators should then begin the process of suspect generation with regard to the evidence available to them and the information known about the victim.

Investigation Stage

It is at the investigation stage that investigators undertake the most challenging work. At this point investigators must attempt to establish a motive for the crime. If this can be done and it is accurate, then this information will greatly assist in reducing the suspect pool. Further to this, signature behaviors also need to be identified because they will again reduce the suspect pool. Turvey (1999, p. 447) defines *signature behavior* as "those acts committed by an offender that are not necessary to complete the offense." The identification of signature behaviors will also allow investigators to link offenses that are being committed by the same offender in the case of serial offenses. If no signature behaviors are present in the crime, then investigators will need to prioritize suspects based on the evidence available and potential motives.

Conversely, by *modus operandi* (MO), we are looking at those acts which the offender had to complete to successfully carry out the crime (Turvey, 1999). Witness accounts also need to be closely examined at this stage and evaluated as to the assistance they can provide in generating a suspect. In this stage investigators should be ensuring that trained experts are evaluating all available physical evidence. Further to this, consideration also needs to be given to any matter that might require reinvestigation as a result of information obtained during this stage. These matters would be dealt with by a feedback loop which allows for reinvestigation of any new leads.

A timeline should also be completed initially in relation to the last 24 hours of the victim; this can be extended if required. This timeline will aid in understanding the movements of the victim and also contribute to potential motives; in addition, it will assist in reducing suspect pools to those with opportunities to commit the offense by comparison with the timeline.

Target Stage

Having carried out a thorough examination of the crime scene, investigators need to generate potential suspects from evidence available during the target stage. The investigators should then test the veracity of this evidence by seeking to establish links between the suspect and the crime. All available evidence needs to be channeled into providing a nexus between the suspect and the victim, both in relation to time and place and also motive.

It is at this point that investigators need to be fully conversant with the investigation as a whole, and they should be evaluating the importance of information gathered by the investigation with regards to generating potential suspects. The investigators should be developing an investigative/interview plan so that when the suspect is confronted, the investigators are clear of the direction and purpose of the action or questioning that they will undertake in the arrest stage.

Arrest Stage

Having generated a suspect during the target stage, the investigators will need to make a decision as to whether they take affirmative action against the potential suspect. This could be in the form of search warrants, surveillance, or bringing in the suspect for questioning. The investigators will have to make a decision on what form of action to take depending on the nature and strength of evidence against the suspect. By this stage the investigators should have sufficient evidence to link the offender to the crime. However, often it is the case that in speaking to the suspect, new evidence or information is gleaned. This information may also require reinvestigation. For example, the suspect indicates that on the day of the offense, he was driving a vehicle the investigators were unaware of; this vehicle would have to be seized and examined.

It has been noted that these stages are organic and fluid in their nature in that they should be able to change to meet the requirements of various types of investigation. For this reason, the preceding explanation of the various stages has been limited to a basic level so as not to detract from this nature. A key facet of the preceding stages is that they are all aimed at gathering and utilizing information that is relevant to the investigation. But how should investigators determine what information is relevant to the investigation and what is not?

THE ABILITY TO COMMUNICATE

The ability to communicate cannot be underestimated. It is here that investigators who have the ability to use social skills to form a relationship with a suspect will come to the fore. While much of criminal investigation could be regarded as a science, it is the crucial ability to form a rapport with the suspect that is an art. As a senior investigator, this author has seen many detectives fail in this regard, and this failure has resulted in a stymied investigation or a weakening of the prosecution case due to the suspect's refusing to be interviewed. The role of rapport building with the suspect is yet another tactical tool that investigators should use in their quest for information about a crime and evidence against a suspect.

With the introduction of the Police Powers and Responsibilities Act in Queensland, Australia, in the late 1990s, suspects were provided with a whole range of safeguards, such as the right to silence and the right to a solicitor, etc. The widely held perception among police at the time was that no longer would they be able to gain interviews with suspects after giving these warnings at the start of an interview. History has shown this is not the case. Experience has shown that good investigators will talk to a suspect about a whole range of issues not related to the crime, whereas inexperienced or bad investigators will talk to the suspect only about the crime, will talk down to the suspect, or worst of all, will even not interact with the suspect. Good investigators who can build a rapport with a suspect will more than likely be able to obtain an interview with the suspect. The reason is that the rapport-building process allows the investigator and suspect to humanize their interaction. No longer is it a clinical transaction taking place in the context of an investigation; rather, it takes on the nature of a conversation between two equals.

Investigative Relevance

All investigations depend on information to proceed to a successful conclusion. But not all information received during an investigation is of use. The Report of the Royal Commission on Police Powers and Procedures (1929, p. 22) stated, "The principal feature of the initial investigation into a crime is usually a widespread search for information." How do investigators determine what information is relevant to an investigation? To answer this question, perhaps we should examine a basic tenet of investigative practice. Many investigators, including this author, were taught that when approaching an investigation, the investigator should be able to answer the following questions at the conclusion of the investigation: who, what, where, when, why, and how. These can be referred to as the six basic investigative questions.

These basic questions can be expanded to ask the following: who did it, what did they do, where did they do it, when did they do it, why did they do it, and how did they do it. In general, most investigators are able to answer what, when, where, and how at an early stage in the majority of investigations. The factors usually unanswered are who did it and why they did it. Canter (1997, p. 486) states that investigators are usually faced with a situation in which the information available to them is constrained. It is constrained by the fact that the investigator has access to "…only an account of what has happened, who the victim is, where it took place and when." It could be suggested that any information or input that assists in answering one of the preceding investigative questions is investigatively relevant and could be useful to investigators. Upon examination of a crime scene, including the victim, the investigator may have some information as to what kind of person committed the offence. Once the evidence at the scene has been collected, referred to as the WHAT of the crime, the investigator may be able to determine the WHY of the crime—that is, the motivation behind each crime scene detail and for the crime itself. A basic premise of investigation is that if the WHAT and the WHY of the crime can be determined, then the WHO will follow.

In its most basic form, information can be said to be of *investigative relevance* if it assists in the identification or apprehension of an offender.

THE MEDIA

The influence of the media cannot be underestimated. In any high-profile investigation, the application of public and political pressure by the media can be enormous. This will be the job of the investigation manager to control and resist. The media are a great investigative tool and should be used as such.

The investigation manager and investigative team will need to decide to what tactical advantage they will use the media. While many investigators refuse to cooperate with the media at all if they can, this is in fact a negative response and fails to utilize a powerful tool. The media can be used to apply great tactical pressure to suspects and can be used to drive the search for information from the public, because more times than not, it is the information from the public rather than great detective work that solves a crime.

CONCLUSION

Criminal investigation is one of the most important functions of policing and is rarely out of the headlines or the public's imagination. Whether it is considered an art or a science, the challenges of a criminal investigation require that the investigator possess a variety of skills that range from the analytical and organizational to the ability to form relationships with people who have committed the most serious of crimes. It is for this reason that detectives are considered to be the elite of police services, and criminal investigation is seen to be one of the most challenging areas of policing in which to perform duty.

SUMMARY

When a crime is committed, investigators usually face the task of determining who did it, what they did, where they did it, why they did it, and how they did it. In many instances, depending on the available evidence, determining who and why are the most difficult questions to answer. Investigators are also charged with determining first and foremost whether a crime was committed, using legally defensible means to identify and locate an offender, as well as demonstrate a nexus between the offender and victim. To do this, investigators must be good communicators, able to establish a rapport with many different types of people, be self-disciplined and professional, and they must have an eye for detail.

In terms of actually carrying out their investigations, most investigators follow a model including a crime scene stage, as well as initial assessment, investigation, target, and arrest stages. Each of these stages also generally involves a feedback loop, where new evidence and information can be incorporated and some elements reinvestigated if necessary. During these stages, and their work in general, it is important that investigators focus on communication, maintaining investigative relevance and utilizing the media in their efforts. With these elements in mind, investigators will be better equipped to answer the questions posed to them in each investigation and to identify and apprehend offenders.

Review Questions

1. What are the crucial questions facing investigators when they first arrive at a crime scene?
2. T/F Great criticism can be/has been leveled at investigators who are overcautious and treat a noncriminal event as a crime scene.
3. What characteristics does it take to be a successful investigator? Why are these characteristics important to the job?
4. What are specialist units? Why are they present in any given jurisdiction?
5. Why is it essential that investigations be undertaken in a legally defensible fashion?
6. Name and describe the six stages of the investigative model.
7. Name and describe the role of each person in an investigative team.
8. What actions may be taken against potential suspects? How do investigators decide which of these actions to carry out?

REFERENCES

Bennett, W., Hess, K., 2000. Criminal Investigation. Wadsworth, Australia.

Bowker, A., 1999. Investigative Planning: Creating a Strong Foundation for White-Collar Crime Cases. FBI Law Enforcement Bulletin 68 (6), 22–25.

Canter, D., 1997. Psychology of Offender Profiling. In: Canter, D., Alison, L. (Eds.), Criminal Detection and Psychology of Crime. Ashgate Publishers, Great Britain.

Duties of the Police in the Investigation of Crimes and Offences—Obtaining of Evidence, The Report of the Royal Commission on Police Powers and Procedures, 1929. London: The Home Office. In: Canter, D., Alison, L. (Eds.), Criminal Detection and Psychology of Crime. Ashgate Publishers, Great Britain, pp. 22–41.

Geberth, V.J., 1996. Practical Homicide Investigation: Tactics Procedures and Forensic Techniques. CRC Press, Boston.

Hagan, M., 1992. Special Issues in Serial Murder. Conference paper presented as part of a group of papers titled The Police Perspective, 12–14 May, Canberra.

Peak, K., Evans, S., Adams, F., Ashby, H., 1998. Recruiting and Testing Criminal Investigators: A Job Related Approach. The Police Chief LXV (4), 165–168.

Rossmo, D., 1997. Place, Space, and Police Investigations: Hunting Serial Violent Criminals. In: Canter, D., Alison, L. (Eds.), Criminal Detection and Psychology of Crime. Ashgate Publishers, Great Britain.

Saferstein, R., 1998. Criminalistics—An Introduction to Forensic Science. Prentice Hall, New York.

Swanson, C., Chamelin, N., Territo, L., 2000. Criminal Investigation. McGraw Hill, Boston.

Turco, R., 1990. Psychological Profiling. Int. J. Offender Ther. Comp. Criminol. 34, 147–154.

Turvey, B., 1999. Criminal Profiling: An Introduction to Behavioural Evidence Analysis. Academic Press, London.

CHAPTER 12

Criminal Defense Investigations

Ronald J. Miller

KEY TERMS

Criminal Defense Investigator (CDI): An individual who performs investigative services for agencies, attorneys, or private clients on their behalf, outside the subordination of law enforcement.

Guilt Phase: The first phase of any trial, including those involving the death penalty, in which the jury decides whether the accused committed the crime and whether the special circumstances for capital murder have been met.

Mitigating Evidence: Any evidence that might provide a reason or rationale for a lighter sentence, including the defendant's character, upbringing, mental status, or circumstances of the crime. Most commonly a feature of death penalty cases because of the legal requirement to treat each defendant as a unique individual with respect punishment for the crime that has been committed.

Mitigation Specialist: A social and psychological biographer of the defendant who investigates, analyzes, and evaluates the life history of the defendant.

Penalty Phase: The second phase of a death penalty trial in which there is a separate jury vote to determine the ultimate sentence in this case, be it death or life without the possibility of parole.

CONTENTS

Much is written regarding the career opportunities associated with criminology, especially those in subspecialty areas such as law enforcement and the forensic sciences. In fact, most of the criminology literature has focused on the roles of government agencies providing services as part of, or on behalf of, the prosecution. Additionally, a dramatically exaggerated role of law enforcement associated crime investigation has been promoted in books, film, and television, both currently and historically. The continued stream

393

of this programming into popular culture, along with the selective nature of the criminology literature, has narrowed the perspective of educational programs and students alike. Colleges and universities teach criminology and criminal justice from a pro-law enforcement and pro-prosecution perspective. They tend to hire educators who perpetuate that view, and students are left without any sense of the careers available in private investigation, let alone that they are valid and necessary components of the criminal justice system.

The result of the current educational and adversarial climate is that criminal defense investigation is generally not taught at university as is police investigation, and that criminal defense investigators tend to be unacknowledged in a legitimate professional sense. The purpose of this chapter is to help correct that oversight; to educate readers regarding the nature and role of criminal defense investigations. Primarily that they exist, who performs them, and how they make a necessary set of contributions to the criminal justice system.

THE CRIMINAL DEFENSE INVESTIGATOR

Criminal defense investigators (CDIs) perform investigative services for agencies, attorneys, or private clients on their behalf. This work is done outside the subordination of law enforcement. Most often their cases involve criminal allegations or charges that have been brought, or may be brought, against a particular individual (e.g., defendants or suspects). There are investigators in civil litigation as well; however, that subspecialty of private investigations is beyond the focus of this effort. This chapter is intended to provide criminology students and professionals with a sense of what criminal defense investigators are, what they do, and why any of it matters.

There is probably no investigative endeavor that is more misunderstood by the general public than the function of criminal defense investigators. All too often, their role is reduced to the ignorant and false accusation that they are "trying to help get the defendant off." It is true that the CDI works for defense attorneys who are ethically bound to vigorously defend their clients and challenge the state's case. However, ethical CDIs are just as dedicated to uncovering fact and truth as their law enforcement counterparts. And, like police investigators, they are not in charge of deciding what happens in court.

As the blind scales of justice indicate, law and society require objective balance—the prosecution on one side and the defense on the other. If one becomes too powerful, the system becomes unbalanced, and justice for all will suffer. Criminal defense investigators are an important component with respect to maintaining this balance. In the United States in particular, their role has a strong historical foundation rooted in the ideals that our country first sought to exemplify. A brief refresher is warranted.

Consider these excerpts from the Constitution of the United States (1787) with its Bill of Rights (emphasis added):

Amendment 4

The right of the people to be secure in their persons, houses, papers, and effects, against unreasonable searches and seizures, shall not be violated, and no Warrants shall issue, but upon probable cause, supported by Oath or affirmation, and particularly describing the place to be searched, and the persons or things to be seized.

Amendment 5

No person shall be held to answer for a capital, or otherwise infamous crime, unless on a presentment or indictment of a Grand Jury, except in cases arising in the land or naval forces, or in the Militia, when in actual service in time of War or public danger; nor shall any person be subject for the same offense to be twice put in jeopardy of life or limb; nor shall be compelled in any criminal case to be a witness against himself, nor be deprived of life, liberty, or property, without due process of law; nor shall private property be taken for public use, without just compensation.

Amendment 6

In all criminal prosecutions, the accused shall enjoy the right to a speedy and public trial, by an impartial jury of the State and district wherein the crime shall have been committed, which district shall have been previously ascertained by law, and to be informed of the nature and cause of the accusation; to be confronted with the witnesses against him; to have compulsory process for obtaining witnesses in his favor, and to have the Assistance of Counsel for his defence.

The 14th Amendment:

...No State shall make or enforce any law which shall abridge the privileges or immunities of citizens of the United States; nor shall any State deprive any person of life, liberty, or property, without due process of law; nor deny to any person within its jurisdiction the equal protection of the laws.

There are, of course, other assurances in the U.S. Constitution besides these. However, it is apparent that the founding fathers specifically intended to protect the rights of those accused of committing crimes. This originated from a healthy fear of suffering abuses at the hands of the State and its less than scrupulous agents.

In 1963, the U.S. Supreme Court held in *Gideon v. Wainwright* that the right to counsel by an indigent defendant extended to all criminal proceedings, not just capital cases. Being poor should not be a factor in whether or not a defendant gets effective representation by counsel. Gideon was charged with breaking and entering in the state of Florida. He was indigent at the time and could not afford to hire a lawyer. He petitioned the court to have an attorney appointed for him at the court's expense; however, he was denied. Gideon was forced to represent himself in the criminal proceedings. He was convicted and sentenced to five years in prison. After a number of appeals, his case made its way to the United States Supreme Court. Upon review of the case, the Supreme Court decided unanimously that the United States Constitution 6th Amendment's guarantee to counsel was a fundamental right and essential to a fair trial. This right was extended to the states through the Due Process Clause of the 14th Amendment.

This right was nothing new at the federal level. However, in the advent of the civil rights movement in the 1960s, the U.S. Constitution was being forced upon many of the states under the provisions of the 14th Amendment. A state's own statutes must guarantee the minimum rights to the individual afforded by the U.S. Constitution, but not all states eagerly abide.

Gideon lays the groundwork for the role of the criminal defense investigator as court-appointed defense counsel requires the services of defense investigators to research and adequately prepare a defense case.

In more recent history, the U.S. Supreme Court has held (*Herring v. New York*, 1975):

> The very premise of our adversary system of criminal justice is that partisan advocacy on both sides of a case will best promote the ultimate objective that the guilty be convicted and the innocent go free.

This is rooted in the 6th Amendment, which guarantees that every criminal defendant be provided with "assistance of counsel" when preparing and presenting a defense. Subsequent to *Herring*, the U.S. Supreme Court further described the effectiveness of this counsel in a pair of landmark opinions requiring that a criminal defendant must receive "assistance of counsel" and that such assistance must be "effective" [See *US v. Cronic* (1984); *Strickland v. Washington* (1984)]. In April of 2004, the Supreme Court of the State of South Carolina succinctly described the functional role of these decisions in the investigation and representation of a criminal defendant (*Nance v. Frederick*, 2004):

> In Cronic, the Court characterized the protection that the Sixth Amendment affords the defendant:

> The right to the effective assistance of counsel is thus the right of the accused to require the prosecution's case to survive the crucible of meaningful adversarial testing. When a true adversarial criminal trial has been conducted—even if defense counsel may have made demonstrable

errors—the kind of testing envisioned by the Sixth Amendment has occurred. But if the process loses its character as a confrontation between adversaries, the constitutional guarantee is violated. As Judge Wyzanski has written: "While a criminal trial is not a game in which the participants are expected to enter the ring with a near match in skills, neither is it a sacrifice of unarmed prisoners to gladiators."

And further:

In Strickland, the Court set forth a two-part test for evaluating the effectiveness of the criminal defendant's attorney. To receive a new trial on the grounds of ineffectiveness of counsel, the petitioner must prove (1) that his counsel's representation was deficient, and (2) that there is a reasonable probability that counsel's deficient conduct prejudiced the outcome of petitioner's trial.

In their continued analysis of these issues in *Nance*, the Court found that (*Nance v. Frederick*, 2004):

The Court stated in Cronic that there are three circumstances in which the defendant's representation is so inadequate that the second element of the Strickland test, the prejudice element, can be presumed. Cronic, 466 U.S. at 658–659, 104 S. Ct. at 2039.

The first scenario in which prejudice is presumed is when there is a "complete denial of counsel," which occurs when a trial is rendered unfair because the defendant is denied assistance of counsel during a "critical stage" of his trial. Id.

In the second scenario, prejudice is presumed if "counsel entirely fails to subject the prosecution's case to a meaningful adversarial testing." When there has been no meaningful adversarial testing, then "the adversary process itself [is] presumptively unreliable." Id. In Bell v. Cone, the U.S. Supreme Court explained further that "the attorney's failure [to test the prosecutor's case] must be complete" for this standard to be met. T. 535 U.S. 685, 697, 122 S. Ct. 1843, 1851, 152 L. Ed. 2d 914 (2002).

Third, prejudice is presumed when circumstances dictate that no attorney could render effective assistance of counsel. Cronic, 466 U.S. at 659–662, 104 S. Ct. at 2047–2048.

Given the language afforded in the U.S. Constitution, and the continued support of the U.S. Supreme Court, the role of the criminal defense investigator is important for the effective administration of justice. Defendants are entitled to defend themselves when accused of crimes by the state. To do this, they need *effective assistance* of counsel and the ability to investigate the charges against them. Despite this reality, criminal defense investigators are rarely held in the same esteem by the courts, or the public, as sworn police officers or federal agents. However, their investigative roles are equally important and a deficit in efforts on either side of the courtroom places justice in a state of imbalance.

THE ROLE OF THE CDI

Keeping in mind the requirements for effective counsel already mentioned, there must also be effective investigation. Criminal investigation does not end with the arrest of a suspect or even with the conviction of a defendant. In fact, each of these events signals a new investigative beginning. In this context, the CDI is ultimately responsible for the reinvestigation of the case that is presented by the state against a defendant. This includes the reinterviewing all key witnesses and reviewing all police reports, crime lab reports, physical evidence, witness statements and statements made by the defendant to police and others. There is, additionally, a never-ending quest for evidence that is being withheld by the state from the defense. As explained in Ciolino (2005, p. 14):

> The first order of business in any old case is to assemble, locate, and organize all available discovery [a.k.a. disclosure] materials. This is much easier said than done. Often it turns into a full time job that will continue throughout your involvement in any specific case. It is a maddening, frustrating, and never-ending quest. But, at the end of the day, it must be accomplished.

Though describing "old" cases, or those inherited from other attorneys and investigators, this advice rings true for new cases as well. Getting the state's evidence assembled and organized must be a priority. Again, this is all done to identify and test the strength of evidence and theories that implicate the defendant. It also provides a foundation for the generation of alternate theories to explain that evidence, when feasible. This is the role of the CDI.

No matter what the case, an attorney cannot adequately represent a criminal defendant without some minimal investigative support. In some instances, that may simply involve an investigator being present to corroborate an interview by an attorney who is talking to witnesses. Because an attorney can't actually be a witness in his or her own cases, it is often necessary to have an independent witness (the investigator) to important events. The CDI can testify about what was observed in the event that a witness changes his or her story after speaking with police, after speaking with prosecutors, or after taking the stand. The more complex case, the more such tasks will be delegated to the CDI.

In 1995, the National Legal Aid and Defender Association published its *Performance Guidelines for Criminal Defense Representation* (NLADA, 1995). These guidelines are the framework constituting the basic "standards of practice" for defense counsel. The criminal defense investigator is a key figure in counsel's compliance to these guidelines. Note that when the word *counsel* is used, one can assume it to mean *counsel and/or his or her investigator*. The attorney has the responsibility to see that things get done, but the investigator is often the one who does all or part of the work to accomplish key tasks. The following was taken from NLADA (1995):

Guideline 4.1 Investigation

Counsel has a duty to conduct an independent investigation regardless of the accused's admissions or statements to the lawyer of facts constituting guilt. The investigation should be conducted as promptly as possible.

Sources of investigative information may include the following:

Charging documents

Copies of all charging documents in the case should be obtained and examined to determine the specific charges that have been brought against the accused. The relevant statutes and precedents should be examined to identify:

the elements of the offense(s) with which the accused is charged;

the defenses, ordinary and affirmative, that may be available;

any defects in the charging documents, constitutional or otherwise, such as statute of limitations or double jeopardy.

The accused

If not previously conducted, an in-depth interview of the client should be conducted as soon as possible and appropriate after appointment or retention of counsel. The interview with the client should be used to:

seek information concerning the incident or events giving rise to the charge(s) or improper police investigative practices or prosecutorial conduct which affects the client's rights;

explore the existence of other potential sources of information relating to the offense;

collect information relevant to sentencing.

Potential witnesses

Counsel should consider whether to interview the potential witnesses, including any complaining witnesses and others adverse to the accused. If the attorney conducts such interviews of potential witnesses, he or she should attempt to do so in the presence of a third person who will be available, if necessary, to testify as a defense witness at trial. Alternatively, counsel should have an investigator conduct such interviews.

The police and prosecution

Counsel should make efforts to secure information in the possession of the prosecution or law enforcement authorities, including police reports. Where necessary, counsel should pursue such efforts through formal and informal discovery unless a sound tactical reason exists for not doing so.

Physical evidence

Where appropriate, counsel should make a prompt request to the police or investigative agency for any physical evidence or expert reports relevant to the offense or sentencing.

The scene

Where appropriate, counsel should attempt to view the scene of the alleged offense. This should be done under circumstances as similar as possible to those existing at the time of the alleged incident (e.g., weather, time of day, and lighting conditions).

Expert assistance

Counsel should secure the assistance of experts where it is necessary or appropriate to:

> the preparation of the defense;
>
> adequate understanding of the prosecution's case;
>
> rebut the prosecution's case.

Additionally, the American Bar Association (ABA) has published similar guidelines for representation in capital cases (ABA, 2003). Although these are meant for cases involving the death penalty, most are applicable to all forms of criminal representation. These recommendations are based on both case law and the U.S. Constitution. The following excerpt from the ABA Guidelines is inclusive of those from the NLADA (ABA, 2003, p.1018):

1. Charging Documents:

Copies of all charging documents in the case should be obtained and examined in the context of the applicable law to identify:

a. the elements of the charged offense(s), including the element(s) alleged to make the death penalty applicable;
b. the defenses, ordinary and affirmative, that may be available to the substantive charge and to the applicability of the death penalty;
c. any issues, constitutional or otherwise, (such as statutes of limitations or double jeopardy) that can be raised to attack the charging documents; and
d. defense counsel's right to obtain information in the possession of the government, and the applicability, extent, and validity of any obligation that might arise to provide reciprocal discovery.

2. Potential Witnesses:

a. Barring exceptional circumstances, counsel should seek out and interview potential witnesses, including, but not limited to:

    (1) eyewitnesses or other witnesses having purported knowledge of events surrounding the alleged offense itself;
    (2) potential alibi witnesses;
    (3) witnesses familiar with aspects of the client's life history that might affect the likelihood that the client committed the charged offense(s), and the degree of culpability for the offense, including:
        (a) members of the client's immediate and extended family
        (b) neighbors, friends, and acquaintances who knew the client or his family
        (c) former teachers, clergy, employers, co-workers, social service providers, and doctors
        (d) correctional, probation, or parole officers;
    (4) members of the victim's family.

b. Counsel should conduct interviews of potential witnesses in the presence of a third person so that there is someone to call as a defense witness at trial. Alternatively, counsel should have an investigator or mitigation specialist conduct the interviews. Counsel should investigate all sources of possible impeachment of defense and prosecution witnesses.

The Police and Prosecution:

Counsel should make efforts to secure information in the possession of the prosecution or law enforcement authorities, including police reports, autopsy reports, photos, video or audio tape recordings, and crime scene and crime lab reports together with the underlying data therefore. Where necessary, counsel should pursue such efforts through formal and informal discovery.

Physical Evidence:

Counsel should make a prompt request to the relevant government agencies for any physical evidence or expert reports relevant to the offense or sentencing, as well as the underlying materials. With the assistance of appropriate experts, counsel should then aggressively re-examine all of the government's forensic evidence, and conduct appropriate analyses of all other available forensic evidence.

The Scene:

Counsel should view the scene of the alleged offense as soon as possible. This should be done under circumstances as similar as possible to those existing at the time of the alleged incident (e.g., weather, time of day, and lighting conditions).

These guidelines give the criminal defense investigator an overlay of the functions and responsibilities encountered in a major case. Just a cursory look reveals how complex and involved these responsibilities can be. In reality, very few individuals have the experience and skill necessary to perform a major case investigation on their own. Often they will have another investigator assist, appointed by the court or hired by the attorney to share the workload.

As already mentioned, the adversarial design of our judicial system requires that a competent defense challenge the prosecution's case. This function is so crucial that it bears repeating: every fact that the state claims in its charges against the defendant must be tested. In this sense, a process akin to the *scientific method* needs to be employed. This method is succinctly described by Turvey (2008, p. 44) as "[a] way to investigate how or why something works or how something happened, through the development of a hypothesis and subsequent attempts at falsification through testing and other accepted means."

The state, by means of indictment or complaint, has formed the hypothesis that the defendant has committed one or more crimes. It is unusual for state investigative agencies to attack their own case theories, a tendency that increases the likelihood of a biased outcome. Evidence that supports their charges is advanced, while other evidence that may not is ignored. In extreme cases it may even be altered or hidden.

This failure of investigative logic is not categorical for all prosecutorial investigations. There are many excellent and professional law enforcement officers and district attorneys who work hard to rule out all possible defects in their hypotheses and ensuing conclusions. The problem is that the defense does not know whether the case at hand was actually subjected to critical thinking or methodical examination. Many cases are sent up from a police agency for prosecution without the benefit of such rigor. It is the duty of the criminal defense investigator to be skeptical and examine all the facts and evidence available in the state's case to be able to disprove their theories. Whether the CDI fails or succeeds, the justice system is more informed for his or her efforts.

THE MITIGATION SPECIALIST

Sandra Lockett was the getaway driver in a pawnshop robbery that resulted in the proprietor's death. Lockett was tried for her involvement in the crime and ultimately convicted and sentenced to death. At issue was whether the State of Ohio had unconstitutionally prohibited Lockett from introducing *mitigating evidence* that could have persuaded a jury to sentence her to another sentence than death. That mitigating evidence would have included the victim's actions contributing to his death, that the offense was committed under duress and coercion, and the offense was the product of mental deficiencies.

In 1978, the U.S. Supreme Court considered the Lockett case and ruled that there is a constitutional right for every defendant in a capital case to be considered as an individual during his or her capital proceedings (*Lockett v. Ohio*, 1978). This meant consideration of mitigating factors. These factors included any aspect of a defendant's character, upbringing, mental status, or circumstances about the crime which might provide a reason for a sentence other than death. This seminal decision has been gradually expanded over the years to include *any factor* which the defendant believes might help a jury decide for a non death sentence. The defendant, the Supreme Court has ruled, must be sentenced as a unique individual in relation to the crime he or she has committed.

As a result of this and related decisions, death penalty trials are divided into two separate phases: the *guilt phase* and the *penalty phase*. In the guilt phase, the jury decides whether or not the defendant committed the crime and whether the special circumstances for capital murder have been met. Each state has different criteria, such as murder during the commission of another felony, murder of a police officer, or murder involving torture, to name just a few. When a capital defendant is found to be guilty, he or she is then entitled to a separate trial to determine what the punishment should be. This is referred to as the *penalty phase*. The options for punishment in the penalty phase include, generally, *death* or *life without the possibility of parole* (a.k.a. L-WOP).

In the landmark case of *Penry v. Lynaugh* (1988), the court re-emphasized that to preserve fairness, trial judges must allow the defense to present mitigation evidence when the death penalty is involved. The court stated that the failure to allow or provide mitigating evidence during the penalty phase can be as devastating as the failure to present proof of innocence in the guilt phase. This decision reinforced a growing recognition in the legal community of the importance of "humanizing" the defendant.

Out of the procedural need mandated in these court decisions has risen the need for the mitigation specialist. The *mitigation specialist* is essentially the social and psychological biographer of the defendant.

The Honorable Helen G. Berrigan perhaps best described the role of the mitigation specialist as follows (2008, p. 827):

> The mitigation specialist must have the skills and experience needed to investigate, analyze, evaluate the life history of the defendant. The specialists are generally trained in the social sciences, with college degrees in social work or psychology, similar to the probation officers and provide background data to judges on non-capital sentencing. They are adept at gathering institutional records, interviewing lay and professional people, and compiling case histories. Significantly, they are trained in uncovering family drama and screening for often subtle mental and psychological disorders. They are likewise experienced in interpersonal communication so they know how to develop trust and rapport with even the most difficult or distrustful of individuals. A criminal investigator is unlikely to have these skills. A typical criminal investigator is likely to have a law enforcement background, but without training in the social sciences. Such investigators are invaluable in preparing for the guilt phase of a capital case—they watch, when, and how the alleged crime occurred ("just the facts, ma'am") but are not skilled and assessing "why" it happened, which is the primary piece of the mitigation defense.
>
> Similarly, a criminal defense lawyer is unlikely to have the necessary skills to amass the mitigation evidence. Lawyers are adept at legal analysis, fitting facts to legal principles, dissecting prior jurisprudence—all essential to an effective defense but often involving abstract concepts far afield from the social sciences. Lawyers are not trained in the communication (particularly listening) skills needed, nor perhaps do they have the time or patience, to delve deeply into the life history of their client. They are not knowledgeable about uncovering

family abuse or assessing for mental illness, nor recognizing other nuanced factors that could be in valuable mitigation evidence. Lawyers are advocates, not investigators and certainly not social workers. On the contrary, lawyers are often perceived by clients and family members as intimidating, and if court appointed, may not even be trusted. Within the criminal justice system, mitigation specialists are needed for the monumental task of investigating, identifying, and developing the evidence needed for a constitutionally effective defense.

In 2003, the American Bar Association published its standards for the representation of capital defendants previously cited. With respect to penalty phase, the ABA (2003) has established the following as the minimal standard for preparation and presentation:

A. ..." In deciding which witnesses and evidence to prepare concerning penalty, the areas counsel should consider include the following:

Witnesses familiar with and evidence relating to the client's life and development, from conception to the time of sentencing, that would be explanatory of the offense(s) for which the client is being sentenced, would rebut or explain evidence presented by the prosecutor, would present positive aspects of the client's life, or would otherwise support a sentence less than death;

Expert and lay witnesses along with supporting documentation (e.g., school records, military records) to provide medical, psychological, sociological, cultural or other insights into the client's mental and/or emotional state and life history that may explain or lessen the client's culpability for the underlying offense(s); to give a favorable opinion as to the client's capacity for rehabilitation, or adaptation to prison; to explain possible treatment programs; or otherwise support a sentence less than death; and/or to rebut or explain evidence presented by the prosecutor;

Witnesses who can testify about the applicable alternative to a death sentence and/or the conditions under which the alternative sentence would be served;

Witnesses who can testify about the adverse impact of the client's execution on the client's family and loved ones.

Demonstrative evidence, such as photos, videos, and physical objects (e.g., trophies, artwork, military medals), and documents that humanize the client or portray him positively, such as certificates

of earned awards, favorable press accounts, and letters of praise
or reference.

Each state has particular statutory sentencing guidelines too numerous to discuss in this chapter. However, in the penalty phase of a capital trial, there are generally four questions that the jury must answer to pass their sentence. Those basic four questions are:

1. Was the conduct that caused the death of the decedent committed deliberately and with the reasonable expectation that the death would occur?
2. Is there a probability that the defendant would commit criminal acts of violence that would constitute a continuing threat to society?
3. Was the conduct of the defendant in killing (the decedents) unreasonable in response to the provocation, if any, by the decedent(s)?
4. Should the defendant receive the death sentence?

The jury of 12 persons votes for each question separately, for a total of 48 votes. If one person votes "no" on any one question, the sentence is automatically life without parole or as defined by state statute.

The fourth question is the focus of the mitigation specialist. One juror can say "no" to the fourth question for any reason, and there is no burden to prove any reason beyond a reasonable doubt.

A mitigation specialist's role is unique in the world of the criminal defense investigator. As described in the ABA's guidelines of 2003, the focus of the mitigation specialist is on the defendant and minimally on the criminal fact case. The mitigation specialist focuses on the following:

Obtaining a complete understanding of the crime with respect to the
defendant's behavior. This includes:

- Complete crime scene reconstruction.
- Roles of other participants, including the victim.
- Physical evidence of any preplanning or attempts to conceal the crime after it occurred.
- Signs or symptoms of altered thinking or perceptual process of the defendant by impairment of mental disorder, brain damage, toxins (drugs and alcohol), dementia, developmental disability.
- Accuracy of the defendant's recollection of events as compared to the physical evidence and/or witness description.

Establishing trust and rapport with family members and those who "know
the family secrets," i.e., physical, emotional, sexual abuse.
Obtaining multiple, in-depth interviews with family members.
Identifying, locating, and interviewing all available teachers, counselors,
doctors, psychologists, and other third parties who would have
witnessed the defendant at various stages of development and

comment on positive traits, situational stressors, or family dysfunction with examples of each.

Locating all educational, counseling, mental health treatment, and medical records, pertaining to the defendant as a youth and adult.

Locating all available prenatal medical records of mother and child and birth records including a birth certificate.

Locating all available medical, mental health, and legal records of all first-order relatives (mother, father, siblings).

Locating all available information leading to identification of all family members going back three generations; create a genogram showing

- Documents and verification of all mental health, abuse, drug and alcohol abuse.
- Criminal records of these family members.
- Allegations of child abuse, sex abuse, emotional abuse.
- Location and interviews of childhood friends and neighbors.
- The identification of potential contemporaneous mental health issues at the time of the crime or in preparation of trial. Ongoing awareness of the defendant's functioning with respect to behavior at the time of the crime and ability to aid and assist (competency to proceed) in his or her own defense.

Identifying appropriate experts for examination of the defendant and providing them with the background materials relevant to their examinations.

Facilitating the examination of the defendant by various psychological and psychiatric experts to evaluate

- Competency and ability to formulate intent.
- Neuropsychological deficits. How does the defendant's brain function with respect to the ability to process information, make decisions, modulate mood and affect, restrain impulsive behavior?
- Drug and alcohol issues with respect to functioning at the time of the crime.

Assembling all the data known about the defendant into a biographical story that can be told by testimony and demonstrative evidence (document exhibits, photos, etc.).

Focusing on the positive worth of the individual to balance the demonization of the defendant that will take place as "aggravating factors" by the prosecution.

Being aware of any factor that might convince a juror to vote "no" to a death sentence.

Having thorough and complete knowledge of all potential aggravating factors as defined by statute in the jurisdiction of trial (i.e., multiple victims, lying in wait, death in the commission of another felony, killing of a police officer, killing of a child under 12, previous felony convictions, etc.) which could be used by the state when seeking the sentence of death.

Assembling this study, arranging the witnesses to testify, and assisting counsel in presenting the mitigation study to the jury.

The mitigation investigation is often inappropriately referred to as providing for the "abuse excuse." This presents a paradox for those who wish to promote the "abuse excuse" as being without merit, as it is evidence of a disingenuous desire for retribution. If our culture doesn't believe that abuse has a dramatic, harmful effect on children and their development to healthy adulthood, why do we so aggressively prosecute child abusers and send child molesters to prison for life? Obviously mitigation is not about generating an "excuse" but rather providing a context with respect to how an individual might come to commit a horrific crime. It is about giving the jury a complete and honest description of a person that they are charged to either kill or let live. There is no greater responsibility for a person than to cast judgment for life or death on another human being. Each juror has the right to know everything that is relevant to his or her decision. Because that decision is personal for each juror, the Supreme Court has said that anything can be a mitigating factor. The mitigation specialist is charged with preparing a case for life instead of death. It is a responsibility not to be taken lightly or by the ill prepared.

As mentioned previously in this chapter, mitigation is an area in which forensic criminologists in particular can provide useful information and insights.

CASE EXAMPLE

Following is an abbreviated example of a mitigation investigation which was presented in the Post Conviction Relief Petition trial of a man on death row on the West Coast. Because this petition was denied at the state circuit court level, it remains in litigation and will likely proceed to the federal courts under a habeas corpus petition. This may take years to litigate.

The names have been changed for the consideration of those involved. The facts are as otherwise presented and in the public record. This "story" is extracted from a report written by a mitigation specialist in this case. It is written in the first person and in the words of the mitigation specialist. The specialist was hired to determine any mitigating circumstances and to testify as an expert witness as to the failure of the original trial counsel to present mitigation evidence to the jury in the penalty phase of the trial. This testimony was presented in a trial for post conviction relief. The defendant is identified as "the Petitioner" because he is petitioning the court for a new penalty phase trial. Guilt is not an issue because he has already finished the guilt phase of the trial and was convicted. The basis for the petition involved numerous claims of what is referred to as "ineffective assistance of counsel" (a.k.a. IAC).

It should be noted that the vast majority of the material presented in this description of the defendant's life was not presented at trial, nor was trial counsel aware of it due to a lack of any mitigation investigation. This information would have been for the benefit of the jury to understand more about the defendant's character and upbringing in a very dysfunctional family. This, of course, does not excuse the defendant's actions but certainly clarifies what led him to such actions. In cases such as this, recall that it takes only one juror, deciding that he or she does not believe the offender should be put to death, to allow for life in prison instead of a death sentence.

The Story of William Hansen

I have worked with and studied families for close to 20 years in clinical practice. I have seen the dynamics at play and how people try to survive. It is not an overnight process. The story evolves from efforts to survive and exercising of choices that cumulatively might result in disaster. This is a likely story which might have helped explain to the jury how this awful crime occurred. It would help explain why a structured, drug-free setting, away from the severe emotional stress and abuse of and by loved ones, such as the penitentiary would be a viable option to death [for this offender]. Every juror knows of someone who has endured similar events in his story and it is likely that at least one juror would identify with the Petitioner and have mercy. This story is based on the insights and observations of those persons who knew the Petitioner and his family. This was the story that was not told [during the original penalty phase] yet all the information was available in 1995 for the asking, assembling and presentation to the jury. There are more details to this story which should have been presented at trial through the testimony of numerous witnesses. It is not an excuse for what William Hansen did on May 10, 1994, but it does help explain how this horrible event may have evolved.

The onset of the circumstances that contributed to the Petitioner's eventual participation of this brutal homicide may have begun at least a generation before. Donna Hansen, mother of the Petitioner, was herself a product and victim of a home in which poverty, abandonment, physical and emotional abuse prevailed. She and her family survived that situation the best that they could. She developed certain coping skills, some of which she learned from her own mother, to move forward in her life. Probably the most obvious of those which she recognizes herself is the ability to stifle emotions and not reveal how she is feeling. Doing so probably protected her from emotional and physical abuse as a young woman. At 17, she became involved with James Hansen and left with him at 18 in a "jailbreak marriage." She was hopeful that such a marriage would provide her an escape from the environment in which she was living. Approximately a year after their marriage, the Petitioner, William Hansen, was born. It is not clear when James Hansen's consumption of alcohol became problematic in their relationship. He maintained a job and along with Donna was able to provide the family with a reasonable standard of living. As time progressed the old coping skill of maintaining a poker face became once again functional for Donna Hansen in her marriage to an alcoholic, angry, and abusive man. As the children grew, they too adopted this style of coping. It is a classic alcoholic family dynamic that the children adopt one of several roles to survive the chaos and unpredictability. In order to cope and avoid the scrutiny of an intoxicated, angry and unpredictable parent, children often develop the skills to become "invisible." They do not express their emotions for fear of retribution, nor do they interact intimately with their parents. If you don't take risks—you don't get hurt.

By the time the Petitioner entered elementary school, he had likely already learned to be very careful in his relationships. As reported by his elementary school teachers, he was cautious in entering into group activities where he had to disclose anything about himself. He also would often become "needy" from some of his teachers, usually women and cautious in his relationships with male teachers. His early struggling in academics could have been a result of situational stress or perhaps a mild learning disability. He had a history of a head injury resulting in a loss of consciousness at a very young age reported by mother to your Affiant in an interview in 2000. It is unknown whether or not this injury may have contributed to his learning difficulties. It may have been prophetic, that as early as the second grade his teachers and school psychologist realized that William needed structure and consistency to be successful. The possibility of a learning disability would only complicate matters if not addressed. William's mother has little recollection or familiarity with his educational history, which is suggestive of a possible emotional "disconnect" with Petitioner and his education and life.

Over time, William Hansen began demonstrating an increased desire to withdraw and disengage from other people. He began retreating into video games and other solo activities. As he became older he withdrew into music and drugs. He began to become increasingly oppositional with his parents. Petitioner's mother stated that she would make William promise not to do drugs and he would agree but that he would then ignore her. There was no follow through discipline by either parent. Along the way, he demonstrated by his art to Marjorie Perry, a dysfunctional and chaotic family. A picture drawn by the Petitioner depicted a family watching chaos on the television. ***Petitioner's Exhibit #100.*** There was no personal connection between the characters in this picture as all one could see were the back of their heads. There was a small animal crawling up a curtain which was described as a rat or a mouse to Ms. Perry by the Petitioner. Petitioner reported to Ms. Perry that his father, James Hansen, shot mice or rats off the curtains with a BB gun in the living room while they were watching TV—a subtle hint of violence in what would normally be considered a peaceful family gathering. This was a family which was very skilled at concealing the events that occurred within the four walls of that home. William Hansen recalls his father drinking beer to intoxication "as far back as he could remember." His mother, Donna Hansen, reported to me that her husband would drink to intoxication and while cleaning his guns express his anger—brandishing the guns to her and himself. He was undoubtedly upset at his wife's described "cold and icy" demeanor and withdrawal from him and the other family members. That was her defense from the abuse. Donna Hansen said that during these drunken episodes with firearms, James Hansen would threaten to kill her, kill William and Jonas, and set the house on fire and then kill himself. He would then threaten to go to the garage and kill himself at which time she would follow him out and talk him out of it. These rants by Mr. Hansen occurred in the home while it was occupied by the Petitioner and his younger brother. I spoke to the neighbor across the street, Nina Olsen, who heard loud noises, apparent yelling, emanating from the Hansen household.

At 14 or 15 years of age, the Petitioner began smoking large quantities of marijuana on a daily basis. He dropped out of school in the 10th Grade and generally rebelled against his father. His father was adamant against drugs yet did not see his own drug addiction to alcohol. ***See Trial Testimony 1509.*** The mother's emotional withdrawal from the family was the model for the Petitioner's own withdrawal from the world.

Approximately one month before the murder at the 7–11 Mini Mart, Donna Hansen decided it was time to leave the marriage and did so a month after the murder. She chose to reduce her stress levels by leaving her husband. It was a matter of survival for her. William, chose to stay with his father, he told your Affiant on one occasion: "I could control him—I made sure he ate." He was acting the classic role of an enabler. The Petitioner himself had been avoiding the emotional conflict by increased amounts of marijuana smoking for several years and large amounts of LSD for several months prior to the murder. Petitioner's mother told your Affiant in an interview that she announced her intention to leave his father several weeks before the 7–11 Mini Mart murder. She testified that she moved out a short time after the murder. *See Trial Testimony 1474.*

The state attempts to present this horrific crime in simplistic terms. As a mitigation expert, I know that it is imperative that in a death penalty case that the Defendant's life be presented in its entirety, with all of its complexities. Unless a thorough examination of the Defendant's life and development are conducted, and presented, the jury is denied all the information they need to render a verdict other than death.

...

The Fourth Question "Should the defendant receive the death sentence?" requires that defense counsel "tell the defendant's story" to enable single or multiple jurors to find a reason not to impose a capital sentence. The process of telling that story and the research and experience needed to do so have been outlined thoroughly through the capital defense literature and numerous state and federal Appellate and Supreme Court decisions. The references provided at the beginning of this affidavit demonstrate that the process has been evolving for years prior to the 1995 trial. In this particular case, it is my opinion as a trained and experienced death penalty investigator and mitigation specialist, that although the defense investigators appointed to both the fact and mitigation investigations had the best of intentions, they were not equipped to adequately recognize salient sociological, psychological, and family systems dynamics to be able to provide trial counsel and the psychological experts retained by defense counsel the information on which to tell the complete story of William Hansen. Capital defendants rarely come from highly functional families. These families are often closed, secretive, and uncooperative and many even sabotage counsel's efforts during the penalty phase. Trial counsel has a responsibility to ensure that the defense team has an individual or individuals trained in the intervention and understanding of complex family dynamics to assist the fact investigators and experts in gathering this valuable information and managing difficult or special needs clients and their families. In the capital trial of William J. Hansen, it is my opinion that trial counsel were clearly deficient and were inadequate in this aspect of preparing for the penalty phase. The Petitioner's due process right to have his story adequately told did not occur and the jury's right to hear his story was denied. The opportunity for a likely sympathetic juror to impose a life sentence was missed.

KNOWLEDGE AND EDUCATION

Criminal defense investigation is equal parts shoe leather, interviewing, and research. Therefore, a host of skills are needed to be successful. But it is also important to accept that no one investigator can do everything. This is why many investigators specialize while finding a broad knowledge base invaluable.

Consider the following examples of the kinds of knowledge that generally prove helpful to CDIs, with the caveat that they are not necessarily trying to become experts in their own right.

Knowledge of Forensic Subjects and Experts

Good CDIs will have an extensive library consisting of reference material developed from every case they've worked. This will include manuals and articles on general criminal procedure and law, as well as textbooks and journals on everything from pharmacology to forensic science and psychology. Albert Einstein prided himself on not knowing the answer to every question but knowing where to find the answer. Any investigator with that kind of skill and humility is a huge asset.

Further still, developing a large database of forensic experts from a wide variety of specialties is crucial. The reason is that most attorneys are not adept at locating experts in areas that they have not explored in previous cases. Investigators must therefore start collecting expert curriculum vitae (or resumes) and business cards very early in their career—sorting the good from the bad, the competent from the inept, and the ethical from the frauds. Many attorneys specifically hire or seek to appoint investigators because of their broad fund of knowledge and reputation in this regard.

Knowledge of Legal and Police Procedures

Criminal defense investigators need a working knowledge of criminal law and police procedures. Consequently, former law enforcement investigators entering the field of private investigation have a distinct advantage. However, this should not dissuade a new investigator who lacks such a background. The reason is that many law enforcement investigators lack this knowledge themselves, and it is not a secret knowable only to a select few.

The law and related legal rulings are publicly available. And, being in or part of a bureaucracy, most law enforcement investigators and their respective agencies are slow to keep up with the changes in the legal landscape—that is, unless such changes involve an issue that has adversely affected their own criminal caseload or departmental liability.

Moreover, in most states, law enforcement agency policy and procedure manuals, as well as training materials, are available pursuant to a public records disclosure request. These materials must be requested at the outset of every case and made part of the investigator's library. In many law enforcement agencies, policy and procedure manuals are read only once, if ever, by employees and then not revisited. Even if employees do read up on their own agency, that is generally the limit of their knowledge.

Given these realities, it is easy to appreciate how CDIs can accumulate manuals and materials from multiple agencies and thereby develop knowledge that is equal to, if not superior to, that of their law enforcement counterparts in this regard.

However, dedicated CDIs will not stop there. The author recommends that investigators should attend the continuing legal education seminars given to defense attorneys by their various professional organizations. There are also numerous resources available from professional investigator organizations. And finally, Perron (1998) and Ciolino (2005) have written excellent guides for criminal offense investigators which essentially outline various approaches to conducting criminal defense investigations. These are excellent references for new investigators and a good review for seasoned CDIs.

A CDI's development of legal and law enforcement procedural knowledge should be viewed as an ongoing process that never ends, as law, policies, and procedures are constantly evolving.

Educational Background

While there are no formal educational background requirements in this profession, CDIs without an education beyond high school are operating at a distinct disadvantage. They must possess the ability to read with comprehension, to perform research on any subject drawing from a variety of databases, and to write their observations clearly. They must also be able to think critically. In terms of subject matter, CDIs must be equally conversant in the law, human behavior, and the forensic sciences. Degrees in criminology, criminal justice, history, psychology, sociology, law, and forensic science are therefore among those most recommended.

Education is a process and not a result; therefore, CDIs must remain current. Typically, this may be accomplished by satisfying the continuing education requirements of investigative professional organizations of any actual merit. Therefore, it is recommended that CDIs join such organizations.

CHALLENGES FOR THE CDI

This brief discussion is presented to prepare aspiring CDIs for some of the realities of being a private or court-appointed investigator.

Income

Some criminal defense investigators work for the government in salaried positions. The federal defender, the state public defender, and the public defender at a county level—each of these may employ full-time criminal investigators shared as a resource among multiple attorneys. Even some large law firms and insurance companies do the same.

However, the vast majority of criminal defense investigators are self-employed, independent contractors. Consequently, they do not have a regular flow of income and must live case-to-case, billing at a preapproved hourly rate. Compensation for one's work at a rate commensurate with one's skill and knowledge requires discipline and perseverance.

When hired by a client through an attorney on a "retained" case (where the accused pays for his or her own defense), CDIs usually are paid by the hour at a rate agreeable to the client and investigator or on a flat "case rate" basis. Smart CDIs will be paid upfront through a "retainer" and continue to work only when there is "money in the account." If clients lose their case, which they often do, they tend not to pay as willingly or in some cases at all.

The hourly rates charged by CDIs vary greatly by jurisdiction, with some regions paying a viable rate and other areas a pittance to the attorney and the investigator. Those areas that are economically depressed and mostly rural tend to provide less assistance. There are many considerations regarding how one establishes a fee schedule. Knowledge, skill, experience, and demand are perhaps the most key determinants to an investigator's rate.

CDIs doing strictly indigent defense cases must work many hours and keep overhead very low to make a living. Most investigators strive to keep a balance of retained and court-appointed cases. The business aspect of private investigators and criminal defense investigators in particular is, to say the least, difficult.

The "Power of the Badge"

Apart from how CDIs are paid, the most significant challenge is the disparity in public recognition between law enforcement investigators and the private investigator community. Police officers or federal agents can walk into just about any business, school, hospital, or other law enforcement agency and, upon displaying their official credentials, can usually count on immediate assistance. This is commonly referred to as the "power of the badge"; a reference to circumstances in which people comply with law enforcement requests whether there is a legal requirement to do so or not.

There is a tradition of cultural deference to law enforcement officials based on their statutory powers and, quite frankly, the resulting public fear. As private investigators, CDIs have no legal authority save those of every other citizen. There is no duty to arrest or to intervene in criminal behavior. Nor is there a statutory obligation for ordinary citizens to comply or cooperate with CDIs unless there is a court order. Therefore, while private CDIs may have state licensure credentials, rarely will these have the same impact with respect to obtaining cooperation as the police badge.

Skilled CDIs soon learn that it is necessary to develop a style and approach that helps obtain cooperation in getting the information being sought. Good people skills are a must. On the other hand, sarcasm, arrogance, and a threatening demeanor will not work the majority of the time, nor is such behavior professional. Good CDIs will have the skill to blend in to the culture in which they are operating and present themselves as genuine, respectful, trustworthy, and assertive persons. Developing a personal style that encourages witnesses and other persons to be willing to talk about subjects and topics about which they do not wish to speak is a critical skill for CDIs.

It is not uncommon for the "power of the badge" and the occasional arrogance that accompany it to make this job easier for CDIs. Such interactions leave a bad taste in the mouths of many. For this reason, a badge is the last symbol that many CDIs want to display.

SUMMARY

Criminal defense investigators are essential to the balance of any adversarial system and are specifically allowed under the U.S. Constitution. These individuals perform investigative services for agencies, attorneys, or private clients on their behalf, outside the subordination of law enforcement. The role of the CDI basically includes reinvestigating the case that will be presented by the state against a defendant. This includes all the general tasks of a police investigator, such as interviewing and reinterviewing witnesses, victims, and suspects; reviewing reports, statements, and physical evidence; as well as undergoing the never-ending quest for evidence that the state wishes to withhold. It is therefore a CDI's job to identify and test the strength of evidence and theories that implicate the defendant, as well as any alternate theories. Specifically, CDIs should examine the charging documents, potential witnesses, the police and prosecution, the physical evidence, and the crime scene in every case they encounter. Their role becomes even more important in death penalty cases.

Similar to CDIs are mitigation specialists who gather evidence for the penalty phase of capital cases. These individuals also work for the defense, in an effort to bring to light mitigating evidence which allows the jury to assess the defendant as a unique individual. Basically, mitigation specialists are biographers of the defendant who gather information about any aspect of his or her history or character that will allow the jury to make a more informed decision in regards to whether this person deserves the death penalty. This role is not about providing excuses; rather, it centers around putting the crime in context in terms of the defendant's life, allowing the jury to understand more about how such a person could come to commit this crime.

To be successful CDIs or mitigation specialists, individuals must have a well-rounded knowledge of forensic subjects, as well as the experts who practice these specialties. They must have a working knowledge of criminal law and police procedures, as well at the ability to interact with many different types of people since they do not have the luxury of simply flashing a badge to get information.

Review Questions

1. Explain how *Gideon v. Wainwright* laid the groundwork for the role of CDIs.
2. What does a CDI's work involve? What is the purpose of a CDI?
3. T/F It is the prosecution's job to test every fact that they are claiming in their charges against the defendant.
4. T/F CDIs should work under the assumption that each case at hand was not subjected to critical thinking or methodical examination.
5. Why is mitigating evidence allowed in death penalty cases?
6. What is a mitigation specialist? How does this role differ from that of the CDI?
7. What are the four questions that the jury must answer during the penalty phase of a death penalty case?
8. Discuss the challenges that face the CDI.

REFERENCES

American Bar Association, 2003. Guidelines for the Appointment and Performance of Defense Counsel in Death Penalty Cases, Revised Edition. Hofstra Law Review 31 (4), Summer.

Berrigan, H.G., 2008. The Indispensable Role of the Mitigation Specialist in a Capital Case: A View from the Federal Bench. Hofstra Law Review 36 (3), 819.

Ciolino, P., 2005. In The Company of Giants: The Ultimate Investigation Guide for Legal Professionals, Journalists & The Wrongly Convicted. iUniverse, Inc., New York.

Gideon v. Wainwright, 1963. 372 U.S. Supreme Court No. 155, March 18.

Herring v. New York, 1975. 422 U.S. Supreme Court 853, No. 73-6587; June 30.

Lockett v. Ohio, 1978. 438 U.S. 586, 98 S.Ct. 2954, 57L.Ed.2d 973.

Nance v. Frederick, 2004. South Carolina Supreme Court, Opinion No. 25814, April 26.

National Legal Aid and Defender Association, 1995. Performance Guidelines for Criminal Defense Representation. Washington, DC; url: http://www.nlada.org/Defender/Defender_Standards/Performance_Guidelines

Penry v. Lynaugh, 1988. 492, U.S. 302, 319, 106 L. Ed. 2d256, 109 S. Ct. 2934.

Perron, B., 1998. Uncovering Reasonable Doubt. Morris Publishing, Kearny, NJ.

Strickland v. Washington, 1984. 466 U.S. Supreme Court 668, No. 82-1554, May 14.

The United States Constitution, 1787. Constitutional Convention. Philadelphia, PA. September 17.

Turvey, B., 2008. Criminal Profiling, third ed. Elsevier Science, San Diego.

United States v. Cronic, 1984. 466 U.S. Supreme Court 648, No. 82-660, May 14.

CHAPTER 13

Forensic Scientists

Brent E. Turvey

KEY TERMS

Bloodstain Pattern Analysis: The examination of the shapes, locations, and distribution patterns of bloodstains for the purpose of interpreting the physical events that caused them (Chisum, 2007).

Bloodstain Patterns: The visible record of the blood shed at a crime scene.

Crime Reconstruction: The determination of the actions and events surrounding the commission of a crime.

Digital Evidence Analysis: The examination of any data stored or transmitted using a computer, or other personal electronic device, that tends to support or refute a theory of how an offense occurred or that addresses critical elements of the offense such as intent or alibi.

Fire Debris Analysis: The examination of material collected at fire scenes for chemical and physical properties related to flammable and combustible liquids that may have been used as accelerants.

Firearms and Tool Mark Examiners: Forensic examiners who use microscopic comparisons of markings to associate an item of evidence with a particular source (Rowe, 2003, p. 327).

Forensic Accountants: Accountants who examine, or audit, financial records to answer investigative questions and help resolve legal disputes.

Forensic Biologists: Scientists such as DNA analysts and serologists who attempt to identify biological material, such as bedily fluids, hair, bones, and tissue.

Forensic Generalists: Forensic scientists who are broadly educated and trained in a variety of forensic specialties.

Forensic Odontology: (a.k.a. *forensic dentistry*) The "application of the arts and sciences of dentistry to the legal system"(Glass, 2003, p. 61).

Forensic Pathologists: Scientists charged with determining cause and manner in cases of violent or unexpected death.

CONTENTS

> *Forensic Science:*   The application of scientific knowledge and principles to the resolution of legal disputes, whether criminal or civil.
>
> *Forensic Specialists:*   Forensic scientists trained in a specific forensic subspecialty, such as an area of criminalistics, forensic toxicology, forensic pathology, or forensic anthropology.
>
> *Forensic Toxicologists:*   Scientists who can collect and examine all manner of biological specimens for testing whether and in what quantity certain substances are present.
>
> *Trace Evidence Analysis:* The examination of the nature of unknown samples and their comparison with others of a similar nature to determine their origins by establishing the physical, microscopic, and chemical characteristics.

Students and professionals alike have a long tradition of approaching those who call themselves "forensic scientists" with awe and deference. The author's experience is that this behavior is largely in response to a historically favorable portrayal in true crime dramas. Since the publication of the first story featuring the fictional detective Sherlock Holmes, books, and later television and film, have depicted forensic scientists as deeply astute crime fighters.[1] They are shown to be capable of rendering a world of dead-on inferences from a drop of blood, a strand of hair, or an object just out of place in a crime scene. They are also presented in near-complete alignment with law enforcement efforts, either as part of the police investigation or the later prosecution of a case.

[1]Sir Arthur Conan Doyle authored the very first Sherlock Holmes mystery, *A Study in Scarlet*, which was published in November 1887 as the main part of Beeton's Christmas Annual.

Unfortunately, this uniformed and embellished view has left a false impression in the minds of those studying and working in the criminal justice system. The media portrayal of infallibility has created a community populated by many who believe themselves to be infallible. In part, this self-perception is sustained for lack of experience with being effectively challenged. As discussed in Cooley (2007, p. 508–509):

> For much of the 20th century, judges, prosecutors, and attorneys infrequently scrutinized the individualizing and reconstructive claims and qualifications of forensic experts. Although various reasons subsist as to why these legal actors did not forcefully and repeatedly challenge such evidence, it is undeniable that this lack of scrutiny has permitted the forensic community to operate below the radar. Left unchecked by the courts, much of the forensic community has grown and evolved believing that it is immune to error, and therefore free from it.

Subsequently, there have been more than a few forensic examiners, and disciplines, that have felt justified in portraying themselves as essentially infallible. This self-congratulatory portrayal has in turn perpetuated the apathetic approach that courts, prosecutors, and defense attorneys have historically taken. These circumstances have also fostered an unsettling and nonscientific atmosphere in which much of the forensic community does not feel obligated to conduct research and substantiate the certainty of their claims. Moreover, these circumstances have created a culture in which forensic examiners feel justified in attesting to statistics, reenactments, and interpretations that often have little, if any, foundation in science or logic.

In February of 2009, however, the climate of unquestioned adulation changed with the publication of a report by the National Academy of Science (a.k.a. the NAS Report), *Strengthening Forensic Science in the United States: A Path Forward* (Edwards and Gotsonis, 2009). The impetus for this systemwide investigation and review of the forensic sciences included the following: the publication of an ongoing series of critical legal reviews regarding the tremendous bias and lack of science in forensic practice (e.g., Cole, 2005; Cooley, 2004; Risinger, Saks, Thompson, and Rosenthal, 2002; Schwartz, 2005), the ongoing occurrence of numerous highly publicized forensic blunders and crime lab scandals across the United States, the ever increasing number of DNA exonerations sourced back to flawed or misleading forensic evidence documented by groups like the Innocence Project,[2] and the publication of Chisum and Turvey (2007),[3] all referenced in the final version of the report. The findings were prepared to inform the U.S. Congress, to help them with related legislative and budgetary decisions, per the role of the NAS.

Judge Harry T. Edwards was the co-chair of the NAS Committee responsible for investigating the forensic science community and the final NAS Report.[4] He testified to the Senate Committee on the Judiciary on March 18, 2009, regarding his role and perspective (Edwards, 2009):

> I started this project with no preconceived views about the forensic science community.... And I do not watch CSI programs on television, so I was not affected by Hollywood's exaggerated views of the capacities of forensic disciplines. Rather, I simply assumed, as I suspect many of my judicial colleagues do, that forensic science disciplines typically are grounded in scientific methodology and that crime laboratories and forensic science practitioners generally are bound by solid practices that ensure that forensic evidence offered in court is valid and reliable. I was surprisingly mistaken in what I assumed. The truth is that the manner in which forensic evidence is presented on television—as invariably conclusive and final—does not correspond with reality.

[2] See http://www.innocenceproject.org

[3] Chisum and Turvey (2007) was the first forensic science textbook authored by practicing scientists to fully embrace the notion of limits with respect to scientific evidence, along with the need to identify bias and separate scientific culture from law enforcement oversight.

[4] The National Academy of Science (NAS) Committee on Identifying the Needs of the Forensic Science Community.

This author would agree, and is of the opinion that the findings of the NAS Report, which have been incorporated into this work, have brought forensic scientists back to earth.

The purpose of this chapter is to define the nature and scope of the service of forensic scientists, their investigative and legal value, and the educational requirements within major subspecialties. It will conclude with recommendations on how forensic criminologists can best utilize the forensic scientists in their cases. In this way we will serve students by showing them career choices and pathways, while at the same time giving practitioners insight into what is available and how to assess its worth.

FORENSIC SCIENCE DEFINED

Forensic science is the application of scientific knowledge and principles to the resolution of legal disputes, whether criminal or civil. This definition, being generally consistent across forensic science textbooks and professional organizations, is quite broad. As defined at the beginning of this text, forensic science in its application is a subdiscipline of criminology.

The relationship between forensic science and criminology may be observed through the lens of higher education. Though many students with chemistry and biology majors go on to work in crime labs, forensic science programs themselves are applied and vocationally oriented. Most such programs, even those with a DNA component, tend to be housed within schools of criminology and criminal justice when found on the college or university campus.

Skeptics may also wish to examine the pages of James and Nordby's *Forensic Science* (2003) or *The Encyclopedia of Forensic Science* by Seigel, Saukko, and Knupfer (2000). Both explore the vast geography of the forensic science community at length, well beyond the borders of a traditional crime laboratory setting. Coverage is given to everything from forensic toxicology to forensic psychology to digital evidence to criminal profiling and more.

It may also be useful to read or reread the preface of this text, where the history of the relationship between criminology and forensic science is expounded.

The Distinguishing Feature

Perhaps the best explanation of what a forensic scientist is comes from Dr. John Thornton, the noted criminalist mentioned in Chapter 1. He writes that the defining quality of forensic scientists is the possibility that they will be called upon to present scientific findings, under penalty of perjury, in a court of law. Subsequently, they will be asked to explain to the court what those findings mean and how they came to them. Those examiners whose work does not bring them into contact with the legal system are not "forensic" in nature. As provided in Thornton and Peterson (2002, p. 148):

> What then, of the forensic scientist? The single feature that distinguishes forensic scientists from any other scientist is the expectation that they will appear in court and testify to their findings and offer an opinion as to the significance of those findings. The forensic scientist will, or should, testify not only to what things are, but to what things mean. Forensic science is science exercised on behalf of the law in the just resolution of conflict. It is therefore expected to be the handmaiden of the law, but at the same time this expectation may very well be the marina from which is launched the tension that exists between the two disciplines.

The unique role of the forensic scientist is ultimately that of an educator to attorneys, judges, and juries. Trust extended to them as an expert by the court under these circumstances is not trivial. The results of their examinations and any related opinions can greatly influence the outcome of a legal proceeding. In civil matters, reputations and fortunes may be lost or won. In criminal matters, nothing less than the life and liberty of the accused is at stake. A convincing forensic scientist can be terribly compelling to a judge or jury, and thus tip the scales of justice for one side of a dispute over the other.

The "Real" Forensic Scientists

As explained in Inman and Rudin (1999), there is much confusion over who precisely the "real" forensic scientists are and who they are not. This is true even within the forensic science community itself. An assessment of the discontinuity is offered in Edwards and Gotsonis (2009, p. S-5):

> The term "forensic science" encompasses a broad range of forensic disciplines, each with its own set of technologies and practices. In other words, there is wide variability across forensic science disciplines with regard to techniques, methodologies, reliability, types and numbers of potential errors, research, general acceptability, and published material. Some of the forensic science disciplines are laboratory based (e.g., nuclear and mitochondrial DNA analysis, toxicology and drug analysis); others are based on expert interpretation of observed patterns (e.g., fingerprints, writing samples, toolmarks, bite marks, and specimens such as hair). The "forensic science community," in turn, consists of a host of practitioners, including scientists (some with advanced degrees) in the fields of chemistry, biochemistry, biology, and medicine; laboratory technicians; crime scene investigators; and law enforcement officers. There are very important differences, however, between forensic laboratory work and crime scene investigations. There are also sharp distinctions between forensic practitioners who have been

trained in chemistry, biochemistry, biology, and medicine (and who bring these disciplines to bear in their work) and technicians who lend support to forensic science enterprises.

[5]Edwards and Gotsonis (2009, p. 1–1): "Not all forensic services are performed in traditional crime laboratories by trained forensic scientists. Some forensic tests might be conducted by a sworn law enforcement officer with no scientific training or credentials, other than experience. In smaller jurisdictions, members of the local police or sheriff's department might conduct the analyses of evidence, such as latent print examinations and footwear comparisons."

Moreover, Edwards and Gotsonis (2009)[5] found the forensic science community poorly focused and badly fragmented, with no clear practice standards, consistent terminology, or standardized means of practitioner certification. Suffice it to say that forensic science is not always practiced in a crime lab, it is not always practiced by someone working for law enforcement (nor should it be, ideally), and, unfortunately, it is not always practiced by scientists.

However, it must also be pointed out that the vast majority of full-time forensic science practitioners in the United States work in police agencies or government-funded crime labs, providing their services exclusively to law enforcement. Edwards and Gotsonis explain that (2009, p. 1–2)

> According to a 2005 census by the Bureau of Justice Statistics (BJS), 389 publicly funded forensic crime laboratories were operating in the United States in 2005: These included 210 state or regional laboratories, 84 county laboratories, 62 municipal laboratories, and 33 federal laboratories, and they received evidence from nearly 2.7 million criminal cases. These laboratories are staffed by individuals with a wide range of training and expertise, from scientists with Ph.D.s to technicians who have been trained largely on the job. No data are available on the size and depth of the private forensic laboratories, except for private DNA laboratories.

This circumstance exists in no small part because forensic science in practice is an applied science (Inman and Rudin, 1999). This means that practitioners borrow from the research and principles of other established scientific disciplines and apply it to their own forensic casework. Because many forensic practitioners are not themselves scientists, especially those in direct police service, the results of their analyses can range from the exceptionally informed to the patently absurd.

Another issue is the distinction that must be made between scientist and technician practitioners of forensic science. The NAS Report goes out of its way to make a clear distinction between forensic scientists and forensic technicians. It provides, among other things, that (Edwards and Gotsonis, 2009, p. S-5)

> There are also sharp distinctions between forensic practitioners who have been trained in chemistry, biochemistry, biology, and medicine (and who bring these disciplines to bear in their work) and technicians who lend support to forensic science enterprises. Many of these differences are discussed in the body of this report.

With the greatest distinction being that of testing versus interpretation (p. 2–4):

> Because of the distinctly different professional tracks within larger laboratories, for example, technicians perform tests with defined protocols, and credentialed scientists conduct specialized testing and interpretation.

The contrast between technician and scientist is both subtle and tremendous. Currently, the trend is to populate government-funded crime labs with forensic technicians who do little more than inject a sample and push a button without knowing the science beneath their analysis. This saves money in terms of having to hire fewer of those with advanced degrees. This also limits the testimony of forensic technicians to results and prevents them from being able to explain the meaning of those results with competence.

This situation provides an interpretative windfall for the police and prosecution—who are left to provide interpretations to the trier of fact with scientists carefully in their pocket or moved entirely to the side. As explained in Chisum and Turvey (2007, pp. xvi–xvii):

> A *technician* is one who is trained in specific procedures, learned by routine or repetition. A forensic technician is trained in the specific procedures related to collecting and even testing evidence found at crime scenes. This is without any need for employing or even understanding the scientific method and the principles of forensic science. This describes the police technicians documenting crime scenes and collecting evidence, and more than a few of the forensic personnel working in government crime labs.
>
> A *scientist* is someone who possesses an academic and clinical understanding of the scientific method and the analytical dexterity to construct experiments that will generate the empirical reality that science mandates. A *forensic scientist* is one who is educated and trained to examine and determine the meaning of physical evidence in accordance with the established principles of forensic science, with the expectation of presenting her findings in court. This describes fewer and fewer of those practicing forensic science in government crime labs. As the authors have experienced on countless cases, it is technicians, investigators, and ultimately attorneys who are actually providing a majority of crime reconstructions in court, often with little understanding of forensic science or the scientific method, to say nothing of the natural limits of physical evidence. Crime lab personnel are performing any necessary laboratory analysis, but police and prosecutors are taking the final step to explain events and their relationships in court. This has the net effect of elevating the lay testimony of investigators and forensic technicians to that of the forensic scientist and of reducing the expert findings of the forensic scientist to the level of the technician.

The position taken by the NAS is that science must be part of both the methods and interpretations of forensic scientists. A technician can collect a sample, extract DNA, or test for the presence or absence of substances. But it takes a scientist to interpret the results of that test in the context in which it was run, with respect to the limits of good science. If others are interpreting evidentiary findings on their behalf or without a scientific background, then there is increased room for misrepresentation and error.

To recap, forensic science is not always practiced in a crime lab, is not always practiced on behalf of law enforcement, and is not always practiced by actual scientists. That is to say, there are an undocumented number of independent forensic scientists in private practice working to provide balance within the criminal justice system. It is, after all, a justice system that is awash with variously qualified law enforcement employed forensic practitioners bound to serve the prosecution and no other. Moreover, the education, training, and experience of forensic practitioners is not fixed or mandated by any one agency or organization. This has resulted in many government and police lab employees who are trained on the job, heralding experience as their only qualification.

A Culture of Science

As already mentioned, the NAS Report provides for the need to separate the current broken forensic science community from law enforcement culture. This is discussed in several sections of the report and all throughout Chapter 6, "Improving Methods, Practice, and Performance in Forensic Science," where it is explained (Edwards and Gotsonis, 2009, p. 6–1):

> The majority of forensic science laboratories are administered by law enforcement agencies, such as police departments, where the laboratory administrator reports to the head of the agency. This system leads to significant concerns related to the independence of the laboratory and its budget. Ideally, public forensic science laboratories should be independent of or autonomous within law enforcement agencies. In these contexts, the director would have an equal voice with others in the justice system on matters involving the laboratory and other agencies. The laboratory also would be able to set its own priorities with respect to cases, expenditures, and other important issues. Cultural pressures caused by the different missions of scientific laboratories vis-à-vis law enforcement agencies would be largely resolved. Finally, the forensic science laboratories would be able to set their own budget priorities and not have to compete with the parent law enforcement agencies.

The NAS Committee's recognition of the incompatibility between scientific and law enforcement/prosecutorial goals, and the bias this can and has created, is perhaps its most significant contribution to the future of the forensic science community. This is consistent with the discussion found in Cooley and Turvey (2007, p. 79):

> To correct institutional bias, which accounts for many of the unwanted observer effects discussed in this chapter, it may be time to consider separating the forensic scientist once and for all from police culture. In other words, it may be time to consider separating all state crime lab systems physically, philosophically, and fiscally from law enforcement and to advocate for the creation of wholly independent state divisions of forensic science that are publicly funded but available to all.
>
> The idea is not new. [Dr. Paul L.] Kirk and [Lowell] Bradford (1965, pp. 22–23) advocated for independent crime labs four decades ago:[*]
>
>> An independent operation, not directly a part of any other law enforcement agency, but available to all, would certainly find it easier to maintain the high degree of scientific objectivity that is so essential to good operation. It is very probable that the quality of service furnished would be higher than is now possible, because there would be no dependence on budgets of the other organization with their inevitable competition for available funds, and there would be no question of comparable rank of personnel, which is a problem in some organizations under the common American system.
>
> [*] Similarly, Professor [James] Starrs (1993) urged that the "inbred bias of crime laboratories affiliated with law enforcement agencies must be breached." Professor [Paul] Gianelli (1997) also advocated for independent crime labs, stating, "These laboratories should be transferred from police control to the control of medical examiner offices, agencies that are already independent of the police."

As forensic scientists and legal scholars agree, and the NAS Report makes clear, science of any kind cannot survive, and therefore does not belong, in the culture of law enforcement. Subsequently, there is an argument to be made that those forensic practitioners employed solely by law enforcement or the prosecution are not forensic scientists at all, but rather police practitioners. In any case, no scientist worth his or her salt wears a badge or a gun, or considers who signs his or her paycheck when rendering results. Therefore, separation of one culture from the other should be painless unless the scientist has become over-identified with law enforcement or the prosecution—which is precisely the problem that needs remedy.

Education for Forensic Scientists

The imposition of basic educational standards is one of the greatest challenges confronting the forensic science community. A major contributing factor to our problem is, again, the alignment of forensic science with the law enforcement community. Many forensic examiners work for or within law enforcement agencies that have very low educational requirements, as do, subsequently, their in-house forensic positions. This is not something that the law enforcement community prefers to acknowledge or be reminded of. Therefore, to remain in the good graces of the many uneducated forensic examiners employed by law enforcement, most forensic professional organizations either do not impose degree requirements or provide exceptions to scientific education for law enforcement experience. This has created one of the core problems that the NAS Report identified: an overall lack of scientific education and training, let alone an absence of scientific culture, in the forensic sciences.

The NAS Report makes clear in its discussion of education reform that at the very least an undergraduate degree in the forensic sciences or some other related science (e.g., biology, chemistry, engineering) is necessary, and that a graduate degree is preferable. It also provides that mere on-the-job training is an inadequate substitute for a scientific education (Edwards and Gotsonis, 2009, p. 8–1):

> Forensic examiners must understand the principles, practices, and contexts of science, including the scientific method. Training should move away from reliance on the apprentice-like transmittal of practices to education at the college level and beyond that is based on scientifically valid principles, as discussed in Chapter 4. For example, in addition to learning a particular methodology through a lengthy apprenticeship or workshop during which a trainee discerns and learns to copy the skills of an experienced examiner, the junior person should learn what to measure, the associated population statistics (if appropriate), biases and errors to avoid, other threats to the validity of the evidence, how to calculate the probability that a conclusion is valid, and how to document and report the analysis. Among many skills, forensic science education and training must provide the tools needed to understand the probabilities and the limits of decision-making under conditions of uncertainty.

> To correct some of the existing deficiencies, the starting place must be better undergraduate and graduate programs, as well as increased opportunities for continuing education. Legitimating practices in the forensic science disciplines must be based on established scientific knowledge, principles, and practices, which are best learned through formal education and training and the proper conduct of research.

This basic scientific observation runs contrary to the views of many law enforcement forensic examiners who have been arguing for generations that experience trumps education and that science can be learned on the job, taught by one police officer to another. It also helps with the task of preventing law enforcement examiners and prosecutors from arguing or suggesting that one must be in law enforcement, or work for law enforcement, to be a forensic scientist.

Additionally, the NAS Report notes that the lack of higher education in forensic science is directly associated with the lack of available scientific research in its many specialties (Edwards and Gotsonis, 2009, p. 8–11):

> Many forensic degree programs are found at small colleges or universities with few graduate programs in science and where research resources are limited. The lack of research funding has discouraged universities in the United States from developing research-based forensic degree programs, which leads to limited opportunities to attract graduate students into such programs. Only a few universities offer Ph.D.-level education and research opportunities in forensic science, and these are chemistry or biology programs with a forensic science focus.

> Most graduate programs in forensic science are master's programs, where financial support for graduate study is limited. In addition, the lack of research funds means that universities are unlikely to develop research programs in forensic science. This lack of funding discourages top scientists from exploring the many scientific issues in the forensic science disciplines. This has become a vicious cycle during which the lack of funding keeps top scientists away and their unavailability discourages funding agencies from investing in forensic science research. Traditional funding agencies have never had a mission to support forensic science research.

This finding provides the argument for establishing Ph.D. forensic science programs to fund and develop much needed research in the forensic sciences. It is something that just about every other scientific discipline enjoys and benefits from. Until this happens, the education available to prospective forensic scientists will be that much less, and research in the forensic sciences will continue to suffer.

FORENSIC SCIENTISTS

There are many different kinds of forensic scientists; as many as there are types of evidence to examine and interpret. There are forensic psychiatrists, forensic psychologists, forensic victimologists, and even forensic criminologists—all of whom are discussed in this text. However, there are also the more traditionally regarded forensic sciences that deal directly with the examination of physical evidence collected in relation to a crime, such as criminalistics and forensic pathology.

In the following sections, we will define the role and education of other the forensic scientists that forensic criminologists are most likely to encounter in their casework. Because of the confusion regarding the certainty of forensic science conclusions, a brief discussion of the limits of some will also be provided.

Generalist vs. Specialists

As in the field of medicine, or any other field for that matter, there are *forensic generalists* and there are *forensic specialists*. The distinction between generalist and specialist forensic practitioners is made clearer by a discussion provided in Chisum and Turvey (2007, pp. ix–x):

> Forensic generalists and forensic specialists alike are a requirement for informed forensic case examination, laboratory testing, and crime reconstruction to occur. A forensic generalist is a particular kind of forensic scientist who is broadly educated and trained in a variety of forensic specialties. They are "big picture"people who can help reconstruct a crime from work performed with the assistance of other forensic scientists and then direct investigators to forensic specialists as needed. They are experts not in all areas, but in the specific area of evidence interpretation. According to DeForest et al. (1983, p. 17):
>
> > Because of the depth and complexity of criminalistics, the need for specialists is inescapable. There can be serious problems, however, with overspecialization. Persons who have a working knowledge of a broad range of criminalistics problems and techniques are also necessary. These people are called generalists. The value of generalists lies in their ability to look at all of the aspects of a complex case and decide what needs to be done, which specialists should be involved, and in which order to carry out the required examinations.
>
> Specialization occurs when a forensic scientist has been trained in a specific forensic subspecialty, such as an area of criminalistics, forensic toxicology, forensic pathology, or forensic anthropology. Specialists are an important part of forensic science casework, with an important role to fill. Traditionally, forensic specialists provide the bricks, and forensic generalists have traditionally provided the blueprints.

The author of this chapter, for example, was educated and trained as a forensic generalist, specializing in crime reconstruction, crime scene analysis, and criminal profiling. One of the author's mentors, and a co-author of *Crime Reconstruction* (2007), W. Jerry Chisum, was also trained as a generalist by the late Dr. Paul Kirk (see Chapter 1). In contrast to the author, Mr. Chisum received his degree in chemistry and then specialized in a number of areas, including serology, crime reconstruction, and bloodstain pattern analysis.

There are fewer and fewer generalists in the forensic science community, and it is not uncommon for forensic scientists to gain employment in government service without a generalist background at all. Rather it is more common for forensic scientists to be narrowly trained as specialists of some sort without the benefit of a general forensic education, and then to learn other subspecialties once employed by a public crime lab. In fact most crime lab employees are cross-trained in multiple areas of evidence, to save having to hire additional personnel.

Criminalists

A criminalist is a particular class of forensic scientist who performs analyses and testing on physical evidence in a crime lab. Indeed, there are more than a few different subspecialties within laboratory criminalistics. As mentioned in Chapter 1, criminalistics traditionally encompasses the following subspecialties:

1. Drug Chemistry Identification and Analysis
   a. Alcohol
   b. Drugs
   c. Toxins
2. Forensic Biology
   a. DNA
   b. Serology
3. Fire Debris Analysis
4. Trace Evidence Analysis
   a. Commercial Materials Analysis
   b. Fiber Analysis
   c. Glass Analysis
   d. Hair Analysis
   e. Soil Analysis

This means that when someone refers to himself or herself as a criminalist, that person is suggesting expertise in one or perhaps more of the preceding areas. Therefore, it may also be necessary to inquire further and determine precisely what kind of criminalist that person is. Most criminalists will be eager to explain their areas of specialty, along with their individual limitations.

General Education

At the forefront of the criminalistics profession is the California Association of Criminalists (CAC).[6] This organization provides that

> A criminalist is a person with a background in science, typically having at least a baccalaureate degree in an area such as chemistry, biology, forensic science, or criminalistics. Some criminalists have degrees in other, similarly related areas. Many criminalists have advanced degrees.

[6]See http://www.cacnews.org/membership/criminalistics.shtml

With the above scientific background and additional training given by his/her employer (either a government or private laboratory) a criminalist applies scientific methods and techniques to examine and analyze evidentiary items and testifies in court as to his or her findings.

The degree requirement provides for the necessity of a scholarly, science-oriented background. The CAC also provides generalist and specialist certification for criminalists. Unfortunately, many "criminalists" working in public crime labs have undergraduate degrees in areas unrelated to scientific endeavor or scholarship, such as music, criminal justice, business, education, or political science. This trend is changing, however, as national hiring practices are being forced to evolve by guidelines such as those provided in the NAS Report.

Analyses

Criminalists specializing in the area of *drug chemistry* test for the presence of particular drugs, alcohol, or toxins; *toxicologists* are specifically looking to establish their level in the human body. Drug identification comprises the bulk of government crime lab work, particularly opiates, amphetamines, cocaine, and cannabinoids associated with marijuana. The questions are related to which drugs are absolutely present, and in what quantities with respect to statutory requirements (a lesser amount may be legal to possess in some jurisdictions, more may be illegal to possess, and still more may demonstrate an intent to sell or distribute).

Forensic toxicologists work in crime labs associated with law enforcement agencies, medical examiners' offices, and private companies. They can collect and examine all manner of biological specimens for testing, including blood, urine, stomach (gastric) contents, vitreous humor (fluid from the eye), liver (and the bile which rains from it), and hair. Depending on the nature of the case, the more invasive samples are typically collected post-mortem.

[7]See http://www.soft-tox.org.

As provided by the Society of Forensic Toxicologists,[7] the educational requirements within this area of criminalistics vary depending on experience. Their membership guidelines demand that

> Applicants for Full membership must have the following education degrees and experience in forensic toxicology:
>
> - Ph.D. and 2 years experience
> - M.S. and 4 years experience
> - B.S. or B.A. and 6 years experience

As one can infer from these requirements, a Ph.D. is the preferred standard. However, the undergraduate degree requirement allowing for a B.A. as opposed to just a B.S. muddies the scientific water a bit. However, it is further reasonable to infer that any undergraduate degree should be related to chemistry or biology, if not held in forensic toxicology itself.

Criminalists specializing in *forensic biology*, such as DNA analysts and serologists (those who examine blood), are interested in forensic identification. Serologists look at blood type, proteins, enzymes, and antibodies. DNA analysts look for genetic material in blood and just about every other biological material they can get their hands on. As explained in Butler and Butler (2004, pp. 166–167):

> Since every living cell contains DNA, any biological material left at a crime scene can potentially be valuable in a DNA test. The most obvious potential sources of DNA that can be obtained from a sexual assault crime scene are semen and vaginal cells.... Other important sources include blood, urine, saliva, skin, hair root, fingernails (often in a struggle a victim will scratch the perpetrator, catching his skin under her fingernails), condoms, clothing, linens, carpet, ligatures, and tape (especially good because tape and ligatures are difficult to work with while wearing gloves, possibly forcing the suspect to temporarily remove them for the task). All can provide biological material that may prove very helpful in solving a case. Even a bite mark on a victim can be swabbed to collect DNA left by the perpetrator's saliva because saliva or "spit" often contains ample cheek cells to perform DNA testing.

DNA analysis was singled out in the NAS Report as having a more solid scientific foundation than any other forensic discipline, with statements such as this throughout (Edwards and Gotsonis, 2009, p. S-5): "With the exception of nuclear DNA analysis, however, no forensic method has been rigorously shown to have the capacity to consistently, and with a high degree of certainty, demonstrate a connection between evidence and a specific individual or source." Such statements are, of course, true.

However, there is an absence of direct criticism from the NAS regarding how DNA is databased and how DNA results are searched for, obtained, calculated, reported, and interpreted by forensic scientists—criticisms that are widely known and understood even by the general public. This includes the FBI's pathological secrecy regarding its DNA databases. It also includes the coordinated threat from the FBI's CODIS director to cut off access to any state that allows database searches it does not approve—which it turns out was a ruse designed to manipulate the court into denying motions from the defense (Dolan and Felch, 2008). All this to say that DNA, while being the forensic science with the most scientific underpinnings, still has a number of shortfalls.

Educational requirements for DNA analysts and other *forensic biologists* vary widely, but undergraduate degrees in chemistry and biology are preferred. However, these persons must also have a strong background in statistics because this is how confidence in findings is expressed in reports and then later in court. A DNA analyst who is unable to explain the statistics behind a "match," how it was derived, and what it means, is no more than a technician. Unfortunately, this is common.

Criminalists specializing in *fire debris analysis* examine material collected at fire scenes for chemical and physical properties related to flammable and combustible liquids that may have been used as accelerants. This includes petroleum products such as gasoline and kerosene, primarily—though not exclusively. Fire debris must be collected in a secure, airtight container that is immune to rust or other forms of chemical erosion, such as a Mason jar, a specially lined paint can, or fire debris evidence bags. Fire debris analysis is a necessary aspect of an investigation into whether or not a fire was caused by arson (intentional fire setting). Given the complexity of fire scene investigation, the mere presence of accelerants does not by itself prove arson (see generally DeHaan, 2007).

Criminalists specializing in *trace evidence analysis* seek to identify the nature of unknown samples and then to compare them with others of a similar nature to determine their origins. Trace evidence identification and comparison are accomplished by establishing the physical, microscopic, and chemical characteristics of a sample. As explained in Thornton and Kimmel-Lake (2007, p. 197):

> For two reasons, the small bits of evidence may have significance beyond that which is commensurate with their size. First, their occurrence may arise from processes that describe the activities that generated them. Fracture, broadcasting of fine particles, and adhesion of foreign particles come to mind. Second, their size makes them inconspicuous. Any actor in the drama that we will call a crime is likely to be oblivious to the existence of this minute evidence, and even if he or she were aware, would be more or less powerless to do anything about it. These traces may provide information by means of which the factual circumstances at the time the crime occurred may be established. We call these materials *trace evidence*. It is an extremely broad category of physical evidence.

Because of the all-encompassing nature of this area, it is best to suggest readers seek out one or more of the learned texts which describes the instrumentation and methodology in the various forms of trace evidence examination, such as *Forensic Analysis on the Cutting Edge: New Methods for Trace Evidence Analysis* by Robert Blackledge (2007); and *Trace Evidence Analysis: More Cases in Mute Witnesses* by Max Houck (2004).

Crime Reconstructionists

Crime reconstruction is the determination of the actions and events surrounding the commission of a crime. A reconstruction may be accomplished by using the statements of witnesses, the confession of a suspect, the statement of a living victim, or by the examination and interpretation of physical evidence. Some refer to this process as crime scene reconstruction; however, the scene is not actually being put back together as it was—only some of the actions and sequences of events are being established.

Crime reconstruction is best conceived as the work of forensic generalists putting together theories of the crime based on the consideration of aggregated results from a variety of forensic disciplines. As explained in Chisum and Turvey (2007, p. xix):

> …[N]o one discipline can truly stand alone in a reconstruction. Each form of evidence must be in agreement with the other forms that are present. Each part must be meticulously established and then considered not just on its own but also in its place as part of the greater whole. What is it, how does it fit, and what does it mean in context—these are the questions asked by a reconstructionist.

> Given this holistic approach, the authors have come to view reconstruction as the work of one who is sufficiently educated, trained, and experienced to understand the total body of forensic evidence and analysis in a case. That is, again, the forensic generalist. The generalist–reconstructionist, it must be understood, need not know how to perform all of the forensic examinations that were conducted. They need not have the ability to operate a camera to view a photograph; they need not have the ability to extract DNA and amplify it to comprehend a DNA analyst's report; they need not have the ability to perform an autopsy to understand the cause and manner of death, and appreciate the trajectory of the projectiles that passed through the body. Rather, they must be able to understand what the results of forensic examinations are, how they were reached, what they mean, and how they may be integrated to create of picture of events. Integration of findings is key because crime is best reconstructed when forged by a collaboration of the forensic evidence, and not a reliance on one single examination or discipline. To rely on one piece of evidence, or one theory, without placing it in context is not only potentially misleading but also a disservice to the justice system that the forensic scientist ultimately serves.

The reconstructionist must therefore have a formal education in the sciences and be trained as a forensic generalist with an appreciation of how the many forensic sciences inform and limit case theories.

Bloodstain Pattern Analysis

Bloodstain pattern analysis (BPA) in a subspecialty of crime reconstruction. In the context of crime and crime scenes, *bloodstain patterns* are the visible record of the bloodshed at a crime scene (Chisum and Turvey, 2007). As explained in

Chisum (2007): "*Bloodstain pattern analysis* is the examination of the shapes, locations, and distribution patterns of bloodstains for the purpose of interpreting the physical events that caused them." It is based on the simple premise that bloodstain patterns are a direct result of the nature of the objects and forces that created them. As provided in the NAS Report (Edwards and Gotsonis, 2009, pp. 5–38):

> Understanding how a particular bloodstain pattern occurred can be critical physical evidence, because it may help investigators understand the events of the crime. Bloodstain patterns occur in a multitude of crime types—homicide, sexual battery, burglary, hit-and-run accidents—and are commonly present. Bloodstain pattern analysis is employed in crime reconstruction or event reconstruction when a part of the crime scene requires interpretation of these patterns.

The NAS Report goes on to advise that (pp. 5–39)

> Scientific studies support some aspects of bloodstain pattern analysis. One can tell, for example, if the blood spattered quickly or slowly, but some experts extrapolate far beyond what can be supported. Although the trajectories of bullets are linear, the damage that they cause in soft tissue and the complex patterns that fluids make when exiting wounds are highly variable. For such situations, many experiments must be conducted to determine what characteristics of a bloodstain pattern are caused by particular actions during a crime and to inform the interpretation of those causal links and their variabilities. For these same reasons, extra care must be given to the way in which the analyses are presented in court. The uncertainties associated with bloodstain pattern analysis are enormous.

Due to the complexity of BPA, a competent bloodstain pattern analyst will have a formal scientific education, as well as working knowledge of forensic pathology, wound pattern analysis, human biology and physiology, and physics. The NAS Report goes further, explaining (Edwards and Gotsonis, 2009, pp. 5–38)

> Interpreting and integrating bloodstain patterns into a reconstruction requires, at a minimum: an appropriate scientific education; knowledge of the terminology employed (e.g., angle of impact, arterial spurting, back spatter, castoff pattern); an understanding of the limitations of the measurement tools used to make bloodstain pattern measurements (e.g., calculators, software, lasers, protractors); an understanding of applied mathematics and the use of significant figures; an understanding of the physics of fluid transfer; an understanding of pathology of wounds; and an understanding of the general patterns blood makes after leaving the human body.

It is important to note that, as described, these minimum requirements would exclude the vast majority of law enforcement bloodstain pattern analysts testifying in court today—for lack of any formal scientific education, lack of applied mathematics, and lack of knowledge regarding applied physics. Most have no science background, and have been trained in BPA by other law enforcement practitioners in a series of short courses. This is far beneath the level of education and training needed to develop expertise or even competency.

Fingerprinting, a.k.a. Friction Ridge Analysis

Fingerprints are used in investigative and legal settings to establish the identity of victims and suspects, and to further establish their presence at a location or their contact with a particular object. Fingerprints are often provided as the sole means of such identifications, a practice that is not as accurate as many believe. As described in the NAS Report (Edwards and Gotsonis, 2009, pp. 5–7):

> Fingerprints, palm prints, and sole prints have been used to identify people for more than a century in the United States. Collectively, the analysis of these prints is known as "friction ridge analysis," which consists of experienced-based comparisons of the impressions left by the ridge structures of volar (hands and feet) surfaces. Friction ridge analysis is an example of what the forensic science community uses as a method for assessing "individualization"—the conclusion that a piece of evidence (here, a pattern left by friction ridges) comes from a single unambiguous source. Friction ridge analysis shares similarities with other experience-based methods of pattern recognition, such as those for footwear and tire impressions, toolmarks, and handwriting analysis....

Consider also the implications of the *one dissimilarity doctrine* in fingerprinting with respect to how prints are "matched" (Thornton, 1977, p. 89):

> Faced with an instance of many matching characteristics and one point of disagreement, the tendency on the part of the examiner is to rationalize away the dissimilarity on the basis of improper inking, uneven pressure resulting in the compression of a ridge, a dirty finger, a disease state, scarring, or superimposition of the impression. How can he do otherwise? If he admits that he does not know the cause of the disagreement then he must immediately conclude that the impressions are not of the same digit in order to accommodate the one-dissimilarity doctrine. The fault here is that the nature of the impression may not suggest which of these factors, if any, is at play. The expert is then in an embarrassing position of having to speculate as to what caused the dissimilarity, and often the speculation is without any particular foundation.

The practical implication of this is that the one-dissimilarity doctrine will have to be ignored. It is, in fact, ignored anyway by virtue of the fact that fingerprint examiners will not refrain from effecting an identification when numerous matching characteristics are observed despite a point of disagreement. Actually, the one dissimilarity doctrine has been treated rather shabbily. The fingerprint examiner adheres to it only until faced with an aberration, then discards it and conjures up some fanciful explanation for the dissimilarity.

Regarding friction ridge analysis, the NAS concludes that it is not an error-free result, nor should it be treated as 100% conclusive with respect to identifications (Edwards and Gotsonis, 2009, pp. 5–12, 5–13):

Historically, friction ridge analysis has served as a valuable tool, both to identify the guilty and to exclude the innocent. Because of the amount of detail available in friction ridges, it seems plausible that a careful comparison of two impressions can accurately discern whether or not they had a common source. Although there is limited information about the accuracy and reliability of friction ridge analyses, claims that these analyses have zero error rates are not scientifically plausible....

Recent legal challenges, *New Hampshire vs. Richard Langill* and *Maryland vs. Bryan Rose*, have also highlighted two important issues for the latent print community: documentation and error rate. Better documentation is needed of each step in the ACE-V process or its equivalent. At the very least, sufficient documentation is needed to reconstruct the analysis, if necessary. By documenting the relevant information gathered during the analysis, evaluation, and comparison of latent prints and the basis for the conclusion (identification, exclusion, or inconclusive), the examiner will create a transparent record of the method and thereby provide the courts with additional information on which to assess the reliability of the method for a specific case. Currently, there is no requirement for examiners to document which features within a latent print support their reasoning and conclusions.

Error rate is a much more difficult challenge. Errors can occur with any judgment-based method, especially when the factors that lead to the ultimate judgment are not documented. Some in the latent print community argue that the method itself, if followed correctly (i.e., by well trained examiners properly using the method), has a zero error rate. Clearly, this assertion is unrealistic, and, moreover, it does not lead to a process of method improvement. The method, and the performance of those who use it, are inextricably linked, and both involve multiple sources of error (e.g., errors in executing the process steps, as well as errors in human judgment).

Some scientific evidence supports the presumption that friction ridge patterns are unique to each person and persist unchanged throughout a lifetime. Uniqueness and persistence are necessary conditions for friction ridge identification to be feasible, but those conditions do not imply that anyone can reliably discern whether or not two friction ridge impressions were made by the same person. Uniqueness does not guarantee that prints from two different people are always sufficiently different that they cannot be confused, or that two impressions made by the same finger will also be sufficiently similar to be discerned as coming from the same source. The impression left by a given finger will differ every time, because of inevitable variations in pressure, which change the degree of contact between each part of the ridge structure and the impression medium. None of these variabilities—of features across a population of fingers or of repeated impressions left by the same finger—has been characterized, quantified, or compared.

Subsequent to the publication of the NAS Report, the International Association for Identification (IAI)[8] overturned a century of forensic practice and declared to its members in a memo that, when responding to challenges during testimony (Garrett, 2009):

[8]The IAI is one of the oldest forensic organizations, consisting primarily of law enforcement practitioners. It certifies, among others, those conducting fingerprint identifications. See http://www.theiai.org.

- It is suggested that members not assert 100% infallibility (zero error rate) when addressing the reliability of fingerprint comparisons.
- Although the IAI does not, at this time, endorse the use of probabilistic models when stating conclusions of identification, members are advised to avoid stating their conclusions in absolute terms when dealing with population issues.

Apart from the NAS Report itself, this memo is perhaps the most significant revelation in the forensic science community in more than 100 years.

It should be noted that the current state of this particular form of analysis exists and has persisted largely because of the fact that the majority of analysts work in law enforcement and have little or no scientific background. Subsequently, it has been accepted uncritically by the courts until recently, and suffered little if any scientific assessment. One hopes this will soon change as a result of the IAI's new mandate.

Firearms and Tool Mark Identification

Firearms and tool mark examiners "use microscopic comparisons of markings to associate an item of evidence with a particular source"(Rowe, 2003, p. 327). Edwards and Gotsonis (2009) explain that (pp. 5–18)

Toolmarks are generated when a hard object (tool) comes into contact with a relatively softer object. Such toolmarks may occur in the commission of a crime when an instrument such as a screwdriver, crowbar, or wire cutter is used or when the internal parts of a firearm make contact with the brass and lead that comprise ammunition. The marks left by an implement such as a screwdriver or a firearm's firing pin depend largely on the manufacturing processes—and manufacturing tools—used to create or shape it, although other surface features (e.g., chips, gouges) might be introduced through post-manufacturing wear. Manufacturing tools experience wear and abrasion as they cut, scrape, and otherwise shape metal, giving rise to the theory that any two manufactured products—even those produced consecutively with the same manufacturing tools—will bear microscopically different marks. Firearms and toolmark examiners believe that toolmarks may be traced to the physical heterogeneities of an individual tool—that is, that "individual characteristics" of toolmarks may be uniquely associated with a specific tool or firearm and are reproduced by the use of that tool and only that tool.

However, the NAS Report offers little enthusiasm for the current state of firearms and tool mark identification efforts, warning that (Edwards and Gotsonis, 2009, pp. 5–21)

Because not enough is known about the variabilities among individual tools and guns, we are not able to specify how many points of similarity are necessary for a given level of confidence in the result. Sufficient studies have not been done to understand the reliability and repeatability of the methods. The committee agrees that class characteristics are helpful in narrowing the pool of tools that may have left a distinctive mark. Individual patterns from manufacture or from wear might, in some cases, be distinctive enough to suggest one particular source, but additional studies should be performed to make the process of individualization more precise and repeatable.

A fundamental problem with toolmark and firearms analysis is the lack of a precisely defined process. As noted above, AFTE [Association of Firearm and Toolmak Examiners] has adopted a theory of identification, but it does not provide a specific protocol. It says that an examiner may offer an opinion that a specific tool or firearm was the source of a specific set of toolmarks or a bullet striation pattern when "sufficient agreement" exists in the pattern of two sets of marks. It defines agreement as significant "when it exceeds the best agreement demonstrated between tool marks known to have been produced by different tools and is consistent with the agreement demonstrated by tool marks known to have been produced by the same tool." The meaning of "exceeds the best agreement" and "consistent with" are not specified, and the examiner is expected to draw on his or her own experience. This AFTE document, which is the best guidance available for the field of toolmark identification, does not even consider, let alone address, questions regarding variability, reliability, repeatability, or the number of correlations needed to achieve a given degree of confidence.

As with friction ridge analysis, the state of this particular form of analysis exists and persists largely because of the fact that the majority of analysts work in law enforcement, and have little or no scientific background. The results of such examinations are therefore to be treated with great caution, as they are too often accepted as firm and final when in fact there is very little if any science behind such opinions (Schwartz, 2005). Again, it is the hope that this will soon change.

Digital Evidence Analysis

Digital evidence analysis refers to the examination of (Casey, 2004, p. 12) "any data stored or transmitted using a computer [or other personal electronic device] that support or refute a theory of how an offense occurred or that addresses critical elements of the offense such as intent or alibi." It includes all kinds of digitally stored data, such as text, images, audio, and video. There are many challenges to collecting digital evidence, as the very act of collection can permanently alter it. For this reason and more, digital evidence is among the least understood and most complex forms of evidence that can be collected in association with a crime.

Law enforcement agencies are only just getting into the habit of collecting digital evidence as a routine matter. However, many agencies lack the expertise or ability to do so. Worse, even when digital evidence is collected, it often goes unexamined unless a private examination is requested by the defense.

As with other areas of forensic examination, many law enforcement officers have taken it upon themselves to become in-house experts with highly varied results. Most, it is fair to say, do not have enough of a background in science or technology to understand the complexity of such evidence, let alone to interpret its meaning objectively. Digital evidence analysis requires a high degree of education and training in the very specialized tasks of collection, processing, and examination/interpretation (Casey, 2004). Consequently, these jobs are often separate, and should be separately credentialed. However, an undergraduate degree in computer science, engineering, or a related subject, is preferred.

For guidelines and practice standards, see generally Eoghan Casey's *Digital Evidence and Computer Crime* (Elsevier, 2004) and *Malware Forensics: Investigating and Analyzing Malicious Code* by Eoghan Casey, Cameron Malin, and James Aquilina (Syngress, 2008).

Forensic Accountant

A *forensic accountant* is a particular kind of accountant who examines, or audits, financial records to answer investigative questions and help resolve legal disputes. Forensic accountants have a high a degree of value to investigative and forensic inquiries. They may be used to answer questions regarding economic losses and financial damages, to resolve issues related to income and lifestyle in disputes over alimony and child custody payments, or to establish the nature and extent of financial fraud and asset ownership in cases where financial crimes are suspected, or those involving organized criminal enterprise.

While there are no firm educational requirements in forensic accounting specifically, it is recommended that practitioners have at least an undergraduate degree in accounting, economics, or a related area, with coursework and further specialized training in auditing, fraud, and forensic accounting. The variety of methods for assessing expertise in forensic accounting are explained in Levanti (2009):

Experience requirements of Forensic Accountants

Unlike many other professional fields, there are no experience requirements necessary to call oneself a Forensic Accountant. When looking for an experienced professional, the length of time someone has spent conducting actual accounting and auditing engagements should be strongly considered. However, accounting and auditing experience is not necessarily enough to qualify one as a Forensic Accountant; one must look at the professional experience of conducting investigations as well. Experience conducting investigations can be gained in many ways, including working in a forensic practice at an accounting firm or working in a law-enforcement capacity. Academia can also provide professionals who have conducted research into fraud-related fields.

Education credentials of Forensic Accountants

Although there are no educational standards for Forensic Accountants, there are standards for other professionals, such as CPAs. When choosing a professional Forensic Accountant, one should be guided by the same professional standards used for other services be it accountant, doctor, or attorney. Lack of education, however, should not be considered solely as a disqualifying factor for a candidate. A candidate may not have an advanced degree, but instead may have many years of experience in auditing, accounting or investigations that makes up for the lack of advanced educational credentials. When hiring a professional from a large, well-known firm, it is highly likely that the person's educational credentials have been verified and that he or she comes with the backing of the firm. When looking at a candidate without backing of a large firm, a request to an educational institution to verify educational credentials may provide needed clarity to make an informed decision. Beware of diploma mills issuing mail-order degrees when inquiring about educational credentials.

Professional credentials of a Forensic Accountant

One of the most effective ways to verify the credentials of a Forensic Accountant is by checking the references that are provided. The Internet is another good source of information, as well as Google, Ask.com and other search engines that offer thousands of sources of information on all types of professionals. Individuals belonging to established professional organizations may be confirmed as active members in good standing.

Regarding professional organizations themselves, there are several organizations that provide accreditations to Forensic Accountants. Some of these organizations have little or no education or experience requirements for their members or established professional standards for their members to follow. When inquiring about professional affiliations, one should seek out the requirements to become a member and/or receive a professional certification. For those organizations that lack satisfactory requirements, it is important to remember that deceptive organizations and certifications exist in every profession, including accounting and fraud investigations.

The lack of educational requirement in this subdiscipline of forensic science makes clear the need for belonging to professional forensic organizations with clearly defined educational requirements, standards of practice, and enforced codes of ethics. When an examiner is unwilling to submit to these, belonging only to those organizations that are essentially large social clubs, this unwillingness telegraphs a lack of professionalism and even a lack of confidence in the examiner's own work.

For guidelines and practice standards, see generally the *Journal of Forensic Accounting: Auditing, Fraud, and Risk* at http://www.rtedwards.com/journals/JFA.

Forensic Anthropologist

Forensic anthropologists apply the science of physical anthropology and human osteology (the study of the human skeleton) to investigative and legal questions. Primarily, they assist in the discernment of human bones from those of animals. If a bone or any set of remains is found to be human, forensic anthropologists proceed to assist with their identification. They are often employed in cases in which human remains are beyond physical recognition as occurs in mass disasters or those cases in which there is advanced decomposition. Forensic anthropologists can also assist with determinations of age, sex, stature, and ancestry, and assess remains for trauma and possible disease.

Practitioners are usually educated at the master's level, if not holding their Ph.D. in anthropology.

For more information, see the American Board of Forensic Anthropology at http://www.theabfa.org.

Readers should also consider referencing Byers (2007), *Introduction to Forensic Anthropology*, 3rd Edition, by Allyn & Bacon publishers.

Forensic Odontology

Forensic odontology, also referred to as forensic dentistry, "is the application of the arts and sciences of dentistry to the legal system,"Glass (2003, p. 61). It involves the identification of individuals by comparison of their teeth with established dental records. This occurs most commonly in cases of accidental death or homicide when human remains are discovered and their identity is unknown. It also involves the comparison of suspect dentition patterns with suspected bite mark patterns for the purposes of helping to establish identity.

Practitioners will typically have a private dental practice of some sort, with forensic work and expertise being something they develop on the side. This means that they must possess a D.D.S., a D.M.D., or the equivalent dental degree from an accredited institution.

For more information, see the American Board of Forensic Odontology, which provides specific standards of forensic practice and uniform terminology for its membership, at http://www.abfo.org.

Readers should also consider referencing Bowers (2004), *Forensic Dental Evidence: An Investigator's Handbook*, by Academic Press.

Forensic Pathologists

Forensic pathologists are those charged with determining cause and manner in cases of violent or unexpected death. They are meant to attend the death scene, gather a history, perform the autopsy, and then assess the nature in which the deceased interacted with the environment in such a manner as to cause his or her demise. They also collect decedent clothing, document injuries, and collect biological samples in accordance with sexual assault kit protocols, as well as those needed for forensic toxicological analysis. Very often, their assessments will determine whether or not a death is the result of crime and also provide the foundation for much of the reconstruction work that may be done regarding the crime. The results of their findings are used in civil and criminal litigation alike.

With respect to the divergent Medical Examiner/ Coroner (ME/C) systems that operate in the United States, the NAS Report concluded (Edwards and Gotsonis, 2009, pp. 9–19)

> ME/C systems function at varying levels of expertise, often with deficiencies in facilities, equipment, staff, education, and training. And, unfortunately, most systems are under budgeted and understaffed. As with other forensic science fields, there are no mandated national qualifications or certifications required for death investigators. Nor is medical expertise always required. In addition, there is no one recognized set of performance standards or best practices for ME/C systems nor are there incentives to implement one recognized set. Also lacking are universally accepted or promulgated methods of quality control or quality assurance. It is clear that the conversion of coroner systems to medical examiner systems as recommended by many studies has essentially halted and requires federal incentives to move forward....

> The shortage of forensic pathologists speaks to the need to provide incentives for young physicians to train in forensic pathology. Systems with authorized positions cannot fill them, because of this shortage and budget deficits.

Practitioners of forensic pathology will have an M.D. and board certification in forensic pathology—that is, unless they are coroners, in which case they need only be 18 and possess a valid driver's license, which can and does happen in some jurisdictions.

For more information, see the National Association of Medical Examiners, which provides specific standards of forensic practice and uniform terminology for its membership, at http://thename.org.

Readers should also consider referencing Dolinak, Matshes, and Lew (2005), *Forensic Pathology: Principles and Practice,* by Academic Press, as well as the National Institute of Justice (NIJ) *Death Investigation: A Guide for the Scene Investigator*[9] (1999) Research Report NCJ 167568, Washington, D.C.

[9]These NIJ Guidelines are available online at http://www.ojp.usdoj.gov/nij/pubssum/167568.htm.

CONSULTING WITH FORENSIC SCIENTISTS

As we have learned, forensic scientists come in many forms, and their numbers include examiners who do not work in crime labs or directly with physical evidence at all. They also lack uniform standards in education and methodology; their conclusions often lack scientific rigor and are overly confident; and they are too often marked by improper alignment with law enforcement and prosecutorial agencies. As a consequence, the forensic science community is fragmented and broken, and does not speak with a single voice. It is also awash with the inept and the biased.

When working with the results of physical evidence examination, forensic criminologists are encouraged to do the following:

1. Check the resumes of purported forensic scientists. Do they actually have the education that they claim? Do they have a formal scientific education? Or does their "science"derive from a series of law-enforcement-sponsored short courses?

2. Learn the practice standards and protocols that individual examiners are operating under when rendering their conclusions. Assess whether their reporting comports with them.

   Learn the ethical codes governing the forensic practitioners that you encounter—if there are any at all. If you learn of unethical conduct, report it. This may not result in any action or sanctions, but it may, and it will at least make a record.

3. Be eager to get a second opinion. Real scientists like having the work checked because they know the validity of their methods and are proud of their efforts.

4. If you have questions regarding a forensic examiner's report (and you will), ask about it. If the examiner refuses to speak with you, that in itself is an answer.

5. Remember that all forensic scientists are not equal; especially true of specialists, they may know only their small piece of the puzzle. Do not assume that they know more or less than they do.

6. Work toward a generalist's level of forensic knowledge. This degree of education is a process rather than a result, so be prepared to make a commitment that is at least the same length as your intended career in forensic service.

7. Develop an extensive forensic library. If a forensic examiner's report doesn't sound right, is overly vague, or seems to lack good science, read up. Repeating this process over and over again on each new case will make you a better forensic examiner.

8. Do not give more weight to scientific findings than they deserve and become proficient with the limits of good science in their areas you routinely encounter.

Forensic scientists have value to investigative and forensic efforts in that they can clearly define the limits of the evidence they have examined—assisting with the support or refutation of case theory. Further still, they can express those limits in both intelligible writing and comprehensible testimony. If they are unable to perform these tasks, then their value is limited. Forensic practitioners who overestimate the significance of their findings or conceal any weaknesses are to be avoided. Whether incompetent or frauds, they place any work which incorporates their findings at risk of being misleading or just plain wrong. Forensic criminologists must therefore become adept in recognizing competent and incompetent forensic practice alike, to maintain the integrity of their own findings.

SUMMARY

Clearly, there are many different types of forensic scientists, with various investigative and legal value and educational experience. The defining quality of forensic scientists is the possibility that they will be called upon to present scientific findings, under penalty of perjury, in a court of law. Scientists then should be prepared to explain to the court what their findings mean and how they came to them. Anyone who cannot or does not do this is not a forensic scientist. The distinction between a forensic scientist and a technician must also be made, where a scientist is educated in the scientific method and uses it to interpret results.

As is clear from the previous discussion, there is a strong argument to be made that those forensic practitioners employed solely by law enforcement or the prosecution are not forensic scientists at all, but rather police practitioners; this is especially true with certain subtypes of forensic scientists, for whom little or no education related to the sciences is necessary.

Although the importance of forensic generalists cannot be understated, it is much more common for forensic scientists to be narrowly trained as specialists of some sort without the benefit of a general forensic background and then to learn other subspecialties once employed by a crime lab. These specialists can take the form of criminalists involved in one area or many: bloodstain pattern analysts, fingerprint or friction ridge analysts, firearms and tool marks identification specialists, forensic anthropologists, forensic odontologists, and forensic pathologists. Each of these specialists will have a different level of education in various fields, each may or may not have a pro-law enforcement bias, and each has the potential to make egregious errors based on lack of scientific knowledge and background education. It is the job of forensic criminologists utilizing these experts to educate themselves on the error rates, problem areas, and necessary qualifications to carry out these examinations and to assess the forensic scientists accordingly.

Review Questions

1. T/F Technicians and scientists are generally viewed as equivalent when it comes to evidence analysis.
2. Describe the different areas of criminalistics and the educational requirements of each.
3. T/F The term *trace evidence* is used to describe a very specific type of physical evidence.
4. Explain what is involved in a crime reconstruction.
5. Name the requirements necessary to be a bloodstain pattern analyst. Where does this leave law enforcement trained pattern analysts?
6. Describe the one-dissimilarity doctrine. What does this mean for the fallibility of fingerprint evidence?
7. Why is it a problem that tool mark and firearms examiners do not have a specific process which they are meant to carry out to determine whether an identification can be made?
8. T/F There are no mandated qualifications or certifications for death investigators in the United States.

REFERENCES

Blackledge, R., 2007. Forensic Analysis on the Cutting Edge: New Methods for Trace Evidence Analysis. John Wiley & Sons, Inc., New Jersey.

Bowers, M., 2004. Forensic Dental Evidence: An Investigator's Handbook. Academic Press, Boston.

Butler, J., Butler, T., 2004. DNA for Detectives. In: Savino, J., Turvey, B. (Eds.), Rape Investigation Handbook. Elsevier Science, Boston.

Byers, S., 2007. Introduction to Forensic Anthropology, third ed. Allyn & Bacon, New Jersey.

Casey, E., 2004. Digital Evidence and Computer Crime. Elsevier Science, Boston.

Casey, E., Malin, C., and Aquilina, J., 2008. Malware Forensics: Investigating and Analyzing Malicious Code. Syngress, Rockland, MA.

Chisum, W.J., 2007. Reconstruction Using Bloodstain Evidence. In: Chisum, W.J., Turvey, B. (Eds.), Crime Reconstruction. Elsevier Science, Boston.

Chisum, W.J., Turvey, B., 2007. Crime Reconstruction. Elsevier Science, Boston.

Cole, S.A., 2005. More Than Zero: Accounting for Error in Latent Fingerprint Identification. Journal of Criminal Law and Criminology 95 (Spring), 985–1078.

Cooley, C., 2004. Reforming the Forensic Science Community to Avert the Ultimate Injustice. Stanford Law and Policy Review 15, 381–446.

Cooley, C., 2007. Reconstructionists in a Post-*Daubert* and Post-DNA Courtroom. In: Chisum, W.J., Turvey, B. (Eds.), Crime Reconstruction. Elsevier Science, Boston.

Cooley, C., and Turvey, B., 2007. Observer Effects and Examiner Bias: Psychological Influences on the Forensic Examiner. In: Chisum, W.J., Turvey, B., (Eds.), Crime Reconstruction. Elsevier Science, Boston.

DeForest, P., Gaennslen, R., Lee, H., 1983. Forensic Science: An Introduction to Criminalistics. McGraw-Hill, New York.

DeHaan, J., 2007. Fire Scene Investigation. In: Chisum, W.J., Turvey, B. (Eds.), Crime Reconstruction. Elsevier Science, Boston.

Dolan, M., Felch, J., 2008. Crime Labs Finding Questionable DNA Matches; FBI Tries to Keep National Database away from Lawyers. Los Angeles Times August 3.

Edwards, H., 2009. Statement before United States Senate, Committee on the Judiciary March 18.

Edwards, H., Gotsonis, C., 2009. Strengthening Forensic Science in the United States: A Path Forward. National Academies Press, Washington, DC.

Garrett, R.J., 2009. Memo from the President of the International Association for Identification to the Membership, February 19.

Giannelli, P.C., 1997. The Abuse of Scientific Evidence in Criminal Cases: The Need for Independent Crime Laboratories. Virginia Journal of Social Policy & Law 4 (Spring), 439–470.

Glass, R., 2003. Forensic Odontology. In: James, S., Nordby, J. (Eds.), Forensic Science: An Introduction to Scientific and Investigative Techniques. CRC Press, Boca Raton.

Gross, H., 1906. Criminal Investigation. G. Ramasawmy Chetty & Co, Madras.

Houck, M., 2004. Trace Evidence Analysis: More Cases in Mute Witnesses. Academic Press, Boston.

Inman, K., Rudin, N., 1999. Principles and Practice of Criminalistics: The Profession of Forensic Science. CRC Press, Boca Raton.

James, S., Nordby, J., 2003. Forensic Science: An Introduction to Scientific and Investigative Techniques. CRC Press, Boca Raton.

Kirk, P., 1953. Crime Investigation. Interscience, New York.

Kirk, P., Bradford, L., 1965. The Crime Laboratory: Organization and Operation. Charles C. Thomas Pub. Ltd., New York.

Levanti, T., 2009. What to Look for in a Forensic Accountant. New York State Society of Certified Public Accounts URL: http://www.nysscpa.org/sound_advice/forensic_acc.htm.

National Institute of Justice (NIJ), 1999. Death Investigation: A Guide for the Scene Investigator. 10 Research Report NCJ 167568, Washington, D.C.

Risinger, D.M., Saks, M.J., Thompson, W.C., Rosenthal, R., 2002. The Daubert/Kumho Implications of Observer Effects in Forensic Science: Hidden Problems of Expectation and Suggestion. California Law Review, 90 (1), 1–56.

Rowe, W., 2003. Firearm and Tool Mark Examinations. In: James, S., Nordby, J. (Eds.), Forensic Science: An Introduction to Scientific and Investigative Techniques, CRC Press, Boca Raton.

Schwartz, A., 2005. A Systemic Challenge to the Reliability and Admissibility of Firearms and Toolmark Identification. The Columbia Science and Technology Law Review 6, 1–42.

Seigel, J., Saukko, P., Knupfer, G., 2000. The Encyclopedia of Forensic Science, vol. 1–3. Academic Press, London.

Starrs, J., 1993. The Seamy Side of Forensic Science: The Mephitic Stain of Fred Salem Zain. Scientific Sleuthing Review 17 (Winter), 1–8.

Thornton, J.I., 1977. The One-Dissimilarity Doctrine in Fingerprint Identification. Int. Crim. Police Rev., 306, 89.

Thornton, J.I., 1983. Uses and Abuses of Forensic Science. In: Thomas, W. (Ed.), Science and Law: An Essential Alliance. Westview Press, Boulder, CO.

Thornton, J., Kimmel-Lake, D., 2007. Trace Evidence in Crime Reconstruction. In: Chisum, W.J., Turvey, B. (Eds.), Crime Reconstruction, Elsevier Science, Boston.

Thornton, J., Peterson, J., 2002. The General Assumptions and Rationale of Forensic Identification. In: Faigman, D.L., Kaye, D.H., Saks, M.J., Sanders, J. (Eds.), Modern Scientific Evidence: The Law and Science of Expert Testimony, vol. 3. West Publishing Co., St. Paul, MN.

CHAPTER 14

Understanding the Role of Forensic DNA: A Primer for Criminologists

Carole McCartney

KEY TERMS

Adventitious Match: A chance match between profiles that do not originate from the same source.

Bayes Theorem: A logical method of weighing different pieces of evidence.

Buccal Swab: A sample of cells taken from the inside of a person's cheek using a swab.

Cold Cases: Those cases which have remained unsolved but open for many years.

Cold Hit: A DNA match which identifies an individual not previously suspected of involvement in a crime.

DNA Profile: A report produced after analysis of a sample of genetic material retrieved either from an individual or from a crime scene exhibit.

Ethnic Inferencing: Trying to predict an offender's ethnic background from his or her DNA profile.

Hypervariable Regions: Those regions of a DNA profile that vary greatly between individuals.

Prosecutor's Fallacy: A misconception committed whenever the recipient of statistical evidence, upon hearing it, believes that he or she has been told the likelihood of guilt or innocence.

Warm Hit: A DNA match which confirms the correct person has been arrested.

CONTENTS

INTRODUCTION

It is now a number of years since it was commented that forensic DNA profiling was an "integral part" of the criminal justice system of England and Wales: a claim that now may easily be made of the majority of the legal systems of developed nations. It may also be convincingly argued that the introduction of DNA profiling into forensic fora has been nothing short of revolutionary,

451

leading to significant legal reform and changes to policing and prosecutorial policy and practice, at the same time as becoming culturally imbued with almost oracle-like qualities. Perhaps most importantly, the use of forensic DNA profiling has undoubtedly saved lives: potential victims not befalling offenders who have been stopped in their criminal tracks, as well as those imprisoned and on death row, exonerated when their innocence was no longer deniable after DNA testing.

In this chapter, the use of DNA in criminal justice matters, and the impact of DNA on the police and courts, will be explored. Those interested in the science behind DNA profiling should read scientific explanations of the process, which will not be covered in any detail here. This chapter relies primarily on data from England and Wales with international comparisons where available and relevant. The United Kingdom is widely considered as leading the international community in the use of forensic DNA and has the largest proportion of its citizenry on the UK National DNA Database (NDNAD). While the chapter concentrates on the utilization of forensic DNA, it will not be possible to guarantee coverage of all possible issues, particularly where a country's size, culture, history, or legal system, for instance, differs significantly from the UK.

FORENSIC DNA ORIGINS

On September 10, 1984, Professor Alec Jeffreys and his team of genetic researchers at Leicester University produced what looked like nothing more than a murky barcode. However, Jeffreys realized that this "barcode" could be used as an identification tool for living organisms—much like barcodes identify the goods on our supermarket shelves. The production of these barcodes was given the moniker "genetic fingerprinting." Such a label was apt for a number of reasons, but importantly, was able to piggy-back on the trust placed in fingerprinting as an identification technique. This label also made it significantly easier to explain to the layman, and it was nonscientists who quickly seized on its usefulness in being able to prove (or disprove) the relatedness of humans. It was this ability—to support claims of biological relationships—that was first put to the test by the authorities who called upon the Leicester laboratory to prove a biological (maternal) link in a disputed immigration case.

After this successful application, the technique continued to be called upon by the Home Office to assist in immigration disputes until in 1985, there were a series of rapes near Leicester, with a local youth confessing. An astute police officer, hearing of Jeffrey's work, realized that they could "test" this confession by comparing the genetic fingerprint of the young man and that of the rapist. The team at Leicester were able to conclusively demonstrate that the youth was, in fact, not the rapist. However, they were unable to assist further without the

DNA of a suspect, prompting Leicester police to set up the first "mass screen" of men in the local area. Though conscientiously and laboriously profiling all these samples, the screen was ultimately fruitless, until it was revealed to the police that a local baker had persuaded a colleague to provide a DNA sample on his behalf. The baker, Colin Pitchfork, immediately became a suspect and had his DNA taken, which matched the crime scene DNA and led to the first criminal conviction using a genetic fingerprint.

Sir Jeffreys' genetic fingerprinting was soon refined and improved upon, developing into the technique known today as DNA profiling (Jobling and Gill, 2004). A *DNA profile* is produced after analysis of a sample of genetic material retrieved either from an individual (usually a *buccal swab* or cheek swab) or from a crime scene exhibit. In 1995, the Second Generation Multiplex (SGM) profiling kit was introduced in the UK, using 6 loci and a gender marker, giving a random match probability for two full profiles, of 1 in 50 million. In 1999, a new improved kit was rolled out: the SGM+ system, which had an additional 4 loci. The SGM+ profiling technique produces a more discriminating profile, giving a random match probability of around 1 in a billion. Countries will vary in their use of proprietary DNA profiling kits; for example, in the United States, they test for 13 loci. The size of the population of the United States demands the use of more loci to make their test even more discriminating.

A forensic DNA profile loaded onto the UK's National DNA Database (NDNAD) will then consist of a series of 20 two-digit numbers and the gender indicator. These numbers represent the peaks noted at the different loci tested using the SGM+ kit, making searching for DNA matches a simple matter of comparing one set of 20 numbers with all the others on the database and seeing which sequences, if any, match. However, the ease of such a computational task belies the actual complexity often involved in actually deciding whether a peak is real or over a chosen threshold, matters of judgment which are complicated by partial or degraded profiles and profiles that are a mixture of more than one individual.

DNA profiling does not examine every single difference between individuals and so can only ever provide probabilistic evidence, though this can be very powerful if it reaches the 1 in 1 billion random match probability. The profiling process simply looks for these 10 loci which are *hypervariable* (also known as hypervariable regions, which vary a great deal between individuals) and also give no indication of anything else such as health information. Matches involving partial profiles (where the DNA sample retrieved may be degraded or only a tiny amount was available) or biological relatives are more likely to occur by chance, reducing discriminatory power considerably. A chance match between profiles that do not originate from the same source is called an *adventitious match*. To date, there has been one reported adventitious match on the UK's NDNAD with two full SGM profiles.

There have been none (that have been reported) with SGM+ profiles, but the risk of adventitious matches inevitably increases as a DNA database grows.

THE FORENSIC DNA "REVOLUTION" IN POLICING

The precision of DNA profiling has made it very attractive to police investigators as a source of incontrovertible evidence. This is a welcome contrast with other, less reliable, evidence such as eyewitness accounts and information from increasingly uncooperative members of the public. DNA is impartial, scientific evidence (it is also increasingly cheap and quick). Indeed, even a decade ago, it was claimed that DNA "has not merely enhanced existing police capacity, but has even begun to replace the slow, tedious, and expensive traditional investigative methods of police interviews" (Watson, 1999, p. 325).[1] In 2004, the British Home Office claimed that not only did science and technology "play a vital role in modern policing," but the National DNA Database was "revolutionizing" crime detection (Home Office, 2004).

[1] For a consideration of the potential issues arising from greater reliance upon DNA during police investigations, see also McCartney (2006a).

It is hard to understate the scale of this revolution in the use of forensic DNA. There is now rarely a police investigation in which the question would not be asked whether DNA could play a role. Indeed, in the United Kingdom, as with many countries, the taking of DNA from individuals by the police is considered routine. While essential in major investigations into violent/sexual crimes, DNA also has significant impact in the investigation of volume (largely property) crime. Periodic initiatives focus on maximizing the use and usefulness of DNA in ever-increasing numbers and types of criminal investigations, the result of a combination of scientific/technological development and significant law reform, as well as substantial government financial investment.

This chapter will review the legal reforms that have enabled the use of DNA in criminal investigations and prosecutions and attempts to gauge the impact of DNA in the criminal process. It will go on to look at the growth of DNA databases before turning to issues that are increasingly coming to the fore, including the issue of the international exchange of DNA data, the raising of ethical questions, and the stretching of the science of DNA profiling.

HOW DNA PROFILES ARE UTILIZED

In Police Investigations

[2] The law differs in Scotland.

While the England, Wales, and Northern Ireland[2] police have the widest powers in the world to obtain, and retain, DNA from suspects, victims, or witnesses in criminal investigations (though perhaps not for much longer), powers to take DNA from suspects and convicted offenders have been written into law in countries across the world. Many countries limit these police powers with regard to the severity of the offense, but while the powers and nomenclature may vary, in general, the police obtain and retain three types of samples:

- *Criminal justice or suspect samples*—samples taken from individuals who have been arrested;
- *Elimination samples*—victim/volunteer samples;
- *Crime scene samples*—samples retrieved from crime scenes and crime scene exhibits.

When a DNA sample is taken, it is immediately[3] subject to a "speculative search"—that is, the DNA profile, once obtained from the sample in the laboratory, is checked against all the DNA profiles already held on a DNA database, including those obtained from scenes of unsolved crimes and all the other DNA profiles held of individuals, checking for duplication. Any matches between newly loaded profiles and retained profiles are then reported to the police who submitted the sample for analysis for further investigation. A match report may not include just one individual; it is not unusual for the police to get a list of named suspects who may have left the DNA sample (or the matches are with replicates on the database). This is more likely where advanced searching or profiling techniques have been used.

The use of scientific investigative methods provides an opportunity to move away from reliance upon less reliable evidence, such as eyewitnesses, confessions, etc. The use of DNA also provides an opportunity to speed up investigations (saving time, money, and resources which can be spent elsewhere) and provide police intelligence where there may be none (or very little) to be garnered using more traditional policing methods. Crimes may be solved years after they occurred (so-called *cold cases*)—or linked together so offenders may be prosecuted for a series of offenses. While the causes of crime are multifaceted and complex, it is accepted that the chances of detection can act (in some cases) as a deterrent. There is then an argument that in time, if most people had their DNA retained by the police, crime would fall because not only would offenders be caught more reliably (and their criminal careers shortened), but other potential offenders would be deterred as they would know the certainty of being caught.

DNA located at a crime scene (or found on a weapon or victim, for example) is very powerful evidence. In some cases it can provide almost incontrovertible "proof" of identity. In rape cases, if there is a full sample left, then the issue of identity is almost undisputable; of course, it does not prove rape, which has further legal elements which require satisfying. Likewise, if a weapon used in a crime is located and DNA found on the weapon, then this will be highly suggestive of involvement with the offense. However, in some instances, the power of DNA lies in being able to exculpate an innocent suspect before locating (sometimes) the real perpetrator. In hundreds of cases, mostly in the United

[3]While it is normally profiled within 48 hours in the United Kingdom, in many countries, particularly the United States, laboratories have severe backlogs, and it may be months, even years, before the DNA is actually profiled, seriously limiting its effectiveness.

States, exculpatory DNA has not been tested until many years after the innocent individual has been in prison—sometimes even on death row. There has been significant (but incomplete) legal reform in the United States to now expedite the use of DNA to exonerate innocent citizens who remain in prison; in many cases, the real perpetrator has also been identified by such testing.[4]

[4]See the Innocence Project—
http://www.innocenceproject.
org.

In the United Kingdom, in over 42% of cases, DNA did not provide a fresh lead (or intelligence)—as the police already had the name of the suspect (and may have had him or her in custody) (Home Office, 2005). Essentially, the DNA match did not then detect the crime, but confirmed the correct person had been arrested and may prove useful in securing his or her conviction. These are sometimes referred to as *warm hits*, as opposed to *cold hits* where the DNA matches with an individual not previously suspected of involvement. The detection rate in which a DNA profile is obtained in connection with a crime is significantly higher—rising to 43% rather than the 26% overall crime detection rate—although it is rare, of course, that the police find DNA in all (or even most) cases, largely because they tend not to look for it too hard (which is costly and timely) rather than because it is not there. Perhaps contrary to expectations, DNA has proven most useful in those crimes that are the most difficult to detect—that is, domestic burglary, rather than the crimes that are the most serious (which tend to have a higher detection rate). For example, the overall detection rate for domestic burglary in England and Wales is 17%, but where DNA is retrieved from a crime scene, this rises to 39%, while theft from a car rises from 9% to 60% (Lake, 2006–2007, p. 16). Similar findings have been recently reported in the United States (Roman et al., 2008).

The success of DNA profiling is determined by the number of samples from crime scenes that can be subsequently linked with a perpetrator. Yet in the United Kingdom, there is wide variation between police forces as to the number of scenes examined, with approximately 17% of all known crime scenes examined, and DNA recovered from just 10% of these examined scenes, while the number of DNA samples sent to forensic laboratories for processing also varies. The reason for this primarily has to do with prioritizing necessary when working with limited budgets. In addition, in many crimes there will be no "scene" or exhibits to examine. Or it will be impossible to search effectively, or the culprit will be obvious. In England and Wales in 2007–2008, just 0.36% of recorded crimes were detected using DNA. This, of course, is an even smaller proportion of all crimes committed (of which only a minority are recorded), meaning that DNA still has a way to go before making a significant impact on crime as a whole. Of course, it can be very helpful in serious crimes, those with no other leads, and those where there was no other hope of detection—but as a general picture of "crime" and its detection, it remains marginal (and still used less often than the humble fingerprint). The most effective way of catching criminals remains asking the public for information. Whether or not they assist the police is an issue of police-community relations. Yet increasing police powers to take and keep DNA may not foster the sort of police-community relations necessary to ensure public cooperation in investigations.

DNA databases are often referred to as a police "intelligence tool"—in that it provides investigators with "intelligence" about offenders and offences, including offender patterns. It is an incredibly powerful resource with new methods continually being developed to further utilize the information stored therein. Two methods include *familial searching* and *ethnic inferencing*—(trying to predict an offender's ethnic background from his or her DNA profile; see later). The police can also trace the offending patterns of *unknown prolifics*—serial offenders who are evading arrest and may be traveling around a country or jurisdiction committing crimes that are not linked by police forces.

The use of DNA requires different policing skills, and lack of training remains a significant issue. In reality, most regular police officers will rarely, if ever, be involved in a crime that requires them to deal with DNA, meaning that if they do, many are ill prepared. It is essential that all police (and emergency services personnel) are forensically aware if DNA is to be successfully obtained and contamination avoided. There are significant issues with the collection of DNA which, if done incorrectly, cannot then be salvaged later (such as in the Duke lacrosse case in the United States). There is no room for error—in the laboratory, but importantly, also at the crime scene. DNA profiling is a sensitive technique, and without the investment of time and resources in proper and thorough crime scene examination, DNA will remain marginal, if not problematic, in police investigations.

Pretrial Issues

The presence of DNA at a crime scene cannot constitute proof of guilt for any crime on its own. In England and Wales, a DNA match is not sufficient evidence upon which to base a criminal charge. Supporting non-DNA evidence must also be submitted to the Crown Prosecution Service (CPS) before they decide to proceed with charging. Most often, a DNA match will lead to further investigations being undertaken by the police, to confirm the match. However, what counts as supporting evidence is a matter for the CPS lawyer, and there is no uniformity in this decision. In some cases, being arrested "close to the scene" is sufficient, or being male and a smoker has been sufficient (with previous convictions). Increasingly, a strong DNA match can be supported by quite weak additional evidence (i.e., lack of an alibi).

In some cases, a DNA match will be very persuasive evidence; for example, in a stranger rape, if a suspect matches the DNA sample and cannot offer an explanation (or produce an alibi, for example), then this will almost inevitably lead to a conviction (most likely from a guilty plea). However, all DNA matches

ted within the case—a match may not actually mean very
killed in her home, and her husband's DNA is found, that
provide evidence because one would expect to find the
s it is found somewhere which may implicate him (like
). Similarly, if there is a bank robbery, a DNA profile
en bank clerks, customers, or robbers (again, if found
it can be more helpful—for instance, on a weapon
ver, there is a danger with DNA matches declared
this information may impact on the direction of
cCartney, 2006a). Research into miscarriages of jus-
wed police investigations are usually characterized by early
made about suspects and the subsequent narrowing of the investiga-
. This has been called "tunnel vision," and early decisions about the guilt
of suspects have been shown to skew police investigations.

There may also be concern over the abbreviation of the criminal process. Often,
the finding of a DNA match can be presented to suspects at a police station,
implying that their conviction is assured, so they would do well to plead guilty
and avoid a trial and perhaps a harsher sentence. Legal advice in this situation is crucial, but it is not clear whether solicitors are able to fully interrogate
the relevance or significance of the DNA match at this early stage; it may be
meaningless, in which case they should probably advise their clients against
pleading guilty. Of course, the police must also disclose all forensic evidence
in a timely fashion to ensure that the defense have a fair chance to assess the
evidence and, if necessary, seek further advice or undertake further testing of
the evidence.

Presentation of DNA Evidence at Court

DNA profiling provides probabilistic evidence and can never provide 100%
proof but is presented as a match probability. As such, it has often been the
source of great confusion at trial, statistics are often widely misunderstood
among the public, and poor reporting by journalists can perpetuate confusion.
The expression *prosecutor's fallacy* was first used by Thompson and Schumann,
but debate concerning the precise definition of the *prosecutor's fallacy* and the
argument that there is a corollary *defender's fallacy* can become highly technical. A simpler way perhaps of understanding the fallacy is as follows: the
statement "If I am a monkey, then I have two arms and two legs" is true, and
yet "If I have two arms and two legs, I am a monkey" is clearly not. Or if you
prefer—imagine being told that there was an elephant outside your house. You
would conceivably presume that the elephant outside had four legs. However,
if you were told that there was an animal outside your house with four legs,
it would be rather odd to jump to the conclusion that the animal must be an
elephant!

The prosecutor's fallacy is committed, then, whenever the recipients of the statistical evidence, upon hearing it, believe that they have been told the likelihood of guilt or innocence. This arises when the rarity of a particular DNA profile (the match probability) is presented as being interchangeable with the probability that the defendant is innocent. For example, a profile with a rarity of "one in a million" produces the false conclusion that the chance of the defendant being innocent is "one in a million" when it actually means that in a country of, say, 60 million people, there may be approximately 60 people with that profile. Without other evidence, the defendant is then no more likely than the other 59 with the same profile to be the actual offender. If there is a full SGM+ match of the suspect's DNA and that recovered from a crime scene, then the rarity is expressed as "of the order of one in a billion." Even though this is very powerful evidence, it still does not, by itself, prove conclusively that the defendant was the source of the crime scene profile. There remains a possibility that somebody else (especially a close relative) may have the same profile.

The leading case in England and Wales on presenting DNA evidence at trial is known as *Doheny and Adams (R v Doheny & Anor,* 1996). In *Doheny,* a DNA expert had testified that it was his opinion that the offender was the defendant. The trial judge directed the jury that if this evidence was to be believed, guilt had been conclusively proved. This was contrary to the proper interpretation of the DNA evidence, that while there was a very small group of other people who could match the DNA profile, the defendant was only one of this small group. In Gary Adams' original trial, both the expert and prosecutor committed the prosecutor's fallacy. The Court of Appeal ruled that it was vital, in light of the increasing use of DNA evidence, that the profiling process be understood and that the manner in which the evidence is presented be made as clear as possible. In *R v Dennis Adams* (1996), the Court of Appeal rejected the argument that the complexity of DNA evidence was a ground upon which such evidence could be excluded. However, the Court ordered a retrial because the defense team's use of the *Bayes theorem* (a logical method of weighing different pieces of evidence) had "plunged the jury into inappropriate and unnecessary realms of theory and complexity deflecting them from their proper tasks."

The courts have further considered the weight of DNA evidence in the cases of *R v Watters* (2000) and *R v Mitchell* (2004). Watters was originally convicted of four burglaries based on a DNA match with samples from cigarette butts found at the scene of burglaries. The prosecution relied on the fact that the defendant was a smoker, lived locally, and was male. On appeal it was argued that the DNA evidence was weak (there was only a partial profile giving a match probability of 1 in 9,000), and the defendant had a brother—which reduced the match probability to 1 in 267. The DNA expert claimed that this DNA evidence should not have been used in isolation at trial, and the Court of Appeal concluded that the case should not have been put before a jury because of the confusion over the brothers. In *R v Mitchell*, the appellant successfully argued that the fact that DNA swabs taken from the victim did *not* match his DNA profile strongly supported his defense of mistaken identity. The trial judge had summed up the DNA evidence at trial, stating that it was entirely neutral and could not assist the jury. The Court of Appeal disagreed, finding that a "non-match" could indeed be powerful evidence, which the jury should consider. The Court concluded that when considering DNA evidence, judges should take great care not to raise scientific speculative possibilities.

There remains a risk that individuals could be charged with a serious criminal offense on the basis of a circumstantial association with the crime scene represented by a DNA match and, if lacking a cast iron defense, it may be very difficult to challenge the DNA evidence. The triers of fact will have to take account of other evidence—for example, alibi evidence (or lack of it), differences in any description of the offender, and the character of the defendant—and decide whether on all the evidence they can be sure of guilt. Special care needs to be taken when DNA is located on a "mobile" object—such as a cigarette butt—which may have originally been dropped somewhere other than where it was found. A corrupt investigator or devious criminal could attempt to deliberately contaminate a crime scene with an innocent person's DNA.

The Impact of DNA at Trial

In the United States, research has shown that prosecution reliance upon DNA evidence resulted in longer sentences (Purcell, Thomas-Winfree, and Mays, 1994). The hypothesis is that judges were "punishing" defendants for wasting time, when the DNA evidence made their conviction almost certain. In Australia, it has been found that juries are 33 times more likely to convict a defendant when the prosecutor produces DNA evidence (Briody, 2002; 2004), and that most jurors had been exposed to DNA through popular culture before trial and anticipated its significance—they went into the courtroom convinced that DNA would be compelling evidence and were happier to convict—even if the DNA evidence was not that significant or helpful in the case (Findlay and Grix, 2003). Such high expectations of DNA makes essential the proper education of legal professionals and jurors.

There has been no equivalent research in England and Wales, but what is clear is that expert opinions can be highly persuasive during both investigations and trials. There have been reported examples of misunderstanding of DNA (and scientific evidence more generally) by judges, lawyers, police, journalists, and even forensic scientists. DNA results may be misleading during both investigations and trials: it being vital that DNA is properly interpreted within the case. However, courts are not the place for scientific debate, making it difficult for all concerned if there are arguments over the DNA results or their significance.

Such difficulties may well result in undeserved acquittals or, perhaps more likely, wrongful convictions.

NATIONAL DNA DATABASES

To maximize the utility of DNA profiling techniques, nearly all developed countries have a DNA database or *databank*. There is huge variety in the laws governing these databases and whose DNA may be stored on them, but their general aim is to store the DNA taken from unsolved crime scenes so that they may be matched with any future suspects, as well as store the DNA of convicted offenders so that their future crimes may be detected more easily. Many countries limit their DNA databases to serious offenders or are time-limited, whereas others can include those who have committed more minor offenses.

The UK National DNA Database

No single legislative instrument or Act of Parliament established the UK National DNA Database (NDNAD), or the police powers to take and retain biological samples from citizens.[5] Instead, the collection, storage, and use of DNA and biological samples has been facilitated piecemeal by successive amendments to the Police and Criminal Evidence Act (PACE) 1984. Over the course of a few years, police sampling powers have been significantly extended by a series of amendments. The Criminal Justice Act 2003 extended sampling powers, permitting the nonconsensual taking of DNA samples upon arrest for a recordable offense. These samples are to be retained on the NDNAD and speculatively searched and used: "for purposes related to the prevention or detection of crime, the investigation of an offence or the conduct of a prosecution" (PACE s.64). However, the European Court of Human Rights has now ruled that these laws breach human rights and are now under review (*S & Marper v UK*, 2008).

[5]The UK NDNAD holds DNA from England, Wales, and Northern Ireland. Scotland has its own national database although the two allow the exchange of DNA profiles for searching.

In 1995 the UK's National DNA Database was established, consisting of electronic records of DNA profiles obtained from individuals and crime scenes (a 20-digit code). In addition, all DNA samples are retained from individuals (the crime scene samples are kept only until the crime has been through the courts). The NDNAD has seen massive growth, so the United Kingdom has the biggest proportion of their population on the database in the world—at nearly 7% of all citizens. By late 2008, there were over 5 million DNA profiles on the database, representing over 4.5 million individuals (there are significant numbers of replicates, estimated to be 14% of the total). Of these individuals, just under 25,000 are from "volunteers" (victims, witnesses, etc.). Currently, 50,000 citizens are added to the NDNAD each month, but this number may drop in light of the European Court ruling. There are also nearly 300,000 crime scene samples stored on the NDNAD. During 2006–2007, over 40,000 matches were made between crime scene and one or more individuals. The database is, not surprisingly, dominated by males (80% of the total) and young people—8% of samples were taken from individuals who were under 14 when their DNA was loaded. There are growing concerns around not only the numbers of "innocent" people on the database (an issue which now has to be addressed), but also the numbers of young people and the disproportionate number of people from ethnic minorities on the database.

The NDNAD is governed by the NDNAD Strategy Board, supported with the creation in late 2007 of an NDNAD Ethics Board. The NDNAD Custodian Unit is responsible for overseeing delivery of NDNAD operations and the Standards of Performance for forensic science laboratories. The Custodian is entrusted with maintaining and safeguarding the integrity of the NDNAD and developing policy. A mix of private organizations and police laboratories are approved to provide DNA profiles from criminal justice and/or crime scene samples to the NDNAD. The UK Accreditation Service (UKAS) accredits laboratories in line with two major standards—ISO/IEC 17025 and ISO 9000:2000—and the Custodian also has stringent quality criteria and checks. In 2007, the role of "Forensic Regulator" was also created, with the Regulator to play a significant role in the future governance of the NDNAD.

The legal parameters for use of the NDNAD are clearly delineated in the Police and Criminal Evidence Act of 1984: the prevention and detection of crime, the investigation of an offense, the conduct of a prosecution, or the identification of a deceased person. This affords some certainty about how the NDNAD may be lawfully used. It precludes the use of the NDNAD in medical or other research, or in paternity disputes. Such terms, however, may be subject to a wide interpretation that expands the range of uses to which the information on the databases may legitimately be put. While, to date, forensic databases have been used primarily to match known suspects with crime scenes, they are increasingly used in efforts to identify unknown suspects: by searching the NDNAD for possible relatives of a perpetrator or for predicting the likely ethnic appearance of an unidentified suspect, for example.

New Zealand and Australia

In 1996, New Zealand was the second country to establish a national forensic DNA database and remains the only country in which the custodian of the database is a private entity. The passing of the Criminal Investigations (Blood Samples) Act 1995 brought together the New Zealand Police and the Institute of Environmental Science and Research to create a national DNA database, with strict rules regarding sampling of individuals. A DNA match can only prompt further police inquiries and is not sufficient to commence a prosecution (Harbison, Hamilton, and Walsh, 2002). The use of DNA testing has not been without controversy, with an inquiry into the investigation of a Christchurch man for murder when his DNA "matched" a sample taken from a murder scene, yet it was subsequently proven that the man had never been to Wellington, where the murders had occurred. A subsequent inquiry in 1999 found that there had been contamination of samples in the laboratory during processing (McCartney, 2006b).

In 1990, the Australian federal government, as well as a number of states and territories, had begun to undertake forensic DNA analysis, and in 1992, the National Institute of Forensic Science (NIFS) began developing national standards for forensic DNA laboratories throughout Australia. In 1999, the Model Forensic Procedures Bill was published, to guide states on the construction of their DNA legislation. While not addressing who such databases may include, it spelled out procedures for sampling and the destruction of samples. Many of the states closely followed the Model Bill when writing their DNA legislation, and others have subsequently amended their legislation to bring it closer into line with the bill, while retaining some variations.

This variation among jurisdictions has led directly to significant problems in creating a national database. In 2001, the federal government established the CrimTrac Agency, a law enforcement agency set up to facilitate national crime fighting initiatives including a DNA database—the National Criminal Investigation DNA Database (NCIDD). Individual states and territories have then had to draw up state-level legislation to enable their voluntary involvement in NCIDD, and the writing of bilateral agreements between each of the states. This has proved to be a slow, painstaking process which has suppressed the ability of states to cross-check DNA samples across the country.[6]

[6]http://www.crimtrac.gov.au/systems_projects/NationalCriminalInvestigationDNADatabase.html

The United States: CODIS

In 1989, Virginia became the first state to create a DNA database which, while limited at its inception to violent and sexual offenders, has subsequently expanded and been joined by DNA databases from all other states in the United States. Every state now collects DNA from offenders, though their sampling powers vary significantly. The FBI were first authorized to establish a national DNA database with the passing of the DNA Identification Act of 1994. This legislation created CODIS, a supra-database consisting of DNA databases at the local (LDIS), state (SDIS), and national levels (NDIS), with over 170 public laboratories contributing to the database. The NDIS has two indexes: a forensic index with profiles obtained from crime scenes and an offender index with profiles of individuals, these profiles consisting of 13 STR loci. A "match" on

[7]http://www.fbi.gov/hq/lab/codis/clickmap.htm

[8]As of October 2008.

[9]See http://www.fbi.gov/hq/lab/codis/clickmap.htm for more information on CODIS. The largest store of DNA in the world is the U.S. military, but this is just DNA samples, not profiles. No military DNA samples are analyzed until required and as such are not held electronically so are not "accessible" for searching as with forensic databases.

[10]http://www.fbi.gov/hq/lab/html/codisbrochure_text.htm

[11]Mitochondrial DNA is generally extracted from biological items of evidence such as hair, bones, and teeth.

the NDIS is reported to the submitting laboratories which then communicate on validating (or refuting) the match and adding the necessary identifiable information (which is not held on the NDIS). As of October 2008, CODIS had produced over 77,700 hits.[7]

Since becoming fully operational in 1998, CODIS has collated 241,685 forensic profiles and 6,384,379 offender profiles,[8] making it the largest DNA database in the world (California alone has the third largest DNA databank in the world).[9] However, an increase in federal funding following the 2003 "President's DNA Initiative," which saw $1 billion poured into training and assistance, and the continued expansion of database laws such as the DNA Fingerprints Act of 2005 mean that CODIS is set to grow dramatically in the coming years.[10] In 2000, the United States also commenced the creation of the National Missing Person DNA Database (NMPDD), which can hold both conventional STR DNA profiles and also mitochondrial (mtDNA) profiles. Mitochondrial DNA is found in the mitochondria of the cell and is inherited only from the mother, making them useful for missing person investigations but not criminal investigations where individuation is necessary.[11]

Europe

The European Council has passed resolutions encouraging member states to develop national DNA databases and permit the exchange of profiles (see Johnson and Williams, 2007). The European Network of Forensic Science Institutes (ENFSI) DNA Working Group report that across the European Union there have been almost universal moves to expand DNA databases, with Ireland remaining one of the last to establish a permanent database of DNA profiles, with legislation intended to be passed in 2009 (*Report on ENFSI*, 2009). However, despite the universal enthusiasm, there are huge variations across Europe with respect to police powers to collect and retain DNA (Williams and Johnson, 2005). At least 20 member states permit the compulsory taking of DNA samples and retaining DNA profiles on databases. However, in many of these states, the power to take samples is limited to certain circumstances, most often being limited to being taken in connection with serious offenses. Further, in most of Europe, DNA is destroyed upon acquittal, although some (e.g., Scotland, Austria) can retain DNA if the suspect continues to be a "risk" for future serious offending. While variations in law governing sampling and retention are many, it may be that in the future, laws will come to more closely align when pressures for data sharing and harmonization grow. The European Court of Human Rights has also recently given a clear steer on when the retention of DNA may be justified, which will lead to modification of the UK's laws to bring them more into line with their European neighbors.

The Future?

The Secretary General of Interpol recently stated that DNA profiling "has benefited mostly the wealthiest of countries" (Noble, 2007), yet policy in this area is developing rapidly and is highly ambitious. There are moves for DNA databases around the world to be compatible and enable searching for DNA matches across borders. The scientific techniques are also continually being refined and improved upon, with mobile DNA testing and automation also a clear aim. However, the use of DNA technology and the relevant enabling legal reforms that have permitted police sampling and databasing have belatedly begun to attract critical attention from different quarters. For example, forensic scientists have conducted research on the scientific principles underpinning DNA profiling, to advance the scientific capabilities of the technique. There has been some examination of forensic identification technologies from a socio-legal perspective (e.g., McCartney, 2006b) and by sociologists (e.g., Williams and Johnson, 2008), examining impacts upon legal systems and social relations. More recently, ethical inquiries have been made by bioethicists (Nuffield Council on Bioethics, 2007), while politicians have inquired into the status of forensic science in the United Kingdom generally (House of Commons, 2005) and, more specifically, the operation and governance of surveillance technologies including the NDNAD (Home Affairs Committee, 2008). There are also serious reasons to suggest that the presumed "infallibility" of DNA requires challenging, in light of continued controversies surrounding DNA.

INTERNATIONAL EXCHANGE

The use of DNA in support of criminal investigations and counterterrorism measures is an important feature of contemporary efforts across the world to ensure security. The use of DNA is also growing among intelligence and other EU-wide security agencies, while rapidly evolving efforts to tackle transnational crime entail the exchange of DNA across jurisdictions and state borders (e.g., Lewis, 2007). Indeed, the international utilization and exchange of forensic DNA is becoming an expectation, with the Schengen Information System (SIS) in Europe, and more recently the Prum Treaty, which stipulate that there should be shared access to law enforcement information across agencies in Europe. Yet there are formidable scientific challenges with harmonization. In Europe, DNA databases in member states are not compatible and cannot be searched against each other meaningfully.[12] Interpol has also attempted to facilitate international transfer of DNA data using the Interpol Standard Set of Loci (ISSOL), and there is an Interpol DNA Charter to monitor transfers, with oversight provided by the DNA Monitoring Group. In 2005, Interpol's DNA database became operational, while more recently, Interpol launched the DNA Gateway, which enables the comparison of DNA profiles to take place online.

[12] ENFSI have agreed on seven common markers for a DNA profile which can be used for exchange, significantly less than the standard used in most countries. There are risks with reliance upon fewer markers, with an increased chance of adventitious matches, demanding that there be further safeguards in place to prevent wrongful convictions.

However, there is a risk that while scientists may attempt to answer the demands of interoperability, scientific developments move faster than legal, ethical, or political regimes can respond. The sending of such "personal" information beyond jurisdictional boundaries is controversial, not least because of a lack of formal procedures and legal guarantees that there will be no scope for unauthorized storage, further manipulation, or exchanges of the data. There are no bodies charged with oversight powers to monitor the international exchange of forensic DNA and no one to whom individuals may direct inquiries or complaints. Such omissions are significant, with continued growth in agreements to exchange forensic DNA data internationally and in proposals for global databases. There have yet to be legal rulings on whether DNA evidence from another country is admissible in domestic courts, which is vital if convictions are to be secured.

ETHICAL ISSUES

The forensic use of citizens' DNA demands the highest operating standards in terms of accountability, security, quality assurance, and ethical standards. Medical databases are strictly governed and subject to laws governing human rights and data protection. However, many DNA databases held by state agencies are not so clearly governed, yet robust ethical governance is vital to ensure "the liberty, autonomy and privacy of those whose details are recorded on such databases, and also to help engender public trust and confidence in their existence and use as part of a criminal justice system" (Nuffield Council on Bioethics, 2007, p. 91) There are imperatives that forensic databases are effective and efficient and their utility maximized at the same time as minimizing risks of abuse or other potential harmful effects. The UK Nuffield Council of Bioethics have found significant room for improvement in the use of DNA and fingerprints while the National Ethics Councils of France and Portugal have highlighted concerns and established principles for the ethical collating and retaining of bioinformation of citizens (French Comité, 2007).

The use of DNA remains sensitive, and the ethical issues involve the police "justifying" that the powers they have are proportionate in the fight against crime. The Nuffield Council 2007 report concluded that there must be a balance between personal liberty and the common good. Many now believe that the popular "no reason to fear if you are innocent" argument commonly used is not a sufficient justification for the full extent of police powers. The European Court of Human Rights in late 2008 agreed (*S & Marper v UK*, 2008), stating that

> ...[T]he blanket and indiscriminate nature of the powers of retention
> of the fingerprints, cellular samples and DNA profiles of persons
> suspected but not convicted of offences... fails to strike a fair balance

between the competing public and private interests and…, constitutes a disproportionate interference with the applicants' right to respect for private life and cannot be regarded as necessary in a democratic society.

The Court also considered that the retention of personal data of juveniles may be especially harmful.

Oversight and management of DNA databases are becoming increasingly important as more ways of using them are found. While most uses can be classified "operational," in that the use is directly related to particular police investigations, there are emerging "research" uses. Research could be conducted using the electronic records (profiles) on the database or the archived biological samples from which the DNA profiles have been generated. Expanding use of the databases beyond "operational" uses makes crucial the need for robust ethical oversight and regulation, particularly in instances in which the research uses the archived biological samples. Advanced levels of ethical and scientific review are necessary because these samples are not initially obtained with consent, unlike those collected in medical settings, and remain easily traceable to named individuals.

STRETCHING THE SCIENCE

In many countries, the focus of debate has been on how to populate DNA databases. However, it is being more widely recognized that the crucial element for DNA databases to be effective in crime detection is the collection of DNA samples from crime scenes, without which the DNA of individuals, whether serious criminals or not, is rendered meaningless. A lot of work has been undertaken on automation, with most modern laboratories now equipped with robots and computerized testing processes. There have also been efforts to create mobile DNA testing capabilities, to enable rapid testing at a crime scene. This has gone so far as attempts to create a "lab-on-a-chip" technology, with visions in the future of police officers able to test DNA on the spot (much as they can now do with fingerprints). So far, trials of mobile DNA analysis laboratories (a Forensic Response Vehicle, or FRV) have demonstrated the feasibility of obtaining profiles at a crime scene, which could speed up investigations. Their significant operating costs have not been justified for standard use to date.

However, there have been significant developments in laboratory methods. The DNA testing now undertaken is far less ambiguous than the original "DNA fingerprint," which left significant room for debate, although DNA profiles still require expert interpretation. This need becomes critical when dealing with mixed samples or partial profiles. Techniques to separate mixed samples and to analyze degraded samples (Mitochondrial DNA Analysis and Y Chromosome Analysis are used in such instances) are becoming more widespread and commonly used.[13]

Partial Profiles

DNA samples may, for a variety of reasons, be degraded or contaminated, requiring a more detailed examination of any resulting profile. Match probabilities will be less decisive than for a full profile and should attract caution. In *R v Bates* (2006) there was a thorough examination of issues arising in cases in which only a partial DNA profile was found at the crime scene, concluding: "We can see no reason why partial profile DNA evidence should not be admissible provided that the jury are made aware of its inherent limitations and are given a sufficient explanation to enable them to evaluate it...."

Mixed Samples

DNA samples originating from more than one person always require interpretation, and a court has to demand evidence of a valid analysis, with interpretation of mixtures heavily dependent on the expert opinion of the reporting officer. Profiles provided by known innocent bystanders can often be subtracted from the mixed profile to identify peaks of unknown origin, and in rape cases, special techniques may identify a male-specific profile from a vaginal swab. Computer programs for identifying individual profiles in mixed samples may be ineffective with very small samples.

Low Template Number DNA

While DNA technology has advanced to be able to analyze ever smaller samples, very small samples give rise to concerns over the presentation of DNA evidence. Concerns about the LTN DNA technique focus on the heightened possibility of contamination when very small amounts of material are amplified to obtain a profile. Contamination, whether deliberate or accidental, is a major issue which is heightened when dealing with very small samples. Samples can easily be contaminated with DNA from one of the police or laboratory team if strict preventive measures are not taken. Elimination databases are maintained, which hold the profiles of potential "innocent donors" of DNA, and hence enable their DNA profiles to be excluded from the investigation.[14] However, many individuals are involved in the transfer of DNA from a crime scene through the process of collection, storage, transport, and laboratory analysis. In the trial of Sean Hoey for a series of bombings in Northern Ireland, the prosecution relied on LTN DNA evidence (*R v Hoey*, 2007). The defense, however, were able to demonstrate that the collection and storage of exhibits had not been undertaken with due diligence. At the time of the investigation, neither the army nor police were cognizant of the concerns that

[13]In the future, STR markers might be superseded by a different type of marker, such as SNIPS—or Single Nucleotide Polymorphisms (SNPs), now used in genetic research. The technology now exists for typing thousands of SNPs from a biological sample in a single automated operation.

[14]The United Kingdom has a Police Elimination Database (PED), which covers the police and Scenes of Crimes Officers, and the Manufacturers Elimination Database (MED), which has the profiles of those who produce the equipment used in DNA analysis because it was found that DNA profiles were being produced of the people who had been involved in the manufacture of the swabbing kits. Each private company also has databases of its staff.

would later arise with regard to DNA collection. This was then compounded by haphazard storage and transportation of exhibits between the police and Forensic Service of Northern Ireland.

Familial Searching

Often, a speculative search on a DNA database may come up with close matches—often from a blood relative. This ability to find partial matches on the database can be used to find the blood relatives of perpetrators, which can provide the police with possible new investigative leads. So-called familial searching has now been used around the world to support serious crime investigations. This ability raises a lot of ethical issues and at times may be of limited use because the search may produce a list of numerous possible relatives. However, in the United Kingdom, there are several cases in which use of the technique has led to the conviction of serious criminals.

A DNA Photofit?

The ultimate in crime-fighting intelligence tools would be for suspect DNA found at a crime scene to be sent to the laboratory and for the scientists to then return a "photofit" of the suspect. The similarity of identical twins clearly demonstrates that physical likeness is influenced by genes, and in principle, physical characteristics might be predictable. At present, this possibility remains incredibly complex, although certain combinations of alleles can give an indication of ethnic origin (inferring ethnicity), a technique that has been used in a number of police investigations into serious crimes when they have stalled in an effort to get as much information as possible on the crime scene stain donor. There have been some developments in identifying redheads (though it cannot tell whether someone is bald or has dyed his or her hair). Several genes have also been identified that contribute to determining eye color, and it is known that skin color is determined by a series of different genes, some of which have been specifically identified. Perhaps even better still than a photofit would be the suspect's name. Since a man's Y chromosome and, most often, his surname are both inherited down the male line, there is some correlation between Y-chromosome markers and surnames. For unusual surnames, the correlation has been sufficient to help narrow a pool of suspects. Such inferences would, of course, be complicated by cases in which individuals had been adopted or otherwise did not share the surname of their biological father.

THE "GOLD STANDARD" OR FOOL'S GOLD?

With the significant investments made around the world in developing forensic DNA capabilities and the continued representations of DNA as the "gold standard" of identification, it is not surprising that many believe DNA to be infallible. However, there are many reasons to believe that there may have been an amount of hype surrounding DNA, and our complete confidence in it may have been misplaced. Where the science cannot be said to have been stretched (as perhaps in the case of Low Template DNA, which remains controversial in forensic assays), there still remain instances in which DNA has failed, normally due to human error or corruption; lack of quality control or regulatory oversight; or simply the misuse or misrepresentation of DNA and its problematic place in an adversarial legal system. In England and Wales, there have been lapses in police processes, one of which saw a serial rapist and murderer evading conviction when the DNA sample that should have been taken would have linked him with a series of offenses, preventing him from killing again.[15] In 2005, it was revealed that there had been nearly 26,200 DNA profiles identified as having errors and were therefore not loaded onto the NDNAD between 1995 and 2004. As a result of the failure to load these profiles, it was determined that 183 crimes had gone undetected (Lords Hansard, 2007).

In addition to problems detailed earlier of DNA matches not being converted into detections, failing to load DNA profiles onto databases has been a perennial issue for laboratories in the United States, with huge backlogs, meaning many laboratories taking months, if not years, to process DNA evidence. In Virginia, investigations in 2006 found that a quarter of the state's sex felons were not on the DNA databank and a further audit undertaken in 2007 found that 20% of felons in that state did not have their DNA loaded onto their DNA databank (Fisher, 2008). Backlogs in state laboratories have become such an issue that federal funding is available to laboratories, to "handle, screen, and analyze backlogged forensic DNA casework samples, as well as to improve DNA laboratory infrastructure and analysis capacity, so that forensic DNA samples can be processed efficiently and cost effectively."[16] Such backlogs, however, do not appear yet to be an historic issue; indeed, many laboratories have now deduced that having a backlog attracts large federal grants, making it in their interest to build up and maintain a backlog to secure extra funds.

In addition to such failures to utilize the DNA evidence available, there have been human errors that have seen individuals wrongly implicated in crimes. In most instances, individual forensic scientists who were dishonest or whose work was incompetent have been discovered, although many not until years had passed, requiring retesting of their casework. However, there have been whole laboratories in the United States whose DNA work has come under critical scrutiny, with laboratories in Virginia, Washington, and North Carolina, among others, being opened to external investigators. The deficiencies in the work at the Houston State Laboratory were such that the serology part of the lab was closed down and a major independent review undertaken (Bromwhich, 2007). In most instances, mistakes arise from cross-contamination and mislabeling of samples. The FBI DNA Advisory Board in 1998 required laboratories

[15]http://www.independent.co.uk/news/uk/crime/rachel-nickell-a-death-foretold-1203679.html

[16]http://www.ncjrs.gov/pdffiles1/nij/sl000831.pdf

to maintain contamination logs and corrective action files. These are required to be updated when contamination is discovered, and they have to "follow procedures for corrective action whenever proficiency testing discrepancies and/or casework errors are detected."[17] When defense attorneys request these documents from the laboratory, it is often surprising just how many episodes of contamination are recorded, raising awkward questions about how frequently contamination/mistakes take place in laboratories and may not be picked up.

Despite the incidence of corruption, errors, police mishandling or omission, legal misinterpretation or misrepresentation, DNA continues to be portrayed as the "gold standard" (NAS, 2009, pp. 5-3):

> DNA typing is now universally recognized as the standard against which many other forensic individualization techniques are judged. DNA enjoys this pre-eminent position because of its reliability and the fact that, absent fraud or an error in labelling or handling, the probabilities of a false positive are quantifiable and often miniscule....

While this may be a valid representation in perfect laboratory conditions, it may be that caution is still required when dealing with forensic DNA analysis. While nearly all other forensic sciences are now under increasing critical scrutiny and often being compared unfavorably to DNA, it may be dangerous to become complacent about DNA and allow no room for doubt when dealing with this powerful evidence.

[17]DNA Advisory Board Quality Assurance Standards for Forensic DNA Testing Laboratories, Standard 14.1.1. Available online at http://www.cstl.nist.gov/div831/strbase/dabqas.htm

CONCLUSION

The advent of forensic DNA profiling has revolutionized the detection of offenders across the world. Thousands of offenders have been caught—many several years after they believed they had escaped detection—while thousands more have been eliminated as suspects in police investigations. Men and women continue to have their wrongful convictions overturned and their innocence proven with DNA tests. The advantages of DNA then are manifold (Lake, 2006–2007, p. 4):

> The benefits... are not only in detecting the guilty, but also in eliminating the innocent from inquiries, focusing the direction of the investigations, which increases police efficiency, and in building public confidence that elusive offenders may be detected and brought to justice as quickly as possible.

The power of DNA has persuaded governments internationally to create national DNA databases, in many cases, being prepared to share this information across jurisdictions and international borders in the fight against crime and terrorism.

[18]In 2006–2007 there were 41,717 matches, which led to 19,949 "detections." Specifically in homicide cases, there were 452 matches declared, leading to just 88 detections.

Yet the use of DNA has perhaps not yet reached its zenith. There remain difficulties in converting DNA matches to actual convictions. The latest figures in the United Kingdom state that over half of DNA matches made between crime scenes and individuals do not result in a crime being solved.[18] Indeed, the use of DNA during the criminal process has been called "a fresh filling between two slices of stale bread" (Leary and Pease, 2002, p. 8). The reason is that the "policing" and "prosecution" slices of bread are still flawed; if they are ineffective and inefficient, then the quality of the whole "sandwich" experience remains poor. A DNA detection still does not mean that an offender will be always be caught or punished for his or her offense.

To improve the effectiveness of DNA databases, improved collection of DNA at crime scenes will prove most fruitful, and limited research has been undertaken in this area. However far the laboratory processes and science may develop, the use of DNA is still restricted to indicating the possible presence of a person at a crime scene or involvement with an offense. How that person's DNA came to be found and what this means in terms of legal liability require much more than a DNA "match." It therefore remains the case that investigators, advocates, judges, and triers of fact cannot rely on DNA alone. If advanced analysis has been undertaken—such as LTN DNA—then it becomes even more vital that the possibility of contamination, misinterpretation, and innocent transfer[19] be given due weight. So while celebrating and encouraging the effective use of DNA in policing, to ignore its limitations could lead to further and greater injustice in the future.

[19]This can occur when we "shed" our DNA and leave it behind us somewhere (which may then later be the scene of a crime) or can be transferred via a third party (or object) to somewhere incriminating. Research has not conclusively ascertained how often or how easily this happens, nor how "innocent" transfer may result in someone's DNA being on or in a place where that person has not physically been himself or herself.

SUMMARY

There have been several legal reforms which have enabled the use of DNA in criminal investigations and prosecutions. The advent of DNA technology in 1984 and the introduction of it into the forensic arena shortly thereafter was revolutionary, leading to changes in policing, prosecutorial policy and procedures, and so on. Once the technology was further refined and improved, DNA profiles were able to be much more discriminatory, thus leading to even greater benefits to the criminal justice system.

Changes to policing which were the result of the advent of DNA technology are many and varied. The most notable change was that DNA evidence was impartial and scientific, varying markedly from traditional investigation methods. It has now become routine to take DNA from individuals and for investigators to ask and determine whether DNA evidence may play a role in solving any given case. Specifically, DNA evidence may be used to speed up investigations, to provide intelligence to police, for the purpose of gaining cold hits, for case linkage, or as a deterrent to other possible criminals.

Although DNA evidence is very convincing, it needs to be reiterated that such evidence is still probabilistic and does not speak toward guilt or innocence. Supporting evidence needs to be gathered for any case involving a DNA match. Moreover, all matches need to be interpreted in the context of the case and presented to the court as such. This is due to the fact that despite DNA being probabilistic evidence, juries are more likely to convict when it is present, and longer sentences may be imposed in these cases due to the high expectations surrounding DNA evidence.

National DNA databases have the aim of storing DNA evidence from convicted offenders so that future crimes can be detected, as well as storing DNA from unresolved cases so they may be matched to future suspects. Many countries around the world utilize these databases, including the United Kingdom, the United States, New Zealand, and Australia as well, as many countries in Europe. In the future, it is hoped that these databases may be compatible with each other and linked to enable international searching. It is anticipated that this would be of great benefit to criminal investigations as well as the war on terror.

The future of DNA technology also involves several ethical issues including security and privacy, as well as mobile testing and automation. Partial profiles, mixed samples, low template number DNA, familial searching, and DNA photofits must also be addressed as ethical problems. Finally, it needs to be addressed that despite its revolutionary effect on the forensic arena and reputation for being infallible, there are cases involving human error and backlogs where DNA evidence has failed.

Review Questions

1. What are the three types of DNA samples obtained by police? How are they used?
2. T/F DNA evidence can and does literally demonstrate guilt or innocence in any given case.
3. T/F Some research has shown that juries are more likely to convict if DNA evidence is present regardless of its probative value.
4. What are some of problems stopping DNA databases from becoming internationally available?
5. Why would automation in DNA testing be beneficial to the forensic community?
6. Name and describe four examples of the science behind DNA evidence being stretched.
7. Describe what a DNA photofit is and how this may benefit those working in a forensic arena.
8. Name and describe the two elements which may lead DNA evidence to fail in any given case.

REFERENCES

Briody, M., 2002. The Effects of DNA Evidence on Sexual Offence Cases in Court. Current Issues in Criminal Justice 14 (2), 159–181.

Briody, M., 2004. The Effects of DNA Evidence on Homicide Cases in Court. Australian and New Zealand Journal of Criminology 37 (2), 231–252.

Bromwich, M.R., 2007, June 13. Final Report of the Independent Investigator for the Houston Police Department Crime Laboratory and Property Room. Available at www.hpdlabinvestigation.org

ENFSI, 2006. Report on ENFSI Member Countries' DNA Database Legislation Survey.

Findlay, M., Grix, J., 2003. Challenging Forensic Evidence? Observations on the Use of DNA in Certain Criminal Trials. Current Issues in Criminal Justice, 14 (3), 276.

Fisher, J., 2008. Forensics Under Fire. Rutgers University Press, New Brunswick.

French Comité consultatif national d'éthique, 2007. Opinion on Biometrics, identifying data and human rights and Portuguese Conselho Nacional de Ética para as Ciências da Vida. Opinion on the legal system for DNA profile databases.

Hansard, L., 2007, June 7. Vol. 692, Part No. 97. Col. HL3859.

Harbison, S., Hamilton, J., Walsh, S., 2002. The New Zealand DNA Databank. Paper presented at the First International Conference on Human Identification in the Millennium.

Home Affairs Committee, 2008. The Surveillance Society? HC 58-1. The Stationery Office Ltd, London.

Home Office, 2004. The Contribution of Shoemark Data to Police Intelligence, Crime Detection and Prosecution, Findings 236. Research and Statistics Directorate, HMSO, London.

Home Office, 2005. DNA Expansion Programme 2000–2005: Reporting Achievement, Forensic Science and Pathology Unit.

House of Commons Select Committee on Science and Technology, 2005. Forensic Science on Trial. HC 96-I, Seventh Report of Session 2004–2005. The Stationery Office Limited, London.

Jobling, M., Gill, P., 2004. October. Encoded Evidence: DNA in Forensic Analysis. Nat. Rev. Genet. 5, 739–751.

Johnson, P., Williams, R., 2007. Internationalizing New Technologies of Crime Control: Forensic DNA Databasing and Datasharing in the European Union. Policing and Society 17, 103–118.

Lake, T., 2007. National DNA Database Annual Report 2006–07. Home Office, National Policing Improvement Agency, UK, p. 16.

Leary, D., Pease, K., 2002. DNA and the Active Criminal Population. Jill Dando Institute of Crime Science, Briefing paper London. p. 8.

Lewis, C., 2007. International Structures and Trans-National Crime. In: Newburn, T., Wiliamson, T., Wright, A. (Eds.), Handbook of Criminal Investigation. Willan Publishing, Cullompton, pp. 175–198.

McCartney, C., 2006a. The DNA Expansion Programme and Criminal Investigation. British Journal of Criminology 46, 175–192.

McCartney, C., 2006b. Forensic Identification and Criminal Justice: Forensic Science, Justice and Risk. Willan, Cullompton.

National Academy of Sciences. 2009 Strengthening Forensic Science in the US. National Academies Press, Washington, DC, p. 5-3.

Noble, R.K., 2007. Opening Remarks at 5th International DNA Users' Conference for Investigative Officers, November 14, Interpol, Lyon, published at www.interpol.int.

Nuffield Council on Bioethics, 2007. The Forensic Use of Bioinformation: Ethical Issues. available at www.nuffieldbioethics.org.uk.

Purcell, N., Thomas-Winfree, L., Mays, G., 1994. DNA Evidence and Criminal Trials: An Exploratory Survey of Factors Associated with the Use of 'Genetic Fingerprinting' in Felony Prosecutions. Journal of Criminal Justice 22 (2), 145–157.

R v Bates, 2006. EWCA Crim 1395.

R v Dennis Adams, 1996. 2 Cr.App.R. 467.

R v Doheny and Anor, 1996. EWCA Crim 728 (31st July, 1996).

R v Hoey, 2007. NICC 49.

R v Mitchell, 2004. EWCA Crim 1928. The Times 8 July.

R v Watters, 2000. EWCA Crim 89.

Roman, J.K., Reid, S., Reid, J., Chalfin, A., Adams, W., Knight, C., 2008. The DNA Field Experiment: Cost-Effectiveness Analysis of the Use of DNA in the Investigation of High-Volume Crimes, final report submitted to the National Institute of Justice, U.S. Department of Justice, Washington, DC (NCJ 222318), available at http://www.ncjrs.gov/pdffiles1/nij/grants/222318.pdf.

S & Marper v UK, 30562/04; 30566/04. European Court of Human Rights, 4th December 2008.

Watson, N., 1999. From Crime Scene to Court, In: P. White (Ed.), The Royal Society of Chemistry, Cambridge.

Williams, R., Johnson, P., 2005. Forensic DNA Databasing: A European Perspective. Interim Report for the Wellcome Trust. available at http://www.dur.ac.uk/sass/projects/research/?mode=project&id=31Williams & Johnson.

Williams, R., Johnson, P., 2008. Genetic Policing: The Use of DNA in Criminal Investigations, Willan, Cullompton.

FURTHER READING

Chalmers, D. (Ed.), 2005. Genetic Testing and the Criminal Law. UCL Press, London.

Genewatch UK—see www.genewatch.org for reports on the National DNA Database, including The Police National DNA Database, Human Rights and Privacy, Balancing Crime Detection, 2005.

Gerlach, N., 2004. The Genetic Imaginary. University of Toronto Press, Toronto.

Lazer, D. (Ed.), 2004. DNA and the Criminal Justice System. MIT Press, Cambridge.

Semikhodskii, A., 2008. Dealing with DNA Evidence: A Legal Guide. Routledge Cavendish, London.

Wall, W., 2004. Genetics and DNA Technology: Legal Aspects, second ed. Cavendish, London.

Williams, R., Johnson, P., 2009. Genetic Policing. Willan Publishing, Cullompton, UK.

CHAPTER 15

Forensic Mental Health Experts

Michael McGrath and Angela N. Torres

KEY TERMS

Actuarial Risk Assessment: The measuring of variables that have been shown to be predictive of future dangerousness while considering the base rates of those behaviors.

Adjusted Actuarial Approach: A risk assessment approach in which actuarial risk measures based on research are used as the framework for the risk assessment, but the predictions may be adjusted to take into account personality and situational variables.

Clinical Risk Assessment: Predictions made by mental health professionals regarding the risk of an individual engaging in some type of criminal behavior based on a clinical interview and collateral information.

Competency to Stand Trial: A defendant's current ability to understand his or her legal situation and to assist his or her attorney with the defense.

Forensic Psychiatrist: Physician who specializes in psychiatry after completing medical school. He or she is able to evaluate patients, diagnose illnesses, and prescribe medication.

Forensic Psychologist: Doctoral-level clinician licensed as a clinical or counseling psychologist who has specialized training and experience in criminal and civil court related issues.

Forensic Social Worker: A professional who applies social work principles to legal issues in civil and criminal cases.

Insanity (Criminal Responsibility): The defendant's mental state at the time of the crime which makes him or her unable to understand that what he or she is doing is wrong or against the law.

Probative: Proving or demonstrating a fact in issue.

Recidivism: The repetition of a criminal act.

Risk Assessment: The prediction of the likelihood that some type of criminal act will be performed by a specific individual in the future.

CONTENTS

INTRODUCTION

Forensic criminologists require expertise in the study of crime and criminals, as well as knowledge of the investigative process and the criminal justice system. As a behavioral science, forensic criminology will necessarily intersect with other behavioral sciences. As a forensic discipline, the forensic criminologist may interact with and/or rely on other behavioral health experts, such as *forensic social workers, forensic psychologists,* and *forensic psychiatrists.* It is important that forensic criminologists have knowledge of what the allied behavioral forensic disciplines have to offer, when to utilize them, and how to judge the quality of the work product.

This chapter will briefly highlight the three professions practicing in forensic mental health: forensic social work, forensic psychology, and forensic psychiatry. We will then discuss some of the more common forensic evaluations performed by these professionals. Finally, this chapter will conclude with discussions related to mental health expertise and law enforcement, as well as issues related to providing mental health services in correctional environments.

Before we move on, some comments about the criminal justice system are in order. Forensic criminologists must be aware of the issues related to the *forensic* behavioral sciences. The behavioral sciences enter the courtroom at their own peril. The goal of science is truth. The goal of the courtroom is justice. Both are very hard to attain. As discussed in previous chapters, facts, truths, and justice are quite different. A person can be found legally guilty when he or she is factually innocent, or found not guilty when he or she is in fact responsible for the crime. The reason is that justice is negotiated in court, as opposed to being the result of objective and careful scientific analysis. Any behavioral scientists wishing to practice in the forensic realm must accept such realities and the common absence of science or scientific in subsequent legal outcomes.

As has been mentioned in previous chapters, adversarial justice depends on "truth" emerging through arguments presented by the prosecution and the defense, as well as the presumption of innocence. Those of us experienced with court can attest that the presumption of innocence is more often than not a legal fiction. It is meant to put the heavy onus of proving a defendant's legal guilt on the state. However, the truth must contend with the very real assumption in the eyes of many jurors that the defendant is guilty for the mere fact that he or she is facing criminal charges. Moreover, the resources available to the defendant pale in comparison to the vast amount of money, manpower, and in-house forensic expertise available to the prosecution—except in the most unusual of circumstances. Few defendants can muster a "dream team" of attorneys, as did O. J. Simpson at his first criminal trial in the mid-1990s. Most defendants would likely trade their presumption of innocence for one of guilt in exchange for the same resources available to the state.

It is into this uneven battle that behavioral scientists enter, sometimes unarmed. There is little, if any, exposure to the forensic side of the behavioral sciences during the education and training of social workers, psychologists, and psychiatrists. It not surprising then that some practitioners do not understand the ethical issues involved in forensic practice, nor the limits of their expertise. For example, a forensic opinion is not a fact. It is an opinion. It is usually couched within "a reasonable degree" of something or other (such as a reasonable degree of psychiatric certainty) to give it *probative* (courtroom) value. There is no agreed-upon level of certainty for forming a forensic opinion. In a criminal case the jury must decide within a reasonable doubt, whatever that may be. Some say this is a 98% threshold. The expert opinion may suggest that such opinion has only to be more likely than not, a 51% threshold, whereas others will hold to a clear and convincing standard, around 85%. Experts are rarely asked in court how certain they are of their opinion, beyond what is considered "reasonable" — probably for good reason.

Just as the courts tend to defer to testimony by law enforcement personnel, eyewitness testimony, fingerprint evidence, and sometimes outrageous prosecutorial behavior, forensic experts are also often allowed great leeway. The weight a judge or jury will give to expert testimony will depend on many factors, most of which are subjective. It will vary between abject deference to experts to completely disregarding proffered opinions. Regardless, although expert witnesses do not make the final legal decision, it is imperative that they remain cognizant of the potential weight their professional opinions can have on the adjudication of defendants. First and foremost, this means that they have an obligation to avoid testimony that would mislead the trier of fact. The most ludicrous testimony can be offered in court by an expert, and it is rare for there to be any repercussions. Even offering fraudulent resumes to the courts is ignored more often than not. This means that forensic examiners of every kind have a responsibility to be alert for diploma mills and those with deficient educational backgrounds to include membership in "professional" associations that grant "certification" in forensic specialties essentially based on paying a fee.

Specific to the mental health community, another issue that must be raised is the fact that social workers, psychologists, and psychiatrists are trained to assess and treat. While they are trained to gather information, they are not trained to question it. They are trained to be empathic, not critical. This professional persona follows many into the forensic arena where they continue to take at face value what they are told and feel uncomfortable making others uncomfortable. While it may seem improbable, some forensic practitioners exhibit marked gullibility when evaluating defendants or plaintiffs. Some believe that the very fact that the defendant committed a major violent crime, such as a murder, is evidence that he or she has a mental disorder. Some do not question when a defendant reports that a voice told him or her to commit the crime. Such individuals do not belong in the forensic arena. This kind of reckless expertise is what brought us the repressed memory debacle, as well as the child abuse hysteria cases, such as the McMartin preschool sex abuse case (Eberle and Eberle, 1993). On this note, one must always be on the alert for personal belief and speculation presented as expert opinion. While the expert behavioral scientist is (usually) entitled to his or her opinions, they must be supportable. If they are not, they are mere speculation. Mental health professionals equipped to perform forensic evaluations for the court are trained to base their conclusions on interviews and corroborating evidence, to clearly support their conclusions, and to always consider that the person they are evaluating may have reasons to be less than truthful. The absence of such measures is a useful way in which actual forensic expertise may be distinguished within the mental health community.

At times it has also been questioned whether those in the mental health community can ethically participate in the adversarial system.[1] As Bursztajn, Scherr, and Brodsky (1993) point out:

> … [A]t the heart of the conundrum of forensic psychiatry is the tension between the legal system's—and people's—wish for simple answers, a wish the psychiatrist (like any other expert) must inevitably disappoint, and a more realistic appreciation of science as offering merely the deepest understanding possible under the circumstances. Once the naive belief in 'exact' science is replaced by a more contextual notion of what scientific knowledge is, it becomes possible to appreciate the numerous ways in which *forensic psychiatrists* deploy this scientific and human understanding in both criminal and civil law.

The authors would agree and argue that the justice system is well educated by competent behavioral scientists of every kind so long as they maintain a clear grasp of their roles, responsibilities, and ethical mandates.

Among such considerations is an appreciation of the fact that forensic mental health practitioners, like forensic behavioral scientists, must not consider themselves a part of any legal team. While certainly expected to be collegial and pleasant to those who have retained them, they must remain independent and unbiased.[2] Too often experts perceive or develop a need to please their clients. This is most unfortunate.

Finally, forensic criminologists should be aware of the credentials and experience of any forensic social workers, psychologists, or psychiatrists whose work product they may rely on. There are practitioners who take on forensic work lacking any expertise in the field and who continue to practice having gained much experience but little knowledge or expertise. Such individuals are easily spotted by credible experts, but are regularly used by the legal arena because they tend to be convenient and user-friendly.

[1] The reader is referred to Bursztajn, H., Scherr, A. and Brodsky, A. (1993) "The Rebirth of Forensic Psychiatry in Light of Recent Historical Trends in Criminal Responsibility," for a pertinent discussion of ethics and forensic psychiatry.

[2] In truth, it is unrealistic to expect experts to have no biases. What is expected, though, is that they are aware of their own biases and do not allow them to affect their professional judgment.

The next part of this chapter is dedicated to distinguishing the major types of forensic mental health professionals along with their backgrounds, roles, and responsibilities.

FORENSIC SOCIAL WORK

It may come as a surprise to those outside the field that a specialty of forensic social work (FSW) exists. Since any forensic field consists of applying the principles of the field to address legal issues, FSW would surely make sense. For example, the National Organization of Forensic Social Work (NOFSW) is a professional organization devoted to applying social work principles to legal issues. Areas involved are both criminal and civil. They include the examination and psychosocial evaluation of divorce issues such as child custody and child abuse, sex offender evaluation and management, substance abuse issues, and sentencing mitigation, among others. A journal in the field is also slated to begin publication sometime in 2010 (Haworth Press, 2008).[3] Although there is literature related to FSW, the authors were unable to locate a current peer-reviewed journal devoted to the field.

[3]Some delay is related to Haworth Press having been bought by the Taylor and Francis Group.

A forensic social worker is expected to be a master's level practitioner, although some social workers go on to earn a doctorate. The NOFSW (2008) notes that social work training (as in other behavioral health disciplines) usually does not include exposure to or instruction on the adversarial legal system. If a social worker should desire to engage in forensic practice, the professional should seek out specialized training, education, and experience to build expertise and competence before engaging in forensic social work. Generally, master's level social workers evaluate and diagnose mental illness and provide treatment within their scope of practice. The practice of social work includes many aspects and levels of interaction with clients. Social workers are licensed or unlicensed, depending on state statutes and regulations, as well as educational and practice level. The NOFSW (2008) commentary on FSW is nicely framed and is applicable to all forensic disciplines:

> Forensic Social Work is based on specialized knowledge drawn from established principles and their application, familiarity with the law, painstaking mental health evaluation, and objective criteria associated with treatment outcomes. What the social worker offers must be of utility and couched in language to which the court can relate. The conclusions and recommendations must withstand critical review and rebuttal from opposing parties.

The National Association of Social Workers (NASW, 2008) Web site[4] lists a code of ethics that includes commentary on various ethical considerations relevant to forensic work in general, such as defining who is the client [section 1.01], the role of informed consent [section 1.03 (d)], dual roles [section 1.6], and statements on the limits of confidentiality [section 1.07 (d)(j)]. The NOFSW (2008) Web site has a code of ethics for FSW.

[4]http://www.nofsw.org/

Barker and Branson (1993) list 10 functions of FSW: (1) providing expert testimony in court; (2) evaluation of individuals for the purpose of court testimony, including competence to stand trial and responsibility; (3) investigation of cases in which criminal activity has taken place, such as physical and sexual abuse; (4) recommendations to courts and other legal authorities regarding sentencing related to criminal acts or civil actions; (5) facilitation of a court-ordered sentence, for example, through monitoring or treatment; (6) mediation of disputes (for example, marital issues) to avoid formal legal proceedings; (7) testimony related to practice standards in malpractice or ethical proceedings; (8) education of colleagues and others about the intersection of law and social work; (9) facilitation of the development and enforcement of laws regulating the profession of social work; and (10) in their own practice FSWs uphold the law and ethics of the profession.

States vary on whether they allow FSWs to perform forensic evaluations for the criminal courts. In Nevada a licensed clinical social worker (LCSW) can perform *competency to stand trial* evaluations on misdemeanor charges, but not felonies (Surface, 2007). Such a distinction makes no clinical sense given that the same criteria for competency to stand trial exist for both misdemeanors and felonies. Stoeson (2006) described a New York State trial court ruling that an LCSW was "qualified to evaluate mental health conditions that may be organic or physical in origin." Civil courts usually allow FSWs to perform evaluations when relevant, such as in family courts and divorce and custody proceedings.

Forensic criminologists will subsequently need to become familiar with the rules and regulations governing the scope and practice of forensic social work in the jurisdictions within which they find themselves working, as they vary a great deal.

FORENSIC PSYCHOLOGY AND PSYCHIATRY

Psychology and psychiatry are two closely related fields but with some important differences. Both fields are part of the behavioral sciences, and can provide group and individual psychotherapy. Psychiatrists are physicians who specialize in psychiatry after completing medical school. They can evaluate patients, diagnose illnesses (both psychological and medical), and prescribe medication. Psychologists are doctoral-level clinicians.[5] They have studied psychology and have various levels of training in conducting research. They also are qualified to perform and interpret psychological measures, such as personality assessments, intelligence tests, and neuropsychological testing. There are practitioners in both forensic psychiatry and psychology who gained their expertise through experience, but currently there is an expectation that one has advanced education and training to qualify as an expert in these fields (Bersoff et al., 1997; Federal Rules of Evidence 702, 2009).

[5]Some with a master's level education in psychology practice under the title of "psychologist," but this is usually under the auspices of an institution, such as a state hospital. They may be referred to as a "psychologist" or "clinical psychologist," as defined by each state.

Both forensic psychiatry and forensic psychology have codes of ethics developed by relevant professional bodies (see AAPL, 2005; Committee on Ethical Guidelines for Forensic Psychologists, 1991).

In the forensic arena, the client can be the court in the form of a court-ordered assessment, or it can be the prosecutor's office, a criminal defense attorney, or a plaintiff's attorney or defense attorney in a civil case. The client is not the individual being examined. In fact, any contractual relationship should be only with the person or party retaining the expert, not the examinee. The person evaluated in the criminal (usually the defendant) or civil (most often the defendant or the plaintiff) forensic context may refuse to cooperate, and the forensic psychologist or forensic psychiatrist may be forced to complete the evaluation based solely on collateral information, as well as expert reports prepared by others, although this is not common. Reliable collateral information is important in clinical evaluations, but is essential in forensic assessments.

A major pitfall for the clinician is to engage in both a treatment and a forensic role with the same person. Ethical guidelines generally recommend avoiding such dual agency (Committee on Ethical Guidelines for Forensic Psychologists, 1991). It is difficult if not impossible to maintain an objective mindset when there is a current or past professional relationship with a client who has a vested interest in one's expert findings. For example, how can a psychiatrist maintain objective neutrality when evaluating his or her own patient for psychological damages when he or she knows the patient is in dire financial straits? How can one provide ongoing psychotherapy to a client who may hold onto symptoms (consciously or unconsciously) that could lead to increased financial gain in a pending lawsuit when he or she is an expert witness for that patient? Such ethical conflicts must be both acknowledged and resolved.

Forensic mental health professionals conduct evaluations in both civil and criminal cases. Civil cases involve matters related to property or torts (i.e., physical or financial injury or some other loss that can be addressed through a lawsuit). Some evaluations involve various risk assessments (general or specific, such as sexual violence risk), child custody evaluations, and competency to sign a will (testamentary competency), to name just a few. Criminal cases by definition involve a criminal act. Some common criminal evaluations are criminal responsibility at the time of offense (also referred to as sanity) and competency to stand trial.

COMPETENCY TO STAND TRIAL AND INSANITY

Incompetency to stand trial is often confused with *insanity*, although they are two different concepts. *Competency to stand trial* relates to a defendant's *current* ability to understand his or her legal situation (e.g., charges, basic court roles, possible legal outcomes) and to assist his or her attorney with the defense (Roesch, Zapf, Golding, and Skeem, 1999). As outlined in *Dusky v. United States* (1960), the defendant must have a factual and rational understanding of the legal proceedings against him or her and possess the capacity to aid his or her attorney in his or her own defense. It is not an assessment of a defendant's mindset at the time the crime was committed, and it is generally not interpreted as a particularly high standard.

Insanity (or *criminal responsibility*) relates to the defendant's mental state at the time of the offense and is thus *retrospective* in nature (Golding, Skeem, Roesch, and Zapf, 1999). There are different standards in different jurisdictions, but, generally, to be found insane or not responsible, a person needs to be have been unable (at the time of the crime) to understand that what he or she was doing was wrong or against the law. The nature of "wrongfulness" is also outlined by the state or federal statutes and case law to be defined either as legal wrongfulness or moral wrongfulness. Some states will also allow an insanity defense if the defendant engaged in the criminal act through an "irresistible impulse." This comes into play if it were determined that a defendant would have engaged in a criminal act even if a police officer was at his or her elbow (Melton et al., 2007). As elegantly stated by the American Psychiatric Association's brief on the subject, "The line between an irresistible impulse and an impulse not resisted is probably no sharper than that between twilight and dusk" (American Psychiatric Association, 1983).

Many assume that a severe mental illness automatically makes a defendant incompetent to stand trial or insane, but that is not the case. While a severe mental illness (such as schizophrenia or bipolar disorder) or a mental defect (such as mental retardation or brain trauma) is considered in assessing competency to stand trial and is a prerequisite in sanity evaluations, such a disorder must then lead to an inability to meet the legal criteria for either competence to stand trial or criminal responsibility.

When an individual is found incompetent to stand trial (sometimes also called *incompetent to proceed*), the legal case is put on hold, depending on the jurisdiction. Each state has different guidelines regarding what happens next. In New York State the charge or charges are dismissed if the crime or crimes are misdemeanors. If the defendant is charged with at least one felony, he or she will be sent to a secure psychiatric hospital for the purpose of treatment with the goal being restoration of competency. In Virginia, the judge may authorize the hospital to continue restoration efforts for most misdemeanors for up to one year, felonies for up to five years, and capital murder cases indefinitely.

It may come as a surprise to many (due to the publicity some notorious cases garner) that the insanity defense is rarely used, and when it is, it rarely results in an acquittal (Hans and Slater, 1993). Also, when it does lead to an acquittal, the acquittee is usually committed to a secure mental health facility for evaluation and often spends more time hospitalized than he or she would have served if sentenced on a plea or even after a guilty verdict (Callahan, McGreery, Cirincione, and Steadman, 1992; Sloat and Frierson, 2005). For example, in Virginia acquittees adjudicated insane at the time of the offense are initially committed to the maximum security forensic hospital where they are evaluated by two independent evaluators, one psychologist and one psychiatrist. The forensic mental health professionals then make recommendations to the judge as to whether the defendant should be released with or without conditions, or committed for more treatment. More often than not, defendants are committed to a psychiatric facility for additional treatment.

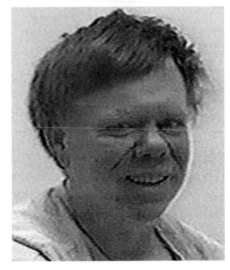

Russell E. Weston, Jr. during his interview with psychiatrist Sally C. Johnson, retained by the defense.

CRIMINAL FORENSIC ASSESSMENT CASE EXAMPLES

Russell E. Weston, Jr.

On July 24, 1998, two U.S. Capitol Hill Police officers were killed by a mentally ill man who had traveled from Illinois with paranoid delusional beliefs related to the federal government. One of the officers wounded the shooter, who was identified as Russell Eugene Weston Jr., a 41-year-old man diagnosed with chronic paranoid schizophrenia. He had been psychiatrically hospitalized in 1996 and was interviewed twice that year by secret service agents due to threats against President Clinton (NY Times, 2002).

Weston was found incompetent to stand trial by a federal district judge. "'Russell Eugene Weston, Jr., presently suffers from a mental disease or defect that renders him incapable of understanding the nature and consequences of the proceedings against him and that precludes him from properly assisting in his defense,' [Judge] Sullivan wrote (Frieden, 1999)." After his return to Butner Federal Correctional Facility, Weston continued to refuse medication to treat his psychosis. Eventually, a court order was obtained to treat him over his objection (NY Times, 2002). He has yet to be brought to trial. If it becomes clear that there is no reasonable expectation that he will ever be restored to competency, his lawyers may move to have the charges dropped, a possibility with *Jackson v. Indiana* [406 US 715 (1972)] as precedent.

Brian D. Mitchell being led into court by sheriff's deputies.

Brian David Mitchell

In the early hours of June 5, 2002, 14-year-old Elizabeth Smart was abducted at knifepoint from her bedroom. A younger sister alerted their parents, setting off a massive search. The manhunt failed to find Elizabeth, and the police targeted a former handyman as a suspect, who later died in jail from a stroke (CNN.com, 2002). In March of 2003, Elizabeth was discovered less than 20 miles from her Salt Lake City home in Sandy, Utah, in the company of a fringe Mormon preacher and his wife. Police charged 51-year-old Brian David Mitchell and his wife, 59-year-old Wanda Eileen Barzee, with kidnapping, sexual assault, and burglary. Both Barzee and Mitchell were found incompetent to proceed. Barzee has so far not regained competency. Mitchell was initially declared incompetent to proceed in 2005. "District Judge Judith Atherton ruled that Brian David Mitchell, 51, was suffering from a delusional disorder based on his religious beliefs, leaving him unable to make decisions in his best interest and assist his defense." Mitchell believed he was a prophet and that God would deliver him from his legal situation. "Two of the three psychiatrists who evaluated Mitchell determined he was delusional and incompetent to stand trial; the third said he was merely narcissistic, not delusional, and was therefore competent." (CNN.com, 2005). It is always problematic attempting to determine where religiosity ends and mental illness begins, especially in a religion patterned on ongoing revelations from a god. Mitchell was declared incompetent to proceed for a second time in December of 2006 after screaming at the judge during a hearing. At the time of this writing, he and his wife have yet to stand trial.

Jeffrey Dahmer

On July 22, 1991, Milwaukee police officers found a handcuffed man who had escaped from an apartment. He told of an encounter with a man that left him very uncomfortable, and he gave police the address of an apartment. The police rang the bell, and 31-year-old Jeffrey Dahmer opened the door. Pictures of bodies and body parts, as well as actual body parts (including heads), were found in the apartment. Subsequent investigation revealed that Jeffrey Dahmer had been on a 13-year killing spree.

At best count, Dahmer had killed 17 victims between 1978 and 1991. His modus operandi was to invite homosexual men or boys to his apartment and drug them. After they were incapacitated, he would strangle them. Dahmer reported having sex with some bodies and occasionally eating body parts. Dahmer eventually pleaded guilty but insane (available in Wisconsin law) and went to trial. He was found guilty (i.e., the jury rejected the insanity portion of the case) in 1992 and sentenced to 15 consecutive life terms. On November 28, 1994, after he had been allowed to enter general population, another inmate at the Columbia Correctional Institute in Wisconsin murdered Dahmer.

Jeffrey Dahmer in court.

The case is notable for the abundance of expert mental health testimony. During the trial, defense and prosecution experts offered opinions as to Dahmer's sanity. Insanity was a hard sell as, although Dahmer was clearly a bizarre individual, he did not appear to have a major diagnosable mental illness to the level of a psychosis. For insanity, it is generally accepted in the field that the mental illness be significant, such as in the case of a psychosis (break with reality) or other thought disorder (Bonnie, 1983; Giorgi-Guarnieri et al., 2002; Hastings and Bonnie, 1981). His crimes and behaviors were all goal directed and not the result of a delusion[6] or other psychotic process.[7]

Eight mental health experts evaluated Dahmer, with seven testifying at his trial.[8] One psychologist, Dr. Kenneth Smail, retained by the defense, evaluated Dahmer and found him competent to stand trial, but offered no opinion on criminal responsibility because his findings regarding responsibility were not "sufficiently supportive" of the defense's case (Smail, 1993, p. 228). Smail did not testify at the trial, but rather at a competency to stand trial hearing. At trial the defense offered three experts. Two experts on sexual disorders opined for the defense that Dahmer could not control himself. Dr. Fred Berlin, a well-known psychiatrist running a sexual disorders clinic at John Hopkins University, diagnosed Dahmer as suffering from necrophilia, a disorder in which one is sexually attracted to corpses and unable to control himself (Masters, 1993). The second defense expert, Dr. Judith Becker, a professor of psychiatry at the University of Arizona, offered testimony that Dahmer was unable to conform his conduct to the requirements of the law (Masters, 1993). The third defense expert, Chicago psychiatrist Dr. Carl Wahlstrom, opined Dahmer suffered from a psychotic disorder, with a primitive personality organization and bizarre delusions related to his desire to create a personal zombie (Masters, 1993).

[6]A delusion is a fixed false belief, such as one is being tormented by radiation from Mars. It is not a culturally sanctioned fixed belief, such as a religion.

[7]A psychotic process is some phenomenon that is a result of faulty reality testing, such as delusional ideation or auditory hallucinations.

[8]For an insightful description of the mental health testimony at Jeffrey Dahmer's trial, the reader is referred to *The Shrine of Jeffrey Dahmer*, by Brian Masters (Masters, 1993). The book's author describes the testimony and the experts both good and bad, although the authors (McGrath and Torres) would not endorse Masters's use of Money's "paraphilic fugue state'"(p. 207) to criticize Park Dietz's testimony. Also, see Ewing, C., and McCann J. (2006) *Minds on Trial: Great Cases in Law and Psychology*. New York: Oxford University Press Inc. pp. 141–152.

Next, two court-appointed psychiatrists, Drs. Palermo and Friedman, testified. These experts were court appointed independent of the prosecution and the defense. While the reason for their being retained by the court (Judge Gram) is not clear, the potential message to the jury was: the experts hired by the defense or the prosecution could not be trusted (Masters, 1993). Dr. Palermo testified that Dahmer was legally sane at the time he committed his murders and not suffering from a major psychiatric illness, labeling him a sexual sadist. Dr. Friedman, while disagreeing with Dr. Palermo around psychodynamic motivations for the killings, did not endorse an insanity defense (Masters, 1993, pp. 196–199).

Two prosecution experts testified. Dr. Fred Fosdal testified Dahmer did not meet the legal definition of insanity. Dr. Park Dietz, the most well known psychiatrist involved in the case, opined Dahmer did not meet criteria for insanity when he committed his crimes. He also did not believe Dahmer was a sadist because, in his view, he did not torture his victims. Giving probably the most detailed testimony of the experts in the trial, Dietz went through each of the murders under consideration. Even Dietz was forced to admit the last two murders were questionable as to whether Dahmer could conform his behavior to the requirements of the law, but he attributed any lack of control to alcohol intoxication (Masters, 1993). Voluntary intoxication at the time of an offense is not a basis for an insanity defense, but goes to *mens rea* and might be a mitigating factor. It will depend on the jurisdiction as to what factor a voluntary intoxication would play in a criminal defense.

Although Dahmer had initially entered a plea of not guilty by reason of insanity, he changed this to a plea of guilty but insane. Unlike a not guilty by reason of insanity adjudication, a guilty but insane adjudication is still technically a guilty verdict. Consequently, this would result in Dahmer having served his sentence in a psychiatric facility under the jurisdiction of the corrections department in Wisconsin. Once "cured" (i.e., not requiring psychiatric hospitalization), he would have been sent to a regular prison. Ironically, Dahmer was killed in prison by an inmate who claimed command auditory hallucinations caused him to kill Dahmer. Christopher Scarver, serving a life sentence, bludgeoned Dahmer and another inmate to death (NY Times, 2008).

Lorena Bobbitt

John Wayne Bobbitt and his wife, Lorena, had a less than idyllic life. He was a handsome ex-marine ne'er do well, and she was an immigrant Ecuadorian, dependent on him. They married in 1989, and after she became pregnant, she stated he insisted she get an abortion. The true facts may be elusive, but it appears that, as reported by Lorena and others, he had cheated on her more than once and did not try to hide his behavior. He was reportedly also physically abusive at times. On June 23, 1993, the 26-year-old ex-marine came

Lorena Bobbitt (left) in court describing abuse at the hands of her husband, John Bobbitt (right) during her 1994 trial. She faced up to 20 years in prison for cutting off his penis. She was found not guilty.

home drunk to their Manassas, Virginia, home and allegedly forced Lorena, 24, to have sex with him, after which he fell asleep. Lorena later reported she could not sleep and went into the kitchen to get a glass of water. She was angry with John, and when she saw a kitchen knife, she took it, went into the bedroom, and cut off his penis. She then ran out of the house and drove around, at one point throwing the severed appendage out the car window. At some point, she called 911. After her arrest, she commented to police: "He always have orgasm and he doesn't wait for me to have orgasm. He's selfish. I don't think it's fair, so I pulled back the sheets then and I did it" (NY Times, 1994).

In 1993 at trial, Lorena was found not guilty due to temporary insanity/irresistible impulse and ordered to undergo a 45-day evaluation, after which she was released. Lorena was portrayed by defense experts as suffering from depression and post-traumatic stress disorder (PTSD) from the spousal abuse and was not responsible for her actions. A prosecution expert opined that she may suffer from PTSD, but the onset was after she assaulted her husband. In any event, as sometimes happens in these cases, she appeared to suffer memory lapses as to what happened. By the time she got to testify, she was unable to remember the incident, which might be surprising to the people she had described it to earlier.

In an interesting postscript, in December 1997, Lorena Bobbitt was charged with assault for allegedly punching her mother as they watched television. Her mother suffered minor injuries, including an abrasion around the eyes and scratches, according to the police report (NY Times, 1997). There is no report on whether she remembers this incident.

RISK ASSESSMENTS

As behavioral scientists, criminologists may be involved in assessing future risk of dangerousness. Though not a diagnostic role, social workers, psychologists, and psychiatrists are also asked to perform risk assessments that aid decision makers. This includes educating judges, probation officers, and correctional staff in deciding whether or not an individual may be released to the community, if she or he should be housed in a prison's general population, or if someone needs restrictive supervised release.

Risk assessments involve the prediction of the likelihood that some type of criminal act will be performed by a specific individual in the future (Bonta, Law, and Hanson, 1998). When a criminal act is repeated, it is referred to as *recidivism*. First, when performing risk assessments, forensic examiners need to define how they are using *recidivism*, how it is defined in research studies they may rely on, and how it is defined in any actuarial assessment tools. It can be defined as a new conviction, a new arrest, or a self-reported criminal act unreported to the police. This does not mean that recidivism statistics are meaningless or inherently unreliable, but it does mean that one must understand the parameters behind the statistics and make sure when making comparisons that one is comparing similar things.

Second, the type of recidivism that will be predicted must be delineated. Risk assessments may include risk for general criminal behavior, violence risk, or sexual violence risk. Certain measures and techniques are appropriate for some but not all types of evaluations. For example, a probation officer might be interested in the risk of general criminal behavior, while a psychiatrist assessing for release from a civil commitment would be more interested in violence risk, while judges ruling on sexually violent predator civil commitments would probably be most interested in predictions of future sexual violence.

There are three main methods of risk assessment: clinical, actuarial, and adjusted actuarial approaches. The oldest approach is the clinical approach. In this method, psychologists, psychiatrists, and social workers make predictions of the risk of an individual engaging in some type of criminal behavior based on a clinical interview and collateral information. However, research demonstrated that clinicians were not good at predicting future violence based on their clinical judgment alone (Monahan, 1981). Even the U.S. Supreme Court was aware of clinicians' limited skills in predicting future risk. In *Barefoot v. Estelle* (1983), the issue of risk prediction was addressed by the Court. Thomas Barefoot was a defendant facing capital murder charges in Texas. At the trial level, the prosecution called two psychiatrists to testify about the future dangerousness of the defendant. Both psychiatrists opined that Barefoot was highly dangerous and very likely to be violent in the future. The case was appealed to the U.S. Supreme Court, and the American Psychiatric Association (APA) submitted an *amicus* brief presenting research and the unreliability of clinical risk prediction. Despite the cautions levied by the APA, the U.S. Supreme Court acknowledged the limitations of *clinical risk assessment* but stated that the Court still relies on forensic mental health professionals to conduct such evaluations. The Court noted that the adversarial legal system, designed to allow for contrasting expert opinions, should be sufficient for aiding the fact finder in decision making. Thomas Barefoot's conviction and death sentence were upheld [*Barefoot v. Estelle*, 463 U.S. 880 (1983)].

Although there are several critiques of the clinical method, the primary weakness is the highly subjective nature of this method. One clinician may evaluate a person and consider him low risk, whereas another may consider that same person high risk, with no difference in the data relied on. The main difference is the threshold for "riskiness" the individual professional has. Also, clinical approaches neglect taking into consideration the base rate, or how often a particular behavior occurs within a specific population (Monahan, 1981). For example, out of 10,000 randomly sampled individuals surveyed a year prior to some type of criminal behavior, only 2% committed a violent act within that year if they did not have a mental illness, 8% if they had schizophrenia, and 21% if they had only substance abuse. The percentage rose to 30% if the person had substance abuse and schizophrenia (Swanson, Holtzer, Granju, and Jono, 1990). Monahan (1981) noted that failing to consider the base rate of how often a particular behavior is performed within a certain population is the single most significant error a clinician can make in predicting future risk.

The actuarial approach was born out of the frustration with the clinical model of risk assessment. Actuarial assessments are measures that use variables which research has shown to be predictive of future dangerousness while considering the base rates of those behaviors. Common violence risk assessment measures are the Violence Risk Appraisal Guide (VRAG) (Harris, Rice, and Quinsey, 1993) and the Historical-Clinical-Risk Management Scheme-20 (HCR-20) (Webster, Douglas, Eaves, and Hart, 1997). Although not initially designed as a *actuarial risk assessment* measure, Hare's Psychopathy Check-list Revised, 2nd Edition, has been found to be of particular utility in violence risk prediction (PCL-R:2; Hare, 2003). Some sexual offense risk assessment measures include the Static-99 (Harris, Phenix, Hanson, and Thornton, 2003) and the RRASOR (Hanson, 1997). There are also more specific risk assessment measures, such as the Spousal Assault Risk Assessment Guide (SARA) (Kropp and Hart, 2000; Kropp, Hart, Webster, and Eaves, 1995). Some researchers recommend that risk assessments should rely more heavily on the actuarial approach to minimize clinical error (Quinsey, Rice, and Harris, 1995), whereas others (Monahan, 1981) cautioned against discarding clinical approaches altogether and instead recommend the integration of the two.

A vast amount of research has been conducted on clinical and actuarial methods of risk assessment. The current professional zeitgeist is to utilize a third method, an *adjusted actuarial approach*, also referred to as *structured clinical judgment* (Jackson and Guyton, 2007). In this approach, actuarial risk measures based on research are used as the framework for the risk assessment. However, these predictions may be adjusted to take into account personality and situational variables, similar to the clinical approach. To use an extreme example, a person who has been convicted of several rapes may be approaching release from prison. A civil commitment hearing may be set to determine whether or not the person requires post-release treatment under a sexually violent predator civil commitment law. Judges and other decision makers utilize a sexually violent predator risk assessment produced by a psychologist. The psychologist may have used several actuarial measures that place the offender in the high range of risk. If the psychologist uses only the actuarial method, he or she may recommend civil commitment. However, if the psychologist also takes into consideration that the man is currently paralyzed from the neck down and is on a ventilator, his or her opinion would most likely change to a very low risk of future sexual offending.

Risk may be communicated to decision makers in various ways. Some professionals prefer to use categorical labels (high, medium, low), whereas others communicate in terms of percentages (i.e., 65% chance of reoffending). Research by Kwartner, Lyons, and Boccaccini (2006) suggests that judges prefer a categorical format to communicate risk over probabilities (Conroy and Murrie, 2007). Most actuarial assessments provide some type of framework to present the prediction of risk. For example, a measure, such as the Classification of Violence Risk (COVR; Monahan et al., 2005), may predict that a civil commitment patient who is released to the community with a certain cluster of risk variables may have a 25% risk of committing a new violent act within one year post-release.

FORENSIC MENTAL HEALTH PROFESSIONALS AND LAW ENFORCEMENT

Psychologists and psychiatrists are sometimes asked by law enforcement to consult on ongoing investigations, to evaluate law enforcement officers pre- and post-employment, and to counsel law enforcement officers after traumatic events or due to cumulative stress. Investigators may consult with psychiatrists and psychologists during active criminal cases because of the professionals' specialized training and experience in human personality, behaviors, and motivations. Mental health professionals may be included in developing potential suspect pools and then prioritizing the suspect list based on offender and victim personality characteristics (McGrath and Torres, 2008). Psychiatrists and psychologists may also aid investigators in methods of interrogation because they are educated in the social psychological principles of social influence, particularly obedience, as well as psychopathy/sociopathy, that may help in an interrogation technique. This area, though, is fraught with ethical issues, especially if the clinician is involved to any degree in the actual interrogation.

Mental health professionals, particularly psychologists who have advanced training in psychometrics and test construction, will sometimes engage in psychological testing for law enforcement. Psychologists are often involved in testing to aid in the selection of appropriate individuals for law enforcement. These tests are largely based on personality characteristics. Testing may also be utilized in Fitness for Duty Evaluations. These evaluations are often performed after an officer has experienced some type of traumatic event such as shooting a criminal suspect, or other situation, such as when an officer has accumulated a large number of complaints related to brutality or an overaggressive policing style. Such an evaluation normally consists of a clinical interview and psychological testing to determine if the officer may return to work or if he or she needs additional treatment and assessment before returning to duty, either full or limited (Psychological Fitness-for-Duty Evaluations, 2004).

Psychiatrists, psychologists, and social workers may be asked to treat law enforcement officers and their families after a traumatic event has occurred. As mentioned previously, these professionals may engage in psychotherapy, while the psychiatrist may choose to prescribe medications, and the psychologist may use psychological tests to aid in diagnosis and treatment. Some police departments will have a mental health professional on staff who is familiar with police culture to help facilitate rapport between officer clients and the therapist. A most difficult area to navigate is that of whether officers can maintain control of their weapons. In most clinically risky situations, psychiatrists, psychologists, and social workers err on the side of caution. Yet to take away the ability of police officers to carry their weapons is akin to stripping them of their professional identity. While such a recommendation may be necessary, the clinician needs to understand the psychological ramifications and ensure that officers understand clearly the reasoning regarding when and how they can expect to get their firearm back if that is the plan.

FORENSIC MENTAL HEALTH IN CORRECTIONS

Psychologists, psychiatrists, and social workers practicing within the criminal justice system (such as in jails, prisons, probation offices, and forensic psychiatric hospitals) must be aware of the unique demands of working in these environments. First, as mentioned previously, determining agency, or who the client is, is very important. For forensic examiners, it is clear the client is the court. For clinicians, their treatment relationship is with the client, yet there may be confidentiality and security issues that interfere with the clinician-patient relationship. Unfortunately, sometimes clinicians are placed in the position of being both forensic examiners and treatment providers, as sometimes happens in forensic hospitals, where the same psychiatrist treating a patient must also offer an opinion as to competency to proceed or dangerousness. When clinicians are in such a situation, it is imperative that they explain the limits of confidentiality clearly to their patients. Another difficult situation occurs when patients are required to participate in court-mandated treatment, even if they appear unwilling to do so. For example, a psychologist working for a probation department may be required to provide court-ordered sexual offender therapy to an individual who does not believe she requires such treatment and does not wish to participate, or who even denies committing the crime in spite of a conviction. The psychologist would have to inform the client of the ramifications of such a decision not to participate in treatment because it could possibly result in the revocation of a supervised release. It is important to understand that while the treatment relationship may appear coerced, the client has agreed to the treatment as part of a plea agreement or a condition of probation or early release or parole. The agreement or mandate is between the patient and the court, not the clinician. Similarly, an inmate convicted of a sex crime may feel coerced into entering into sex offender treatment in prison to gain an early release, but any "coercion" is between the inmate and the criminal justice system and not the mental health clinician providing the treatment.

It is important to outline many of the common limits of confidentiality and mandatory reporting scenarios before therapy commences in criminal justice settings. Common instances when confidentiality must be breached occur when there is discussion of abuse of a child (including "consensual" sex with an adult by legal minors), an elderly or disabled person's abuse, or threats to institution security. Although most of what is said in therapy in these contexts is confidential, each institution may have specific rules about what should be reported to authorities. Mental health professionals must use their personal discretion to determine whether certain infractions require a breach in confidentiality. For example, a psychiatrist who is informed during a therapy session that his "client" is making a homemade weapon for protection is required to breach confidentiality and inform correctional staff because having such a weapon is a threat to the safety of all at the prison. The psychiatrist should discuss with the individual that he must report him to officers and why this is important, but must also take his or her own personal safety into account before engaging in the discussion.

On the other hand, a therapist may choose to use some discretion in reporting violations of minor rules to further the goals of therapy. For example, a social worker may be told by a prisoner that he won some homemade liquor (a.k.a.., "hooch") after gambling one night. Gambling and making alcohol, as well as the theft of alcohol-making items, are against prison rules. Since the infraction already occurred, the social worker may refrain from reporting such behavior in lieu of using the situation as a point of discussion to explore issues of antisocial thinking and brainstorming about how to better deal with a similar situation in the future. Of course, it is perfectly within the social worker's purview to report this behavior if he or she chooses to do so. However, the mental health professional should carefully weigh the therapeutic strength of this situation against the common behavior by inmates to "case people out" and try to manipulate professionals who fail to report certain behaviors. Choosing when to and when not to break confidentiality in correctional settings is often difficult to determine, so the professional must examine his or her own level of expertise in working with inmate populations before making these ethical decisions and the preceding social worker example does not apply to every situation.

Privacy in general is sometimes difficult to extend to therapy clients in prisons and jails. When people come to clinics for outpatient therapy, they are provided a relatively private setting to discuss delicate matters. In corrections, there may be correctional staff present for the safety of the therapist; doors may be left wide open during therapy sessions for security; or quick evaluations may be performed under poorly defined conditions, such as shouting through a hole in a door with other inmates within earshot. Correctional officers and other inmates are not bound to keep confidential what they hear, and often view mental health interventions as coddling inmates. Obviously, such conditions are less than ideal for fostering the typical therapeutic relationship, but they are oftentimes an unfortunate necessity for work in correctional settings.

Boundaries are always important to establish in any professional and therapeutic relationship, but absolutely essential in correctional work. A professional who works in these environments must take careful stock in what he or she is comfortable with personally, professionally, and ethically. Inmates have a lot of time on their hands and will often engage in criminal thinking and manipulative games with mental health professionals acting as unwitting accomplices. As mentioned previously, inmates will often "case out" professionals, determining who they may target for future manipulation. Inmates will try to manipulate professionals by getting them to engage in some type of small infraction that can then be used against those professionals to obtain greater favors in the future. Also, some inmates will feign or exaggerate mental health symptoms in an attempt to be released from work details, to gain additional attention in segregation units, or to use therapy sessions as a "safe" way to snitch against other inmates and staff. Not to be forgotten, just about any medication inmates can get a psychiatrist to prescribe for them will have a "street" value in the prison or jail setting. On the other hand, the fact that a medication was prescribed to an inmate could make that inmate a target by others who want the medication for themselves or to sell, or may identify that mentally ill inmate as a vulnerable individual to prey upon. Often in prisons, inmates who need medications must attend "pill line," which makes it nearly impossible to maintain privacy. Making roles and boundaries clear with inmates immediately is absolutely essential, and astute clinicians are on the alert for incremental boundary creep.

Finally, the scope of practice is somewhat limited in most correctional settings. Clients may not wish to write down thought logs as commonly used in cognitive-behavior therapies, for fear of them being discovered by other inmates or officers. Certain behavioral activation techniques commonly used in the treatment of depression may not be feasible in the regimented day of the typical inmate. Issues of power, control over one's life, and issues of hopelessness are common themes that are difficult to address in a correctional environment. Similarly, psychiatrists are often greatly limited by the medications available in correctional setting formularies, as well as the timing and administration of dosing, including attempting to offer a medication *prn* (as needed).

SUMMARY

Psychologists, psychiatrists, and social workers are behavioral health professionals that criminologists can expect to encounter in the forensic arenas of court, corrections, and investigations. Behavioral health professionals have extensive training, education, and experience in personality and behavior that may be directly relevant to the work of criminologists. Behavioral health professionals may conduct criminal and civil forensic evaluations for the courts, such as a civil assessment for child custody or a criminal evaluation of competency to stand trial or criminal responsibility. Forensic evaluators and clinicians may be asked to conduct risk assessments to aid decision makers in decisions related to placement, supervision, and/or treatment. In addition, mental health professionals may consult with law enforcement during active investigations or help in the selection, retention, and treatment of law enforcement officers. Finally, social workers, psychiatrists, and psychologists are prominent in corrections in the areas of assessment and treatment.

It is important that forensic criminologists have knowledge of what the allied behavioral forensic disciplines have to offer, when to utilize them, and how to judge the quality of the work product. First and foremost, forensic criminologists must be aware of the fact that the goals of mental health professionals differ greatly from those of the court, where mental health professionals are more interested in treatment-oriented goals, and the court is interested specifically in justice. Despite expert behavioral scientists being interested in separate goals from the court and being entitled to their professional opinions, these opinions must be supportable. Forensic criminologists should be aware that these individuals should be basing their conclusions on interviews and corroborating evidence, not on speculation. It is with this recognition of the importance of supporting evidence, objectivity, and critical thought that criminologists can determine actual forensic expertise from everything else in the mental health community.

The issue of risk assessment was also addressed here in some detail. Actuarial methods were compared with clinical assessments, as well as adjusted actuarial approaches. We noted that actuarial approaches often do not consider individual differences, whereas clinical methods do not take into account base rates. A combination of these two methods has therefore been deemed the most accurate.

Finally, forensic criminologists need to aware of mental health professionals and their roles relating to law enforcement and corrections. Issues relating to developing suspect pools, interrogation strategies, psychological testing for both suspects and officers, treatment of officers, privacy and security, confidentiality, boundaries, mandatory reporting, and the professional's discretion are all pertinent.

Review Questions
1. What is the difference between the role of a forensic psychiatrist and a forensic psychologist?
2. Define competency to stand trial.
3. T/F Forensic psychiatrists are qualified to make medical diagnoses.
4. T/F Insanity defenses are commonly used to gain acquittals in criminal trials.
5. T/F Those found not guilty by reason of insanity are usually sent to minimum security prisons.
6. Describe the differences between actuarial, clinical and adjusted actuarial risk assessment techniques.
7. Describe some of the issues mental health professionals working in corrections need to be aware of.
8. How can mental health professionals assist law enforcement?

REFERENCES

AAPL (American Academy of Psychiatry and the Law), 2005. Code of Ethics. Available online at http://www.aapl.org/ethics.htm (Last accessed 01/04/2009).

American Psychiatric Association, 1983. American Psychiatric Association Statement on the Insanity Defense. Am. J. Psychiatry 140, 681–688.

Barefoot v. Estelle, 1983. 463 U. S. 880.

Barker, R.L., Branson, D.B., 1993. Forensic Social Work: Legal Aspects of Professional Practice, The Haworth Press, Inc., Binghamton, New York.

Bersoff, D., Goodman-Delahunty, J., Grisso, T., Hans, V., Poythrees, N., Roesch, R., 1997. Training in Law and Psychology: Models from the Villanova Conference. Am. Psychol. 52 (12), 1301–1310.

Bonnie, R.J., 1983. The Moral Basis of the Insanity Defense. American Bar Association Journal 69, 194–197.

Bonta, J., Law, M., Hanson, R.K., 1998. The Prediction of Criminal and Violent Recidivism among Mentally Disordered Offenders: A Meta-Analysis. Psychol. Bull. 123, 123–142.

Bursztajn, H., Scherr, A., Brodsky, A., 1993. The Rebirth of Forensic Psychiatry in Light of Recent Historical Trends in Criminal Responsibility. Available online at http://www.forensic-psych.com/articles/artRebirth.php last accessed 01/10/09

Callahan, L.A., McGreery, M.A., Cirincione, C., Steadman, H.J., 1992. Measuring the Effects of the Guilty but Mentally Ill (GBMI) Verdict: Georgia's 1982 GBMI Reform. Law Hum. Behav. 16, 447–462.

CNN. com, 2002, September 2. Daughter's Abductor Likely Had Help, Father Says. Available online at http://archives.cnn.com/2002/US/09/02/missing.girl/index.html (Last accessed 01/04/09).

CNN. com, 2005, July 27. Smart's Accused Kidnapper Ruled Incompetent. Available online at http://www.cnn.com/2005/LAW/07/26/smart.suspect/index.html. (Last accessed 12/07/08).

Committee on Ethical Guidelines for Forensic Psychologists, 1991. Specialty Guidelines for Forensic Psychologists. Law Hum. Behav. 15 (6), 655–665.

Conroy, M.A., Murrie, D.C., 2007. Forensic Assessment of Violence Risk: A Guide for Risk Assessment and Risk Management. John Wiley and Sons, Hoboken, NJ.

Dusky v. United States, 1960. 362 U. S. 402.

Eberle, P., Eberle, S., 1993. The Abuse of Innocence: The McMartin Preschool Trial, Prometheus Books, Buffalo, New York.

Ewing, C., McCann, J., 2006. Minds on Trial: Great Cases in Law and Psychology, Oxford University Press Inc., New York.

Federal Rules of Evidence 702, 2009. Available online at http://www.law.cornell.edu/rules/fre/rules.htm#Rule702 (Last accessed 12/13/08).

Freiden, T., 1999, April 2. Weston Found Incompetent to Stand Trial for Capitol Shooting. CNN. com. http://www.cnn.com/ALLPOLITICS/stories/1999/04/22/capitol.shooting/ (Last accessed 12/07/08).

Giorgi-Guarnieri, D., Janofsky, J., Kerman, E., et al., 2002. AAPL Practice Guideline for Forensic Psychiatric Evaluation of Defendants Raising the Insanity Defense. J. Am. Acad. Psychiatry Law 30 (Suppl.).

Golding, S.L., Skeem, J.L., Roesch, R., Zapf, P.A., 1999. The Assessment of Criminal Responsibility. In: Hess, A.K., Weiner, I.B. (Eds.), The Handbook of Forensic Psychology, second ed. John Wiley and Sons, New York, pp. 379–408.

Hans, P., Slater, D., 1983. John Hinckley, Jr., and the Insanity Defense: The Public's Verdict. Public Opin. Q. 47 (2), 202–212.

Hanson, R.K., 1997. The Development of a Brief Actuarial Risk Scale for Sexual Offense Recidivism (User report no. 1997004). Corrections Research, Ministry of the Solicitor General of Canada, Ottawa, Canada. Access online from: http://ww2.ps-sp. gc.ca/publications/corrections/199704_e.pdf. (Last accessed 1/1/09).

Hare, R.D., 2003. Manual for the Revised Psychopathy Checklist, second ed. Multi-Health Systems, Toronto, Ontario, Canada.

Harris, A., Phenix, A., Hanson, R.K., Thornton, D., 2003. Static-99 Coding Rules, Revised 2003. Available online at http://www.static99.org/pdfdocs/static-99-coding-rules_e.pdf (Last accessed on 1/1/09).

Harris, G.T., Rice, M.E., Quinsey, L., 1993. Violent Recidivism of Mentally Disordered Offenders: The Development of a Statistical Prediction Instrument. Criminal Justice and Behavior 20, 315–335.

Hastings, D., Bonnie, R.J., 1981. A Survey of Pretrial Psychiatric Evaluations in Richmond, Virginia. Developments in Mental Health Law 1, 9.

Haworth Press: Journal of Forensic Social Work Haworth Press. Accessed online at: http://www. haworthpress.com/store/product.asp?sid=8NSJRQ392PE58LT3N0TK3 TLBDG2TBSWFandsku=J203andAuthType=4. (Last accessed 12/06/08).

Jackson v. Indiana, 1972. 406 US 715.

Jackson, R.L., Guyton, M.R., 2007. Violence Risk Assessment. In: Jackson, R. (Ed.), Learning Forensic Assessment. CRC Press, Boca Raton, FL.

Kropp, P.R., Hart, S.D., Webster, C.D., Eaves, D., 1995. Manual for the Spousal Assault Risk Assessment Guide, second ed. The British Columbia Institute Against Family Violence, Vancouver, BC.

Kropp, R., Hart, S.D., 2000. The Spousal Assault Risk Assessment Guide (SARA): Reliability and Validity in Adult Male Offenders. Law Hum. Behav. 24, 101–118.

Kwartner, P.K., Lyons, P.M., Boccaccini, M.T., 2006. Judges' Risk Communication Preferences in Risk for Future Violence Cases. International Journal of Forensic Mental Health 5 (2), 185–194.

Masters, B., 1993. The Shrine of Jeffrey Dahmer. BCA, New York.

McGrath, M., Torres, A., 2008. The Mental Health Professional's Contribution to Criminal Profiling. In: Turvey, B. (Ed.), Criminal Profiling: An Introduction to Behavioral Evidence Analysis, third ed. Academic Press, London, pp. 113–132.

Melton, G.B., Petrila, J., Poythress, N.G., Slobogin, C., Lyons, P.M., 2007. Psychological Evaluations for the Courts: A Handbook for Mental Health Professionals and Lawyers, third ed. Guilford Press, New York.

Monahan, J., 1981. Predicting Violent Behavior: An Assessment of Clinical Technique. Sage Publications, London.

Monahan, J., Steadman, H.J., Appelbaum, P.S., Grisso, T., Mulvey, E.P., Roth, L.H., et al., 2005. Classification of Violence Risk (COVR). Psychological Assessment Resources, Lutz, FL.

National Association of Social Workers, 2008. http://www.socialworkers.org/pubs/ Code/code.asp (Last accessed 12/06/08).

National Organization of Forensic Social Work, 2008. http://www.nofsw.org/html/forensic_social_work.html (Last accessed 12/06/08).

NY Times, 2008, December 20. Inmate Bludgeoned with Jeffrey Dahmer on Work Detail Dies. Available online at http://query.nytimes.com/gst/fullpage.html?res=9405E3DC1130F932A35751C1A962958260 (Last accessed 12/20/08).

NY Times, 1994, January 4. Lorena Bobbitt Acquitted in Mutilation of Husband. Available online at http://query.nytimes.com/gst/fullpage.html?res=980DE5D71230F931A15752C0A962958260andsec=andspon=andpagewanted=all (Last accessed on 01/04/09).

NY Times, 1997, December 8. Bobbitt's Ex-Wife Charged in Assault. Available online at http://query.nytimes.com/gst/fullpage.html?sec=healthandres=9C00E1DA163CF93BA35751C1A961958260. (Last accessed 12/07/08).

NY Times, 2002, August 2. Judge Rules Capitol Gunman Can Be Forced to Take Medicine. Available online at http://query.nytimes.com/gst/fullpage.html?res=9F07E5DE153BF930A3575BC0A9649C8B63. (Last accessed 12/07/08).

Psychological Fitness-for-Duty Evaluations, 2004. Ratified by the International Association of Chiefs of Police (IACP) Police Psychological Services Center, Los Angeles, California. Available online at http://www.theiacp.org/div_sec_com/sections/PsychologicalFitnessforDutyEvaluation.pdf. (Last accessed 12/22/08).

Quinsey, L., Rice, M.E., Harris, G.T., 1995. Actuarial Prediction of Sexual Recidivism. J. Interpers. Violence 10 (1), 85–105.

Roesch, R., Zapf, P.A., Golding, S.L., Skeem, J.L., 1999. Defining and Assessing Competency to Stand Trial. In: Hess, A.K., Weiner, I.B. (Eds.), The Handbook of Forensic Psychology. second ed. John Wiley and Sons, New York, pp. 327–349.

Sloat, S.M., Frierson, R.L., 2005. Juror Knowledge and Attitudes Regarding Mental Illness Verdicts. J. Am. Acad. Psychiatry Law 33 (2), 208–213.

Smail, K., 1993. Postscript: The Insanity Defence. In: Masters, B. (Ed.), The Shrine of Jeffrey Dahmer. BCA, New York, pp. 226–234.

Surface, D., 2007. State of Mind: Evaluating Competency to Stand Trial. Social Work Today, 7 (4), 17. Available online at http://www.socialworktoday.com/archive/julyaug2007p17.shtml (Last accessed on 12/19/08).

Stoeson, L., 2006. NY State Court Rules on Forensic Expertise. NASW News March Available online at www.socialworkers.org/pubs/news/2006/03/default.asp

Swanson, J.W., Holtzer III, C.E., Granju, K., Jono, R.T., 1990. Violence and Psychiatric Disorder in the Community: Evidence from the Epidemiological Catchment Area Surveys. Hosp. Community Psychiatry 176, 324–331.

Webster, C.D., Douglas, K.S., Eaves, D., Hart, S.D., 1997. HCR-20: Assessing Risk for Violence, version 2. Simon Fraser University, Burnaby, British Columbia, Canada.

Forensic Criminology in Practice

CHAPTER 16

Writing Forensic Reports

Wayne A. Petherick and Brent E. Turvey[1]

[1]Select portions of this chapter have been inspired by or adapted from Chisum and Turvey (2007), Chapter 4. "Practice Standards for the Reconstruction of Crime."

KEY TERMS

Operationalize: To define a term with multiple meanings as it is being used in a given report or publication, in order to prevent misunderstanding or misinterpretation.

Peer Review: The appraisal of work and research by others in the same discipline or profession. Refers to publications, the results of examinations, or the application of methodology with respect to either.

Reliability: In reference to scientific testing, the ability to give consistent results over time.

Sufficiency: In reference to scientific examinations, the determination of whether there is enough evidence of the necessary quality for forensic examiners to conduct a meaningful examination.

CONTENTS

The majority of forensic examination reports do not meet acceptable scientific standards. In fact, it is common for such reports to "contain only identifying and agency information, a brief description of the evidence being submitted, a brief description of the types of analysis requested, and a short statement of the results," and "[t]he norm is to have no description of the methods or procedures used, and most reports do not discuss measurement uncertainties or confidence limits" (Edwards and Gotsonis, 2009, p. 6–3). In other words, most forensic examination reports do not explain how results were achieved or interpretations were rendered, and tend to leave readers with a false sense of overconfidence regarding the findings presented.

The authors have seen autopsy reports in complex homicide cases that average 3 pages long from one forensic pathologist and 30 pages from another. We have seen DNA reports from criminalists that are a half page long in one jurisdiction and three to four pages for similar evidence tested in another. We have

503

seen criminal profiles that are a single page (or less), and we have seen them at 45 pages or more. Consistently, the primary difference between these reports has been the amount of space spent explaining what was actually examined, precisely what it means, and the nature of any limitations.

Short reports are not generally created by accident. Often the reason for an absence of content in forensic reporting is combination of ignorance, concern for liability, a desire for brevity, or unmitigated duplicity. Many examiners are poorly trained and lack good writing skills; their lack of writing is a genuine reflection of what they believe to be adequate practice because nobody has ever corrected them. Still, some examiners fear revealing too much about what they did or what their efforts mean within a given case; theirs is a genuine concern about revealing ignorance or being wrong. Other examiners simply do not have the time, or do not wish to take the time, to make a full reporting. Also, there are instances in which examiners wish to hold determinations close to the vest so as to preserve their ability to change them. In such cases, reports are short, and terminology is either confusing or equivocal.

Whatever the case, not one of these reasons provides a legitimate justification for deficient reporting. Even claiming ignorance is actually a proclamation that one is inexpert and has no business rendering forensic reports at all. As explained by Dr. John Thornton (Kirk and Thornton, 1970, pp. v–vi): "When the liberty of an individual may depend in part on physical evidence, it is not unreasonable to ask that the expert witnesses who are called upon to testify, either against the defendant or in his behalf, know what they are doing."

The purpose of this chapter is to help alleviate the epidemic of substandard reporting that currently plagues the forensic community. While forensic criminology must be featured, it is universal in its application to any endeavor where scientific results are being rendered for court-related purposes. It provides a practical foundation regarding the necessary philosophy of forensic reporting and basic outline for how such reports should be prepared.

PHILOSOPHY

In previous chapters, we have discussed the need for an appropriate forensic character, or *ethos*. It should go without saying that forensic practitioners require a predisposition for objectivity, competence, and professionalism in their work (Thornton, 1997). Professionalism involves an acceptance that forensic practitioners bear the burden of ensuring conclusions are effectively communicated to intended recipients, including investigators, attorneys, and the court. This means writing them down. This also means that they must be competent at the task of intelligible writing, and their reports must be comprehensive with regard to examinations performed, findings, and conclusions.

The suggestion that report writing has a particular value when rendering forensic conclusions is not at all new. Dr. Hans Gross (see Chapter 1) wrote, for example, of the critical role that exact, deliberate, and patient forensic examination efforts play in investigative and forensic contexts. Specifically, he stated that just looking at evidence and forming opinions are the best practice. He argued that there is utility in reducing one's opinions to the form of a report to identify problems in the logic of one's theories (Gross, 1906, p. 439):

> So long as one only looks on the scene, it is impossible, whatever the care, time, and attention bestowed, to detect all the details, and especially note the incongruities: but these strike us at once when we set ourselves to describe the picture on paper as exactly and clearly as possible.
>
> ...
>
> The "defects of the situation" are just those contradictions, those improbabilities, which occur when one desires to represent the situation as something quite different from what it really is, and this with the very best intentions and the purest belief that one has worked with all of the forethought, craft, and consideration imaginable.

The experiences of the authors concur with those of Hans Gross. The act of preparing opinions in a written format, gathering references, forming supportive argumentation, and rendering deliberately crafted conclusions is a valuable step in the analytical process. It allows errors and omissions in any of these areas to be realized and helps to identify breaks in the logic of misinformed interpretation.

Conversely, verbal conclusions should be viewed as a form of substandard work product. They are susceptible to conversions, alterations, and misrepresentations. They may also become lost to time. Written conclusions are fixed in time, easy to reproduce, and are less susceptible to accidental or intentional conversion, alteration, and misrepresentation. An analyst who prefers verbal conclusions as opposed to written conclusions reveals his or her preference for conclusive mobility.

However, the forensic criminologist is often in a bind on this point. As mentioned in Chapter 3, the prosecution and their agents must follow different rules of conduct than the accused. This has to do with the forensic landscape: the laws of discovery (a.k.a. disclosure) are not the same for both sides. Forensic examiners employed by the prosecution must document their involvement in every case and write reports regarding their findings or face very serious penalties. However, those who work for defense attorneys are bound by the attorney-client privilege; they may be asked by their clients to refrain from writing a report of their findings for any number of legitimate reasons. In such cases, forensic criminologists should take scrupulous notes to augment the absence of a written report and be prepared to share them with the court upon request.

As explained in Chisum and Turvey (2007), if a conclusion cannot be written down in a logical form, easily understood by all, then apart from having no forensic value, it is also likely to be wrong.

TERMINOLOGY

It has been said that language is a cumbersome engine for thought. No truer words have been spoken. This has certainly been the case in the forensic disciplines, where there has been little or no standardization of terms or their intended meaning. Each agency, each lab, each practitioner, it seems, uses its/his/her own language. As explained in Edwards and Gotsonis, 2009 (p. 6–3):

> …[M]any terms are used by forensic examiners in reports and in court testimony to describe findings, conclusions, and the degrees of association between evidentiary material (e.g., hairs, fingerprints, fibers) and particular people or objects. Such terms include but are not limited to "match," "consistent with," "identical," "similar in all respects tested," and "cannot be excluded as the source of." The use of such terms can have a profound effect on how the trier of fact in a criminal or civil matter perceives and evaluates evidence. Yet the forensic science disciplines have not reached agreement or consensus on the precise meaning of any of these terms. Although some disciplines have developed vocabulary and scales to be used in reporting results, they have not become standard practice. This imprecision in vocabulary stems in part from the paucity of research in forensic science and the corresponding limitations in interpreting the results of forensic analyses.

Given these limitations, it is currently the onus of forensic criminologists to use plain language in report writing and to *operationalize* all significant terms used. They have a responsibility to become familiar with and write at the level of their intended audience, and they must define any key terms as they are being used to relate findings. Without precise definitions, and in the absence of forensic examiners to explain their word usage, the meaning of forensic reports is too often found in the eye of the beholder. In most instances, this involves a stakeholder in the outcome (i.e., an attorney) rather than a neutral party, making misinterpretation and misunderstanding a predictable hazard.

REPORT STRUCTURE

Apart from their relative permanence, written conclusions also provide forensic practitioners with the best chance to memorialize methods, interpretations, arguments, and the relevant underlying facts of a case as they understand them. However, forensic examiners are often bound by convention and policy. For example, those who work for the government will have specific policies to follow and forms to use when preparing their reports. These policies and forms vary widely with respect to relevance, content, and quality.

The purpose of this section is to assist with the development of policies and standards which conform with best practice, as provided in the recently published National Academy of Science (NAS) report: *Strengthening Forensic Science in the United States: A Path Forward*. Adapted from Chisum and Turvey (2007), and consistent with the recommendations of the NAS Report (Edwards and Gotsonis, 2009), a written forensic report should include, but need not be limited to, the following information:

1. Name(s) and date(s) of examination, with signature.
2. A preliminary background section, describing the forensic examiner's involvement in the case.
3. A chain of custody section, describing and detailing the evidence (material) that was examined or included in the examination.
4. A descriptive section, in which the forensic examiner thoroughly describes his or her examination and consideration of the facts and evidence.
5. A results section, in which the examiner lists any results and conclusions, including their significance and limitations.

Name, Date, and Signature

It is a safe bet that most of those reading this text were taught the need for providing both name and date on every homework assignment, research paper, and exam during the first days of primary school. It is a habit that we either learn or suffer the consequences for ignoring. For a variety of reasons, many forensic reports lack one or both elements.

In every forensic report, the examiner's name must be provided so that readers may be certain who did the work. Dates of various examinations must be provided so that readers may learn at which point they occurred within a given case, and their timing with respect to any other case activity or examinations. A dated signature line also is necessary so that readers may verify the author of the report and when it was completed or submitted.

Without this basic information, it is not possible for the readers to know who did what or when relative to anything else that happened. The lack of this information also allows for inaccurate suggestions that examinations were performed sooner or later than they should have been. And finally, on days when examiner testimony is needed, failing to include this information on a report allows agencies to send available personnel to court rather than those who actually did the work. This circumstance leads to testimony in which the court or the trier of fact may assume that the examiner (or a supervisor) on the witness stand performed work that he or she actually didn't.

Preliminary Background Section

The preliminary background section of a report provides the forensic examiner's involvement in the case. It should include who hired the examiner, under what circumstances, and when that hiring occurred. The reason is that it is important to know which side was providing the examiner with information and whether the examiner's involvement was secured before or after certain events took place, such as an arrest or a previous conviction. For example, a forensic criminologist performing a postconviction review of a capital murder case for the defense deals with a completely different set of facts and evidence than one who is brought in by the police during the investigation before an arrest has been made.

This section of the report may also include basic background information regarding the case, including the type of crime involved; the date, time, and location of the offense; and any relevant victim information not otherwise mentioned in the report. This information is meant to provide a quick thumbnail sketch of the case that is useful to those glancing at the report for its context. It also has utility to forensic examiners, who may use this information to refresh their memory while testifying on the stand with report in hand.

Chain of Custody Section

The chain of custody section of the report provides the materials examined, where they came from, and when. In this section, examiners make clear which facts and evidence they are relying on, and where they might be found, so that others may check their work if necessary.

At this point, it is necessary to distinguish between *legal* and *scientific sufficiency* of evidence. Legal standards have no hold over scientific methods of examination. In other words, what is sufficiently reliable for legal purposes may not be sufficiently reliable for inclusion in a forensic examiner's report, and the opposite is also true. It is the forensic criminologist's responsibility to know the difference to make it clear to the court when necessary.

As Thornton explains (1994, p. 476):

> Although there is a forensic science profession in the United States, and although many of us spend much of our time in courts of law, we have for the most part been passive spectators to the court decisions that deal

with the admissibility of scientific evidence. In one sense, this is as it should be. It is the job of the law, and not of science, to determine how science is to be used in the courts. But in another sense, our passivity has served both ourselves and the legal system poorly. It is the job of science, and not of law, to determine what is good science and what is not.

And as Thornton further notes (1994, p. 483):

> Every scientist understands that there are courts of law. By and large, they are accorded respect. I am not as certain that every lawyer understands that there are courts of science as well. They are not as easily identified because they do not exist in a particular point in space, nor is there one man or woman in a black robe that symbolizes the court, nor a marble anteroom outside smelling of urine and industrial strength disinfectant. Courts of science are constructs of the mind, which bring clarity and coherency to scientific and technical matters. They are built not of marble, but from the scientific method. Every scientist is expected to serve as his or her own presiding judge, and if a costume is necessary, it is a white lab coat instead of a black robe. But these courts have certain rules also, just as courts of law. And the scientist who declines to practice his or her profession by the rules of science will soon find that he or she has earned only the derision of his or her colleagues, and eventually finds that he or she cannot continue to practice at all.

Ultimately, forensic examiners must determine whether evidence is *sufficient* and *reliable* for their examinations. That is to say, is there enough evidence of sufficient quality to examine, and are the results of the examination going to be reliable enough to carry any conclusions? The courts, at a later point, will determine whether or not this is admissible. One does not necessarily hinge on the other, nor should it.

Descriptive Section

In the descriptive section of the report, the forensic examiner should describe the types of examinations performed and the steps involved before results were achieved. This description may require a single sentence, a short paragraph, or several pages. Failure to provide this information deprives third-party reviewers of knowing precisely how evidence was handled by the examiner and potentially filtered or even altered.

Results

In the results section of the report, forensic examiners should describe the nature and extent of ANY findings subsequent to their examinations—not just the findings they like or can explain clearly, but ALL findings from EVERY examination performed.

In the presentation of findings, forensic criminologists will find themselves using statements that suggest varying degrees of confidence. They may even become accustomed to using vague terms or terms of art such as *probably, likely, identify, match, consistent with,* and *reasonable degree of scientific certainty,* to qualify the probability of findings. Without proper limits, this language can be misleading to those it is intended to assist.

Conclusions expressed with confidence statements must be qualified and explained to the point of absolute clarity (Turvey, 2008). Without a high degree of internal clarification, findings may be misunderstood, misrepresented, and misapplied. Edwards and Gotsonis (2009) provide the following general advisory (p. 6–3):

> Forensic science reports, and any courtroom testimony stemming from them, must include clear characterizations of the limitations of the analyses, including associated probabilities where possible. Courtroom testimony should be given in lay terms so that all trial participants can understand how to weight and interpret the testimony. In order to enable this, research must be undertaken to evaluate the reliability of the steps of the various identification methods and the confidence intervals associated with the overall conclusions.

When forensic criminologists have given findings, written or otherwise, there must remain no question as to whether the findings are certain and no question as to how certainty was established. After all, the purpose of presenting findings is to clarify the evidence, not muddle it.

As mentioned in Chapter 3, a common *Brady* violation, often committed out of nothing more than ignorance, is related to the forensic practice of labeling a finding or report "inconclusive." There are forensic practitioners employed by the government, from fingerprint analysts to DNA technicians, who erroneously believe that inconclusive or indeterminate findings are not an actual result. Therefore, they feel comfortable withholding the existence of such tests and related findings by virtue of failing to write them up in a report or failing to disclose those kinds of reports to the defense.

Inconclusive findings are, however, relevant to the reconstruction of a crime, the nature and extent of examinations performed, the evidence they were performed on, the quality of any testing, the competency of the examiner, and the legal proceedings that hinge upon the weight the court places on evidence of every kind. They are a result, just not one that is expected or even desired—and they must not be ignored.[2]

[2]For a more complete discussion of inconclusive findings, refer to Chapter 3.

FACT CHECKING

Before preparing the final draft of a forensic report, forensic examiners should take care to check that facts relied upon are accurate and up to date. When they are working for the government, this means relying on supervisors, colleagues, and law enforcement investigators. However, when they are working privately, forensic examiners may rely on their clients (the attorneys) and their investigators, either of which may have a more accurate and even encyclopedic knowledge of the case facts. It is therefore proper to allow either the clients or their investigators to fact-check the final report. They may even suggest questions that the forensic examiners failed to answer. It is improper, however, for attorneys or investigators to suggest changes as to final conclusions. Forensic examiners must stand behind their methods and results and not be swayed by those who have a stake in the outcome of legal proceedings that will be informed by them.

PEER REVIEW

Ultimately, the purpose of report writing is to make findings clear and to make a record of them. A secondary goal for scientists is to allow for peer review. *Peer review* refers to the appraisal of work and research by others in the same discipline or profession. It can happen when a report is in draft form, or when scholarly writing is in prepublication, so as to allow for refinement based on feedback. Or this process can take place after a final report or publication is rendered. Textbooks and journal articles are regularly critiqued in like formats, while forensic reports must be peer reviewed as part of the adversarial process by experts retained by opposing counsel.

With respect to report writing in particular, Edwards and Gotsonis (2009) explain (p. 6–3):

> Although it is not appropriate and practicable to provide as much detail as might be expected in a research paper, sufficient content should be provided to allow the nonscientist reader to understand what has been done and permit informed, unbiased scrutiny of the conclusion.

Good scientific practice invites peer review; it wants to suffer the crucible of peer examination and critique. In this way it becomes more informed of its own weaknesses and becomes better. Poor scientific practice avoids peer review and even chastises those who would deign to engage in it.

In any case, it is strongly recommended that forensic examiners submit draft reports to one or more peers for review—to identify any shortcomings, failures in logic, or lapses in practice. When examiners are working for government agencies, a supervisor will likely perform this task. When they are engaged in defense work, peer review requires a trusted colleague. It should be done without identifying information to protect attorney-client privilege, and always with the client's permission. If the client says no, that is his or her call. However, it should be made clear that the very act of writing the report and supplying it to the state affords the opportunity for peer review should the client desire it.

SAMPLE REPORT

Forensic Examination Report

To: Shari Greenberger, Sara Zalkin, Attorneys

From: Brent E. Turvey, MS, P.O. Box 2175, Sitka, AK 99835

Date: October 17, 2005

Re: Kirstin "Blaise" Lobato case

On July 8, 2001, the deceased body of Duran Bailey was found behind a garbage dumpster in an unlocked, three sided cement enclosure on West Flamingo Road in Las Vegas, Nevada. According to witness statements, he was homeless and slept in this location at night. Kirstin "Blaise" Lobato is charged with his murder.

In August of 2005, this examiner was asked by Attorneys Greenberger and Zalkin to examine the forensic evidence in this case with respect to both a possible reconstruction of events and a motivational analysis of the offense behavior.

Between September 16th and October 3rd of 2005, this examiner received material related to this case from Attorney Shari Greenberger, including, but not limited to:

1. Las Vegas Metro Police Department (LVMPD) crime scene evidence list
2. LVMPD crime scene diagram
3. LVMPD Arrest and Incident Reports
4. LVMPD Crime Scene and Evidence Reports
5. LVMPD Investigator's Reports
6. LVMPD Voluntary Statements of Witnesses
7. LVMPD Forensic Laboratory Reports of Examination
8. Crime scene and autopsy photos
9. Autopsy report of Duran Bailey
10. Autopsy Evidence Form
11. APL toxicology report

12. Preliminary hearing testimony
13. Trial testimony of Dr. Larry Simms
14. Clark County Coroner's Investigation reports
15. Reports and Testimony of Criminalist Tom Wahl, LVMPD Forensic Lab
16. Report and Testimony of Joel Gellere, fingerprint examiner
17. Report and Testimony of Defense reconstructionist, George Schiro
18. LVMPD Reports and witness statements related to the sexual assault w/ weapon of Diann Parker on 7/1/01

On October 1 of 2005, this examiner visited the crime scene in Las Vegas, NV during both daylight hours and evening hours with Attorneys Greenberger and Zalkin, and Investigator James Aleman.

On October 5th, 2005, Investigator James Aleman faxed this examiner an undated copy of "FOLLOW-UP NOTES" from the Clark County Coroner's Office by Investigative Staff Supervisor William Gaza relating to the death of Duran Bailey. It was advised that these notes had just been sent from the Coroner's office, and had not been discovered previously.

FINDINGS

After a careful review of the facts and information provided, it is the opinion of this examiner that:

1. There is no physical evidence associating Kirstin "Blaise" Lobato, or her vehicle (a red 1984 Fiero), to the crime scene.
2. The offender in this case would have transferred bloodstains to specific areas of any vehicle they entered and operated.
3. The failure of Luminol to luminesce at any of the requisite sites in the defendant's vehicle is a reasonably certain indication that blood was not ever present, despite any conventional attempts at cleaning.
4. There are several items of potentially exculpatory evidence that were present on or with the body at the crime scene but subsequently not submitted to the crime lab for analysis.
5. A primary motive in this case is directed anger expressed in the form of brutal injury, overkill and sexual punishment to the victim's genitals.
6. The wound patterns in this case may be used to support a theory of multiple assailants.

DISCUSSION

1. There is no physical evidence associating Kirstin "Blaise" Lobato to the crime scene.

According to LVMPD Forensic Lab Reports by Criminalist Thomas Wahl, all of the evidence from the body or the crime scene that he was asked to examine excluded Ms. Lobato. This includes:

- TAW 1, item 1O & 1P: DNA from left and right fingernail clippings of Duran Bailey.
- TAW 3, item 16: DNA from saliva on a wad of chewing gum found at the scene with victim's blood on it.
- TAW 10, items 7, 8, & 9: DNA from blood sample and control swabs from sandal at scene.
- TAW 6, item 2: a pair of Nike Air shoes collected from Ms. Lobato were negative for blood.
- TAW 7, item 2: an aluminum baseball bat collected from Ms. Lobato was negative for blood.
- TAW 8, item 2: a seat cover collected from Ms. Lobato's vehicle was negative for blood.
- TAW 11, item 10: small pieces of unknown wax like trace evidence with "silver colored paper" collected from Duran Bailey's rectum at autopsy were not associated with Ms. Lobato's vehicle or any item associated with her.

None of the footwear seized from Ms. Lobato by the LVMPD could be associated with the crime scene or the bloody footwear impressions found leading out of the crime scene area.

None of the tire tracks found at the scene by the LVMPD were associated with Ms. Lobato's vehicle.

None of the fingerprint examinations performed by the LVMPD associated Ms. Lobato with the scene or the crime.

2. The offender in this case would have transferred bloodstains to specific areas of any vehicle they entered and operated.

After stabbing the victim so many times, cutting off the victim's penis, moving the victim, and walking around in the victim's blood in such a confined space, the offender would have had blood on their hands and feet at the very least.

This would necessarily result in bloody footwear impressions on the ground leading away from body, which was the case. It would also necessarily result in bloody transfer to the interior and exterior door handles, the steering wheel, the gearshift, the driver's side floor pads, and any of the foot pedals. This transfer, even if wiped or washed away with conventional cleaning agents, would be detectable using Luminol.

3. **The failure of Luminol to luminesce at any of the requisite sites in the defendant's vehicle would be a reasonably certain indication that blood was not ever present, despite any conventional attempts at cleaning.**

Consider the following scientific facts regarding Luminol testing in a forensic context:

- When Luminol oxidizes, it glows in a process called chemiluminescence.
- It's not the blood that glows in a positive Luminol reaction, but the iron in the blood that makes the Luminol glow.
- Luminol oxidation is catalyzed by the presence of metal ions such as copper, iron, and cyanide.
- As blood dries, it turns brownish and rusty colored; Fe(2) oxidizes to Fe(3). Consequently, the older the bloodstain, the more intense the reaction with Luminol.
- Luminol is extremely sensitive; studies have shown that it can detect blood in 1 parts per million (1:1,000,000). This includes blood that may be found in urine.
- Luminol is sensitive enough to pick up minute traces of blood even when attempts have been made to wash it away with various cleaning agents such as bleach and ammonia.
- Luminol tests cannot distinguish between human blood and animal blood.
- Brass, bronze, and similar alloys containing copper can give false positives for blood when using Luminol.
- Luminol reacts with some cleaning agents, including certain bleaches, *Fast Orange*, *The Works*, *Fantastic* and *Babo Cleanser*.
- Luminol reacts with many difference kinds of vegetation.

What this all means is that it takes considerable effort to clean any visible bloodstain from clothing to such a degree that Luminol would fail to detect evidence of its presence. This is in no small part why *Gaennslen* (1983) reports that (pp. 247–248):

A number of compounds have been used for the [presumptive] tests, and in particular the test is often named after the chemical compound that is used. Some of the compounds are: benzidine, phenolphthalein, leucomalachite green, ortho-tolidine, tetramethylbenzidine, ortho-dianisidine, and luminol.

...

Most authorities agree that positive presumptive tests alone should not be taken to mean that blood is definitely present. A positive test suggests that the sample could be blood and indicates [the need for] confirmatory testing. On the other hand, a negative presumptive test is a reasonably certain indication that blood is absent, although in rare circumstances an inhibiting chemical could be present.

This is in agreement with the testimony of LVMPD Criminalist Thomas Wahl (pp. 964–965):

Luminol is used primarily to determine or to detect the possibility of blood being present on something that cannot be seen with the naked visual eye. And perpetrators do attempt, have been known to attempt to wash out blood from certain items such that they cannot be seen visually with the naked eye and that's why Luminol is an important tool in crime scene investigation to try to be able to detect blood that's not visually apparent and may have been washed out or diluted.

According to Criminalist Wahl, the vehicle seat cover (TAW 8, item 5) and the interior left door panel (TAW 9) of Ms. Lobato's vehicle:

…yielded weak positive presumptive tests for the presence of blood in one area of each item. Human blood could not be confirmed from either item. Human DNA was not detected in extracts prepared from swabbings collected from both items.

Consequently, it is most accurate to say that no blood of any kind was found in Ms. Lobato's vehicle. Furthermore, it is a reasonable scientific certainty that no blood was ever transferred to those areas in or on the car where Luminol results were negative. This precludes the possibility that the person who committed this crime also entered and operated Ms. Lobato's vehicle immediately after its commission.

4. **There are several items of potentially exculpatory evidence that were present on or with the body at the crime scene, but subsequently not submitted to the crime lab for analysis.**

Item No. 01032493 1; EV# 0107082410

"SEXUAL ASSAULT KIT, DOE, JOHN"

This item appears to be a sexual assault kit performed on the victim in this case, Duran Bailey. According to the Autopsy Evidence Form by CSA Maria Thomas, this sexual assault kit contains combed pubic hair and a penile swab. At the very least, the penile swab and any pubic combings should be tested for DNA in order to confirm or refute the theory that any particular person had sexual contact with the victim prior to death.

It must be noted that the victim's actual penis was not collected and retained as an item of evidence, and was apparently buried with the victim's body (re: communication with Investigator James Aleman on October 5, 2005).

Item No. 01034392 1; EV# 0107082410

3—"CIGARETTE BUTTS"

These items may or may not be the cigarette butts evident in photo 40400012.jpg. The cigarettes in that photograph are located on the victim's right abdomen, left thigh, and left hand.

The cigarettes in that photograph are associated with a single expended paper match (Item 1034392 2) located on his right thigh.

The cigarettes in that photograph are associated with what appears to be ash in the same area.

The cigarettes in that photograph may also be associated with dark injuries described vaguely under Chest and Abdomen; Item 1 as "scattered irregular and curvilinear pressure marks" (see p. 4 of the autopsy report).

As evident in photograph 40400009.jpg, these cigarette butts were located under a plastic bag that shielded them from the garbage that was subsequently placed on top of the body. This associates them more directly with the crime and any related activity. Each cigarette could be examined for latent prints and tested for DNA to confirm or refute the theory that any particular person was at that location after the victim's pants were pulled down, but before the plastic bag was placed over the victim's body.

Uncollected Item

"White Paper Towels"

According to the recently discovered FOLLOW-UP NOTES from the Clark County Coroner's Office by William Gazza, referencing observations at the scene on 07/09/01 on the first page:

> The decedent's penis had been cut off, but the testicles remained. There were what appeared to be white paper towels stuffed in the open wound in this area.

This examiner is unable to locate any reference to white paper towels (or any other paper towels) having been collected from the body at the scene, or submitted to the lab for latent or bloody print examination. This item, having been placed into the wound by the offender, could have contained valuable exculpatory evidence that is now apparently irrecoverable.

5. **A primary motive in this case is directed anger expressed in the form of brutal injury, overkill and sexual punishment to the victim's genitals**.

According to Turvey (2002, p. 307) motives are the "emotional, psychological, and material needs that impel and are satisfied by behavior."

There is no profit motivation evident in this case as, the victim is homeless, has no valuables, is indigent and obviously so to all.

There are no power motivations evident in this case, as these involve only the force necessary to commit the offense (a robbery, rape or homicide). They do not involve overkill.

Intense, directed anger is evidenced in this case by the combination of brutal force, lethal force, overkill, and the time spent with the victim inflicting superficial cuts and performing peri/post-mortem sexual mutilation.

Brutal and lethal force is evidenced in this case by repeated injuries that inflict tremendous damage until death results: the cumulative blunt force trauma, stab wounds, and incise wounds to the victim's face, neck and head. These include, but are not necessarily limited to:

- The contusion to the back of the scalp;
- The 4.5-inch superficial incised wound to the left neck.
- Multiple abrasions and contusions to the left side of the face and head;
- Multiple abrasions and contusions to the right side of the face and head;
- The 1.2-inch stab wound to the anterolateral right forehead;
- The superficial incised wound group to the left lateral neck;
- The pre-mortem stab wound evident to the remaining scrotum;
- The stab wound and associated 2.5-inch incise wound on the anterolateral left neck;
- The stab would to the left chin;
- The 0.6-inch stab wound to the anterior neck;
- The 1.2-inch incise wound above the right eye;
- The multiple superficial incise wounds in near the left eye and eyelids.
- The multiple lacerations of the lips, associated with the fractures and avulsions of the teeth;
- The .75-inch incise wound on the chin;
- The 2.8-inch incise wound to the left upper chest.

Overkill is evidenced by injury that goes beyond what is needed to kill the victim, including, but not limited to:

- the postmortem removal of the penis and associated partial removal of the scrotum;
- the incise wound to the rectum;
- the incise wound to the perineum;
- the four postmortem stab wounds to the upper abdomen.

It is a common misapprehension that this kind of sexual mutilation (cutting off the victim's penis; incising the victim's rectum) may suggest a female attacker.

In the context of a homicide, this form of sexual mutilation is almost exclusively associated with male victims killed by male offenders. In such cases, one or more male offenders kill a male victim and remove his penis in the peri/ post-mortem interval to:

- satisfy jealousy, spite or rage relating to real or perceived sexual rivalry;
- punish or torture the victim for a real or perceived wrong—retribution;
- collect a trophy;
- feminize a victim in an attempt to "normalize" a sexual assault.

Moreover, a nationwide *Westlaw* search of state and federal appellate cases revealed only 16 homicides where an adult victim's penis was actually cut off. In all but one case it was a male, or a group of two or more males, who committed the murder and the ultimate removal of the victim's penis.

- Most of the cases involved brutal attacks to the victim prior to death, even torture in some cases, and evidence of overkill.
- 7 of the cases involved multiple male offenders (2–8).
- More than 1/3 of the cases involved homosexual offenders.

Notably, the alleged circumstances in only one case involved a female acting alone to attack, subdue, and remove the penis of an adult male victim—*Nv v. Kirstin Blaize Lobato*.

6. **The wound patterns in this case may be used to support a theory of multiple assailants.**

The wound patterns and bloodstains in this case evidence that the victim was attacked in the location where he was found, that he fought back at first given the defensive injuries on his hands and forearms, but that he was ultimately overpowered and unable to physically resist.

The victim was subsequently beaten, cut, and stabbed repeatedly all over the face, head, neck, and abdomen from all directions and with multiple weapons (at least one blunt force object and one sharp force object).

It would be irresponsible not to suggest the theory that more than one person was involved in the attack on the victim given the following:

- Evidence of multiple weapons;
- multiple injuries at a wide variety of locations from multiple directions; and
- stab and incise wounds of varying lengths and depths.

It is important to note that the available physical evidence does not disprove this possibility. Nor does the case material suggest that this issue has been seriously explored or properly addressed by any of the forensic experts in this case.

Please do not hesitate to contact me with any questions.

Brent Turvey, MS—Forensic Science

REFERENCES

Creamer, J.I., Quickenden, T.I., Crichton, L.B., Robertson, P., Ruhayel, R.A., 2005. "Attempted Cleaning of Bloodstains and Its Effect on the Forensic Luminol Test," Luminescence June 20.

Gaennslen, R.E., 1983. Sourcebook in Forensic Serology, Immunology, and Biochemistry, National Institute of Justice Publication, USDOJ.

Kent, E.J., Elliot, D.A., Miskelly, G.M., 2003. "Inhibition of Bleach-Induced Luminol Chemiluminescence," Journal of Forensic Science January, 48 (1), 64–67.

Quickenden, T.I., Ennis, C.P., Creamer, J.I., "The Forensic Use of Luminol Chemiluminescence to Detect Traces of Blood Inside Motor Vehicles," Luminescence 2004 September-October; 19 (5), 271–277.

Turvey, B., 2002. Criminal Profiling: An Introduction to Behavioral Evidence Analysis, Elsevier Science, London.

SUMMARY

Depending on the expert asked to opine on a given case, reports of various types can range in length and quality. This can be the result of many factors, including a lack of education on how to write a report properly, the format to be used, what to include, and so on. No matter the reasoning, though, there is no excuse for deficient reporting at any time, let alone when the opinions given should be of court quality. To serve their purpose then, forensic criminologists must be competent at the task of intelligible writing, and their reports must be comprehensive with regard to examinations performed, findings, and conclusions. It is also critically important for criminologists to operationalize the terms which they are using to explain their findings, to use a standard format when writing their reports, as well as to include their name, signature, and the date.

When conducting their analyses for court, forensic examiners must determine whether evidence is sufficient and reliable. That is, is there enough evidence of sufficient quality to examine, and are the results of the examination going to be reliable enough to carry any conclusions? The courts, at a later point, will determine whether or not this is admissible. When forensic criminologists have given findings, written or otherwise, there must remain no question as to whether the findings are certain and no question as to how certainty was established. Forensic criminologists and other examiners should also make themselves open to and seek out opportunities for fact checking and peer review. These are crucial components of any robust examination.

Review Questions

1. Why is it important for forensic criminologists to write down their conclusions?
2. What does it mean to *operationalize* the terminology which is being used? Why is this important?
3. Describe some of the necessary sections in a forensic report.
4. Why might forensic examiners prefer not to include their name and signature on a given report tenured to the court?
5. What is involved in the chain of custody section of a forensic report? Why is this important information for the court?
6. What is the difference between *legal* and *scientific sufficiency* of evidence?
7. T/F Forensic examiners should include all findings from every examination performed in their report.
8. What is fact checking? Why is it important to fact check before submitting a report?

REFERENCES

Chisum, W.J., Turvey, B., 2007. Crime Reconstruction. Elsevier Science, Boston.

Edwards, H., Gotsonis, C., 2009. Strengthening Forensic Science in the United States: A Path Forward. National Academies Press, Washington DC. url: http://nationalacademies. org/morenews/20090218.html

Gross, H., 1906. Criminal Investigation. Ramaswamy, Madras.

Kirk, P., Thornton, J. (Eds.), 1970. Crime Investigation, second ed. Wiley, New York.

Thornton, J.I., 1994. Courts of Law v. Courts of Science: A Forensic Scientist's Reaction to Daubert. Shepard's Expert Scientific Evidence Quarterly 1 (3), 475–485.

Thornton, J.I., 1997. The General Assumptions and Rationale of Forensic Identification. In: Faigman, D., Kaye, D., Saks, M., Sanders, J. (Eds.), Modern Scientific Evidence: The Law and Science of Expert Testimony, vol. 2. West, St. Paul, MN.

Turvey, B.E., 2008. Criminal Profiling: An Introduction to Behavioral Evidence Analysis, third ed. Elsevier Science, San Diego.

CHAPTER 17

The Nature and Role of Expert Forensic Testimony

David Field

There will probably always be tension between trial advocates and expert witnesses of all disciplines. The reason is that each of them speaks a different language, and each of them is regarded as an "expert" in what he or she does. It is important for the "expert" criminologist to appreciate that professional trial advocates do not take kindly to other so-called experts trespassing on their turf and parading another expertise before the jury or trial judge. Call it professional arrogance, but in a courtroom, trial advocates tend to regard themselves as the *only* experts who should be seen and heard.

There is also the problem created by the fact that trial lawyers, on the whole, are not comfortable in other disciplines. They are in fact likely to know as much about some forensic specialities (e.g., DNA, forensic anatomy, psychopharmacology, and so forth) as they do about ancient history or spoken Mandarin. In those circumstances, they are in all probability defensive and tend toward reductive displays of behavior designed to simplify the evidence of the forensic expert to language that they, as lawyers, can understand. They also share this discomfort over expert subject matter with the members of the jury and will often play on that unfamiliarity in an attempt to make the expert witness seem like a pompous irrelevance—that is, unless, of course, the witness is one whom *they* have called.

Perhaps worse than ignorant advocates are the semi-educated. Some lawyers have taken the trouble to acquire *limited* knowledge in the subject area of the expert and may then seek to show it off before the jury. This is a particular hazard for criminologists, since many law students these days take a course in criminology as part of their degree studies or include criminology texts among their leisure-time reading lists. The result is the worst of all critics—the one with only a smattering of knowledge, which gets in the way of a true understanding of the depth of the subject and the many conflicting layers of professional opinion within it.

CONTENTS

523

These tensions, and those associated with them, arise and persist regardless of country, courtroom, or jurisdiction. Every adversarial system suffers from these constraints in one form or another. Consequently, though specifics in this chapter are drawn from the author's knowledge and experience with Australian law and courts, they are representative of issues encountered just about everywhere else.

Against this unpromising background, we may now examine the *formal* relationship between trial lawyer and expert witness.

WHO NEEDS EXPERTS?

The short answer to the (usually rhetorical) question "Who needs experts?" is "the court." As society becomes more complex and more technology driven, courts of law, which are called upon to make important decisions about the lives and financial interests of others, require increased guidance in areas where they have no knowledge or expertise of their own. The history of the courts' use of expert witnesses mirrors very closely the history of the availability of technical expertise to assist in that decision making.

In the sphere of criminal law, for example, since the dawn of the twentieth century we have known of the possibility of identifying perpetrators of crime by means of the individual "ridge characteristics" of their finger-ends. This technique became familiar to Australian criminal lawyers, crime fiction writers, and TV court drama buffs as "expert fingerprint evidence" after its official welcome into the Australian justice process as early as 1912. As the century progressed, we also learned how to identify people by means of their blood groups, and "forensic serology" dominated our criminal courts until the advent of the "generic fingerprint" of DNA in the 1990s.

Civil law went down a similar road. As reported by Smith and Bace (2002, pp. 116–117):

> Throughout the twentieth century there was one constant trend in the litigation of cases involving new technologies—that is, the increased use of technical and scientific expert witnesses. During that period, auto mechanics, accident reconstruction specialists, engineers of all kinds, and hundreds if not thousands of other speciality technical experts were required to testify in hundreds of thousands of cases... health care professionals have experienced an explosive growth in the number of lawsuits that allege both human and technical failures resulting in death or injury... Construction failures have also generated a large number of experts who frequently testify about the poor construction of bridges, highways, and buildings and also

about their failures or collapses… Since World War II, both the private and commercial airplane industries have needed to identify experts to testify in hundreds of cases that are litigated based on claims of technical or human failures, or both.

As human knowledge has been developed, along with resulting technologies, so has the ability and then ultimately the need to use that knowledge in the resolution of legal disputes. As long as technology and scientific theory are a part of the lives we lead, the crimes we commit or suffer, and liabilities we incur, the justice system will have need of experts to explain how they work and apply.

WHEN DO WE NEED EXPERTS?

An expert is required whenever courts are asked to reach a decision based on facts that are not within their general life experience to interpret. This begs a supplementary question: "Is this something which might reasonably be expected to lie within the everyday knowledge of the average jury member or judge, or is it something which requires years of training and experience to fully appreciate and interpret?"

As one would expect, such distinctions and determinations routinely call for "line-ball" decisions. Even when the case involves a jury, it will ultimately be the judge who makes that call. Very often, he or she will be doing so at the request of counsel for one side in a case, who has access to the testimony of an expert who may be expected to give evidence favorable to the party whom he or she represents. Equally, counsel against whose client such evidence will operate will be seeking to argue that the matter in hand is one which may be safely left to the court to determine, without the need to call for expert testimony. Such is the adversarial process: each side touts the value and merits of experts when expert opinions are favorable and marginalizes them when the opposite is true.

The problem is more acute when the issue in question is not obviously one of scientific specialty (such as DNA or forensic pathology), but rather comes close to the "everyday" life experience of those who will be making the final decision. As explained in the High Court's ruling in *Murphy v. Regina*[1] (1989, pp. 130–131):

> Admission of [expert] evidence carries with it the implication that the jury are not equipped to decide the relevant issue without the aid of expert opinion and thus, if it is wrongly admitted, it is likely to divert them from their proper task which is to decide the matter for themselves using their own common sense.

[1] In this case, it was held that expert evidence *would* have assisted a jury in deciding whether or not the vocabulary and sentence structures employed during the course of an alleged confession by a youth were appropriate for someone with a "literacy age" of 10, since child psychology is not a matter in which we are all proficient.

Fairly and squarely within the "everyday" category come matters of human emotion, and in *Regina v. Turner* (1975), the English High Court held that a jury was perfectly capable of assessing, from its own "life experience," the likely emotional effect on a young man of being told by his girlfriend that she had been unfaithful to him. Expert testimony from a psychologist was therefore not necessary to assist the jury.

Criminologists are likely to run into this problem on a fairly regular basis because their subject matter is one on which just about everyone has a point of view. Just about everyone who reads the news or watches television thinks he or she understands crime and criminals. This delusion persists to the point where professionals untrained in criminology, and even some laypersons, consider its practice a matter of common sense. For example, consider a proposal to call an expert criminologist to testify in the local Planning and Environment Court regarding the likely impact on a local residential community of having a brothel (legal in many parts of Australia and in some parts of the United States), or perhaps a strip club, operating from business premises in the center of a busy street. If this were to be near a primary school or church, the "other side" can be almost guaranteed to argue, "We don't need experts, Your Honor—everyone knows that the local residents are likely to have their 'quality of life' diminished by this proposal, and we shall be calling local residents to testify to this effect."

Likewise, the proposal to call, as an expert witness, some university professor who has just completed a three-year research program on the deterrent effects of close-circuit television (CCTV) cameras installed in shopping malls, is likely to be met with derisive comments such as "What a waste of public money *that* was; we all know that we behave differently when we're being watched."

The problem in such cases is the failure to be aware of the depth of research that has been conducted into areas of social activity in which nonexperts may *believe* they are well informed and experienced but in fact are not.

The situation comes down, in the end, to whether or not the subject matter at hand has been treated by those who earn their livings from it as a "specialist" area, and, if so, whether or not it is "safe" to allow nonspecialists to hear what the specialists have to say. This is for the very important reason that (Morling, 1987):[2]

[2]Morling, J. (1987) in the *Royal Commission of Inquiry into the Chamberlain Convictions* report. The Chamberlain case is now regarded as one in which a jury was seriously misled by so-called "expert forensic evidence" that was seriously flawed.

> Juries may attach great weight to the opinions of experts on matters outside the competence of the layman to understand. It is essential that everything possible be done to ensure that opinions expressed by experts, especially Crown experts, be soundly based and correct.

Ultimately, if the judge in a given case remains unconvinced that an expert's opinions are beyond his or her ability to comprehend without assistance, then the expert's testimony will likely be deemed unnecessary and inadmissible—regardless of its quality. If, however, the advocate proposing expert testimony makes a compelling argument to the court, then such testimony may be admitted for the jury to hear. In this fashion, forensic experts of every kind are very much at the mercy of their attorney clients.

THE SAFEGUARDS

Like most advances in the use (and the corresponding risk of abuse) of expert evidence, the first "threshold tests" controlling its admissibility were introduced in the United States, in the so-called Frye-Daubert rulings of their Supreme Court.[3] One of Australia's leading judges, J. A. Heydon (now Justice Heydon of the High Court), in *Makita (Australia) Pty Ltd v. Sprowles* (2001) rolled all these tests together when he ruled that (pp. 743–744):

> ...[I]f evidence tendered as expert opinion evidence is to be admissible, it must be agreed or demonstrated that there is a field of "specialised knowledge"; there must be an identified aspect of that field in which the witness demonstrates that by reason of specified training, study or experience, the witness has become an expert; the opinion proffered must be "wholly or substantially based on the witness's expert knowledge"; so far as the opinion is based on facts "observed" by the expert, they must be identified and admissibly proved by the expert, and so far as the opinion is based on "assumed" or "accepted" facts, they must be identified and proved in some other way; it must be established that the facts on which the opinion is based form a proper foundation for it; and the opinion of an expert requires demonstration or examination of the scientific or other intellectual basis of the conclusions reached: that is, the expert's evidence must explain how the field of "specialised knowledge" in which the witness is expert by reason of "training, study or experience," and on which the opinion is "wholly or substantially based," applies to the facts assumed or observed so as to produce the opinion propounded. If all these matters are not made explicit, it is not possible to be sure whether the opinion is based wholly or substantially on the expert's specialised knowledge. If the court cannot be sure of that, the evidence is strictly speaking not admissible, and, in so far as it is admissible, of diminished weight.

[3]*Frye v. United States*, 293 F 1013 at 1014 D.C.Cir, 1923 and *Daubert v. Merrill Dow Pharmaceuticals*, 509 U.S. 579 (1993).

Since these are the accepted tests for the admissibility of expert evidence, they are also the grounds upon which the proposal to adduce expert testimony will be attacked by opposing counsel during the *voir dire*.[4] Additionally, in the United States, these are guidelines that judges may follow and be held accountable for by appeals courts, but they are by no means uniformly adopted or enforced even when it is suggested otherwise. That is to say, judges in the United States

[4]This legal term, which is French for "speak the truth," refers to the challenges made against the suitability of jurors or the credibility of witnesses.

are perfectly within their authority to disregard these guidelines at will and do so routinely as it suits their purpose. We may now examine them one by one.

1. There must be a field of "specialized knowledge."

This issue has already been fully considered previously. The first line of attack of any counsel seeking to have proposed expert testimony excluded will be to allege that it does not originate in any area of knowledge which is not within the capability and experience of those (i.e., the jury, or the judge in the increasing number of cases in which judges decide matters without a jury) with the responsibility of making the ultimate decision on the facts. The examples cited earlier, involving brothels in residential areas and the deterrence value of CCTV equipment, serve to illustrate the sorts of challenges which criminologists may expect to face in practice, given the number of amateur criminologists who seem to exist within our midst.

2. The witness must demonstrate that he or she has become an expert in an "identified aspect of that field" by virtue of "specified training, study, or experience."

This guideline does not in practice give rise to much difficulty, given that contemporary professional practice is for the proposed expert to attach a copy of his or her curriculum vitae (CV, a.k.a. expert resume) to his or her report. But sometimes counsel for the opposing side prove themselves to be particularly adept at nit-picking their way through that CV and pointing out that, for example, while the proposed expert may have a Ph.D. in Molecular Biology, he or she has no laboratory experience in the isolation and comparison of DNA segments. In some areas of medical science, practical experience and postgraduate publications are regarded as more important than formal academic qualifications, and unless the proffered expert can point to recent research and/or publication in precisely the narrow field in which he or she is proposing to testify, that expert will be challenged regarding his or her expertise.

For example, in *Regina v. Parenzee* (2007), in which Parenzee sought to adduce expert testimony tending to challenge the widely accepted belief that unprotected sex can lead to the spread of the HIV virus, the trial judge rejected the evidence of the witness in question ("E") in the following terms:

> A person's practical experience must be relevant. If a person has work experience and has developed their knowledge from learning from others and being taught, that may be sufficient to qualify the person as an expert. In many disciplines, practical experience is essential... Simply reading about the subject may not be sufficient.... [E] has no practical experience. She has never worked with patients who are said to be infected with HIV, or with any virus. She has never treated

or diagnosed patients who have viruses. She has never worked in laboratories or conducted research. She has no practical experience. She has given evidence on the topics of virology, immunology, epidemiology, microbiology and microscopy. She has no practical experience and she has never worked in any of the areas.

In such ways, the judge may step in and limit expert testimony or exclude it entirely.

3. The opinion which is given must be "wholly or substantially based on the witness's expert knowledge."

The major risk in this context is of the witness being coaxed out of the area in which he or she is truly expert, into a field in which his or her knowledge, although far superior to that of the layman, does not really qualify as being based on practical and current expertise.

A good illustration of this process in action arose in the late 1990s with regard to the evidence given by a clinical and forensic psychologist in a New South Wales case that became the subject of a High Court appeal. The case in question was *HG v. Regina* (1999). HG had been convicted of two counts of sexual abuse of his de facto wife's 8-year-old daughter. This occurred following the refusal of the trial judge to admit evidence from a psychologist, Dr. M., to whom the girl had been referred for assessment by her general practitioner (GP) after the offenses had come to light. Dr. M. had experience in counseling emotionally disturbed children and in counseling child victims of sexual abuse, and the GP referring the child to him had done so because of alleged "internal inconsistencies" in the child's allegations.

Dr. M. therefore began his assessment of the child with some cynicism, which only increased when he learned that the child had experienced a disturbed earlier childhood at the hands of a violent, drug-abusing father who had received treatment in a psychiatric hospital before his death. The father had also had custody of the child for a period of a month, following which the child, on her return to her mother, experienced emotional difficulties both at home and at school, including frequent nightmares in which she would call out "Stop it, Daddy." These behaviors ceased before her mother entered into her relationship with the accused, and by contrast there were no substantial changes in her behavior after the alleged sexual assaults on her by the accused.

Not surprisingly, Dr M. reached certain conclusions that were favorable to the defense, namely that the child *had* been the victim of sexual abuse, but not by the accused when she was 8 and 9 years old. Rather, her own natural father had victimized her when she was less than 5 years of age. It was this portion of

Dr. M.'s report, which, it will be recalled, had been compiled for the victim's GP and which the defense subsequently sought to rely upon.

In upholding the trial judge's decision to exclude this evidence, the High Court had this to say (*HG v. Regina*, 1999, pp. 41–44):

> If all that [M] had said was that, based on his study, training and experience, he considered that the behaviour of the complainant during 1992 and 1993, as recounted to him by others, appeared to be inconsistent with her having been sexually abused during that time… then that might have been one thing. It would have required identification of the facts he was assuming to be true, so that they could be measured against the evidence; and it would have required or invited demonstration of examination of the scientific basis of the conclusion. However, that was not what the defence wanted from him… What defence counsel wanted was evidence of his opinion that, although the complainant had been abused, the abuse had occurred back in 1987 when, for a period of a month, she was in the custody of her father, and that it was her father who was the abuser. That opinion was not shown to have been based, either wholly or substantially, on [M's] specialised knowledge as a psychologist. On the contrary, a reading of his report… reveals that it was based on a combination of speculation, inference, personal and second-hand views as to the credibility of the complainant, and a process of reasoning which went well beyond the field of expertise of a psychologist…

> Logically, there were a number of competing possibilities. The complainant may have been sexually abused by nobody; she may have been abused, as she claimed, by the appellant; she may have been abused by her father; she may have been abused by both her father and the appellant; she may have been abused by some person or persons unknown. It was not demonstrated, and it is unlikely, that it is within the field of expertise of a psychologist to form and express an opinion as to which of those alternatives was to be preferred.

> … Experts who venture an opinion (sometimes merely their own inference of fact), outside their field of specialised knowledge may invest those opinions with a spurious appearance of authority, and legitimate processes of fact-finding may be subverted. The opinions which [M] was to be invited to express appear to provide a good example of the mischief which is to be avoided.

The appeal was dismissed. Part of the court's concern, expressed in the portion of the judgment cited here, is that an expert was asked to decide questions of fact which more properly may be thought of as being the function of the jury.

Moreover, the expert was being led not just up to that line but well over it by counsel. The expert was being asked to be more specific and more certain than the court was comfortable with, especially given the expert's lack of expertise.

Let us revert back to the example of the criminologist called as an expert witness on the deterrent effect of CCTV cameras in public places on the basis of recently completed research the criminologist had conducted into the subject. A similar outcome (i.e., a rejection of the evidence) might be expected were he or she to be asked to comment on the potential deterrent effect of the alternative strategy of increasing the visible police presence on the same streets. Unless the criminologist has a sufficient amount of the relevant expertise, the court will likely be unwilling to let him or her go further.

4. That opinion must, if based on facts, either be based on facts "observed" by the expert which are "identified and admissibly proved by that expert," or be based on "assumed" or "accepted" facts identified and proved in some other way.

The opinions of an expert witness are no better than the facts upon which they are based. As a consequence, the easiest course open to counsel seeking to destroy that evidence is to undermine those facts. For example, "time of death" in a murder trial may be heavily dependent upon the ambient air temperature in the vicinity in which the body lay before it was discovered. Therefore, evidence to the effect that the temperature in question was a degree or two over or under that assumed by any forensic scientist when compiling his or her report and reaching a conclusion can convert that report into so much waste paper. It can also have the same effect on any expert reports that rely on such a forensic scientist's findings.

Similarly, consider the criminologist who has conducted a series of street surveys investigating the number and description of persons passing by the front entrance of a building that is proposed to convert into a brothel. If it can be proved that those surveys were conducted solely during school holidays when there are more young people in evidence, then the conclusions reached in the subsequent report may be seriously undermined. This is in no small way a warning to criminologists that research must be not just relevant but representative.

One of the most dramatic examples on record of expert evidence being trashed by a fundamental undermining of assumed facts, in Australia, was that which occurred in *Regina v. Ryan* (2002), in which the Victorian Court of Appeal quashed a rape conviction based entirely on DNA samples allegedly taken from the accused. When matched with DNA material allegedly taken from the crime scene, the DNA from the accused put him in the same "one in 1.5 billion" population group as the perpetrator. Although this explanation sounds very convincing, the problem was that the expert who gave the DNA matching evidence was not responsible for collecting either sample, but based his opinion entirely on computer-generated printouts. As explained in Corn (2006, p. 350):

> In *R v Ryan* [2002] VSCA 176, the accused was charged with rape. The case was purely circumstantial. The key prosecution evidence was an alleged DNA match between the accused and a sample found at the scene. Expert evidence regarding the DNA results was given by the relevant forensic scientist, based on statistical data provided to him by other staff at the Forensic Science Centre. In effect, the expert's opinion was based wholly on hearsay evidence and as there were no applicable exceptions to the hearsay rule, the entirety of the expert's opinion should not have been admitted. In the absence of that evidence, a verdict of guilty could not be sustained. On appeal against conviction, the majority of the Victorian Court of Appeal stated (at [15]):
>
> > Where it is evident to an appeal court after the completion of a criminal trial that on the evidence adduced before the trial court, the prosecution was doomed to failure, only in rare situations would a retrial be ordered. The simple failure of the prosecution to adduce crucial evidence which may have been available to it would not satisfy this requirement.
>
> The court ordered that a verdict of acquittal be entered. The court also took into account the fact that the accused had already served a significant part of the sentence, the fact that key items of forensic evidence had been destroyed and that two years had elapsed between the trial and the appeal.

In the absence of any other evidence relating to the collecting of the samples (which had since been destroyed), and their connection with the accused, the conviction had to be overturned. This is among the gravest outcomes related to the conduct of any forensic expert. However, in this particular case, it was entirely preventable.

5. It must be shown that the facts upon which the opinion is based form a "proper foundation for it."

Another popular line of attack from opposing trial lawyers is to challenge the logical connection between the facts upon which the expert report has been based, and the conclusions that have been drawn from it. Consider our example regarding the deterrent effect of CCTV cameras. If the expert criminologist has based his or her conclusion that such cameras are "effective in reducing crime" on a reduction in the number of reported crimes during the survey period after the installation of the cameras, the criminologist's entire thesis could be simply destroyed by pointing to some alternative explanation for the reduced reporting rate (such as the increased presence of uniformed police in the same area during the same period).

A common hazard currently faced by DNA experts giving evidence in court is not the primary conclusion regarding the "match" between the DNA profile of the accused and that found at the crime scene (which it is usually beyond the scientific skill of the lawyer to challenge), but rather the statistical conclusions regarding the strength of that match using population databases. Consider the case of *California v. Michael Pizarro* (2003). Mr. Pizarro was initially convicted of rape largely on the basis of a DNA match determined and explained in court by the FBI Crime Laboratory. As detailed in Jarvis (2003):

> A 1990 murder case, the first one in Madera County to use DNA evidence to help gain a conviction, was overturned by the Fifth District Court of Appeal in July and will be retried in Madera County Superior Court.
>
> "The conviction was overturned because of the DNA calculations the FBI used," District Attorney Ernie LiCalsi said.
>
> LiCalsi prosecuted the case that occurred June 10, 1989 in the mountain community of North Fork. According to reports, Michael Pizarro, then 20 years old, brought his wife and their 5-month-old son to North Fork to visit his mother, Chris Conston. The couple lived in Clovis.
>
> The victim was 13-year-old Amber Barfield, Pizarro's half sister, LiCalsi said.
>
> "This was the first case when DNA (evidence) was used in Madera County," LiCalsi said. "In fact, it was one of the first (cases) in the state (to use DNA evidence)."
>
> Pizarro attended a party that night, got into an argument with his wife, Sandy Pizarro, and left on foot. He admitted during the trial that he was heavily intoxicated. He walked in front of the truck Sandy Pizarro was driving, and at one point even laid in the roadway.
>
> Unable to get Pizarro into the truck, Sandy Pizarro drove to Conston's home, picked up Amber Barfield and returned at about 2:30 a.m. to try and locate Pizarro.
>
> Sandy Pizarro lost track of Amber, who climbed out of the truck to try and find Pizarro.

Sandy Pizarro reportedly testified that she heard a scream, a muffled sound, and then silence. She returned to Conston's house, and Conston contacted the sheriff's department.

Deputies joined Sandy Pizarro and Conston in the search, and shortly after 4 a.m. the search was temporarily called off.

It wasn't until 5:50 a.m. that Michael Pizarro returned to Conston's house. According to the appellate courts opinion, Pizarro was "dirty, sleepy and appeared ... to be drunk."

About 7 a.m. deputies continued the search. But it wasn't until they questioned Pizarro at about 8 a.m. that they learned they were looking in the wrong area.

Pizarro told deputies to look about one-tenth of a mile farther west. It was there they found Amber's body. She had been raped, beaten and suffocated.

Samples of bodily fluid found on the body and Pizarro's blood were sent to the FBI laboratory in Washington, DC for testing.

"At that time, the FBI was the only one doing these tests," LiCalsi said.

According to FBI Special Agent Dr. Dwight Adams,[5] who performed the DNA analysis, the fluid found on the victim's body matched the blood sample taken from Pizarro.

[5]In 2002, Dr. Dwight Adams was appointed Director of the FBI Crime Laboratory, subsequent to being the Chief of the DNA Unit.

The appellate court ruled that, "despite the prosecution's 'strong circumstantial case' against (Pizarro), the DNA identification evidence clearly 'sealed (his) fate'."

The court ruled that the scientific issues surrounding the DNA findings were "straightforward evidentiary issues disguised by technicality" and when those issues were exposed, it became clear that they were "plagued by a persistent and insidious tendency to assume the defendant's guilt."

The test conducted by the FBI used an ethnic data base, which excluded any suspects who were not Hispanic, according to the appellate court opinion. The court also said that the evidence did not show that the "perpetrator in this ... case was Hispanic based solely upon the ... (DNA) pattern found in the evidence ... left at the crime scene by the perpetrator."

Pizarro is half Hispanic.

A Hispanic database had been used by the FBI in preparing their calculations solely because Pizarro was Hispanic. The fallacy here, of course, is in the basic assumption that the *perpetrator* must also be Hispanic. There was in fact no direct evidence to support such an assumption other than the fact that Pizarro himself was the prime suspect.

The relevant testimony of Dr. Dwight Adams, Director of the FBI Crime Lab from 2002–2006, is provided and discussed in *California v. Michael Pizarro* (2003, pp. 623–626):

> At trial, there was evidence that the victim was last seen as she approached the area where defendant, who was half Hispanic, had been not long before. This was the extent of the evidence offered to establish that the perpetrator was Hispanic (or half Hispanic).
>
> Adams, who conducted the scientific work in Pizarro's case in 1989, was the sole scientific witness at trial. He testified that "[t]he likelihood of finding another unrelated Hispanic individual" with a profile similar to the perpetrator's and defendant's profiles was approximately 1 in 250,000. His 1990 testimony follows:
>
> [PROSECUTOR:] What is your opinion as to the chances of another Hispanic male having the same DNA profile as Mr. Pizarro?
>
> [ADAMS:] The likelihood of finding another unrelated Hispanic individual with a similar profile as Mr. Pizarro is one in approximately 250,000.
>
> [PROSECUTOR:] And this would also be the same statistic for the probability of a match of a DNA profile between the [perpetrator's DNA] obtained from the vaginal swab?
>
> [ADAMS:] That is correct.
>
> [PROSECUTOR:] Same statistic?
>
> [ADAMS:] Yes.
>
> [PROSECUTOR:] And, again, this is only with Hispanic men?
>
> [ADAMS:] Hispanics, not broken down into gender. [¶] ... [¶]
>
> [PROSECUTOR:] Dr. Adams, we have been talking about the chance for a match within the Hispanic community. Would the statistics for a match within the Caucasian community be different?
>
> [ADAMS:] Yes, generally there are going to be some differences in the population data from the different populations. So that's why we keep them separate. That's why we have a Caucasian and a Black and a Hispanic, American Indian population because there are differences. [¶] So if I were to compare one person in each of those different populations

I would come up—I'm sure I would come up with somewhat different results because in one population that pattern may be very rare, and another population that same pattern may be very common.

[PROSECUTOR:] Have you done any of the calculations necessary to determine what the chances are of having matches of this particular DNA profile within the Caucasian community?

[ADAMS:] Yes.

[PROSECUTOR:] And what are those statistics?

[ADAMS:] The statistics in those cases—in that case comparing the same profile to the Caucasians is much greater. It would be one in 10,000,000.

[PROSECUTOR:] But within the Hispanic group alone it is according to your testimony one in 250,000?

[ADAMS:] Yes, ma'am.

[PROSECUTOR:] What about a situation where someone is half Hispanic and half Caucasian?

[ADAMS:] Well, there is nothing we can do other than to compare them to the two populations and we would use only the smaller of the two in our report. [Adams referred to the number with the smaller denominator.]

[PROSECUTOR:] Why do you use only the smaller of the two?

[ADAMS:] We attempt to be as conservative as possible. The smaller number is less detrimental to the defendant.

...

Dr. Adams did not testify and, as we understand the evidence, could not testify that the perpetrator in the instant case was Hispanic based solely upon the allele pattern found in the evidence which was left at the crime scene by the perpetrator.

...

If the only way you can conclude the perpetrator fits a racial/ethnic category is to assume the perpetrator was the same race/ethnic background as the suspect then the reasoning is circular, i.e.: proof of the racial/ethnic background of the perpetrator depends on the racial/ethnic background of the suspect from which we infer a statistical probability that the perpetrator is the suspect.

The Californian Court of Appeals ruled in part that (*California v. Michael Pizarro*, 2003, p. 632):

> in the absence of sufficient evidence of the perpetrator's ethnicity, *any* particular ethnic frequency is irrelevant. The problem is again one of preliminary fact—now occurring multiply and simultaneously. It does not matter how many Hispanics, Caucasians, Blacks, or Native Americans resemble the perpetrator if the perpetrator is actually Asian. If various ethnic frequencies are presented to the jury, each will have been admitted without adequate foundation.

Ultimately, the Court of Appeals hammered the bias demonstrated by the FBI Crime Lab, put forth by the prosecution, which suffered from what they referred to as "logical infractions" (p. 634):

> The scientific issues in this case are straightforward evidentiary issues disguised by technicality. When the evidentiary issues are exposed, it also becomes clear that those issues are plagued by a persistent and insidious tendency to assume the defendant's guilt. The logical and evidentiary infractions in such an exercise are stunning in scope and consequence.

They found such practices and testimony well beyond harmless error and subsequently reversed Mr. Pizarro's conviction.

The lesson for criminologists here is that research and findings presented in support of a theory must actually be relevant to supporting it. Merely assuming the validity of an untested theory as part of one's analysis, regardless of how great the resulting statistics appear, is scientifically bankrupt. While at the trial level, prosecutors and judges may be eager to accept such evidence and any accompanying circular reasoning when it is helpful to a prosecution, the Court of Appeals patiently waits to reveal such infractions.

6. The expert's evidence must explain how the field of "specialized knowledge" in which the witness is "expert," and on which the opinion is "wholly or substantially based," applies to the facts assumed or observed so as to produce the opinion given.

This is basically a combination of the factors already considered. The "constructive alignment" between the facts observed by or reported to the expert and his or her eventual conclusion can, as we have seen, be attacked at any point during that process. It is therefore essential that the expert, in his or her report, "joins up the dots" at every stage, and leaves nothing unsaid.

To consider a simple example, the pathologist who simply reports "I noted the presence of water in the lungs of the deceased, from which I conclude that cause of death was drowning" is leaving out that vital link in the chain from observation to conclusion which explains that "The standard literature on forensic pathology with which I am familiar reveals that the presence of water in the lungs is a strong indicator that the deceased aspirated that water prior to death. In layman's terms, it means that he or she died from drowning."

CHEAP SHOTS FROM THE BAR TABLE

Even assuming that the expert witness has carefully established comportment with all the preceding considerations, his or her ordeal is probably far from over. The desperate counsel against whose client that expert evidence is aimed may then be forced back into performing "lawyer's tricks." These are designed to discredit the witness for no good reason other than to suggest to a jury, which knows no more about the subject matter (and possibly even less) than the trial counsel, that the expert should not be believed. The members of the jury who are silently baffled by what the expert has been saying and who are hoping that it will all go away may well grab gratefully at any straw thereby offered to them to *make* it go away.

The following are just a few of the standard "cheap shots" from counsel's locker.

1. "You are being paid to be here today, aren't you?"

Some expert witnesses of my acquaintance are so familiar, and comfortable, with this lawyer's trick that their standard response is to smile sweetly at the idiot asking the question and reply, "Yes, and so are you." Only the less experienced expert will become defensive when asked this question and may display a demeanor which the jury regard as one of guilt. The appropriate response is something along the lines of "Of course. Like all experts in my field, I have to earn a living, but the ultimate conclusions in my report are based on proven fact and scientific certainty. Because they support the case for *X*, I was asked to come here today and deliver my report. If they supported your client, no doubt you would have asked me the same."

2. "Please answer my next question with a simple 'yes' or 'no.'"

Chances are, the question which follows is highly misleading, in the sense that the expert cannot answer in the simple affirmative or negative without qualifying his or her answer. Thus, the question "A brothel has been operating in the premises directly across the street from my client's proposed establishment for the past two years, has it not?," if simply confirmed by the witness, does not give him or her the opportunity to explain that (a) it has been a constant source of complaint, or (b) it operates only between 9 p.m. and 6 a.m.

Expert witnesses should never allow themselves to be tied down in this manner, if the court will be left with the wrong impression. Nor can they necessarily rely on their own counsel, in "re-examination," to dig them out of the hole they have created for themselves.

One of the most devastating uses of this technique has passed into the enduring legend of one of England's finest criminal advocates, Lord (then plain Norman) Birkett. His client was accused of murdering a man and then leaving his corpse in a blazing car to make it appear that the man had died in a car accident. A chief Crown witness was an expert metallurgist whose evidence against the accused threatened to be most telling, until Birkett stood up in cross-examination and asked, "What is the co-efficient of expansion of brass?" Instead of replying that this information was not something he carried in his head, but that he could easily look up the point, should it be important, the witness simply replied, "I don't know," and Birkett sat down again with a triumphant smirk on his face.

3. "It's a simple enough question, witness—why can't you answer it?"

This trick is more of the same. The chances are that the question was *far* from simple, and it may even have been compounded, in the sense that it asked more than one question. Questions like that deserve the acid response which they sometimes get from the expert, along the lines of "It may be simple to you, but to someone who knows anything about the subject, it is anything but simple." The witness should then go on to explain *why* and leave counsel wishing that he or she had never opened his or her mouth in the first place.

APPEARANCES ARE EVERYTHING

Reference has already been made to the fact that most juries are ill equipped to understand the scientific significance of what expert witnesses are testifying to. This is normally less of a problem for criminologists, but even in their case it is as well to bear in mind that juries often assess the truthfulness of witnesses by their *demeanor*. This means that if the expert looks and sounds confident and relaxed, then regardless of what he or she actually says, that expert is more likely to be thought credible by the jury. By the same token, no amount of brilliance in what the expert actually says will convince the jury to believe him or her if he or she appears nervous, uncertain, defensive, arrogant, or overaggressive in response to taunts from counsel. And some counsel *will* sink so low as to attempt to goad the expert into losing his or her "cool," bursting into tears or showing other signs of stress, which the jury may well then interpret against the credibility of the evidence the expert is there to give.

Part of the same "sales technique" for the expert's evidence also requires that, when answering a question, he or she make eye contact, not with the questioner, but with the person for whom the answers are intended, namely the judge and/or the jury.

COPING WITH THE OPPOSING EXPERT

If the matter on which expert evidence has been called for one side is sufficiently significant in a case, it may almost be guaranteed that the other side will arm itself with its own expert. This then leads to a phenomenon known to trial lawyers as that of "dueling experts," and whether those who will ultimately decide on the facts consist of a jury or a judge sitting alone, their task is the same: somehow they have to *choose* between their conflicting expert opinions, even though the very reason expert evidence was called for in the first place is that the subject matter is deemed to be beyond the everyday experience of that "tribunal of fact."

The ultimate horror story in this context may well have been the English trial, in the 1980s, of the so-called Yorkshire Ripper, Peter Sutcliffe. Sutcliffe was accused of the multiple murders of several women whom he believed to have been prostitutes, and whom he believed he had been commanded by God to kill. Not surprisingly, the question of his sanity at the time was raised at the trial, and the jury were required to listen to the expert testimony of no fewer than 38 forensic psychiatrists before they decided that he was sane. Nineteen of them had testified as to his insanity, and 19 as to his sanity, and if nothing else, that reveals something about the nature of forensic psychiatry.

More recently, in Australia, a jury was asked to rule in a case in which a man was ultimately found guilty of the murder of his wife, from whom he had been separated at the time. The essential question for the jury had been whether or not, at the time he stabbed her to death, he had been suffering from what, in that state, is known as "a mental impairment," but which at common law is more commonly referred to as "insanity." A psychiatrist called for the Crown gave his opinion that G [the defendant] was not suffering from such an impairment at the time, while a psychiatrist for the defense gave his professional opinion that he was.

In response to a series of questions from the jury as to how they should approach this conflict, the trial judge gave this direction, which was subsequently upheld on appeal *Regina v. Gemmill* (2004):

This is a trial by jury, not by experts. In the end, you have to form your own conclusions as to the facts on the evidence as a whole, and in particular, it is a question of fact whether you are satisfied that the accused man suffered from mental impairment at the time he killed his wife… [use] your common sense and experience of life to assess [the evidence as a whole]. So you use your experience in helping you decide what you accept were the relevant facts and what you think was important about those facts, and ultimately you have to come to a conclusion as a matter of fact… you are entitled to do that as a jury, and the advantage you have in doing it as a jury is that you have the experience and the combined common sense, if you like, of 12 of you to apply to the problem… you can use your life experience, but you can't substitute it for the evidence. You must decide the case on the evidence you've heard in this court.

In such cases, not only does the expert witness have to cope with the antics of counsel for the party against whom he is testifying, but also the opposing opinion of the expert for the other side, who may be an academic or professional colleague. This is no time for settling old scores or academic enmities, and each expert must remain calm, dignified, and confident in manner even when his or her carefully researched report is being trashed and ridiculed by a fellow expert. Each will also get his or her opportunity to explain why he or she disagrees with the opinion expressed by the rival expert, and then of course the roles are reversed; but even then, good grace and dignity must be preserved.

The employment of dueling experts has the tendency to slow down the trial process and add to the expense of the proceedings, to the point at which most states and territories in Australia now have what are called "Practice Directions," which are designed to regulate, and to an extent control, the proliferation of expert testimony in appropriate cases. Also, more and more jurisdictions are now experimenting with a process known as "hot tubbing," under which conflicting experts are brought together in a process not dissimilar to a mediation process, and asked to identify what they can agree on and where their points of difference are and why.

"CONFERENCES" WITH COUNSEL

The quaint expression "conferences" refers to the firmly established professional practice of counsel meeting in advance with each of the witnesses whom he or she intends to call in his or her client's case and going carefully through the evidence they are to give. This process serves a number of functions, one of which is to develop a rapport between counsel and witnesses, but in the case

[6] That is, when *he* or *she* is the "friendly" one taking the witness through his or her professional report.

[7] This is the part in the trial when the "unfriendly" one for the other side seeks to challenge the evidence that the expert has given.

of the professional expert witness, it can also be valuable in ensuring that all the bases have been covered. Reverting back to the "pitfalls" referred to earlier, a good trial counsel will ensure that his or her expert witness can deal confidently and fluently with the following issues that may arise, which counsel calling that witness will hope to cover "in chief,"[6] but which may arise only during cross-examination.[7]

Qualifications

Determining an expert's qualifications, as explained previously, is more than just a matter of the expert's formal degree and postgraduate academic medals. It covers what the expert has done since, and in particular why the research and other activities in which he or she has recently engaged qualifies him or her to speak as an expert on the subject. This information should either be in the expert's formal curriculum vitae, attached to his or her report, or brought out in a series of questions asked by counsel calling him or her, which need to be "rehearsed."

There is nothing dishonest or unethical about counsel priming a witness in advance with something along the lines of "When I ask you if you have any experience in the workings of the security industry, I want you to respond by listing all the research projects you have conducted for 'Acme Homeguard,' and in particular the one relating to closed-circuit TV installations."

Materials to Be Tendered to the Court

At the final court hearing, the expert's evidence will usually take the form of a report that he or she has prepared for the party calling him or her, in which the expert will explain what he or she has done, why, using what scientific or other processes, and what conclusions he or she has drawn, using his or her training and experience. It is essential that counsel calling the expert is very precise in the instructions given to the expert (usually by the instructing solicitor who has briefed counsel in the first place) so that his or her report exactly fits the requirements of the client.

It is also essential that, ahead of the court hearing, the expert *also* briefs counsel on where, in his or her report, are the essential factors which have to be brought out in evidence. Counsel may then constructively align questions to those factors. The following example might apply:

> "Dr X, if I may take you to page 4 of your report. You carried out a public survey—why did you do that?" *[The witness answers.]*
> "If I may take you now to page 8 of your report, what were the results of that survey?" *[The witness answers.]*
> "If we go now to page 10 of your report, there are references there to various experiments conducted in Canada and the United States in the

late 1990s. How are these relevant to the survey results?" *[The witness answers.]*

"Finally, Dr. X, on page 23 of your report—which is the final page— you have arrived at certain conclusions, based both on your survey results and on the previous experiments conducted in the 1990s which you have already told the court about. Could you explain to the court how your conclusions are based on both your survey results and the results of the previous experiments?" *[The witness answers.]*

Preparing for the Voir Dire

As already explained, preparing for the voir dire is the first challenge the proposed expert will face, during which counsel for the other side will attempt to prevent the expert's evidence going before the court. Counsel calling that expert will need to prepare him or her very well for this ordeal, and one of the best ways in which to achieve this in practice is for counsel calling the witness to role-play counsel for the other side during a pretrial conference. The expert thereby gets his or her first taste of (a) having his or her expertise challenged; (b) dealing with the suggestion that what he or she has spent months preparing is something within the everyday knowledge of the average juror, and (c) being goaded into being "The Expert Witness from Hell."

THE EXPERT WITNESS FROM HELL

The assessment of the expert as being "The Expert Witness from Hell" comes from his or her *own* client and counsel, as they break every rule in the book. To qualify for this epithet, the expert must perform *all* the following activities, although not necessarily in the suggested order:

1. Admit that he or she has deliberately discounted views which do not confirm with his or her own.
2. Admit that he or she has skewed the conclusions in his or her report to meet the known expectations of the party commissioning his or her services.
3. Admit that there are recent publications, survey outcomes, learned journal articles, and conflicting opinions of which he or she is not aware.
4. Admit that the area in which he or she is testifying is not one with which he or she is fully familiar.
5. Allow counsel for the other side to draw ludicrous and totally unjustified conclusions from his or her report, which make the expert who wrote it look like an amateur.

6. Become increasingly petulant and defensive, abuse the reputation of the expert on the other side (e.g., "Everyone knows that he was sacked from his Deanship at X University because he was having an affair with one of his junior colleagues, whom he promoted to full professor"), lose his or her temper, and storm out of court in tears.

THE BOTTOM LINE

In summary, we are required to go back to the primary point made at the start of this chapter. This is that lawyers do not like other experts on their turf and do not understand the specialist material which experts normally deliver in report form. They will therefore argue against the need to call experts in the first place, challenge the expertise of individual witnesses, call their own experts with contrary views, and attempt to discredit the experts in the witness box by any means which does not involve actually engaging those experts in their own specialist area.

Any criminologist entering this fraught arena would be well advised to engage in as many conferences as possible with the counsel who is calling him or her as a witness. After all, the expert is venturing into a world in which he or she is *not* expert.

SUMMARY

Aside from becoming familiar with the practice and procedures of the court, forensic criminologists need to be aware of what they are up against when venturing into this arena. First and foremost, criminologists must be aware of the fact that, when coming in as experts, they are not the only experts in the room, and that those whose toes they may be stepping upon will not always be impressed by their presence.

Forensic criminologists should be aware of when they will be needed in court, who they will be called by, and what they are meant to be doing. It is also helpful for them to be familiar with the stringent guidelines they themselves, as well as their evidence, must meet for it to be allowed in court. First, the area in which they purport to be expert must be a field of specialized knowledge, and they must show that they are expert in some aspect of that field. Second, the opinion that they give must be based on their expertise in that field and must be based on proven facts which form a proper foundation for that opinion. Third, they must demonstrate how their opinion applies to the facts of the case.

If they meet all these requirements and actually make it into court, forensic criminologists must be ready for cheap shots from the bar table, they must be keenly aware that appearances are everything to a judge and jury, and they may have to go up against a colleague in the field working as an opposing expert. To be prepared for this, experts should confer with their clients as much as possible to prepare to defend their qualifications, the materials they will be tenuring to the court, as well as for the voir dire. Namely, experts have to know what is expected of them, what they can and cannot say based on their expertise, and how to maintain their professionalism on the stand.

Review Questions

1. Why are experts used in criminal or civil cases?
2. When can an expert be called?
3. Discuss the importance of experts demonstrating that they have become expert in their field of specialized knowledge.
4. Why is it important that expert evidence be based on proven facts?
5. Name three cheap shots experts may expect from the bar table and how they should respond.
6. T/F Juries assess the truthfulness of witnesses by their demeanor.
7. T/F Conferences with counsel should not rehearse what to say about an expert's qualifications.
8. T/F An expert witness can be petulant and defensive or storm out of court if necessary.

REFERENCES

California v. Michael Pizarro, 2003. No. F030754, 110 Cal.App.4th 530, 3 Cal.Rptr.3d 21.

Corn, C., 2006. The Discretion of a Court of Appeal to Order a New Trial or a Verdict of Acquittal. Criminal Law Journal 30, 343–356.

HG v. Regina, 1999. HCA 2.

Jarvis, G., 2003. Accused Murderer to Get New Trial. The Madera Tribune Thursday, October 30.

Makita (Australia) Pty Ltd v. Sprowles, 2001. 52 NSWLR 705.

Morling, J., 1987. Report of the Commissioner. Royal Commission of Inquiry into the Chamberlain Convictions, Government Printer of the Northern Territory, Northern Territory, Australia.

Murphy v. Regina, 1989. 167 CLR 94.

Regina v. Gemmill, 2004. VSCA 72.

Regina v. Parenzee, 2007. SASC 143.

Regina v. Ryan, 2002. VSCA 176.

Regina v. Terence Turner, 1975. 61 Cr App R 67; QB 834.

Smith, F., Bace, R., 2002. A Guide to Forensic Testimony: The Art and Practice of Presenting Testimony as an Expert Technical Witness. Addison-Wesley, Boston.

CHAPTER 18

Ethics for the Forensic Criminologist

Wayne A. Petherick and Claire E. Ferguson

CONTENTS

INTRODUCTION

Most fields of professional endeavor involve a code of ethics that dictates acceptable and unacceptable conduct of members of the profession. Medicine, psychology and psychiatry, and law, to name but a few, enjoy full and well-defined codes of ethics that restrain members within those professions. What's more, these disciplines are well regulated, and to be a practitioner, one must meet certain educational and experiential criteria. By extension, any individual who wishes to ply his or her trade must not only meet these criteria, but must also subscribe to the relevant organization's code of ethics.

Criminology, however, despite belonging to the broad class of disciplines within the social and behavioral sciences, isn't regulated at all. Despite a number of organizations around the world dedicated to the professionalization of criminology, none strictly regulates its members by mandating particular levels of education or experience. As a result, one can practice as a criminologist without having to be a member of any organization or having met any specific criteria. This also means that one needn't subscribe to a code of ethics of any organization, such as the Australian and New Zealand Society of Criminology, The British Society of Criminology, or the American Society of Criminology. While the British Society of Criminology's code specifically cites membership as implicit acceptance of the code,[1] an individual can still practice as a criminologist without having to belong to one of these groups, and by extension may not subscribe to a code of ethics.

[1]"Membership…is taken to imply acceptance of these general principles and the need to be aware of ethical issues and issues regarding professional conduct that may arise in people's work" (British Society of Criminology, 2006).

547

It is the purpose of this chapter to discuss a range of issues related to ethics in criminology and criminal justice, and to propose a code of ethics for forensic criminologists to employ in their work.

WHAT ARE ETHICS?

Before considering a range of issues relating to ethics in criminology, we need to define the nature and role of ethics so as to provide direction to the forthcoming discussions. Siegel (2008, pp. 18–19) provides the following on the importance of ethics, both for students and in general, and this sets the stage for the remainder of the chapter:

> A critical issue facing criminology students involves recognizing the field's political and social consequences. All too often criminologists forget the social responsibility they bear as experts in the area of crime and justice. When government agencies request their views of issues, their pronouncements and opinions may become the basis for sweeping social policy.
>
> The lives of millions of people can be influenced by criminological research data. Debates over gun control, capital punishment, and mandatory sentences are ongoing and contentious. Some criminologists have argued successfully for social services, treatment, and rehabilitation programs to reduce the crime rate; others consider these a waste of time, suggesting instead that a massive prison construction program coupled with tough criminal sentences can bring the crime rate down. By accepting their roles as experts on law-violating behavior, criminologists place themselves in positions of power. The potential consequences of their actions are enormous. Therefore, they must be both aware of the ethics of their profession and prepared to defend their work in the light of public scrutiny. Major ethical issues include what to study, whom to study, and how to conduct those studies.

Ethics and *morals* are terms that are used interchangeably and may be used in ways that mean the same thing. Pollock (2007) suggests this makes sense because both words share the same root meaning; *ethos* is Greek and relates to custom or character, whereas *morals* is Latin and has a similar meaning.

Other takes on the subject suggest that ethics refer to the normative behavior of groups, while morals operate on a more personal level. For instance, Inman and Rudin (2000, p. 311) suggest

> One definition of ethics is:
>
> The rules of conduct recognized in respect to a particular class of human actions or a particular group, culture, etc.: medical ethics, Christian ethics (Webster's Unabridged, 1996).

In other words, individuals that choose to associate themselves with a particular group make a personal decision to abide by rules of conduct espoused by that community. These rules of conduct are, by definition, codified into a written code of ethics along with instructions for enforcement. Specifications for determining whether a member has committed an ethical violation, and specific direction regarding the consequences of that violation, must accompany the code. The community must have the means and the courage to enforce its code of ethics.

So not just providing a definition for ethics, Inman and Rudin further suggest that this code must be written and there must be rules for enforcement.

But further distinction must be made between ethics and morals. A man might have a personal moral code dictating that lying to his wife is a bad thing, though he has no compunction whatsoever in lying on the stand while under oath, to further the needs or wants of his group or organization. So, what happens on a personal level may have very little to do with what happens on a professional level. This is also canvassed by Inman and Rudin (2000, p. 312):

Ethics and morals don't necessarily intersect. An individual might be highly moral, according to her own personal code, and still violate some particular rule of ethics. Conversely, someone might act immorally, by his own standards or someone else's, and remain in compliance with a specific ethical code.

For something to be considered unethical, a number of criteria need to be met. This ensures that we are in fact talking about an ethical dilemma, and not something that has occurred by accident, or falls outside the realm of ethics, or alternatively that an ethical problem can be justly treated as such. Pollock (2007, pp. 11–12) suggests that there are four elements to ethical standards. They are:

1. **Act:** There must be some act to judge.
2. **Only human acts:** Ethics are directed specifically at human acts; the acts of lower order animals cannot be considered unethical.
3. **Free will:** Only behavior stemming from free will and free action can be judged unethical; behavior of individuals that is done under duress or threat is not unethical.
4. **Effects on others:** Unethical behavior must have some significant effect on other people.

So, a code of ethics is more than simply feeling good about the craft or about the individuals involved in it. A code of ethics proscribes behaviors that are unacceptable and offers an accepted set of sanctions that members abide by when they sign up. A code of ethics broadcasts subscription to a set standard and acknowledges that the code goes beyond the individual members or the sanctity of the group. It broadcasts that all members have agreed to and subscribed to it; that the needs of the individual are superseded by the needs of the group and the community.

ADVOCACY AND THE FORENSIC CRIMINOLOGIST

Forensic criminologists should be impartial voices in the arbitration of facts. They should strive to be devoid of emotion during their examinations and immune to pressures when rendering conclusions. Forensic criminologists, after all, are not interested in the outcome of a case; they are not advocates for either side. This is their primary value to any forensic enterprise.

However, it is necessary to add some confusion at this point. Forensic criminologists are advocates for the evidence they examine. They are advocates for objective examination and good scientific practice. Subsequently, they are also advocates for their findings once they have been rendered.

Conversely, forensic examiners' speaking of their cases in such a way as to suggest alignment with a team (by referring to their lawyer client when stating "we are going to win this case") should be avoided at all costs. These and similarly oriented statements telegraph an inherent bias in disposition and suggest that these experts have been anything but nonpartisan in their analyses.

THE MEDIA, ETHICS, AND THE FORENSIC CRIMINOLOGIST

As a forum for social issues, the media are often responsible for shaping the way that crime and justice issues are broadcast to both public and professional communities. They are often responsible for what is discussed, what is portrayed, the way it is portrayed, and even who may be responsible for a given criminal event. As discussed by Hinds (2009, p. 6):

> It is important to be aware that the media constructs a version of crime for a number of reasons. First, as the media is the primary public source of information about crime and criminals, it is the primary storyteller of crime events. The media has the capacity to inform the public about the reality of crime, by providing a statistical or research-based account of the number and types of crimes, and how to prevent victimization. The media also has the capacity to escalate public fear of crime by selectively focusing on crime generally, and in particular, certain types of crime as more prevalent and threatening.

The media can take many forms, and it is necessary to distinguish between them. The news media have the responsibility of reporting current affairs in a variety of ways to the public, both as it happens and later when new developments arise. This can be in print—newspapers and bulletins—or as electronic media—the television or various permutations on the Internet or anywhere else. *Media*, as a broad-brush term, may also include a wide variety of true-crime sources, from Internet resources through to print media such as memoirs or case-based works.

It may be argued, by some at least, that criminologists have less of an ethical obligation to the media. After all, the media are purveyors of supposition and not necessarily fact, so the obligation of criminologists is reduced because they are dealing with a less discriminating audience. However, this is the exact reason that forensic criminologists have to be more on guard, more discriminating, and more aware of what they are saying and the impact this voice may have on the target audience. To be fair to consumers of the mainstream media, this is not to say they are stupid or ignorant, but as a general rule they will be less educated in the intricacies of criminal behavior and its interpretation. To be equally fair, many professionals actively involved in the criminal justice field (whether police officers, prison guards, educators, or private security officers) may be similarly disengaged with the reality of criminal behavior.

The criminologists' duty to the media is to educate and inform. A useful parallel can be drawn with voting. In democracies where voting is not compulsory, nonvoters almost surrender their right to complain about the elected government simply by virtue of their nonaction. In the same way, criminologists virtually surrender their right to complain about the media when they do not view it as their responsibility to inform and to educate. All the while media outlets are reporting on crime without an educated voice, they will continue to report on matters of criminological interest without an informed viewpoint to provide balance and objectivity. Therefore, it is the immediate responsibility of forensic examiners to provide this as and when appropriate. The fact that our words are not always conveyed accurately is a separate issue of considerable import, but will not be given further attention here.

As experts in crime and criminal behavior, criminologists are oft-sought-out consultants to the media, especially in high profile, extremely violent, or unusual crimes. This will often place great strain on criminologists, who may be tempted to stray outside their area of expertise, especially in cases where journalists apply pressure to "assist the public" in their understanding of these types of crimes. Further, they may be tempted to engage in unethical practices because of the media buy-in; the more they are cited by news outlets, the more "real" they become. Turvey (2008) suggests the reason is that media attention is, inappropriately, viewed as a form of professional validation.

The first author has experienced firsthand the pressures placed on criminologists by media outlets to provide some—any—commentary on cases in which they have an interest. This pressure may be subtle in the form of carefully worded questions, with answers restated or reworded to suit a purpose; or it may be overt, by claims that if a particular expert won't comment on an issue, the reporter will just have to find someone else who will comment no matter the cost. But it is not the job of criminologists to pander to the media. Instead, they should be there to provide an objective analysis of what is known (not assumed or surmised) and to act as a buffer between the news producer and the news consumer in what is usually a very emotive or sensational grab at the chance to influence public opinion.

In all this, there is one very important point to remember: the media need criminologists more than criminologists need the media.

Turvey (2008, p. 723) provides the following commentary on the potential conflicts of interest that may occur between commentator and media outlets. While the discussion relates specifically to profiling, one could just as easily replace the word *profiler* with *criminologist*:

> Because of the high amount of emotional and sexual voyeurism inherent in the criminal profiling process, it has an equally high entertainment value. This attracts not only a large number of consumers to profiling-related media but arguably a high number of students to college courses on the subject as well. In any case, criminal profilers are constantly being asked to contribute to, consult on, or opine for media-related projects on real or fictional offenders and offenses.
>
> The relationship between the criminal profiler and the media should be the same as any other—the profiler should be there to educate. Not to alarm. Not to sensationalize. Not to judge. Not to condemn. Not to assume facts or guess about whether or not a missing child is dead or whether a suspect is guilty. The profiler is either a source of competent and informed knowledge based on objective forensic practice or serving no valid professional purpose whatsoever.

So, before commenting on any cases, new, old, cold, or otherwise, criminologists must ask themselves a number of questions:

1. Am I qualified to opine on this specific issue?
2. Is the opinion warranted?
3. Is the evidence that is currently in the public domain sufficient to form an opinion?
4. Will I possibly hurt the case and any subsequent investigation into it by offering commentary (for example, through contempt of court laws by commenting on a case currently before the courts)?

Criminologists must also ensure they do the following in providing opinions to the media:

1. Be clear in stating the difference between fact, opinion, and assumption.
2. Be clear in differentiating between opinions of the extant case and opinions of a general variety (for example, discussing the specifics of a murder case versus general knowledge or information about murder as a crime type).
3. Make every effort to correct misinformation or misinterpretation of any opinion provided.

One case that highlights the potential problems of the nexus between the news media and criminologists is the homicide of Lisa Marie Kimmell. The background to the case is discussed by Lohr (2007):

> In the spring of 1988, Lisa Marie Kimmell's future was full of promise, and at only 18 years old, she had her whole life ahead of her. Friends and family knew Lisa as "Lil Miss," a nickname she received when her grandmother began calling her Little Miss Marie years before.
>
> After graduating from Billings Senior High, Lisa Marie moved to Denver where she worked as manager of an Arby's Restaurant. Life was great for Lisa, but it was all about to change on a fateful spring day in 1988.
>
> On the morning of March 25, 1988, Lisa Marie Kimmell got into her new black Honda CRX with a personalized license plate that read "LILMISS" and started out on a trip from Denver to Billings, Montana, to visit family. She planned to stop in Cody, Wyoming, along the way to pick up her boyfriend, Ed Jaroch. Lisa was excited at the prospect of introducing Ed to her family. Unfortunately, Lisa never made it that far.
>
> After leaving Denver, the last verified account of Lisa's whereabouts would come from Wyoming State Highway Patrolman Al Lesco, who stopped her for speeding near Douglas. Though unverified, some witnesses reported seeing her later that evening, near Casper.
>
> Panicked by the uncharacteristic disappearance of their oldest child, Lisa Marie's parents, Ron and Sheila Kimmell, began a relentless search to discover what had happened to her. Lisa's father chartered a plane to search for any signs of his daughter's black car from the air and, at one point, drove the route from Denver to Billings himself in hopes of spotting her. The family also created posters with Lisa's picture and distributed them widely in hopes of getting a lead on her whereabouts. Unfortunately, there was no sign of Lisa. She had seemingly vanished into thin air.

On April 2, 1988, William Greg Bradford was with a friend on the North Platte River when they happened upon the partially clothed body of a young woman, just downstream from Government Bridge. The body was later identified as that of Lisa Marie Kimmell. The teenager had been found, but there was no trace of her black Honda CRX with the unique license plate. The mysterious case would soon become known as the "Lil Miss murder," and investigators asked for the public's help in locating her black sports car.

In the following weeks, police received several tips from people who thought they'd spotted Lisa's car, though none of them resulted in any solid leads.

Despite the fact that Lisa had been missing for eight days, the autopsy revealed that she had only been dead a short time. Lisa had apparently been kept captive for several days before she was murdered and, until years later, only investigators would know the horrible details of Lisa's murder and how she likely spent her last days.

The ensuing investigation would bring out several possible suspects, including the highway patrolman who stopped her for speeding and the sheriff of Natrona County, although all the initial suspects were eventually cleared. A year after Lisa disappeared, someone placed a mysterious note on her grave that said Lisa would be missed and that she'd "always live in me." The note was signed as the fictional character Stringfellow Hawke from the 1980s TV series "Airwolf." The clues led nowhere, and as the months and years sped by, the "Lil Miss" case went cold.

The case was later solved by a cold hit from a DNA database that matched Dale Eaton, who was in federal custody at the time. Later, the case was to become the focus of a new cable television show to air on TruTV. However, not everyone was happy to see the case receive the coverage it did, in the way it did. Sheila Kimmell, the victim's mother, was less than impressed with the way TruTV handled the case, or the commentary provided by retired Florida Department of Law Enforcement criminal profiler, Dayle Hinman. As discussed in Tuttle (2008):

> A woman whose daughter was murdered in 1988 said she is disappointed and angered by a new reality television show about her family's case.

> Sheila Kimmell, who used to live in Billings, Mont., said she is considering legal action against the producers of the TruTV cable show "Body of Evidence." The program features Dayle Hinman, an FBI-trained criminal profiler.

The season premiere of the show aired Saturday and included a 30-minute segment on the murder of Lisa Marie Kimmell, who was abducted, raped and killed in Wyoming while driving between Denver and Billings.

...

The case has long captured public interest, and it has been featured on such television shows as "Eye on America," "Unsolved Mysteries" and "Cold Case Files." In 2005, Sheila Kimmell, who now lives in Colorado, wrote a book about her family's loss and experience with the criminal justice system.

Kimmell said in a telephone interview she believes the latest television version of her daughter's case is misleading because Hinman appears in the show as if she was involved from the beginning. Hinman never played a role in the investigation of her daughter's murder, Kimmell said, and she said the show is a "disservice" to the law enforcement officers who were involved.

"I'm not going to stand behind it and endorse it," Kimmell said. "I'm not going to be used, and I'm not going to let them use my daughter. This is not what Lisa's life and legacy are about, and I'm not going to prostitute my daughter. I'm not going to prostitute my family."

Kimmell said she agreed to be interviewed and filmed at her home for the program last summer. She said she agreed to participate after a producer assured her the show would be factual.

"He described it as an educational program, reality-based, about criminal profiling," Kimmell said.

Shortly after the film crew left, Kimmell said, she grew concerned. Others close to the investigation had not agreed to participate, she said, and it appeared as if Hinman, whom she has never spoken with, was injecting herself into the closed investigation.

"There is nothing she did to contribute to the solving of this case," Kimmell said.

Similar concerns were expressed by Billings resident Don Flickinger, a retired ATF agent who spent nearly a decade investigating the Kimmell murder. Flickinger said he also agreed to be filmed for the Hinman show. After watching it, Flickinger said he disagrees with how the program presented the investigation.

"The FBI agent who did the actual (criminal) profile shortly after the murder was never even mentioned in the program," Flickinger said. "It's pretty easy to do a program like that and act like you are profiling the individual involved when that person has already been convicted and is on death row."

Bryan Ranharter, an associate producer for Story House Productions, said Thursday the company would have no comment about the complaints by Kimmell and Flickinger.

Kimmell said she is most concerned that viewers will be deceived into believing that Hinman was responsible for solving her daughter's murder. She is considering legal action to halt any future broadcast of the segment, but she acknowledged there may be little chance of winning such case.

"Anybody can write a book, and I can't stop them," Kimmell said. "But I can expose them. The same goes for a TV program."

Hinman has essentially been accused of taking credit for work she didn't do, by virtue of the nature of the television show she was involved with. This show leaves a false impression in the mind of the viewer that she was somehow involved, which also provides her with the opportunity to trade on the broadcast perception that she was at ground-zero with the case. No efforts to retract this perception and to correct the false impression have been located.

Forensic examiners at all times should be clear in reporting on any matter in which they were involved, and the exact degree and nature of their involvement. Whether this involves opining to the media on an open or solved case, consulting with detectives as to the "profile" of an offender, or in the provision of expert testimony, examiners must be honest about what has been done, with what, and how.

ETHICS IN REPORTING AND REPORT WRITING

In 1992, Paula Gilfoyle's body was found in the garage of her home in Merseyside, England. A suicide note was found with the body, and police sought out the advice of Dr. David Canter, an "investigative psychologist" from the University of Liverpool in assessing the note for its potential as a fake written by her husband to conceal a homicide. Based on his assessment of the written note, Canter suggested that it didn't contain the hallmarks of Paula Gilfoyle's own writings and wasn't in keeping with a woman who intended to take her own life. Interestingly, he was also to suggest that the writings were not in keeping with Eddie Gilfoyle's other writings, even though this was the contention of the Crown Prosecution Service. As discussed in Kennedy (2008a):

The pioneer of criminal profiling in Britain has switched sides to say that a man he helped to jail for life for murdering his wife is innocent.

Eddie Gilfoyle was prosecuted after David Canter, a psychology professor, told police that his hanged wife's suicide note betrayed signs of having been faked. But research prompted by the case into the difference between genuine and false suicide notes has persuaded Professor Canter that Paula Gilfoyle, 32, was, indeed, the sole author of her final words.

Now campaigners for the jailed husband are hoping to use Professor Canter's analysis of the suicide note as part of a fresh appeal.

On a June evening in 1992, Paula Gilfoyle's body was found hanged in the garage of the home in Upton, Wirral, Merseyside, that she shared with her husband.

Mrs Gilfoyle, who worked in a local factory, was eight months pregnant and presented a cheery front to the world. But the long suicide note that she left spoke of a feeling of failure and unhappiness, and hinted at strains in her marriage. She told her husband not to blame himself, and even suggested that the baby was not his. There is an overwhelming feeling of guilt and self-blame in the note.

Friends and relatives refused to believe that she could have killed herself. They insisted that she had no cares and was looking forward to the birth of her first baby. Suspicion soon turned on her husband. Some work-mates told police that she had said that her husband, a hospital porter, had persuaded her to write a bogus suicide note as part of a course that he was taking on suicide. No such course existed.

However, Professor Canter points out, in a 10,000-word report on the case, that for the bogus suicide plot to have worked Gilfoyle would have had to persuade his wife to climb a ladder in the garage and allow a noose to be placed around her neck. There were no signs of force on her body.

Gilfoyle has always protested his innocence of what was portrayed as a calculated, evil plot to make his pregnant wife's killing look like suicide.

When Merseyside police began to investigate Mrs Gilfoyle's death, they consulted Professor Canter, who had been the first psychological profiler to be used by British police and who shared their doubts about the note.

His evidence formed part of the prosecution case, though it was never heard by the jury. He nonetheless believes that it helped to reinforce prosecutors' determination to press ahead against Gilfoyle, who was convicted unanimously of murder in July 1993.

Professor Canter used a technique of linguistic analysis to try to establish whether Mrs Gilfoyle had composed her note. Police suspected that her husband had dictated it to her. But studies since, including one supervised by Professor Canter, have shown that errors can be produced by using simple word counts as the main basis for deciding authorship.

By chance, a couple of years after the conviction, Professor Canter moved to Merseyside, taking a post at the University of Liverpool. There, he came into contact with Gilfoyle's relatives and eventually met the prisoner himself. "He wasn't that creative an individual," Professor Canter said. The academic then began looking closer into the science of suicide notes.

The most pertinent study was conducted 50 years ago by the founders of the Los Angeles Suicide Prevention Centre, Edwin Schneidman and Norman Farberow. The two psychologists, pioneers in suicide prevention, compared genuine suicide notes with artificial ones written by people who had never been suicidal.

Their purpose was to look for ways to stop people taking their own lives. But Professor Canter made a study of those 1950s notes, along with other samples, to seek clues to how a genuine suicide note could be distinguished from an imagined one. It became clear that it is difficult to simulate the elements in a real suicide note. Professor Canter now uses Mrs Gilfoyle's final handwritten lines, beginning "Dear Eddie" and ending "Goodnight and God bless, love Paula," in his lectures.

"It is my opinion that the suicide note was written, unaided, by Paula Gilfoyle," he said. "That this intention was genuine is difficult to determine, but the way in which the note appears to be the culmination of months of thinking of various possibilities for dealing with her situation, and indicates so directly that Paula could see no other way, is consistent with a very real determination to kill herself."

Gilfoyle's brother-in-law, Paul Caddick, a retired police sergeant who found Mrs Gilfoyle's body and now runs the miscarriage of justice campaign, praised Professor Canter.

"He is a brave man," Mr Caddick said. "We are very pleased he has come on to the defence side because he is a man of integrity. Obviously, for a long time, Eddie didn't like him. When he came on to our side he said, 'The bastard, he should've said the right thing in the first place.' But now he realises it was a dreadful mistake."

Gilfoyle has already lost two appeals against conviction but his new legal team at Birnberg Peirce is preparing evidence to bring before the Criminal Cases Review Commission.

Merseyside Police said: "There was a lot of other evidence heard by the jury and he was convicted on that evidence."

Regarding the admissibility of the evidence put forth by Canter, Freckleton and Selby (2002, p. 403) state:

The most substantial English analysis of the admissibility of psychological profiling took place in Gilfoyle [2001] 2 Cr App R 57. It dealt with the admissibility of evidence by Professor Canter regarding the likelihood that a deceased person had committed suicide. The Court of Appeal declined the evidence, accepting Professor Canter as an expert but finding that he had never embarked on evaluating suicidality of a deceased person previously and on the basis that "his reports identify no criteria by reference to which the court could test the quality of his opinions: there is no database comparing real and questionable suicides and there is no substantial body of academic writing approving his methodology": at [67]. It found, too, that Professor Canter's views were based on "one-sided information" provided by the defendant.

While the court didn't put much faith in the evidence, not allowing Canter to testify, the Crown Prosecution Service certainly paid close attention to his opinion. In fact, it guided their case to closure cementing their position that they had their man. But the reasoning was circular: Professor Canter was told what the police theories were; these were then fed back to prosecutors; the prosecutors used these theories to guide and mount their case.

Later, Canter was to write his own op-ed piece regarding his involvement in the case. Curiously, he admits that there was no strong evidence supporting the theory that Paula Gilfoyle had been the victim of a staged homicide (Canter, 2008):

My report was never presented to the court but apparently had an influence behind the scenes. But I had always been curious about how a pregnant woman would write a suicide note under dictation from her husband with whom she had had a strained relationship, and then put her head in a noose with him standing behind her. So when the opportunity arose a few years later for me to talk to Eddie and his family (an option I had been denied as a prosecution expert) I jumped at it. The picture that emerged from these discussions was much less clear than the original story. There was no strong evidence that Eddie had ever dictated a suicide note, or even claimed that he was doing a course as a paramedic, just hearsay from friends of Paula, which was never presented to the court.

So how could such a prominent and experienced psychologist become so embroiled in something so clearly inconsistent with the evidence and his reported methodology involving empirical, objective, and purportedly scientific analysis? Using a method that was untested, largely hypothetical, and lacking any empirical foundation, Canter appears to have been the victim of observer effects and examiner bias. This is evident in his own admissions regarding the Gilfoyle case (Canter, 2008):

> The police officer leading the inquiry presented the suicide note to me with the fascinating thesis that it had been dictated to Paula by her husband, Eddie, who was believed then to have encouraged Paula to put her neck in a noose while he stood behind her, after which he killed her by lifting her legs to hang her.

> I was told that it was believed that Eddie had murdered Paula, who was eight and a half months pregnant, after tricking her into writing the suicide note on the pretext that he needed it for a paramedical evening class he was taking. His motive, in the crime novel tradition, was hinted at being an affair that he was having.

Basing an opinion solely on the suicide note in this case was sheer folly, especially given the wealth of evidentiary problems evident. And these didn't just relate to those things done later in the investigation. Kennedy (2008b) discusses the range of errors that were present in this investigation:

> "Incorrect prioritising of the call out by the divisional control room staff"

> The first constable asked for CID and scenes of crime. But control room called coroner's officer and police surgeon, who arrived before detectives

> "Lack of scene-preservation and destruction of potential evidence"

> Mrs Gilfoyle was said to have been found hanging with her feet resting on a pair of step ladders. But the ladders were taken from the garage into the house before a detective arrived. Sand by the door was trampled, destroying possible footprints

> "The coroner's officer making crucial decisions about the investigation and mode of death before the arrival of the CID"

> The first policeman to arrive was the coroner's officer, who decided that Mrs Gilfoyle took her own life

> "The cutting down of the body by the coroner's officer"

> He lay Mrs Gilfoyle on the floor to "preserve her dignity"

No detective saw her hanging, although exact details would be important to establish murder or suicide

"The decision of the coroner's officer with regards to photographic evidence"

He said there was no need for photos as the coroner did not require them

"The lack of consideration to the advanced pregnant condition of the deceased"

This should have been suspicious enough for a full inquiry

"The lack of communication"

When the detective inspector did arrive, he was mistakenly told that photographs had been taken

"The destruction of the ligature following post-mortem"

No officer attended the post-mortem examination. The ligature was burnt by the mortuary assistant. Experts could have deduced who tied the knot

"The initial officer allowing Edward Gilfoyle and his parents to leave before the arrival of the CID"

No one was questioned

Clearly in this case the massive and numerous errors meant any investigative theories were substantially set back by the destruction of evidence which may have supported or refuted them. In fact, investigative blunders from the outset meant that it would be virtually impossible to tell what anything meant, unless these errors were accounted for and, one hopes, corrected.

ETHICS IN PUBLISHING

Most legal systems around the world require that witnesses who give opinion evidence in court actually be experts in their respective area. One way this expertise might be established is through the publication of research and scholarly thought in textbooks and journal articles. For forensic criminologists who also work in the tertiary education sector, publishing may be a requirement of the position, and absolutely necessary for promotion, advancement, and other financial incentives such as bonuses and pay raises. Indeed, anyone who has ever set foot in a university will probably be well aware of the saying "publish or perish."

Because the courts and education sector may require this of forensic criminologists, there is a great pressure to publish as much as possible, as frequently as possible, in the highest tier journals possible. Some are more than capable of maintaining a standard and holding fast in their ethical responsibilities to themselves, to the community, and to their craft. Others opt for the path of least resistance, exploiting colleagues and subordinates; plagiarizing; engaging in outright theft of material, thoughts, and ideas; or adopting an inappropriate research methodology.

However, these are not the only problems confronting authors/academics/practitioners. For some, to make a publication fit an idea, they may have to assume certain propositions or conditions; otherwise, their writings may not be accepted or as valued. For instance, assuming rather than establishing a particular state of affairs may provide an easy shortcut to getting a publication under one's belt. The temptation is great, but the problems presented are even greater.

But we cannot for an instant assume that such behavior is isolated, rare, or unique. For example, Turvey (2008) gives one example of a problem of ethics in publishing where the guilt of a suspect had to be assumed to establish the purported validity of a profiling method and the subsequent article that arose from it.

A further search found at least one other article where such an assumption has been made, but the exact extent of the problem cannot be known until a more thorough examination has been undertaken. While it is not the province of this chapter to delve further into this issue, such a task would make an excellent research project for any graduate or research student.

In 2005, McCabe and Wauchope published "Behavioural Characteristics of Men Accused of Rape: Evidence for Different Types of Rapists." The purpose of this article was to "determine whether the behavioral characteristics demonstrated by rapists clustered together into groups that were similar to the common rapist typology in the literature" (p. 241). The study was broken into two parts: the first was an analysis of 130 men charged with sexual assault, while the second examined court transcripts from 50 tried rape cases. Only the first study is relevant to the current discussion and will be discussed here.

In the first study (McCabe and Wauchope, 2005, p. 242):

> Data were collected over a three year period on 130 men who had been charged with rape, using information in the form of a violent crime analysis report, gathered by the Victorian police ... in the course of their investigations of these alleged sexual assaults.

Study 1, therefore, assessed whether an alleged offender fit within the rapist typology developed by Hazelwood and Burgess (1987). To be clear, these suspects had not been unequivocally convicted of the offenses for which they had been charged; rather, their involvement was the result of allegations that they had sexually assaulted someone. This is a problem because of the false reporting involved in the crime of rape, but we shall turn to this in a moment.

To be able to use the results of the study, that is, whether these suspects (men only *accused* of rape) fit within an established rape typology (rape being a penal classification that implies guilt), the researchers had to assume the guilt of these suspects. At the least the reader is required to do this to agree that the results are in any way valid or meaningful.

There is a greater problem here that needs to be canvassed though. Beyond the grave problem of assuming guilt to give the data meaning, there is the much graver problem of falsely accusing another of the crime of rape. What this means is that there is a great probability that some of the "rapists" studied in this article are not in fact guilty of rape, and are in fact victims themselves of false accusations and/or overzealous police and prosecutors who place too much faith in the words of those who present as victims and not enough effort into investigation. Savino and Turvey (2004) provides an excellent review of the major studies in false reporting of rape, showing the rate to be between approximately 13% to approximately 40%, depending on the study.

If these figures can be transposed onto the McCabe sample, this would suggest that anywhere between 17 and 52 of the 130 "participants" in the study are not actually rapists but are in fact victims. Assessing the degree to which those accused of a crime fit within offender typologies, of any type, is therefore wholly inappropriate.

ETHICAL GUIDELINES FOR THE FORENSIC CRIMINOLOGIST

In conducting research for this chapter, the authors became more than a little concerned about the absence of a code of ethics for criminologists, even in the works published on ethics in criminology and criminal justice.

While some professional organizations have a code of ethics, they frequently lack any explanation of consequences for violating the code. This too is a significant problem because it potentially signals a lack of consequences for the unethical practitioner and removes the ability of the organization to sanction misconduct in a substantive or meaningful way. This essentially gives a green light to the unethical examiner and effectively rewards bad behavior.

While some issues are very clear in their ethical status (e.g., "don't lie under oath while giving evidence"), other areas may be less well defined and are far less clear in terms of being ethical or unethical. For the initiate or the student, having a clearly defined code of ethics to refer to in times of doubt will go a long way to professionalizing the field and raising the bar of practice.

But having a code of ethics is only half of the battle. As noted, if there are no accompanying consequences for breaches, there is little that an organization can do to control the behavior of any member or members. It should also be noted that the code should be designed not only to sanction errant behavior, but also to advance the discipline and to protect it from unethical individuals. It should not be the purpose of the code to protect the organization, as is evident in the American Academy of Forensic Sciences code of ethics:

> Article II. CODE OF ETHICS AND CONDUCT
>
> SECTION 1—THE CODE: As a means to promote the highest quality of professional and personal conduct of its members and affiliates, the following constitutes the Code of Ethics and Conduct which is endorsed by all members and affiliates of the American Academy of Forensic Sciences:
>
> **a.** Every member and affiliate of the Academy shall refrain from exercising professional or personal conduct adverse to the best interests and objectives of the Academy. The objectives stated in the Preamble to these bylaws include: promoting education for and research in the forensic sciences, encouraging the study, improving the practice, elevating the standards and advancing the cause of the forensic sciences.
>
> **b.** No member or affiliate of the Academy shall materially misrepresent his or her education, training, experience, area of expertise, or membership status within the Academy.
>
> **c.** No member or affiliate of the Academy shall materially misrepresent data or scientific principles upon which his or her conclusion or professional opinion is based.
>
> **d.** No member or affiliate of the Academy shall issue public statements that appear to represent the position of the Academy without specific authority first obtained from the Board of Directors.

Along with a clear intent to protect the organization, it should be noted that no consequences or sanctions for breaking the American Academy of Forensic Science code of conduct are given.

Perhaps a more useful touchstone for a code of ethics for Forensic Criminologists is the Academy of Behavioral Profiling (ABP) guidelines designed for criminal profilers. This code is general enough to apply to criminological settings and specific enough to identify component behaviors and exceptions. The ABP code and the sanctions for violating the code are as follows (Academy of Behavioral Profiling, 1999):

Applicants, Students, Affiliates, and Members of the ABP shall:

- Maintain an attitude of professionalism and integrity.
- Conduct all research in a generally accepted scientific manner.
- Assign appropriate credit for the ideas of others that are used.
- Treat all information (not in the public domain) from a client or agency in a confidential manner, unless specific permission to disseminate information is obtained.
- Maintain an attitude of independence and impartiality in order to ensure an unbiased analysis and interpretation of the evidence.
- Strive to avoid preconceived ideas or biases regarding potential suspects or offenders from influencing a final profile or crime analysis when appropriate.
- Render opinions and conclusions strictly in accordance with the evidence in the case.
- Not exaggerate, embellish, or otherwise misrepresent qualifications when testifying, or at any other time, in any form.
- Testify in an honest, straightforward manner and refuse to extend their opinion beyond their field of competence, phrasing testimony in a manner intended to avoid misinterpretation of their opinion.
- Not use a profile or crime analysis (the inference of Offender or Crime Scene characteristics) for the purposes of suggesting the guilt or innocence of a particular individual for a particular crime.
- Make efforts to inform the court of the nature and implications of pertinent evidence if reasonably assured that this information will not be disclosed in court.
- Maintain the quality and standards of the professional community by reporting unethical conduct to the appropriate authorities or professional organizations.

Sanctions for Violations of the Ethical Guidelines for Professional Conduct

There are three (3) types of sanctions for Applicants, Students, Affiliates, and Members of the ABP who have been found to have violated the ethical guidelines of this Academy:

Advisement: A written notification to the individual responsible for the violation to cease their unethical conduct. Two advisements result in an automatic warning.

Warning: A written warning to the individual responsible for the violation to cease their unethical conduct immediately or risk expulsion. Warnings will be made known to ABP membership. Two warnings result in automatic expulsion.

Expulsion: A written notification of expulsion from the Academy of Behavioral Profiling to the individual responsible for the violation. Expulsions will be made public.

The purpose of these sanctions is not necessarily to simply punish those responsible for unethical behavior, but to educate them, and give them an opportunity to make changes before more serious sanctions are levied. This provides a mechanism for identifying well intentioned individuals who err in judgment versus those whose ethics are at odds with those of the Academy.

Formal reports of ethics violations, with proper documentation, should be presented to the Ethics Committee within the Board of Directors. The Chair of the Ethics Committee shall investigate complaints regarding potential unethical conduct within the membership and then pass a recommendation along to the Board of Directors for an official vote.

No sanctions shall be given before those members involved are provided an opportunity to defend themselves.

If one is bound to a code of ethics, and has it ready at hand should questions arise, then it becomes easier to guard against unethical behavior and other unethical practitioners. Indeed, a printed code close by, out for all others to see, would surely be a safeguard even against a request that one should go to the "dark side." To be sure, one lapse in judgment is a precursor to further errors in professional practice, opening the door to a swath of further requests or temptations.

Thornton (2007, p. 48) provides the following canon of ethics for reconstructionists that could be easily adopted by forensic criminologists:

One simple device that may assist the crime reconstructionist in the maintenance of the proper professional stance against external pressure is a printed statement of ethical behavior posted conspicuously in his or her office. A consulting reconstructionist could have it posted on his or her Web site. This may read something along the lines of:

1. As a practicing crime reconstructionist, I pledge to apply the principles of science and logic and to follow the truth courageously wherever it may lead.
2. As a practicing crime reconstructionist, I acknowledge that the scientific spirit must be inquiring, progressive, logical, and unbiased.
3. I will never knowingly allow a false impression to be planted in the mind of anyone availing themselves of my services.

4. As a practicing crime reconstructionist, it is not my purpose to present only that evidence which supports the view of one side. I have a moral and professional responsibility to ensure that everyone concerned understands the evidence as it exists and to present it in an impartial manner.

5. The practice of crime reconstruction has a single professional demand—correctness. It has a single ethical demand—truthfulness. To these I commit myself, totally and irrevocably.

6. The exigencies of a particular case will not cause me to depart from the professionalism that I am required to exercise.

For the sake of those on whom this may be lost (italics added):

1. As a practicing *forensic criminologist*, I pledge to apply the principles of science and logic and to follow the truth courageously wherever it may lead.

2. As a practicing *forensic criminologist*, I acknowledge that the scientific spirit must be inquiring, progressive, logical, and unbiased.

3. I will never knowingly allow a false impression to be planted in the mind of anyone availing themselves of my services.

4. As a practicing *forensic criminologist*, it is not my purpose to present only that evidence which supports the view of one side. I have a moral and professional responsibility to ensure that everyone concerned understands the evidence as it exists and to present it in an impartial manner.

5. The practice of *forensic criminologist* has a single professional demand—correctness. It has a single ethical demand—truthfulness. To these I commit myself, totally and irrevocably.

6. The exigencies of a particular case will not cause me to depart from the professionalism that I am required to exercise.

While sanctions are necessary, they are only useful if (1) there is a code of ethics to hold people accountable to, and (2) if there is a professional group to hold them accountable to that code of ethics. At the time of writing, no such professional group exists for the forensic criminologist. However, at the time of this writing, things are underway to rectify this situation.

SUMMARY

Forensic criminologists have a great duty to ensure that the result of their analysis not only comports to the evidence, but that the results of their analysis are ethical and subscribe to ethical standards. These standards have, to date, been poorly defined and prescribed. These standards relate to all areas of professional practice, including any expert reports or testimony, and also to commentary provided to the media or other public forums.

There is often great pressure placed on forensic criminologists to provide results one way or the other, for whatever side may employ them. It is their sole responsibility to ensure that they remain impartial, regardless of the pressure, and to provide an analysis that benefits nothing but the facts of the case and the decider of those facts, be they judge, jury, or panel.

A code of ethics goes a long way to helping forensic criminologists remain impartial and ensuring that their analysis is helpful to the trier of fact in no other way than it paints a clearer picture of what happened. In addition, an ethical canon provides cover for ethical criminologists from all others, especially those who would see them alter their opinion out of fear or favor.

Review Questions

1. According to Pollock (2007), what are the four elements to ethical standards?
2. What is the difference between ethics and morals?
3. T/F Forensic criminologists, when working for a defense team, may take on the role of advocate for the accused.
4. What must forensic criminologists consider before opining to the media on any given case?
5. T/F For research purposes, it is standard practice to assume the guilt of suspects.
6. Why is it necessary to provide not only ethical guidelines, but also the sanctions which will be handed down if the guidelines are broken?
7. Discuss some of the ethical guidelines which are necessary for any forensic criminologist.

REFERENCES

Academy of Behavioral Profiling, 1999. Ethical Guidelines. Available fromhttp://www. profiling.org/abp_conduct.html (Accessed on 12 March, 2009).

British Society of Criminology, 2006. Code of Ethics for Researchers in the Field of Criminology. Available from http://www.britsoccrim.org/ethical.htm (Accessed on 12 March, 2009).

Canter, D., 2008. Yes, I Got It Wrong—and Then an 'Innocent' Man Was Jailed for Life. Available from http://www.timesonline.co.uk/tol/news/uk/crime/article3427717. ece (Accessed on 24 March, 2009).

Freckleton, I., Selby, H., 2002. Expert Evidence: Law, Practice, Procedure and Advocacy, second ed. The Lawbook Co., Sydney.

Hazelwood, R., Burgess, A., 1987. Practical Aspects of Rape Investigation: A Multidisciplinary Approach. Elsevier, New York.

Hinds, L., 2009. Media and Crime. In: Hayes, H., Prenzler, T. (Eds.), Crime and Criminology, second ed. Pearson Education, Frenchs Forest.

Inman, K., Rudin, N., 2000. Principles and Practice of Criminalistics: The Profession of Forensic Science. CRC Press, Boca Raton.

Kennedy, D., 2008a. CPS to Reconsider Eddie Gilfoyle Murder Conviction After Police Notes Uncovered. Available from http://www.timesonline.co.uk/tol/news/uk/crime/article5774189.ece?token=null&offset=0&page=1 (Accessed on 24 March, 2009).

Kennedy, D. 2008b. Inquiry Reveals Errors in Investigation of Eddie Gilfoyle. Available from http://www.timesonline.co.uk/tol/news/uk/crime/article3784886.ece (Accessed on 24 March, 2009).

Lohr, D., 2007. Lisa Marie Kimmell: DNA Helps Solve Fifteen-Year-Old 'Lil Miss' Case. Available from http://blogs.discovery.com/criminal_report/2007/12/lisa-marie-kimm.html (Accessed on 30 March 2009).

McCabe, M.P., Wauchope, M., 2005. Behavioural Characteristics of Men Accused of Rape: Evidence for Different Types of Rapists. Arch. Sex Behav. 34, (2), 241–253.

Pollock, J.M., 2007. Ethical Dilemmas and Decisions in Criminal Justice, fifth ed. Thompson Wadsworth, Belmont.

Savino, J., Turvey, B.E., 2004. Rape Investigation Handbook. Elsevier Science, Boston.

Siegel, L.J., 2008. Criminology: The Core, third ed. Wadsworth Thompson, Belmont.

Thornton, J.I., 2007. Crime Reconstruction—Ethos and Ethics. In: Chisum, W.J., Turvey, B.E. (Eds.), Crime Reconstruction. Academic Press, Burlington, MA.

Turvey, B.E., 2008. Criminal Profiling: An Introduction to Behavioral Evidence Analysis, third ed. Academic Press, Boston.

Tuttle, G., 2008. Kimmell's Mom Is Angry About Reality Crime Show. Available from http://www.jacksonholestartrib.com/articles/2008/01/13/news/casper/833b99aba4012af2872573ce00268888.txt (Accessed on 30 March 2009).

Index